HARRAP'S BOOK OF FILM DIRECTORS AND THEIR FILMS

HARRAP'S BOOK OF FILM DIRECTORS AND THEIR FILMS

A Comprehensive Guide from 1924 to the Present Day

ALISON J. FILMER
ANDRE GOLAY

LONDON

First published in Great Britain 1989
by HARRAP BOOKS LIMITED
26 Market Square, Bromley, Kent BR1 1NA

ISBN 0 245-54942-0

Printed and bound in Great Britain
at the Bath Press, Avon

CONTENTS

PREFACE

Welcome to *Harrap's Book of Film Directors and Their Films* – the most comprehensive guide to directors of full-length English-language feature films ever published in the UK or the USA, running from the sound era's commencement (1924) right up to the present day. Also included are some noted foreign directors, but only if (like Truffaut) they have made one or more films in English. A complete work on foreign directors would obviously require a large volume in its own right.

In modern times the director has justifiably become accepted as the major influence in film-making. The study of a director's past achievements, therefore, is probably the most informative and entertaining way of assessing the quality of any given film. It is hoped that this book will be of invaluable service to the casual filmgoer and the expert alike, and will be used continually in conjunction with other cinema, video and television reference books. Every effort has been made to be as accurate and up-to-the-minute as is humanly possible, but contributions and corrections for the next edition are welcomed, particularly in regard to new directors.

Finally, acknowledgements are genuinely too numerous to mention, but special credit must be given to the following for their invaluable assistance: The British Film Institute Library, The American Film Institute, The BFI Monthly Film Bulletin, Variety and Screen International.

Tunbridge Wells
August 1989

ALISON J. FILMER
ANDRE GOLAY

EXPLANATORY NOTES

BIOGRAPHY

Emphasis has been placed on the director's work, so biographical details are kept to a minimum. The amount of detail included on each director varies in accordance with career success, while information is as yet unavailable to those who have only recently emerged from total obscurity. The dates in brackets denote each director's lifespan, and are followed by either his/her place of birth or nationality. Unfortunately, show-business vanity may prevent some of the birth dates from being totally accurate. In some cases a reference has been made to autobiographies or biographies for further in-depth reading.

FILMOGRAPHY

A director's filmography consists of full-length feature films intended for theatrical release in the UK or USA. Documentaries, animations, serials (serialized B pictures), shorts (less than 60 minutes), TV movies (films made exclusively for television) and mini-series are not included. However, if any of these categories form a substantial part of a director's career, his/her filmography contains a footnote. When a film has more than one director, any directors are bracketed after the film's title(s). A co-director who has never been the sole director of a film is listed only in this capacity. A handful of prolific foreign directors (denoted by an asterisk) have had films omitted if these were relseased only in the country of their origin.

TITLE

A film may change its title when remarketed in different countries or re-released at a later date, so to assist in recognition alternative titles have been included in italics unless the variations are only slight. Also included are a number of working titles by which films became known during production. Foreign films are given only their English-language title if it is a direct translation of the original.

DATE

The intention is to give the initial theatrical release date (many films can take a year or more to be exported). Dates of films not yet released at the time of going to press are projections, and therefore subject to last-minute alterations.

AWARDS

The American Academy (Oscar) award nominees and winners in best director and film categories are denoted thus:

Best Director	Nomination:	D*
	Winner:	D**
Best Film	Nomination:	F*
	Winner:	F**

INDEX

'A', 'An' and 'The' are ignored in the indexing of titles (although foreign titles are to be found under their respective definite and indefinite articles). Titles commencing with numbers are thrown to the beginning of the Index. Main titles and alternative titles are indexed separately, and cross-referenced; however, a few very lengthy main titles have been abbreviated, and one or two similarly lengthy alternatives have been omitted altogether.

AARON, Paul
1978 A Different Story
1979 A Force of One
1983 Deadly Force
1985 Maxie / *Free Spirit*
1987 Home Front / *Morgan Stewart's Coming Home*

ABBOTT, George
(1887–) Forestville, New York, USA. Autobiography: Mister Abbott.
1929 Why Bring That Up?
1929 Half-Way to Heaven
1930 Manslaughter
1930 The Sea God
1931 Stolen Heaven
1931 Secrets of a Secretary
1931 My Sin
1931 The Cheat
1940 Too Many Girls
1957 The Pajama Game **(Stanley DONEN)**
1958 Damn Yankees / *What Lola Wants* **(Stanley DONEN)**

ABBOTT, Norman
1966 Last of the Secret Agents

ABRAHAMS, Derwin
1941 Border Vigilantes
1941 Secrets of the Vigilantes
1941 Secrets of the Wasteland
1944 Cattle Call
1944 Phantom Outlaws
1944 Renegade Roundup
1944 Return of the Durango Kid
1944 Rough Riders' Justice
1944 Texas Rifles
1945 Both Barrels Blazing
1945 Northwest Trail
1945 Rustlers of the Badlands
1945 Drifting Along
1945 The Haunted Mine
1946 Fighting Frontiersman
1946 Frontier Gunlaw
1946 South of the Chisholm Trail
1947 Prairie Riders
1947 Riders of the Lone Star
1947 The Stranger from Ponca City
1947 Smoky River Serenade
1948 Docks of New Orleans
1948 Cowboy Cavalier
1948 The Rangers Ride
1948 Steamboat Rhythm
1949 Mississippi Rhythm
1950 The Girl from San Lorenzo
1951 The Whistling Hills

ABRAHAMS, Jim
(1944–) Milwaukee, Wisconsin, USA.
1980 Airplane **(David ZUCKER, Jerry ZUCKER)**
1984 Top Secret **(David ZUCKER, Jerry ZUCKER)**
1986 Ruthless People **(David ZUCKER, Jerry ZUCKER)**
1988 Big Business

ABULADZE, Tengiz
1988 Repentance

ACIN, Jovan
1986 Hey Babu Riba
1988 Paratrooper

ACKLAND, Rodney
(1908–)
Autobiography: The Celluloid Mistress.
1942 Thursday's Child

ACOMBA, David
1973 Slipstream
1982 Hank Williams: The Show He Never Gave
1989 Night Life

ADAMS, Catlin
1987 Sticky Fingers

ADAMS, Neal
1988 Death to the Pee-Wee Squad

ADAMSON, Al
1964 Two Tickets to Terror
1969 Gun Riders
1969 Blood of Dracula's Castle
1970 Satan's Sadists
1970 Hell's Bloody Devils / *The Fakers*
1971 Five Bloody Graves
1971 Horror of the Blood Monsters
1971 The Female Bunch
1971 The Last of the Comancheros
1972 Blood of Ghastly Horror
1972 The Brain of Blood
1972 Doomsday Voyage
1973 Dracula Versus Frankenstein
1974 The Dynamite Brothers
1974 Girls for Rent
1975 The Naughty Stewardesses
1975 Stud Brown
1975 Blazing Stewardesses
1976 Jessie's Girls
1976 Black Heat
1977 Cinderella 2000
1977 Black Samurai
1978 Sunset Cove
1978 Death Dimension
1978 Nurse Sherri
1980 Freeze Bomb
1981 Black Heat
1982 Carnival Magic

ADAMSON, Victor
(1890–1972) American.
1930 Sagebrush Politics
1930 Sweeping Against the Winds
1930 Desert Vultures
1931 Fighting Romance
1931 Lightning Bill
1931 Rawhide Romance
1931 Ridin' Speed
1932 Boss Cowboy
1932 Circle Canyon
1932 Lightning Range
1932 The Fighting Cowboy
1932 Range Busters
1934 Arizona Trail
1936 Desert Mesa
1938 Mormon Conquest
1963 Halfway to Hell

ADDISS, Jud
1958 The Cry Baby Killer

ADLER, Lou
1978 Up in Smoke
1982 Ladies and Gentlemen...The Fabulous Stains

ADLON, Percy
(1935–) Munich, Germany.
1981 Celeste
1982 Five Last Days
1983 The Swing
1985 Sugarbaby
1988 Bagdad Café / *Out of Rosenheim*

ADLUM, Ed
1976 Invasion of the Blood Farmers

ADOLFI, John G
(1888–1933) American.
1924 Chalk Marks
1925 The Phantom Express
1926 The Checkered Flag
1927 Husband Hunters
1927 What Happened to Father?
1928 The Little Snob
1928 The Midnight Taxi
1929 Evidence
1929 Fancy Baggage
1929 In the Headlines
1929 Show of Shows
1930 College Lovers
1930 Dumbbells in Ermine
1930 Recaptured Love
1930 Sinners' Holiday
1931 Alexander Hamilton
1931 Compromised
1931 The Millionaire
1932 A Successful Calamity
1932 Central Park
1932 The Man Who Played God / *The Silent Voice*
1933 The King's Vacation
1933 The Working Man
1933 Voltaire

ADREON, Franklin
(1902–) American.
1955 No Man's Woman
1956 The Man Is Armed
1956 Terror at Midnight
1956 Hell's Crossroads
1962 The Nun and the Sergeant
1966 Cyborg 2087
1966 Dimension Five

AGRAZ, Jose Luis Garcia
(1952–) Mexico City, Mexico.
1984 Nocout
1985 Dreams of Gold **(Eric WESTON)**
1986 Las Noches del Califas
1987 Approved Exam
1988 Treasure of the Moon Goddess

AHEARN, Charlie
1983 Wild Style

AINSWORTH, John
1963 The Bay of St Michel

AKKAD, Moustapha
1977 The Message / *Mohammad, Message of God*
1981 Lion of the Desert

ALDA, Alan
(1938–) New York, New York, USA. Biographies: An Unauthorised Biography by Jason Bonderoff. A Biography by Raymond Strait.
1981 The Four Seasons
1986 Sweet Liberty
1988 A New Life

ALDRICH, Robert
(1918–1983) Cranston, Rhode Island, USA.
1953 The Big Leaguer
1954 Apache
1954 Vera Cruz
1954 World for Ransom
1955 The Big Knife
1955 Kiss Me Deadly
1956 Attack!
1956 Autumn Leaves
1957 The Garment Jungle **(Vincent SHERMAN)**
1959 The Angry Hills
1959 Ten Seconds to Hell
1961 The Last Sunset
1962 Whatever Happened to Baby Jane?
1962 Sodom and Gomorrah
1963 Four for Texas
1965 Hush, Hush, Sweet Charlotte
1966 Flight of the Phoenix
1967 The Dirty Dozen
1968 The Killing of Sister George
1968 The Legend of Lylah Clare
1970 Too Late the Hero
1971 The Grissom Gang
1972 Ulzana's Raid
1973 Emperor of the North Pole
1974 The Longest Yard / *The Mean Machine*
1975 Hustle
1977 The Choirboys
1977 Twilight's Last Gleaming
1979 The Frisco Kid
1981 California Dolls / *All the Marbles...*

ALIX, Steven
1988 Channel One **(David BRADY)**

ALLAND, William
(1916–) American.
1961 Look in Any Window

ALLEGRET, Marc *
(1900–1973) Basel, Switzerland.
1932 Fanny
1937 Heart of Paris / *Gribouille*
1938 The Curtain Rises / *Entrée des Artistes*
1942 Twilight / *La Belle Aventure*
1948 Blanche Fury
1949 The Naked Heart / *Maria Chapdelaine*
1950 Blackmailed
1955 Sweet Sixteen / *Futures Vedettes*
1956 Mam'zelle Striptease / *Please Mr Balzac / En Effeuillant la Marguerite*
1958 Blonde for Danger / *Sois Belle et Tais-Toi*

ALLEN, Corey
(1934–) Cleveland, Ohio, USA.
1971 Pinocchio
1977 Thunder and Lightning
1978 Avalanche
(also many TV movies)

ALLEN, Fred (John F Sullivan)
(1894–1956) American.
Autobiography: Much Ado About Me.
1931 Freighters of Destiny
1932 Ride Him Cowboy
1933 The Mysterious Rider
1933 Beyond the Rockies
1933 Ghost Valley
1933 Partners
1933 Saddle Buster

ALLEN, Irving
(1905–) Polish-American.
1946 Avalanche
1946 High Conquest
1946 Strange Voyage
1948 Sixteen Fathoms Deep
1951 Slaughter Trail

ALLEN, Irwin
(1916–) New York, New York, USA.
1957 The Story of Mankind
1960 The Lost World
1961 Voyage to the Bottom of the Sea
1962 Five Weeks in a Balloon
1974 The Towering Inferno *(Fire sequences only)* **F***
1978 The Swarm
1979 Beyond the Poseidon Adventure

ALLEN, Lewis
(1905–) British.
1944 Our Hearts Were Young and Gay
1944 The Uninvited
1945 The Unseen
1945 Those Endearing Young Charms
1946 Desert Fury
1946 The Imperfect Lady / *Mrs Loring's Secret*
1946 The Perfect Marriage
1948 Sealed Verdict
1948 So Evil My Love
1949 Chicago Deadline
1951 Appointment with Danger
1951 Valentino
1952 At Sword's Point / *Sons of the Musketeers*
1954 Suddenly
1955 A Bullet for Joey
1955 Illegal
1958 Another Time, Another Place
1959 Whirlpool
1965 Decision at Midnight

ALLEN, Woody (Allen Stewart Konigsberg)
(1935–) Brooklyn, New York, USA.
Biographies: An Illustrated Biography by Myles Palmer; A Biography by Lee Guthrie; Joking Aside by Gerald McKnight.
1966 What's Up Tiger Lily?
1968 Take the Money and Run
1971 Bananas
1972 Everything You Always Wanted to Know About Sex
1973 Sleeper
1975 Love and Death
1977 Annie Hall **D** F****
1978 Interiors **D***
1979 Manhattan
1980 Stardust Memories
1982 A Midsummer Night's Sex Comedy
1983 Zelig
1983 Broadway Danny Rose **D***
1985 The Purple Rose of Cairo
1986 Hannah and Her Sisters **D* F***
1987 Radio Days
1987 September
1989 Another Woman
1989 New York Stories **(Francis Ford COPPOLA, Martin SCORSESE)**
1989 Brothers

ALMODOVAR, Pedro
1984 What Have I Done to Deserve This?
1987 Law of Desire
1988 Women on the Verge of a Nervous Breakdown

ALMOND, Paul
(1931–) Montreal, Quebec, Canada.
1962 Backfire
1968 Isabel
1970 Act of the Heart
1972 Journey
1980 Final Assignment
1983 Ups and Downs
1987 Captive Hearts

ALONZO, John A
(1934–) Dallas, Texas, USA.
1978 FM / *Citizen's Band*
(also many TV movies)

ALSTON, Emmett
1981 New Year's Evil
1985 Deadly Warriors / *Nine Deaths of the Ninja*
1987 Tiger Shark
1988 Demonwarp
1989 Force of the Ninja

ALTMAN, Herbert S
1971 Dirtymouth

ALTMAN, Robert
(1925–) Kansas City, Missouri, USA.
1957 The Delinquents
1968 Countdown
1969 That Cold Day in the Park
1970 M*A*S*H* **D* F***
1970 Brewster McCloud
1971 McCabe and Mrs Miller
1972 Images
1973 The Long Goodbye
1974 Thieves Like Us
1974 California Split
1976 Nashville **D* F***
1976 Buffalo Bill and the Indians, or Sitting Bull's History Lesson
1977 Three Women
1978 A Wedding
1979 A Perfect Couple

1979 Quintet
1979 Health
1980 Popeye
1982 Come Back to the Five and Dime Jimmy Dean, Jimmy Dean
1983 Streamers
1984 Secret Honour
1985 O.C. and Stiggs
1985 Fool for Love
1987 Beyond Therapy
1987 Aria **(Bruce BERESFORD, Bill BRYDEN, Jean-luc GODARD, Derek JARMAN, Franc RODDAM, Nicolas ROEG, Ken RUSSELL, Charles STURRIDGE, Julien TEMPLE)**
1989 The Room
1989 The Dumb Waiter

ALTON, Robert (Robert Alton Hart)
(1897–1957) American.
1947 Merton of the Movies
1950 Pagan Love Song

ALVES, Joe
(1938–) San Leandro, California, USA.
1983 Jaws 3-D
1990 Adventure 1

AMATEAU, Rodney
(1923–) New York, New York, USA.
1951 The Bushwhackers
1952 Monsoon
1970 Pussycat, Pussycat I Love You
1971 The Statue
1972 Where Does It Hurt?
1976 Drive-In
1978 The Seniors
1978 Hitler's Son
1984 Lovelines
1987 Garbage Pail Kids
(also many TV comedy shorts)

AMENTA, Pinto
1988 Boulevard of Broken Dreams

AMIEL, Jon
1989 Queen of Hearts

AMIR, Gideon
1986 P.O.W. The Escape / *Behind Enemy Lines*

AMY, George J
(1903–) American.
1933 She Had to Say Yes **(Busby BERKELEY)**
1939 Kid Nightingale
1940 Gambling on the High Seas
1940 Granny Get Your Gun

AMYES, Julian
(1917–) British.
1956 A Hill in Korea / *Hell in Korea*
1957 Miracle in Soho

ANDERSON, Andy
1987 Positive I.D.

ANDERSON, Lindsay
(1923–) Bangalore, India.
1963 This Sporting Life
1968 If. . .
1973 O Lucky Man!
1974 In Celebration
1982 Britannia Hospital
1987 The Whales of August
(also many documentaries)

ANDERSON, Michael
(1920–) London, England.
1949 Private Angelo **(Peter USTINOV)**
1950 Waterfront
1951 Hell Is Sold Out
1951 Night Was Our Friend
1953 Will Any Gentleman?
1955 The House of the Arrow
1956 The Dam Busters
1956 1984
1956 Around the World in Eighty Days **(Kevin McCLORY) D* F****
1957 Yangtse Incident / *Battle Hell / Escape of the Amethyst*
1958 Chase a Crooked Shadow
1959 The Wreck of the Mary Deare
1960 All the Fine Young Cannibals
1961 The Naked Edge
1964 Flight from Ashiya
1964 Wild and Wonderful
1964 Operation Crossbow / *The Great Spy Mission*
1965 The Quiller Memorandum
1968 The Shoes of the Fisherman
1972 Pope Joan / *The Devil's Imposter*
1975 Doc Savage, The Man of Bronze
1975 Conduct Unbecoming
1975 Logan's Run
1976 Orca — Killer Whale
1979 Dominique
1983 Murder By Phone
1984 Second Time Lucky
1985 Separate Vacations
1988 The Goldsmith's Shop
1989 Millenium

ANDERSON, Robert
1975 Swiss Bank Account

ANNAKIN, Ken
(1914–) Beverley, Yorkshire, England.
1947 Holiday Camp
1948 Miranda
1948 Broken Journey
1948 Here Come the Huggetts
1948 Quartet **(Arthur CRABTREE, Harold FRENCH, Ralph SMART)**
1949 Vote for Huggett
1949 The Huggetts Abroad
1949 Landfall
1950 Trio **(Harold FRENCH)**
1951 Hotel Sahara
1952 The Story of Robin Hood and His Merry Men **(Alex BRYCE)**
1952 The Planter's Wife / *Outpost in Malaya*
1953 The Sword and the Rose
1953 Double Confession
1954 You Know What Sailors Are
1955 The Seekers / *Land of Fury*

1956 Loser Takes All
1957 Value for Money
1958 Three Men in a Boat
1958 Across the Bridge
1958 Third Man on the Mountain
1959 Nor the Moon By Night / *Elephant Gun*
1960 Swiss Family Robinson
1962 The Hellions
1962 Very Important Person / *A Coming Out Party*
1962 The Fast Lady
1962 Crooks Anonymous
1962 The Longest Day **(Andrew MARTON, Bernard WICKI)** **F***
1965 Those Magnificent Men in Their Flying Machines, or How I Flew from London to Paris in Twenty-Five Hours and Eleven Minutes
1965 Battle of the Bulge
1966 The Informers
1967 The Long Duel
1968 The Biggest Bundle of them All
1969 Those Daring Young Men in Their Jaunty Jalopies / *Monte Carlo or Bust*
1975 Call of the Wild
1976 Paper Tiger
1979 The Fifth Musketeer
1980 Cheaper to Keep Her
1982 The Pirate Movie
1988 The Adventures of Pippi Longstocking
(also many documentary shorts)

ANNAUD, Jean-Jacques
(1943–) Jurisy, France.
1978 Black and White in Colour / *La Victoire en Chantant*
1980 Hothead / *Coup de Tête*
1982 Quest for Fire
1986 The Name of the Rose
1988 The Bear

ANNETT, Paul
1974 The Beast Must Die

ANSPAUGH, David
1986 Hoosiers / *Best Shot*
1988 Fresh Horses

ANTHONY, Joseph (J A Deuster)
(1912–) Milwaukee, Wisconsin, USA.
1956 The Rainmaker
1958 The Matchmaker
1959 Career
1961 All in a Night's Work
1966 Conquered City
1972 Tomorrow

ANTONIONI, Michelangelo
(1912–) Ferrara, Italy.
1950 Story of a Love Affair
1952 The Vanquished / *I Vinti*
1953 Camille / *The Lady with Camellias*
1953 Love in the City **(Federico FELLINI, Alberto LATTUADA, Carlo LIZZANI, Francesco MASELLI, Dino RISI)**
1957 The Cry
1961 L'Avventura
1961 The Night
1962 Eclipse
1965 Red Desert
1964 I Tre Volti **(Mauro BOLOGNINI)**
1966 Blow Up **D***
1970 Zabriskie Point
1975 The Passenger / *Professione: Reporter*
1981 Il Mistero di Oberwald
1982 Identification of a Woman

APTED, Michael
(1941–) Aylesbury, Buckinghamshire, England.
1972 Triple Echo
1974 Stardust
1977 The Squeeze
1978 Agatha
1980 Coal Miner's Daughter **F***
1981 Confidential Divide
1983 P'Tang Yang Kipperbang
1983 Gorky Park
1984 Firstborn
1987 Critical Condition
1988 Gorillas in the Mist
(also many TV movies)

ARBUCKLE, Roscoe (Fatty Arbuckle)
(1887–1933) Smith Center, Arkansas, USA.
Biography: The Day the Laughter Stopped by David A Yallop.
Pseudonym: William Goodrich.
1927 The Red Mill
(also many educational films, shorts and TV comedy shorts)

ARCAND, Denys
(1941–) Deschambault, Quebec, Canada.
1984 The Crime of Ovide Plouffe **(Gilles CARLE)**
1986 The Decline of the American Empire
(also many documentaries)

ARCHAINBAUD, George
(1890–1959) France.
1924 The Flaming Forties
1924 Christine of the Hungry Heart
1924 For Sale
1924 The Plunderer
1924 The Mirage
1924 Single Wives
1924 Shadow of the East
1924 The Storm Daughter
1925 Enticement
1925 The Necessary Evil
1925 The Scarlet Saint
1925 What Fools Men
1926 Puppets
1926 Men of Steel
1926 The Silent Lover
1927 Easy Pickings
1927 Night Life
1928 The Tragedy of Youth
1928 Woman Against the World
1928 Ladies of the Night Club
1928 Bachelor Paradise
1928 The Grain of Dust
1928 George Washington Cohen
1929 The Broadway Hoofer / *Dancing Feet*
1929 College Coquette
1929 Broadway Scandals

1929 Man in Hobbles
1929 Two Men and a Maid
1929 Voice Within
1930 Shooting Straight
1930 Framed
1930 Alias French Gertie / *Love Finds a Way*
1930 The Silver Horde
1930 The Lady Refuses
1931 Three Who Loved
1932 Men of Chance
1932 State's Attorney / *Cardigan's Last Chance*
1932 The Lost Squadron
1932 The Penguin Pool Murder
1932 Thirteen Women
1933 After Tonight / *Sealed Lips*
1933 The Big Brain / *Enemies of Society*
1934 Keep 'Em Rolling
1934 Murder on the Blackboard
1935 My Marriage
1935 Thunder in the Night
1936 The Return of Sophie Lang
1937 Blonde Trouble
1937 Clarence
1937 Hideaway Girl
1937 Hotel Haywire
1937 Thrill of a Lifetime
1938 Boy Trouble
1938 Campus Confessions / *Fast Play*
1938 Her Jungle Love
1938 Thanks for the Memory
1939 Night Work
1939 Some Like It Hot
1940 Comin' Round the Mountain
1940 Opened By Mistake
1940 Untamed
1942 Flying with Music
1943 False Colours
1943 Hoppy Serves a Writ
1943 The Kansan
1943 The Woman of the Town
1944 Alaska
1944 Mystery Man
1944 Texas Masquerade
1945 Girls of the Big House
1945 The Big Bonanza
1946 Fool's Gold
1946 The Devil's Playground
1946 Unexpected Guest
1947 Dangerous Adventure
1947 Hoppy's Holiday
1947 King of the Wild Horses
1947 The Millerson Case
1948 False Paradise
1948 Silent Conflict
1948 Strange Gamble
1948 The Dead Don't Dream
1950 Border Treasure
1950 Hunt the Man Down
1952 Apache Country
1952 Barbed Wire / *False News*
1952 Blue Canadian Rockies
1952 Night Stage to Galveston
1952 The Old West
1952 The Rough, Tough West
1952 Wagon Team
1953 Goldtown Ghost Riders
1953 On Top of Old Smoky
1953 Pack Train
1953 Saginaw Trail
1953 Winning of the West
1953 Last of the Pony Riders

ARCHER, Ted (Nello Rossati)
1987 Djano Strikes Again

ARDOLINO, Emile
1987 Dirty Dancing
1988 Chances Are / *Life After Life*

ARGENTO, Dario
(1943–) Rome, Italy.
1970 The Bird with Crystal Plumage / *The Gallery Murders*
1970 One Night at Dinner
1971 Cat O'Nine Tails
1972 Four Flies on Grey Velvet
1973 Le Cinque Giornate
1976 Deep Red
1977 Suspiria
1981 Inferno
1982 Unsane / *Tenebrae*
1985 Phenomena / *Creepers*
1987 Opera

ARISTARAIN, Adolfo
(1943–) Buenos Aires, Argentina.
1987 The Stranger

ARKIN, Alan
(1934–) New York, New York, USA.
1970 Little Murders
1977 Fire Sale

ARKLESS, Robert
1975 The Man Who Would Not Die

ARKUSH, Allan
(1948–) New York, New York, USA.
1976 Hollywood Boulevard **(Joe DANTE)**
1978 Deathsport **(Henry SUSO)**
1979 Rock 'n' Roll High School
1981 Heartbeeps
1983 Get Crazy
1988 Caddyshack II

ARLISS, Leslie
(1901–) British.
1940 The Farmer's Wife **(Norman Lee ARLISS)**
1942 The Night Has Eyes / *Terror House*
1943 The Man in Grey
1944 Love Story / *A Lady Surrenders*
1945 The Wicked Lady
1947 A Man About the House
1948 Idol of Paris
1948 Saints and Sinners
1952 The Woman's Angle
1955 Miss Tulip Stays the Night
1955 See How They Run
(also many TV movies)

ARMITAGE, George
1972 Private Duty Nurses
1972 Hit Man
1976 Vigilante Force
1989 Miami Blues

ARMSTRONG, Gillian
(1950–) Melbourne, Australia.

1976 The Singer and the Dancer
1979 My Brilliant Career
1982 Starstruck
1984 Mrs Soffel
1987 High Tide

ARMSTRONG, Michael
(1944–) Bolton, Lancashire, England.
1970 Horror House / *The Haunted House of Horror*
1970 Mark of the Devil

ARNER, Gwen
1981 My Champion

ARNO, Eddie
1988 Murder Story

ARNOLD, Jack
(1916–) New Haven, Connecticut, USA.
1953 Girls in the Night / *Life After Dark*
1953 It Came from Outer Space
1953 The Glass Web
1954 The Creature from the Black Lagoon
1955 Revenge of the Creature
1955 The Man from Bitter Ridge
1955 Tarantula
1956 Outside the Law
1956 Red Sundown
1957 The Incredible Shrinking Man
1957 The Tattered Dress
1958 Man in the Shadow / *Pay the Devil*
1958 The Lady Takes a Flyer
1958 The Space Children
1958 Monster on the Campus
1959 The Mouse That Roared
1959 No Name on the Bullet
1961 Bachelor in Paradise
1964 The Lively Set
1964 A Global Affair
1969 Hello Down There
1974 Black Eye
1975 The Games Girls Play
1975 Boss Nigger / *The Black Bounty Killer*
1977 The Swiss Conspiracy
1981 When the Snow Bled

ARNOLD, Newton
1962 Hands of a Stranger
1988 Bloodsport

ARTHUR, Karen
(1941–) Omaha, Nebraska, USA.
1976 Legacy
1979 The Mafu Cage
1987 Lady Beware
1989 Bridge to Silence
(also many TV movies)

ARTZI, Ami
1988 Purgatory

ARZNER, Dorothy
(1900–1979) San Francisco, California, USA.
1927 Fashions for Women
1927 Get Your Man
1927 Ten Modern Commandments
1928 Manhattan Cocktail
1929 The Wild Party
1930 Behind the Makeup **(Robert MILTON)**
1930 Anybody's Woman
1930 Sarah and Son
1931 Honour Among Lovers
1931 Working Girls
1932 Merrily We Go to Hell
1933 Christopher Strong
1934 Nana / *Lady of the Boulevards*
1936 Craig's Wife
1937 The Bride Wore Red
1940 Dance, Girl, Dance
1943 First Comes Courage

ASHBURNE, Derek
1970 The Politicians

ASHBY, Hal
(1936–1988) Ogden, Utah, USA.
1970 The Landlord
1971 Harold and Maude
1973 The Last Detail
1975 Shampoo
1976 Bound for Glory **F***
1978 Coming Home **D* F***
1979 Being There
1981 Second Hand Hearts
1982 Lookin' to Get Out
1985 The Slugger's Wife
1986 Eight Million Ways to Die

ASHCROFT, Ronnie
1957 The Astounding She-Monster / *Mysterious Invader*

ASHE, Richard
1976 Track of the Moon Beast

ASHER, Robert
(1915–) British.
1959 Follow a Star
1960 Make Mine a Mink
1960 The Bulldog Breed
1962 On the Beat
1963 A Stitch in Time
1965 The Early Bird
1965 The Intelligence Men / *Spylarks*
1966 Press for Time

ASHER, William
(1919–) American.
1948 Leather Gloves **(Richard QUINE)**
1956 The Shadow on the Window
1956 The 27th Day
1963 Beach Party
1963 Johnny Cool
1963 Muscle Beach Party
1964 Bikini Beach
1965 Beach Blanket Bingo
1965 How to Stuff a Wild Bikini
1966 Fireball 500
1981 Butcher, Baker, Nightmare Maker
1985 Movers and Shakers / *Dreamers*

ASHWORTH, Piers
1990 National Lampoon's Family Dies

ASKEY, David
1973 Take Me High

ASLANIAN, Samson
1986 Torment **(John HOPKINS)**

ASQUITH, Anthony
(1902–1968) London, England. Biographies: The Films of Anthony Asquith by A.S. Barnes; 'Puffin' Asquith by R.J. Minney.
1927 Shooting Stars
1928 Boadicea
1928 Underground
1928 The Runaway Princess
1929 A Cottage on Dartmoor / *Escaped from Dartmoor*
1931 Tell England / *The Battle of Gallipoli* **(Gerald BARKAS)**
1931 Dance Pretty Lady
1933 The Lucky Number
1934 Unfinished Symphony / *Lover Divine*
1935 Moscow Nights / *I Stand Condemned*
1938 Pygmalion **(Leslie HOWARD) F***
1940 Freedom Radio / *Voice in the Night*
1940 Quiet Wedding
1940 Channel Incident
1941 Rush Hour
1941 Cottage to Let / *Bombsite Stolen*
1942 Uncensored
1943 We Dive at Dawn
1943 The Demi-Paradise / *Adventure for Two*
1943 Welcome to Britain
1944 Fanny By Gaslight / *Man of Evil*
1944 Two Fathers
1945 The Way to the Stars / *Johnny in the Clouds*
1947 While the Sun Shines
1948 The Winslow Boy
1950 The Woman in Question / *Five Angles on Murder*
1950 The Browning Version
1951 The Importance of Being Earnest
1952 The Net / *Project M7*
1952 The Final Test
1955 The Young Lovers / *Chance Meeting*
1955 On Such a Night
1956 Carrington VC / *Court-Martial*
1958 Orders to Kill
1958 The Doctor's Dilemma
1959 Libel
1960 The Millionairess
1960 Zero
1961 Two Living, One Dead
1962 Guns of Darkness
1963 The VIP's
1963 An Evening with the Royal Ballet
1964 The Yellow Rolls Royce

ATKINS, Thomas
1934 The Silver Streak
1934 Mutiny Ahead
1946 Hi Gaucho

ATTENBOROUGH, Sir Richard
(1923–) Cambridge, Cambridgeshire, England.
1969 Oh! What a Lovely War
1972 Young Winston
1977 A Bridge Too Far **(Sidney HAYERS)**
1978 Magic
1982 Gandhi **D** F****
1985 A Chorus Line
1987 Cry Freedom / *Asking for Trouble*

ATTIAS, Daniel
1985 Silver Bullet

AUDLEY, Michael
1958 The Mark of the Hawk

AUER, John H
(1906–1975) Hungary.
1934 The Pervert
1934 Rest in Peace
1935 The Crime of Dr Crespi
1937 A Man Betrayed
1937 Circus Girl
1937 Rhythm in the Clouds
1938 A Desperate Adventure
1938 Invisible Enemy
1938 I Stand Accused
1938 Orphans of the Street
1938 Outside of Paradise
1939 Calling All Marines
1939 Forged Passport
1939 S.O.S. Tidal Wave
1939 Smuggled Cargo
1940 The Hit Parade of 1941
1940 Thou Shalt Not Kill
1940 Women in War
1941 The Devil Pays Off
1942 Johnny Doughboy
1942 Moonlight Masquerade
1942 Pardon My Stripes
1943 Gangway for Tomorrow
1943 Tahiti Honey
1944 Music in Manhattan
1944 Seven Days Ashore
1945 Pan Americana
1947 Beat the Band
1947 The Flame
1948 I, Jane Doe / *Diary of a Bride*
1948 Angel on the Amazon / *Drums Along the Amazon*
1950 Hit Parade of 1951
1950 The Avengers
1952 Thunderbirds
1953 The City That Never Sleeps
1954 Hell's Half Acre
1957 Johnny Trouble

AUGUST, Bille
(1948–) Danish.
1978 Honeymoon
1983 Zappa
1984 Twist and Shout
1985 Buster's World
1987 Pelle the Conqueror

AURTHER, Robert Alan
(1922–1978) American.
1969 The Lost Man

AUSTIN, Ray
(1932–) London, England.
1970 It's the Only Way to Go
1971 Fun and Games
1972 The Virgin Witch
1973 House of the Living Dead
(also many TV movies)

AUZINS, Igor
1977 High Rolling
1983 We of the Never-Never
1984 Coolangatta Gold
1989 The Gold and the Glory

AVAKIAN, Aram
(1926–) New York, New York, USA.
1961 Lad: A Dog **(Leslie H MARTINSON)**
1970 End of the Road
1973 Cops and Robbers
1974 11 Harrowhouse

AVEDIS, Howard Hikmet
1973 The Stepmother
1974 The Teacher
1975 Dr Minx
1975 The Specialist
1976 Scorchy
1978 Texas Detour
1980 The Fifth Floor
1981 Separate Ways
1983 Mortuary
1984 They're Playing with Fire
1987 Kidnapped

AVERBACK, Hy
(1925–) American.
1966 Chamber of Horrors
1968 Where Were You When the Lights Went Out?
1968 I Love You, Alice B Toklas
1969 The Great Bank Robbery
1970 Suppose They Gave a War and Nobody Came
1984 Where the Boys Are
(also many TV movies and Comedy TV shorts)

AVILDSEN, John G
(1937–) Chicago, Illinois, USA.
1969 Turn on to Love
1970 Guess What We Learned in School Today?
1970 Joe
1971 Cry Uncle! / *Super Dick*
1972 Okay Bill
1972 The Stoolie
1973 Save the Tiger
1975 Fore Play **(Robert McCARTY, Bruce MALMUTH)**
1975 W.W. and the Dixie Dancekings
1976 Rocky **D** F****
1978 Slow Dancing in the Big City
1980 The Formula
1982 Neighbours
1983 A Night in Heaven
1984 The Karate Kid
1986 The Karate Kid II
1987 Happy New Year
1988 For Keeps / *Maybe Baby*
1988 Guardian Angels
1989 Lean on Me
1989 The Karate Kid III

AVILDSEN, Tom
1982 Things Are Tough All Over

AXEL, Gabriel
1988 Babette's Feast
1989 Martin

AXELROD, George
(1922–) New York, New York, USA.
1966 Lord Love a Duck
1968 The Secret Life of an American Wife

AYRES, Lew (Lewis Ayer)
(1908–) Minneapolis, Minnesota, USA.
1936 Hearts in Bondage
1955 Altars of the East

AZZOPARDI, Mario
1987 Nowhere to Hide

BABENCO, Hector
1975 King of the Night
1978 Lucio Flavio
1981 Pixote
1985 Kiss of the Spider Woman **D* F***
1988 Ironweed
1988 The Second Killing of the Dog

BACON, Lloyd
(1890–1955) San Jose, California, USA.
1926 Private Izzy Murphy
1926 Broken Hearts of Hollywood
1927 Finger Prints
1927 White Flannels
1927 The Heart of Maryland
1927 A Sailor's Sweetheart
1927 Brass Knuckles
1928 The Lion and the Mouse
1928 Pay As You Enter
1928 Women They Talk About
1928 The Singing Fool
1929 Honky Tonk
1929 No Defense
1929 Say It with Songs
1929 Stark Mad
1930 A Notorious Affair
1930 Moby Dick
1930 She Couldn't Say No
1930 So Long Lefty
1930 The Office Wife
1930 The Other Tomorrow
1931 Fifty Million Frenchmen
1931 Gold Dust Gertie
1931 Honour of the Family
1931 Kept Husbands
1931 Sit Tight
1932 Crooner
1932 Fireman, Save My Child
1932 Manhattan Parade
1932 Miss Pinkerton
1932 The Famous Ferguson Case
1932 You Said a Mouthful
1933 42nd Street **F***
1933 Mary Stevens, M.D.
1933 Picture Snatcher
1933 Son of a Soldier
1933 Footlight Parade
1934 A Very Honourable Guy
1934 Here Comes the Navy **F***
1934 He Was Her Man
1934 Six-Day Bike Rider
1935 Wonder Bar
1935 Broadway Gondolier

1935 Devil Dogs of the Air
1935 Frisco Kid
1935 In Caliente
1935 The Irish in Us
1936 Cain and Mabel
1936 Gold Diggers of 1937
1936 Sons o' Guns
1937 Ever Since Eve
1937 Marked Woman
1937 San Quentin
1937 Submarine
1938 A Slight Case of Murder
1938 Boy Meets Girl
1938 Cowboy from Brooklyn / *Romance and Rhythm*
1938 Racket Busters
1939 Espionage Agent
1939 Indianapolis Speedway
1939 The Oklahoma Kid
1939 Wings of the Navy
1940 A Child Is Born
1940 Brother Orchid
1940 Knute Rockne, All American / *A Modern Hero*
1940 Invisible Stripes
1940 Three Cheers for the Irish
1941 Affectionately Yours
1941 Footsteps in the Dark
1941 Honeymoon for Three
1941 Navy Blues
1942 Larceny, Inc.
1942 Silver Queen
1943 Action in the North Atlantic
1943 Sunday Dinner for a Soldier
1944 The Sullivans
1945 Captain Eddie
1946 Home Sweet Homicide
1946 Wake Up and Dream
1947 I Wonder Who's Kissing Her Now
1948 Don't Trust Your Husband
1948 Give My Regards to Broadway
1948 You Were Meant for Me
1949 It Happens Every Spring
1949 Miss Grant Takes Richmond / *Innocence Is Bliss*
1949 Mother Is a Freshman / *Mother Knows Best*
1950 The Fuller Brush Girl / *The Affairs of Sally*
1950 The Good Humour Man
1950 Kill the Umpire
1951 Call Me Mister
1951 The Golden Girl
1951 The Frogmen
1953 The Great Sioux Uprising
1953 The I Don't Care Girl
1953 Walking My Baby Back Home
1954 She Couldn't Say No / *Beautiful But Dangerous*
1954 The French Line
(also many silent shorts)

BADAT, Randall
1983 Surf II / *The Nerds Strike Back*

BADGER, Clarence
(1880–1964) San Francisco, California, USA.
1924 The Shooting of Dan McGrew
1924 Painted People
1924 One Night in Rome
1925 New Lives for Old
1925 Paths to Paradise
1925 The Golden Princess
1926 Miss Brewster's Millions
1926 The Campus Flirt
1926 Hands Up
1926 The Rainmaker
1927 Manpower
1927 Senorita
1927 It
1927 Swim Girl Swim
1927 She's a Sheik
1927 A Kiss in the Taxi
1928 The Fifty-Fifty Girl
1928 Hot News
1928 Red Hair
1928 Three Weekends
1928 Paris
1929 No, No, Nanette
1929 Murder Will Out
1930 The Bad Man
1931 Sweethearts and Wives
1931 The Hot Heiress
1931 Woman Hungry / *The Challenge*
1931 Party Husband
1933 When Strangers Marry
1939 Rangle River
1941 That Certain Something
(also many silent shorts)

BADHAM, John
(1939–) England. American.
1976 The Bingo Long Travelling All Stars and Motor Kings
1977 Saturday Night Fever
1979 Dracula
1981 Whose Life Is It Anyway?
1983 Blue Thunder
1983 Wargames
1985 American Flyers
1986 Short Circuit
1987 Stakeout
(also many TV movies)

BADIYI, Reza
(1936–) Iran.
1972 Death of a Stranger
1973 Trader Horn
(also many TV movies)

BAER jnr, Max
(1937–) Oakland, California, USA.
1975 The Wild McCullochs
1976 Ode to Billy Joe
1979 Hometown USA.

BAFALOUKOS, Ted
(1946–) Athens, Greece.
1979 Rockers

BAGGOTT, King
(1874–1948) St Louis, Missouri, USA.
1924 The Gaiety Girl
1924 The Whispered Name
1925 Tumbleweeds
1925 The Home-Maker
1925 Raffles, the Amateur Cracksman
1926 Lovely Mary
1927 Down the Stretch

1927 Perch of the Devil

BAIL, Chuck
1974 Black Samson
1975 Casino of Gold
1976 The Gumball Rally
1986 On Dangerous Grounds / *Choke Canyon*

BAILEY, Patrick
(1947–) Crawfordsville, Indiana, USA.
1984 Door to Door

BAILEY, Rex
1953 Mexican Manhunt
1953 Fangs of the Arctic
1953 Northern Patrol

BAILEY, Richard
1975 Win, Place or Steal

BAIN, Bill
1971 What Became of Jack and Jill?

BAKER, Fred
1986 Murder She Sings

BAKER, Graham
1981 The Final Conflict
1984 Impulse
1988 Alien Nation / *Outer Heat*

BAKER, Robert S
(1916–) British.
1950 Blackout **(Monty BERMAN)**
1952 13 East Street
1953 The Steel Key
1956 Passport to Treason
1959 Jack the Ripper **(Monty BERMAN)**
1960 The Siege of Sidney Street **(Monty BERMAN)**
1960 The Hellfire Club **(Monty BERMAN)**
1961 The Treasure of Monte Cristo **(Monty BERMAN)**

BAKER, Roy Ward
(1916–) London, England.
1947 The October Man
1948 The Weaker Sex
1949 Paper Orchid
1950 Morning Departure / *Operation Disaster*
1951 Highly Dangerous
1951 The House in the Square / *I'll Never Forget You*
1952 Don't Bother to Knock
1952 Night Without Sleep
1953 Inferno
1955 Passage Home
1956 Jacqueline
1956 Tiger in Smoke
1958 The One That Got Away
1958 A Night to Remember
1962 The Singer Not the Song
1962 Flame in the Streets
1962 The Valiant **(Giorgio CAPITANI)**
1963 Two Left Feet
1968 Quatermass and the Pit / *Five Million Years to Earth*
1968 The Anniversary
1970 Moon Zero Two
1970 The Vampire Lovers
1971 The Scars of Dracula
1972 Dr Jekyll and Sister Hyde
1972 Asylum
1973 The Vault of Horror
1973 And Now the Screaming Starts
1979 The Legend of the Seven Golden Vampires / *The Seven Brothers Meet Dracula*
1981 The Monster Club

BALABAN, Bob
1988 Parents

BALABAN, Burt
(1922–1965) American.
1954 Stranger from Venus
1957 Lady of Vengeance
1958 High Hell
1960 Murder Inc. **(Steven ROSENBERG)**
1961 Mad Dog Coll
1966 The Gentle Rain

BALDI, Ferdinando
1960 David and Goliath **(Richard POTTIER)**
1961 Duel of Champions **(Terence YOUNG)**
1972 Blindman
1976 Get Mean
1976 My Name Is Guilty
1977 The Sicilian Connection
1981 Comin' at Ya!
1983 Treasure of the Four Crowns

BALDWIN, Tom
1988 Order of the Eagle
1989 Invasion Force

BALLARD, Carroll
(1937–) Los Angeles, California, USA.
1979 The Black Stallion
1983 Never Cry Wolf
1986 The Nutcracker

BALLARD, John
1979 The Orphan

BANCROFT, Anne (Anna Maria Louise Italiano)
(1931–) Bronx, New York, USA.
Biography: Seesaw by William Holzman.
1980 Fatso

BAND, Albert (Alfredo Antonini)
(1924–) Paris, France.
1956 The Young Guns
1957 I Bury the Living
1959 Face of Fire
1962 The Avenger
1965 Massacre at the Grand Canyon
1966 The Tramplers
1977 Dracula's Dog / *Zoltan, Hound of Dracula*
1979 She Came to the Valley
1987 Ghoulies II

BAND, Charles
(1952–) Los Angeles, California, USA.
1977 Crash
1982 Parasite
1983 Metalstorm: The Destruction of Jared-Syn
1985 The Dungeonmaster / *Ragewar* **(David ALLEN, John BUECHLER, Peter MANOOGIAN, Ted NICOLAOU, Stephen STAFFORD, Rose-Marie TURKO)**
1985 Trancers / *Future Cop*
1988 Pulse Pounders: The Evil Clergyman; Trancers II: The Return of Jack Deth; Dungeonmaster II: A Sorceror's Nightmare
1989 Primevals **(David ALLEN)**

BANK, Mirra
1985 Enormous Changes at the Last Minute **(Ellen HOVDE)**

BANKS, Monty (Mario Bianchi)
(1897–1950) Italian.
1928 Cocktails
1929 Eve's Fall
1929 The Compulsory Husband
1929 Not So Quiet in the Western Front
1930 Why Sailors Leave Home
1930 Almost a Honeymoon
1930 Old Soldiers Never Die
1931 What a Night
1931 My Wife's Family
1932 Tonight's the Night
1932 Money for Nothing
1933 Heads We Go
1933 You Made Me Love You
1934 Falling in Love
1934 The Girl in Possession
1934 Father and Son
1935 No Limit
1935 This Woman Is Mine
1935 So You Won't Talk?
1935 Hello Sweetheart
1935 The Church Mouse
1935 Man of the Moment
1936 Keep Your Seats Please
1936 Queen of Hearts
1938 We're Going to Be Rich
1938 Keep Smiling / *Smiling Along*
1939 Shipyard Sally
1941 Great Guns

BARABASH, Uri
1983 Stigma
1985 Beyond These Walls
1988 Unsettled Land / *Once We Were Dreamers*

BARAN, Jack
1971 Roommates

BARDEW, J A
1969 The Last Day of the War

BARE, Richard I
(1909–) American.
1948 Smart Girls Don't Talk
1949 Flaxy Martin
1949 The House Across the Street
1950 This Side of the Law
1950 Return of the Frontiersman
1953 Prisoners of the Casbah
1956 The Outlanders
1956 The Storm Riders
1957 The Travellers
1957 Shoot-Out at Medicine Bend
1958 Girl on the Run
1960 This Rebel Breed
1973 Wicked, Wicked
1986 Sudden Target
1987 The Toolbox Murders II

BARKER, Clive
1987 Hellraiser
1989 Nightbreed

BARKER, Reginald
(1886–1937) Scotland.
1924 The Great Divide
1924 The Dixie Handicap
1925 The White Desert
1925 When the Door Opened
1926 The Flaming Forest
1927 The Frontiersman
1929 Seven Keys to Baldpate
1929 New Orleans
1929 The Mississippi Gambler
1930 The Great Divide
1930 Hide-Out
1934 The Moonstone
1935 The Healer
1935 Women Must Dress
1936 Forbidden Heaven

BARNARD, Michael
1985 Shopping Mall
1987 Nights in White Satin

BARNETT, Ivan
1949 The Fall of the House of Usher

BARNETT, William H
1975 Nothing By Chance

BARNWELL, John
1956 Huk!
1959 Surrender, Hell!

BARON, Allen
(1935–) New York, New York, USA.
1961 Blast of Silence
1964 Pie in the Sky
1966 Terror in the City
1970 Red, White and Blue
1972 Outside In
1981 Fox Fire Light

BARRETO, Bruno *
1977 Dona Flor and Her Two Husbands
1983 Gabriela
1983 Happily Ever After
1989 Show of Force

BARRETT, Lezli-An
1987 Business As Usual

BARRIS, Chuck
1980 The Gong Show

BARRON, Arthur
1973 Jeremy
1977 Brothers

BARRON, Steven
(1956–) Dublin, Republic of Ireland.
1984 Electric Dreams
1989 Teenage Mutant Ninja Turtles

BARRON, Zelda
1984 Secret Places
1988 Shag
1989 The Bulldance

BARROWS, Nicholas
1937 Dangerous Holiday

BARRY, Donald (Donald Barry d'Acosta)
(1912–1980) American.
1954 Jesse James' Woman

BARRY, Ian
1988 Outback

BARRY, Michael
1974 The Second Coming of Suzanne

BARRY, Wesley
1952 The Steel Fist
1954 Racing Blood
1954 The Outlaw's Daughter

BARRYMORE, Dick
1969 Last of the Ski Bums

BARRYMORE, Lionel (Lionel Blythe)
(1878–1954) Philadelphia, Pennsylvania, USA.
Autobiography: We Barrymores.
1929 Confession
1929 His Glorious Night / *Breath of Scandal*
1929 Madame X **D***
1929 The Unholy Night
1930 The Rogue Song
1931 Ten Cents a Dance

BARSHA, Leon
1937 One Man Justice
1937 Trapped
1937 Two Fisted Sheriff
1937 Two Gun Law
1938 Who Killed Gail Preston?
1938 Convicted
1939 Manhattan Shakedown
1939 Special Inspector
1952 The Place That Thrills

BARTEL, Paul
(1938–) Brooklyn, New York, USA.
1972 Private Parts
1975 Death Race 2000
1976 Cannonball / *Carquake*
1982 Eating Raoul
1984 Not for Publication
1985 Lust in the Dust
1986 The Longshot
1988 Frankencar
1988 Scenes from the Class Struggle in Beverly Hills

BARTLETT, Hall
(1922–) Kansas City, Missouri, USA.
1955 Unchained
1957 Drango **(Jules BRICKEN)**
1957 Zero Hour
1960 All the Young Men
1963 The Caretakers / *Borderlines*
1969 Changes
1972 The Wild Pack / *The Sandpit Generals*
1973 Jonathan Livingston Seagull
1978 The Children of Sanchez
1986 Leaving Home

BARTLETT, Richard
1955 The Lonesome Trail
1955 The Silver Star
1956 I've Lived Before
1956 Rock, Pretty Baby
1956 Two Gun Lady
1957 Joe Dakota
1957 Slim Carter
1958 Money, Women and Guns

BARTMAN, William S
1982 O'Hara's Wife

BARTON, Charles T
(1902–1981) American.
1934 Wagon Wheels
1935 Car No 99.
1935 Rocky Mountain Mystery
1935 The Last Outpost **(Louis J GASNIER)**
1936 And Sudden Death
1936 Nevada
1936 Murder with Pictures
1936 Rose Bowl / *O'Brien's Luck*
1936 Timothy's Quest
1937 Forlorn River
1937 The Crime Nobody Saw
1937 Thunder Train
1938 Born to the West
1939 Behind Prison Gates
1939 Five Little Peppers and How They Grew
1940 Babies for Sale
1940 Five Little Peppers at Home
1940 Five Little Peppers in Trouble
1940 Island of Doomed Men
1940 My Son Is Guilty / *Crime's End*
1940 Nobody's Children
1940 Out West with the Peppers
1941 Harmon of Michigan
1941 Honolulu Lu
1941 Sing for Your Supper
1941 The Latins from Manhattan
1941 The Big Boss
1941 The Phantom Submarine
1941 The Richest Man in Town
1942 A Man's World
1942 Hello Annapolis / *Personal Honour*
1942 Lucky Legs
1942 Laugh Your Blues Away
1942 Parachute Nurse
1942 Shut My Big Mouth
1942 Sweetheart of the Fleet
1942 The Spirit of Stanford / *Fighting Spirit*
1942 Tramp, Tramp, Tramp
1943 Is Everybody Happy?
1943 Let's Have Fun
1943 Reveille with Beverly

1943 She Has What It Takes
1943 What's Buzzin' Cousin?
1944 Beautiful But Broke
1944 Hey, Rookie
1944 Jam Session
1944 Louisiana Hayride
1945 Men in Her Diary
1945 The Beautiful Cheat / *What a Woman!*
1946 Smooth As Silk
1946 The Time of Their Lives
1946 White Tie and Tails
1946 The Ghost Steps Out
1947 Buck Private Come Home
1947 The Wistful Widow of Wagon Gap
1948 Abbott and Costello Meet Frankenstein / *Abbott and Costello Meet the Ghosts*
1948 Mexican Hayride
1948 The Noose Hangs High
1949 Abbott and Costello Meet the Killer
1949 Africa Screams
1949 Free for All
1950 Double Crossbones
1950 The Milkman
1952 Ma and Pa Kettle at the Fair
1956 Dance with Me, Henry
1959 The Shaggy Dog
1960 Toby Tyler
1962 Swingin' Along

BARTON, Don
1975 Blood Waters of Dr Z

BARWOOD, Hal
1985 Biohazard / *Warning Sign*

BASKIN, Richard
1988 Sing

BASS, Saul
(1920–) New York, New York, USA.
1973 Phase IV

BASSOFF, Lawrence
1984 Weekend Pass
1987 Hunk

BAT-ADAM, Michal
1979 Moments / *Each Other*
1980 The Thin Line
1983 Young Love
1986 The Lover

BATTERSBY, Roy
1970 The Body
1984 Winter Flight

BAVA, Lamberto
(1944–) Italian.
1986 Demons
1987 Demons II: The Nightmare Returns
1988 Demons III: The Ogre
1988 Delirium

BAXLEY, Craig
1988 Action Jackson
1988 Man to Man
1989 Dark Angel

BAXTER, John
(1896–1975) British.
1933 Doss House
1933 Song of the Plough
1933 Taking Ways
1934 Lest We Forget
1934 Say It with Flowers
1934 Music Hall
1934 Floodtide
1934 Kentucky Minstrels
1935 A Real Bloke
1935 Jimmy Boy
1935 The Small Man
1935 Birds of a Feather
1936 Men of Yesterday
1936 Hearts of Humanity
1937 The Academy Decides
1937 Talking Feet
1937 Song of the Road
1938 Stepping Toes
1939 What Would You Do Chums?
1939 Secret Journey / *Among Human Wolves*
1940 Old Mother Riley in Society
1940 Laugh It Off
1940 Crook's Tour
1940 Old Mother Riley in Business
1941 Love on the Dole
1941 The Common Touch
1942 Let the People Sing
1942 We'll Smile Again
1943 Theatre Royal
1943 The Shipbuilders
1943 When We Are Married
1944 Dreaming
1945 Here Comes the Sun
1946 The Grand Escapade
1947 Fortune Lane
1947 When You Come Home
1948 Nothing Venture
1948 The Last Load
1950 The Dragon of Pendragon Castle
1950 The Second Mate
1950 Judgment Deferred
1956 Ramsbottom Rides Again

BAYLY, Stephen
1987 Coming Up Roses
1988 Just Ask for Diamond / *The Falcon's Malteser*

BEAIRD, David
1984 Octavia
1984 Party Animal
1985 My Chauffeur
1988 Pass the Ammo
1988 It Takes Two / *My New Car*

BEAL, Scott R
1935 Straight from the Heart
1938 Convicts at Large **(David FRIEDMAN)**

BEAN, Robert B
1971 Made for Each Other

BEARDE, Chris
1983 Hysterical

BEATTIE, Alan
1981 Delusion

1984 The House Where Death Lives
1985 Stand Alone

BEATTY, Warren (Warren Beaty)
(1937–) Richmond, Virginia, USA. Biography: Warren Beatty by Jim Burke.
1978 Heaven Can Wait **(Buck HENRY) D* F***
1981 Reds **D** F***
1990 Dick Tracy

BEAUDINE, William
(1892–1970) New York, New York, USA.
1924 Cornered
1925 Little Annie Rooney
1925 The Narrow Street
1925 A Broadway Butterfly
1925 How Baxter Butted In
1926 The Social Highwayman
1926 The Canadians
1926 Hold That Lion
1926 That's My Baby
1927 Frisco Sally Levy
1928 The Irresistible Lover
1928 Give and Take
1928 The Cohens and the Kellys in London
1928 Home James
1928 Do Your Duty
1929 Fugitives
1929 Hard to Get
1929 The Girl from Woolworths
1929 Two Weeks Off
1930 The Road to Paradise
1930 Those Who Dance
1930 Wedding Rings
1931 Misbehaving Ladies
1931 Penrod and Sam
1931 The Lady Who Dared
1931 The Mad Parade
1931 The Men in Her Life
1931 Father's Son
1932 Make Me a Star!
1932 Three Wise Girls
1933 Her Bodyguard
1933 The Crime of the Century
1934 The Old-Fashioned Way
1935 Boys Will Be Boys
1935 Dandy Dick
1935 Get Off My Foot
1935 Two Hearts in Harmony
1936 Educated Evans
1936 It's in the Bag
1936 Mr Cohen Takes a Walk
1936 Where There's a Will
1936 Windbag the Sailor
1937 Take It from Me
1937 Feather Your Nest
1937 Transatlantic Trouble
1938 Said O'Reilly to McNab
1938 Torchy Gets Her Man
1940 Misbehaving Husbands
1941 Desperate Cargo
1941 Emergency Landing
1941 Federal Fugitives
1941 Mr Celebrity
1941 The Blonde Comet
1942 Duke of the Navy
1942 Foreign Agent
1942 Gallant Lady
1942 Men of San Quentin
1942 One Thrilling Night
1942 Phantom Killer
1942 The Broadway Big Shot
1942 The Living Ghost / *Lend Me Your Ear*
1942 The Miracle Kid
1942 The Panther's Claw
1942 Professor Creeps
1942 Prison Girls
1943 Clancy Street Boys
1943 Ghosts on the Loose
1943 Here Comes Kelly
1943 Mr Muggs Steps Out
1943 Spotlight Scandals
1943 The Ape Man / *Lock Your Doors*
1943 The Mystery of the Thirteenth Guest
1944 Bowery Champs
1944 Crazy Knights
1944 Detective Kitty O'Day
1944 Follow the Leader
1944 Hot Rhythm
1944 Leave It to the Irish
1944 Mom and Dad / *A Family Story*
1944 Oh, What a Night
1944 Shadow of Suspicion
1944 Voodoo Man
1944 What a Man!
1945 Black Market Babies
1945 Blonde Ransom
1945 Come Out Fighting
1945 Fashion Model
1945 Swingin' on a Rainbow
1945 The Adventures of Kitty O'Day
1946 Below the Deadline
1946 Don't Gamble with Strangers
1946 Girl on the Spot
1946 Mr Hex / *Pride of the Bowery*
1946 One Exciting Week
1946 Spook Busters
1947 Bowery Buckaroos
1947 Gas House Kids Go West
1947 Hard Boiled Mahogany
1947 Killer at Large
1947 News Hounds
1947 Philo Vance Returns
1947 The Chinese Ring
1947 Too Many Winners
1948 Angel's Alley
1948 Incident
1948 Jiggs and Maggie in Court **(Edward CLINE)**
1948 Jinx Money
1948 Kidnapped
1948 Smuggler's Cove
1948 The Feathered Serpent
1948 The Golden Eye
1948 The Shanghai Chest
1949 Forgotten Women
1949 Jackpot Jitters
1949 Tough Assignment
1949 Tuna Clipper
1950 Again Pioneers!
1950 Blue Grass of Kentucky
1950 Blues Buster
1950 Blonde Dynamite
1950 Country Fair
1950 Jiggs and Maggie Out West
1950 Lucky Losers
1950 Second Chance
1951 Bowery Battalion

1951 Crazy Over Horses
1951 Cuban Fireball
1951 Ghost Chasers
1951 Havana Rose
1951 Let's Go Navy
1951 The Prince of Peace **(Harold DANIELS)**
1952 Bela Lugosi Meets a Brooklyn Gorilla
1952 Feudin' Fools
1952 Here Come the Marines
1952 Hold That Line
1952 Rodeo
1952 The Rose Bowl Story
1953 For Every Child
1953 Jalopy
1953 Murder Without Tears
1953 Roar of the Crowd
1953 The Hidden Heart
1954 More for Peace
1954 Paris Playboys
1954 Pride of the Blue Grass
1954 Yukon Vengeance
1955 Each According to His Own Faith
1955 High Society / *Bowery Boys*
1955 Jail Busters
1957 In the Money
1957 Up in Smoke
1957 Westward Ho the Wagons!
1960 Ten Who Dared
1963 Lassie's Great Adventure
1966 Billy the Kid Versus Dracula
1966 Jesse James Meets Frankenstein's Daughter
(also many silent shorts)

BEAUMONT, Gabrielle
1980 The Godsend
1987 He's My Girl / *Pulling It Off*
(also many TV movies)

BEAUMONT, Harry
(1888–1966) American.
1924 Babbitt
1924 Beau Brummell
1924 The Lover of Camille
1924 Don't Doubt Your Husband
1925 A Lost Lady
1925 Recompense
1925 His Majesty: Bunker Bean
1925 Rose of the World
1926 Sandy
1926 Womanpower
1927 One Increasing Purpose
1928 Forbidden Hours
1928 Our Dancing Daughters
1928 A Single Man
1929 Speedway
1929 The Broadway Melody **D* F****
1930 The Floradora Girl / *The Gay Nineties!*
1930 Our Blushing Brides
1930 Lord Byron of Broadway / *What Price Melody?* **(William NIGH)**
1930 Those Three French Girls
1930 Children of Pleasure
1931 Dance, Fools, Dance
1931 Laughing Sinners
1931 The Great Lover
1932 Faithless
1932 Unashamed
1932 Are You Listening?
1932 West of Broadway
1933 When Ladies Meet
1933 Made on Broadway / *The Girl I Made*
1933 Should Ladies Behave?
1934 Murder in the Private Car / *Murder on the Runaway Train*
1935 Enchanted April
1936 The Girl on the Front Page
1944 When's Your Birthday?
1944 Maisie Goes to Reno / *You Can't Do That to Me*
1945 Twice Blessed
1946 Up Goes Maisie
1946 The Show-Off
1947 Undercover Maisie
1948 Alias a Gentleman

BEAVER, Lee W *see* **Carlo LIZZANI**

BECHARD, Gorman
1984 Disconnected
1985 And Then?
1987 Psychos in Love
1988 Galactic Gigolo / *Club Earth*
1988 Assault of the Killer Bimbos
1988 Hack 'Em High
1988 Pand Evil

BECK, George
1951 Behave Yourself!

BECK, Martin
1974 Challenge
1975 The Brass Ring

BECKER, Harold
1972 The Ragman's Daughter
1979 The Onion Field
1980 The Black Marble
1981 Taps
1985 Vision Quest
1988 The Boost
1989 Sea of Love

BECKER, Terry
1975 The Thirsty Dead

BEDFORD, Terry
1983 Slayground

BEEBE, Ford
(1888–) American.
1932 The Pride of the Legion
1933 Laughing at Life
1935 Law Beyond the Range
1935 The Man from Guntown
1936 Stampede
1937 Trouble at Midnight
1937 Westbound Limited
1939 Oklahoma Frontier
1940 Son of Roaring Dan
1941 The Masked Rider
1942 The Night Monster / *House of Mystery*
1943 Frontier Badmen
1944 Enter Arsène Lupin
1944 The Invisible Man's Revenge
1945 Easy to Look At
1946 My Dog Shep
1947 Six Gun Serenade
1948 Courtin' Trouble
1948 Shep Comes Home

1949 Bomba, the Jungle Boy
1949 Bomba on Panther Island
1949 Red Desert
1949 Satan's Cradle
1949 The Dalton Gang
1950 Bomba and the Hidden City
1950 The Lost Volcano
1951 Bomba and the Elephant Stampede
1951 Bomba and the Lion Hunters
1952 Bomba and the African Treasure
1952 Bomba and the Jungle Girl
1952 Wagons West
1953 Bomba and the Safari Drums
1954 Killer Leopard
1954 The Golden Idol
1956 Lord of the Jungle
(also many serials)

BEEMAN, Greg
1988 Licence to Drive

BEINEIX, Jean-Jacques
1982 Diva
1983 The Moon in the Gutter
1986 Betty Blue / *37.2 Degrés le Matin*

BELL, Monta
(1891–1958) American.
1924 Broadway After Dark
1924 How to Educate a Wife
1924 Lady of the Night
1924 The Snob
1925 Lights of Old Broadway
1925 Pretty Ladies
1925 The Torrent
1925 The King on Main Street
1926 The Boyfriend
1926 Upstage
1927 Man, Son and Sin
1928 The Bellamy Trial
1930 East is West
1930 Young Man of Manhattan
1931 Fires of Youth
1931 Personal Maid
1931 Up for Murder
1932 Downstairs
1933 The Worst Woman in Paris?

BELLAMY, Earl
(1917–) Minneapolis, Minnesota, USA.
1955 Seminole Uprising
1956 Blackjack, Ketchum, Desperado
1958 Toughest Gun in Tombstone
1962 Stagecoach to Dancers' Rock
1965 Fluffy
1966 Incident at Phantom Hill
1966 Gunpoint
1966 Munster Go Home
1968 Three Guns for Texas **(David Lowell RICH, Paul STANLEY)**
1969 Backtrack
1975 Seven Alone
1975 Sidecar Racers
1975 Part II, Walking Tall
1975 Against a Crooked Sky
1977 Sidewinder One
1978 Speedtrap
1981 Magnum Thrust

BELLISARIO, Dan
1988 Last Rites / *Sanctuary*

BELLOCCHIO, Marco *
(1939–) Piacenza, Italy.
1965 Fist in His Pocket
1967 China Is Near
1974 Fit to Be Untied
1976 Victory March
1979 Leap into the Void
1983 The Eyes, the Mouth
1984 Henry IV / *Enrico IV*
1986 Devil in the Flesh
1987 The Visions of Sabbah

BELSON, Jerry
1982 Jekyll and Hyde. . . Together Again
1987 Surrender

BEMBERG, Maria Luisa
1981 Momentos
1982 Senora de Nadie
1984 Camila
1986 Miss Mary

BENDER, Joel
1979 Gas Pump Girls
1989 The Immortalizer

BENEDEK, Laslo (Laszlo Benedek)
(1907–) Budapest, Hungary.
1948 The Kissing Bandit
1949 Port of New York
1951 Death of a Salesman
1952 Storm Over the Tiber
1954 The Wild One
1954 Bengal Brigade / *Bengal Rifles*
1955 Kinder, Mütter und ein General
1957 Affair in Havana
1959 Malaga / *Moment of Danger*
1960 Recours en Grâce
1966 Namu, the Killer Whale
1968 Daring Game
1971 The Night Visitor
1976 Assault on Agathon

BENEDICT, Richard (Riccardo Benedetto)
(1923–) American.
1965 Winter a Go-Go
1969 Impasse

BENETT, Bill *
1985 A Street to Die
1986 Backlash
1986 Dear Cardholder
1988 Jilted
1988 Coast to Coast
1988 Sebastian and the Sparrow

BENJAMIN, Richard
(1938–) New York, New York, USA.
1982 My Favourite Year
1984 Racing with the Moon
1984 City Heat
1986 The Money Pit
1988 Little Nikita
1988 My Stepmother Is an Alien

BENNER, Richard
1977 Outrageous

1980 Happy Birthday Gemini
1987 Too Outrageous

BENNERT, Walter
1987 Young Love: Lemon Popsicle 7

BENNET, Gordon Spencer
(1893–1987) American.
1929 Hawk of the Hills
1930 Rogue of the Rio Grande
1933 Justice Takes a Holiday
1933 The Midnight Warning
1934 Badge of Honour
1934 Fighting Rookie / *Dangerous Enemy*
1934 Night Alarm
1934 The Oil Raider
1935 Calling All Cars
1935 Get That Man
1935 Heir to Trouble
1935 Lawless Riders
1935 Rescue Squad
1936 Western Courage
1936 Avenging Waters
1936 Heroes of the Range
1936 Ranger Courage
1936 The Cattle Thief
1936 The Fugitive Sheriff / *Law and Order*
1936 The Unknown Ranger
1936 Rio Grande Ranger
1937 The Law of the Ranger
1937 The Rangers Step In
1939 Reckless Ranger
1939 Oklahoma Terror
1939 Across the Plains
1939 Riders of the Frontier
1940 Cowboy from Sundown
1940 Westbound Stage
1941 Arizona Bound
1941 Gunman from Brodie
1941 Ridin' the Cherokee Trail
1942 They Raid By Night
1943 Calling Wild Bill Elliott
1943 Canyon City
1944 Beneath Western Skies
1944 California Joe
1944 Code of the Prairie
1944 Mojave Firebrand
1944 Tucson Raiders
1945 Lone Texas Ranger
1952 Brave Warrior
1952 Voodoo Tiger
1953 Killer Ape
1953 Savage Mutiny
1955 Devil Goddess
1959 Submarine Seahawk
1965 Requiem for a Gunfighter
1965 The Bounty Killer
(also many serials)

BENNETT, Charles
(1899–) British.
1949 Madness of the Heart
1953 No Escape

BENNETT, Chester
1924 The Painted Lady
1924 The Ancient Mariner **(Henry OTTO)**
1925 The Champion of the Lost Causes
1926 Honesty — The Best Policy

BENNETT, Compton (Robert Compton-Bennett)
(1900–1974) British.
1945 The Seventh Veil
1946 Daybreak
1946 The Years Between
1948 My Own True Love
1949 That Forsyte Woman
1950 King Solomon's Mines **(Andrew MARTON) F***
1952 The Gift Horse / *Glory at Sea*
1952 It Started in Paradise
1952 So Little Time
1953 Desperate Moment
1957 After the Ball
1957 The Flying Scot / *Mailbag Robbery*
1957 That Woman Opposite / *City After Midnight*
1960 Beyond the Curtain

BENNETT, Geoffrey
1989 The Boy in the Island

BENNETT, Hugh
1941 Henry Aldrich for President
1942 Henry Aldrich, Editor
1942 Henry Aldrich and Dixie
1943 Henry Aldrich Gets Glamour
1943 Henry Aldrich Haunts a House
1943 Henry Aldrich Swings It
1944 Henry Aldrich, Boy Scout
1944 Henry Aldrich Plays Cupid
1944 Henry Aldrich's Little Secret
1944 National Barn Dance

BENNETT, Richard C
1978 Harper Valley PTA
1986 A State of Emergency

BENSON, Leon
1964 Flipper's New Adventure

BENSON, Robby (Robert Segal)
(1957–) Dallas, Texas, USA.
1988 Crack in the Mirror / *White Hot*
1990 Modern Man

BENTLEY, Thomas
(1880–1953) London, England.
1924 Old Bill Through the Ages
1924 Chappy That's All
1924 A Romance of Mayfair
1925 Money Isn't Everything
1926 White Heat
1927 The Silver Lining
1928 Not Quite a Lady
1929 The American Prisoner
1929 Young Woodly
1930 Harmony Heaven
1930 Compromising Daphne
1931 Keepers of Youth
1931 Hobson's Choice
1931 After Office Hours
1932 The Last Coupon
1932 Sleepless Nights
1933 The Hawleys of High Street
1933 The Love Nest
1933 The Scotland Yard Mystery
1934 Those Were the Days
1934 The Old Curiosity Shop

1934 The Great Defender
1935 Royal Cavalcade **(Herbert BRENON, William KELLINO, Norman LEE, Walter SUMMERS, Marcel VARNEL)**
1935 Music Hath Charms **(Alexander ESWAY, Walter SUMMERS, Arthur WOODS)**
1936 She Knew What She Wanted
1937 The Last Chance
1937 Silver Blaze / *Murder at the Baskervilles*
1937 The Angelus
1938 A Night Alone
1938 Marigold
1939 Me and My Pal
1939 Dead Man's Shoes
1939 Lucky Me
1940 The Middle Watch
1940 Three Silent Men
1940 Cavalcade of Variety
1941 Old Mother Riley's Circus
(also many silent shorts)

BENTON, Robert
(1932–) Waxahachie, Texas, USA.
1972 Bad Company
1976 The Late Show
1979 Kramer Versus Kramer **D** F****
1982 Still of the Night
1984 Places in the Heart / *The Texas Project* **D* F***
1987 Nadine

BERCOVICI, Luca
1985 Ghoulies
1989 Rockula

BERESFORD, Bruce
(1940–) Sydney, New South Wales, Australia.
1972 The Adventures of Barry McKenzie
1974 Barry McKenzie Holds His Own
1976 Don's Party
1977 The Getting of Wisdom
1978 Money Movers
1980 Breaker Morant
1981 The Club
1982 Puberty Blues
1983 Tender Mercies **D* F***
1985 King David
1986 The Fringe Dwellers
1986 Crimes of the Heart
1987 Aria **(Robert ALTMAN, Bill BRYDEN, Jean-Luc GODARD, Derek JARMAN, Franc RODDAM, Nicolas ROEG, Ken RUSSELL, Charles STURRIDGE, Julien TEMPLE)**
1988 Her Alibi
(also many documentaries)

BERGER, Ludwig (Ludwig Bamberger) *
(1892–1969) German.
1926 The Waltz Room
1928 The Woman from Moscow
1928 Sins of the Fathers
1929 The Vagabond King
1930 Playboy of Paris
1933 Three Waltzes
1940 Ballerina
1940 The Thief of Bagdad **(Michael POWELL, Tim WHELAN)**

BERGER, Pamela
1989 The Imported Bridegroom

BERGMAN, Andrew
(1945–) New York, New York, USA.
1981 So Fine

BERGMAN, Ingmar (Ernst Ingmar Bergman)
(1918–) Uppsala, Sweden.
Biographies: Ingmar Bergman by Peter Cowie; Ingmar Bergman by Robin Wood.
1945 Crisis
1946 It Rains on Our Love
1947 The Land of Desire
1947 A Ship to India / *Frustration*
1948 Night Is My Future
1948 Port of Call
1948 The Devil's Wanton / *The Prison*
1949 Three Strange Loves / *Thirst*
1950 To Joy
1951 This Can't Happen Here
1951 Illicit Interlude / *Sommarlek*
1952 Secrets of Women / *Waiting Women*
1953 Monika
1953 Sawdust and Tinsel / *The Naked Night*
1954 A Lesson in Love
1955 Dreams / *Journey into Autumn*
1955 Smiles of a Summer Night
1957 The 7th Seal
1957 Wild Strawberries
1958 So Close to Life
1958 The Magician / *The Face*
1960 The Virgin Spring
1960 The Devil's Eye
1961 Through a Glass Darkly
1961 Winter Light
1963 The Silence
1964 All These Women
1966 Persona
1968 Hour of the Wolf
1968 Shame
1969 The Ritual
1969 The Passion of Anna
1971 The Touch
1972 Cries and Whispers **D* F***
1973 Scenes from a Marriage
1975 The Magic Flute
1976 Face to Face **D***
1978 The Serpent's Egg
1978 Autumn Sonata
1980 From the Life of Marionettes
1983 Fanny and Alexander **D***
1983 After the Rehearsal

BERGMAN, Robert
1988 A Scream to a Whisper
1989 Night of Retribution

BERKE, William
(1903–1958) American.
1935 The Pecos Kid
1935 Toll of the Desert
1936 Desert Justice
1936 Gun Grit
1942 Badmen of the Hills
1942 Down Rio Grande Way
1942 Lawless Plainsmen

1942 Overland to Deadwood
1942 Riders of the Northland
1942 The Lone Prairie
1942 A Tornado in the Saddle
1943 The Fighting Buckaroo
1943 Hail to the Rangers
1943 Law of the Northwest
1943 Pardon My Gun
1943 Riding Through Nevada
1943 Robin Hood of the Range
1943 Tornado
1943 Frontier Fury
1943 Minesweeper
1943 Silver City Raiders
1943 Riders of the Northwest Mounted
1943 Saddles and Sagebrush
1944 Double Exposure
1944 The Falcon in Mexico
1944 Riding West
1944 The Girl in the Case
1944 The Navy Way
1944 Sailor's Holiday
1944 That's My Baby
1944 The Vigilantes Ride
1944 Wyoming Hurricane
1944 The Last Horseman
1944 Dark Mountain
1944 Dangerous Passage
1945 Betrayal from the East
1945 Dick Tracy, Detective / *Splitface*
1945 Why Girls Leave Home
1945 High Powered
1946 The Falcon's Adventure
1946 Sunset Pass
1946 Ding Dong Williams
1947 Shoot to Kill
1947 Code of the West
1947 Renegade Girl
1948 Rolling Home
1948 Caged Fury
1948 Jungle Jim
1948 Highway 13
1948 Racing Luck
1948 Speed to Spare
1948 Waterfront at Midnight
1949 The Lost Tribe
1949 Zamba
1949 Deputy Marshal
1949 Arson Inc.
1949 Sky Liner
1949 Treasure of Monte Cristo
1950 Captive Girl
1950 Gunfire
1950 Pigmy Island
1950 Mark of the Gorilla
1950 On the Isle of Samoa
1950 Operation Haylift
1950 I Shot Billy the Kid
1950 Border Rangers
1950 Bandit Queen
1950 Everybody's Dancing
1950 Train to Tombstone
1951 FBI Girl
1951 Fury of the Congo
1951 Savage Drums
1951 Smuggler's Gold
1951 Danger Zone
1951 Pier 13
1951 Roaring City
1952 The Jungle
1953 The Marshal's Daughter
1953 Valley of the Headhunters
1957 Four Boys and a Gun
1957 Street of Sinners
1958 Cop Hater
1958 Island of Women
1958 The Muggers
1958 The Lost Missile

BERKELEY, Busby (William Berkeley Enos)
(1895–1976) Los Angeles, California, USA.
1932 Night World
1933 She Had to Say Yes
1935 Bright Lights / *Funny Face*
1935 Gold Diggers of 1935
1935 I Live for Life
1936 Stage Struck
1937 Hollywood Hotel
1937 The Go Getter
1938 Garden of the Moon
1938 Men Are Such Fools
1938 Comet Over Broadway
1939 Babes in Arms
1939 They Made Me a Criminal
1939 Fast and Furious
1940 Forty Little Mothers
1940 Strike Up the Band
1941 Babes on Broadway
1941 Blonde Inspiration
1942 For Me and My Gal
1942 Born to Sing **(Edward LUDWIG)**
1943 The Gang's All Here / *The Girls He Left Behind*
1946 Cinderella Jones
1949 Take Me Out to the Ball Game / *Everybody's Cheering*
(Busby Berkeley also choreographed many other feature films)

BERLATSKY, David
1977 The Farmer

BERLIN, Abby
1945 Leave It to Blondie
1945 Life with Blondie
1946 Blondie Knows Best
1946 Blondie's Lucky Day
1946 Blondie's in the Dough
1947 Blondie's Anniversary
1947 Blondie's Big Moment
1947 Blondie's Holiday
1948 Blondie's Reward
1949 Mary Ryan, Detective
1950 Double Deal
1950 Father Is a Bachelor **(Norman FOSTER)**

BERMAN, Monty
(1913–) British.
1950 Blackout **(Robert S BAKER)**
1956 Jack the Ripper **(Robert S BAKER)**
1960 The Hellfire Club **(Robert S BAKER)**
1960 The Siege of Sidney Street **(Robert S BAKER)**
1961 The Treasure of Monte Cristo **(Robert S BAKER)**

BERMAN, Shelley
(1926–) American.
1975 Keep Off! Keep Off!

BERN, Paul (Paul Levy)
(1889–1932) American.
Biography: A Dozen and One by Jim Tully.
1924 Worldly Goods
1924 Open All Night
1925 The Dressmaker from Paris
1925 Grounds for Divorce
1925 Tomorrow's World
1925 Flower of the Night

BERNARD, Chris
1985 A Letter to Brezhnev / *Kirby's Girls*
1987 Southie

BERNDS, Edward
(1905–) American.
1948 Blondie's Secret
1949 Blondie's Big Deal
1949 Blondie Hits the Jackpot
1949 Feudin' Rhythm
1950 Beware of Blondie
1950 Blondie's Hero
1951 Corky of Gasoline Alley
1951 Gasoline Alley
1951 Gold Raiders
1952 The Harem Girl
1953 Clipped Wings
1953 Hot News
1953 Loose in London
1953 Private Eyes
1954 Jungle Gents
1954 The Bowery Boys Meet the Monsters
1955 Spy Chasers
1956 Calling Homicide
1956 Dig That Uranium
1956 Navy Wife / *Mother, Sir!*
1956 World Without End
1957 Reform School Girl
1957 The Storm Rider
1958 Escape from Red Rock
1958 Joy Ride
1958 Quantrill's Raiders
1958 Queen of Outer Space
1958 Space Master
1959 Alaska Passage
1959 High School Hellcats
1959 Return of the Fly
1961 Valley of the Dragons
1962 The Three Stooges in Orbit
1962 The Three Stooges Meet Hercules
1966 Prehistoric Valley

BERNE, Joseph
1934 Dawn to Dawn
1944 They Live in Fear
1969 Down Missouri Way

BERNHARD, Jack
(1913–) American.
1946 Decoy
1946 Sweetheart of Sigma Chi
1946 Violence
1947 In Self Defense
1948 Appointment with Murder
1948 The Hunted
1948 Unknown Island
1948 Blond Ice
1948 Perilous Waters
1949 Search for Danger
1949 Alaska Patrol
1950 The Second Face

BERNHARDT, Curtis (Kurt Bernhardt) *
(1899–1981) Worms, Germany.
1927 The Prince of Rogues / *Schinderhannes*
1930 Three Loves
1930 Thirteen Men and a Girl
1937 The Beloved Vagabond
1938 The Girl in the Taxi
1938 Crossroads
1940 Lady with Red Hair
1940 My Love Came Back
1941 Million Dollar Baby
1942 Juke Girl
1943 Happy Go Lucky
1945 Conflict
1946 My Reputation
1946 Devotion
1946 A Stolen Life
1947 Possessed
1947 High Wall
1949 The Doctor and the Girl
1951 Payment on Demand
1951 Sirocco
1951 The Blue Veil
1952 The Merry Widow
1953 Miss Sadie Thompson
1954 Beau Brummell
1955 Interrupted Melody
1956 Gaby
1963 Stephanie in Rio
1964 Kisses for My President

BERNSTEIN, Armyan
1984 Windy City / *All the Sad Young Men*
1987 American Date / *Cross My Heart*

BERNSTEIN, Walter
(1929–) Chicago, Illinois, USA.
1980 Little Miss Marker

BERRI, Claude (Claude Langmann)
(1934–) Paris, France.
1968 The Two of Us / *Le Vieil Homme et L'Enfant*
1968 Marry Me! Marry Me! / *Mazel Tov ou le Mariage*
1970 The Man with Connections / *Le Pistonne*
1970 Le Cinéma de Papa
1973 Sex Shop
1975 Male of the Century
1976 The First Time
1978 One Wild Moment
1981 Le Maitre d'Ecole
1983 Tchao Pantin
1986 Jean de Florette
1986 Manon des Sources

BERRY, Bill
1987 Crazy Legs

BERRY, John
(1917–) New York, New York, USA.
1945 Miss Susie Slagle's
1946 From This Day Forward
1946 Cross My Heart
1948 Casbah

1949 Tension
1950 Robinson Crusoeland / *Atoll K / Escapade/ Utopia* **(Leo JOANNON)**
1951 He Ran All the Way / *Menaces dans la Nuit*
1952 C'est Arrivé à Paris
1954 Ca Va Barder
1955 Je suis un Sentimental
1956 Pantaloons / *Don Juan*
1957 Tamango
1958 OK Mambo
1966 Maya
1967 A Tout Casser
1974 Claudine
1977 Thieves
1978 Sparrow
1978 The Bad News Bears Go to Japan
1985 Le Voyage à Paimpol
1987 Bad Deal

BERRY, Tom
1987 Down Home
1988 Something About Love
1989 Blind Fear / *A Long Dark Night*
1990 The Amityville Curse

BERTHOMIEU, André *
(1903–1960) French.
1937 The Girl in the Taxi

BERTOLUCCI, Bernardo
(1940–) Parma, Italy.
1962 The Grim Reaper
1964 Before the Revolution
1968 Partner
1969 Love and Anger
1970 The Spider's Stratagem
1971 The Conformist
1973 Last Tango in Paris **D***
1977 1900
1977 Luna
1982 Tragedy of a Ridiculous Man
1987 The Last Emperor **D** F****
1989 The Sheltering Sky

BERWICK, Irwin
1958 The Monster of Piedras Biancas
1979 Malibu High

BERZ, Michael
1987 Snow White and the Seven Dwarfs

BESHEARS, James
1982 Homework

BESSIE, Dan
1986 Hard Travelling

BESSON, Luc
(1959–) French.
1983 Le Dernier Combat
1985 Subway
1988 The Big Blue

BETTMAN, Gill
1986 Never Too Young to Die
1987 Crystal Heart

BETUEL, Jonathan
1985 My Science Project

BEYMER, Richard
(1939–) American.
1974 The Interview

BIANCHI, Edward
(1942–)
1981 The Fan

BIBERMAN, Abner
(1909–1977) American.
1954 The Golden Mistress
1955 The Looters
1955 Running Wild
1955 Behind the High Wall
1956 The Price of Fear
1957 Gun for a Coward
1957 The Night Runner
1958 Flood Tide

BIBERMAN, Herbert J
(1900–1971) Philadelphia, Pennsylvania, USA.
1935 One Way Ticket
1936 Meet Nero Wolfe
1944 The Master Race
1954 Salt of the Earth
1969 Slaves

BIERMAN, Robert
1988 Vampire's Kiss

BIGELOW, Kathryn
1981 The Loveless / *Breakdown* **(Monty MONTGOMERY)**
1987 Near Dark
1989 Blue Steel

BILL, Tony
(1940–) San Diego, California, USA.
1980 My Bodyguard
1982 Six Weeks
1988 Five Corners

BILLINGTON, Kevin
(1933–) British.
1968 Interlude
1970 The Rise and Rise of Michael Rimmer
1971 The Light at the Edge of the World
1973 Voices
(also many TV movies)

BILSON, Bruce
(1928–) New York, New York, USA.
1978 The North Avenue Irregulars / *Hill's Angels*
1984 Chattanooga Choo Choo
(also many TV movies)

BILSON, Danny
1985 Zone Troopers
1988 Wrong Guys **(Paul DEMEO)**
1989 Journey Through the Darkzone

BINDER, John
1984 Uforia

BING, Mack
1969 All the Loving Couples
1972 Class of '74 **(Arthur MARKS)**
1974 Gabriella

BINNEY, Josh
1933 Across the Rio Grande
1933 My Gypsy Sweetheart
1933 Rangers at War
1933 Where Cattle Is King
1947 The Good Shepherd
1947 Hi Di Ho
1947 The Producer's Dilemma
1948 Boardin' House Blues
1948 Killer Diller

BINYON, Claude
(1905–1978) American.
1948 Family Honeymoon
1948 The Saxon Charm
1950 Mother Didn't Tell Me
1950 Stella
1951 Aaron Slick from Punkin' Crick / *Marshmallow Moon*
1952 Dreamboat
1953 Here Come the Girls

BIRCH, Patricia
1982 Grease II

BIRD, Richard
(1894–) British.
1938 The Terror

BIRD, Stewart
1984 Home Free All

BIRDWELL, Russell J
1929 Masquerade
1933 Flying Devils
1956 The Come-On
1957 The Girl in the Kremlin

BIRKENSHAW, Alan
1989 Death on Safari

BIRKIN, Andrew
1988 The Burning Secret

BIRT, Daniel
(1907–1955) British.
1948 The Three Weird Sisters
1948 No Room at the Inn
1949 The Interrupted Journey
1950 She Shall Have Murder
1952 The Night Won't Talk
1953 Circumstantial Evidence
1953 Three Steps in the Dark
1953 Background / *Edge of Divorce*
1953 Meet Mr Malcolm
1955 Third Party Risk
1956 Laughing in the Sunshine

BISCHOFF, Samuel
(1890–1975) American.
1932 The Last Mile

BISHOP, Terry
(1917–1981) British.
1952 You're Only Young Twice
1954 Jim Driscoll's Donkey
1957 Light Fingers
1958 Model for Murder
1959 Cover Girl Killer
1960 Danger Tomorrow
1961 The Unstoppable Man
(also many TV movies)

BLACHE, Herbert
1920 The Saphead
1924 High Speed
1925 The Calgary Stampede
1925 Head Winds
1925 Secrets of the Night
1926 The Mystery Club

BLACK, Noel
(1937–) Chicago, Illinois, USA.
1968 Pretty Poison
1970 Cover Me Baby
1977 Jennifer on My Mind
1978 Mirrors
1979 A Man, a Woman and a Bank
1983 Private School
(also many TV movies)

BLACKTON, Stuart J
(1875–1941) Sheffield, Yorkshire, England.
1921 The Glorious Adventure
1926 Bride of the Storm
1926 Hell-Bent for Heaven
1926 The Gilded Highway

BLACKWOOD, Michael
1988 Retracing Steps

BLAINE, Cullen
1988 R.O.T.O.R

BLAIR, George
(1906–1970) American.
1944 Silent Partner
1944 Secrets of Scotland Yard
1944 End of the Road
1945 Scotland Yard Investigator
1945 A Sporting Chance
1946 GI War Bride
1946 Gay Blades
1946 Affairs of Geraldine
1946 That's My Girl
1947 The Ghost Goes Wild
1947 Exposed
1947 The Trespasser
1948 Daredevils of the Clouds
1948 Homicide for Three
1948 King of the Gamblers
1948 Lightning in the Forest
1948 Madonna of the Desert
1948 Show Time
1949 Alias the Champ
1949 Daughter of the Jungle
1949 Duke of Chicago
1949 Flaming Fury
1949 Post Office Investigator
1949 Rose of the Yukon
1949 Streets of San Francisco
1950 Under Mexicali Stars
1950 Unmasked
1950 Federal Agents at Large
1950 Destination Big House
1950 Woman from Headquarters
1950 Lonely Hearts Bandits
1950 The Missourians
1951 Thunder in God's Country

1951 Insurance Investigator
1951 Silver City Bonanza
1951 Secrets of Monte Carlo
1952 Desert Pursuit
1952 Woman in the Dark
1953 Perils of the Jungle
1955 The Twinkle in God's Eye
1956 Fighting Trouble
1956 Jaguar
1957 Sabu and the Magic King
1957 Spook Chasers
1960 The Hypnotic Eye

BLAIR, Les
(1941–) Manchester, Lancashire, England.
1984 Number One

BLAKELEY, John
(1889–1958) British.
1936 Dodging the Dole
1940 Somewhere in England
1942 Somewhere in Camp
1942 Somewhere on Leave
1944 Demobbed
1946 Under New Management
1946 Home Sweet Home
1948 Cup Tie Honeymoon
1948 Holiday with Pay
1949 Somewhere in Politics
1949 What a Carry On
1949 School for Randal
1950 Over the Garden Wall
1950 Let's Have a Murder
1953 It's a Grand Life

BLAKEMORE, Michael
(1928–) Sydney, NSW, Australia.
1983 Privates on Parade

BLANCATO, Ken
1986 Stewardess School

BLANCHARD, John
1987 Screwball Academy / *Loose Ends*

BLANGSTED, Folmar
(1904–1982) American.
1937 The Old Wyoming Trail
1937 Westbound Mail

BLATT, Edward A
(1905–) American.
1944 Between Two Worlds
1945 Escape in the Desert
1948 Smart Woman

BLATTY, William Peter
(1928–) New York, New York, USA.
1980 The Ninth Configuration / *Twinkle, Twinkle 'Killer' Kane*

BLECKNER, Jeff
1987 Rites of Summer / *White Water Summer*

BLIER, Bertrand
(1939–) Paris, France.
1963 Hitler, Connais Pas
1967 Si J'Etais un Espion
1974 Going Places / *Les Valseuses*
1976 Calmos
1978 Get Out Your Handkerchiefs
1979 Buffet Froid
1981 Beau-Père
1983 My Best Friend's Girl
1984 Separate Rooms / *Notre Histoire*
1986 Menage

BLOCK, Bruce
1987 Princess Academy

BLOOM, Jeffrey
1974 Dog-Pound Shuffle / *Spot*
1977 The Stick Up
1981 Blood Beach
1987 Flowers in the Attic

BLOOMFIELD, George
1970 Jenny
1971 To Kill a Clown
1975 Child Under a Leaf
1979 Riel
1980 Nothing Personal
1981 Double Negative

BLOT, Philippe
1987 Sylvia Kristel's Desires / *The Arrogant*

BLYSTONE, John G
(1892–1938) American.
1924 Ladies to Board
1924 Oh You Tony
1924 Teeth
1925 The Best Bad Man
1925 The Everlasting Whisper
1925 Dick Turpin
1925 The Last Man on Earth
1925 Lucky Horseshoe
1926 The Family Upstairs
1926 Hardboiled
1926 My Old Pal
1926 Wings of a Storm
1927 Ankles Preferred
1927 Pyjamas
1927 Slaves of Beauty
1928 Mother Knows Best
1928 Sharpshooters
1929 Thru Different Eyes
1929 The Sky Hawks
1929 Captain Lash
1930 So This Is London
1930 Tol'able David
1930 The Big Party
1931 Mr Lemon of Orange
1931 Young Sinners
1931 Men on Call
1932 The Painted Woman
1932 Too Busy to Work
1932 Charlie Chan's Chance
1932 She Wanted a Millionaire
1932 Amateur Daddy
1933 Hot Pepper
1933 Shanghai Madness
1933 My Lips Betray
1934 Change of Heart
1934 Coming-Out Party
1934 Hell in the Heavens
1935 The County Chairman
1935 Bad Boy

1936 Great Guy / *Pluck of the Irish*
1936 Gentle Julia
1936 Little Miss Nobody
1936 The Magnificent Brute
1937 23½ Hours Leave
1937 Woman Chases Man
1937 Music for Madame
1938 Block-Heads
1938 Swiss Miss

BLYTH, David
1984 Death Warmed Up
1988 Exurbia
1990 Red Blooded American Girl

BOASBERG, Al
1934 Myrt and Marge

BOETTICHER, Budd (Oscar Boetticher Jnr.)
(1916–) Chicago, Illinois, USA.
Autobiography: When in Disgrace.
1944 One Mysterious Night / *Behind Closed Doors*
1944 The Missing Juror
1945 A Guy, a Gal and a Pal
1945 Escape in the Fog
1945 Youth on Trial
1946 The Fleet That Came to Stay
1948 Assigned to Danger
1948 Behind Locked Doors
1949 The Wolf Hunters
1949 Black Midnight
1950 Killer Shark
1951 The Bullfighter and the Lady
1951 The Sword of D'Artagnan
1951 The Cimarron Kid
1952 Red Ball Express
1952 Bronco Buster
1952 Horizons West
1953 City Beneath the Sea
1953 Seminole
1953 The Man from the Alamo
1953 East of Sumatra
1953 Wings of the Hawk
1955 The Magnificent Matador / *The Brave and the Beautiful*
1956 The Killer Is Loose
1956 Seven Men from Now
1957 The Tall T
1957 Decision at Sundown
1958 Buchanan Rides Alone
1959 Ride Lonesome
1959 Westbound
1960 Comanche Station
1960 The Rise and Fall of Legs Diamond
1971 A Time for Dying

BOGART, Paul
(1919–) New York, New York, USA.
1968 Halls of Anger
1969 Marlowe
1971 Skin Game
1973 Class of '44
1974 Cancel My Reservation
1975 Mr Ricco
1977 The Three Sisters
1984 Oh,God! You Devil
1988 Torch Song Trilogy
(also many TV movies)

BOGAYEVICZ, Yurek
1987 Anna

BOGDANOVICH, Peter
(1939–) Kingston, New York, USA.
1968 Targets
1971 The Last Picture Show **D* F***
1972 What's Up Doc?
1973 Paper Moon
1974 Daisy Miller
1975 At Long Last Love
1976 Nickelodeon
1979 Saint Jack
1982 They All Laughed
1985 Mask
1988 Illegally Yours

BOGLE, Andrew
1980 Dark Water
1985 Haunters of the Deep

BOGLE, James
1988 Stones of Death / *Kadaicha*

BOGNER, Willy
1987 Fire and Ice / *Ski Dance*

BOKOVA, Jana
1985 Hotel du Paradis

BOLESLAWSKI, Richard (Boleslaw Ryszart Srzednicki)
(1889–1937) Warsaw, Poland.
1930 Last of the Lone Wolf
1931 Woman Pursued
1931 Gay Diplomat
1932 Rasputin and the Empress
1932 Storm at Daybreak
1932 Beauty for Sale
1934 Hollywood Party **(Allan DWAN, Roy ROWLAND)**
1934 Fugitive Lovers
1934 Men in White
1934 Operator 13 / *Spy 13*
1934 The Painted Veil
1935 Clive of India
1935 Les Misérables **F***
1935 O'Shaughnessy's Boy
1935 Metropolitan
1936 The Three Godfathers
1936 Theodora Goes Wild
1936 The Garden of Allah
1937 The Last of Mrs Cheyney **(George FITZMAURICE)**

BOLOGNINI, Mauro *
(1923–) Pistoia, Italy.
1955 Wild Love
1957 Newlyweds / *Young Husbands*
1959 On Any Street / *Bad Girls Don't Cry / La Notte Brava*
1960 From a Roman Balcony / *A Crazy Day / Pickup in Rome*
1960 The Love Makers
1964 I Tre Volti **(Michelangelo ANTONIONI)**
1966 The Queens / *Le Fate* **(Mario MONICELLI, Antonio PIETRANGELI, Luciano SALCE)**
1967 The Oldest Profession **(Claude AUTANT-LARA, Philippe DE BROCA,**

Jean-Luc GODARD, Franco INDOVINA, Michael PFLEGHAR)
1976 Down the Ancient Stairs
1977 Black Journal / *La Signora degli Orrori*
1981 The True Story of Camille
1987 Goodbye Moscow

BOLT, Ben
(1952–) English.
1987 The Big Town / *The Arm*

BOLT, Robert
(1924–) Sale, Cheshire, England.
1972 Lady Caroline Lamb

BOND, Jack
1988 It Couldn't Happen Here
1989 Ocean Point

BONDARCHUK, Sergei (Sergei Bondartchouk)
(1920–) Belozersk, Ukraine, USSR.
1961 Fate of a Man
1968 War and Peace
1971 Waterloo
1974 They Fought for Their Motherland
1977 The Steppe
1982 Red Bells: Mexico in Flames
1983 Red Bells: I've Seen the Birth of the New World
1986 Boris Godounov

BONERZ, Peter
(1938–) Portsmouth, New Hampshire, USA.
1981 Nobody's Perfekt
1989 Police Academy VI: City Under Siege

BONNER, Lee
1987 The Adventure of the Action Hunters / *Two for the Money*

BOORMAN, John
(1933–) Shepperton, Middlesex, England.
1965 Catch Us If You Can / *Having a Wild Weekend*
1967 Point Blank
1968 Hell in the Pacific
1970 Leo the Last
1972 Deliverance **D* F***
1974 Zardoz
1977 The Heretic: Exorcist II
1981 Excalibur
1985 The Emerald Forest
1987 Hope and Glory **D* F***

BOOTH, Harry
1960 Blitz on Britain
1965 A King's Story
1971 On the Buses
1972 Go for a Take

BORAU, José Luis *
(1929–) Zaragoza, Spain.
1986 On the Line

BORDEN, Lizzie
1984 Born in Flames
1987 Working Girls

BORG, Peter
1988 Scorched Heat

BORIS, Robert
1984 Oxford Blues
1987 Steele Justice
1988 Buy and Cell

BORRIS, Clay
1986 Quiet Cool

BORSOS, Phillip
1983 The Grey Fox
1985 The Mean Season
1985 One Magic Christmas
1988 Bethune, the Making of a Hero

BORZAGE, Frank
(1893–1962) Salt Lake City, Utah, USA.
1924 Secrets
1925 The Lady
1925 Lazybones
1925 Daddy's Gone a-Hunting
1925 Wages for Wives
1925 The Circle
1926 Marriage Licence / *The Pelican*
1926 The Dixie Merchant
1926 Early to Wed
1926 The First Year
1927 Seventh Heaven **D** F***
1928 Street Angel
1929 The River
1929 Lucky Star
1929 They Had to See Paris
1930 Song O' My Heart
1930 Liliom
1931 Doctors' Wives
1931 As Young As You Feel
1931 Bad Girl **D** F***
1931 A Farewell to Arms **F***
1932 After Tomorrow
1932 Young America / *We Humans*
1933 Man's Castle
1933 Secrets
1934 Flirtation Walk **F***
1934 No Greater Glory
1934 Little Man, What Now?
1935 Living Velvet
1935 Shipmates Forever
1935 Stranded
1936 Desire
1936 Hearts Divided
1936 The Big City
1937 Green Light
1937 History Is Made at Night
1937 Mannequin
1938 The Shining Hour
1938 Three Comrades
1939 Disputed Passage
1940 Flight Command
1940 The Mortal Storm
1940 Strange Cargo
1941 Smilin' Through
1941 The Vanishing Virginian
1942 Seven Sweethearts
1943 His Butler's Sister
1943 Stage Door Canteen
1943 Till We Meet Again
1944 The Spanish Main
1946 I've Always Loved You / *Concerto*

1946 Magnificent Doll
1947 That's My Man / *Will Tomorrow Ever Come?*
1948 Moonrise
1958 China Doll
1959 The Big Fisherman

BOSNICK, Ned
1970 Imago
1972 To Be Free

BOULTING, John
(1913–1985) Bray, Berkshire, England.
1945 Journey Together
1947 Brighton Rock / *Young Scarface*
1950 Seven Days to Noon
1952 The Magic Box
1954 Seagulls Over Sorrento / *Crest of the Wave* **(Roy BOULTING)**
1956 Private's Progress
1957 Lucky Jim
1960 I'm All Right, Jack
1961 Suspect / *The Risk* **(Roy BOULTING)**
1963 Heavens Above!
1965 Rotten to the Core

BOULTING, Roy
(1913–) Bray, Berkshire, England.
1938 Consider Your Verdict
1939 Trunk Crime / *Design for Murder*
1939 Inquest
1940 Pastor Hall
1942 Thunder Rock
1948 The Guinea Pig / *Single Handed*
1954 Seagulls Over Sorrento / *Crest of the Wave* **(John BOULTING)**
1955 Josephine and Men
1956 Brothers-in-Law
1959 Happy Is the Bride
1960 Carlton-Browne of the F.O. / *Man in a Cocked Hat* **(Jeffrey DELL)**
1960 A French Mistress
1961 Suspect / *The Risk* **(John BOULTING)**
1967 The Family Way
1969 Twisted Nerve
1970 There's a Girl in My Soup
1971 Mr Forbush and the Penguins / *Cry of the Penguins*
1975 Soft Beds and Hard Battles / *Undercover Hero*
1979 The Last Word

BOURGUIGNON, Serge
(1928–) French.
1962 Sundays and Cybele
1965 The Reward
1967 Two Weeks in September / *A Coeur Joie*
1969 The Picasso Summer
1987 The Fascination

BOWEN, Jenny
1982 Street Music
1985 Animal Behavior
1988 Wizard of Loneliness

BOWEN, John
1989 Nudity Required

BOWER, Dallas
(1907–) British.
1950 Alice in Wonderland
1952 The Second Mrs Tanqueray
1957 Doorway to Suspicion

BOWERS, George
1980 The Hearse
1981 Body and Soul
1983 My Tutor
1985 Private Resort

BOWSER, Kenneth
1987 In a Shallow Grave

BOX, Muriel (Muriel Baker)
(1905–) Tolworth, Surrey, England. Autobiography: Odd Woman Out.
1952 The Happy Family
1953 Street Corner / *Both Sides of the Law*
1954 The Beachcomber
1955 Simon and Laura
1956 Eye Witness
1956 The Passionate Stranger / *A Novel Affair*
1956 Cash on Delivery / *To Dorothy a Son*
1957 The Truth About Women
1958 Subway in the Sky
1959 Too Young to Love
1964 Rattle of a Simple Man

BOYD, Don
1976 East of Elephant Rock

BOZZACCHI, Gianni
1987 I Love N.Y.

BRABIN, Charles R
(1883–1957) British.
1925 So Big
1925 Stella Maris
1926 Twinkletoes
1927 Hard Boiled Haggerty
1927 Framed
1927 The Valley of the Giants
1928 Burning Daylight
1928 The Whip
1929 The Bridge of San Luis Rey
1930 The Ship from Shanghai
1930 Call of the Flesh
1931 The Great Meadow
1931 Sporting Blood
1932 The Mask of Fu Manchu **(Charles VIDOR)**
1932 The Beast of the City
1932 New Morals for Old
1932 The Washington Masquerade
1933 The Secret of Madame Blanche
1933 Stage Mother
1933 Day of Reckoning
1934 A Wicked Woman
(also many silent shorts)

BRACKEN, Bert
1932 The Face on the Barroom Floor

BRADBURY, Robert North
(1895–) American.
1924 The Galloping Ace
1924 The Phantom Horseman

1924 The Man from Wyoming
1925 Hidden Loot
1926 The Border Sheriff
1926 Looking for Trouble
1928 The Phantom Flyer
1931 Dugan of the Bad Lands
1931 Son of the Plains
1932 Hidden Valley
1932 Man from Hell's Edges
1932 Riders of the Desert
1932 Texas Buddies
1932 Law of the West
1932 Son of Oklahoma
1933 Breed of the Border
1933 Gallant Fool
1933 Galloping Romeo
1933 Ranger's Code
1934 Riders of Destiny
1934 The Star Packer
1934 Blue Steel
1934 The Lucky Texan
1934 The Man from Utah
1934 West of the Divide
1934 Happy Landing
1935 Between Men
1935 Courageous Avenger
1935 The Dawn Rider
1935 The Lawless Frontier
1935 Rainbow Valley
1935 Smoky Smith
1935 Texas Terror
1935 Westward Ho
1935 Kid Courage
1935 Rider of the Law
1935 Western Justice
1936 The Lawless Range
1936 Valley of the Lawless
1936 Cavalry
1936 Headin' for the Rio Grande
1936 The Last of the Warrens
1936 Sundown Saunders
1937 Trouble in Texas
1937 The Gun Ranger
1937 The Trusted Outlaw
1937 Hittin' the Trail
1937 Riders of the Dawn
1937 Riders of the Rockies
1937 Stars Over Arizona
1937 Where Trails Divide
1937 Sing, Cowboy, Sing
1937 Danger Valley
1942 Forbidden Trails

BRADLEY, David
(1919–) American.
1941 Peer Gynt
1941 Treasure Island
1946 Macbeth
1950 Julius Caesar
1952 Talk About a Stranger
1958 Dragstrip Riot
1960 Twelve to the Moon
1964 Madmen of Mandoras

BRADY, David
1988 Channel One **(Steven ALIX)**

BRADY, John (Hans Brahm)
(1898–1984) Hamburg, Germany.
1935 Scrooge
1936 The Last Journey
1937 Counsel for Crime
1937 Broken Blossoms
1938 Penitentiary
1938 Girls' School
1939 Let Us Live
1939 Rio
1940 Escape to Glory / *Submarine Zone*
1941 Wild Geese Calling
1942 The Undying Monster / *The Hammond Mystery*
1943 Tonight We Raid Calais
1943 Wintertime
1944 Guest in the House
1944 The Lodger
1945 Hangover Square
1946 The Locket
1947 The Brasher Doubloon / *The High Window*
1947 Singapore
1951 The Thief of Venice
1952 Face to Face **(Bretaigne WINDUST)**
1952 The Miracle of Our Lady of Fatima
1953 The Diamond Queen
1954 The Mad Magician
1955 Bengazi
1955 Special Delivery
1967 Hot Rods to Hell

BRAME, Bill
(1928–) American.
1970 Cycle Savages
1976 Jive Turkey

BRAND, Larry
1988 The Drifter

BRANDAUER, Klaus Maria
1989 The Artisan

BRANDER, Richard
1986 Sizzle Beach USA

BRANDO, Marlon
(1924–) Omaha, Nebraska, USA. Biographies: Brando by René Jordan; Portrait of the Rebel as an Artist by Bob Thomas.
1961 One-Eyed Jacks

BRANDON, Phil
1942 We'll Meet Again

BRANNON, Fred
(1901–) American.
1949 Bandit King of Texas
1949 Frontier Investigator
1950 Salt Lake Raiders
1950 Code of the Silver Sage
1950 Gunmen of Abilene
1950 Rustlers on Horseback
1950 Vigilante Hideout
1951 Night Riders of Montana
1951 Rough Riders of Durango
1951 Arizona Manhunt
1952 Captive of Billy the Kid
1952 Wild Horse Ambush
1958 Satan's Satellites
1958 Missile Monsters
(also many serials)

BRASCIA, Dominic
1988 Evil Laugh

BRASON, John
1969 Walk a Crooked Path

BRASS, Tinto (Giovanni Tinto Brass) *
(1933–) Milan, Italy.
1966 Yankee
1972 Dropout
1976 Salon Kitty
1977 Caligula
1979 Action
1985 The Key
1985 Miranda
1987 Letter from Capri / *Caprice*
1988 Snack Bar Budapest

BRAUNSTEIN, Joseph
1988 Edge of the Axe

BRAVERMAN, Charles
(1944–) Los Angeles, California, USA.
1982 Hit and Run / *Revenge Squad*

BRAVMAN, Jack
1987 Zombie Nightmare

BREAKSTON, George
(1922–1973) France.
1948 Urubu
1950 Jungle Stampede
1954 The Scarlet Spear
1955 Golden Ivory
1956 Escape in the Sun
1957 The Woman and the Hunter
1966 The Boy Cried Murder
1968 Blood River

BRECHER, Irving S
(1914–) American.
1949 The Life of Riley
1952 Somebody Loves Me
1961 Sail a Crooked Ship

BREEN, Richard L
(1919–1967) American.
1957 Stop-Over Tokyo

BREN, Milton
1952 Three for Bedroom C

BRENON, Herbert (Alexander Herbert Reginald St John Brenon)
(1880–1958) Dublin, Republic of Ireland.
1924 The Side Show of Life
1924 Shadows in Paris
1924 The Breaking Point
1924 Peter Pan
1925 The Alaskan
1925 Street of Forgotten Men
1925 The Little French Girl
1925 A Kiss for Cinderella
1926 The Great Gatsby
1926 The Song and Dance Man
1926 Dancing Mothers
1926 God Save My Twenty Cents
1927 Beau Geste
1927 The Telephone Girl
1927 Sorrell and Son **D***
1928 Laugh Clown Laugh
1929 The Rescue
1930 The Case of Sergeant Grischa
1930 Lummox
1931 Beau Ideal
1931 Transgression
1932 Girl of the Rio / *The Dove*
1933 Wine, Women and Song
1935 Royal Cavalcade **(Thomas BENTLEY, William KELLINO, Norman LEE, Walter SUMMERS, Marcel VARNEL)**
1935 Honours Easy
1936 Living Dangerously
1936 Someone at the Door
1937 The Dominant Sex
1937 The Spring Handicap
1937 The Live Wire
1938 Housemaster
1938 Yellow Sands
1939 Black Eyes
1939 The Flying Squad

BRESCIA, Alfonso
1987 Iron Warrior

BRESLOW, Hugh
1951 You Never Can Tell / *You Never Know*

BRESSON Jnr., Arthur
1983 Abuse
1985 Buddies

BRESSON, Robert
(1907–) Bromont-la-Mothe, France.
1943 Les Affaires Publiques
1943 Angels of the Streets
1945 The Ladies of the Park
1950 Diary of a Country Priest
1956 A Man Escaped
1959 Pickpocket
1962 The Trial of Joan of Arc
1966 Balthazar
1969 A Gentle Creature
1967 Mouchette
1972 Four Nights of a Dreamer
1975 Lancelot of the Lake
1977 The Devil, Probably
1983 Money

BREST, Martin
(1951–) New York, New York, USA.
1977 Hot Tomorrows
1979 Going in Style
1984 Beverly Hills Cop
1988 Midnight Run
1990 Death Takes a Holiday

BRETHERTON, Howard
(1896–1969) American.
1926 While London Sleeps
1927 Hills of Kentucky
1927 The Black Diamond Express
1927 One-Round Hogan
1927 The Bush Leaguer
1927 The Silver Slave
1928 Across the Atlantic
1928 Caught in the Fog
1929 From Headquarters

1929 Greyhound Limited
1929 The Time, the Place and the Girl
1929 The Redeeming Sin
1930 Second Choice
1930 Isle of Escape
1932 The Match King **(William KEIGHLEY)**
1933 Ladies They Talk About **(William KEIGHLEY)**
1934 Return to Terror
1935 Dinky **(Ross D LEDERMAN)**
1935 Bar 20 Rides Again
1935 The Eagle's Brood
1935 Hopalong Cassidy
1936 The Leathernecks Have Landed
1936 Three on the Trail
1936 King of the Royal Mounted
1936 Call of the Prairie
1936 Heart of the West
1936 Girl from Mandalay
1936 Wild Brian Kent
1936 Secret Valley
1937 It Happened Out West
1937 County Fair
1937 Western Gold
1938 Wanted By the Police
1939 Boys' Reformatory
1939 Danger Flight
1939 Irish Luck
1939 Navy Secrets
1939 Sky Patrol
1939 Tough Kid
1939 Undercover Agent
1940 The Showdown
1940 Chasing Trouble
1940 Laughing at Danger
1940 Midnight Limited
1940 On the Spot
1940 Up in the Air
1941 In Old Colorado
1941 Outlaws of the Desert
1941 Twilight on the Trail
1941 Sign of the Wolf
1941 You're Out of Luck
1942 Below the Border
1942 Ghost Town Law
1942 Down Texas Way
1942 Riders of the West
1942 West of Tombstone
1942 Dawn on the Great Divide
1942 Rhythm Parade **(Dave GOULD)**
1943 Beyond the Last Frontier
1943 Wagon Trails West
1943 Whispering Footsteps
1943 Carson City Cyclone
1943 Fugitive from Sonora
1943 Riders of the Rio Grande
1944 Hidden Valley Outlaws
1944 Law of the Valley
1944 The San Antonio Kid
1944 Outlaws of Santa Fe
1944 The Girl Who Dared
1945 Gun Smoke
1945 The Navajo Trail
1945 Renegades of the Rio Grande
1945 The Topeka Terror
1945 The Big Showoff
1947 The Trap
1947 Ridin' Down the Trail
1948 The Prince of Thieves
1948 Where the North Begins
1948 Triggerman
1952 Night Raiders

BRICE, Monte
1927 Casey at the Bat
1933 Take a Chance **(Lawrence SCHWAB)**
1935 Sweet Surrender

BRICKMAN, Marshall
1980 Simon
1983 Lovesick
1986 The Manhattan Project
1987 Deadly Game

BRICKMAN, Paul
1983 Risky Business
1989 Men Don't Leave

BRIDGES, Alan
(1928–) Liverpool, England.
1964 Act of Murder
1966 Invasion
1970 The Lie
1973 The Hireling
1975 Out of Season
1977 Age of Innocence
1981 Very Like a Whale
1982 The Return of the Soldier
1984 The Shooting Party
1988 Apt Pupil

BRIDGES, Beau (Lloyd Bridges III)
(1941–) Los Angeles, California, USA.
1987 Devil's Odds
1988 Seven Hours to Judgement

BRIDGES, James
(1936–) Paris, Arkansas, USA.
1970 The Baby Maker
1973 The Paper Chase
1977 September 30th 1955
1979 The China Syndrome
1980 Urban Cowboy
1984 Mike's Murder
1985 Perfect!
1988 Bright Lights, Big City

BRINCKERHOFF, Burt
(1936–) American.
1977 Dogs
1978 Acapulco Gold
(also many TV movies)

BROCK, Deborah
1987 Don't Let Go
1988 Andy Colby's Incredible Adventure

BROCKA, Lino *
(1940–) San Jose, Nuevo Ecija, Philippines.
1970 Wanted: Perfect Mother
1970 Santiago
1971 Now
1971 Stardoom
1972 Cherry Blossoms
1972 Villa Miranda
1974 You Are Weighed in the Balance But Are Found Lacking

1975 Manila in the Claws of Light
1979 Jaguar
1981 Hello, Young Lovers
1982 P.X.
1982 In This Corner
1982 Caught in the Act
1982 Mother Dear
1983 Experience
1983 Strangers in Paradise
1984 Hot Property

BRODERICK, John
1976 Bad Georgia Road
1984 The Warrior and the Sorceress

BRODIE, Kevin
1984 Mugsy's Girls / *Delta Pi*

BRODY, Hugh
1985 1919

BROMFIELD, Rex
1977 Love at First Sight
1981 Tulips **(Mark WARREN, Al WAXMAN)**
1983 Melanie
1987 Home Is Where the Hart Is

BROMLY, Alan
1954 The Angel Who Pawned Her Harp

BROOK, Clive (Clifford Brook)
(1887–1974) London, England.
1943 On Approval

BROOK, Peter
(1925–) London, England.
Biography: Peter Brook by J.C. Trewin.
1953 The Beggar's Opera
1963 Lord of the Flies
1967 The Persecution and Assassination of Jean-Paul Marat as Performed by the Inmates of the Asylum of Charenton Under the Direction of the Marquis de Sade
1968 Tell Me Lies
1971 King Lear
1979 Meetings with Remarkable Men
1989 The Mahabharata

BROOKNER, Howard
1989 Bloodhounds of Broadway

BROOKS, Adam
(1956–) Toronto, Ontario, Canada.
1984 Almost You
1987 Little Red Riding Hood

BROOKS, Albert
(1947–) Los Angeles, California, USA.
1979 Real Life
1981 Modern Romance
1985 Lost in America

BROOKS, Bob
(1927–) Philadelphia, Pennsylvania, USA.
1981 Tattoo

BROOKS, James L
(1940–) Brooklyn, New York, USA.
1983 Terms of Endearment **D** F****
1987 Broadcast News **F***

BROOKS, Joseph
1977 You Light Up My Life
1978 If Ever I See You Again
1980 Headin' for Broadway
1984 Invitation to a Wedding

BROOKS, Mel (Melvin Kaminsky)
(1926–) New York, New York, USA.
Biography: The Irreverent Funny Man by Billy Alder.
1968 The Producers
1970 The Twelve Chairs
1973 Blazing Saddles
1974 Young Frankenstein
1976 Silent Movie
1977 High Anxiety
1981 History of the World, Part 1
1987 Spaceballs

BROOKS, Richard
(1912–) Philadelphia, Pennsylvania.
1950 Crisis
1951 The Light Touch
1952 Deadline USA
1953 Battle Circus
1953 Take the High Ground
1954 The Last Time I Saw Paris
1954 Flame and the Flesh
1955 The Blackboard Jungle
1956 The Catered Affair / *Wedding Breakfast*
1956 The Last Hunt
1957 Something of Value
1958 The Brothers Karamazov
1958 Cat on a Hot Tin Roof **D* F***
1960 Elmer Gantry **F***
1962 Sweet Bird of Youth
1965 Lord Jim
1966 The Professionals **D***
1967 In Cold Blood **D***
1969 The Happy Ending
1972 Dollar / *The Heist*
1975 Bite the Bullet
1977 Looking for Mr Goodbar
1982 Wrong Is Right / *The Man with the Deadly Lens*
1985 The Fever

BROOKS, Thor
1958 Legion of the Doomed
1959 Arson for Hire

BROOMFIELD, Nicholas
1989 Diamond Skulls

BROWER, Otto
1928 Avalanche
1929 Stairs of Sand
1929 The Sunset Pass
1930 The Light of Western Stars **(Edwin H KNOPF)**
1930 The Santa Fe Trail **(Edwin H KNOPF)**
1930 The Border Legion **(Edwin H KNOPF)**
1931 Fighting Caravans **(David BURTON)**
1931 Clearing the Range
1931 The Hard Hombre

1932 Gold
1932 The Local Bad Man
1932 Spirit of the West
1932 Pleasure
1932 Lure of the Sea
1933 Headline Shooter
1933 Crossfire
1933 Scarlet River
1933 Fighting for Justice
1934 Speed Wings
1934 Straightaway
1934 I Can't Escape
1935 The Outlaw Deputy
1936 Sins of Man **(Gregory RATOFF)**
1936 Postal Inspector
1938 Speed to Burn
1938 Road Demon
1939 Stop, Look and Love
1939 Too Busy to Work
1939 Winner Takes All
1940 The Gay Caballero
1940 Youth Will Be Served
1940 Girl from Avenue A
1940 Men with Steel Faces **(B Reeves EASON)**
1940 On Their Own
1942 Little Tokyo, USA
1943 Dixie Dugan
1946 Behind Green Lights

BROWN, Alastair
1987 Last Chance

BROWN, Barry
1970 The Way We Live Now
1977 Cloud Dancer

BROWN, Clarence
(1890–1987) Clinton, Massachusetts, USA.
1924 Butterfly
1924 Smouldering Fires
1924 The Signal Tower
1925 The Goose Woman
1925 The Eagle
1926 Kiki
1928 Flesh and the Devil
1928 A Woman of Affairs
1929 Trail of '98
1929 Navy Blues
1929 Wonder of Woman
1930 Romance
1930 Anna Christie **D***
1931 A Free Soul **D***
1931 Inspiration
1931 Possessed
1932 The Son-Daughter
1932 Emma
1932 Letty Lynton
1933 Looking Forward / *Service*
1933 Night Flight
1934 Chained
1934 Sadie McKee
1935 Ah, Wilderness
1935 Anna Karenina
1936 The Gorgeous Hussy
1936 Wife Versus Secretary
1937 Conquest / *Marie Walewska*
1938 Of Human Hearts
1939 Idiot's Delight
1939 The Rain Comes
1940 Edison, the Man
1941 Come Live with Me
1941 They Met in Bombay
1943 The Human Comedy **D***
1944 National Velvet **D***
1944 The White Cliffs of Dover
1946 The Yearling **F***
1947 Song of Love
1949 Intruder in the Dust
1950 To Please a Lady
1951 Angels in the Outfield / *Angels and the Pirates*
1952 It's a Big Country **(Don HARTMAN, John STURGES, Richard THORPE, Charles VIDOR, Don WEIS, William A WELLMAN)**
1952 When in Rome
1952 Plymouth Adventure

BROWN, Edwin
1982 Irresistible

BROWN, Harry Joe
(1892–1972) American.
1929 The Lawless Legion
1929 The Royal Rider
1929 The Wagon Master
1929 Señor Americano
1930 Lucky Larkin
1930 Parade of the West
1930 The Squealer
1930 The Fighting Legion
1930 Mountain Justice
1930 Song of the Caballero
1930 Sons of the Saddle
1931 A Woman of Experience
1932 Madison Square Garden
1933 Sitting Pretty
1933 The Billion Dollar Scandal
1933 I Love That Man
1944 Knickerbocker Holiday

BROWN, Jim (James Nathaniel Brown)
(1935–) St Simons Island, New York, USA.
1986 Slam-Dunk

BROWN, Larry
1987 Final Cut

BROWN, Melville
1926 The Buckaroo Kid
1927 Fast and Furious
1927 Taxi! Taxi!
1928 Red Lips
1928 The Washington Square
1929 Geraldine
1929 Jazz Heaven
1929 The Love Doctor
1929 Dance Hall
1929 Lovin' the Ladies
1930 She's My Weakness
1930 Check and Double Check
1931 Behind Office Doors
1931 White Shoulders
1931 Fanny Foley Herself
1934 Redhead
1934 Lost in the Stratosphere
1934 The Nut Farm

1935 Champagne for Breakfast
1935 Forced Landing
1938 He Loved an Actress

BROWN, Rigg
1987 Thinking Big

BROWN, Robert
1988 Two Wrongs Make a Right

BROWN, Rowland V
(1901–1963) American.
1931 Quick Millions
1932 Hell's Highway
1933 Blood Money

BROWNING, Ricou
(1930–) American.
1966 Around the World Under the Sea **(Andrew MARTON)**
1975 Salty
(Ricou Browning specializes in underwater direction)

BROWNING, Tod (Charles Browning)
(1882–1962) Louisville, Kentucky, USA.
1924 The Dangerous Flirt
1924 Silk Stocking Sal
1925 Dollar Down
1925 The Mystic
1925 The Unholy Three
1926 The Black Bird
1926 Road to Mandalay
1927 The Unknown
1927 The Show
1927 London After Midnight / *The Hypnotist*
1928 The Big City
1928 West of Zanzibar
1929 Where East Is East
1929 The Thirteenth Chair
1930 Outside the Law
1930 Dracula
1931 Iron Man
1932 Freaks
1933 Fast Workers
1935 Mark of the Vampire
1936 The Devil Doll
1939 Miracle for Sale
(also many silent shorts)

BROWNRIGG, S F
1973 Don't Look in the Basement
1976 Poor White Trash: Part II

BRUCE, George
(1898–) American.
1939 King of the Turf

BRUCE, James
1987 Still Life
1988 The Suicide Club

BRUCKMAN, Clyde
(1895–1955) California, USA.
1926 The General **(Buster KEATON)**
1927 A Perfect Gentleman
1927 Horse Shoes
1929 Welcome Danger
1930 Feet First
1930 Everything's Rosie
1932 Movie Crazy
1935 Spring Tonic
1935 The Man on the Flying Trapeze / *The Memory Expert*
(also many silent shorts)

BRUNEL, Adrian
(1892–1958) British.
1927 Blighty
1927 The Vortex
1928 The Constant Nymph
1928 A Light Woman / *Dolores*
1929 The Crooked Billet
1930 Elstree Calling **(Alfred HITCHCOCK, Jack HULBERT, Paul MURRAY)**
1933 Taxi to Paradise
1933 I'm an Explosive
1933 Follow the Lady
1933 The Laughter of Fools
1933 Two Wives for Henry
1933 Little Napoleon
1934 Important People
1934 Badger's Green
1934 Menace / *While London Sleeps*
1934 Variety
1935 The City of Beautiful Nonsense
1935 Vanity
1936 Prison Breaker
1936 Love at Sea
1936 The Invader / *An Old Spanish Custom*
1938 The Rebel Son **(Alexis GRANOWSKY)**
1939 The Lion Has Wings **(Brian Desmond HURST, Michael POWELL)**
1939 The Girl Who Forgot
(also many shorts)

BRUSATI, Franco *
(1922–) Milan, Italy.
1968 Tenderly
1978 Bread and Chocolate
1980 To Forget Venice
1982 The Good Soldier

BRYAN, James
1983 Don't Go into the Woods
1984 The Executioner Part II
1985 Hell Riders

BRYANT, Baird
1971 Celebration of Big Sur

BRYANT, Gerald
1957 Rock Around the World

BRYCE, Alan
1936 The End of the Road

BUCHANAN, Larry
1963 Free, White and Twenty-One
1964 Under Age
1964 The Trial of Lee Harvey Oswald
1966 Zontar — The Thing from Venus
1967 Creature of Destruction
1968 Hell Raiders
1968 Mars Needs Women
1970 Strawberries Need Rain
1970 A Bullet for Pretty Boy
1976 Goodbye, Norma Jean
1978 Hughes and Harlow: Angels in Hell

1982 The Loch Ness Horror
1984 Down on Us
1988 Goodnight, Sweet Marilyn

BUCHOWETZKI, Dimitri
(1895–1932) Russian.
1924 Men
1924 Lily of the Dust
1925 The Swan
1925 Graustark
1926 The Crown of Lies
1926 The Midnight Sun
1926 Valencia

BUCKINGHAM, Thomas
1924 Arizona Express
1924 The Cyclone Rider
1926 Tony Runs Wild
1932 Cock of the Air

BUCKSEY, Colin
1989 Dealers

BUCQUET, Harold S
(1891–1946) London, England.
1938 Young Dr Kildare
1939 Calling Dr Kildare
1939 On Borrowed Time
1939 The Secret of Dr Kildare
1940 Dr Kildare's Strange Case
1940 We Who Are Young
1940 Dr Kildare Goes Home
1940 Dr Kildare's Crisis
1941 The Penalty
1941 The People Versus Dr Kildare
1941 Dr Kildare's Wedding Day
1941 Kathleen
1942 Calling Dr Gillespie
1942 The War Against Mrs Hadley
1943 The Adventures of Tartu
1944 Dragon Seed **(Jack CONWAY)**
1945 Without Love
(also many shorts)

BUECHLER, John
1985 The Dungeonmaster / *Ragewar* **(David ALLEN, Charles BAND, Peter MANOOGIAN, Ted NICOLAOU, Stephen STAFFORD, Rose-Marie TURKO)**
1986 Troll
1987 Cellar Dweller
1988 Friday the 13th Part VII — New Blood

BULGAKOV, Leo
1934 White Lies
1935 I'll Love You Always
1935 After the Dance

BUNTZMAN, Mark
1984 Exterminator II

BURGE, Robert A
1986 Vasectomy, a Delicate Matter
1989 Keaton's Cop

BURGE, Stuart
(1918–) Brentwood, Essex, England.
1960 There Was a Crooked Man
1963 Uncle Vanya
1965 Othello
1967 The Mikado
1969 Julius Caesar

BURKE, Edwin
1934 Now I'll Tell / *When New York Sleeps*

BURKE, Martyn
1976 The Clown Murders
1978 Power Play
1981 The Last Chase

BURMAN, Tom
1989 Life on the Edge

BURNAMA, Jopi
1987 The Intruder

BURNETT, Charles
1983 My Brother's Wedding

BURNS, Allan
1986 Just Between Friends

BURR, Jeff
1987 From a Whisper to a Scream / *The Offspring*
1989 Stepfather II

BURROWES, Geoff
1987 The Man from Snowy River

BURROWES, Michael *see* **Robert HARTFORD-DAVIS**

BURROWS, James
(1940–) Los Angeles, California, USA.
1982 Partners
(also many TV comedy shorts)

BURSTALL, Tim
(1929–) England.
1969 Two Thousand Weeks
1971 Stork
1973 Libido **(David BAKER, John B MURRAY, Fred SCHEPISI)**
1973 Alvin Purple
1974 Petersen
1976 Eliza Fraser
1976 End Play
1979 The Last of the Knucklemen
1981 Duet for Four
1982 Attack Force Z
1985 The Naked Country
1986 Kangaroo
1987 Great Expectations — The Untold Story

BURTON, David
(1890–) American.
1930 The Bishop Murder Case **(Nick GRINDE)**
1930 Strictly Unconventional
1931 Fighting Caravans **(Otto BROWER)**
1931 Confessions of a Co-Ed **(Dudley MURPHY)**
1932 Dancers in the Dark
1933 Brief Moment
1934 Lady By Choice

1934 Let's Fall in Love
1934 Sister Under the Skin
1935 Princess O'Hara
1935 The Melody Lingers On
1936 Make Way for a Lady
1940 The Man Who Wouldn't Talk
1940 Manhattan Heartbeat
1941 Private Nurse

BURTON, Tim
1985 Pee-Wee's Big Adventure
1988 Beetlejuice
1989 Batman

BUSHELL, Anthony
(1904–) British.
1949 The Angel with the Trumpet
1951 The Long Dark Hall **(Reginald BECK)**
1960 The Terror of the Tongs

BUSHELMAN, John
1961 The Silent Call
1961 Sniper's Ridge
1962 The Broken Land
1965 Day of the Nightmare
1975 Cruisin' High
1976 High Seas Hijack

BUSHNELL Jnr., William J
1973 Prisoners
1974 The Four Deuces

BUSSMAN, Tom
1987 Whoops Apocalypse

BUTLER, David
(1894–1979) San Francisco, California, USA.
1927 High School Hero / *Just Lads*
1928 News Parade
1928 Prep and Prep / *Tiger's Son*
1928 Win That Girl
1929 Fox Movietone Follies of 1929 **(Marcel SILVER)**
1929 Masked Emotions **(Kenneth HAWKS)**
1929 Chasing Through Europe **(Alfred L WERKER)**
1929 Salute **(John FORD)**
1929 Sunny Side Up
1930 High Society Blues
1930 Just Imagine
1931 A Connecticut Yankee
1931 Delicious
1931 Business and Pleasure
1932 Down to Earth
1932 Handle with Care
1933 Hold Me Tight
1933 My Weakness
1934 Bottoms Up
1934 Handy Andy
1934 Have a Heart
1934 Bright Eyes
1935 The Little Colonel
1935 Doubting Thomas
1935 The Littlest Rebel
1936 Captain January
1936 White Fang
1936 Pigskin Parade / *The Harmony Parade*
1937 Ali Baba Goes to Town
1937 You're a Sweetheart
1938 Kentucky Moonshine / *Three Men and a Girl*
1938 Straight, Place and Show / *They're Off*
1939 Kentucky
1939 East Side of Heaven
1939 That's Right, You're Wrong
1940 If I Had My Way
1940 You'll Find Out
1941 Caught in the Draft
1941 Playmates
1942 Road to Morocco
1943 They Got Me Covered
1943 Thank Your Lucky Stars
1944 Shine on Harvest Moon
1944 The Princess and the Pirate
1945 San Antonio
1946 Two Guys from Milwaukee / *Royal Flush*
1946 The Time, the Place and the Girl
1947 My Wild Irish Rose
1948 Two Guys from Texas
1949 John Loves Mary
1949 Look for the Silver Lining
1949 It's a Great Feeling
1949 The Story of Seabiscuit / *Pride of Kentucky*
1950 The Daughter of Rosie O'Grady
1950 Tea for Two
1951 The Lullaby of Broadway
1951 Painting the Clouds with Sunshine
1952 Where's Charley?
1952 April in Paris
1953 By the Light of the Silvery Moon
1953 Calamity Jane
1954 The Command
1954 King Richard and the Crusaders
1955 Jump into Hell
1956 Glory
1956 The Girl He Left Behind
1961 The Right Approach
1967 C'mon, Let's Live a Little

BUTLER, Robert
(1927–) Los Angeles, California, USA.
1968 Guns in the Heather
1970 The Computer Wore Tennis Shoes
1971 The Barefoot Executive
1971 Scandalous John
1972 Now You See Him, Now You Don't
1974 The Ultimate Thrill
1978 Hot Lead and Cold Feet
1980 Night of the Juggler
1981 Underground Aces
1983 Up the Creek
(also many TV movies)

BUZBY, Zane
1986 Club Sandwich / *Last Resort*

BUZZELL, Edward
(1897–1985) Brooklyn, New York, USA.
1932 The Big Timer
1932 Hollywood Speaks
1932 Virtue
1933 Child of Manhattan
1933 Ann Carver's Profession
1933 Love, Honour and Oh, Baby!
1933 Cross Country Cruise

1934 The Human Side
1935 The Girl Friend
1936 Transient Lady / *False Witness*
1936 Three Married Men
1936 The Luckiest Girl in the World
1937 As Good as Married
1938 Paradise for Three / *Romance for Three*
1938 Fast Company
1939 Honolulu
1939 At the Circus
1940 The Marx Brothers Go West
1941 The Get-Away
1941 Married Bachelor
1942 Ship Ahoy
1942 The Omaha Trail
1943 The Young Profession
1943 Best Foot Forward
1945 Keep Your Powder Dry
1946 Easy to Wed
1946 Three Wise Fools
1947 Song of the Thin Men
1949 Neptune's Daughter
1950 A Woman of Distinction
1950 Emergency Wedding / *Jealousy*
1953 Confidentially Connie
1955 Ain't Misbehavin'
1961 Mary Had a Little...
(also many silent shorts)

BYERS, Mark
1988 Tunnels
1988 The Most Dangerous Woman Alive

BYRNE, David
1986 True Stories

BYRON, Paul
1966 Lt Robin Crusoe USN

BYRUM, John
(1947–) Evanston, Illinois, USA.
1976 Inserts
1979 Heart Beat
1984 The Razor's Edge
1986 The Whoopee Boys
1989 Edie / *The Girl of the Year / The War at Home*

CAAN, James
(1939–) Bronx, New York, USA.
1980 Hide in Plain Sight

CABANNE, William Christy
(1888–1950) St Louis, Missouri, USA.
1924 The Sixth Commandment
1924 The Spitfire
1924 Lend Me Your Husband
1924 Youth for Sale
1924 Is Love Everything?
1925 The Midshipman
1925 The Masked Bride
1926 Monte Carlo
1926 Altars of Desire
1928 Restless Youth / *Wayward Youth*
1928 Driftwood
1928 Nameless Men
1928 Annapolis
1930 Conspiracy
1931 The Sky Raiders
1931 Graft
1931 Hotel Continental
1932 Midnight Patrol
1932 Hearts of Humanity
1932 The Western Limited / *The Night Express*
1932 Red Haired Alibi
1932 The Unwritten Law
1933 Daring Daughters
1933 The World Gone Mad / *The Public Be Hanged*
1933 Midshipman Jack
1934 Money Means Nothing
1934 Jane Eyre
1934 A Girl of the Limberlost
1934 When Strangers Meet
1934 Behind Green Lights
1935 Rendezvous at Midnight
1935 One Frightened Night
1935 The Keeper of Bees
1935 Storm Over the Andes
1935 Another Face / *It Happened in Hollywood*
1935 The Last Outlaw
1936 We Who Are About to Die
1936 Criminal Lawyer
1937 Don't Tell Your Wife
1937 The Outcasts of Poker Flat
1937 You Can't Beat Love
1937 Annapolis Salute / *Salute to Romance*
1937 The Westland Case
1937 Everybody's Doing It
1938 Night Spot
1938 The Marriage Business
1939 Smashing the Spy Ring
1939 Mutiny on the Black Hawk
1939 Tropic Fury
1939 Legion of the Lost Flyers
1940 Man from Montreal
1940 Danger on Wheels
1940 Alias the Deacon
1940 Hot Steel
1940 The Mummy's Hand
1940 The Devil's Pipeline
1941 Scattergood Baines
1941 Scattergood Pulls the Strings
1942 Scattergood Meets Broadway
1942 Scattergood Rides High
1942 Drums of the Congo
1942 Timber
1942 Top Sergeant
1942 Scattergood Survives a Murder
1943 Cinderella Swings It
1943 Keep 'Em Slugging
1944 Dixie Jamboree
1945 The Man Who Walked Alone
1946 Sensation Hunters
1947 Scared to Death
1947 Robin Hood of Monterey
1947 King of the Bandits
1948 Silver Trails
1948 Back Trail
(also many silent shorts)

CACOYANNIS, Michael (Mikhalis Kakogiannis)
(1922–) Cyprus.
1953 Windfall in Athens
1955 Stella
1958 The Final Lie

1959 Our Last Spring
1959 A Girl in Black
1960 The Wastrel
1962 Electra
1964 Zorba the Greek **D* F***
1967 The Day the Fish Came Out
1971 The Trojan Women
1977 Iphigenia
1987 Sweet Country

CAGNEY, Jimmy (James Cagney)
(1899–1986) New York, USA.
Autobiography: Cagney by Cagney.
1957 Short Cut to Hell

CAHN, Edward L
(1899–1963) American.
1931 Homicide Squad **(George MELFORD)**
1932 Law and Order
1932 Radio Patrol
1932 Afraid to Talk
1933 Laughter in Hell
1933 Emergency Call
1935 Confidential
1937 Bad Guy
1941 Redhead
1944 Mainstreet After Dark
1945 Dangerous Partners
1947 Born to Speed
1947 Gas House Kids in Hollywood
1948 The Chequered Coat
1948 Bungalow 13
1949 I Cheated the Law
1949 Prejudice
1950 The Great Plane Robbery
1950 Destination Murder
1950 Experiment Alcatraz
1951 Two Dollar Bettor
1955 The Creature with the Atom Brain
1955 Betrayed Women
1956 Girls in Prison
1956 The She-Creature
1956 Flesh and Spur
1956 Runaway Daughters
1956 Shake, Rattle and Roll
1957 Voodoo Woman
1957 Zombies of Mora-Tau / *The Dead That Walk*
1957 Dragstrip Girl
1957 Invasion of the Saucer Men
1957 Motorcycle Gang
1958 Jet Attack
1958 Suicide Battalion
1958 It! The Terror from Beyond Space
1958 The Curse of the Faceless Man
1959 Hong Kong Confidential
1959 Guns, Girls and Gangsters
1959 Riot in Juvenile Prison
1959 Invisible Invaders
1959 The Four Skulls of Jonathan Drake
1959 Pier 5, Havana
1959 Inside the Mafia
1959 Vice Raid
1960 Gunfighters of Abilene
1960 A Dog's Best Friend
1960 Oklahoma Territory
1960 Three Came to Kill
1960 Twelve Hours to Kill
1960 Noose for a Gunman
1960 The Music Box Kid
1960 Cage of Evil
1960 The Walking Target
1961 The Police Dog Story
1961 Frontier Uprising
1961 Operation Bottleneck
1961 Five Guns to Tombstone
1961 The Gambler Wore the Gun
1961 Gun Fight
1961 When the Clock Strikes
1961 You Have to Run Fast
1961 Secret of Deep Harbour
1961 Boy Who Caught a Crook
1961 Incident in the Alley
1962 Gun Street
1962 The Clown and the Kid
1962 Beauty and the Beast

CAHN, Phil
1935 I've Been Around

CAIN, Christopher
(1943–) Sioux Falls, South Dakota, USA.
1976 Brother, My Song
1976 Grand Jury
1976 The Buzzard
1977 Sixth and Main
1984 The Stone Boy
1985 That Was Then, This Is Now
1986 Where the River Runs Black / *Lazaro*
1987 The Principal
1988 Young Guns

CALLAHAN, Jerry
1935 Gunners and Guns

CALLAS, John
1987 Lone Wolf

CAMERON, James
(1954–) Kapuskasing, Ontario, Canada.
1983 Piranha II: The Spawning
1984 The Terminator
1986 Aliens
1989 The Abyss

CAMERON, Ken
1982 Monkey Grip
1985 Fast Talking
1987 The Good Wife

CAMMELL, Donald
1970 Performance **(Nicolas ROEG)**
1977 Demon Seed
1987 White of the Eye
1989 Jericho

CAMP, Joe
(1939–) St Louis, Missouri, USA.
1974 Benji
1976 Hawmps
1978 For the Love of Benji
1979 The Double McGuffin
1980 Oh Heavenly Dog
1987 Benji, the Hunted

CAMPBELL, Graeme
1988 Into the Fire / *The Legend of the Wolf Lodge*

1988 Murder One
1988 Blood Relations
1989 A Red Blooded American Girl

CAMPBELL, Martin
1988 Criminal Law

CAMPBELL, Norman
1983 The Magic Show

CAMPBELL, Sterling
1947 Bush Pilot

CAMPION, Jane
1989 Sweetie

CAMPUS, Michael
1971 Zero Population Growth
1973 The Mack
1974 The Education of Sonny Carson
1977 The Passover Plot

CANNON, Raymond
1929 Why Leave Home?
1929 Joy Street
1929 Red Wine
1930 Ladies Must Play
1931 Night Life in Reno
1931 Swanee River
1932 Hotel Variety
1934 Two Brothers
1934 The Treasure of Wong Low
1937 Swing It, Sailor
1937 Behind Prison Bars

CANTRELL, Ray
1987 The Warrior

CANUTT, Yakima (Enos Edward Canutt)
(1895–1986) American.
Autobiography: Stunt Man.
1945 Sheriff of Cimarron
1948 Carson City Raiders
1948 Oklahoma Badlands
1948 Son of Adventure
1954 The Lawless Rider
1957 Zarak
(also many serials)

CAPETANOS, Leon
1974 Summer Run

CAPRA, Frank
(1897–) Palermo, Sicily.
Autobiography: The Name Above the Title.
1926 The Strong Man
1927 Long Pants
1927 For the Love of Mike
1928 That Certain Thing
1928 So This Is Love
1928 The Matinee Idol
1928 The Way of the Strong
1928 Say It with Sables
1928 Submarine
1928 The Power of the Press
1929 The Younger Generation
1929 The Donovan Affair
1929 Flight
1930 Ladies of Leisure
1930 Rain or Shine
1931 Dirigible
1931 The Miracle Woman
1932 Forbidden
1932 American Madness
1933 The Bitter Tea of General Yen
1933 Lady for a Day **D* F***
1934 It Happened One Night **D** F****
1934 Broadway Bill / *Strictly Confidential*
1936 Mr Deeds Goes to Town **D** F***
1937 Lost Horizon **F***
1938 You Can't Take It with You **D** F****
1939 Mr Smith Goes to Washington **D* F***
1941 Meet John Doe
1944 Arsenic and Old Lace
1946 It's a Wonderful Life **D* F***
1948 State of the Union / *The World and His Wife*
1950 Riding High
1951 Here Comes the Groom
1959 A Hole in the Head
1961 Pocketful of Miracles
(also many documentaries)

CARAX, Léos
1984 Boy Meets Girl
1986 The Night Is Young / *Mauvais Song*

CARD, Lamar
(1942–) Lookout Mountain, Tennessee, USA.
1977 The Clones
1980 Supervan
1982 Disco Fever

CARDIFF, Jack
(1914–) Great Yarmouth, Norfolk, England.
1959 Intent to Kill
1959 Beyond This Place / *Web of Evidence*
1960 Scent of Mystery / *Holiday in Spain*
1960 Sons and Lovers **D* F***
1962 My Geisha
1962 The Lion
1964 The Long Ships
1965 Young Cassidy
1966 The Liquidator
1968 Dark of the Sun / *The Mercenaries*
1968 The Girl on the Motorcycle / *Naked Under Leather*
1973 Penny Gold
1974 The Mutations

CARDONE, J S
1982 The Slayer
1985 Thunder Alley

CARDOS, John (Bud Cardos)
1972 The Red, White and Black / *Soul Soldier*
1974 Drag Racer
1977 Kingdom of the Spiders
1979 The Dark
1979 The Day Time Ended
1983 Other Realms
1984 Mutant / *Night Shadows*
1987 Outlaw
1987 Skeleton Coast
1989 Act of Piracy

CARDOZA, Anthony
1979 Smokey and the Hotwire Gang

CAREW, Topper (Colin A Carew)
(1943–) Boston, Massachusetts, USA.
1985 Breakin' and Enterin'

CAREWE, Edwin
(1883–1940) American.
1929 Evangeline
1930 The Spoilers
1931 Resurrection
1934 Are We Civilized?

CARLE, Gilles *
(1929–) Maniwaki, Quebec, Canada.
1970 Red
1977 The Angel and the Woman
1980 Fantastica
1981 The Plouffe Family
1983 Maria Chapdelaine
1984 The Crime of Ovide Plouffe **(Denys ARCAND)**
1985 Scalp

CARLINO, John Lewis
(1912–) New York, New York, USA.
1976 The Sailor Who Fell from Grace with the Sea
1980 The Great Santini / *The Ace*
1983 Class

CARLSEN, Henning
(1927–) Aalborg, Denmark.
1962 Dilemma
1963 How About Us?
1964 The Cats
1966 Hunger
1967 People Meet and Sweet Music Fills the Heart
1969 We Are All Demons
1971 Are You Afraid? Of What?
1972 Oh to Be on the Bandwagon!
1974 Un Divorce Heureux
1976 When Svante Disappeared
1978 Did Somebody Laugh?
1978 A Street Under the Snow
1982 Your Money or Your Life
1987 Wolf at the Door

CARLSON, Richard (Albert Lea)
(1912–1977) Minnesota, USA.
1954 Four Guns to the Border
1954 Riders to the Stars
1958 Appointment with a Shadow / *The Big Story*
1958 The Saga of Hemp Brown
1966 Kid Rodelo
1968 Island of the Lost

CARON, Glen Gordon
1988 Clean and Sober

CARPENTER, Horace B
1929 West of the Rockies

CARPENTER, John
(1948–) Bowling Green, Kentucky, USA.
1974 Dark Star
1976 Assault on Precinct 13
1978 Halloween
1981 Escape from New York
1981 The Fog
1982 The Thing
1983 Christine
1984 Starman
1986 Big Trouble in Little China
1987 Prince of Darkness
1988 They Live

CARPENTER, Stephen
1982 The Dorm That Dripped Blood / *Pranks* **(Jeffrey OBROW)**
1983 The Power **(Jeffrey OBROW)**
1987 The Kindred **(Jeffrey OBROW)**

CARPI, Fabio
(1925–) Italian.
1971 Carpo d'Amore
1974 Eta Della Pace
1984 Quatuor Basileus
1987 Blue Beard, Blue Beard

CARR, Bernard
1947 Curley
1947 The Fabulous Joe **(Harve FOSTER)**
1947 The Hal Roach Comedy Carnival
1948 Who Killed "Doc" Robbin?

CARR, Terry
1986 Welcome to 18

CARR, Thomas
(1907–) American.
1944 The Cherokee Flash
1945 Santa Fe Saddlemates
1945 Oregon Trail
1945 Bandits of the Badlands
1945 Rough Riders of Cheyenne
1946 Days of Buffalo Bill
1946 The Undercover Woman
1946 Alias Billy the Kid
1946 The El Paso Kid
1946 Red River Renegades
1946 Rio Grande Rivers
1947 Song of the Wasteland
1947 Code of the Saddle
1950 Hostile Country
1950 Marshal of Heldorado
1950 Crooked River
1950 Colorado Ranger
1950 West of the Brazos
1950 Fast on the Draw
1950 Outlaws of Texas
1952 Man from the Black Hills
1952 Wyoming Roundup
1952 The Maverick
1953 The Star of Texas
1953 Rebel City
1953 Topeka
1953 Captain Scarlett
1953 The Fighting Lawman
1954 Bitter Creek
1954 The Forty-Niners
1954 The Desperado
1955 Bobby Ware Is Missing
1956 Three for Jamie Dawn
1957 Dino

1957 The Tall Stranger
1958 Gunsmoke in Tucson
1959 Cast a Long Shadow
1967 Sullivan's Empire **(Harvey HART)**
(also many serials)

CARRADINE, David (John Arthur Carradine)
(1936–) Hollywood, California, USA.
1975 You and Me
1983 Americana

CARRAS, Anthony
1963 Operation Bikini

CARRE, Bartlett
1935 Gunsmoke on the Guadalupe

CARRERAS, Michael
(1927–) London, England.
1958 The Steel Bayonet
1961 Passport to China / *Visa to Canton*
1962 The Savage Guns
1963 Maniac
1963 What a Crazy World
1965 The Curse of the Mummy's Tomb
1966 Slave Girls / *Prehistoric Women*
1968 The Lost Continent
1975 Call Him Mr Shatter

CARRIER, Rick
1962 Strangers in the City

CARROLL, J Larry
1984 Swordkill / *Ghost Warrior*

CARROLL, Robert M
1988 Sonny Boy

CARRUTH, William
1936 Love Letters of a Star **(Lewis R FOSTER)**
1936 Breezing Home
1936 The Man in Blue
1937 Reported Missing
1937 Some Blondes Are Dangerous
1937 The Lady Fights Back
1937 She's Dangerous **(Lewis R FOSTER)**

CARSTAIRS, John Paddy (John Keys)
(1910–1970) London, England. Autobiographies: Honest Injun; Hadn't We Gaiety; Kaleidoscope and a Jaundiced Eye.
1934 Paris Plane
1936 Holiday's End
1937 Night Ride
1937 Incident in Shanghai
1937 Missing Believed Married
1937 Double Exposure
1938 Lassie from Lancashire
1939 The Saint in London
1939 The Second Mr Bush
1939 Meet Maxwell Archer
1940 Spare a Copper
1941 He Found a Star
1947 Dancing with Crime
1948 Sleeping Car to Trieste
1949 Fools Rush In
1949 The Chiltern Hundreds
1950 Tony Draws a Horse
1951 Talk of a Million
1952 Treasure Hunt
1953 Made In Heaven
1953 Trouble in Store
1953 Top of the Form
1954 One Good Turn
1954 Up to His Neck
1956 The Big Money
1957 Just My Luck
1958 The Square Peg
1959 Tommy the Toreador
1960 Sands of the Desert
1961 Weekend with Lulu
1962 The Devil's Agent / *Im Namen des Teufels*

CARTER, Peter
1978 High Ballin'

CARTIER, Rudolph
1958 Passionate Summer

CARVER, H P
1930 The Silent Enemy

CARVER, Steve
(1945–) Brooklyn, New York, USA.
1974 The Arena
1974 Big Bad Mama
1975 Capone
1976 Drum
1979 Fast Charlie. . The Moonbeam Rider
1980 Steel / *Look Down and Die*
1981 An Eye for an Eye
1983 Lone Wolf McQuade
1987 Jocks / *Road Trip*
1987 Bulletproof
1988 River for Death
1989 Split Lightning

CASDEN, Ron
1987 Campus Man

CASS, Henry
(1902–) British.
1937 Lancashire Luck
1945 29, Acacia Avenue / *The Facts of Love*
1949 The Glass Mountain
1949 No Place for Jennifer
1950 Last Holiday
1951 Young Wives' Tale
1952 Castle in the Air
1952 Father's Doing Fine
1955 The Reluctant Bride / *Two Grooms for a Bride*
1955 No Smoking
1956 Bond of Fear
1956 Breakaway
1956 The High Terrace
1957 The Crooked Sky
1957 Booby Trap
1957 Professor Tim
1958 Blood of the Vampire
1960 Boyd's Shop
1960 The Hand
1960 The Man Who Couldn't Walk
1966 Mr Brown Comes Down the Hill
1967 Give a Dog a Bone
1969 Happy Deathday
(also many documentaries)

CASSAVETES, John
(1929–1989) New York, New York, USA.
1961 Shadows
1962 Too Late Blues
1963 A Child Is Waiting
1968 Faces
1970 Husbands
1971 Minnie and Moskowitz
1974 A Woman Under the Influence **D***
1976 The Killing of a Chinese Bookie
1979 Opening Night
1980 Gloria
1984 Love Streams
1985 Big Trouble

CASTELLARI, Enzo
1987 Sinbad of the Seven Seas

CASTLE, Nick
(1947–) Los Angeles, California, USA.
1982 Tag
1984 The Last Starfighter
1986 The Boy Who Could Fly
1988 Tap

CASTLE, William (William Schloss)
(1914–1977) New York, USA.
Autobiography: Step Right Up I'm Gonna Scare the Pants Off America.
1943 The Chance of a Lifetime
1943 Klondike Kate
1944 The Whistler
1944 When Strangers Marry / *Betrayed*
1944 She's a Soldier, Too
1944 The Mark of the Whistler / *The Marked Man*
1945 Voice of the Whistler
1945 Crime Doctor's Warning
1946 Just Before Dawn
1946 The Mysterious Intruder
1946 The Return of Rusty
1946 The Crime Doctor's Man Hunt
1947 The Crime Doctor's Gamble
1948 Texas, Brooklyn and Heaven / *The Girl from Texas*
1948 The Gentleman from Nowhere
1949 Johnny Stool Pigeon
1949 Undertow
1950 It's a Small World
1951 The Fat Man
1951 Hollywood Story
1951 Cave of Outlaws
1953 Serpent of the Nile
1953 Fort Ti
1953 Conquest of Cochise
1954 Slaves of Babylon
1954 Charge of the Lancers
1954 Drums of Tahiti
1954 Jesse James Versus the Daltons
1954 Battle of Rogue River
1954 The Iron Glove
1954 The Saracen Blade
1954 The Law Versus Billy the Kid
1954 Masterson of Kansas
1955 The Americano
1955 New Orleans Uncensored / *Riot on Pier 6*
1955 The Gun That Won the West
1955 Duel on the Mississippi
1956 The Houston Story
1956 Uranium Boom
1958 Macabre
1958 The House on Haunted Hill
1959 The Tingler
1960 Thirteen Ghosts
1961 Homicidal
1961 Mr Sardonicus
1962 Zotz!
1963 Thirteen Frightened Girls
1963 The Old Dark House
1964 Strait-Jacket
1964 The Nightwalker
1965 I Saw What You Did
1966 Let's Kill Uncle
1967 The Busy Body
1967 The Spirit Is Willing
1968 Project X
1974 Shanks

CASTLEMAN, William Allen
1973 Bummer
1975 Johnny Firecloud

CASTON, Hoite
1985 The Dirt Bike Kid

CATES, Gilbert (Gilbert Katz)
(1934–) New York, New York, USA.
1970 I Never Sang for My Father
1973 Summer Wishes, Winter Dreams
1976 One Summer Love / *Dragonfly*
1979 The Promise / *Face of a Stranger*
1980 The Last Married Couple in America
1980 Oh God! Book II
1987 Backfire
(also many TV movies)

CATES, Joseph
(1924–) American.
1960 Girl of the Night
1965 Who Killed Teddy Bear?
1966 Fat Spy

CATO, Don
1988 Dixie Lanes / *Indian Summer*

CATON-JONES, Michael
1989 Scandal

CAVALCANTI, Alberto (Alberto de Almeida Cavalcanti) *
(1897–1982) Rio de Janeiro, Brazil.
1927 Sea Fever
1935 Coalface
1936 Message from Geneva
1937 We Live in Two Worlds
1937 The Line to Tschierva
1937 Who Writes to Switzerland
1938 Four Barriers
1938 The Chiltern Country
1939 Alice in Switzerland
1939 Midsummer Day's Work
1940 Yellow Caesar / *The Heel of Italy*
1941 Young Veteran
1941 Master of the Sea
1942 Went the Day Well? / *Forty-Eight Hours*
1943 Watertight

1944 Champagne Charlie
1945 Dead of Night **(Charles CRICHTON, Basil DEARDEN, Robert HAMER)**
1947 Nicholas Nickleby
1947 They Made Me a Fugitive / *I Became a Criminal*
1948 For Them That Trespass
1948 The First Gentleman / *Affairs of a Rogue*
1952 Simon the One-Eyed
1953 The Song of the Sea
1954 A Real Woman
1960 The Monster of Highgate Ponds
(also many documentaries)

CAVANI, Liliana
(1936–) Capri, Italy.
1968 Galileo
1969 The Year of the Cannibals
1971 L'Ospite
1973 Milarepa
1974 The Night Porter
1977 Beyond Good and Evil
1981 Le Pelle
1982 The Secret Beyond the Door
1986 Berlin Affair
1988 San Francesco

CAVARA, Paolo *
(1926–) Italian.
1972 The Black Belly of the Tarantula
1972 Deaf Smith and Johnny Ears

CAYTON, William
1965 Knockout
1970 AKA Cassius Clay

CEDAR, Ralph
1928 Wife Savers
1932 A Fool's Advice
1934 She Had to Choose
1935 Captain Bill
1938 Meet the Major
1940 West of Abilene

CELLAN-JONES, James
(1931–) Swansea, Wales.
1973 A Bequest to the Nation / *The Nelson Affair*
(also many TV movies)

CHABROL, Claude
(1930–) Paris, France.
Autobiography: Et pourtant je tourne.
1958 Le Beau Serge
1959 The Cousins
1959 Web of Passion / *A Double Tour / Leda*
1960 Les Bonnes Femmes
1960 Les Godelureaux
1961 The Third Lover / *L'Oeil du Malin*
1962 Seven Capital Sins **(Philippe DEBROCA, Jacques DEMY, Sylvaine DHOMME, Jean-Luc GODARD, Edouard MOLINARO, Marie-José NAT, Dominique PATUREL, Perrette PRADIER, Jean-Marc TENNBERG, Roger VADIM)**
1962 Ophelia
1962 Bluebeard / *Landru*
1964 The Tiger Likes Fresh Blood
1965 An Orchid for the Tiger
1965 Maria Chantal contre le Docteur Kha
1966 The Champagne Murders / *Le Scandale*
1966 La Ligne de Démarcation
1967 The Road to Corinth / *Who's Got the Black Box*
1968 The Does
1968 La Femme Infidèle
1969 This Man Must Die / *The Beast Must Die / Killer*
1969 The Butcher
1970 The Breakup
1971 Just Before Nightfall
1971 Ten Days' Wonder
1972 High Heels / *Scoundrel in White / Docteur Popaul*
1973 Wedding in Blood / *Red Wedding*
1974 The Nada Gang
1975 Innocents with Dirty Hands
1975 Les Magiciens
1976 The Twist
1977 Alice ou la Dernière Fugue
1977 Blood Relatives
1978 Violette
1980 Splintered
1980 Le Cheval d'Orgeuil
1982 Les Fantômes du Chapelier
1985 Poulet au Vinaigre
1987 Inspecteur Lavardin
1987 Masques
1988 A Story of Women

CHAFFEY, Don
(1917–) British.
1950 The Mysterious Poacher
1951 The Case of the Missing Scene
1953 Skid Kids
1954 Time Is My Enemy
1956 The Secret Tent
1957 The Girl in the Picture
1957 The Flesh Is Weak
1958 A Question of Adultery
1958 The Man Upstairs
1959 Danger Within / *Breakout*
1960 Dentist in the Chair
1960 Lies My Father Told Me
1961 Nearly a Nasty Accident
1961 Greyfriars Bobby
1962 A Matter of Who
1962 The Prince and the Pauper
1963 The Webster Boy / *Middle of Nowhere*
1963 The Horse Without a Head
1963 Jason and the Argonauts
1963 They All Died Laughing / *A Jolly Bad Fellow*
1963 The Three Lives of Thomasina
1963 The Crooked Road
1967 One Million Years B.C.
1967 The Viking Queen
1968 A Twist of Sand
1971 Creatures the World Forgot
1972 Clinic Xclusive
1973 Charley-One-Eye
1974 Persecution / *The Terror of Sheba*
1975 The Fourth Wish
1976 Harness Fever
1976 Ride a Wild Pony / *Born to Run*
1977 Surf
1977 Pete's Dragon

1978 The Magic of Lassie
1979 C.H.O.M.P.S.
(also many TV movies)

CHAMBERS, Everett
(1926–) Montrose, California, USA.
1959 Run Across the River
1964 The Lollipop Cover

CHAMPION, Gower
(1919–1981) American.
1965 My Six Loves
1974 The Bank Shot

CHAMPION, John
(1923–) American.
1976 Mustang Country

CHAN, Jackie (Chen Yuan-Long)
(1954–) Hong Kong.
1979 The Fearless Hyena
1980 Young Master
1982 Dragon Lord
1983 Project A
1985 Police Story
1986 The Armour of God
1987 Project A Part II
1988 Police Story II

CHANEY, Warren
1987 The Lamp

CHAPLIN, Charlie (Sir Charles Spencer Chaplin)
(1889–1977) London, England.
Autobiographies: My Trip Abroad; My Wonderful Visit; My Autobiography; My Life in Pictures.
1920 The Kid
1923 The Pilgrim
1923 A Woman of Paris
1925 The Gold Rush
1926 A Woman of the Sea
1927 The Circus **D***
1931 City Lights
1935 Modern Times
1940 The Great Dictator **F***
1947 Monsieur Verdoux
1952 Limelight
1957 A King in New York
1967 A Countess from Hong Kong
(also many silent shorts)

CHAPMAN, Matthew
(1950–) British.
1979 Hussy
1984 Strangers Kiss
1989 Heart of Midnight

CHAPMAN, Michael
(1935–) Maine, USA.
1983 All the Right Moves
1985 The Clan of the Cave Bears
1987 The Juryman

CHAREF, Mehdi
1985 Tea in the Harem

CHARON, Jacques
(1920–1978) French.
1968 A Flea in Her Ear

CHARREL, Erik
(1895–1974) German.
1931 Congress Dances
1934 Caravan

CHAUDHRI, Amin Q
1986 Once Again
1988 Tiger Warsaw

CHEECH, Richard
1987 Born in East L.A.

CHEEK, Douglas
1984 C.H.U.D.

CHERRY, John
1985 Dr Otto and the Riddle of the Gloom Beam
1987 Ernest Goes to Camp
1988 Ernest Saves Christmas
1989 Ernest Meets the Voodoo Queen

CHETWYND, Lionel
(1940–) London, England.
1977 Two Solitudes
1987 Hanoi Hilton

CHINN, Robert C
1976 Panama Red

CHIODO, Steve
1987 Killer Klowns from Outer Space

CHOMSKY, Marvin J
(1929–) New York, New York, USA.
1972 Evel Knievel
1975 Mackintosh and T.J.
1975 Live a Little, Steal a Lot / *Murph the Surf*
1979 Good Luck, Miss Wyckoff
1984 Tank
(also many TV movies)

CHONG, Thomas
1980 The Next Cheech and Chong Movie
1981 Cheech and Chong's Nice Dreams
1983 Cheech and Chong: Still Smokin'
1984 Cheech and Chong's the Corsican Brothers

CHOOLUCK, Leon
(1920–) American.
1960 Three Blondes in His Life

CHOPRA, Joyce
1985 Smooth Talk
1988 The Lemon Sisters

CHOURAQUI, Elie
(1950–) French.
1978 Mon Premier Amour
1981 Qu'est-çe-que fait courir David?
1986 Love Songs / *Paroles et Musique*
1987 Man on Fire

CHRISTENBERRY, Chris
1973 Little Cigars

CHRISTENSEN, Benjamin
(1879–1959) Viborg, Denmark.
1925 The Woman Who Died
1926 The Devil's Circus
1927 Mockery
1928 The Haunted House
1929 Seven Footsteps to Satan
1929 The House of Horror
1929 The Mystery Island
1939 Children of Divorce
1940 The Child
1941 Come Home with Me
1942 The Lady with the Coloured Gloves

CHRISTIAN, Roger
(1944–) London, England.
1981 The Dollar Bottom
1982 Sender
1986 Lorca and the Outlaws / *Starship Redwing / 2084*

CHRISTIE, Al
(1886–1951) Ontario, Canada.
1930 Charley's Aunt
1938 Birth of a Baby
1940 Half a Sinner

CHRISTY, Howard
1933 Sing, Sinner, Sing

CHUDNOW, Byron
1973 The Doberman Gang
1973 The Daring Dobermans
1976 The Amazing Dobermans

CHUNG, David
1987 Magnificent Warriors
1987 In the Line of Duty

CICCORITTI, Gerard
1986 Psycho Girls
1987 Graveyard Shift
1989 Graveyard Shift II: The Understudy

CIMBER, Matt (Mateo Ottaviano)
1968 Single Room Furnished
1970 Man and Wife
1971 Calliope
1974 The Black Six
1975 The Candy Tangerine Man
1975 Gemini Affair
1975 Lady Cocoa
1976 The Witch Who Came from the Sea
1981 Butterfly
1983 Fake Out
1983 A Time to Die
1984 Hundra
1984 Yellow Hair and the Fortress of Gold

CIMINO, Michael
(1940–) New York, New York, USA.
1974 Thunderbolt and Lightfoot
1978 The Deer Hunter **D** F****
1980 Heaven's Gate
1985 Year of the Dragon
1987 The Sicilian
1988 Santa Anna Winds

CIUPKA, Richard
1983 Curtains

CLAIR, René (René-Lucien Chomette)
(1898–1981) Paris, France.
1927 The Italian Straw Hat / *The Horse Ate the Hat*
1928 Les Deux Timides
1930 Under the Roofs of Paris
1931 Le Million
1931 A Nous la Liberté
1932 July 14th
1934 Le Dernier Milliardaire
1936 The Ghost Goes West
1938 Break the News
1941 The Flame of New Orleans
1942 I Married a Witch
1943 Forever and a Day **(Edmund GOULDING, Cedric HARDWICKE, Frank LLOYD, Victor SAVILLE, Robert STEVENSON, Herbert WILCOX)**
1944 It Happened Tomorrow
1945 And Then There Were None / *Ten Little Niggers*
1947 Man About Town / *Le Silence est d'Or*
1947 Beauty and the Beast
1952 Beauties of the Night
1955 The Grand Manoeuvre
1957 Gates of Paris
1961 All the Gold in the World
1962 Three Fables of Love
1965 Les Fêtes Galantes

CLARK, Bob
(1941–) New Orleans, Louisiana, USA.
1972 Deathdream
1972 Children Shouldn't Play with Dead Things
1974 Dead of Night
1975 Black Christmas / *Silent Night, Evil Night / Stranger in the House*
1976 Breaking Point
1979 Murder by Decree
1980 Tribute
1982 Porky's
1983 Porky's II: The Next Day
1983 A Christmas Story
1984 Rhinestone
1985 Turk 182
1987 From the Hip
1988 The Von Metz Incident / *Face Off*
1989 Loose Cannons

CLARK, Bruce
1969 Naked Angels
1971 The Ski Bum
1972 Hammer
1981 Galaxy of Terror

CLARK, Frank C
1981 Beyond the Reef

CLARK, Greydon
(1943–) American.
1973 Tom
1976 Black Shampoo
1976 The Bad Bunch
1977 Satan's Cheerleaders
1978 Hi-Riders
1980 Angels Brigade
1980 Without Warning

1981 The Return
1982 Joysticks
1983 Wacko
1985 Final Justice
1988 Uninvited
1989 Skinheads

CLARK, James B
(1908–) American.
1957 Under Fire
1958 Sierra Baron
1958 Villa!
1958 The Sad Horse
1958 A Dog of Flanders
1960 One Foot in Hell
1961 The Big Show
1961 Misty
1963 Flipper
1963 Drums of Africa
1964 Island of the Blue Dolphins
1966 And Now Miguel
1969 My Side of the Mountain
1971 The Little Ark

CLARK, John
1984 Fast Lane Fever

CLARK, Matt
1988 Da
1989 Roots in a Parched Ground

CLARK, Richard
1989 Dr Hackenstein

CLARK, Ron
1983 The Funny Farm

CLARKE, Alan
(1935–) Liverpool, England.
1979 Scum
1986 Billy the Kid and the Green Baize Vampire
1987 Rita, Sue and Bob Too

CLARKE, James Kenelm
(1941–) Gloucestershire, England.
1973 Got It Made
1975 Exposé
1977 Let's Get Laid
1978 The Music Machine
1982 Funny Money
1985 Yellow Pages / *Going Undercover*

CLARKE, Malcolm
1990 Nobody's Children

CLARKE, Shirley (Shirley Brimberg)
(1925–) New York, New York, USA.
1953 Dance in the Sun
1954 In Paris Parks
1955 Bullfight
1957 A Moment of Love
1958 Loops
1959 Bridges-Go-Round
1960 A Scary Time
1962 The Connection
1964 The Cool World

CLAUSEN, Erik
1987 The Dark Side of the Moon

CLAVELL, James
(1924–) Sydney, New South Wales, Australia.
1959 Five Gates to Hell
1960 Walk Like a Dragon
1967 To Sir, with Love
1968 The Sweet and the Bitter
1969 Where's Jack?
1971 The Last Valley

CLAXTON, William F
(1914–) California, USA.
1948 Half Past Midnight
1949 Tucson
1951 All That I Have
1956 Stagecoach to Fury
1957 The Quiet Gun
1957 Young and Dangerous
1957 Rockabilly Baby
1957 God Is My Partner
1960 Desire in the Dust
1960 Young Jesse James
1963 Law of the Lawless
1964 Stage to Thunder Rock
1972 Night of the Lepus

CLAYTON, Jack
(1921–) Brighton, West Sussex, England.
1956 The Bespoke Overcoat
1958 Room at the Top **D* F***
1962 The Innocents
1964 The Pumpkin Eater
1967 Our Mother's House
1974 The Great Gatsby
1983 Something Wicked This Way Comes
1987 The Lonely Passion of Judith Hearne

CLEGG, Tom
1970 Love Is a Splendid Illusion
1978 Sweeney II
1980 McVicar
1984 The Inside Man
1988 Any Man's Death

CLEMENS, William
(1905–) American.
1936 Manhunt
1936 The Law in Her Hands
1936 The Case of the Velvet Claws
1936 Down the Stretch
1936 Here Comes Carter! / *The Voice of Scandal*
1937 Once a Doctor
1937 The Case of the Stuttering Bishop
1937 Talent Scout
1937 The Footloose Heiress
1937 Missing Witnesses
1938 Torchy Blane in Panama
1938 Accidents Will Happen
1938 Mr Chump
1938 Nancy Drew, Detective
1939 Nancy Drew, Reporter
1939 Nancy Drew, Trouble Shooter
1939 Nancy Drew, and the Hidden Staircase
1939 The Dead End Kids on Dress Parade
1940 Calling Philo Vance
1940 King of the Lumberjacks
1940 Devil's Island
1941 She Couldn't Say No

1941 Knockout
1941 The Night of January 16th
1942 A Night in New Orleans
1942 Sweater Girl
1943 Lady Bodyguard
1943 The Falcon in Danger
1943 The Falcon and the Co-Eds
1944 The Falcon Out West
1944 Crime by Night
1947 The Thirteenth Floor

CLEMENT, Dick
(1937–) Westcliff-on-Sea, Essex, England.
1969 Otley
1971 A Severed Head
1971 Catch Me a Spy
1979 Porridge
1983 Bullshot!
1984 Water

CLEMENT, René
(1913–) Bordeaux, France.
1945 La Bataille du Rail
1946 Mr Orchid / *Le Père Tranquille*
1946 The Damned
1949 The Walls of Malapaga
1950 Le Château de Verre
1952 Forbidden Games
1954 Lovers, Happy Lovers / *Knave of Hearts / Monsieur Ripois*
1955 Gervaise
1958 This Angry Age / *The Sea Wall*
1960 Purple Noon
1961 Quelle Joie de Vivre
1962 The Day and the Hour
1964 Joy House / *The Love Cage*
1966 Is Paris Burning?
1970 Rider on the Rain
1971 The Deadly Trap / *La Maison sous les Arbres*
1972 And Hope to Die / *La Course du Lièvre à travers les Champs*
1975 Wanted: Baby-Sitter
(also many documentaries)

CLIFFORD, Bill
1952 Birthright

CLIFFORD, Graeme
1982 Frances
1985 Burke and Wills
1988 Gleaming the Cube

CLIFT, Denison
(1892–1961) American.
1924 This Freedom
1924 Honour Among Men
1925 Flames of Desire
1925 Ports of Call
1935 The Mystery of the Marie Celeste / *Phantom Ship*

CLIFTON, Elmer
(1890–1949) Chicago, Illinois, USA.
1924 Daughters of the Night
1924 The Warrens of Virginia
1935 Captured in Chinatown
1935 Rip Roaring Riley
1935 Skull and Crown
1935 Pals of the Range
1935 Saddle Courage
1935 Fighting Caballero
1935 Rough Riding Rangers
1935 Border Patrol
1935 Cyclone of the Saddle
1936 Wildcat Trooper
1936 Gambling with Souls
1937 Crusade Against Rackets
1937 Assassin of Youth
1937 Death in the Air
1937 Mile a Minute Lover
1938 California Frontier
1938 Crashin' Thru
1938 Law of the Texan
1938 Stranger from Arizona
1938 Wolves of the Sea
1938 Paroled from the Big House
1938 Crime Afloat
1940 Isle of Destiny
1941 Swamp Woman
1941 Hard Guy
1941 City of Missing Girls
1941 I'll Sell My Life
1942 Deep in the Heart of Texas
1942 The Old Chisholm Trail
1943 The Sundown Kid
1943 Frontier Law
1944 Boss of Rawhide
1944 Dead or Alive
1944 Gangsters of the Frontier
1944 Guns of the Law
1944 The Pinto Bandit
1944 Return of the Rangers
1944 Seven Doors to Death
1944 Spook Town
1944 Whispering Skull
1945 Youth Aflame
1945 Marked for Murder
1949 The Judge
1949 Not Wanted

CLINE, Edward F (Eddie Cline)
(1892–1961) Wisconsin, USA.
1924 Captain January
1924 When a Man's a Man
1924 Little Robinson Crusoe
1924 Good Bad Boy
1924 Along Came Ruth
1925 The Rag Man
1925 Old Clothes
1927 Let It Rain
1927 Soft Cushions
1928 Ladies' Night in a Turkish Bath
1928 The Head Man
1928 Broadway Fever
1928 The Crash
1929 His Lucky Day
1929 The Forward Pass
1930 Leathernecking / *Present Arms*
1930 In the Next Room
1930 Sweet Mama / *Conflict*
1930 Hook, Line and Sinker
1930 The Widow from Chicago
1931 Cracked Nuts
1931 The Naughty Flirt
1932 The Girl Habit
1932 Million Dollar Legs
1933 Parole Girl
1933 So This Is Africa

1934 Peck's Bad Boy
1934 The Dude Ranger
1935 When a Man's a Man
1935 The Cowboy Millionaire
1935 It's a Great Life
1936 F-Man
1937 On Again, Off Again
1937 Forty Naughty Girls
1937 High Flyers
1938 Hawaii Calls
1938 Go Chase Yourself
1938 Breaking the Ice
1938 Peck's Bad Boy with the Circus
1940 My Little Chickadee
1940 The Villain Still Pursued Her
1940 The Bank Dick
1941 Meet the Chump
1941 Hello Sucker
1941 Cracked Nuts
1941 Never Give a Sucker an Even Break / *What a Man!*
1942 Snuffy Smith
1942 The Yard Bird
1942 What's Cookin'? / *Wake Up and Dream*
1942 Private Buckaroo
1942 Give Out, Sisters
1942 Behind the Eight Ball / *Off the Beaten Track*
1943 He's My Guy
1943 Crazy House
1944 Hat Check Honey
1944 Swingtime Johnny
1944 Slightly Terrific
1944 Ghost Catchers
1944 Moonlight and Cactus
1944 Night Club Girl
1945 See My Lawyer
1945 Penthouse Rhythm
1946 Bringing Up Father
1948 Jiggs and Maggie in Society
1948 Jiggs and Maggie in Court **(William BEAUDINE)**
(also many silent shorts)

CLOCHE, Maurice *
(1907–) Commercy, France.
1951 Never Take No for an Answer **(Ralph SMART)**
1967 The Viscount
(also many documentaries)

CLOUSE, Robert
1970 Darker Than Amber
1970 Dreams of Glass
1973 Enter the Dragon
1974 Black Belt Jones
1974 Golden Needles
1976 The Ultimate Warrior
1978 The Amsterdam Kill
1978 The Pack
1979 Game of Death
1980 The Big Brawl
1981 Force: Five
1983 Night Eyes / *The Rats*
1984 Dark Warrior
1985 Gymkata
1989 China O'Brien

CLURMAN, Harold
(1901–1980) American.
Autobiography: All People Are Famous.
1946 Deadline at Dawn

COATES, Lewis (Luigi Cozzi) *
1979 Starcrash
1980 Alien Contamination
1983 Hercules
1983 The Adventures of Hercules II

COCHRAN, Steve (Robert Cochran)
(1917–1965) American.
1966 Tell Me in the Sunlight

COE, Fred
(1914–1979) American.
1965 A Thousand Clowns **F***
1969 Me, Natalie

COE, Peter
(1929–1987) London, England.
1969 Lock Up Your Daughters

COEN, Joel
1984 Blood Simple
1987 Raising Arizona
1989 Miller's Crossing

COHEN, Bennett
1931 Law of the Rio Grande **(Forrest SHELDON)**
1934 Rainbow Riders

COHEN, David
1986 Hollywood Zap

COHEN, Howard R
1981 Saturday the 14th
1983 Space Raiders
1988 Saturday the 14th Strikes Back
1989 Time Trackers

COHEN, Larry
(1938–) New York, New York, USA.
1972 Bone / *Dial Rat for Terror*
1973 Black Caesar / *Godfather of Harlem*
1973 Hell Up in Harlem
1974 It's Alive
1977 God Told Me To / *Demon*
1978 It Lives Again
1978 The Private Files of J. Edgar Hoover
1981 Full Moon High
1982 Q, the Winged Serpent
1985 Blind Alley / *Perfect Strangers*
1985 Special Effects
1985 The Stuff
1987 Island of the Alive: It's Alive III
1987 Return to Salem's Lot
1987 Deadly Illusion / *Love You to Death* **(William TANNEN)**
1989 Apparatus
1989 Wicked Stepmother
1990 Ambulance

COHEN, Norman
(1936–1983) Irish.
1967 Brendan Behan's Dublin
1967 The London Nobody Knows
1968 Till Death Us Do Part
1971 Dad's Army

1972 Adolf Hitler - My Part in His Downfall
1977 Stand Up Virgin Soldiers

COHEN, Robert
(1949–) Cornwall-on-the-Hudson, New York, USA.
1980 A Small Circle of Friends
1984 Scandalous

COKLISS, Harley
(1945–) San Diego, California, USA.
1979 That Summer
1982 Battlestruck / *Warlords of the 21st Century*
1985 Black Moon Rising
1987 Malone
1988 The Dream Demon

COLEMAN Jnr., C C
1934 Voice in the Night
1936 Legion of Terror
1936 Code of the Range
1936 Dodge City Trail
1937 Parole Racket
1937 Criminals of the Air
1937 Paid to Dance
1937 The Shadow
1937 A Fight to the Finish
1938 When G-Men Step In
1938 Highway Patrol
1938 Squadron of Honour
1938 Flight to Fame
1939 Homicide Bureau
1939 Missing Daughters
1939 Outpost of the Mounties
1939 Spoilers of the Range
1939 My Son Is a Criminal

COLEMAN, Clifford
1989 The Ice Runner

COLEMAN, Herbert
1961 Battle of Bloody Beach
1961 Posse from Hell

COLE, John
1989 Signs of Life

COLLA, Richard A
(1918–) Milwaukee, Wisconsin, USA.
1970 Zigzag / *False Witness*
1972 Fuzz
1978 Olly Olly Oxen Free
1979 Battlestar Galactica
(also many TV movies)

COLLECTOR, Robert
1984 Red Heat
1987 Nightflyers

COLLIER, James F
1966 For Pete's Sake!
1967 His Land
1967 Two a Penny
1970 Catch a Pebble
1972 Time to Run
1975 The Hiding Place
1980 Joni
1984 The Prodigal
1985 Cry from the Mountain
1987 Caught

COLLINS, Arthur Greville
(1897–1980) American.
1935 Personal Maid's Secret
1935 The Widow of Monte Carlo
1936 Thank You Jeeves
1936 Nobody's Fool
1937 Paradise Isle
1938 Saleslady

COLLINS, Lewis D
(1889–1954) American.
1930 Devil's Pit
1930 Young Desire
1931 Law of the Tong
1933 Gun Law
1933 Via Pony Express
1933 Trouble Busters
1933 Skyways
1933 Ship of Wanted Men
1934 Sing Sing Nights
1934 The Man from Hell
1934 Public Stenographer
1934 Brand of Hate
1934 Ticket to a Crime
1935 Make a Million
1935 The Desert Rail
1935 Hoosier Schoolmaster
1935 Spanish Cape Mystery
1935 Manhattan Butterfly
1935 Along Came a Woman
1936 Down to the Sea
1936 Return of Jimmy Valentine
1936 The Leavenworth Case
1936 Doughnuts and Society
1936 Timber Wolves
1937 Fury and the Woman
1937 Trapped By G-Men
1937 Under Suspicion
1937 The Wildcatter
1937 River of Missing Men
1937 Mighty Treve
1938 Making the Headlines
1938 Flight into Nowhere
1938 Reformatory
1938 Crime Takes a Holiday
1938 The House of Mystery
1938 Outside the Law
1938 The Strange Case of Dr Meade
1939 Hidden Power
1939 Fugitive at Large
1939 Trapped in the Sky
1939 Whispering Enemies
1940 Outside the Three-Mile Limit
1940 Passport to Alcatraz
1940 Prison Camp
1940 The Great Plane Robbery
1941 The Great Swindle
1941 Borrowed Hero
1942 Little Joe, the Wrangler
1942 Danger in the Pacific
1943 Raiders of San Joaquin
1943 Tenting Tonight on the Old Camp Ground
1944 The Old Texas Trail
1944 Trigger Trail
1944 Sweethearts of the USA
1944 Oklahoma Raiders
1946 Danger Woman

1947 Heading for Heaven
1947 Killer Dill
1948 Jungle Goddess
1949 Fighting Redhead
1949 Ride, Ryder, Ride
1949 Thunder Roll
1950 Cherokee Uprising
1950 Law of the Panhandle
1950 Cowboy and the Prizefighter
1950 Hot Rod
1951 Canyon Raiders
1951 Nevada Badmen
1951 Abilene Trail
1951 Lawless Cowboys
1951 Stage from Blue River
1951 Colorado Ambush
1951 The Longhorn
1951 Man from Sonora
1951 Oklahoma Justice
1951 Texas Lawman
1952 Dead Man's Trail
1952 Fargo
1952 Kansas Territory
1952 Texas City
1952 Waco
1952 Wild Stallion
1952 The Gunman
1952 Montana Incident
1952 Texas Marshal
1953 The Marksman
1953 Canyon Ambush
1953 The Homesteaders
1953 Texas Badmen
1953 Vigilante Terror
1954 Two Guns and a Badge
(also many serials)

COLLINS, Robert
1979 Walk Proud
1981 Savage Harvest
(also many TV movies)

COLLINSON, Peter
(1938–1980) Cleethorpes, Lincolnshire, England.
1967 The Penthouse
1967 Up the Junction
1968 The Long Day's Dying
1969 The Italian Job
1970 You Can't Win 'Em All
1971 Fright
1972 Innocent Bystanders
1972 Straight on Till Morning
1973 The Man Called Noon
1974 And Then There Were None
1974 Open Season
1975 The Sellout
1975 The Spiral Staircase
1977 Tomorrow Never Comes
1977 Tigers Don't Cry
1980 The Earthling

COLMES, Walter
1945 Identity Unknown
1945 The Woman Who Came Back
1946 The French Key
1947 The Burning Cross
1947 Road to the Big House

COLOMO, Fernando
1986 Star Knight

COLOSIMO, Rosa
1988 Lay Off

COLUMBUS, Chris
1987 Adventures in Babysitting / *A Night on the Town*
1988 Heartbreak Hotel

COMENCINI, Luigi *
(1916–) Salo, Brescia, Italy.
1952 Heidi
1953 Bread, Love and Dreams
1954 Frisky / *Pane, Amore e Gelosia*
1960 Everybody Go Home!
1963 Bebo's Girl
1968 Italian Secret Service
1976 Sunday Woman
1979 Traffic Jam
1980 They All Loved Him
1987 A Boy from Calabria
1988 History
1989 La Bohème

COMFORT, Lance
(1908–1967) British.
1941 Hatter's Castle
1941 Penn of Pennsylvania / *The Courageous Mr Penn*
1941 Those Kids from Town
1942 Squadron Leader X
1943 Escape to Danger
1943 When We Are Married
1943 Old Mother Riley Detective
1944 Hotel Reserve **(Max GREENE, Victor HANBURY)**
1945 Great Day
1946 Bedelia
1946 Temptation Harbour
1947 Daughter of Darkness
1947 Silent Dust
1950 Portrait of Clare
1953 The Girl on the Pier
1954 Bang, You're Dead / *Game of Danger*
1954 Eight O'Clock Walk
1956 The Man in the Road
1957 Face in the Night
1957 The Man from Tangier / *Thunder Over Tangier*
1957 At the Stroke of Nine
1959 The Ugly Duckling
1959 Make Mine a Million
1961 The Breaking Point / *The Great Armoured Car Swindle*
1961 Rag Doll / *Young, Willing and Eager*
1961 Pit of Darkness
1961 The Painted Smile / *Murder Can Be Deadly*
1962 The Break
1962 Tomorrow at Ten
1963 Touch of Death
1963 Live It Up / *Swing and Swing*
1963 Blind Corner
1964 Devils of Darkness
1965 Be My Guest
(also many TV shorts)

COMMERFORD, Joe
1988 Reefer and the Model

COMMONS, David
1969 The Angry Breed

COMPTON, Richard
1970 Angels Die Hard
1972 Welcome Home Soldier Boys
1973 Macon County Line
1975 Return to Macon County
1977 Maniac
1979 Ravages

CONDON, William
1987 Sister, Sister

CONNELL, James a
1989 Retreads

CONNELL, Merle W
1952 Untamed Woman
1956 The Flesh Merchants

CONNOLLY, Robert (Bobby Connelly)
1937 The Devil's Saddle Legion
1937 Expensive Husbands
1938 The Patient in Room 18 **(Crane WILBUR)**

CONNOR, Kevin
(1937–) London, England.
1975 From Beyond the Grave
1975 The Land That Time Forgot
1976 At the Earth's Core
1976 Trial By Combat / *Choice of Weapons / Dirty Knight's Work*
1977 The People That Time Forgot
1978 Warlords of Atlantis
1979 Arabian Adventure
1980 Motel Hell
1982 The House Where Evil Dwells

CONRAD, Mikel
1950 The Flying Saucer

CONRAD, Patrick
1987 Mascara

CONRAD, William
(1920–) Louisville, Kentucky, USA.
1964 The Man from Galveston
1965 Two on the Guillotine
1965 My Blood Runs Cold
1985 Brainstorm

CONSIDINE Jnr, John W
(1898–) American.
1932 Disorderly Conduct

CONTE, Richard (Nicholas Conte)
(1911–1975) Italian-American.
1969 Operation Cross Eagles

CONVY, Bert
(1933–) St Louis, Missouri, USA.
1986 Weekend Warriors / *Hollywood Airforce Base*

CONWAY, Jack
(1887–1952) Graveville, USA.
1924 The Trouble Shooters
1924 The Rough Neck / *Thorns of Passion*
1924 The Heartbusters
1925 The Hunted Woman
1925 The Only Thing
1926 Soul Mates
1926 Brown of Harvard
1927 Twelve Miles Out
1927 The Understanding Heart
1928 Bringing Up Father
1928 The Smart Set
1928 While the City Sleeps
1928 Quicksands
1929 Alias Jimmy Valentine
1929 Untamed
1929 Our Young Maidens
1930 The Unholy Three
1930 They Learned About Women **(Sam WOOD)**
1930 New Moon
1931 The Easiest Way
1931 Just a Gigolo / *The Dancing Partner*
1932 Arsène Lupin
1932 Red Headed Woman
1932 But the Flesh Is Weak
1933 Hell Below
1933 The Nuisance / *Accidents Wanted*
1933 The Solitaire Man
1934 The Gay Bride
1934 The Girl from Missouri / *One Hundred Per Cent Pure*
1934 Tarzan and His Mate **(Cedric GIBBONS)**
1934 Viva Villa! **(Howard HAWKS)** **F***
1935 A Tale of Two Cities **F***
1935 One New York Night / *The Trunk Mystery*
1936 Libeled Lady **F***
1937 Saratoga
1938 Too Hot to Handle
1938 A Yank at Oxford
1938 Lady of the Tropics
1939 Let Freedom Ring
1940 Boom Town
1941 Honky Tonk
1941 Love Crazy
1942 Crossroads
1943 Assignment in Brittany
1944 Dragon Seed **(Harold S BUCQUET)**
1947 High Barbaree
1947 The Hucksters
1947 Desire Me **(George CUKOR, Mervyn LE ROY)**
1948 Julia Misbehaves

CONWAY, James l
(1950–) New York, New York, USA.
1976 In Search of Noah's Ark
1977 The Lincoln Conspiracy
1978 Beyond and Back
1979 The Fall of the House of Usher
1980 Hangar 18
1981 Earthbound
1981 The Boogens
1981 The President Must Die

CONWAY, Kevin
(1942–) New York, New York, USA.

1986 The Violins Came with the Americans
1988 Sun and Moon

CONYERS, Darcy
(1919–1973) British.
1952 Ha'penny Breeze
1959 The Night We Dropped a Clanger
1960 The Night We Got the Bird
1961 In the Doghouse

COOK, Bruce
1984 The Census Taker
1988 Line of Fire

COOK, Fielder
(1923–) Atlanta, Georgia, USA.
1958 Patterns
1961 Home Is the Hero
1966 A Big Hand for the Little Lady / *Big Deal at Dodge City*
1968 How to Save a Marriage and Ruin Your Life
1968 Prudence and the Pill
1972 Eagle in a Cage
1973 The Hideaways
(also many TV movies)

COOK, Philip
1988 Beyond the Rising Moon

COOKE, Alan
(1935–) London, England.
1962 Flat Two
1970 The Mind of Mr Soames
(also many TV movies)

COOLIDGE, Martha
(1946–) New Haven, Connecticut, USA.
1976 Not a Pretty Picture
1983 Valley Girl
1984 Joy of Sex
1984 The City Girl
1985 Real Genius
1988 Plain Clothes / *Glory Days*

COOPER, George A
1932 This World, the Flesh, the Devil
1933 The Man Outside
1933 His Grace Gives Notice
1934 Home Sweet Home
1934 The Roof
1934 Mannequin
1934 The Black Abbot
1934 Tangled Evidence
1935 Anything Might Happen

COOPER, Jackie
(1921–) Los Angeles, California, USA.
1971 Stand Up and Be Counted
1984 Go for the Gold
(also many TV movies and TV shorts)

COOPER, Merian C
(1893–1973) Jacksonville, Florida, USA.
1925 Grass **(Ernest B SCHOEDSACK)**
1927 Chang **(Ernest B SCHOEDSACK)**
1929 The Four Feathers **(Lothar MENDES, Ernest B SCHOEDSACK)**
1933 King Kong **(Ernest B SCHOEDSACK)**
1933 The Last Days of Pompeii **(Ernest B SCHOEDSACK)**

COOPER, Peter H
1986 Ordinary Heroes

COOPER, Stuart
(1942–) Hoboken, New Jersey, USA.
1974 Little Malcolm and His Struggle Against the Eunuchs
1975 Overlord
1977 The Disappearance

COPELAN, Jodie
1958 Ambush at Cimarron Pass

COPELAND, Jack
1958 Hell's Five Hours

COPPOLA, Chris
1987 Dracula's Widow

COPPOLA, Francis Ford
(1939–) Detroit, Michigan, USA.
1961 Tonight for Sure
1963 Dementia 13 / *The Haunted and the Hunted*
1966 You're a Big Boy Now
1968 Finian's Rainbow
1969 The Rain People
1972 The Godfather **D* F****
1974 The Conversation **F***
1974 The Godfather, Part II **D** F****
1979 Apocalypse Now **D* F***
1982 One from the Heart
1983 The Outsiders
1983 Rumble Fish
1984 The Cotton Club
1986 Peggy Sue Got Married
1987 Gardens of Stone
1988 Tucker, the Man and His Dream
1989 New York Stories **(Woody ALLEN, Martin SCORSESE)**

CORBUCCI, Bruno *
(1931–) Italian.
1982 Thieves and Robbers
1985 Miami Super Cops
1987 Aladdin

CORBUCCI, Sergio *
(1927–) Rome, Italy.
1961 Two Colonels
1961 Duel of the Titans / *Romolo and Remo*
1961 Goliath and the Vampires / *Maciste Contro il Vampiro*
1962 The Slave / *Il Figlio di Spartacus*
1965 Minnesota Clay
1966 Django
1966 Navajo Joe / *Un Dollaro a Testa*
1966 Johnny Oro
1966 The Hellbenders
1969 The Mercenary
1980 I Don't Understand You Anymore
1981 I'm Getting Myself a Yacht
1981 Super Fuzz
1982 My Darling, My Dearest
1982 Three Wise Kings

1982 Count Tacchia
1983 Sing Sing

CORMAN, Roger (William CORMAN)
(1926–) Detroit, Michigan, USA.
1955 Five Guns West
1955 The Apache Woman
1956 The Day the World Ended
1956 Swamp Woman
1956 The Oklahoma Woman
1956 Gunslinger
1956 It Conquered the World
1957 Not of This Earth
1957 The Undead
1957 Naked Paradise
1957 Attack of the Crab Monsters
1957 Rock All Night
1957 Teenage Doll
1957 Carnival Rock
1957 Sorority Girl / *The Bad One*
1957 The Viking Woman and the Sea Serpent
1958 War of the Satellites
1958 The She Gods of Shark Reef
1958 Machine Gun Kelly
1958 Teenage Caveman / *Out of the Darkness*
1959 I, Mobster
1959 A Bucket of Blood
1959 The Wasp Woman
1960 Ski Troop Attack
1960 The House of Usher
1960 The Little Shop of Horrors
1960 The Last Woman on Earth
1961 Creature from the Haunted Sea
1961 Atlas
1961 The Pit and the Pendulum
1962 The Intruder / *I Hate Your Guts / The Stranger*
1962 The Premature Burial
1962 Tales of Terror
1962 Tower of London
1963 The Raven
1963 The Terror
1963 'X' - The Man with the X-Ray Eyes
1963 The Haunted Palace
1963 The Young Racers
1964 The Secret Invasion
1964 The Masque of the Red Death
1965 The Tomb of Ligeia
1966 The Wild Angels
1967 The St Valentine's Day Massacre
1967 The Trip
1968 Target: Harry / *How to Make It*
1970 Bloody Mama
1970 Gas-s-s-s!. . . Or It Became Necessary to Destroy the World in Order to Save It!
1971 Von Richthofen and Brown / *The Red Baron*

CORNELIUS, Henry
(1913–1958) South Africa.
1949 Passport to Pimlico
1951 The Galloping Major
1954 Genevieve
1955 I Am a Camera
1958 Next to No Time
1958 Law and Disorder **(Charles CRICHTON)**

CORNELL, John
1988 Crocodile Dundee II

CORNFIELD, Hubert
(1929–) Istanbul, Turkey.
1955 Sudden Danger
1957 Lure of the Swamp
1957 Plunder Road
1959 The Third Voice
1961 Angel Baby **(Paul WENDKOS)**
1962 Pressure Point
1969 The Night of the Following Day

CORNSWEET, Harold
1975 Return to Campus

CORONA, Alfonso
1988 Deathstalker III

CORR, Eugene
1977 Over-Under, Sideways-Down **(Peter GESSNER, Steve WAX)**
1985 Desert Bloom

CORRIGAN, Lloyd
(1900–1969) American.
1930 Follow Thru **(Lawrence SCHWAB)**
1930 Along Came Youth **(Norman McLEOD)**
1931 Daughter of the Dragon
1931 The Beloved Bachelor
1932 No One Man
1932 The Broken Wing
1932 He Learned About Women
1934 By Your Leave
1935 Murder on a Honeymoon
1936 Dancing Pirate
1937 Night Key
1937 Lady Behave

CORTEZ, Ricardo (Jake Kranz)
(1899–1977) American.
1938 Inside Story
1939 Heaven with a Barbed Wire Fence
1939 Chasing Danger
1939 The Escape
1940 City of Chance
1940 Free, Blonde and Twenty-One
1940 Girl in 313

COSBY, Bill (William H Cosby Jnr)
(1937–) Philadelphia, Pennsylvania, USA.
1983 Bill Cosby, Himself

COSCARELLI, Don
(1954–) Tripoli, Libya.
1976 Jim — The World's Greatest
1976 Kenny and Company
1979 Phantasm
1982 The Beastmaster
1987 The Survival Game / *The Survival Quest*
1988 Phantasm II

COSMATOS, George Pan
(1941–) Greek.
1973 Massacre in Rome / *Rappresaglia*
1977 The Cassandra Crossing
1978 Restless
1979 Escape to Athena

1983 Of Unknown Origin
1985 Rambo: First Blood Part II
1986 Cobra
1989 Leviathan

COSTA-GAVRAS, Constantin (Konstantinos Gavras)
(1933–) Athens, Greece.
1966 The Sleeping Car Murders
1968 Shock Troops
1969 Z **D* F***
1970 The Confession
1973 State of Siege
1975 Special Section
1982 Missing **F***
1983 Hanna K
1985 Family Business
1988 Summer Lightning / *Sundown*
1988 Betrayed
1989 Music Box

COUFFER, Jack
(1922–) American.
1961 Nikki, Wild Dog of the North
1969 Ring of Bright Water
1972 Living Free
1972 The Darwin Adventure

COURTLAND, Jerome
(1926–) Knoxville, Tennessee, USA.
1972 Run, Cougar, Run
1972 Diamonds on Wheels

COWAN, Will
1958 The Big Beat
1958 The Thing That Couldn't Die

COWARD, Sir Noel
(1899–1973) Teddington, Middlesex, England.
Autobiography: Present Indicative. Future Indefinite.
1942 In Which We Serve **(David LEAN) F***

COWEN, William J
(1883–1964) American.
1932 Kongo
1933 Oliver Twist
1934 Woman Unafraid

COX, Alex
(1954–) Birkenhead, Cheshire, England.
1984 Repo Man
1986 Sid and Nancy
1987 Straight to Hell
1987 Walker

COX, Nell
1985 The Roommate

COX, Paul
1976 Illuminations
1977 Inside Looking Out
1979 Kostas
1982 Lonely Hearts
1983 Man of Flowers
1984 My First Wife
1985 Cactus
1988 Vincent

1989 Island

CRABTREE, Arthur
(1900–1975) British.
1944 Madonna of the Seven Moons
1945 They Were Sisters
1946 Caravan
1947 Dear Murderer
1949 Quartet **(Ken ANNAKIN, Harold FRENCH, Ralph SMART)**
1949 The Calendar
1949 Don't Ever Leave Me
1951 Lilli Marlene
1952 Hindle Wakes / *Holiday Week*
1953 The Wedding of Lilli Marlene
1957 Death Over My Shoulder
1957 East of Suez
1957 Morning Call / *The Strange Case of Dr Manning*
1958 The Fiend Without a Face
1959 Horror of the Black Museum

CRABTREE, Gary L
1974 Gettin' Back

CRAFT, William James
1924 Big Timber
1927 A Hero for a Night
1927 Painting the Town
1928 How to Handle a Woman
1928 The Gate Crasher
1928 Hot Heels
1929 The Kid's Clever
1929 The Cohens and the Kellys in Atlantic City
1929 Skinner Steps Out
1930 The Cohens and the Kellys in Scotland
1930 Dames Ahoy!
1930 See America Thirst
1930 Czar of Broadway
1930 Embarrassing Moments
1930 Little Accident
1930 One Hysterical Night
1931 Honeymoon Lane

CRAIN, William
(1943–) American.
1972 Blacula
1976 Dr Black, Mr Hyde
1979 The Watts Monster
1982 The Kid from Not-So-Big
1984 Standing in the Shadows of Love

CRANE, Peter
1972 Hunted
1973 Assassin
1974 Moments
1984 Cover Up

CRAVEN, Frank
(1875–1945) American.
1934 That's Gratitude

CRAVEN, Wes
(1949–) Cleveland, Ohio, USA.
1973 Last House on the Left
1977 The Hills Have Eyes
1981 Deadly Blessing
1982 Swamp Thing
1984 A Nightmare on Elm Street

1985 The Hills Have Eyes, Part II
1986 Deadly Friend
1988 Serpent and the Rainbow
1989 No More, Mr Nice Guy

CRICHTON, Charles
(1910–) Wallasey, Cheshire, England.
1944 For Those in Peril
1945 Painted Boots / *The Girl on the Canal*
1945 Dead of Night **(Alberto CAVALCANTI, Basil DEARDEN, Robert HAMER)**
1947 Hue and Cry
1948 Against the Wind
1948 Another Shore
1948 Train of Events **(Basil DEARDEN, Sidney COLE)**
1950 Dance Hall
1951 The Lavender Hill Mob
1952 Hunted / *The Stranger in Between*
1953 The Titfield Thunderbolt
1953 The Lover Lottery
1954 The Divided Heart
1956 The Man in the Sky
1958 Law and Disorder **(Henry CORNELIUS)**
1958 Floods of Fear
1959 The Battle of the Sexes
1960 The Boy Who Stole a Million
1964 The Third Secret
1966 He Who Rides a Tiger
1988 A Fish Called Wanda **D***
(also many TV shorts)

CRICHTON, Michael
(1942–) Chicago, Illinois, USA.
1973 Westworld
1978 Coma
1979 The Great Train Robbery
1981 Looker
1984 Runaway
1989 Physical Evidence / *Smoke*

CRISP, Donald
(1880–1974) Aberfeldy, Scotland.
1924 The Navigator **(Buster KEATON)**
1925 Don Q Son of Zorro
1930 The Runaway Bride
(many silent shorts)

CROFT, David
1972 Not Now, Darling **(Ray COONEY)**

CROMBIE, Donald
1976 Caddie
1978 The Irishman
1979 Cathy's Child
1981 The Killing of Angel Street
1982 Kitty and the Bagman
1984 Robbery Under Arms **(Ken HANNAM)**
1986 Playing Beatie Bow

CROMWELL, John (Elwood Dager Cromwell)
(1887–1979) Toledo, Ohio, USA.
1929 Close Harmony **(Edward A SUTHERLAND)**
1929 The Dance of Life **(Edward A SUTHERLAND)**
1929 The Mighty
1930 Street of Chance
1930 The Texan / *The Big Race*
1930 Tom Sawyer
1930 For the Defence
1930 Seven Days' Leave / *Medals* **(Richard WALLACE)**
1931 Scandal Sheet
1931 Unfaithful
1931 The Vice Squad
1931 Rich Man's Folly
1932 The World and the Flesh
1933 Sweepings
1933 The Silver Cord
1933 Double Harness
1933 Ann Vickers
1934 The Fountain
1934 Of Human Bondage
1934 Spitfire
1934 This Man Is Mine
1935 I Dream Too Much
1935 Jalna
1935 Village Tale
1936 Banjo on My Knee
1936 Little Lord Fauntleroy
1936 To Mary with Love
1937 The Prisoner of Zenda
1938 Algiers
1939 In Name Only
1939 Made for Each Other
1940 Abe Lincoln in Illinois / *Spirit of the People*
1940 Victory
1941 So Ends Our Night
1942 Son of Fury
1944 Since You Went Away **F***
1945 The Enchanted Cottage
1946 Anna and the King of Siam
1947 Dead Reckoning
1947 Night Song
1950 Caged
1950 The Company She Keeps
1951 The Racket
1958 The Goddess
1961 A Matter of Morals
1963 The Scavengers

CRONE, George
1930 Reno
1930 What a Man!
1930 Blaze of Glory **(Renaud HOFFMAN)**
1931 Get That Girl
1931 Speed Madness

CRONENBERG, David
(1943–) Toronto, Ontario, Canada.
1969 Stereo
1970 Crimes of the Future
1976 They Came from Within / *Shivers / The Parasite Murders*
1977 Rabid
1979 The Brood
1979 Fast Company
1981 Scanners
1983 Videodrome
1983 The Dead Zone
1986 The Fly
1988 Dead Ringers / *Twins*

CROSLAND, Alan
(1894–1936) New York, New York, USA.
1924 Miami

1924 Three Weeks / *The Romance of a Queen*
1924 Unguarded Woman
1924 Sinners in Heaven
1925 Compromise
1925 Contraband
1925 Bobbed Hair
1926 Don Juan
1926 When a Man Loves / *His Lady*
1927 The Beloved Rogue
1927 Old San Francisco
1927 The Jazz Singer
1928 Glorious Betsy
1928 The Scarlet Lady
1929 On with the Show
1929 General Crack
1930 The Furies
1930 Son of the Flames
1930 Big Boy
1930 Viennese Nights
1931 Captain Thunder
1931 Children of Dreams
1931 The Silver Lining
1932 Weekends Only
1933 Hello Sister / *Walking Down Broadway*
1934 Massacre
1934 Midnight Alibi
1934 The Personality Kid
1934 The Case of the Howling Dog
1935 It Happened in New York
1935 Mr Dynamite
1935 Lady Tubbs / *The Gay Lady*
1935 King Solomon of Broadway
1935 The Great Impersonation

CROUNSE, Avery
1984 Eyes of Fire / *Crying Blue Sky*
1987 The Invisible Kid

CROW, Dean
1987 Geek / *Backwoods*
1988 Twice Under

CROWE, Cameron
1989 Say Anything

CROWE, Christopher
1988 Saigon Off Limits

CRUMP, Owen
1955 Cease Fire
1956 The River Changes
1962 The Couch

CRUZE, James (Jens Cruz Bosen) *(1884–1942) Five Points, Near Ogden, Utah, USA.*
1923 The Covered Wagon
1923 Hollywood
1923 Ruggles of Red Gap
1924 Merton of the Movies
1924 The Fighting Coward
1924 The Enemy Sex
1924 The City That Never Sleeps
1924 The Garden of Weeds
1925 Welcome Home
1925 Wake Up the Town
1925 Beggar on Horseback
1925 The Pony Express
1925 Marry Me
1925 The Goose Hangs High
1926 Old Ironside / *Sons of the Sea*
1926 Mannequin
1927 On to Reno
1927 We're All Gamblers
1927 The City Gone Wild
1928 Excess Baggage
1928 The Mating Call
1928 The Red Mark
1929 The Great Garbo
1929 The Duke Steps Out
1929 A Man's a Man
1930 Once a Gentleman
1930 She Got What She Wanted
1931 Salvation Nell
1932 If I Had a Million **(Bruce H HUMBERSTONE, Ernst LUBITSCH, Norman Z MCLEOD, Stephen ROBERTS, William A SEITER, Norman TAUROG)**
1932 Washington Merry-Go-Round / *Invisible Power*
1933 I Cover the Waterfront
1933 Mr Skitch
1933 Sailor Be Good
1933 Racetrack
1934 David Harum
1934 Their Big Moment / *Afterwards*
1935 Helldorado
1935 Two Fisted
1936 Sutter's Gold
1937 The Wrong Road
1938 Prison Nurse
1938 Gangs of New York
1938 Come On, Leathernecks

CUKOR, George (George Dewey Cukor) *(1899–1983) New York, New York, USA.*
1930 The Royal Family of Broadway / *Theatre Royal* **(Cyril GARDNER)**
1930 The Virtuous Sin / *Cast Iron*
1930 Grumpy
1931 Tarnished Lady
1931 Girls About Town
1932 One Hour with You **(Ernst LUBITSCH) F***
1932 A Bill of Divorcement
1932 Rockabye
1932 What Price Hollywood?
1933 Dinner at Eight
1933 Little Women **D* F***
1933 Our Betters
1935 David Copperfield **F***
1935 Sylvia Scarlett
1936 Romeo and Juliet **F***
1937 Camille
1938 Holiday / *Free to Live / Unconventional Linda*
1939 Zaza
1939 The Women
1939 Gone with the Wind **(Victor FLEMING, Sam WOOD) D** F****
1940 The Philadelphia Story **D* F***
1940 Susan and God / *The Gay Mrs Trexel*
1941 Two-Faced Woman
1941 A Woman's Place
1942 Her Cardboard Lover
1942 Keeper of the Flame
1944 Gaslight / *The Murder in Thornton*

Square **F***
1944 Winged Victory
1947 Desire Me **(Jack CONWAY, Mervyn LE ROY)**
1948 A Double Life **D***
1949 Adam's Rib
1949 Edward, My Son
1950 Born Yesterday **D* F***
1950 A Life of Her Own
1951 The Model and the Marriage Broker
1952 The Marrying Kind
1952 Pat and Mike
1953 The Actress
1954 It Should Happen to You
1954 A Star Is Born
1956 Bhowani Junction
1957 Les Girls
1957 Wild Is the Wind
1960 Heller in Pink Tights
1960 Let's Make Love
1960 Song Without End **(Charles VIDOR)**
1962 The Chapman Report
1964 My Fair Lady **D** F****
1969 Justine
1972 Travels with My Aunt
1976 The Blue Bird
1981 Rich and Famous

CULP, Robert
(1930–) Berkeley, California, USA.
1972 Hickey and Boggs

CUMMINGS, Irving
(1888–1959) New York, USA.
1924 Stolen Secrets
1924 In Every Woman's Life
1924 The Dancing Cheat
1924 Fools' Highway
1924 Riders Up
1924 The Rose of Paris
1924 The Desert Flower
1925 As Man Desires
1925 Just a Woman
1925 One Year to Live
1925 Infatuation
1926 The Midnight Kiss
1926 Bertha, the Sewing Machine Girl
1926 The Country Beyond
1926 Rustling for Cupid
1926 The Johnstown Flood
1927 The Brute
1927 Port of Missing Girls
1928 Dressed to Kill
1928 Romance of the Underworld
1929 Behind the Curtain
1929 In Old Arizona **(Raoul WALSH) D* F***
1930 A Devil with Women
1930 Not Quite Decent
1930 Cameo Kirby
1930 On the Level
1931 A Holy Terror
1931 The Cisco Kid
1932 Attorney for the Defence
1932 The Night Club Lady
1932 Man Against Woman
1933 Man Hunt
1933 The Woman I Stole
1933 The Mad Game
1934 I Believe in You
1934 Grand Canary
1934 The White Parade **F***
1935 It's a Small World
1935 Curly Top
1936 The Poor Little Rich Girl
1936 Girls' Dormitory
1936 White Hunter
1937 Vogues of 1938
1937 Merry-Go-Round of 1938
1938 Little Miss Broadway
1938 Just Around the Corner
1939 The Story of Alexander Graham Bell / *The Modern Miracle*
1939 Hollywood Cavalcade
1939 Everything Happens at Night
1940 Lillian Russell
1940 Down Argentine Way
1941 That Night in Rio
1941 Belle Starr
1941 Louisiana Purchase
1942 My Gal Sal
1942 Springtime in the Rockies
1943 Sweet Rosie O'Grady
1943 What a Woman! / *The Beautiful Cheat*
1944 The Impatient Years
1945 The Dolly Sisters
1951 Double Dynamite / *It's Only Money*

CUMMINGS, Jack
(1900–) American.
1941 Love Crazy

CUNNINGHAM, Sean s
(1941–) New York, New York, USA.
1971 Together
1974 Case of the Full Moon Murders / *Case of the Smiling Stiffs / Sex on the Groove Tube.*
1978 Here Come the Tigers
1979 Manny's Orphans
1980 Friday the 13th
1982 A Stranger Is Watching
1983 Spring Break
1985 The New Kids
1987 Dating Delilah
1988 Deep Star Six

CURRIE, Anthony
1987 Pink Chiquitas

CURTIN, Lawrence
1988 One Minute to Midnight

CURTIS, Dan
(1928–) Bridgeport, Connecticut, USA.
1970 House of Dark Shadows
1971 Night of Dark Shadows
1976 Burnt Offerings
(also many TV movies)

CURTIZ, Michael (Michael Courtice or Mihaly Kertesz)
(1888–1962) Budapest, Hungary.
1924 Moon Over Israel
1925 Red Heels / *Das Spielzeug von Paris*
1926 The Road to Happiness
1926 The Third Degree
1927 The Desired Woman
1927 A Million Bid
1927 Good Time Charley

1928 Tenderloin
1929 Noah's Ark
1929 The Glad Rag Doll
1929 Madonna of Avenue A
1929 The Gamblers
1929 Hearts of Exile
1930 Mammy
1930 Under The Texas Moon
1930 The Matrimonial Bed
1931 The Mad Genius
1931 Bright Lights
1931 River's End
1931 God's Gift to Women / *Too Many Women*
1931 The Woman from Monte Carlo
1931 Soldier's Plaything
1932 Cabin in the Cotton
1932 Doctor X
1932 The Strange Love of Molly Louvain
1932 Alias the Doctor
1933 Kennel Murder Case
1933 Mystery of the Wax Museum
1933 20,000 Years in Sing Sing
1933 The Keyhole
1933 Private Detective 62
1933 Female
1933 Goodbye Again
1933 British Agent
1934 Jimmy the Gent
1934 Mandalay
1934 The Key
1935 Black Fury
1935 Captain Blood **F***
1935 Front Page Woman
1935 The Case of the Curious Bride
1935 Little Big Shot
1936 The Charge of the Light Brigade
1936 The Walking Dead
1937 Kid Galahad / *Battling Bellhop*
1937 Stolen Holiday
1937 Mountain Justice
1937 The Perfect Specimen
1938 The Adventures of Robin Hood **(William KEIGHLEY) F***
1938 Four Daughters **D* F***
1938 Gold Is Where You Find It
1938 Angels with Dirty Faces **D***
1939 Daughters Courageous
1939 Dodge City
1939 Four Wives
1939 The Private Lives of Elizabeth and Essex
1940 Santa Fe Trail
1940 The Sea Hawk
1940 Virginia City
1941 Dive Bomber
1941 The Sea Wolf
1941 Captains of the Clouds
1942 Yankee Doodle Dandy **D* F***
1942 Casablanca **D** F****
1943 Mission to Moscow
1943 This Is the Army
1944 Janie
1944 Passage to Marseilles
1945 Mildred Pierce **F***
1945 Roughly Speaking
1946 Night and Day
1947 Life with Father
1947 The Unsuspected
1948 Romance on the High Seas / *It's Magic*
1948 Flamingo Road
1949 The Lady Takes a Sailor
1949 My Dream Is Yours
1950 The Breaking Point
1950 Bright Leaf
1950 Young Man with a Horn / *Young Man of Music*
1951 Force of Arms
1951 I'll See You in My Dreams
1951 Jim Thorpe, All American / *Man of Bronze*
1952 The Story of Will Rogers
1953 The Jazz Singer
1953 Trouble Along the Way
1954 The Boy from Oklahoma
1954 The Egyptian
1954 White Christmas
1955 We're No Angels
1956 The Best Things in Life Are Free
1956 The Scarlet Hour
1956 The Vagabond King
1957 The Helen Morgan Story / *Both Ends of the Candle*
1958 King Creole
1958 The Proud Rebel
1959 The Hangman
1959 The Man in the Net
1960 The Adventures of Huckleberry Finn
1960 A Breath of Scandal
1961 The Comancheros
1961 Francis of Assisi
(also many foreign silent films)

CUTTS, Graham (Jock G Cutts)
(1885–1958) Brighton, Sussex, England.
1924 Woman to Woman
1924 The White Shadow
1924 The Prude's Fall
1924 The Passionate Adventure
1925 The Blackguard
1925 The Rat
1926 The Sea Urchin
1926 The Triumph of the Rat
1927 The Rolling Road
1927 Confetti
1927 The Queen Was in the Parlour
1928 God's Clay
1929 Glorious Youth
1929 The Return of the Rat
1931 The Temperance Fete
1932 The Sign of Four **(Rowland V LEE)**
1932 Love on the Spot
1932 Looking on the Bright Side
1933 As Good As New
1933 Three Men in a Boat
1935 Oh Daddy!
1936 Aren't Men Beasts!
1937 Let's Make a Night of It
1937 Over She Goes
1939 She Couldn't Say No

CZINNER, Paul *
(1890–1972) Budapest, Hungary.
1930 The Woman He Scorned
1934 Catherine the Great
1936 As You Like It
1937 Dreaming Lips **(Lee GARMES)**
1939 A Stolen Life

DAALDER, Renee
1969 De Blanke Slavin
1976 Massacre at Central High
1985 Population: One

DA COSTA, Morton (Morton Tecosky)
(1914–) Philadelphia, Pennsylvania, USA.
1958 Auntie Mama **F***
1962 The Music Man **F***
1963 Island of Love

DAHLIN, Bob
1987 The Incredible Closet Monster

DALEY, Tom
1987 The Lamp / *The Outing*

DALRYMPLE, Ian
(1903–) British.
1937 Storm in a Teacup **(Victor SAVILLE)**
1940 Old Bill and Son
1947 Esther Waters **(Peter PROUD)**

DALVA, Robert
(1942–) New York, New York, USA.
1983 The Black Stallion Returns

DAMIANI, Damiano *
(1922–) Pasiano, Italy.
1962 Arturo's Island
1964 The Empty Canvas
1968 Mafia / *Il Giorno della Civetta*
1968 A Bullet for the General / *Quien Sabe?*
1975 The Devil Is a Woman
1977 I Am Afraid
1978 Goodbye and Amen
1980 Time of the Jackals
1982 Amityville II: The Possession
1985 Pizza Connection
1986 The Enquiry

DAMSKI, Mel
(1946–) New York, New York, USA.
1983 Yellowbeard
1985 Mischief / *Heart and Soul*
1988 Happy Together
(also many TV movies)

DANE, Lawrence
1985 Heavenly Bodies

DANIEL, Rod
1985 Teen Wolf
1987 Like Father, Like Son
1989 K-9

DANIELS, Harold
1948 The Woman from Tangier
1949 Daughter of the West
1951 Roadblock
1951 The Prince of Peace **(William BEAUDINE)**
1953 Port Sinister
1953 Sword of Venus
1956 Bayou **(E I FESSLER)**
1958 Terror in the Haunted House / *My World Dies Screaming*

DANIELS, Marc
1957 The Big Fun Carnival
1971 Squeeze a Flower
(also many TV movies)

DANIELS, Stan
1988 Sketch Life

DANSKA, Herbert
1967 Sweet Love Bitter / *It Won't Rub Off Baby*
1970 Right On!

DANTE, Joe
(1948–) American.
1976 Hollywood Boulevard **(Allan ARKUSH)**
1978 Piranha
1980 The Howling
1983 Twilight Zone — The Movie **(John LANDIS, George MILLER, Steven SPIELBERG)**
1984 Gremlins
1985 Explorers
1987 Innerspace
1987 Amazon Women on the Moon **(Carl GOTTLIEB, Peter HORTON, John LANDIS, Robert k WEISS)**
1989 The 'Burbs

DANTINE, Helmut
(1917–1982) Austria.
1958 Thundering Jets

DANTON, Ray
(1931–) New York, New York, USA.
1972 The Deathmaster
1973 Crypt of the Living Dead
1975 Psychic Killer

D'ANTONI, Phil
(1929–) New York, New York, USA.
1973 The Seven Ups

DARE, Danny
1938 The Main Event

DARLING, Joan
(1935–) Boston, Massachusetts, USA.
1977 First Love
1984 The Check Is in the Mail

D'ARREST, Harry d'abbadie
(1893–1968) Argentina.
1927 Service for Ladies
1927 A Gentleman in Paris
1927 Serenade
1928 The Magnificent Flirt
1928 Dry Martini
1930 Raffles **(George FITZMAURICE)**
1930 Laughter
1933 Topaze
1934 The Three Cornered Hat / *It Happened in Spain*

DASSIN, Jules (Julius Dassin)
(1911–) Middletown, Connecticut, USA.
Biography: I Was Born a Greek by Melina Mercouri.

1942 Nazi Agent
1942 The Affairs of Martha / *Once Upon a Thursday*
1942 Reunion in France / *Mademoiselle France*
1943 Young Ideas
1944 The Canterville Ghost
1945 A Letter for Evie
1946 Two Smart People
1947 Brute Force
1948 The Naked City
1949 Thieves' Highway
1950 Night and the City
1954 Rififi
1957 He Who Must Die
1960 Where the Hot Wind Blows / *The Law*
1960 Never on Sunday **D***
1962 Phaedra
1964 Topkapi
1966 10.30pm Summer
1968 Survival '67
1968 Up Tight
1970 Promise at Dawn
1978 A Dream of Passion
1981 Circle of Two

DAUGHERTY, Herschel
(1909–) American.
1958 The Light in the Forest
1963 The Raiders
(also many TV movies)

DAUMERY, John
1930 Rough Waters
1932 Help Yourself
1932 Blind Spot
1933 Naughty Cinderella
1933 Little Miss Nobody
1933 The Thirteenth Candle
1933 Call Me Mame
1933 Head of the Family
1933 The Acting Business
1933 Mr Quincey of Monte Carlo

DAVES, Delmer
(1904–1977) San Francisco, California, USA.
1943 Destination Tokyo
1944 Hollywood Canteen
1944 The Very Thought of You
1945 Pride of the Marines / *Forever in Love*
1947 The Red House
1947 Dark Passage
1948 To the Victor
1949 A Kiss in the Dark
1949 Task Force
1950 Broken Arrow
1951 Bird of Paradise
1952 Return of the Texan
1953 Never Let Me Go
1953 Treasure of the Golden Condor
1954 Demetrius and the Gladiators
1954 Drum Beat
1956 Jubal
1956 The Last Wagon
1957 3.10 to Yuma
1958 The Badlanders
1958 Cowboy
1958 Kings Go Forth
1959 The Hanging Tree
1959 A Summer Place
1961 Parrish
1961 Susan Slade
1962 Rome Adventure / *Lovers Must Learn*
1963 Spencer's Mountain
1964 Youngblood Hawke
1965 The Battle of the Villa Fiorita
1965 I Was Happy Here

DAVID, Charles
1945 Lady on a Train
1945 River Gang

DAVID, Harold
1959 Career Girl

DAVIDSON, Boaz
(1943–) Tel Aviv, Palestine.
1972 Azit the Paratrooper Dog
1973 Charlie and a Half
1977 Lupo Goes to New York
1981 Lemon Popsicle
1981 Going Steady: Lemon Popsicle II
1981 Seed of Innocence / *Ten Mothers*
1981 X-Ray / *Hospital Massacre*
1981 Hot Bubblegum: Lemon Popsicle III
1982 The Last American Virgin
1982 Private Popsicle: Lemon Popsicle IV
1986 Alex Falls in Love
1987 Dutch Treat
1987 Going Bananas / *My American Adventure*
1988 Army Brats
1988 What Do Women Want?
1988 Salsa: The Motion Picture

DAVIDSON, Carson
1975 The Wrong Damn Film

DAVIDSON, Gordon
(1933–) New York, New York, USA.
1972 The Trial of the Catonsville Nine

DAVIDSON, Martin
(1939–) New York, New York, USA.
1974 The Lords of Flatbush **(Stephen F VERONA)**
1978 Almost Summer
1980 Hero at Large
1983 Eddie and the Cruisers
1989 Heart of Dixie

DAVIES, Ray
1985 Return to Waterloo

DAVIES, Terence
1987 Distant Voices, Still Lives

DAVIES, Valentine
(1905–) American.
1955 The Benny Goodman Story
1956 The Goddess

DAVIS, Allan
1953 Rogue's March

DAVIS, Andrew
1980 Stony Island
1983 The Final Terror
1985 Code of Silence

1988 Above the Law
1989 The Package

DAVIS, B J
1988 White Ghost
1988 Fair Trade / *Flight to Hell*
1989 The Streets of Hollywood

DAVIS, Charles
1962 Get Out of Town
1973 Happy As the Grass Was Green
1978 Hazel's People

DAVIS, Desmond
(1927–) London, England.
1964 The Girl with Green Eyes
1966 Time Lost and Time Remembered / *I Was Happy Here*
1966 The Uncle
1967 Smashing Time
1969 A Nice Girl Like Me
1981 Clash of the Titans
1983 The Sign of Four
1983 The Country Girls
1984 Ordeal By Innocence

DAVIS, Eddie
1967 Panic in the City
1969 Colour Me Dead
1969 It Takes All Kinds

DAVIS, Kate
1988 Girltalk

DAVIS, Ossie
(1917–) Cogdell, Georgia, USA.
1970 Cotton Comes to Harlem
1972 Black Girl
1973 Kongi's Harvest
1973 Gordon's War
1976 Countdown at Kusini

DAVISON, Robert W
1979 Cry of the Wind

DAVISON, Tito
(-1985) American.
1969 The Big Cube

DAWN, Norman
(1904–) American.
1936 Tundra
1939 Taku
1949 Arctic Fury
1950 Two Lost Worlds

DAWSON, Anthony M (Antonio Margheriti) *
(1930–) Rome, Italy.
1960 Space-men / *Assignment Outer Space*
1961 The Outsider
1962 The Golden Arrow
1965 Lightning Bolt
1966 Wild, Wild Planet
1966 War Between the Planets
1966 Planet on the Prowl
1966 Snowman
1968 The Young, the Evil and the Savage
1973 Decameron 3
1974 Blood Money
1977 The Stranger and the Gunfighter
1976 The Squeeze / *Rip-Off*
1977 House of 1000 Pleasures
1978 Killer Fish
1980 Cannibals in the Street
1980 The Last Hunter / *Hunter of the Apocalypse*
1981 Car Crash
1982 The Hunters of the Golden Cobra
1983 Yor, The Hunter from the Future
1983 Tornado
1984 Ark of the Sun God
1984 Codename: Wildgeese

DAWSON, Ralph
(1897–) American.
1929 The Girl in the Glass Cage
1934 The Bermondsey Kid
1934 The Life of the Party

DAY, Ernest
1981 Green Ice
1983 Waltz Across Texas

DAY, Robert
(1922–) Sheen, Surrey, England.
1957 The Green Man
1957 Strangers' Meeting
1958 Grip of the Strangler / *The Haunted Strangler*
1958 Corridors of Blood / *Doctor from Seven Dials*
1959 First Man into Space
1959 Life in Emergency Ward 10
1960 Bobbikins
1960 Two-Way Stretch
1960 Tarzan the Magnificent
1961 The Rebel / *Call Me Genius*
1962 Operation Snatch
1963 Tarzan's Three Challenges
1965 She
1966 Tarzan and the Valley of Gold
1967 Tarzan and the Great River
1967 I Think We're Being Followed
1980 The Man with Bogart's Face / *Sam Marlow, Private Eye*
(also many TV movies)

DAYTON, Lyman D
1976 Baker's Hawk
1976 Rivals
1981 The Avenging
1984 Solo
1985 The Red Fury

DEAN, Basil
(1888–1978) Croydon, Surrey, England.
Autobiography: Mind's Eye.
1929 The Return of Sherlock Holmes
1931 The Perfect Alibi / *Birds of Prey*
1931 Escape
1932 Nine Till Six
1932 The Impassive Footman / *Woman in Chains*
1933 Loyalties
1933 The Constant Nymph
1934 Autumn Crocus
1934 Sing as We Go
1935 Lorna Doone
1935 Look Up and Laugh

1936 Whom the Gods Love / *Mozart*
1937 The Show Goes On
1937 Twenty-One Days / *The First and the Last*

DE ANTONIO, Emile
(1920–) Scranton, Pennsylvania, USA.
1983 In the King of Prussia
(also many documentaries)

DEAR, William
1976 The North Cemetery Massacre
1983 Timerider
1987 Harry and the Hendersons / *Bigfoot and the Hendersons*

DEARDEN, Basil (Basil Dear)
(1911–1971) Westcliff-on-Sea, Essex, England.
1941 The Black Sheep of Whitehall **(William HAY)**
1942 The Goose Steps Out
1943 The Bells Go Down
1944 The Halfway House
1944 They Came to the City
1945 Dead of Night **(Alberto CAVALCANTI, Charles CRICHTON, Robert HAMER)**
1946 The Captive Heart
1947 Frieda
1948 Saraband for Dead Lovers **(Michael RELPH)**
1949 The Blue Lamp
1949 Train of Events **(Sidney COLE, Charles CRICHTON)**
1950 Cage of Gold
1950 Pool of London
1952 The Gentle Gunman
1952 I Believe in You
1953 The Square Peg
1954 Out of the Clouds **(Michael RELPH)**
1954 The Rainbow Jacket
1955 The Ship That Died of Shame / *PT Raiders* **(MIchael RELPH)**
1956 Who Done It?
1957 The Smallest Show on Earth / *Big Time Operators*
1958 Violent Playground
1959 Sapphire
1960 Man in the Moon
1960 The League of Gentlemen
1961 All Night Long
1961 The Secret Partner
1961 Victim
1962 Life for Ruth / *Walk in the Shadow*
1963 The Mind Benders
1963 A Place to Go
1964 Woman of Straw
1965 Masquerade
1966 Khartoum
1968 The Assassination Bureau
1968 Only When I Larf
1970 The Man Who Haunted Himself

DEARDEN, James
(1949–) London, England.
1988 Pascali's Island

DEASY, Frank
1988 The Courier **(Joe LEE)**

DE BELLO, John
1978 Attack of the Killer Tomatoes
1987 Sour Grapes / *Happy Hour*
1987 Return of the Killer Tomatoes

DE BOSIO, Gianfranco
(1924–) Verona, Italy.
1976 Moses

DeBROCA, Philippe *
(1933–) Paris, France.
1959 The Love Game
1961 The Joker
1961 The Five Day Lover
1962 Swords of Blood / *Cartouche*
1962 Seven Capital Sins **(Claude CHABROL, Jacques DEMY, Sylvaine DHOMME, Jean-Luc GODARD, Edouard MOLINARO, Marie-José NAT, Dominique PATUREL, Perrette PRADIER, Jean-Marc TENNBERG, Roger VADIM)**
1964 That Man from Rio
1966 Male Companion
1966 Up to His Ears / *Les Tribulations d'un Chinois en Chine*
1966 The King of Hearts
1968 The Oldest Profession **(Claude AUTANT-LARA, Mauro BOLOGNINI, Jean-Luc GODARD, Franco INDOVINA, Michael PFLEGHAR)**
1969 The Devil By the Tail
1970 Give Her the Moon / *Les Caprices de Marie*
1971 Touch and Go / *La Route au Soleil*
1973 How to Destroy the Reputation of the Greatest Secret Agent / *La Magnifique*
1975 Incorrigible
1978 Dear Detective / *Tendre Poulet*
1980 Practice Makes Perfect
1980 Jupiter's Thigh
1981 Psy

DE CORDOVA, Frederick
(1910–) American.
1945 Too Young to Know
1946 Her Kind of Man
1947 That Way with Women
1947 Love and Learn
1947 Always Together
1948 Wallflower
1948 For the Love of Mary
1948 The Countess of Monte Cristo
1949 Illegal Entry
1949 The Gal Who Took the West
1950 Buccaneer's Gal
1950 Peggy
1950 The Desert Hawk
1951 Bedtime for Bonzo
1951 Katie Did It
1951 Little Egypt / *Chicago Masquerade*
1951 Finders Keepers
1952 Here Come the Nelsons
1952 Bonzo Goes to College
1952 Yankee Buccaneer
1953 Column South
1965 I'll Take Sweden
1966 Frankie and Johnny

DE CORDOVA, Leander
1930 After the Fog
1931 Trails of the Golden West

DE COTEAU, David
1987 Dreamaniac
1987 Creepozoids
1987 Bitchin' Sorority Babes
1987 Lady Avenger
1988 Space Sluts in the Slammer
1988 I Was a Teenage Sex Mutant
1988 The Dirty Filthy Slime
1988 American Rampage
1989 Deadly Embrace

DE COURVILLE, Albert
(1887–1960) London, England.
1930 Wolves / *Wanted Men*
1931 77 Park Lane
1931 Night Shadows
1932 There Goes the Bride
1932 The Midshipmaid
1933 This Is the Life
1934 Wild Boy
1934 Things Are Looking Up
1935 The Case of Gabriel Perry
1935 Charing Cross Road
1936 Strangers on a Honeymoon
1936 Seven Sinners / *Doomed Cargo*
1937 Clothes and the Woman
1937 Oh Boy
1938 Star of the Circus
1938 Crackerjack
1938 The Rebel Son
1939 The Lambeth Walk
1939 An Englishman's Home / *Madmen of Europe*

DEHLAUI, Jamil
1986 The Master Musician
1987 Born of Fire

DEIMEL, Mark
1988 The Perfect Match

DEIN, Edward
1945 Swing Out Sister
1955 Shack Out in 101
1957 Calypso Joe
1958 Seven Guns to Mesa
1959 Curse of the Undead
1960 The Leech Woman

DEITCH, Donna
(1945–) San Francisco, California, USA.
1984 Desert of the Heart

DE JARNATT, Steve
1986 Cherry 2000
1988 Miracle Mile

DEKKER, Fred
(1959–) San Francisco, California, USA.
1986 Night of the Creeps / *Homecoming Night*
1987 The Monster Squad

DE LACEY, Robert
1929 Idaho Red
1930 Pardon My Gun

DE LEON, Gerry
1959 Terror Is a Man
1964 The Walls of Hell
1972 Women in Cages

DELIA, Francis
1988 Freeway

DELL, Jeffrey
(1904–) British.
1943 The Flemish Farm
1944 Don't Take It to Heart
1948 It's Hard to Be Good
1950 The Dark Man
1958 Carlton-Browne of the F.O. / *Man in a Cocked Hat* **(Roy BOULTING)**

DELMAN, Jeffrey
1986 Dead Time Stories

DEL MONTE, Peter *
(1943–) San Francisco, California, USA.
1988 Julia and Julia

DELON, Natalie
1987 Sweet Lies

DEL RUTH, Roy
(1895–1961) Philadelphia, Pennsylvania, USA.
1925 Eve's Lover
1925 Hogan's Alley
1926 The Man Upstairs
1926 The Little Irish Girl
1926 Across the Pacific
1926 Three Weeks in Paris
1926 The Footloose Woman / *Fine Feathers*
1927 Wolf's Clothing
1927 The First Auto
1927 If I Were Single
1927 Ham and Eggs at the Front
1928 The Terror
1928 Beware of Bachelors
1928 Powder My Back
1928 Five and Ten Cent Annie / *Ambitious Annie*
1929 Conquest
1929 The Desert Song
1929 The Hottentot
1929 Gold Diggers of Broadway
1929 The Aviator
1930 Hold Everything
1930 The Second Floor Mystery
1930 Three Faces East
1930 The Life of the Party
1931 My Past
1931 Divorce Among Friends
1931 The Maltese Falcon
1931 Side Show
1931 Blonde Crazy / *Larceny Lane*
1932 Taxi !
1932 Beauty and the Boss
1932 Winner Takes All
1932 Blessed Event
1933 Employees Entrance

1933 The Mind Reader
1933 The Little Giant
1933 Captured
1933 Bureau of Missing Persons
1933 Lady Killer
1934 Bulldog Drummond Strikes Back
1934 Upper World
1934 Kid Millions
1935 Folies Bergère
1935 Broadway Melody of 1936 **F***
1935 Thanks a Million
1936 It Had to Happen
1936 Private Number / *Secret Interlude*
1936 Born to Dance
1937 On the Avenue
1937 Broadway Melody of 1938
1937 They Won't Forget
1938 Happy Landing
1938 My Lucky Star
1939 Tail Spin
1939 The Star Maker
1939 Here I Am a Stranger
1940 He Married His Wife
1941 Topper Returns
1941 The Chocolate Soldier
1942 Maisie Gets Her Man
1943 DuBarry Was a Lady
1944 Broadway Rhythm
1944 Barbary Coast Gent
1947 It Happened on Fifth Avenue
1948 The Babe Ruth Story
1949 Red Light
1949 Always Leave Them Laughing
1950 The West Point Story / *Fine and Dandy*
1951 On Moonlight Bay
1951 Starlift
1951 Quo Vadis
1952 About Face
1952 Stop, You're Killing Me
1953 Three Sailors and a Girl
1954 Phantom of the Rue Morgue
1959 The Alligator People
1960 Why Must I Die? / *Thirteen Steps to Death*
(also many shorts)

DE LUCA, Rudy
1985 Transylvania 6–5000

DE LUISE, Dom
(1933–) Brooklyn, New York, USA.
1979 Hot Stuff

DE MARTINO, Alberto
1977 Holocaust 2000 / *The Chosen*

DEMBO, Richard
(1948–) French.
1984 Dangerous Moves

DEMCHUK, Bob
1986 Whatever It Takes

DeMILLE, Cecil B (Cecil Blount DeMille)
(1881–1959) Ashfield, Massachusetts, USA.
Autobiography: Autobiography of Cecil B. DeMille.
1923 Adam's Rib
1923 The Ten Commandments
1924 Triumph
1924 Feet of Clay
1925 The Golden Bed
1925 The Road to Yesterday
1926 The Volga Boatman
1928 King of Kings
1928 The Godless Girl
1929 Dynamite
1930 Madam Satan
1931 The Squaw Man / *The White Man*
1932 The Sign of the Cross
1933 This Day and Age
1934 Four Frightened People
1935 The Crusades
1936 The Plainsman
1936 Cleopatra **F***
1938 The Buccaneer
1939 Union Pacific
1940 Northwest Mounted Police
1942 Reap the Wild Wind
1944 The Story of Dr Wassell
1947 Unconquered
1949 Samson and Delilah
1952 The Greatest Show on Earth **D* F****
1956 The Ten Commandments **F***

DE MILLE, William C (William Churchill De Mille)
(1875–1955) Washington, USA.
1924 The Fast Set
1924 The Bedroom Window
1924 Icebound
1925 Lost — a Wife
1925 Men and Women
1925 New Brooms
1925 The Splendid Crime
1925 Locked Doors
1926 The Runaway
1929 The Doctor's Secret
1929 The Idle Rich
1930 This Mad World
1930 Passion Flower
1932 Two Kinds of Women
1934 His Double Life **(Arthur HOPKINS)**

DEMME, Jonathan
(1944–) Rockville Center, New York, USA.
1974 Caged Heat
1975 Crazy Mama
1976 Fighting Mad
1977 Citizen's Band / *Handle with Care*
1979 Last Embrace
1980 Melvin and Howard
1983 Swing Shift
1986 Something Wild
1987 Swimming to Cambodia
1988 Married to the Mob
1988 Famous All Over Town

DE MORO, Pierre
1983 Savannah Smiles
1985 Hell Hole

DEMY, Jacques
(1931–) Pontchâteau, Loire-Atlantique, France.
1961 Lola
1962 Seven Capital Sins **(Claude CHABROL, Philippe DeBROCA, Sylvaine**

DHOMME, Jean-Luc GODARD, Edouard MOLINARO, Marie-Jose NAT, Dominique PATUREL, Perrette PRADIER, Jean-Marc TENNBERG, Roger VADIM)
1964 Bay of Angels
1964 The Umbrellas of Cherbourg
1968 The Young Girls of Rochefort
1969 Model Shop
1971 Donkey Skin / *The Magic Donkey*
1972 The Pied Piper
1973 L'Evénément le plus Important depuis que l'Homme a marché sur la Lune
1977 A Slightly Pregnant Man
1978 Lady Oscar
1982 Une Chambre en Ville
1985 Parking
(also many shorts)

DENHAM, Reginald
1933 Called Back **(Jack HARRIS)**
1934 Death at Broadcasting House
1935 The Silent Passenger
1936 The Crimson Circle
1938 Kate Plus Ten
1939 Blind Folly
1939 Flying Fifty-Five
1958 Anna of Brooklyn **(Carlo LASTICATI)**

DENNY, Craig
1975 The Astrologer

DENNY, Reginald (Reginald Leigh Daymore)
(1891–1967) British.
1933 The Big Bluff

DENSHAM, Pen
1985 The Zoo Gang **(John WATSON)**
1988 The Host

DENTON, Lawrence
1988 Purgatory

DEODATO, Ruggero *
1980 Cannibal Holocaust
1984 Atlantis Interceptors
1984 The House on the Edge of the Park
1986 Cut and Run
1987 The Barbarians
1987 Lone Runner
1988 Body Count

DE OLIVEIRA, Manoel (Manoel Cándido Pinto de Oliveira) *
(1908–) Oporto, Portugal.
1972 Past and Present
1975 Benilde: Virgin and Mother
1978 Ill-Fated Love
1981 Francesca
1982 Memories and Confessions *(to be released only after Manoel de Oliveira's death)*
1983 Cultural Lisbon
1985 The Satin Slipper
(also many documentaries and shorts)

DE OLIVEIRA, Oswaldo
1987 Bare Behind Bars

DE PALMA, Brian
(1940–) Newark, New Jersey, USA.
1968 Murder à la Mode
1968 Greetings
1969 The Wedding Party **(Wilford LEACH, Cynthia MUNROE)**
1970 Dionysus in '69 **(Robert FIORE, Bruce RUBIN)**
1970 Hi Mom!
1972 Get to Know Your Rabbit
1973 Sisters
1974 Phantom of the Paradise
1976 Obsession
1976 Carrie
1978 The Fury
1980 Home Movies
1980 Dressed to Kill
1981 Blow Out
1983 Scarface
1984 Body Double
1986 Wise Guys
1987 The Untouchables
1988 Home Movies
1989 Casualties of War

DE PALMA, Frank
1989 Operation: Paratrooper
1989 Private War

DERAY, Jacques (J Deray-Desraymond) *
(1929–) Lyons, France.
1961 Rififi in Tokyo
1965 Symphony for a Massacre
1966 That Man George! / *L'Homme de Marrakech*
1970 The Swimming Pool / *The Sinners*
1971 Easy Down There!
1973 The Outside Man / *Un Homme est Mort*
1974 Blood on the Streets / *Borsalino and Co*
1975 Flic Story
1986 He Died with His Eyes Open
1989 Les Bois Noirs

DEREK, John (Derek Harris)
(1926–) Hollywood, California, USA.
1966 Once Before I Die
1968 A Boy.. A Girl
1969 Childish Things
1973 And Once Upon a Time / *Fantasies*
1981 Tarzan the Ape Man
1984 Bolero
1987 A Knight of Love
1989 Ghosts Don't Do It

DESCHANEL, Caleb
(1944–) Philadelphia, Pennsylvania, USA.
1982 The Escape Artist
1988 Crusoe

DE SICA, Vittorio *
(1902–1974) Sora, near Rome, Italy. Biography: Un Amour Obstiné: Ma Vie avec Vittorio de Sica by Maria Mercader.
1941 Doctor Beware / *Teresa Venerdi*
1943 The Children Are Watching Us
1948 Bicycle Thieves

1950 Miracle in Milan
1954 Indiscretion of an American Wife / *Terminus Station*
1954 The Roof
1955 Gold of Naples
1960 Two Women
1961 The Last Judgement
1963 Yesterday, Today and Tomorrow
1964 Marriage Italian Style
1966 After the Fox
1967 Woman Times Seven
1969 A Place for Lovers
1969 Sunflower
1971 The Garden of the Finzi-Continis
1974 The Voyage

DeSIMONE, Tom
1977 Chatter-box
1981 Hell Night
1982 The Concrete Jungle
1987 Reform School Girls
1988 Angel III: The Final Chapter

DESTEIN, Joseph
1987 The Method

DE TOTH, Andre (Sasvrai Farkasfawi Tothfalusi Antai Mihaly) *
(1910–) Mako, Hungary.
1942 The Jungle Book **(Zoltan KORDA)**
1943 Passport to Suez
1944 None Shall Escape
1944 Dark Waters
1947 Ramrod
1947 The Other Lover
1948 Pitfall
1949 Slattery's Hurricane
1951 Man in the Saddle / *The Outcast*
1952 Carson City
1952 Springfield Rifle
1952 Last of the Comanches / *Sabre and the Arrow*
1953 House of Wax
1953 The Stranger Wore a Gun
1953 Thunder Over the Plains
1954 Riding Shotgun
1954 Crime Wave / *The City Is Dark*
1954 The Bounty Hunter
1954 Tanganyika
1955 The Indian Fighter
1957 Monkey on My Back
1957 Hidden Fear
1959 The Two-Headed Spy
1959 Day of the Outlaw
1960 Man on a String / *Confessions of a Counterspy*
1960 Morgan the Pirate
1961 The Mongols
1962 Gold for the Caesars
1968 Play Dirty

DEUTCH, Howard
1986 Pretty in Pink
1987 Some Kind of Wonderful
1988 The Great Outdoors / *Big Country*

DEVENISH, Ross
1974 Boesman and Lena
1977 The Guest at Steenkampskraal
1980 Marigolds in August

DEVILLE, Michel *
(1931–) Boulogne-sur-Seine, France.
1968 Benjamin
1969 Bye Bye Barbara
1970 The Bear and the Doll
1974 The French Way
1985 Peril
1986 Death in a French Garden

DeVITO, Danny
(1944–) Asbury Park, New Jersey, USA.
1987 Throw Momma from the Train
1989 War of the Roses

DEXTER, John
(1935–) English.
1969 The Virgin Soldiers
1970 The Sidelong Glances of a Pigeon Kicker
1971 I Want What I Want

DEXTER, Maury
(1927–) American.
1960 The High Powered Rifle
1960 Walk Tall
1961 The Purple Hills
1961 Woman Hunt
1962 The Firebrand
1962 Air Patrol
1962 The Day Mars Invaded Earth
1962 House of the Damned
1963 Harbour Lights
1963 The Young Swingers
1963 Police Nurse
1963 Young Guns of Texas
1963 Surf Party
1964 Raiders from Beneath the Sea
1965 Wild on the Beach
1965 The Naked Brigade
1968 Maryjane
1968 The Mini-Skirt Mob
1968 Born Wild
1969 Hell's Belles

DICK, Nigel
1987 Dead End
1987 Private Investigations
1988 Deadly Intent

DICKENSON, Thorold
(1903–1984) Bristol, Avon, England.
1936 The High Command
1939 The Arsenal Stadium Mystery
1939 Gaslight / *Angel Street*
1940 The Prime Minister
1942 Next of Kin
1946 Men of Two Worlds / *Kisenga, Man of Africa / Witch Doctor*
1948 The Queen of Spades
1951 The Secret People
1954 Hill 24 Doesn't Answer
(also many documentaries)

DICKSON, Paul
(1920–) British.
1956 Satellite in the Sky
1957 The Depraved

DIEGE, Samuel
1938 Water Rustlers
1938 Singing Cowboys
1938 Ride 'Em Cowboy
1939 Ride 'Em Cowgirl
1939 The Singing Cowgirl

DIETERLE, William (Wilhelm Dieterle)
(1893–1972) Ludwigshafen, Germany.
1927 Behind the Altar / *Das Geheimnis des Abbé*
1928 Sex in Fetters
1929 Triumph of Love / *Ich Lebe Für Dich*
1930 The Dance Goes On
1931 Her Majesty Love
1931 The Last Flight
1932 Jewel Robbery
1932 Lawyer Man
1932 Six Hours to Live
1932 The Crash
1932 Scarlet Dawn
1932 Man Wanted
1933 The Devil's in Love
1933 Grand Slam
1933 Adorable
1933 From Headquarters
1934 Fashions of 1934
1934 Fog Over Frisco
1934 Madame DuBarry
1934 The Firebird
1935 Dr Socrates
1935 A Midsummer Night's Dream **(Max REINHARDT) F***
1935 Secret Bride / *Concealment*
1935 Men on Her Mind
1936 Satan Met a Lady
1936 The Story of Louis Pasteur **F***
1936 The White Angel
1937 Another Dawn
1937 The Great O'Malley
1937 The Life of Emile Zola **D* F****
1938 Blockade
1939 The Hunchback of Notre Dame
1939 Juarez
1940 A Dispatch from Reuters / *This Man Reuter*
1940 Dr Ehrlich's Magic Bullet
1941 All That Money Can Buy / *Daniel and the Devil / Here Is a Man*
1942 Syncopation
1942 Tennessee Johnson / *The Man on America's Conscience*
1944 I'll Be Seeing You
1944 Kismet / *Oriental Dream*
1945 Love Letters
1945 This Love Is Ours
1946 The Searching Wind
1946 Duel in the Sun *(with many others)*
1948 The Accused
1948 Portrait of Jennie
1949 Rope of Sand
1950 Dark City
1950 Paid in Full
1950 September Affair
1951 Peking Express
1951 Red Mountain
1952 Boots Malone
1952 The Turning Point
1953 Salome
1954 Elephant Walk
1956 Magic Fire
1957 Omar Khayyam
1959 Mistress of the World
1964 Quick, Let's Get Married / *The Confession / Seven Different Ways*

DILEO, Mario
1989 Final Alliance

DILLON, John Francis
(1887–1934) American.
1926 Love's Blindness
1928 Scarlet Seas
1929 Children of the Ritz
1929 Careers
1929 Fast Life
1929 Sally
1930 Bride of the Regiment
1930 Spring Is Here
1930 The Girl of the Golden West
1930 Kismet
1930 One Night at Susie's
1931 Millie
1931 The Finger Points
1931 The Reckless Hour
1931 The Pagan Lady
1932 The Cohens and Kellys in Hollywood
1932 Behind the Mask
1932 Man About Town
1932 Call Her Savage
1933 Humanity
1934 The Big Shakedown

DILTZ, Charles
1932 Wild Women of Borneo

DINGWALL, John
1989 Phobia

DINNER, Michael
1983 Miss Lonelyhearts
1985 Catholic Boys / *Heaven Help Us*
1986 Off Beat
1988 Hot to Trot
1988 Dogfight

DITTRICH, Scott
1976 Freewheelin'

DIXON, Ivan
(1931–) New York, New York, USA.
1972 Trouble Man
1973 The Spook Who Sat By the Door

DIXON, John
1988 Running from the Guns

DMYTRYK, Edward
(1908–) Grand Forks, British Columbia, Canada.
Autobiography: It's a Hell of a Life but not a Bad Living.
1935 The Hawk
1939 Television Spy
1940 Emergency Squad
1940 Mystery Sea Raiders
1940 Golden Gloves
1940 Her First Romance
1940 The Devil Commands
1941 Under Age

1941 Sweethearts of the Campus / *Broadway Ahead*
1941 The Blonde from Singapore / *Hot Pearls*
1941 Confessions of Boston Blackie
1941 Secrets of the Lone Wolf
1942 Counter Espionage
1942 Seven Miles from Alcatraz
1942 The Falcon Strikes Back
1943 Hitler's Children
1943 Captive Wild Woman
1943 Behind the Rising Sun
1943 Tender Comrade
1945 Cornered
1945 Murder My Sweet / *Farewell My Lovely*
1945 Back to Bataan
1945 Till the End of Time
1947 Crossfire **D* F***
1947 So Well Remembered
1949 Obsession / *The Hidden Room*
1949 Give Us This Day / *Salt to the Devil*
1952 Mutiny
1952 The Sniper
1952 Eight Iron Men
1953 The Juggler
1954 The Caine Mutiny **F***
1954 Broken Lance
1954 The End of the Affair
1955 Soldiers of Fortune
1955 The Left Hand of God
1956 The Mountain
1957 Raintree Country
1958 The Young Lions
1959 Warlock
1959 The Blue Angel
1962 Walk on the Wild Side
1962 The Reluctant Saint
1963 The Carpetbaggers
1964 Where Love Has Gone
1965 Mirage
1966 Alvarez Kelly
1968 Anzio
1968 Shalako!
1972 Bluebeard
1974 The Human Factor
1976 He Is My Brother

DOBBS, Frank Q
1975 Disciples of Death
1986 Uphill All the Way

DOBKIN, Larry
1974 Like a Crow on a June Bug

DODSON, James
1988 Deadlock

DOHENY, Lawrence
1961 Teenage Millionaire

DOLGY, Mike
1988 Secret Weapon

DOMARADZKI, Jerzy
1983 The Tailor's Planet
1986 White Dragon

DONALDSON, Roger
(1945–) Ballarat, Australia.
1977 Sleeping Dogs
1981 Smash Palace
1984 The Bounty
1985 Marie
1987 No Way Out / *Deceit*
1988 Cocktail

DONAT, Robert
(1905–1958) Manchester, Lancashire, England.
Biography: Robert Donat by J.C. Trewin.
1949 The Cure for Love

DONEHUE, Vincent J
(1916–1966) American.
1958 Lonelyhearts
1960 Sunrise at Campobello

DONEN, Stanley
(1924–) Columbia, South Carolina, USA.
1949 On the Town **(Gene KELLY)**
1951 Royal Wedding / *Wedding Bells*
1952 Singin' in the Rain **(Gene KELLY)**
1952 Love Is Better Than Ever / *The Light Fantastic*
1952 Fearless Fagan
1952 Give a Girl a Break
1954 Seven Brides for Seven Brothers **F***
1954 Deep in My Heart
1955 It's Always Fair Weather **(Gene KELLY)**
1957 Funny Face
1957 The Pajama Game **(George ABBOTT)**
1957 Kiss Them for Me
1958 Indiscreet
1958 Damn Yankees / *What Lola Wants* **(George ABBOTT)**
1960 Once More, with Feeling
1960 Surprise Package
1961 The Grass Is Greener
1964 Charade
1966 Arabesque
1967 Two for the Road
1967 Bedazzled
1969 Staircase
1974 The Little Prince
1975 Lucky Lady
1978 Movie Movie
1980 Saturn 3
1984 Blame It on Rio

DONIGER, Walter
(1917–) New York, New York, USA.
1953 Duffy of San Quentin / *Men Behind Bars*
1954 The Steel Cage
1955 The Steel Jungle
1958 Unwed Mother
1960 House of Women
1962 Safe at Home!
1977 Mad Bull **(Len STECKLER)**
1983 Kentucky Woman

DONNELLY, Tom
1985 Quicksilver

DONNER, Clive
(1926–) London, England.
1957 The Secret Place

1958 Heart of a Child
1961 Marriage of Convenience
1961 The Sinister Man
1963 Some People
1963 The Caretaker / *The Guest*
1964 Nothing But the Best
1965 What's New Pussycat?
1967 Luv
1968 Here We Go Round the Mulberry Bush
1969 Alfred the Great
1975 Vampira / *Old Dracula*
1980 The Nude Bomb
1980 Charlie Chan and the Curse of the Dragon Queen
1988 Arthur the King
1989 Stealing Heaven
(also many TV movies)

DONNER, Richard
(1930–) New York, USA.
1961 X-15
1968 Salt and Pepper
1970 Twinky / *Lola*
1976 The Omen
1978 Superman
1980 Inside Moves
1982 The Toy
1985 Ladyhawke
1985 Goonies
1987 Lethal Weapon
1988 Scrooged
1989 Lethal Weapon II

DONOHUE, Jack
(1912–1984) American.
1948 Close-Up
1950 The Yellow Cab Man
1950 Watch the Birdie
1954 Lucky Me
1961 Babes in Toyland / *March of the Wooden Soldiers*
1965 Marriage on the Rocks
1966 Assault on a Queen

DONOVAN, Paul
1980 Torpedoed
1983 Self Defence / *Siege* **(Mauro O'CONNELL)**
1985 Def Con 4 / *Ground Zero*
1988 Caribe
1988 A Switch in Time

DONOVAN, Terence
1973 Yellow Dog

DONOVAN, Tom
1981 Tristan and Isolt

DORNHELM, Robert
1982 She Dances Alone
1983 Digital Dreams
1985 Echo Park
1989 Cold Feet

DORRIE, Doris
(1955–) Germany.
1983 Straight Through the Heart
1984 The Belly of the Whale
1986 Men
1986 Paradies

1988 Me and Him

DOUGHTON Jnr, Russell S
1967 The Hostage
1968 Fever Heat

DOUGLAS, Bill
1987 Comrades

DOUGLAS, Gordon
(1909–) New York, New York, USA.
1936 General Spanky **(Fred NEWMEYER)**
1939 Zenobia / *Elephants Never Forget*
1940 Saps at Sea
1941 Road Show **(Hal ROACH, Hal ROACH Jnr)**
1941 Broadway Limited / *The Baby Vanishes*
1941 Niagara
1942 The Devil with Hitler
1943 The Great Gildersleeve
1943 Gildersleeve's Bad Day
1943 Gildersleeve on Broadway
1944 Gildersleeve's Ghost
1944 A Night of Adventure
1944 Girl Rush
1944 The Falcon in Hollywood
1945 Zombies on Broadway / *Loonies on Broadway*
1945 First Yank in Tokyo / *Mask of Fury*
1946 Dick Tracy Versus Cueball
1946 San Quentin
1948 If You Knew Susie
1948 The Black Arrow
1948 Walk a Crooked Mile
1949 Mr Soft Touch / *House of Settlement* **(Harry LEVIN)**
1949 The Doolins of Oklahoma / *The Great Manhunt*
1950 The Nevadan
1950 Fortunes of Captain Blood
1950 Rogues of Sherwood Forest
1950 Kiss Tomorrow Goodbye
1950 Between Midnight and Dawn
1951 The Great Missouri Raid
1951 Once the Valiant
1951 I Was a Communist for the FBI
1951 Come Fill the Cup
1952 Maru Maru
1952 The Iron Mistress
1953 She's Back on Broadway
1953 The Charge of Feather Creek
1953 So This Is Love / *The Grace Moore Story*
1954 Them
1954 Young at Heart
1955 The McConnell Story / *Tiger in the Sky*
1955 Sincerely Yours
1956 Santiago / *The Gun Runner*
1957 The Big Land / *Stampeded!*
1957 Bombers B-52 / *No Sleep Till Dawn*
1958 Fort Dobbs
1958 The Fiend Who Walked the West
1959 Up Periscope
1959 Yellowstone Kelly
1961 Gold of the Seven Saints
1961 The Sins of Rachel Cade
1961 Claudelle Inglish / *Young and Eager*
1962 Follow That Dream
1963 Call Me Bwana

1964 Robin and the Seven Hoods
1964 Rio Conchos
1965 Sylvia
1965 Harlow
1966 Stagecoach
1966 Way..Way Out!
1967 In Like Flint
1967 Chuka
1967 Tony Rome
1968 The Detective
1968 Lady in Cement
1970 Skullduggery
1970 Barquero
1970 They Call Me Mr Tibbs!
1978 Viva Knievel!
(also many shorts)

DOUGLAS, Kirk (Issur Danielovitch Demsky)
(1916–) Amsterdam, New York, USA.
Biography: Kirk Douglas by Robert Munn.
1973 Scalawag
1975 Posse

DOUGLAS, Peter
1988 A Tiger's Tale

DOWD, Nancy
(1944–) Framingham, Massachusetts, USA.
1982 Love **(Annette COHEN, Liv ULLMANN, Mai ZETTERLING)**

DOWDEY, Kathleen
(1949–) Washington DC, USA.
1984 Blue Heaven

DOWNEY, Robert
(1936–) American.
1963 Babo 73
1965 Chafed Elbows
1968 No More Excuses
1969 Putney Swope
1970 Pound
1972 Greaser's Palace
1980 Up the Academy
1984 Moonbeam
1986 America
1988 Rented Lips

DOYLE, Julian
1987 Love Potion

DRAGIN, Bert I
1987 The Butterfly Revolution / *Summer Camp Nightmare*
1988 Twice Dead

DRAGOTI, Stan
(1932–) New York, New York, USA.
1972 Dirty Little Billy
1979 Love at First Bite
1983 Mr Mom
1985 The Man with One Red Shoe
1988 Crack
1989 Daddy's Little Girl
1990 Love at Second Bite

DRAKE, Jim
1987 Police Academy IV: Citizens on Patrol
1989 Speedzone Fever / *One for the Money*

DRAKE, Oliver
1934 Texas Tornado
1942 Today I Hang **(George M MERRICK)**
1943 Border Buckaroos
1944 Trail of Terror
1946 Moon Over Montana
1946 Trail to Mexico
1946 West of the Alamo
1946 Ginger
1947 Deadline
1947 Fighting Mustang
1947 Shootin' Irons
1947 Son of the Sierras
1947 Sunset Carson Rides Again
1949 Across the Rio Grande
1949 Brand of Fear
1949 Lawless Code
1949 Roaring Westwards
1957 The Parson and the Law
1957 A Lust to Kill

DREAM, Rinse
1986 Café Flesh

DREIFUSS, Arthur
(1908–) Frankfurt am Main, Germany.
1939 Double Deal
1940 Mystery in Swing
1941 Murder on Lenox Avenue
1941 Sunday Sinners
1941 Reg'lar Fellers
1942 Baby Face Morgan
1942 The Boss of Big Town
1942 The Pay Off
1943 Sarong Girl
1943 Melody Parade
1943 Campus Rhythm
1943 Nearly Eighteen
1944 The Sultan's Daughter
1944 Ever Since Venus
1945 Eddie Was a Lady
1945 Boston Blackie Booked on Suspicion
1945 Boston Blackie's Rendezvous
1945 The Gay Señorita
1945 Prison Ship
1946 Junior Prom
1946 Freddie Steps Out
1946 High School Hero
1947 Vacation Days
1947 Betty Co-Ed / *The Melting Pot*
1947 Little Miss Broadway
1947 Two Blondes and a Redhead
1947 Sweet Genevieve
1948 Glamour Girl / *Night Club*
1948 Mary Lou
1948 I Surrender Dear
1948 An Old-Fashioned Girl
1948 Manhattan Angel
1948 All American Pro
1949 Shamrock Hill
1949 There's a Girl in My Heart
1955 Secret File
1956 Assignment Abroad
1958 Life Begins at 17
1959 The Last Blitzkrieg

1959 Juke Box Rhythm
1962 The Quare Fellow
1967 Riot on Sunset Strip
1967 The Love-Ins
1968 For Singles Only
1968 A Time to Sing
1968 The Young Runaways

DREW, Di
1987 The Right Hand Man

DRISCOLL, Richard
1987 The Comic
1988 The Silent Hero

DRIVER, Donald
1973 The Naked Ape

DRIVER, Sara
(1956–) New York, New York, USA.
1986 Sleepwalk

DROVE, Antonio
1987 The Tunnel

DRURY, David
1984 Forever Young
1985 Defence of the Realm
1988 Split Decisions / *Kid Gloves*
1989 The Krays

DUBIN, Charles S
(1919–) New York, New York, USA.
1957 Mister Rock and Roll
1976 Moving Violation
(also many TV movies)

DUFFELL, Peter
(1924–) British.
1961 Partners in Crime
1970 The House That Dripped Blood
1972 England Made Me
1975 Inside Out / *Hitler's Gold / The Golden Heist*
1983 Experience Preferred But Not Essential

DUGAN, Michael
1983 Mausoleum

DUIGAN, John
1975 The Firm Man
1976 The Trespassers
1979 Dimboola
1981 Winter of Our Dreams
1983 Far East
1984 One Night Stand
1988 The Year My Voice Broke
1989 Romero

DUKE, Daryl
(c1935–) Vancouver, Canada.
1972 Payday
1978 The Silent Partner
1981 Hard Feelings
1986 Tai-Pan
(also many TV movies)

DUNCAN, Pat
1988 84 Charlie Mopic

DUNLAP, Scott R
(1892–1970) American.
1926 Desert Valley
1927 Whispering Sage
1927 Good as Gold
1929 One Stolen Night

DUNNE, Philip
(1908–) New York, USA.
1955 Prince of Players
1955 The View from Pompey's Head / *Secret Interlude*
1956 Hilda Crane
1957 Three Brave Men
1958 In Love and War
1958 Ten North Frederick
1959 Blue Denim / *Blue Jeans*
1961 Wild in the Country
1962 Lisa / *The Inspector*
1966 Blindfold

DUPONT, E A (Ewald André Dupont)
(1891–1956) Zeitz, Saxony, Germany.
1925 Variety / *Vaudeville*
1928 Love Me and the World Is Mine
1928 Moulin Rouge
1929 Atlantic
1929 Piccadilly
1930 Two Worlds
1930 Cape Forlorn / *Love Storm*
1931 Trapeze
1932 Peter Voss
1933 Der Laüfer von Marathon
1933 Ladies Must Love
1935 The Bishop Misbehaves / *The Bishop's Misadventures*
1936 Forgotten Faces
1936 A Son Comes Home
1937 Night of Mystery
1937 On Such a Night
1938 Love on Toast
1939 Hell's Kitchen **(Lewis R SEILER)**
1951 The Scarf
1953 Problem Girls
1953 The Neanderthal Man
1953 The Steel Lady
1954 Return to Treasure Island

DURAND, Rudy
1979 Tilt

DURAS, Marguerite (Marguerite Donnadieu)
(1914–) Giadinh, French Indochina.
1969 Destroy, She Said
1975 India Song

DURSTON, David
1970 I Drink Your Blood
1972 Stigma
1972 Blue Sextet

DUVALL, Robert
(1931–) San Diego, California, USA.
1983 Angelo, My Love

DUVIVIER, Julien *
(1896–1967) Lille, France.
1930 David Golder
1934 Maria Chapdelaine / *The Naked Heart*
1935 Escape from Yesterday / *La Bandera*

1936 They Were Five / *La Belle Equipe*
1936 The Golem
1938 The Great Waltz
1940 The Heart of a Nation / *Untel Père et Fils*
1941 Lydia
1942 Tales of Manhattan
1943 Flesh and Fantasy
1944 The Imposter / *Strange Confession*
1944 Destiny **(Reginald LeBORG)**
1946 Panic
1947 Anna Karenina
1949 The Sinners / *Au Royaume des Cieux*
1950 Captain Black Jack
1951 The Little World of Don Camillo
1952 Henrietta's Holiday
1953 The Return of Don Camillo
1953 On Trial / *L'Affaire Maurizius*
1955 Deadlier Than the Male / *Voici le Temps des Assassins*
1956 The House of Lovers / *Pot-Bouille*
1960 Boulevard
1961 The Curse and the Coffin
1962 The Devil and the Ten Commandments
1963 Highway Pickup
1967 Diabolically Yours
(also many documentaries)

DWAN, Allan (Joseph Aloysius Dwan)
(1885–1981) Toronto, Canada. Biography: Allan Dwan: The Last Pioneer by Peter Bogdanovich.
1922 The Hidden Woman
1923 Robin Hood
1923 The Glimpses of the Moon
1923 Lawful Larceny
1923 Zaza
1923 Big Brother
1924 A Society Scandal
1924 Manhandled
1924 Her Love Story
1924 Her Wages of Virtue
1924 Argentine Love
1924 Night Life of New York
1924 The Coast of Folly
1924 Stage Struck
1926 Sea Horses
1926 Padlocked
1926 Tin Gods
1926 Summer Bachelors
1927 Music Master
1927 The Joy Girl
1927 East Side, West Side
1927 French Dressing / *Lessons for Wives*
1928 The Big Noise
1929 The Iron Mask
1929 Tide of Empire
1929 The Far Call
1929 Frozen Justice
1929 South Sea Rose
1930 What a Widow!
1931 Man to Man
1931 Chances
1931 Wicked
1932 While Paris Sleeps
1933 Her First Affair
1933 Counsel's Opinion
1934 The Morning After / *I Spy*
1934 Hollywood Party **(Richard BOLESLAWSKI, Roy ROWLAND)**
1935 Black Sheep
1935 Navy Wife
1936 Song and Dance Man
1936 Human Cargo
1936 High Tension
1936 15 Maiden Lane
1937 Woman Wise
1937 That I May Live
1937 One Mile from Heaven
1937 Heidi
1938 Rebecca of Sunnybrook Farm
1938 Josette
1938 Suez
1939 The Three Musketeers / *The Singing Musketeer*
1939 The Gorilla
1939 Frontier Marshal
1940 Sailor's Lady
1940 Young People
1940 Trail of the Vigilantes
1941 Rise and Shine
1941 Look Who's Laughing
1942 Friendly Enemies
1942 Here We Go Again
1943 Around the World
1944 Up in Mabel's Room
1944 Abroad with Two Yanks
1945 Brewster's Millions
1946 Getting Gertie's Garter
1946 Rendezvous with Annie
1947 Northwest Outpost / *End of the Rainbow*
1947 Calendar Girl
1947 Driftwood
1948 The Inside Story
1948 Angel in Exile **(Philip FORD)**
1949 The Sands of Iwo Jima
1950 Surrender
1951 Belle le Grand
1952 The Wild Blue Yonder / *Thunder Across the Pacific*
1952 I Dream of Jeanie
1952 Montana Belle
1953 The Woman They Almost Lynched
1953 Sweethearts on Parade
1954 Flight Nurse
1954 Silver Lode
1954 Passion
1955 Cattle Queen of Montana
1955 Escape to Burma
1955 Pearl of the Pacific
1955 Tennessee's Partner
1956 Slightly Scarlet
1956 Hold Back the Night
1957 The River's Edge
1957 The Restless Breed
1958 Enchanted Island
1961 The Most Dangerous Man Alive
(also a multitude of silent shorts)

DWYER, John
1986 The Texas Serial Killings

DYAL, Kay L
1974 Memory of Us

DYKE, Robert
1988 Moontrap

DYLAN, Bob (Robert Zimmerman)
(1941–) Hibbing, Minnesota, USA.
1978 Renaldo and Clara

EADY, David
(1924–) British.
1954 Three Cases of Murder **(George More O'FERRALL, Wendy TOYE)**
1960 Faces in the Dark
1960 In the Wake of a Stranger

EASON, B Reeves (Breezy Eason)
(1886–1956) American.
1924 Trigger Finger
1924 Women First / *The Turf Sensation*
1924 Flashing Spurs / *Spider's Web*
1925 Border Justice
1925 The Texas Bearcat
1925 Fighting Youth
1925 Fighting the Flames
1925 The New Champion
1925 The Shadow on the Wall
1925 A Fight to the Finish
1925 Lone Hand Saunders
1926 The Test of Donald Norton
1926 The Sign of the Claw
1927 The Denver Dude
1927 The Prairie King
1927 Painted Ponies
1927 Johnny Get Your Hair Cut **(Archie L MAYO)**
1927 Through Thick and Thin
1927 Galloping Fury
1928 The Flyin' Cowboy
1928 Ridin' for Fame
1928 A Trick of Hearts
1928 Clearing the Trail
1929 The Lariat Kid
1929 The Winged Horseman **(Arthur ROSSON)**
1930 Troopers Three **(Norman TAUROG)**
1930 The Roaring Ranch **(Arthur ROSSON)**
1930 Trigger Tricks
1930 Spurs
1931 The Sunset Trail
1931 Honour of the Press / *The Scoop*
1932 The Heart Punch
1933 Cornered
1933 Behind Jury Doors
1933 Alimony Madness
1933 Revenge at Monte Carlo / *Mystery at Monte Carlo*
1933 Her Resale Value
1933 Dance Hall Hostess
1933 Neighbours' Wives
1936 Red River Valley
1937 Land Beyond the Law
1937 Empty Holsters
1937 Prairie Thunder
1938 Sergeant Murphy
1938 The Kid Comes Back
1938 The Daredevil Drivers
1938 Call of the Yukon **(John T COYLE)**
1939 Blue Montana Skies
1939 Mountain Rhythm
1940 Men with Steel Faces **(Otto BROWER)**
1942 Murder in the Big House / *Born for Trouble*
1942 Spy Ship
1943 Truck Busters
1943 Murder on the Waterfront
1946 North of the Border
1946 'Neath Canadian Skies
1949 Rimfire
1952 The Singapore Story
1952 Kamong Sentosa
1953 Paper Tiger
1953 Jungle Justice
(also many serials and silent shorts)

EASTMAN, Alan
1987 The War Boy
1987 Crazy Moon

EASTMAN, Charles
1973 The All-American Boy

EASTMAN, Gordon
1976 The Savage World

EASTWOOD, Clint
(1930–) San Francisco, California, USA.
Biography: The Man Behind the Myth by Patrick Agan.
1971 Play Misty for Me
1972 High Plains Drifter
1973 Breezy
1975 The Eiger Sanction
1976 The Outlaw Josey Wales
1977 The Gauntlet
1980 Bronco Billy
1982 Firefox
1982 Honkytonk Man
1983 Sudden Impact
1985 Pale Rider
1986 Heartbreak Ridge
1988 Bird

EBERHARDT, Thomas
1984 Sole Survivor
1984 Night of the Comet
1988 The Night Before
1988 Without a Clue / *Sherlock and Me*

EBERSON, Drew
1938 The Overland Express
1939 The Phantom Stage

EDMONDS, Don
1974 Tender Loving Care
1983 Terror on Tour
1985 Striker

EDWARDS, Blake (William Blake McEdwards)
(1922–) Tulsa, Oklahoma, USA.
1955 Bring Your Smile Along
1956 He Laughed Last
1957 Mister Cory
1958 This Happy Feeling
1959 The Perfect Furlough / *Strictly for Pleasure*
1959 Operation Petticoat
1960 High Time
1961 Breakfast at Tiffany's
1962 Experiment in Terror / *The Grip of Fear*
1962 Days of Wine and Roses
1964 The Pink Panther

1964 A Shot in the Dark
1965 The Great Race
1966 What Did You Do in the War, Daddy?
1967 Gunn
1968 The Party
1970 Darling Lili
1971 Wild Rovers
1972 The Carey Treatment
1974 The Tamarind Seed
1975 Return of the Pink Panther
1976 The Pink Panther Strikes Again
1978 Revenge of the Pink Panther
1979 10
1981 S.O.B.
1982 Victor Victoria
1982 Trail of the Pink Panther
1983 Curse of the Pink Panther
1983 The Man Who Loved Women
1984 Micki and Maude
1986 A Fine Mess / *The Music Box*
1986 That's Life / *Crisis*
1987 Blind Date
1988 Sunset
1989 Skin Deep

EDWARDS, George
1984 The Attic

EDWARDS, Henry
(1882–1952) British.
1926 Tramp, Tramp, Tramp
1931 Stranglehold
1933 The Flag Lieutenant
1934 Lord Edgware Dies
1934 The Lash
1935 The Rock of Valpre
1935 The Private Secretary
1935 Scrooge
1936 In the Soup
1936 Juggernaut
1937 The Vicar of Bray

EDWARDS, Vincent (Vincento Edouardo Zoine)
(1928–) New York, New York, USA.
1973 The Maneater

EDZARD, Christine
1979 Stories from a Flying Trunk
1983 Biddy
1986 Little Dorrit: Nobody's Fault
1987 Little Dorrit: Little Dorrit's Story

EGGLESTON, Colin
1984 Innocent Prey
1986 Sky Pirates
1987 Cassandra
1987 The Prince at the Court of Yarralumla
1989 Conspiracy

EGLESON, Jan
1979 Billy in the Lowlands
1981 The Dark End of the Street

ELDRIDGE, John
(1917–1960) British.
1951 Brandy for the Parson
1952 Laxdale Hall / *Scotch on the Rocks*
1953 Conflict of Wings / *Fuss Over Feathers*
(also many documentaries)

ELEASARI, Jacob
1987 Walk in Beauty
1988 Obsession

ELFSTROM, Robert
1973 The Gospel Road
(also many documentaries)

ELLES, Fred
1939 Mrs Pym of Scotland Yard

ELLIOT, Clyde E
1932 Bring 'Em Back Alive
1934 Devil Tiger
1934 China Roars
1938 Booloo

ELLIOT, Grace
1931 The Three Racketeers
1931 10,000 and Broke
1931 Him Who Has
1931 Marriage à la Carte
1931 The Spice of Life
1931 Devil's Marriage
1931 Splurge

ELLIOTT, Lang
(1950–) Los Angeles, California, USA.
1980 The Private Eyes
1989 Cage

ELLIS, Robert
1974 The Girl from Petrovka
1987 Warm Nights on a Slow Moving Train

ELLISON, Joseph
1980 Don't Go in the House
1985 Joey

ELVEY, Maurice (William Seward Folkard)
(1887–1967) Darlington, England.
1924 Henry, King of Navarre
1924 Slaves of Destiny
1924 The Love Story of Ailette Brunton
1924 My Husband's Wives
1925 Folly of Vanity **(Henry OTTO)**
1925 Curlytop
1925 She Wolves
1925 Everyman's Wife
1926 Woman Tempted
1926 Human Law
1926 The Flag Lieutenant
1926 Mademoiselle from Armentières
1927 Hindle Wakes
1927 Roses of Picardy
1927 The Flight Commander
1927 The Glad Eye
1927 Quinneys
1927 Mademoiselle Parley Voo
1927 Palais de Danse
1927 You Know What Sailors Are
1929 High Treason
1930 The School for Scandal
1931 A Honeymoon Adventure
1931 Sally in Our Alley
1931 Potiphar's Wife / *Her Strange Desire*
1932 The Water Gypsies
1932 Diamond Cut Diamond / *Blame the Woman* **(Fred NIBLO)**

1932 Frail Woman
1932 In a Monastery Garden
1932 The Lodger / *The Phantom Fiend*
1932 The Marriage Bond
1933 The Lost Chord
1933 I Lived with You
1933 This Week of Grace
1933 The Wandering Jew
1933 Soldiers of the King / *The Woman in Command*
1934 Love, Life and Laughter
1934 Road House
1934 Princess Charming
1934 The Clairvoyant
1935 The Tunnel / *Transatlantic Tunnel*
1936 The Man in the Mirror
1936 Spy of Napoleon
1937 Change for a Sovereign
1937 Who Killed John Savage?
1937 For Freedom
1940 Under Your Hat
1942 Salute John Citizen
1943 The Gentle Sex **(Leslie HOWARD)**
1943 The Lamp Still Burns
1944 Medal for a General / *The Gay Intruder*
1944 Strawberry Roan
1946 Beware of Pity
1951 The Late Edwina Black / *Obsessed*
1952 The Great Game
1954 The Gay Dog
1954 The Happiness of Three Women
1956 Dry Rot
1957 Second Fiddle
(also many silent shorts)

ELWYN, Robert
1953 That Man from Tangier

EMES, Ian
(1949–) Birmingham, England.
1986 Knights and Emeralds

EMMERICH, Roland
1984 The Noah's Ark Principle
1985 Making Contact
1988 Ghost Chase
1989 Moon 44

EMSHWILLER, Ed
1970 Image, Flesh and Voice
1971 Branches

ENDELSON, Robert
1979 Staying Alive

ENDERS, Robert
1978 Stevie

ENDFIELD, C Raker (Cy Endfield)
(1914–) Scranton, Pennsylvania, USA.
Pseudonym: Hugh Raker.
1946 Gentleman Joe Palooka
1947 Stork Bites Man
1948 The Argyle Secrets
1949 Joe Palooka in the Big Fight
1950 The Underworld Story
1950 The Sound of Fury / *Try and Get Me*
1952 Tarzan's Savage Fury
1953 Colonel March Investigates
1954 The Master Plan
1955 The Secret
1956 Child in the House
1957 Hell Drivers
1958 Sea Fury
1959 Jet Storm
1961 Mysterious Island
1964 Hide and Seek
1964 Zulu
1965 Sands of the Kalahari
1969 De Sade
1971 Universal Soldier

ENGEL, Morris
(1918–) American.
1956 Lovers and Lollipops **(Ruth ORKIN)**
1960 Weddings and Babies

ENGELBACH, David
1986 America 3000 / *Thunder Warriors*

ENGLISH, John
(1903–1969) British.
1935 His Fighting Blood
1935 Red Blood of Courage
1937 Arizona Days
1937 Whistling Bullets
1938 Call the Mesquiteers
1941 Gangs of Sonora
1942 Code of the Outlaw
1942 The Yukon Patrol **(Charles WITNEY)**
1942 Valley of Hunted Men
1942 Westward Ho
1942 Phantom Plainsmen
1942 Shadows on the Range
1942 Raiders of the Range
1943 Death Valley Manhunt
1943 The Man from Thunder River
1943 Overland Mail Robbery
1943 Dead Man's Gulch
1943 The Black Hill's Express
1943 Thundering Trails
1944 Grissly's Millions
1944 San Fernando Valley
1944 The Port of Missing Thieves
1944 Call of the South Seas
1944 The Laramie Trail
1944 Faces in the Fog
1944 Silver City Kid
1945 Utah
1945 Don't Fence Me In
1945 The Phantom Speaks
1945 Behind City Lights
1946 Murder in the Music Hall / *Midnight Melody*
1947 Trail to San Antone
1947 The Last Round-Up
1948 The Strawberry Roan
1949 The Cowboy and the Indians
1949 Loaded Pistols
1949 Riders of the Sky
1949 Riders of the Whistling Pines
1949 Rim of the Canyon
1950 Beyond the Purple Hills
1950 The Blazing Sun
1950 Cow Town
1950 Indian Territory
1950 Mule Train
1950 Sons of New Mexico

1950 The Whipped
1951 Gene Autry and the Mounties
1951 Hills of Utah
1951 Silver Canyon
1951 Valley of Fire
1951 Whirlwind
(also many serials)

ENGLUND, George H
(1926–) Washington DC. USA.
1962 The Ugly American
1964 Signpost to Murder
1970 Zachariah
1972 The Ski Raiders / *Snow Job*

ENGLUND, Robert
1988 976 Evil / *Horoscope*

ENRICO, Robert *
(1931–) Lievin, France.
1965 The Wise Guys
1969 The Last Adventure
1969 Zita
1976 The Old Gun
1980 Heads or Tails
1983 For Those I Loved
1986 Zone Rouge
1989 The French Revolution **(Richard HEFFRON)**

ENRIGHT, Ray (Raymond E Enright)
(1896–1965) Anderson, Indiana, USA.
1927 Traced By the Police
1927 Jaws of Steel
1927 The Girl from Chicago
1928 Domestic Trouble
1928 Land of the Silver Fox
1929 Little Wildcat
1929 Stolen Kisses
1929 Kid Gloves
1929 Skin Deep
1930 Song of the West
1930 Golden Dawn
1930 Dancing Sweeties
1930 Scarlet Pages
1932 Play Girl
1932 The Tenderfoot
1933 Blondie Johnson
1933 The Silk Express
1933 Tomorrow at Seven
1933 Havana Widows
1934 I've Got Your Number
1934 Twenty Million Sweethearts
1934 The Circus Clown
1934 Dames
1934 The St Louis Kid / *A Perfect Weekend*
1935 While the Patient Slept
1935 Travelling Saleslady
1935 Alibi Ike
1935 We're in the Money
1935 Miss Pacific Fleet
1936 Snowed Under
1936 Earthworm Tractors / *A Natural Born Salesman*
1936 Sing Me a Love Song / *Come Up Smiling*
1936 China Clipper
1937 Ready Willing and Able
1937 Slim, the Singing Marine
1937 Back in Circulation
1938 Swing Your Lady
1938 Gold Diggers in Paris / *The Gay Imposters*
1938 Going Places
1939 Naughty But Nice
1939 Angels Wash Their Faces
1939 On Your Toes
1940 Brother Rat and a Baby / *Baby Be Good*
1940 An Angel from Texas
1940 The River's End
1941 The Wagons Roll at Night
1941 Thieves Fall Out
1941 Bad Men of Missouri
1941 Law of the Tropics
1941 Wild Bill Hickok Rides
1942 The Spoilers
1942 Men of Texas
1942 Sin Town
1943 Good Luck, Mr Yates
1943 The Iron Major
1943 Gung Ho!
1945 China Sky
1945 Man Alive
1946 One Way to Love
1947 Trail Street
1948 Albuquerque / *Silver City*
1948 Return of the Bad Men
1948 Coroner Creek
1949 South of St Louis
1950 Montana
1950 Kansas Raiders
1951 Flaming Feathers
1953 The Man from Cairo / *Crime Squad*
(also many documentaries)

EPHRON, Henry
(1912–) American.
1958 Sing, Boy, Sing

EPSTEIN, Jerome
1968 The Adding Machine

EPSTEIN, Marcelo
1984 Body Rock

ERDMAN, Richard
(1925–) Enid, Oklahoma, USA.
1971 Bleep
1973 The Brothers O'Toole

ERICKSON, A F
1929 The Woman from Hell
1930 Lone Star Ranger
1930 Rough Romance
1930 Under Suspicion
1932 This Sporting Age

ERIKSEN, Dan
1966 A Midsummer Night's Dream

ERLER, Rainer
1987 The Nuclear Conspiracy

ERMAN, John
1971 Making It
1973 Ace Eli and Rodger of the Skies
1989 Stella
(also many TV movies)

ERSKINE, Chester
(1905–1986) American.
1934 Midnight / *Call It Murder*
1935 Frankie and Johnnie
1947 The Egg and I
1949 Take One False Step
1952 Androcles and the Lion
1952 A Girl in Every Port
1972 Irish Whiskey Rebellion

ESPER, Dwain
1934 Maniac

ESSEX, Harry
(1910–) American.
1953 I, the Jury
1955 Mad at the World

ESTABROOK, Howard
(1884–1978) American.
1944 Heavenly Days

ESTEVEZ, Emilio
(1962–) New York, New York, USA.
1986 Wisdom
1990 Men at Work

ESWAY, Alexander
1931 Shadows
1935 Music Hath Charms **(Thomas BENTLEY, Walter SUMMERS, Arthur WOODS)**
1945 Steppin' in Society

EVANS, John
1974 Black Godfather

EVANS, Warren
1980 Love at First Gulp

EVERETT, D S *see* **Donald SHEBIB**

EVERS, Jason (Herbert Evers)
(1922–) American.
1963 The Brain That Wouldn't Die

EYRE, Richard
1983 The Ploughman's Lunch
1983 Loose Connections

FAIMAN, Peter
1986 Crocodile Dundee
(also many Australian TV shorts)

FAIRCHILD, William
(1918–) British.
1955 John and Julie
1956 The Extra Day
1958 The Silent Enemy

FAIRFAX, Ferdinand
(1944–) London, England.
1983 Nate and Hayes / *Savage Islands*
1988 The Rescue
(also many TV movies)

FAITHFULL, Geoffrey
(1894–1979) British.
1944 For You Alone

FANAKA, Jamaa
1975 Welcome Home, Brother Charles
1977 Emma Mae
1980 Penitentiary
1982 Penitentiary II
1987 Penitentiary III

FARALDO, Claude *
(1936–) French.
1986 Flagrant Desire / *A Certain Desire*

FARGO, James
(1938–) Washington DC, USA.
1976 The Enforcer
1978 Every Which Way But Loose
1979 Caravans
1980 Game for Vultures
1982 Forced Vengeance
1984 Voyage of the Rock Aliens / *When the Rain Begins to Fall*
1988 Born to Race
1988 Riding on the Edge

FARKAS, Michael
1985 Prime Risk

FARKAS, Nicolas
(1891–1982) Hungarian.
1934 The Battle / *Hara Kiri* / *Thunder in the East*
1935 Variétés
1936 Port-Arthur

FARMER, Dan
1987 Cannibal Hookers

FARRIS, John
1975 Dear Dead Delilah

FARROW, John Villiers
(1904–1963) Sydney, New South Wales, Australia.
1937 Men in Exile
1937 West of Shanghai
1937 The Invisible Menace
1938 She Loved a Fireman
1938 Little Miss Thoroughbred
1938 My Bill
1938 Broadway Musketeers
1939 Woman in the Wind
1939 The Saint Strikes Back
1939 Sorority House / *That Girl from College*
1939 Five Came Back
1939 Full Confession
1939 Reno
1940 Married and in Love
1940 A Bill of Divorcement / *Never to Love*
1942 Wake Island **D* F***
1942 Commandos Strike at Dawn
1943 China
1944 The Hitler Gang
1945 You Came Along
1946 Two Years Before the Mast
1946 California
1947 Easy Come, Easy Go
1947 Blaze of Noon
1947 Calcutta
1948 The Big Clock
1948 The Night Has a Thousand Eyes

1948 Beyond Glory
1949 Alias Nick Beale / *The Contact Man*
1949 Red Hot and Blue
1951 His Kind of Woman
1951 Submarine Command
1953 Ride, Vaquero
1953 Plunder of the Sun
1953 Botany Boy
1953 Hondo
1954 A Bullet Is Waiting
1955 The Sea Chase
1956 Back from Eternity
1957 The Unholy Wife
1959 John Paul Jones

FASANO, John
1986 Edge of Hell / *Rock 'n' Roll Nightmare*
1988 Black Roses

FEFERMAN, Lina
1986 Seven Minutes in Heaven

FEINSTEIN, Barry
1968 You Are What You Eat

FEIST, Felix E
(1906–1965) New York, USA.
1932 Stepping Sisters
1933 The Deluge
1943 All By Myself
1943 You're a Lucky Fellow, Mr Smith
1944 This Is the Life
1944 Pardon My Rhythm
1944 Reckless Age
1945 George White's Scandals
1947 The Devil Thumbs a Ride
1948 The Winner's Circle
1949 The Threat
1949 Guilty of Treason
1950 The Golden Gloves Story
1950 The Man Who Cheated Himself
1951 Tomorrow Is Another Day
1951 The Basketball Fix / *The Big Decision*
1952 This Woman Is Dangerous
1952 The Big Trees
1952 The Man Behind the Gun
1953 Donovan's Brain
1953 Battles of Chief Pontiac
1955 Pirates of Tripoli
(also many shorts)

FEJOS, Paul (Pál Fejös)
(1897–1963) Budapest, Hungary.
Biography: The Several Lives of Paul Fejos by John Dodds.
1928 Lonesome
1929 Broadway
1929 The Last Performance / *The Last Call*
1930 Captain of the Guard **(John S ROBERTSON)**
1930 The Big House
1932 Marie
1932 Storm at Balaton
1934 Flight from the Millions
1935 Prisoner Number One
1935 The Golden Smile
1951 Jungle of Chan **(Gunnar SKOGLUND)**
(also many documentaries)

FEKE, Steve
1989 Keys to Freedom

FELDMAN, Dennis
1987 Real Men

FELDMAN, Marty
(1933–1982) London, England.
1977 The Last Remake of Beau Geste
1980 In God We Trust

FELIX, Seymour
(1892–1961) American.
1931 Girls Demand Excitement
1932 Stepping Sisters
(Seymour Felix also choreographed many films)

FELLINI, Federico
(1920–) Rimini, Italy.
Biographies: Fellini by Liliana Betti; Fellini the Artist by Edward Murray.
1950 Variety Lights **(Alberto LATTUADA)**
1952 The White Sheik
1953 The Loafers / *Spivs*
1953 Love in the City **(Michelangelo ANTONIONI, Alberto LATTUADA, Carlo LIZZANI, Francesco MASELLI, Dino RISI)**
1954 The Road
1955 The Swindle
1957 Night of Cabiria
1960 La Dolce Vita **D***
1963 ½ **D***
1965 Juliet of the Spirits
1969 Spirits of the Dead / *Histoires Extraordinaires* **(Louis MALLE, Roger VADIM)**
1970 Fellini — Satyricon **D***
1971 The Clowns
1972 Fellini's Roma
1974 Amarcord **D***
1977 Fellini's Casanova
1979 Orchestra Rehearsal
1981 City of Women
1983 And the Ship Sails On
1986 Ginger and Fred
1987 The Interview

FELTHAM, Kerry
(1939–) Edmonton, Alberta, Canada.
1970 The Great Chicago Conspiracy Circus

FENADY, Georg J
(1930–) Toledo, Ohio, USA.
1973 Arnold
1973 Terror in the Wax Museum

FENTON, Leslie
(1902–1978) British.
1939 Tell No Tales
1939 Stronger Than Desire
1940 The Man from Dakota / *Arouse and Beware*
1940 The Golden Fleecing
1941 The Saint's Vacation
1943 There's a Future in It
1944 Tomorrow the World!
1946 Pardon My Past
1948 On Our Merry Way / *A Miracle Can*

Happen **(King VIDOR)**
1948 Saigon
1948 Lulu Belle
1948 Whispering Smith
1949 Streets of Laredo
1950 The Redhead and the Cowboy

FERGUSON, Norman
1945 The Three Caballeros

FERRARA, Abel
1979 Driller Killer
1981 M S 45
1985 Fear City
1987 China Girl
1989 Cat Chaser

FERRARI, Stefano
1987 Dead Heat

FERRER, José (José Vincente Ferrer y Cintron)
(1912–) Santurce, Puerto Rico.
1955 The Shrike
1956 The Cockleshell Heroes
1956 The Great Man
1958 I Accuse!
1958 The High Cost of Living
1961 Return to Peyton Place
1962 State Fair

FERRER, Mel (Melchoir Gaston Ferrer)
(1917–) Elberton, New Jersey, USA.
1945 The Girl of the Limberlost
1950 Vendetta
1950 The Secret Fury
1959 Green Mansions
1966 Every Day Is a Holiday

FERRERI, Marco *
(1928–) Milan, Italy.
1963 The Conjugal Bed / *Una Storia Moderna*
1964 The Ape Woman
1965 Kiss the Other Sheik / *Oggi, Domani e Dopodomani* **(Edouardo DeFILIPPO, Luciano SALCE)**
1968 The Man with the Balloons
1970 The Seed of Man
1976 The Last Woman
1978 Bye Bye Monkey
1980 No Child's Land
1983 Tales of Ordinary Madness
1983 The Story of Piera
1987 I Love You

FERRETTI, Robert
1988 Fear / *Honor Betrayed / Flashback*

FERRIN, Frank
1955 Sabaka

FEYDER, Jacques (Jacques Frédérix)
(1885–1948) Ixelles, Belgium.
1926 Carmen
1928 Shadows of Fear / *Thérèse Raquin*
1928 Les Nouveaux Messieurs
1929 The Kiss
1930 The Unholy Night
1930 Anna Christie
1930 Olympia
1930 His Glorious Night
1931 Son of India
1931 Daybreak
1933 Le Grand Jeu
1934 Pension Mimosas
1935 Carnival in Flanders / *La Kermesse Héroique*
1937 Knight Without Armour
1941 Une Femme Disparaît
1942 La Loi de Nord
(also many foreign shorts)

FIEGELSON, Julius
1971 The Windsplitter

FIELDS, Leonard
1934 Manhattan Love Song
1934 King Kelly of the USA
1935 Streamline Express

FIELDS, Michael
1987 Geraldine

FIGGIS, Mike
1988 Stormy Monday
1989 Hot Spot

FINBOW, Colin
1984 Dark Enemy
1985 Mister Skeeter
1986 Daemon
1987 School for Vandals

FINCH, Charles
1987 Priceless Beauty

FINEGAN, John P
1986 Girl School Screamers

FINK, Michael
1975 Force Four
1976 Velvet Smooth

FINKLEMAN, Ken
1982 Airplane II: The Sequel
1986 Head Office

FINNEY, Albert
(1936–) Salford, Lancashire, England.
1968 Charlie Bubbles

FINNEY, Edward
1941 Silver Stallion
1941 Riot Squad
1942 King of the Stallions
1947 Queen of the Amazons

FIRSTENBERG, Sam
(1950–) Israel.
1981 One More Chance
1983 Revenge of the Ninja
1984 Ninja III: The Domination
1984 Breakin' 2 Electric Boogaloo
1985 American Ninja
1986 Avenging Force / *Night Hunter*
1987 American Ninja II: The Confrontation
1988 The Prank

FIRTH, Michael
1977 Off the Edge
1984 Heart of the Stag
1985 Sylvia
1988 The Leading Edge

FISCHA, Michael
1988 Death Spar
1989 My Mom's a Werewolf

FISCHER, Max
1980 The Lucky Star
1983 The Man in 5A / *Killing 'Em Softly*

FISHELSON, David
1983 City News **(Joe ZINMAN)**

FISHER, David
(1948–) Nashville, Tennessee, USA.
1982 Liar's Moon
1984 Toy Soldiers

FISHER, Jack
1989 Forbidden Love

FISHER, Terence
(1904–1980) London, England.
1947 To the Public Danger
1948 A Song for Tomorrow
1948 Colonel Bogey
1948 Portrait from Life / *The Girl in the Painting*
1949 Marry Me
1950 So Long at the Fair **(Anthony DARNBOROUGH)**
1951 Home to Danger
1952 Four Sided Triangle
1952 Stolen Face
1952 The Last Page / *Manbait*
1952 Wings of Danger / *Dead on Course*
1953 Mantrap / *Man in Hiding*
1953 Spaceways
1953 Blood Orange
1954 The Stranger Came Home / *The Unholy Four*
1954 Final Appointment
1954 Face the Music / *The Black Glove*
1954 Mask of Dust / *Race for Life*
1954 Children Galore
1955 Stolen Assignment
1955 The Flaw
1955 Murder By Proxy / *Blackout*
1956 The Gelignite Gang
1956 The Last Man to Hang
1957 The Astonished Heart **(Anthony DARNBOROUGH)**
1957 The Curse of Frankenstein
1957 Kill Me Tomorrow
1958 The Revenge of Frankenstein
1958 Dracula
1959 The Hound of the Baskervilles
1959 The Man Who Could Cheat Death
1959 The Mummy
1959 The Stranglers of Bombay
1960 The Brides of Dracula
1960 Sword of Sherwood Forest
1960 The Two Faces of Dr Jekyll / *House of Fright*
1961 The Curse of the Werewolf
1962 The Phantom of the Opera
1964 Sherlock Holmes and the Deadly Necklace
1964 The Horror of It All
1964 The Earth Dies Screaming
1964 The Gorgon
1965 Dracula, Prince of Darkness
1965 Frankenstein Created Woman
1966 Island of Terror
1967 The Devil Rides Out / *The Devil's Bride*
1967 Night of the Big Heat / *Island of the Burning Damned*
1969 Frankenstein Must Be Destroyed
1973 Frankenstein and the Monster from Hell
(also many TV shorts)

FISHMAN, William
1988 Tapeheads

FISK, Jack
(1945–) Ipava, Illinois, USA.
1981 Raggedy Man
1985 Violets Are Blue

FITZMAURICE, George
(1885–1941) Paris, France.
1924 Cytherea
1924 Tarnish
1925 A Thief in Paradise
1925 His Supreme Moment / *The Dark Angel*
1927 The Tender Hour
1927 The Son of the Sheik
1927 The Night of Love
1927 The Love Mart
1927 Rose of the Golden West
1928 The Barker
1928 Lilac Time / *Love Never Dies*
1929 The Locked Door
1929 His Captive Woman
1929 Man and the Moment
1929 Tiger Rose
1930 The Bad One
1930 One Heavenly Night
1930 The Devil to Pay
1930 Raffles **(Harry d'abbadie D'ARRAST)**
1931 Strangers May Kiss
1931 The Unholy Garden
1932 Mata Hari
1932 As You Desire Me
1934 All Men Are Enemies
1936 Petticoat Fever
1936 Suzy
1937 The Last of Mrs Cheyney **(Richard BOLESLAWSKI)**
1937 The Emperor's Candlesticks
1937 Live, Love and Learn
1938 Arsène Lupin Returns
1938 Vacation from Love
1940 Adventure in Diamonds

FITZPATRICK, James
(1902–1980) American.
1930 The Lady of the Lake
1945 Song of Mexico
(also many documentary shorts)

FLAHERTY, Paul
1988 18 Again
1989 Who's Harry Crumb?

FLAHERTY, Robert J
(1884–1951) Iron Mountain, Michigan, USA.
Biography: Robert J Flaherty: A Biography by Paul Rotha.
1921 Nanook of the North
1926 Moana
1937 Elephant **(Zoltan KORDA)**
1948 Louisiana Story
(also many documentaries)

FLEISCHER, Richard O
(1916–) Brooklyn, New York, USA.
1946 Child of Divorce
1947 Banjo
1948 Design for Death
1948 So This Is New York
1948 Bodyguard
1949 Make Mine Laughs
1949 The Clay Pigeon
1949 Follow Me Quietly
1949 Trapped
1950 Armoured Car Robbery
1952 The Narrow Margin
1952 The Happy Time
1953 Arena
1954 20,000 Leagues Under the Sea
1955 Violent Saturday
1955 The Girl in the Red Velvet Swing
1956 Bandido
1956 Between Heaven and Hell
1958 The Vikings
1959 These Thousand Hills
1959 Compulsion
1959 Crack in the Mirror
1961 The Big Gamble **(Elmo WILLIAMS)**
1966 Fantastic Voyage
1967 Dr Dolittle **F***
1968 The Boston Strangler
1969 Che!
1970 Tora! Tora! Tora! **(Kinji FUKASAKU, Toshio MASUDA)**
1971 10, Rillington Place
1971 Blind Terror / *See No Evil*
1971 The Last Run
1972 The New Centurions / *Precinct 45 / Los Angeles Police*
1972 Soylent Green
1973 The Don Is Dead
1974 The Spikes Gang
1974 Mr Majestyk
1975 Mandingo
1976 The Incredible Sarah
1978 The Prince and the Pauper / *Crossed Swords*
1980 Ashanti
1980 The Jazz Singer
1983 Tough Enough
1983 Amityville 3-D
1984 Conan the Destroyer
1985 Red Sonja
1987 Million Dollar Mystery

FLEISCHMANN, Peter
1987 Hard to Be God

FLEMING, Andrew
1988 Bad Dreams

FLEMING, Victor
(1883–1949) Pasadena, California, USA.
1924 The Code of the Sea
1924 Empty Hands
1925 Adventure
1925 The Devil's Cargo
1925 Lord Jim
1926 A Son and His Father
1926 Mantrap
1926 The Blind Goddess
1927 Hula
1927 The Rough Riders / *The Trumpet Call*
1927 Abie's Irish Rose **(Jules FURTHMAN)**
1929 The Way of All Flesh **F***
1929 Wolf Song
1929 The Virginian
1930 Renegades
1930 Common Clay
1931 Around the World in Eighty Minutes **(Douglas FAIRBANKS)**
1932 Red Dust
1932 The Wet Parade
1933 Bombshell
1933 The White Sister
1934 Treasure Island
1935 The Farmer Takes a Wife
1935 Reckless
1937 Captain Courageous **F***
1938 Test Pilot **F***
1939 Gone with the Wind **(George CUKOR, Sam WOOD) D** F****
1939 The Wizard of Oz **F***
1941 Dr Jekyll and Mr Hyde
1942 Tortilla Flat
1943 A Guy Named Joe
1945 Adventure
1948 Joan of Arc

FLEMYNG, Gordon
(1934–) Glasgow, Scotland.
1962 Sold for Sparrow
1963 Five to One
1963 Just for Fun
1965 Dr Who and the Daleks
1966 Daleks — Invasion Earth 2150AD
1968 The Split
1968 Great Catherine
1969 The Last Grenade
(also many TV movies)

FLICKER, Theodore J
(1930–) Freehold, New Jersey, USA.
1964 The Troublemaker
1967 The President's Analyst
1970 Up in the Cellar
1978 Jacob Two-Two Meets the Hooded Fang
1981 Soggy Bottom USA
(also many TV movies)

FLOCKER, James T
1976 Secret of Navajo Cave

FLOOD, James
(1895–1953) American.
1924 The Tenth Woman
1925 The Man Without a Conscience
1925 The Woman Hater
1925 The Woman Who Wasn't Wanted

1925 Satan in Sables
1926 Why Girls Go Back Home
1926 The Honeymoon Express
1928 The Count of Ten
1929 Midstream
1929 Mister Antonio
1930 Sisters
1930 Swellhead
1931 She-Wolf
1931 Mother's Millions
1932 Life Begins / *A Dream of Life* **(Elliot NUGENT)**
1932 Undercover Man
1932 The Mouthpiece **(Elliot NUGENT)**
1934 All of Me
1934 Such Women Are Dangerous
1934 Wings in the Dark
1935 Shanghai
1936 We're Only Human
1936 Everybody's Old Man
1937 Midnight Madonna
1937 Scotland Yard Commands
1939 Off the Record
1947 Stepchild

FLOREA, John
(1916–) American.
1972 Pickup on 101
1987 Hot Child in the City

FLOREY, Robert
(1900–1979) Paris, France.
Pseudonym: Florian Roberts.
1927 One Hour of Love
1927 The Romantic Age
1927 Face Value
1927 Hollywood Extra **(Slavko VORKAPICH)**
1927 Johann the Coffin Maker
1927 The Loves of Zero
1929 The Hole in the Wall
1929 Pusher-in-the-Face
1929 The Cocoanuts **(Joseph STANLEY)**
1929 Battle of Paris
1932 Murders in the Rue Morgue
1932 The Man Called Back
1932 Those We Love
1933 Girl Missing
1933 Ex-Lady
1933 The House on 56th Street
1934 Bedside
1934 Smarty / *Hit Me Again*
1934 Registered Nurse
1934 I Sell Anything
1935 I Am a Thief
1935 The Woman in Red
1935 The Florentine Dagger
1935 Don't Bet on Blondes
1935 Going Highbrow
1935 Ship Café
1935 The Pay-Off
1936 The Preview Murder Mystery
1936 'Til We Meet Again
1936 Hollywood Boulevard
1937 Outcast
1937 King of the Gamblers / *Czar of the Slot Machines*
1937 Mountain Music
1937 This Way Please
1937 Daughter of Shanghai / *Daughter of the Orient*
1938 Dangerous to Know
1938 King of Alcatraz
1939 Disbarred
1939 The Magnificent Fraud
1939 Death of a Champion
1940 Women Without Names
1940 Parole Fixer
1941 The Face Behind the Mask
1941 Meet Boston Blackie
1941 Two in a Taxi
1941 Dangerously We Live
1942 Lady Gangster
1943 The Desert Song
1944 Man from Frisco
1944 Roger Touhy, Gangster / *The Last Gangster*
1945 God Is My Co-Pilot
1945 Danger Signal
1946 The Beast with Five Fingers
1948 Tarzan and the Mermaids
1948 Rogues Regiment
1949 Outpost in Morocco
1949 The Crooked Way
1950 Johnny One-Eye
1950 The Vicious Years / *The Gangster We Made*
(also many silent shorts and TV movies)

FLYNN, Emmett J
1924 The Man Who Came Back
1925 The Dancers
1925 East Lynne
1925 Gerald Cranston's Lady
1925 The Winds of Youth
1926 The Palace of Pleasure
1926 The Yankee Señor
1926 Yellow Fingers
1927 Married Alive
1929 The Veiled Woman
1929 Hold Your Man
1929 The Shannons of Broadway

FLYNN, John
1968 The Sergeant
1971 The Jerusalem File
1973 The Outfit
1978 Rolling Thunder
1980 Defiance
1983 Touched
1987 Best Seller / *Hard Cover*
1989 Escape

FOLDES, Lawrence D
(1959–) Los Angeles, California, USA.
1979 Malibu High
1981 Don't Go Near the Park
1982 The Great Skycopter Rescue
1983 Young Warriors
1987 Nightforce

FOLEY, James
1984 Reckless
1986 At Close Range
1987 Who's That Girl / *Slammer*

FONDA, Peter
(1939–) New York, New York, USA.
1971 The Hired Hand

1975 Idaho Transfer
1979 Wanda Nevada

FONG, Allen (Fang Yu Ping)
1983 Father and Son

FONTAINE, Richard
1975 The Sins of Rachel

FORBES, Bryan (John Clarke)
(1926–) Stratford-atte-Bow, England.
Autobiography: Notes for a Life.
1962 Whistle Down the Wind
1963 The L-Shaped Room
1964 Seance on a Wet Afternoon
1965 King Rat
1966 The Wrong Box
1967 The Whisperers
1968 Deadfall
1969 The Madwoman of Chaillot
1971 The Raging Moon / *Long Ago Tomorrow*
1975 The Stepford Wives
1976 The Slipper and the Rose
1978 International Velvet
1981 Sunday Lovers **(Edouard MOLINARO, Dino RISI, Gene WILDER)**
1983 Better Late Than Never
1985 The Naked Face

FORCIER, Andrew
1987 Kalamazoo

FORD, John (Sean Aloysius O'Fearna or John Augustine Feeney)
(1895–1973) Cape Elizabeth, Maine, USA.
Biography: The Cinema of John Ford by John Baxter.
1924 The Iron Horse
1924 Hearts of Oak
1924 Hoodman Blind
1924 North of Hudson Bay
1925 The Fighting Heart / *Once to Every Man*
1925 Kentucky Pride
1925 Lightnin'
1925 Thank You
1926 The Blue Eagle
1926 The Shamrock Handicap
1926 Three Bad Men
1927 Upstream / *Footlight Glamour*
1928 Hangman's House
1928 Four Sons
1928 Mother Mackree
1928 Riley the Cop
1929 Salute **(David BUTLER)**
1929 Strong Boy
1929 The Black Watch
1930 Men Without Women
1930 Born Reckless
1930 Up the River
1931 The Brat
1931 Arrowsmith **F***
1931 The Seas Beneath
1932 Airmail
1932 Flesh
1933 Dr Bull
1933 Pilgrimage
1934 The Lost Patrol
1934 The World Moves On
1934 Judge Priest
1935 The Informer **D****
1935 Steamboat 'Round the Bend
1935 The Whole Town's Talking / *Passport to Fame*
1936 Mary of Scotland
1936 The Plough and the Stars
1936 The Prisoner of Shark Island
1937 The Hurricane
1937 Wee Willie Winkie
1938 Four Men and a Prayer
1938 Submarine Patrol
1939 Drums Along the Mohawk
1939 Stagecoach **D* F***
1939 Young Mr Lincoln
1940 The Grapes of Wrath **D** F***
1940 The Long Voyage Home **F***
1941 How Green Was My Valley **D** F****
1941 Tobacco Road
1945 They Were Expendable
1946 My Darling Clementine
1947 The Fugitive
1948 Fort Apache
1948 Three Godfathers
1949 She Wore a Yellow Ribbon
1950 Rio Grande
1950 Wagonmaster
1950 When Willie Comes Marching Home
1952 The Quiet Man **D** F***
1952 What Price Glory?
1953 Mogambo
1953 The Sun Shines Bright
1955 The Long Gray Line
1955 Mr Roberts **(Mervyn LE ROY) F***
1956 The Searchers
1957 The Rising of the Moon
1957 The Wings of Eagles
1958 The Last Hurrah
1959 The Horse Soldiers
1959 Gideon of Scotland Yard
1960 Sergeant Rutledge
1961 Two Rode Together
1962 The Man Who Shot Liberty Valence
1963 Donovan's Reef
1963 How the West Was Won **(Henry HATHAWAY, George MARSHALL) F***
1964 Cheyenne Autumn
1966 Seven Women
(also many shorts and documentaries)

FORD, Philip
(1902–1976) American.
1945 The Tiger Woman
1946 Valley of the Zombies
1946 The Last Crooked Mile
1946 Crime of the Century
1946 The Invisible Informer
1946 The Inner Circle
1946 The Mysterious Mr Valentine
1947 The Wild Frontier
1947 Bandits of Dark Canyon
1947 The Web of Danger
1948 Angel in Exile **(Allan DWAN)**
1948 The Bold Frontiersman
1948 The Denver Kid
1948 California Firebrand
1948 Desperadoes of Dodge City
1948 Marshal of Amarillo

1948 The Timber Trail
1948 Train to Alcatraz **(Gerald GERAGHTY)**
1949 Law of the Golden West
1949 The Wyoming Bandit
1949 Hideout
1949 Outcasts of the Trail
1949 Pioneer Marshal
1949 Powder River
1949 Prince of the Plains
1949 Ranger of Cherokee Strip
1949 San Antone Ambush
1949 South of Rio
1950 Buckaroo Sheriff of Texas
1950 The Old Frontier
1950 Prisoners in Petticoats
1950 Redwood Forest Trail
1950 Trial Without Jury
1950 The Vanishing Westerner
1951 Wells Fargo Gunmaster
1951 The Dakota Kid
1951 Missing Woman
1951 Pride of Maryland
1951 Rodeo King and the Señorita
1951 Utah Wagon Train
1952 Bal Tabarin
1952 Desperadoes' Outpost

FORD, Wesley
1933 Her Forgotten Past
1933 Secret Sinners
1935 $20 a Week

FORDE, Eugene J
(1898–) American.
1928 Hello Cheyenne
1928 Daredevil's Reward
1928 Painted Post
1929 Outlawed
1929 Big Diamond Robbery
1933 Smoky
1934 Charlie Chan in London
1935 Mystery Woman
1935 The Great Hotel Murder
1935 Your Uncle Dudley
1936 The Country Beyond
1936 Thirty-Six Hours to Kill
1937 Midnight Taxi
1937 Step Lively, Jeeves!
1937 The Lady Escapes
1937 Charlie Chan on Broadway
1937 Charlie Chan at Monte Carlo
1938 International Settlement
1938 One Wild Night
1938 Meet the Girls
1939 Inspector Hornleigh
1939 The Honeymoon's Over
1940 Charlie Chan's Murder Cruise
1940 Pier 13
1940 Michael Shayne, Private Detective
1940 Charter Pilot
1941 Sleepers West
1941 Dressed to Kill
1941 Buy Me That Town
1941 Man at Large
1942 Right to the Heart
1942 Berlin Correspondent
1943 The Crime Doctor's Strangest Case
1944 Shadows in the Night
1947 Backlash
1947 Jewels of Brandenburg
1947 The Crimson Key
1947 The Invisible Wall

FORDE, Walter (Thomas Seymour)
(1896–) Yorkshire, England.
1920 Fishing for Trouble
1922 Walter's Trying Frolics
1922 Walter Makes a Move
1922 Walter Wants Work
1926 Walter the Sleuth
1928 Wait and See
1928 What Next?
1929 The Silent House
1929 Would You Believe It?
1930 Red Pearls
1930 You'd Be Surprised!
1930 The Last Hour
1930 Lord Richard in the Pantry
1930 Bed and Breakfast
1931 Third Time Lucky
1931 The Ringer
1931 The Ghost Train
1931 Splinters in the Navy
1932 Condemned to Death
1932 Lord Babs
1932 Jack's the Boy / *Night and Day*
1932 Roman Express
1932 Orders Is Orders
1934 Jack Ahoy!
1934 Chu Chin Chow
1934 Bulldog Jack / *Alias Bulldog Drummond*
1935 King of the Damned
1935 Brown on Revolution / *Born to Glory / Forever England*
1936 Land Without Music / *Forbidden Music*
1938 Kicking the Moon Around / *Millionaire Merry-Go-Round / The Playboy*
1938 The Gaunt Stranger / *The Phantom Strikes*
1939 Let's Be Famous
1939 The Four Just Men / *The Secret Four*
1939 Cheer Boys Cheer
1939 Happy Families
1939 Inspector Hornleigh on Holiday
1940 Charley's Big-Hearted Aunt
1940 Saloon Bar
1940 Sailors Three / *Three Cockeyed Sailors*
1940 Inspector Hornleigh Goes to It / *Mail Train*
1941 The Ghost Train
1941 Atlantic Ferry / *Sons of the Sea*
1942 Go to Blazes
1942 Flying Fortress
1942 The Peterville Diamond
1942 It's That Man Again
1943 Time Flies
1944 One Exciting Night
1947 Master of Bankdam
1949 Cardboard Cavalier

FORDER, Timothy
1987 Indian Summer

FOREMAN, Carl
(1914–1984) Chicago, Illinois, USA.
1963 The Visitors

FORLONG, Michael
1961 The Green Helmet

FORMAN, Milos
(1932–) Caslav, Czechoslovakia. Biography: The Milos Forman Stories by Antonin Liehm.
1963 Competition / *If It Weren't for Music*
1964 Black Peter / *Peter and Pavla*
1966 Loves of a Blonde
1968 The Fireman's Ball
1971 Taking Off
1976 One Flew Over the Cuckoo's Nest **D** F****
1979 Hair
1981 Ragtime
1984 Amadeus **D** F****
1989 Valmont

FORSTER, Robert
(1941–) Rochester, New York, USA.
1985 Hollywood Harry

FORSYTH, Bill
(1947–) Glasgow, Scotland.
1979 That Sinking Feeling
1980 Gregory's Girl
1983 Local Hero
1984 Comfort and Joy
1987 Housekeeping / *Sylvie's Ark*
1988 Breaking In
1989 Rebecca's Daughter

FORSYTH, Ed
1973 Superchick

FORZANO, Andrea *see* **Joseph LOSEY**

FOSSE, Bob (Robert Louis Fosse)
(1927–1987) Chicago, Illinois, USA.
1969 Sweet Charity
1972 Cabaret **D** F***
1974 Lenny **D* F***
1979 All That Jazz **D* F***
1983 Star 80
(Bob Fosse also choreographed many films)

FOSTER, Giles
1988 Consuming Passions
1989 The Tree of Hands

FOSTER, Harry
(1906–1985) American.
1958 Let's Rock

FOSTER, Harve
1946 Song of the South
1947 The Fabulous Joe **(Bernard CARR)**

FOSTER, Lewis R
(1899–1974) American.
1936 Two in a Crowd
1936 Love Letters of a Star **(Milton CARRUTH)**
1937 She's Dangerous **(Milton CARRUTH)**
1937 Armoured Car
1937 The Man Who Cried Wolf
1949 The Lucky Stiff
1949 El Paso
1949 Manhandled
1950 Captain China
1951 The Eagle and the Hawk
1951 The Last Outpost
1951 Passage West / *High Venture*
1951 Crosswinds
1951 Hong Kong
1953 Tropic Zone
1953 Jamaica Run
1953 Those Redheads from Seattle
1955 Crashout
1955 Top of the World
1956 The Bold and the Brave
1956 Dakota Incident
1958 Tonka
1960 The Sign of Zorro **(Norman FOSTER)**
(also many shorts)

FOSTER, Norman (Norman Hoeffer)
(1900–1976) Richmond, Indiana, USA.
1936 I Cover Chinatown
1937 Fair Warning
1937 Think Fast, Mr Moto
1937 Thank You, Mr Moto
1938 Walking Down Broadway
1938 Mysterious Mr Moto
1938 Mr Moto Takes a Chance
1939 Mr Moto's Last Warning
1939 Charlie Chan in Reno
1939 Mr Moto Takes a Vacation
1939 Charlie Chan at Treasure Island
1940 Charlie Chan in Panama
1940 Viva Cisco Kid
1940 Ride, Kelly, Ride
1941 Scotland Yard
1942 Journey into Fear **(Orson WELLES)**
1946 Song of the Siren
1948 Rachel and the Stranger
1948 Kiss the Blood Off My Hands
1949 Tell It to the Judge
1950 Father Is a Bachelor **(Abby BERLIN)**
1950 Woman on the Run
1952 Navajo
1952 Sky Full of Moon
1953 Sombrero
1955 Davy Crockett, King of the Wild Frontier
1960 The Sign of Zorro **(Lewis R FOSTER)**
1966 Indian Paint
1967 Brighty of the Grand Canyon

FOWLER Jnr, Gene
1957 I Was a Teenage Werewolf
1958 Gang War
1958 Showdown at Boot Hill
1958 I Married a Monster from Outer Space
1959 Here Come the Jets
1959 The Rebel Set
1959 The Oregon Trail

FOWLER, Robert
1980 Below the Belt

FOWLEY, Douglas
(1911–) American.
1960 Macumba Love

FOX, Wallace W
(1898–1958) American.
1929 Come and Get It
1929 The Amazing Vagabond
1929 Laughing at Death
1931 Partners of the Trail

1932 The Cannonball Express
1932 Devil on Deck
1935 Red Morning
1935 Powdersmoke Range
1936 Yellow Dust
1936 The Last of the Mohicans **(George B SEITZ)**
1937 Racing Lady
1938 The Mexicali Kid
1938 The Gun Packer
1941 The Lone Star Vigilantes
1941 Bowery Blitzkrieg
1942 Bullets for Bandits
1942 The Corpse Vanishes
1942 Let's Get Tough!
1942 Smart Alecks
1942 Bowery at Midnight
1942 'Neath Brooklyn Bridge
1943 Kid Dynamite
1943 The Ghost Rider
1943 Outlaws of Stampede Pass
1943 The Girl from Monterey
1943 Career Girl
1944 Men on Her Mind
1944 The Great Mike
1944 Riders of Santa Fe
1944 Pride of the Plains
1944 Block Busters
1944 Song of the Range
1944 Million Dollar Kid
1945 Mr Muggs Rides Again
1945 Bad Men of the Border
1945 Code of the Lawless
1945 Trail to Vengeance
1945 Pillow of Death
1946 Gun Town
1946 Rustler's Round-Up
1946 Wild Beauty
1946 Lawless Breed
1946 Gunman's Code
1948 Docks of New York
1948 The Valiant Hombre
1949 The Gay Amigo
1949 The Daring Caballero
1949 Western Renegades
1950 Fence Riders
1950 West of Wyoming
1950 Over the Border
1950 Gunslingers
1950 Six-Gun Mesa
1950 Arizona Territory
1950 Silver Raiders
1950 Outlaw Gold
1951 Montana Desperado
1951 Blazing Bullets

FOY, Bryan
(1896–1977) American.
1928 The Home Towners
1928 Lights of New York
1929 Queen of the Nightclubs
1929 The Royal Box
1931 The Gorilla

FRAKER, William A
(1923–) Los Angeles, California, USA.
1970 Monte Walsh
1971 Reflection of Fear
1981 The Legend of the Lone Ranger

FRANCIS, Freddie
(1917–) London, England.
1962 Two and Two Make Six
1962 Vengeance / *The Brain*
1964 Paranoiac
1964 Nightmare
1964 The Evil of Frankenstein
1964 Traitor's Gate
1965 Dr Terror's House of Horrors
1965 Hysteria
1965 The Skull
1966 The Psychopath
1967 The Dead Bees
1967 They Came from Beyond Space
1968 Torture Garden
1969 Dracula Has Risen from the Grave
1970 Mumsy, Nanny, Sonny and Girly
1970 Trog
1971 The Happening of the Vampire
1972 Tales from the Crypt
1973 Tales That Witness Madness
1973 The Creeping Flesh
1974 Son of Dracula
1974 Craze
1974 The Ghoul
1975 Legend of the Werewolf
1986 The Doctor and the Devils
1987 Dark Tower

FRANCIS, Karl
1981 The Mouse and the Woman
1982 Giro City / *And Nothing But the Truth*
1984 The Happy Alcoholic
1986 Boy Soldier

FRANCO, Giraldi
1967 Dead or Alive / *A Minute to Pray, a Second to Die*

FRANCO, Jesse
1971 Venus in Furs

FRANCO, Ricardo
1986 In 'n Out / *St Jude of the Border*
1988 Berlin Blues

FRANK, A M
1987 Angel of Death

FRANK, Carol
1986 Sorority House Massacre

FRANK, Charles
(1910–) British.
1947 Uncle Silas / *The Inheritance*

FRANK, Ernest L
1933 Nagana
1934 One Exciting Adventure

FRANK, Melvin
(1913–) Chicago, Illinois, USA.
1950 The Reformer and the Redhead **(Norman PANAMA)**
1951 Callaway Went Thataway / *The Star Said No* **(Norman PANAMA)**
1951 Strictly Dishonourable **(Norman PANAMA)**
1952 Above and Beyond **(Norman PANAMA)**

1954 Knock on Wood **(Norman PANAMA)**
1956 The Court Jester **(Norman PANAMA)**
1956 That Certain Feeling **(Norman PANAMA)**
1959 The Jayhawkers
1959 Li'l Abner
1960 The Facts of Life
1965 Strange Bedfellows
1968 Buona Sera, Mrs Campbell
1973 A Touch of Class **F***
1975 The Prisoner of Second Avenue
1976 The Duchess and the Dirtwater Fox
1979 Lost and Found
1987 Walk Like a Man / *Bobo*

FRANK, Robert
1988 Candy Mountain **(Rudolph WURLITZER)**

FRANKEL, Cyril
(1921–1973) British.
1954 Devil on Horseback
1954 Make Me an Offer
1956 It's Great to Be Young
1957 No Time for Tears
1958 Alive and Kicking
1958 She Didn't Say No!
1961 Don't Bother to Knock
1961 On the Fiddle / *Operation Snafu*
1962 The Very Edge
1966 The Trygon Factor
1966 The Witches / *The Devil's Own*
1975 Permission to Kill

FRANKENHEIMER, John
(1930–) Malba, New York, USA.
1957 The Young Stranger
1961 The Young Savages
1962 All Fall Down
1962 Birdman of Alcatraz
1962 The Manchurian Candidate
1964 Seven Days in May
1965 The Train
1966 Seconds
1966 Grand Prix
1968 The Fixer
1969 The Extraordinary Seaman
1969 The Gypsy Moths
1970 I Walk the Line
1971 The Horsemen
1973 The Iceman Cometh
1973 Impossible Object
1974 99 and 44 / 100% Dead / *Call Harry Crown*
1974 French Connection II
1976 Black Sunday
1979 Prophecy
1982 The Challenge
1985 The Holcroft Covenant
1986 52 Pick Up
1987 Across the River and into the Trees
1989 Dead Bang
1989 The Fourth War

FRANKLIN, Carl
1988 K.I.A. Killed in Action
1989 Eye of the Eagle II
1989 Caddo Lake

FRANKLIN, Chester M
(1890–1948) American.
1924 The Silent Accuser
1924 Behind the Curtain
1927 The Thirteenth Hour
1928 Detectives
1932 File No. 113
1932 The Stoker
1932 Vanity Fair
1932 A Parisian Romance
1933 The Iron Master
1935 Sequoia
1936 Tough Guy

FRANKLIN, Richard
(1948–) Melbourne, Victoria, Australia.
1972 Belinda
1973 Loveland
1975 The True Story of Eskimo Nell / *Dick Down Under*
1977 Fantasm
1979 Patrick
1981 Road Games
1983 Psycho II
1984 Cloak and Dagger
1986 Link

FRANKLIN, Sidney
(1893–1972) San Francisco, California.
1924 Her Night of Romance
1925 Her Sister from Paris
1925 Learning to Love
1926 Beverly of Graustark
1926 The Duchess of Buffalo
1927 Quality Street
1928 The Actress / *Trelawney of the Wells*
1929 Devil May Care
1929 Wild Orchids
1929 The Last of Mrs Cheyney
1930 A Lady's Morals / *Jenny Lind*
1930 The Lady of Scandal / *The High Road*
1930 Soul Kiss
1931 The Guardsman
1931 Private Lives
1932 Smilin' Through
1933 Reunion in Vienna
1934 The Barretts of Wimpole Street / *Forbidden Alliance* **F***
1935 The Dark Angel
1937 The Good Earth **D* F***
1946 Duel in the Sun (also many others)
1957 The Barretts of Wimpole Street
(also co-directed many silent shorts)

FRANKLIN, Wendell James
1971 The Bus Is Coming

FRASER, Harry L
1931 Montana Kid
1931 Oklahoma Jim
1932 From Broadway to Cheyenne
1932 Land of Wanted Men
1932 Ghost City
1932 The Reckoning
1932 Texas Pioneers
1932 Mason of the Mountain
1932 Law of the North
1932 Honour of the Mountain
1932 The Savage Girl

1933 The Fighting Parson
1933 The Fugitive
1933 Diamond Trail
1933 Rainbow Ranch
1934 Fighting Through
1934 'Neath Arizona Skies
1934 Randy Rides Alone
1935 Rustlers' Paradise
1935 Wagon Trail
1935 Wild Mustang
1935 Fighting Pioneers
1935 Saddle Acres
1935 Last of the Clintons
1936 Aces Wild
1936 Feud of the West
1936 Ghost Town
1936 The Riding Avenger
1936 Hair-Trigger Casey
1936 Cavalcade of the West
1936 Romance Rides the Range
1937 Heroes of the Alamo
1937 Spirit of Youth
1937 Galloping Dynamite
1938 Six Shootin' Sheriff
1938 Fury Below
1938 Songs and Saddles
1939 Lightning Strikes West
1940 The Phantom Rancher
1941 Jungle Man
1943 The Old Chisholm Trail
1944 Brand of the Devil
1944 Gunsmoke Mesa
1944 Outlaw Roundup
1945 Enemy of the Law
1945 Flaming Bullets
1945 Frontier Fugitives
1945 Navajo Kid
1945 Three on the Saddle
1946 Ambush Trail
1946 Six-Gun Man
1947 The White Gorilla
1949 Stallion Canyon

FRAWLEY, James
(1937–) American.
1971 The Christian Licorice Store
1973 Kid Blue
1976 The Big Bus
1979 The Muppet Movie
1985 Wendell / *Fraternity Vacation*
(also many TV movies)

FREARS, Stephen
(1931–) Leicester, Leicestershire, England.
1971 Gumshoe
1984 The Hit
1985 My Beautiful Laundrette
1987 Prick Up Your Ears
1987 Sammy and Rosie Get Laid
1989 Dangerous Liaisons **F***

FREED, Herb
1972 Awol
1977 Haunts
1980 Beyond Evil
1981 Graduation Day
1985 Tomboy
1987 Survival Game
1987 Johnny Blade

FREEDMAN, Jerrold
1972 Kansas City Bomber
1980 Borderline
1986 Native Son
(also many TV movies)

FREEDMAN, Robert
1982 Goin' All the Way

FREELAND, Thornton
(1898–) American.
1929 Three Live Ghosts
1930 Be Yourself
1930 Whoopee
1931 Six Cylinder Love
1931 The Secret Witness
1931 Terror By Night
1932 They Call It Sin / *The Way of Life*
1932 Weekend Marriage
1932 The Unexpected Father
1932 Love Affair
1933 Flying Down to Rio
1934 George White's Scandals
1935 Skylark
1935 Brewster's Millions
1935 The Amateur Gentleman
1936 Accused
1936 The Gaiety Girls / *Paradise for Two*
1937 Dark Sands / *Jericho*
1937 Over the Moon **(William K HOWARD)**
1939 The Gang's All Here / *The Amazing Mr Forrest*
1940 So This Is London
1941 Marry the Boss's Daughter
1941 Too Many Blondes
1947 The Brass Monkey / *Lucky Mascot*
1948 Meet Me at Dawn / *The Gay Duellist*
1949 Dear Mr Prohack

FREEMAN Jnr, Al
(1934–) American.
1971 A Fable

FREEMAN, Joan
1985 Streetwalkin'
1988 Satisfaction / *Sweet Little Rock and Roller*

FREGONESE, Hugo
(1908–1987) Buenos Aires, Argentina.
1943 Pampa Barbara **(Lucas DEMARE)**
1946 Where Words Fail
1947 Live in Fear / *Hardly a Criminal*
1950 One Way Street
1950 Saddle Tramp
1951 Apache Drums
1951 Mark of the Renegade
1952 My Six Convicts
1952 Untamed Frontier
1953 Blowing Wild
1953 Decameron Nights
1954 The Man in the Attic
1954 The Raid
1954 Black Tuesday
1957 The Beast of Marseilles / *Seven Thunders*
1958 Harry Black and the Tiger
1962 Marco Polo
1967 Shatterhand! / *Apache's Last Battle*
1967 Savage Pampas

FRENCH, Harold
(1897–) British.
Autobiographies: I Swore I Never Would; I Thought I Never Could.
1937 Cavalier of the Streets
1939 Dead Men Are Dangerous
1940 The House of the Arrow
1941 Major Barbara **(David LEAN, Gabriel PASCAL)**
1941 Jeannie / *Girl in Distress*
1942 Secret Mission
1942 Unpublished Story
1942 The Day Will Dawn / *The Avengers*
1942 Talk About Jacqueline
1943 Dear Octopus / *The Randolph Family*
1943 English Without Tears / *Her Man Gilbey*
1944 Mr Emmanuel
1944 Quiet Weekend
1946 My Brother Jonathan
1947 White Cradle Inn / *High Fury*
1948 The Blind Goddess
1949 Adam and Evelyne
1949 The Dancing Years
1949 Quartet **(Ken ANNAKIN, Arthur CRABTREE, Ralph SMART)**
1950 Trio **(Ken ANNAKIN)**
1951 Encore **(Pat JACKSON, Anthony PELISSIER)**
1952 The Hour of Thirteen
1952 Isn't Life Wonderful?
1952 The Man Who Watched Trains Go By / *Paris Express*
1953 Rob Roy the Highland Rogue
1954 Forbidden Cargo
1954 The Man Who Loved Redheads

FREND, Charles
(1909–1977) Pulborough, England.
1941 The Big Blockade
1941 The Foreman Went to France / *Somewhere in France*
1943 San Demetrio London
1945 Johnny Frenchman
1945 Return of the Vikings
1947 The Loves of Joanna Godden
1948 Scott of the Antarctic
1949 A Run for Your Money
1950 The Magnet
1952 The Cruel Sea
1954 Lease of Life
1956 The Long Arm / *The Third Key*
1957 Barnacle Bill / *All at Sea*
1960 Cone of Silence / *Trouble in the Sky*
1962 Girl on Approval
1962 Torpedo Bay
1967 The Sky Bike

FRENKE, Eugene
1934 Girl in the Cage
1934 Life Returns
1936 A Woman Alone / *Two Who Dared*
1954 Miss Robinson Crusoe

FRESHMAN, William
1948 The Plot to Kill Roosevelt

FREUND, Karl
(1890–1969) Königinhoff, Czechoslovakia.
1932 The Mummy
1933 Moonlight and Pretzels / *Moonlight and Melody*
1934 Madame Spy
1934 Countess of Monte-Cristo
1934 Uncertain Lady
1934 Give My Love
1934 Gift of the Gab
1935 Mad Love / *The Hands of Orlac*

FRIEDBERG, Rick
1980 Pray TV / *K-God*
1983 Off the Wall

FRIEDENBERG, Richard
1974 The Life and Times of Grizzly Adams
1976 The Adventures of Frontier Fremont
1979 The Bermuda Triangle

FRIEDKIN, Dave
1957 Hot Summer Night
1958 Handle with Care

FRIEDKIN, William
(1939–) Chicago, Illinois, USA.
1967 Good Times
1968 The Birthday Party
1968 The Night They Raided Minsky's
1970 The Boys in the Band
1971 The French Connection **D** F****
1973 The Exorcist **D* F***
1977 Sorcerer / *Wages of Fear*
1978 The Brink's Job
1980 Cruising
1983 Deal of the Century
1985 To Live and Die in LA
1987 Rampage

FRIEDMAN, Ken
1988 Made in USA / *USA Today*

FRIEDMAN, Richard
1987 Scared Stiff
1988 Doom Asylum
1989 Phantom of the Mall

FRIEDMAN, Seymour
(1917–) American.
1948 Trapped By Boston Blackie
1949 Boston Blackie's Chinese Venture
1949 Crime Doctor's Diary
1949 The Devil's Hangman
1949 Prison Warden
1949 Chinatown at Midnight
1949 Rusty's Birthday
1949 Rusty Saves a Life
1950 Bodyhold
1950 Customs Agent
1950 Rookie Fireman
1950 Counterspy Meets Scotland Yard
1951 Criminal Lawyer
1951 Her First Romance
1951 The Son of Dr Jekyll
1952 Loan Shark
1952 Escape Route **(Peter GRAHAM)**
1953 Flame of Calcutta
1953 I'll Get You
1954 Khyber Patrol
1954 The Saint's Girl Friday
1955 African Manhunt

1956 Secret of Treasure Mountain

FRIEDMANN, Anthony
1970 Bartleby

FRIEND, Robert
1970 Tarzan's Deadly Silence

FRITCH, Gunther
1944 The Curse of the Cat People **(Robert WISE)**
1947 Cigarette Girl

FROEHLICH, Bill
1987 Return to Horror High

FROST, Lee
1971 Chrome and Hot Leather
1971 The Scavengers
1972 The Thing with Two Heads
1974 Policeman
1975 The Black Gestapo
1976 Dixie Dynamite

FRUET, William
(1948–) Canadian.
1973 Wedding in White
1977 The House By the Lake / *Death Weekend*
1979 Search and Destroy / *Striking Back*
1981 Funeral Home / *Cries in the Night*
1982 Baker County USA / *Trapped*
1983 Spasms / *Death Bite*
1984 Bedroom Eyes
1985 April Fool / *Fool's Night / Killer Party*
1987 Green Monkey / *Blue Monkey*
1988 Insect

FUEST, Robert
(1927–) London, England.
1966 Just Like a Woman
1970 And Soon the Darkness
1971 Wuthering Heights
1971 The Abominable Dr Phibes
1972 Dr Phibes Rises Again
1974 The Last Days of Man on Earth / *The Final Programme*
1975 The Devil's Rain
1982 Aphrodite

FUHR, Charles
1943 Bomber's Moon

FUKASAKU, Kinji
1969 The Green Slime
1970 Tora! Tora! Tora! **(Richard O FLEISCHER, Toshio MASUDA)**
1973 The Yakuza Papers
1978 Message from Space
1979 The Shogun's Samurai
1980 Virus
1980 Devil Resuscitation
1980 Kamata March
1982 The Fall Guy
1982 Under the Flag of the Rising Sun
1984 Shanghai Vance King
1984 Legend of the Dogs of Satomi

FULLER, Lester
1944 You Can't Ration Love

FULLER, Samuel
(1911–) Worcester, Massachusetts, USA.
1949 I Shot Jesse James
1950 The Baron of Arizona
1951 The Steel Helmet
1951 Fixed Bayonets!
1952 Park Row
1953 Pickup on South Street
1954 Hell and High Water
1955 House of Bamboo
1957 Run of the Arrow
1957 Forty Guns
1957 China Gate
1958 Verboten!
1959 The Crimson Kimono
1961 Underworld USA
1962 Merrill's Marauders
1963 Shock Corridor
1964 The Naked Kiss
1970 Shark!
1972 Dead Pigeon of Beethoven Street
1980 The Big Red One
1982 White Dog
1983 Thieves After Dark

FULLER, Tex
1987 Shock Wave / *Stranded*
1988 Street of No Return

FUNT, Allen
(1914–) New York, New York, USA.
1970 What Do You Say to a Naked Woman?
1971 Money Talks

FURIE, Sidney J
(1933–) Toronto, Canada.
1959 A Dangerous Age
1959 A Cool Sound from Hell
1960 Dr Blood's Coffin
1961 The Snake Woman
1961 Night of Passion / *During One Night*
1961 Three on a Spree
1961 Wonderful to Be Young / *The Young Ones*
1962 The Boys
1964 The Leather Boys
1964 Swingers' Paradise / *Wonderful Life*
1965 The Ipcress File
1966 The Appaloosa / *Southwest to Senora*
1967 The Naked Runner
1970 The Lawyer
1970 Little Fauss and Big Halsy
1972 Lady Sings the Blues
1973 Hit!
1975 Sheila Levine Is Dead and Living in New York
1976 Gable and Lombard
1978 The Boys in Company C
1983 The Entity
1984 Purple Hearts
1986 Iron Eagle
1987 Superman IV: Quest for Peace
1988 Day By Day
1988 Iron Eagle II: Battle Beyond the Flag

FURY, Lewis
1988 Shadow Dancing / *Stage Fright*

GABEL, Martin
(1912–1986) Philadelphia, Pennsylvania, USA.
1947 The Lost Moment

GABOR, Pal
(1932–1987) Hungarian.
1968 Forbidden Ground
1973 Journey with Jacob
1978 Epidemic
1979 Angi Vera
1982 Wasted Lives
1984 Brady's Escape / *The Long Run*

GABOURIE, Mitchell
1988 Buying Time

GADE, Svend *
(1877–1952) Copenhagen, Denmark.
1925 Siege
1925 Peacock Feathers
1925 Fifth-Avenue Models
1926 The Blonde Saint
1926 Watch Your Wife
1926 Into Her Kingdom
1928 Jazz Mad
1928 The Masks of the Devil

GADNEY, Alan
(1941–) Dayton, Ohio, USA.
1973 West Texas
1974 Moonchild

GAFFNEY, Robert
(1931–) American.
1965 Frankenstein Meets the Space Monster

GAGE, George
1977 Skateboard
1984 Fleshburn / *Fear In a Handful of Dust*

GAGE, John
1948 The Velvet Touch

GAGE, Nicholas
1987 The Godfather Part III

GALFAS, Timothy
(1934–) Atlanta, Georgia, USA.
1975 Bogard
1976 The Black Streetfighter
1977 Black Fist
1979 Sunnyside

GALLAGHER, John A
(1955–) New York, New York, USA.
1972 Beach House
1986 Hell Soldier

GALLAHER, Donald
1929 Nix on Dames
1930 Temple Tower

GALLICO, Paul
(1891–1955) American.
1960 Next to No Time

GANNAWAY, Albert C
(1920–) American.
1956 Hidden Guns
1956 Daniel Boone, Trail Blazer **(Ismael RODRIGUEZ)**
1957 The Badge of Marshal Brennan
1957 Raiders of Old California
1958 Man or Gun
1958 No Place to Land
1959 Plunderers of Painted Flats

GANZER, Alvin
1953 The Girls of Pleasure Island **(Hugh F HERBERT)**
1955 The Leather Saint
1958 Country Music Holiday
1965 When the Boys Meet the Girls
1966 Three Bites of the Apple

GARDNER, Cyril
1930 The Royal Family of Broadway / *Theatre Royal* **(George CUKOR)**
1930 Only Saps Work **(Edwin KNOPF)**
1931 Reckless Living
1932 The Doomed Battalion
1933 Perfect Understanding
1934 Big Business
1935 Widow's Might

GARDNER, Herb
1984 The Goodbye People

GARDNER, Richard
1988 Deadly Daphne's Revenge

GARDOS, Peter
1989 Whooping Cough

GAREN, Leo
1973 Hex

GARFEIN, Jack
(1930–) Mukacevo, Czechoslovakia.
1957 The Strange One / *End As a Man*
1961 Something Wild

GARGIULO, Mike
1970 It's Your Thing

GARLAND, Patrick
(1936–) London, England.
1973 A Doll's House

GARMES, Lee
(1898–1978) Peoria, Illinois, USA.
1937 Dreaming Lips **(Paul CZINNER)**
1937 The Sky's the Limit **(Jack BUCHANAN)**
1940 Angels Over Broadway **(Ben HECHT)**
1953 Outlaw Territory **(John IRELAND)**

GARNETT, Tay (William Taylor Garnett)
(1894–1977) Los Angeles, California, USA.
Autobiography: Light Up Your Torches and Pull on Your Tights.
1928 Celebrity
1929 The Spellbinder / *The Spieler*
1929 The Flying Fool
1930 Officer O'Brien
1930 Her Man
1930 Bad Company
1932 Destination Unknown

1932 One Way Passage
1932 Okay America / *Paying the Penalty*
1932 Prestige
1933 SOS Iceberg
1935 China Seas
1935 Professional Soldier
1935 She Couldn't Take It / *Woman Tamer*
1937 Love Is News
1937 Slave Ship
1937 Stand-In
1938 Joy of Living
1938 Trade Winds
1939 Eternally Yours
1940 Seven Sinners / *Doomed Cargo*
1940 Slightly Honourable
1941 Cheers for Miss Bishop
1942 My Favourite Spy
1943 Bataan
1943 The Cross of Lorraine
1944 Mrs Parkington
1945 The Valley of Decision
1946 The Postman Always Rings Twice
1947 Wild Harvest
1949 A Connecticut Yankee in King Arthur's Court
1950 The Fireball
1951 Cause for Alarm
1951 Soldiers Three
1952 One Minute to Zero
1953 Main Street to Broadway
1954 The Black Knight
1956 Seven Wonders of the World
1960 Night Fighters / *A Terrible Beauty*
1963 Cattle King / *Guns of Wyoming*
1970 The Delta Factor
1972 The Mad Trapper
1973 Timber Tramp
1976 Challenge to Be Free

GARNETT, Tony
(1936–) Birmingham, England.
1981 Prostitute
1984 Deep in the Heart / *Handgun*

GARRETT, Oliver J P
(1897–1952) American.
1942 Careful, Soft Shoulders

GARRETT, Otis
(c1895–1941) American.
1937 The Black Doll
1938 The Last Express
1938 Personal Secretary
1938 Danger on the Air
1938 Lady in the Morgue / *The Case of the Missing Blonde*
1939 The Witness Vanishes
1939 Mystery of the White Room
1939 Exile Express
1940 Margie **(P G SMITH)**
1941 Sandy Gets Her Man **(P G SMITH)**

GARRIS, Mike
1989 Critters 2: The Main Course

GARRISON, Greg
1961 Hey, Let's Twist
1962 Two Tickets to Paris

GARY, Jerome
1986 Stripper
1988 Traxx

GASNIER, Louis J
(1882–1963) Paris, France.
1924 Wine
1929 Darkened Rooms
1930 Slightly Scarlet **(Edwin KNOPF)**
1930 The Shadow of the Law **(Max MARCIN)**
1930 The Virtuous Sin / *Cast Iron* **(George CUKOR)**
1931 The Lawyer's Secret **(Max MARCIN)**
1931 Silence **(Max MARCIN)**
1932 The Strange Case of Clara Deane **(Max MARCIN)**
1932 Forgotten Commandments **(William SCHORR)**
1933 Gambling Ship **(Max MARCIN)**
1935 The Last Outpost **(Charles T BARTON)**
1937 The Gold Racket
1937 Bank Alarm
1940 The Burning Question
1940 Murder on the Yukon
1941 Stolen Paradise
1942 Fight On, Marines

GAVALDON, Roberto *
(1909–) Mexican.
1948 Adventures of Casanova
1955 The Littlest Outlaw

GAVER, Eleanor
1988 Slipping into Darkness / *Taken By Force*

GAYTON, Joe
1989 Warm Summer Rain

GELDOF, Bob
1989 Cowboys

GELLER, Bruce
1973 Harry in Your Pocket

GENOCK, Edward
1950 Cassino to Korea

GEORGE, Leslie
1984 Screw Loose

GEORGE, Peter
1987 Surf Nazis Must Die

GEORGIAS, Andrew
1976 Bigtime

GERAGHTY, Maurice
(1908–1987) American.
1951 Sword of Monte Cristo

GERING, Marion
(1901–1977) Polish-Russian.
1931 I Take This Woman **(Slavko VORKAPICH)**
1931 Twenty-Four Hours
1932 Ladies of the Big House
1932 Devil and the Deep
1932 Madame Butterfly

1933 Pick Up
1933 Jennie Gerhardt
1934 Good Dame
1934 Thirty-Day Princess
1934 Ready for Love
1935 Rumba
1936 Rose of the Rancho
1936 Lady of Secrets
1937 Thunder in the City
1938 She Married an Artist
1950 Sarumba
1963 Violated Paradise

GERRARD, Gene (Eugene O'Sullivan)
(1892–1971) British.
1931 Out of the Blue **(John ORTON)**
1932 Let Me Explain Dear
1937 Wake Up Famous
1938 It's in the Blood

GERRETSEN, Peter
1987 The Kidnapping of Baby John Doe
1987 A Cry from the Heart
1988 Night Friend

GERSHUNY, Theodore
1973 Love, Death
1974 Silent Night, Bloody Night
1977 Sugar Cookies
1981 Deathouse

GERSTAD, Harry
1960 Thirteen Fighting Men

GESSNER, Nicolas
(1932–) French.
1965 Un Milliard dans un Billard
1968 The Blonde from Peking
1971 Someone Behind the Door / *Two Minds for Murder*
1977 The Little Girl Who Lives Down the Lane
1978 Deux Affreux dans le Sable
1981 It Rained All Night the Day I Left
1988 Quicker Than the Eye
1989 Tennessee Waltz
1989 Day of the Hunter

GIANNONE, Joe
1982 Madman

GIBBINS, Duncan
1986 Fire with Fire / *Captive Hearts*

GIBBONS, Cedric
(1893–1960) Dublin, Republic of Ireland.
1934 Tarzan and His Mate **(Jack CONWAY)**
(also a multitude of films as the art director)

GIBBONS, Pamela
1987 Belinda

GIBSON, Alan
(1938–) Canadian.
1969 Crescendo
1970 Goodbye Gemini
1972 Dracula AD 1972
1973 The Satanic Rites of Dracula / *Dracula Is Alive and Well and Living in London*
1978 Checkered Flag or Crash
1985 Martin's Day

GIBSON, Brian
1980 Breaking Glass
1986 Poltergeist II: The Other Side

GIBSON, Tom
1937 The Singing Buckaroo
1937 Santa Fe Rides

GIEVE, Andrew
1987 On the Black Hill

GILBERT, Brian
1984 Sharma and Beyond
1985 French Lesson / *The Frog Prince*
1988 Vice Versa

GILBERT, Lewis
(1920–) London, England.
1947 The Little Ballerina
1950 Once a Sinner
1951 There Is Another Side / *Wall of Death*
1951 The Scarlet Thread
1952 Emergency Call / *Hundred Hour Hunt*
1952 Time Gentlemen Please!
1953 The Slasher / *Cosh Boy*
1953 Johnny on the Run **(Vernon HARRIS)**
1953 Albert RN / *Break to Freedom*
1954 The Good Die Young
1954 The Sea Shall Not Have Them
1955 Cast a Dark Shadow
1956 Reach for the Sky
1957 The Admirable Crichton / *Paradise Lagoon*
1958 Carve Her Name with Pride
1959 A Cry from the Streets
1959 Ferry to Hong Kong
1960 Sink the Bismarck!
1960 Light Up the Sky / *Skywatch*
1961 The Greengage Summer / *Loss of Innocence*
1962 HMS Defiant / *Damn the Defiant*
1964 The Seventh Dawn
1966 Alfie **F***
1967 You Only Live Twice
1970 The Adventurers
1971 Friends
1974 Paul and Michelle
1975 Operation Daybreak
1976 Seven Nights in Japan
1977 The Spy Who Loved Me
1979 Moonraker
1983 Educating Rita
1985 Not Quite Jerusalem / *Not Quite Paradise*
1989 Shirley Valentine
(also many documentaries)

GILBERT, Philip
1971 Blood and Lace

GILBERT, Terry
1952 You're Only Young Twice

GILER, David
1975 The Black Bird

GILES, David
1968 The Dance of Death

GILLARD, Stuart
1982 Paradise
1988 A Man Called Sarge

GILLIAM, Terry
(1940–) Minneapolis, Minnesota, USA.
1975 Monty Python and the Holy Grail **(Terry JONES)**
1977 Jabberwocky
1981 Time Bandits
1985 Brazil
1988 The Adventures of Baron Munchausen

GILLIAT, Sidney
(1908–) Edgeley, England.
1943 Millions Like Us **(Frank LAUNDER)**
1944 Waterloo Road
1945 The Rake's Progress / *The Notorious Gentleman*
1946 Green for Danger
1948 London Belongs to Me / *Dulcimer Street*
1950 State Secret / *The Great Manhunt*
1953 The Story of Gilbert and Sullivan
1954 The Constant Husband
1956 Fortune Is a Woman / *She Played with Fire*
1959 Left, Right and Centre
1962 Only Two Can Play
1966 Robbery **(Frank LAUNDER)**
1971 Endless Night

GILLING, John
(1912–1985) British.
1948 Escape from Broadway
1950 A Matter of Murder
1950 The Quiet Woman
1950 No Trace
1950 The Frightened Woman
1952 Mother Riley Meets the Vampire / *My Son the Vampire*
1952 The Voice of Merrill / *Murder Will Out*
1953 Recoil
1953 Three Steps to the Gallows / *White Fire*
1953 Deadly Nightshade
1953 Escape By Night
1954 Double Exposure
1954 The Embezzler
1954 The Gilded Cage
1955 Tiger By the Tail
1955 The Gamma People
1956 Odongo
1957 High Flight
1957 Interpol / *Pickup Alley*
1958 The Man Inside
1959 Idle on Parade
1959 The Bandit of Zhobe
1959 The Flesh and the Fiends / *Mania*
1959 The Challenge / *It Takes a Thief*
1960 Fury at Smuggler's Bay
1961 Pirates of Blood River
1961 The Shadow of the Cat
1963 The Scarlet Blade / *The Crimson Blade*
1963 Panic
1965 The Brigand of Kandahar
1965 The Night Caller / *Blood Beast from Outer Space*
1966 Where the Bullets Fly
1966 The Reptile
1966 The Mummy's Shroud
1974 The Devil's Cross

GILMORE, Stuart
(1913–1971) American.
1946 The Virginian
1951 Hot Lead
1952 Captive Woman
1952 The Half-Breed
1952 Target

GILROY, Frank D
(1925–) New York, New York, USA.
1971 Desperate Characters
1976 From Noon Till Three
1978 Once in Paris
1985 The Gig
(also many TV movies)

GINNANE, Tony
1988 Savage Sarah
1988 White Fire

GINSBERG, Milton Moses
1969 Coming Apart
1973 The Werewolf of Washington

GIOVINAZZO, Buddy
1986 Combat Shock / *American Nightmare*

GIRALDI, Bob
1982 National Lampoon's Movie Madness **(Henry JAGLOM)**
1987 Hiding Out / *Adult Education*

GIRARD, Bernard
(1929–) American.
1957 The Green-Eyed Blonde
1958 Ride Out for Revenge
1958 As Young As We Are
1958 The Party Crashers
1962 A Public Affair
1966 Dead Heat on a Merry-Go-Round
1969 Mad Room
1972 The Happiness Cage / *The Mind Snatchers*
1975 Gone with the West

GIRDLER, William
(1947–1978) American.
1971 Asylum of Satan
1972 Three on a Meathook
1974 The Zebra Killer
1974 Abby
1975 Sheba Baby
1975 Asylum of Satan
1976 The Day of the Animals
1976 Grizzly
1978 The Manitou

GIST, Robert
(1924–) American.
1966 An American Dream / *See You in Hell, Darling*

GITTENS, Wyndham
1938 Forbidden Valley

GLADWELL, David
(1935–) Gloucester, Gloucestershire, England.
1977 Requiem for a Village
1981 Memoirs of a Survivor

GLASER, Paul Michael
(1943–) Cambridge, Massachusetts, USA.
1986 Band of the Hand
1987 The Running Man

GLAZER, Benjamin
(1887–1958) American.
1929 Strange Cargo **(Arthur GREGOR)**
1948 Song of My Heart

GLEASON, Michie
1981 Broken English
1987 Summer Heat

GLEN, John
(1932–) Sunbury on Thames, Surrey, England.
1981 For Your Eyes Only
1983 Octopussy
1985 A View to a Kill
1987 The Living Daylights
1989 License To Kill

GLENDON, Frank
1935 Circle of Death

GLENN, Jack
1950 Cry Murder

GLENNON, Bert
(1893–1967) Anaconda, Montana, USA.
1929 Syncopation
1930 Girl of the Port
1930 Around the Corner
1930 Paradise Island
1931 In Line of Duty
1932 South of Santa Fe

GLENVILLE, Peter
(1913–) London, England.
1955 The Prisoner
1958 Me and the Colonel
1961 Summer and Smoke
1963 Term of Trial
1964 Becket **D* F***
1966 Hotel Paradiso
1967 The Comedians

GLICKENHAUS, James
(1950–) New York, New York, USA.
1979 The Astrologer
1980 The Exterminator
1982 The Soldier
1985 The Protector
1988 Shakedown / *Blue Jean Cop*
1989 Room at the End of the Universe

GLOWNA, Vadim
1981 Desperado City
1987 The Devil's Paradise

GODARD, Jean-Luc
(1930–) Paris, France.
Autobiography: Godard on Godard.
1960 Breathless
1961 A Woman Is a Woman
1962 Seven Capital Sins **(Claude CHABROL, Philippe DeBROCA, Jacques DEMY, Sylvaine DHOMME, Edouard MOLINARO, Marie-José NAT, Dominique PATUREL, Perrette PRADIER, Jean-Marc TENNBERG, Roger VADIM)**
1962 My Life to Live
1962 Rogopag
1963 The Little Soldier
1963 The Soldiers
1964 Contempt
1964 Band of Outsiders
1964 The Married Woman
1965 Six in Paris
1965 Alphaville
1965 Pierrot le Fou
1966 Masculine Feminine
1966 Made in USA
1967 Two or Three Things I Know About Her
1967 The Oldest Profession **(Claude AUTANT-LARA, Mauro BOLOGNINI, Philippe DeBROCA, Franco INDOVINA, Michael PFLEGHAR)**
1967 La Chinoise
1968 Weekend
1968 Un Film comme les Autres
1969 One A.M.
1969 Communications
1969 Sympathy for the Devil -1 +1
1969 Wind from the East **(Jean-Pierre GORIN)**
1971 Vladimir et Rosa **(Jean-Pierre GORIN)**
1972 Tout Va Bien **(Jean-Pierre GORIN)**
1972 Letter to Jane: Investigation of a Still
1980 Everyman for Himself / *Sauve qui peut la Vie*
1983 Passion
1983 First Name: Carmen
1985 Hail Mary
1985 Detective
1987 Soigne ta Droite
1987 Aria **(Robert ALTMAN, Bruce BERESFORD, Bill BRYDEN, Derek JARMAN, Franc RODDAM, Nicolas ROEG, Ken RUSSELL, Charles STURRIDGE, Julien TEMPLE)**
1987 King Lear

GODDARD, Gary
1987 Masters of the Universe

GODDARD, Jim
(1936–) London, England.
1984 The Black Stuff
1985 Parker
1986 Shanghai Surprise
1988 Reasonable Force
(also many TV movies)

GODFREY, Peter
(1899–1970) British.

1930 Thread o' Scarlet
1931 Down River
1939 The Lone Wolf Spy Hunt
1941 Unexpected Uncle
1942 Highways By Night
1944 Make Your Own Bed
1945 Hotel Berlin
1945 Christmas in Connecticut / *Indiscretion*
1946 One More Tomorrow
1947 The Two Mrs Carrolls
1947 Cry Wolf
1947 That Hagen Girl
1947 Escape Me Never
1948 The Woman in White
1948 The Decision of Christopher Blake
1949 The Girl from Jones Beach
1949 One Last Fling
1950 Barricade
1950 The Great Jewel Robbery
1950 He's a Cockeyed Wonder
1952 One Big Affair
1956 Please Murder Me

GODMILOW, Jill
1987 Waiting for the Moon / *On the Trail of the Lonesome Pine*

GODWIN, Frank
1984 Break Out

GOLAN, Menahem (Menahem Globus)
(1929–) Tiberias, Israel.
1963 El Dorado
1967 Trunk to Cairo
1967 The Girl from the Dead Sea
1968 Tevye and His Seven Daughters
1969 Fortuna
1969 What's Good for the Goose
1970 Margo
1970 Lupo!
1970 Queen of the Road
1971 Katz and Karasso
1972 The Great Telephone Robbery
1972 Escape to the Sun
1973 Kazablan
1975 Lepke
1975 Diamonds
1976 The Ambassador
1978 Operation Thunderbolt
1978 The Uranium Conspiracy
1979 The Magician of Lublin
1980 The Apple
1981 Enter the Ninja
1984 Over the Brooklyn Bridge
1986 The Delta Force
1987 Over the Top
1988 Hannah's War / *Innocent Heroes*
1989 The Three-Penny Opera
1989 What Do Women Want?

GOLD, Gregg
1987 House of the Rising Sun

GOLD, Jack
(1930–) London, England.
1968 The Bofors Gun
1969 The Reckoning
1973 The National Health
1975 Who?
1975 Man Friday
1977 Aces High
1978 The Medusa Touch
1978 The Sailor's Return
1980 Charlie Muffin
1982 Praying Mantis
1983 Red Monarch
1985 The Chain
(also many TV movies)

GOLD, Jeffrey
1989 Bottom Line

GOLDBECK, Willis
(1899–1979) American.
1942 Dr Gillespie's New Assistant
1943 Dr Gillespie's Criminal Case / *Crazy to Kill*
1944 Rationing
1944 Three Men in White
1944 Between Two Women
1945 She Went to the Races
1946 Love Laughs at Andy Hardy
1947 Dark Delusion / *Cynthia's Secret*
1949 Johnny Holiday
1951 Ten Tall Men

GOLDBERG, Dan
1988 Feds

GOLDBERG, Gary D
1989 Dad

GOLDBERG, Jack
1944 We've Come a Long Way

GOLDBLATT, Mark
1988 Dead Heat
1989 The Punisher

GOLDEN, John
1986 Fat Guy Goes Nutzoid
1988 The Big Giver

GOLDING, Paul
1988 Pulse
1989 Breakfast of Champions

GOLDMAN, Martin
1972 The Legend of Nigger Charley

GOLDMAN, Michael
1988 A Jumpin' Night in the Garden of Eden

GOLDMAN, Stuart
1987 Senior Week

GOLDSCHMIDT, John
1984 She'll Be Wearing Pink Pyjamas
1987 Maschenka

GOLDSTEIN, Scott
1985 Flanagan / *Walls of Glass*

GOLDSTONE, James
(1931–) Los Angeles, California, USA.
1968 Jigsaw
1969 A Man Called Gannon
1969 Winning
1971 Brother John

1971 Red Sky at Morning
1971 The Gang That Couldn't Shoot Straight
1972 They Only Kill Their Masters
1976 Swashbuckler / *The Scarlet Buccaneer*
1977 Rollercoaster
1980 When Time Ran Out
(also many TV movies)

GOLDSTONE, Phil
1933 The Sin of Nora Moran
1936 Marriage Forbidden

GOLDSTONE, Richard
(1929–) American.
1958 South Seas Adventure **(many others)**
1962 No Man Is an Island / *Island Escape* **(John MONKS Jnr)**

GOLDWYN Jnr, Samuel
(1926–) American.
1964 The Young Lovers

GOLLINGS, Franklin
1969 Connecting Rooms

GOMER, Steve
1987 Sweet Lorraine

GOODMAN, Edward
1931 Women Love Once

GOODRICH, Wiliam *see* **Roscoe ARBUCKLE**

GOODWIN, Robert L
1971 Black Chariot

GOODWINS, Leslie
(1899–1969) British.
1936 With Love and Kisses
1937 Anything for a Thrill
1937 Headline Crasher
1937 Young Dynamite
1938 Crime Ring
1938 Fugitives for a Night
1938 Mr Doodle Kicks Off
1938 Tarnished Angel
1939 The Girl from Mexico
1939 Mexican Spitfire
1939 The Day the Bookies Wept
1939 Almost a Gentleman
1939 Sued for Libel
1940 Men Against the Sky
1940 Millionaire Playboy / *Glamour Boy*
1940 Pop Always Pays
1940 Let's Make Music
1940 Mexican Spitfire Out West
1941 Parachute Battalion
1941 They Met in Argentina **(Jack HIVELY)**
1941 Mexican Spitfire's Baby
1942 Mexican Spitfire at Sea
1942 Mexican Spitfire Sees a Ghost
1942 Mexican Spitfire's Elephant
1943 Silver Skates
1943 Ladies' Day
1943 Gals, Inc.
1943 Mexican Spitfire's Blessed Event
1943 The Adventures of a Rookie
1943 Rookies in Burma
1944 Casanova in Burlesque
1944 The Mummy's Curse
1944 Murder in the Blue Room
1944 The Singing Sheriff
1944 Goin' to Town
1944 Hi, Beautiful / *Pass to Romance*
1945 I'll Tell the World
1945 Radio Stars on Parade
1945 What a Blonde
1945 An Angel Comes to Brooklyn
1946 Genius at Work
1946 Riverboat Rhythm
1946 Vacation in Reno
1947 The Lone Wolf in London
1947 Dragnet
1952 Gold Fever
1954 Fireman Save My Child
1955 Fresh from Paris
1955 Paris Follies of 1956
1967 Tammy and the Millionaire **(Sidney MILLER, Ezra STONE)**
(also many shorts)

GORDON, Bert I
(1922–) Kenosha, Wisconsin, USA.
1955 King Dinosaur
1957 Beginning of the End
1957 Cyclops
1957 The Amazing Colossal Man
1958 Attack of the Puppet People / *Six Inches Tall*
1958 War of the Colossal Beast / *The Terror Strikes*
1958 The Spider
1960 The Boy and the Pirates
1960 Tormented
1962 The Magic Sword
1965 Village of the Giants
1966 Picture Mommy Dead
1970 How to Succeed with Sex
1972 Necromancy
1973 The Mad Bomber
1973 The Police Connection / *Detective Geronimo*
1976 The Food of the Gods
1977 Empire of the Ants
1981 The Coming
1984 Doing It
1986 The Big Bet

GORDON, Gerard
1973 So Long Blue Boy

GORDON, Keith
1988 The Chocolate War
1989 The Uncle Bob Show

GORDON, Lewis H *see* **Herschell G LEWIS**

GORDON, Michael
(1909–) Baltimore, Maryland, USA.
1942 Boston Blackie Goes to Hollywood
1942 Underground Agent
1943 One Dangerous Night
1943 Crime Doctor
1947 The Web
1948 Another Part of the Forest
1948 An Act of Murder / *Live Today for Tomorrow*
1949 The Lady Gambles
1950 Woman in Hiding

1950 Cyrano de Bergerac
1951 I Can Get It for You Wholesale / *This Is My Affair*
1951 The Secret of Convict Lake
1953 Wherever She Goes
1959 Pillow Talk
1960 Portrait in Black
1962 Boys' Night Out
1963 For Love or Money
1963 Move Over, Darling
1965 A Very Special Favour
1966 Texas Across the River
1968 The Impossible Years
1970 How Do I Love Thee?

GORDON, Robert
1947 Black Eagle
1947 Blind Spot
1947 Sport of Kings
1953 The Joe Louis Story
1955 It Came from Beneath the Sea
1958 Damn Citizen
1958 The Rawhide Trail
1963 Black Zoo
1968 Tarzan and the Jungle Boy
1972 The Gatling Gun

GORDON, Steve
(1938–1982) American.
1981 Arthur

GORDON, Stuart
1985 Re-Animator
1986 From Beyond
1986 Dolls
1988 Robojox
1989 Hotel Dick
1990 The Pit and the Pendulum

GORDY, Berry
(1929–) American.
1975 Mahogany

GORETTA, Claude *
(1929–) Geneva, Switzerland.
1975 The Wonderful Crook / *Pas si méchant que ça....*
1977 The Lacemaker
1981 The Girl from Lorraine / *La Provinciale*
1983 The Death of Mario Ricci

GORMELY, Charles
1986 Heavenly Pursuits / *Gospel According to Vic*

GORNICK, Michael
1987 Creepshow II

GOSHA, Hideo
1970 Hunter in the Dark
1972 The Wolves
1985 Cracked
1985 The Paddle
1985 Fireflies of the North

GOTHAR, Peter
(1947–) Pecs, Hungary.
1979 A Priceless Day
1982 Time Stands Still
1986 Time

1987 Pure America / *Just Like America*

GOTTLIEB, Alex
1941 Dark Streets of Cairo

GOTTLIEB, Carl
(1938–) American.
1981 Caveman
1987 Amazon Women on the Moon **(Joe DANTE, Peter HORTON, John LANDIS, Robert K WEISS)**

GOTTLIEB, Lisa
1985 Just One of the Guys

GOTTLIEB, Michael
1987 Mannequin / *Perfect Timing*

GOULDER, Stanley
1975 Naked Evil

GOULDING, Alfred
(1896–1972) American.
1925 Don't
1928 All at Sea
1936 Everything Is Rhythm
1939 A Chump at Oxford
1939 Honeymoon Merry-Go-Round

GOULDING, Edmund
(1891–1959) London, England.
1925 Sun-Up
1925 Sally, Irene and Mary
1926 Paris
1927 Women Love Diamonds
1927 Love
1929 The Trespasser
1930 The Devil's Holiday
1931 The Night Angel
1931 Reaching for the Moon
1932 Blondie of the Follies
1932 Grand Hotel **F****
1934 Riptide
1935 The Flame Within
1937 That Certain Woman
1938 The Dawn Patrol
1938 White Banners
1939 Dark Victory **F***
1939 The Old Maid
1939 We Are Not Alone
1940 'Til We Meet Again
1941 The Great Lie
1943 Claudia
1943 The Constant Nymph
1943 Forever and a Day **(René CLAIR, Cedric HARDWICKE, Frank LLOYD, Victor, SAVILLE, Robert STEVENSON, Herbert WILCOX)**
1946 The Razor's Edge **F***
1946 Of Human Bondage
1947 Nightmare Alley
1949 Everybody Does It
1950 Mister 880
1952 We're Not Married
1953 Down Among the Sheltered Palms
1956 Teenage Rebel
1958 Mardi Gras

GOVER, Victor M
1946 The Curse of the Wraydons

GOVERNOR, Richard
1988 Ghost Town

GRAEFF, Tom
(1929–) American.
1959 Teenagers from Outer Space

GRAHAM, Bob
1981 The End of August

GRAHAM, Jo
1942 Always in My Heart
1942 You Can't Escape Forever
1943 The Good Fellows

GRAHAM, William A
(1928–) American.
1967 Waterhole Three
1968 Change of Habit
1969 Submarine X-1
1972 Honky
1972 Count Your Bullets
1974 Where the Lilies Bloom
1974 Together Brother
1976 Part 2 Sounder
1983 Harry Tracy
(also many TV movies)

GRAND, Richard
1976 The Commitment
1979 Fyre

GRANT, James Edward
(1902–1966) American.
1947 Angel and the Badman
1954 Ring of Fear

GRANT, Lee (Lyova Rosenthal)
(1927–) New York, New York, USA.
1980 Tell Me a Riddle
1989 Staying the Same / *Boy's Life*
(also many TV movies)

GRANT, Michael
1980 Fatal Attraction / *Head On*
1987 China Run

GRASSHOFF, Alex
(1930–) Boston, Massachusetts, USA.
1960 The Jailbreakers
1978 Smokey and the Goodtime Outlaws
1978 JD and the Salt Flat Kid
1982 Wacky Taxi
1985 A Billion for Boris

GRAUMAN, Walter
(1922–) Milwaukee, Wisconsin, USA.
1957 The Disembodied
1964 Lady in a Cage
1964 633 Squadron
1965 A Rage to Live
1966 I Deal in Danger
1970 The Last Escape
(also many TV movies and shorts)

GRAVER, Gary
1963 The Great Dream
1967 The Embracers
1970 The Hard Road
1970 Erika's Hot Summer
1970 Sandra, The Making of a Woman
1973 There Was a Little Girl
1981 Texas Lightning
1983 Trick or Treat
1987 Party Camp
1987 Moon in Scorpio
1989 Crossing the Line

GRAY, John
1987 Billy Galvin

GRAY, Mike
1983 Wavelength

GRAYSON, Godfrey
1949 Meet Simon Cherry
1953 The Fake
1959 An Honourable Murder

GREEK, Janet
Pseudonym: A.K. Allen.
1985 Violated / *Ladies Club*
1989 Spellbinder / *Witching Hour*

GREEN, Alfred E
(1889–1960) American.
1924 In Hollywood with Potash and Perlmutter / *So This Is Hollywood*
1924 Pied Piper Malone
1924 Inez from Hollywood / *The Good Bad Girl*
1925 Sally
1925 The Man Who Found Himself
1926 Irene
1926 Ella Cinders
1926 The Girl from Montmartre
1926 It Must Be Love
1926 Ladies at Play
1927 Two Girls Wanted
1927 The Auctioneer
1927 Is Zat So?
1927 Come to My House
1928 Honour Bound
1929 Making the Grade
1929 Disraeli **F***
1930 The Green Goddess
1930 The Man from Blankley's
1930 Sweet Kitty Bellairs
1931 Smart Money
1931 Men of the Sky
1931 The Road to Singapore
1932 Union Depot / *Gentleman for a Day*
1932 It's Tough to Be Famous
1932 The Rich Are Always with Us
1932 The Dark Horse
1932 Silver Dollar
1933 Parachute Jumper
1933 The Narrow Corner
1933 Baby Face
1933 I Loved a Woman
1934 As the Earth Turns
1934 Dark Hazard
1934 The Merry Frinks / *The Happy Family*
1934 Housewife
1934 Side Streets / *Woman in Her Thirties*
1934 A Lost Lady
1934 Gentlemen Are Born
1935 Sweet Music
1935 The Girl from 10th Avenue / *Men on*

Her Mind
1935 Here's Romance
1935 The Goose and the Gander
1935 Dangerous
1936 Colleen
1936 The Golden Arrow
1936 Two in a Crowd
1936 They Met in a Taxi
1936 More Than a Secretary
1937 Let's Get Married
1937 The League of Frightened Men
1937 Mr Dodds Takes the Air
1937 Thoroughbreds Don't Cry
1938 Ride a Crooked Mile / *Escape from Yesterday*
1938 Duke of West Point
1939 The King of the Turf
1939 The Gracie Allen Murder Case
1939 20,000 Men a Year
1940 Shooting High
1940 South of Pago Pago
1940 Flowing Gold
1940 East of the River
1941 Adventure in Washington / *Female Correspondent*
1941 Badlands of Dakota
1942 The Major of 44th Street
1942 Meet the Stewarts
1943 Appointment in Berlin
1943 There's Something About a Soldier
1944 Mr Winkle Goes to War / *Arms and the Woman*
1944 Strange Affair
1945 A Thousand and One Nights
1946 Tars and Spars
1946 The Jolson Story
1947 The Fabulous Dorseys
1947 Copacabana
1948 Four Faces West / *They Passed This Way*
1948 The Girl from Manhattan
1949 Cover-Up
1950 Sierra
1950 The Jackie Robinson Story
1951 Two Gals and a Guy
1953 Invasion USA
1953 Paris Motel
1953 The Eddie Cantor Story
1954 Top Banana

GREEN, David
(1948–) London, England.
1985 Car Trouble
1988 Buster
1989 Wings of the Apache
(also many TV movies)

GREEN, Guy
(1913–) Somerset, England.
1954 River Boat
1955 Portrait of Alison / *Postmark for Danger*
1956 Lost / *Tears for Simon*
1956 House of Secrets / *Triple Deception*
1958 Snorkel
1958 Sea of Sand / *Desert Patrol*
1960 S O S Pacific
1960 The Angry Silence
1961 The Mark
1962 Light in the Piazza
1963 Diamond Head
1965 A Patch of Blue
1968 Pretty Polly / *A Matter of Innocence*
1968 The Magus
1970 A Walk in the Spring Rain
1974 Luther
1975 Jacqueline Susann's Once Is Not Enough
1978 The Devil's Advocate
(also many TV movies)

GREEN, Joseph
1986 The Perils of P.K.

GREEN, Terry
1989 Father Jim

GREENAWAY, Peter
(1942–) England.
1980 The Falls
1981 Act of God
1982 Draughtsman's Contract
1985 A Zed and Two Noughts
1987 The Belly of an Architect
1988 Drowning By Numbers
1989 The Cook, the Thief, His Wife and Her Lover

GREENBERG, Richard
1989 Little Monsters

GREENE, Danford B
1984 The Secret Diary of Sigmund Freud

GREENE, David
(1921–) Manchester, England.
1966 The Shuttered Room
1968 Sebastian
1968 The Strange Affair
1969 I Started Counting
1970 The People Next Door
1973 Godspell
1978 Grey Lady Down
1981 Hard Country
(also many TV movies)

GREENE, Don Fox
1988 Blindside / *From Father to Son*

GREENE, Herbert
1959 The Cosmic Man

GREENE, Max (Mutz Greenbaum)
(1896–1968) German.
1944 The Man from Morocco
1944 Hotel Reserve **(Lance COMFORT, Victor HANBURY)**

GREENE, Sparky
(1948–) Chicago, Illinois, USA.
1984 The Oasis / *A Savage Hunter*

GREENGRASS, Paul
1989 Resurrected

GREENWALD, Robert
(1945–) New York, New York, USA.
1980 Xanadu
1988 Sweethearts Dance
(also many TV movies)

GREENWALT, David
1985 Secret Admirer
1989 Rude Awakening

GREENWOOD, Edwin
1929 The Co-Optimists **(Laddie CLIFF)**
1929 To What Red Hell

GREFE, William
1964 Racing Fever
1969 Hooked Generation
1973 Stanley
1975 Impulse
1976 The Jaws of Death

GREGG, Colin
(1947–) Cheltenham, Gloucestershire, England.
1986 Lamb
1988 We Think the World of You
(also many TV movies)

GREVILLE, Edmond T *
(1906–1966) France.
1936 Gypsy Melody
1937 Brief Ecstasy
1937 Mademoiselle Docteur
1937 What a Man
1937 Secret Lives / *I Married a Spy*
1939 Menaces
1948 But Not in Vain
1949 The Romantic Age / *Naughty Arlette*
1954 The House on the Waterfront / *Le Port du Désir*
1956 Guilty?
1958 Temptation Island
1960 Beat Girl / *Wild for Kicks*
1960 The Hands of Orlac
1961 The Liars / *Twisted Lives*

GRIES, Tom
(1922–1977) American.
1955 Hell's Horizon
1958 Girl in the Woods
1968 Will Penny
1969 100 Rifles
1969 Number One
1970 Hawaiians / *Masters of the Islands*
1970 Fools
1971 Earth II
1972 Journey Through Rosebud
1973 Lady Ice
1975 Dynamite Man
1975 Breakout
1976 Breakheart Pass
1976 Helter Skelter
1977 The Greatest
(also many TV movies)

GRIFFITH, Charles B
1959 Forbidden Island
1976 Eat My Dust
1979 Up from the Depths
1980 Dr Heckle and Mr Hype
1981 Smokey Bites the Dust
1989 Wizards of the Lost Kingdom II

GRIFFITH, D W (David Wark Griffith)
(1875–1948) Oldham County Farm, Centerfield, Kentucky, USA.
Autobiography: The Man Who Invented Hollywood, the Autobiography of W.G. Griffith edited by James Hart.
1915 The Birth of a Nation
1916 Intolerance
1918 Hearts of the World
1919 Broken Blossoms
1919 True Heart Susie
1920 Way Down East
1921 Dream Street
1921 Orphans of the Storm
1924 Isn't Life Wonderful?
1924 America / *Love and Sacrifice*
1925 Sally of the Sawdust
1925 That Royle Girl
1926 The Sorrows of Satan
1929 Lady of the Pavements
1930 Abraham Lincoln
1931 The Struggle
1940 One Million B.C. / *The Cave Dwellers / Man and His Mate* **(Hal ROACH, Hal ROACH Jnr.)**
(also a multitude of silent shorts 1908–1916)

GRIFFITH, Edward H
(1894–) Virginia, USA.
1924 Another Scandal
1924 Weekend Husbands
1925 Headlines
1925 Bad Company
1926 White Mice
1926 Atta Boy!
1927 Alias the Lone Wolf
1927 The Price of Honour
1927 Afraid to Love
1927 Hold 'Em, Yale!
1927 The Opening Night
1928 Love Overnight
1928 Captain Swagger
1929 The Shady Lady
1929 Rich People
1930 Holiday
1931 Rebound
1932 The Animal Kingdom / *The Woman in His House*
1932 Lady with a Past / *Reputation*
1933 Another Language
1935 Biography of a Bachelor Girl
1935 No More Ladies
1936 Next Time We Love
1937 I'll Take Romance
1937 Café Metropole
1939 Honeymoon in Bali / *Husbands or Lovers*
1939 Café Society
1939 Safari
1941 One Night in Lisbon
1941 Virginia
1943 The Sky's the Limit
1943 Young and Willing
1946 Perilous Holiday

GRIFFITHS, Mark
1984 Running Hot
1984 Hardbodies
1986 Hardbodies II

GRILLO, Gary
1986 American Justice / *Jackals*

GRINDE, Nick (Harry A Grindé)
(1893–1979) American.
1925 Excuse Me
1926 Upstage
1928 Beyond the Sierras
1928 Riders of the Dark
1929 Morgan's Last Raid
1929 The Desert Rider
1930 The Bishop Murder Case **(David BURTON)**
1930 Good News **(Edgar J McGREGOR)**
1930 Remote Control **(Malcolm ST CLAIR)**
1931 This Modern Age
1932 Shopworn
1932 Vanity Street
1935 Stone of Silver Creek
1935 Border Brigands
1935 Ladies Crave Excitement
1936 Jailbreak / *Murder in the Big House*
1936 Public Enemy's Wife / *G Man's Wife*
1937 Fugitive in the Sky
1937 The Captain's Kid
1937 White Bondage
1937 Public Wedding
1937 Love Is in the Air / *The Radio Murder Mystery*
1937 Exiled to Shanghai
1938 Down in Arkansas
1939 Federal Man-Hunt / *Flight from Justice*
1939 King of Chinatown
1939 Sudden Money
1939 Million Dollar Legs
1939 The Man They Could Not Hang
1939 A Woman Is the Judge
1940 Scandal Sheet
1940 Convicted Woman
1940 The Man with Nine Lives / *Behind the Door*
1940 Men Without Souls
1940 Girls of the Road
1940 Before I Hang
1940 Friendly Neighbours
1941 Mountain Moonlight / *Moving in Society*
1942 The Girl from Alaska
1943 Hitler, Dead or Alive
1943 We've Never Been Licked / *Texas to Tokyo*
1945 Road to Alcatraz
(also many shorts)

GRISSELL, Wallace A
(1904–) American.
1944 Marshal of Reno
1944 Vigilantes of Dodge City
1945 Wanderer of the Wasteland **(Edward KILLY)**
1945 Corpus Christi Bandits
1947 Wild Horse Mesa
1948 Western Heritage
1952 A Yank in Indo-China
(also many serials)

GRISSMER, John
1976 Scalper
1987 Nightmare at Shadow Woods / *Complex*

GROFE Jnr, Ferde
1968 Warkill
1972 The Proud and the Damned

GROSBARD, Ulu
(1929–) Antwerp, Belgium.
1968 The Subject Was Roses
1971 Who Is Harry Kellerman and Why Is He Saying Those Terrible Things About Me?
1978 Straight Time
1981 True Confessions
1984 Falling in Love
1988 A Likely Story

GROSS, Jerry
1968 Teenage Mother

GROSS, Larry
1986 3.15

GROSSMAN, Douglas
1988 Real Trouble / *Raging Fury*

GRUNE, Karl
(1890–1962) Vienna, Austria.
1935 Abdul the Damned
1936 The Marriage of Corbal
1936 Pagliacci / *A Clown Must Laugh*

GUENETTE, Robert
(1935–) Holyoke, Mass., USA.
1969 The Tree
1976 The Mysterious Monsters
1976 The Amazing World of Psychic Phenomena
1981 The Man Who Saw Tomorrow

GUERCIO, James William
1973 Electra Glide in Blue

GUEST, Christopher
1989 The Big Picture

GUEST, Val (Valmond GUEST)
(1911–) London, England.
1943 Miss London Ltd.
1944 Bees in Paradise
1944 Give Us the Moon
1945 I'll Be Your Sweetheart
1947 Just William's Luck
1948 William Comes to Town
1949 Murder at the Windmill
1950 Miss Pilgrim's Progress
1950 The Body Said No
1951 Mister Drake's Duck
1952 Penny Princess
1954 Life with the Lyons / *A Family Affair*
1954 The Runaway Bus
1954 Men of Sherwood Forest
1954 Dance Little Lady
1955 They Can't Hang Me
1955 The Lyons in Paris
1955 Break in the Circle
1955 The Quatermass Experiment / *The Creeping Unknown*
1956 It's a Wonderful World
1956 The Weapon
1957 Carry On Admiral / *The Ship Was Loaded*

1957 Quatermass II / *Enemy from Space*
1957 The Abominable Snowman of the Himalayas
1958 The Camp on Blood Island
1958 Up the Creek
1958 Further Up the Creek
1958 Expresso Bongo
1959 Yesterday's Enemy
1960 Life Is a Circus
1960 Hell Is a City
1961 The Full Treatment / *Stop Me Before I Kill*
1962 The Day the Earth Caught Fire
1962 Jigsaw
1963 80,000 Suspects
1964 The Beauty Jungle / *Contest Girl*
1965 Where the Spies Are
1967 Casino Royale **(Ken HUGHES, Joseph McGRATH, Robert PARRISH)**
1968 Assignment K
1969 When Dinosaurs Ruled the Earth
1970 Tomorrow
1971 The Persuaders
1972 Au Pair Girls
1974 Confessions of a Window Cleaner
1975 Killer Force / *The Diamond Mercenaries*
1980 The Shillingbury Blowers / *... And the Band Played On*
1980 Dangerous Davies - The Last Detective
1983 The Boys in Blue

GUILFOYLE, Paul
(1902–1961) American.
1960 Tess of the Storm Country

GUILLERMIN, John
(1923–) London, England.
1949 Torment / *Paper Gallows*
1951 Smart Alec
1951 Two on the Tiles
1951 Four Days
1952 Bachelor in Paris / *Song of Paris*
1952 Miss Robin Hood
1953 Operation Diplomat
1954 Adventure in the Hopfields
1954 The Crowded Day
1955 Dust and Gold
1955 Thunderstorm
1957 Town on Trial
1958 The Whole Truth
1958 I Was Monty's Double / *Hell, Heaven and Hoboken*
1959 Tarzan's Greatest Adventure
1960 The Day They Robbed the Bank of England
1960 Never Let Go
1962 Waltz of the Toreadors
1962 Tarzan Goes to India
1964 Guns at Batasi
1965 Rapture
1966 The Blue Max
1968 P J / *New Base in Hell*
1969 House of Cards
1969 The Bridge at Remagen
1970 El Condor
1972 Skyjacked
1973 Shaft in Africa
1974 The Towering Inferno F*
1976 King Kong
1978 Death on the Nile
1980 Mr Patman
1983 Crossover
1984 Sheena, Queen of the Jungle
1986 King Kong Lives
1988 Dead or Alive
1989 The Favourite
1989 The French Revolution

GUIOL, Fred
(1898–1964) American.
1934 What's Your Racket?
1935 The Rainmakers
1936 Silly Billies
1936 Mummy's Boys
1941 Tanks a Million
1941 Miss Polly
1942 Hay Foot
1946 Here Comes Trouble
1951 As You Were

GUNN, Bill
1970 Stop
1973 Ganja and Hess

GUNN, Gilbert
(c1912–) British.
1951 The Elstree Story
1953 Valley of Song
1957 The Strange World of Planet X
1959 Operation Bullshine
1962 What a Whopper
(also many documentaries)

GUTIERREZ ALEA, Tomas *
(1928–) Havana, Cuba.
1968 Memories of Underdevelopment
1976 The Last Supper
1984 Up to a Point

GUTMAN, Amos
1984 Drifting / *Nagua*
1986 Bar 51
1987 Hemo, King of Jerusalem

GUTMAN, Nathaniel
1987 War Zone / *Deadline*

GUTTFREUND, André
1984 Breach of Contract

GUZMAN, Claudio
1973 Antonio
1975 Linda Lovelace for President

GYLLENHAAL, Steve
(1949–) Cleveland, Ohio, USA.
1985 A Certain Jury

HAAS, Charles
(1918–) American.
1956 Star in the Dust
1956 Screaming Eagles
1956 Showdown in Abilene
1958 Summer Love
1958 Wild Heritage
1959 The Beat Generation / *This Rebel Age*
1959 Girls, Town
1960 Platinum High School / *Rich, Young and Deadly*

HAAS, Hugo
(1901–1968) Czechoslovakia.
1939 Our Combat
1951 Pickup
1951 The Girl on the Bridge
1952 Strange Fascination
1953 One Girl's Confession
1953 Thy Neighbour's Wife
1954 Bait
1954 The Other Woman
1955 Hold Back Tomorrow
1956 Edge of Hell
1957 Lizzie
1957 Hit and Run
1959 Night of the Quarter Moon
1959 Born to Be Loved
1962 Paradise Alley
1967 The Crazy Ones

HACKFORD, Taylor
1980 The Idolmaker
1982 An Officer and a Gentleman
1984 Against All Odds
1985 White Nights
1989 Everybody's All-American

HADDEN, George
1943 Charlie Chan's Courage

HAGEN, Ross
1979 The Glove

HAGG, Russell
1977 Raw Deal

HAGGARD, Piers
(1939–) Scotland.
1970 Wedding Night / *I Can't. . I Can't*
1971 The Blood on Satan's Claw / *Satan's Skin*
1979 The Quatermass Conclusion
1980 The Fiendish Plot of Dr Fu Manchu
1982 Venom
1988 A Summer Story
(also many TV movies)

HAGGIS, Paul
1989 Red Hot

HAGMAN, Larry
(1931–) Weatherford, Texas, USA.
1971 Beware: The Blob / *Son of Blob*

HAGMANN, Stuart
(1942–) Sturgeon Bay, Wisconsin, USA.
1970 The Strawberry Statement
1971 Believe in Me

HAINES, Fred
1974 Steppenwolf

HAINES, Randa
1986 Children of a Lesser God **F***
(also many TV movies)

HALE, Sonnie (Robert Hale Monro)
(1902–1959) British.
1937 Head Over Heels
1937 Gangway
1938 Sailing Along

HALE, William (Billy Hale)
(1928–) American.
1959 The Naked Hunt
1966 Journey to Shiloh
1967 Gunfight in Abilene
(also many TV movies)

HALEY Jnr, Jack
(1933–) Los Angeles, California, USA.
1969 Norwood
1971 The Love Machine
(also many documentaries)

HALICKI, H B (Toby Halicki)
1974 Gone in 60 Seconds
1982 The Junkman
1983 Deadline Auto Theft

HALL, Alexander
(1894–1968) American.
1932 Sinners in the Sun
1932 Madame Racketeer / *The Sporting Widow* **(Harry WAGSTAFF)**
1933 The Girl in 419 **(George SOMNES)**
1933 Midnight Club **(George SOMNES)**
1933 Torch Singer / *Broadway Singer* **(George SOMNES)**
1934 Miss Fane's Baby Is Stolen / *Kidnapped*
1934 Little Miss Marker / *The Girl in Fawn*
1934 The Pursuit of Happiness
1934 Limehouse Blues / *East End Chant*
1935 Goin' to Town
1935 Annapolis Farewell / *Gentlemen of the Navy*
1936 Give Us This Night
1936 Yours for the Asking
1937 Exclusive
1938 There's Always a Woman
1938 I Am the Law
1938 There's That Woman Again / *What a Woman!*
1939 The Lady's from Kentucky
1939 Good Girls Go to Paris
1939 The Amazing Mr Williams
1940 The Doctor Takes a Wife
1940 He Stayed for Breakfast
1940 This Thing Called Love / *Married But Single*
1940 Here Comes Mr Jordan **D* F***
1940 Bedtime Story
1942 They All Kissed the Bride
1942 My Sister Eileen
1943 The Heavenly Body
1944 Once Upon a Time
1945 She Wouldn't Say Yes
1945 Over Twenty-One
1947 Down to Earth
1949 The Great Lover
1950 Love That Brute
1950 Louisa
1951 Up Front
1952 Because You're Mine
1956 Forever Darling

HALL, Ivan
1988 Bush Shrink

HALL, Jon (Charles Locher)
(1913–1979) American.
1965 Monster from the Surf / *The Beachgirls and the Monster*

HALL, Kenneth
1987 Evil Spawn

HALL, Sir Peter
(1930–) Bury St Edmunds, Suffolk, England.
Publication: Peter Hall's Diaries.
1968 Work Is a Four Letter Word
1968 A Midsummer Night's Dream
1969 Three Into Two Won't Go
1970 Perfect Friday
1973 The Homecoming

HALLER, Daniel
(1926–) Los Angeles, California.
1965 Die, Monster, Die! / *Monster of Terror*
1967 Devil's Angels
1968 The Wild Racers
1970 Paddy / *Goodbye to the Hill*
1970 Pieces of Dreams
1970 The Dunwich Horror
1979 Buck Rogers in the 25th Century
1981 Follow That Car
(also many TV movies)

HALLOWELL, Todd
1989 Love or Money

HALLSTROM, Lasse
1987 My Life As a Dog **D***
1989 Once Around

HALPERIN, Victor Hugh
(1895–) American.
1924 Greater Than Marriage
1924 When a Girl Loves
1925 The Unknown Lover
1925 School for Wives
1926 In Borrowed Plumes
1927 Dance Magic
1930 Party Girl
1931 Ex-Flame
1932 White Zombie
1933 Supernatural
1936 I Conquer the Sea
1937 Nation Aflame
1939 Torture Ship
1940 Buried Alive
1942 Girls' Town

HAMER, Robert
(1911–1963) Kidderminster, Worcestershire, England.
1945 Dead of Night **(Alberto CAVALCANTI, Charles CRICHTON, Basil DEARDEN)**
1945 Pink String and Sealing Wax
1949 Kind Hearts and Coronets
1949 The Spider and the Fly
1951 His Excellency
1952 The Long Memory
1954 Father Brown / *The Detective*
1954 To Paris with Love
1959 The Scapegoat
1960 School for Scoundrels

HAMILTON, Guy
(1922–) Paris, France.
1952 The Ringer
1953 The Intruder
1954 An Inspector Calls
1955 The Colditz Story
1956 Charley Moon
1957 Manuela / *Stowaway Girl*
1959 The Devil's Principle
1960 A Touch of Larceny
1962 The Best of Enemies
1964 Man in the Middle
1964 Goldfinger
1966 The Party's Over
1966 Funeral in Berlin
1969 Battle of Britain
1971 Diamonds Are Forever
1973 Live and Let Die
1974 The Man with the Golden Gun
1978 Force 10 from Naverone
1980 The Mirror Crack'd
1982 Evil Under the Sun
1985 Remo.. Unarmed and Dangerous / *Remo Williams: The Adventure Begins*
1989 Try This One for Size

HAMILTON, Strathford
1988 Blueberry Hill

HAMILTON, William
1935 Freckles **(Edward KILLY)**
1935 Seven Keys to Baldpate **(Edward KILLY)**
1936 Murder on the Bridal Path **(Edward KILLY)**
1936 Bunker Bean **(Edward KILLY)**
1941 Call Out the Marines **(Frank RYAN)**

HAMMOND, Peter
(1923–) British.
1970 Spring and Port Wine

HANBURY, Victor
1933 Dick Turpin **(John STAFFORD)**
1933 No Funny Business **(John STAFFORD)**
1935 Admirals All
1936 The Crouching Beast
1936 Ball at the Savoy
1936 The Beloved Imposter
1936 The Avenging Hand
1937 Second Bureau
1937 Return of the Stranger
1944 Hotel Reserve **(Lance COMFORT, Max GREENE)**

HANBURY, Victor *see* **Joseph LOSEY**

HANCOCK, John
(1939–) Kansas City, Missouri, USA.
1971 Let's Scare Jessica to Death
1973 Bang the Drum Softly
1976 Baby Blue Marine
1979 California Dreaming
1987 Weeds / *Honour Among Thieves*
1989 Steal the Sky

HANNANT, Brian
1988 The Time Guardian

HANOOKA, Itzhak
1987 Red Nights

HANSELL, Marion
1986 Dust
1987 The Cruel Embrace

HANSON, Curtis
1976 The Arousers
1980 The Little Dragons
1983 Losin' It
1987 The Bedroom Window

HANSON, John
1978 Northern Lights **(Rob NILSSON)**
1984 Wildrose

HANSON, Mark *see* **Herschell G LEWIS**

HANWRIGHT, Joseph C
1979 Uncle Joe Shannon

HARDWICKE, Sir Cedric (Cedric Webotes Hardwicke)
(1896–1964) Stourbridge, Worcestershire, England.
Biography: A Victorian in Orbit by James Brough.
1943 Forever and a Day **(René CLAIR, Edmund GOULDING, Frank LLOYD, Victor SAVILLE, Robert STEVENSON, Herbert WILCOX)**

HARDY, Jonathan
1988 Backstage

HARDY, Robin
1973 The Wicker Man
1987 The Fantasist
1988 The Bulldance

HARE, David
(1947–) Sussex, England.
1985 Wetherby
1988 Paris By Night
1989 Strapless

HARGROVE, Dean
(1938–) Iola, Kansas, USA.
1975 The Manchu Eagle Murder Caper Mystery

HARLAN, Richard
1938 Radio Troubador
1938 Bachelor Father
1938 Papa Soltero
1940 Mercy Plane

HARLIN, Renny
1986 Born American
1987 Prison
1988 Nightmare on Elm Street IV: The Dream Master

HARLOW, John
(1896–) British.
1933 Songbirds
1933 My Lucky Star
1934 Master and Man
1934 Bagged
1940 Spellbound / *Passing Clouds / The Spell of Amy Nugent*
1941 This Was Paris
1943 Headline
1943 The Dark Tower
1944 Candles at Nine
1944 Meet Sexton Blake
1944 The Agitator
1945 The Echo Murders
1945 Appointment with Crime
1947 Green Fingers
1948 While I Live / *The Dream of Olwen*
1949 Old Mother Riley's New Venture
1950 Old Mother Riley Headmistress
1952 Those People Next Door
1953 The Blue Parrot
1954 Dangerous Cargo
1954 Delayed Action

HARMON, Robert
1986 The Hitcher
1989 The Tender

HARPER, Max
1989 Corpses Never Lie

HARRINGTON, Curtis
(1928–) Los Angeles, California, USA.
1961 Night Tide
1966 Queen of Blood
1967 Games
1971 What's the Matter with Helen?
1972 Who Slew Auntie Roo?
1974 The Killing Kind
1985 Mata Hari
(also many shorts and TV movies)

HARRIS, Damien
1989 The Rachel Papers

HARRIS, Denny
1980 Silent Scream

HARRIS, Frank
1984 Killpoint
1986 Savage Sunday / *Low Blow*
1986 The Patriot
1989 Aftershock / *If We Knew Then*

HARRIS, James B
(1928–) New York, New York, USA.
1965 The Bedford Incident
1973 Some Call It Moving
1982 Fast-Walking
1988 Cop / *Blood on the Moon*

HARRIS, Richard
(1932–) Limerick, Republic of Ireland.
1972 Bloomfield / *The Hero*

HARRISON, Jules
1985 Exterminators of the Year 3000

HARRISON, Ken
(1942–) Poetry, Texas, USA.

1985 1918
1986 On Valentine's Day

HARRISON, Paul
1974 The House of Seven Corpses

HARRY, Lee
1987 Silent Night, Deadly Night II

HART, Chris
1986 Eat and Run / *Mangia*

HART, Harvey
(1928–) Toronto, Canada.
1965 Bus Riley's Back in Town
1965 Dark Intruder
1967 Sullivan's Empire **(Thomas CARR)**
1968 The Sweet Ride
1971 Fortune and Men's Eyes
1973 The Pyx
1976 Shoot
1981 The High Country
1983 Getting Even
(also many TV movies)

HARTFORD, Ken
1984 Hell Squad

HARTFORD-DAVIS, Robert
(1923–1977) British.
Pseudonym: Michael Burrowes.
1961 Crosstrap
1962 That Kind of Girl
1963 The Yellow Teddy Bear
1963 Saturday Night Out
1964 The Black Torment
1966 The Sandwich Man
1966 Press for Time
1967 Corruption
1969 The Smashing Bird I Used to Know
1971 Nobody Ordered Love
1971 The Fiend
1972 Black Gunn
1974 The Take

HARTMAN, Don (Samuel Hartman)
(1901–1958) American.
1947 It Had to Be You **(Rudolph MATE)**
1948 Every Girl Should Be Married
1949 Holiday Affair
1951 It's a Big Country **(Clarence BROWN, John STURGES, Richard THORPE, Charles VIDOR, Don WEIS, William A WELLMAN)**
1951 Mr Imperium / *You Belong to My Heart*

HARTMAN, Rivka
1987 Once Upon a Weekend

HARVARD, Emile
1975 Fugitive Killer

HARVEY, Anthony
(1931–) London, England.
1966 Dutchman
1968 The Lion in Winter **D* F***
1972 They Might Be Giants
1974 The Abdication
1979 Players
1979 Eagle's Wing
1981 Richard's Things
1984 The Ultimate Solution of Grace Quigley
(also many TV movies)

HARVEY, Laurence (Larushka Mischa Skikne)
(1928–1973) Janiskis, Lithuania.
Biographies: The Laurence Harvey Story by Hans Borgett; One Tear Is Enough by Pauline Stone.
1963 The Ceremony
1973 Welcome to Arrow Beach

HASKIN, Byron
(1899–1984) Portland, Oregon, USA.
1927 Irish Hearts
1927 Matinee Ladies
1927 The Siren
1927 Ginsberg the Great / *The Broadway Kid*
1947 I Walk Alone
1948 Man-Eater of Kumaon
1949 Too Late for Tears
1950 Treasure Island
1951 Warpath
1951 Silver City / *High Vermillion*
1951 Tarzan's Peril / *Tarzan and the Jungle Queen*
1952 Denver and Rio Grande
1953 The War of the Worlds
1953 His Majesty O'Keefe
1954 The Naked Jungle
1955 Conquest of Space
1955 Long John Silver
1956 The First Texan
1956 The Boss
1958 From the Earth to the Moon
1959 The Little Savage
1960 Jet Over the Atlantic
1960 September Storm
1961 Armoured Command
1963 Captain Sinbad
1964 Robinson Crusoe on Mars
1968 The Power

HATHAWAY, Henry (Marquis Henri Leopold de Frennes)
(1898–1985) Sacramento, California, USA.
1932 Heritage of the Desert
1932 Wild Horse Mesa
1933 Under the Tonto Ridge
1933 Sunset Pass
1933 Man of the Forest
1933 To the Last Man
1933 The Thundering Herd
1934 The Last Round-Up
1934 Come on Marines!
1934 The Witching Hour
1934 Now and Forever
1935 The Lives of a Bengal Lancer **D* F***
1935 Peter Ibbetson
1936 The Trail of the Lonesome Pine
1936 Go West, Young Man
1937 Souls at Sea
1938 Spawn of the North
1939 The Real Glory
1940 Johnny Apollo

1940 Brigham Young, Frontiersman
1941 The Shepherd of the Hills
1941 Sundown
1942 Ten Gentlemen from West Point
1942 China Girl
1944 Home in Indiana
1944 Wing and a Prayer
1945 Knob Hill
1945 The House on 92nd Street
1946 The Dark Corner
1947 13 Rue Madeleine
1947 Kiss of Death
1948 Call Northside 777
1949 Down to the Sea in Ships
1950 The Black Rose
1951 You're in the Navy Now / *USS Teakettle*
1951 Fourteen Hours
1951 Rawhide
1951 The Desert Fox
1952 Diplomatic Courier
1953 Niagara
1953 White Witch Doctor
1954 Prince Valiant
1954 Garden of Evil
1955 The Racers / *Such Men Are Dangerous*
1956 The Bottom of the Bottle / *Beyond the River*
1956 23 Paces to Baker Street
1957 Legend of the Lost
1958 From Hell to Texas / *Manhunt*
1959 Woman Obsessed
1959 Seven Thieves
1960 North of Alaska
1963 How the West Was Won **(John FORD, George MARSHALL) F***
1964 Circus World / *The Magnificent Showman*
1964 Of Human Bondage **(Ken HUGHES)**
1965 The Sons of Katie Elder
1966 Nevada Smith
1967 The Last Safari
1968 Five Card Stud
1969 True Grit
1971 Raid on Rommel
1971 Shoot-Out
1974 Hangup

HATTON, Maurice
1988 American Roulette

HAWES, Michael
1988 Family Reunion

HAWKES, Steve
1975 Steve, Samson and Delilah

HAWKS, Howard (Howard Winchester Hawks)
(1896–1977) Goshen, Indiana, USA. Biography: The Cinema of Howard Hawks by Peter Bogdanovich.
1926 Fig Leaves
1926 The Road to Glory
1927 The Cradle Snatchers
1927 Paid to Love
1928 Fazil
1928 A Girl in Every Port
1929 Trent's Last Case
1929 Masked Emotions **(David BUTLER)**
1930 The Dawn Patrol
1931 The Criminal Code
1932 The Crowd Roars
1932 Tiger Sharks
1932 Scarface / *The Shame of a Nation*
1932 Today We Live
1933 The Prizefighter and the Lady **(W S VAN DYKE)**
1934 Twentieth Century
1934 Viva Villa! **(Jack CONWAY) F***
1934 Barbary Coast
1935 Ceiling Zero
1936 Come and Get It **(William WYLER)**
1936 The Road to Glory
1936 Bringing Up Baby
1938 Only Angels Have Wings
1940 His Girl Friday
1940 Ball of Fire
1941 Sergeant York **D* F***
1941 Airforce
1943 The Outlaw **(Howard HUGHES)**
1943 To Have and Have Not
1944 The Big Sleep
1946 Red River
1948 A Song is Born
1949 I Was a Male War Bride / *You Can't Sleep Here*
1951 The Thing **(Christian NYBY)**
1952 The Big Sky
1952 Monkey Business
1953 Gentlemen Prefer Blondes
1955 Land of the Pharaohs
1959 Rio Bravo!
1962 Hatari!
1964 Man's Favourite Sport?
1965 Red Line 7000
1966 El Dorado
1970 Rio Lobo

HAYDEN, Jeffrey
1957 The Vintage

HAYDN, Richard
(1905–1985) London, England.
1948 Miss Tatlock's Millions
1949 Dear Wife
1950 Mr Music

HAYERS, Sidney
(1921–) Edinburgh, Scotland.
1959 Violent Moment
1959 The White Trap
1960 Circus of Horrors
1960 The Malpas Mystery
1961 Echo of Barbara
1961 Payroll
1962 Night of the Eagle / *Burn, Witch, Burn*
1963 This Is My Street
1965 Three Hats for Lisa
1966 The Trap / *The Baited Trap*
1967 Finders Keepers
1969 The Southern Star
1971 Assault / *In the Devil's Garden*
1971 The Firechasers
1972 All Coppers Are...
1973 Revenge / *Inn of the Frightened People*
1974 Deadly Strangers
1975 Diagnosis: Murder
1976 What Changed Charley Farthing?
1976 One Way

1977 A Bridge Too Far **(Richard ATTENBOROUGH)**

HAYES, Michael
1969 Promise

HAYES, Robert
1988 Phoenix the Warrior

HAYNES, Stanley
1946 Carnival

HAZAN, Jack
1975 A Bigger Splash
1980 Rude Boy **(David MINGAY)**

HEARD, Paul F
1958 Hong Kong Affair

HEATH, Simon
1984 Bullamakanka
1986 Charley's Web

HEAVENER, David
1988 Outlaw Force
1989 The Reactor
1989 Kill Crazy

HECHT, Ben
(1894–1964) New York, USA. Autobiographies: A Child of the Century; Gaily, Gaily.
1934 Crime Without Passion **(Charles MacARTHUR)**
1935 The Scoundrel **(Charles MacARTHUR)**
1936 Soak the Rich **(Charles MacARTHUR)**
1936 Once in a Blue Moon **(Charles MacARTHUR)**
1940 Angels Over Broadway **(Lee GARMES)**
1946 Specter of the Rose
1952 Actors and Sin

HECKERLING, Amy
(1954–) Bronx, New York, USA.
1982 Fast Times at Ridgemont High
1984 Johnny Dangerously
1985 National Lampoon's European Vacation
1989 Daddy's Home

HEERMAN, Victor
(1892–) Anglo-American.
1924 The Confidence Man
1925 Irish Luck
1925 Old Home Week
1927 Rubber Heels
1927 Ladies Must Dress
1928 Love Hungry
1930 Animal Crackers
1930 Sea Legs

HEFFRON, Richard T
(1930–) Chicago, Illinois, USA.
1974 Newman's Law
1976 Trackdown
1976 Futureworld
1977 Outlaw Blues
1978 Foolin' Around
1982 I, the Jury
(also many TV movies)

HEINZ, Russell Ray
1935 Blazing Guns
1935 Border Vengeance
1936 Just My Luck

HEISLER, Stuart
(1894–1979) Los Angeles, California, USA.
1936 Straight from the Shoulder
1937 The Hurricane **(John FORD)**
1940 The Biscuit Eater / *God Gave Him a Dog*
1941 Among the Living
1941 The Monster and the Girl
1942 The Glass Key
1942 The Remarkable Andrew
1945 Along Came Jones
1946 Blue Skies
1947 Smash-Up: The Story of a Woman / *A Woman Destroyed*
1949 Tokyo Joe
1949 Tulsa
1950 Chain Lightning
1950 Dallas
1950 Storm Warning
1950 Vendetta
1951 Journey into Light
1952 Island of Desire / *Saturday Island*
1953 The Star
1954 Beachhead
1954 This Is My Love
1955 I Died a Thousand Times
1956 The Burning Hills
1956 The Lone Ranger
1962 Hitler

HELLMAN, Jerome
(1928–) New York, New York, USA.
1979 Promises in the Dark

HELLMAN, Monte
(1932–) New York, New York, USA.
1959 Beast from Haunted Cave
1964 Back Door to Hell
1965 Flight to Fury
1966 The Shooting
1966 Ride in the Whirlwind
1971 Two-Lane Black Top
1971 Cockfighter / *Born to Kill*
1974 China 9 Liberty 37
1987 The Typhoon Shipments
1988 The Day of the Iguana

HELLMAN, Oliver
1977 Tentacles

HELMAN, Henri
1977 Le Coeur Froid
1984 Where Is Parsifal?

HELPERN Jnr, David
1979 Something Short of Paradise

HEMMINGS, David
(1941–) Guildford, Surrey, England.
1972 Running Scared
1973 The 14
1979 Just a Gigolo
1981 The Survivor
1981 Race to the Yankee Zephyr

HENABURY, Joseph E
(1888–1976) American.
1924 The Guilty One
1924 A Sainted Devil
1924 The Stranger
1924 Tongues of Flame
1925 Cobra
1929 Clear the Decks
1929 Red Hot Speed
1929 Light Fingers
1930 The Love Trader
1943 The Leather Burners

HENENLOTTER, Frank
1982 Basket Case
1987 Brain Damage
1989 Basket Case II
1989 Frankenhooker

HENLEY, Hobart
1924 A Lady of Quality
1924 The Tornado
1924 The Turmoil
1924 Sinners in Silk
1925 An Exchange of Wives
1925 A Slave to Fashion
1925 The Auction Block
1925 His Secretary
1925 The Denial
1926 A Certain Young Man
1927 Wickedness Preferred
1927 Tillie the Toiler
1928 His Tiger Lady
1929 The Lady Lies
1930 The Big Pond
1930 Roadhouse Nights
1930 Mothers Cry
1930 Free Love
1931 Captain Applejack
1931 Bad Sisters
1931 Expensive Women
1932 Night World
1934 Unknown Blonde

HENREID, Paul (Paul George Julius Von Henreid)
(1907–) Trieste, Austria.
1952 For Men Only
1956 A Woman's Devotion
1958 Girls on the Loose
1958 Live Fast, Die Young
1964 Dead Ringer / *Dead Image*
1965 Ballad in Blue / *Blues for Lovers*

HENRY, Buck (B. Zuckerman)
(1930–) New York, New York, USA.
1978 Heaven Can Wait **(Warren BEATTY) D* F***
1980 First Family

HENSON, Jim
(1936–) Greenville, North Carolina, USA.
1981 The Great Muppet Caper
1982 The Dark Crystal **(Frank OZ)**
1986 Labyrinth

HERBERT, F Hugh
(1897–1957) American.
1930 He Knew Women
1930 Danger Lights
1948 Scudda Hoo, Scudda Hay / *Summer Lightning*
1953 The Girls of Pleasure **(Alvin GANZER)**

HERBERT, Henry
1973 Malachi's Cove / *The Seaweed Children*

HERBERT, Martin
1976 Blazing Magnum
1977 Strange Shadows in an Empty Room

HEREK, Stephen
1986 Critters
1987 Bill and Ted's Excellent Adventure

HERMAN, Albert
1931 Sporting Chance
1932 Exposed
1933 The Big Chance
1935 Western Frontier
1935 Danger Ahead
1935 Gun Play
1935 Hot Off the Press
1935 Trail's End
1935 What Price Crime?
1935 Twisted Rails
1935 Cowboy and the Bandit
1935 Big Boy Rides Again
1936 Blazing Justice
1936 Outlaws of the Range
1936 Bars of Hate
1937 Renfrew of the Royal Mounted
1937 Valley of Terror
1938 Starlight Over Texas
1938 Where the Buffalo Roam
1938 Rollin' Plains
1938 On the Great White Trail
1938 Utah Trail
1939 Down the Wyoming Trail
1939 Roll, Wagons, Roll
1939 Song of the Buckaroo
1939 Sundown on the Prairie
1939 Rollin' Westward
1939 Man from Texas
1940 Arizona Frontier
1940 The Golden Trail
1940 Rainbow Over the Range
1940 Rhythm of the Rio Grande
1940 Take Me Back to Oklahoma
1941 Rolling Home to Texas
1941 Pioneers
1941 Gentlemen from Dixie
1942 Nazi Spy Ring
1942 A Yank in Libya
1943 The Rangers Take Over
1943 Miss V from Moscow / *Intrigue in Paris*
1944 Delinquent Daughters
1944 Shake Hands with Murder
1945 The Missing Corpse
1945 The Phantom of 42nd Street
1945 Rogue's Gallery

HERRINGTON, Rowdy
1988 Jack's Back / *Red Rain*
1989 Road House

HERTZ, Nathan
1958 Attack of the Fifty Foot Woman

HERZ, Michael
(1949–) New York, New York, USA.
1980 Squeeze Play! **(Sam WEIL)**
1982 Waitress! **(Sam WEIL)**
1983 Stuck on You! **(Sam WEIL)**
1984 The First Turn On! **(Sam WEIL)**
1984 The Toxic Avenger **(Sam WEIL)**
1988 Troma's War! **(Sam WEIL)**
1989 The Toxic Avenger II **(Sam WEIL)**

HERZFELD, John
1983 Two of a Kind

HERZOG, Werner (Werner Stipetic)
(1942–) Sachrang, Germany.
1968 Signs of Life
1971 Even Dwarfs Started Small
1973 Aguirre, the Wrath of God
1974 The Mystery of Kaspar Hauser / *Everyman for Himself and God Against All*
1976 Heart of Glass
1977 Stroszek
1978 Fata Morgana
1979 Woyzeck
1979 Nosferatu the Vampyre
1982 Fitzcarraldo
1984 Where the Green Ants Dream
1987 Cobra Verde

HESS, Jon
1988 The Lawless Land
1989 Watchers

HESSLER, Gordon
(1930–) Berlin, Germany.
1965 Catacombs / *The Woman Who Wouldn't Die*
1969 The Oblong Box
1969 The Last Shot You Hear
1970 Scream and Scream Again
1970 Cry of the Banshee
1971 Murders in the Rue Morgue
1973 Embassy
1974 The Golden Voyage of Sinbad
1974 Medusa
1983 Escape from El Diablo
1985 Pray for Death
1987 Rage of Honour / *Way of the Ninja*
1987 Wheels of Terror / *The Misfit Brigade*
1989 Retaliator II: Out on Bail
1989 The Girl on the Swing
(also many TV movies)

HESTON, Charlton (John Charlton Carter)
(1924–) Evanston, Illinois, USA.
Autobiography: An Actor's Life.
1973 Antony and Cleopatra
1982 Mother Lode

HEWITT, David
1967 Journey to the Centre of Time
1967 Return from the Past

HEWITT, Rod
1987 Gangland: The Verne Miller Story

HEYES, Douglas
(1923–) American.
1964 Kitten with a Whip
1966 Beau Geste
(also many TV movies)

HIBBS, Jesse
(1906–1985) American.
1953 The All American / *The Winning Way*
1954 Ride Clear of Diablo
1954 Black Horse Canyon
1954 Rails into Laramie
1954 The Yellow Mountain
1955 To Hell and Back
1955 The Spoilers
1956 World in My Corner
1956 Walk the Proud Lane
1957 Joe Butterfly
1958 Ride a Crooked Trail

HICKEY, Bruce
1987 Necropolis

HICKOX, Anthony
1988 Waxwork
1989 Sundown

HICKOX, Douglas
(1929–1988) London, England.
1959 The Giant Behemoth **(Eugene LOURIE)**
1963 It's All Over Town
1963 Just for You / *Disk-o-tek Holiday*
1970 Entertaining Mr Sloane
1972 Sitting Target
1973 Theatre of Blood
1975 Brannigan
1976 Sky Riders
1979 Zulu Dawn
1983 The Hound of the Baskervilles
(also many shorts and TV movies)

HIGAN, James
1943 The Mad Ghoul

HIGGIN, Howard
(1893–1937) American.
1929 Sal of Singapore
1929 The Leatherneck
1929 High Voltage
1930 The Racketeer
1931 The Painted Desert
1932 The Last Man
1932 The Final Edition
1932 Hell's House
1933 Carnival Lady
1933 Marriage on Approval
1934 The Line Up
1937 Battle of Greed

HIGGINS, Colin
(1941–) New Caledonia.
1978 Foul Play
1980 Nine to Five
1982 The Best Little Whorehouse in Texas

HIKEN, Nat
1969 The Love God

HILL, George Roy
(1922–) Minneapolis, Minnesota, USA.
1962 Period of Adjustment
1963 Toys in the Attic

1964 The World of Henry Orient
1966 Hawaii
1967 Thoroughly Modern Millie
1969 Butch Cassidy and the Sundance Kid **D* F***
1971 Slaughterhouse-Five
1973 The Sting **D** F****
1975 The Great Waldo Pepper
1977 Slap Shot
1979 A Little Romance
1982 The World According to Garp
1984 The Little Drummer Girl
1988 Funny Farm

HILL, George William
(1895–1934) Douglas, Kansas, USA.
1924 The Hill Billy
1924 The Midnight Express
1924 Through the Dark
1924 The Foolish Virgin
1925 The Limited Mail
1925 Zandar the Great
1926 The Barrier
1926 Tell It to the Marines
1927 Buttons
1927 The Callahans and the Murphys
1928 The Cossacks
1929 The Flying Fleet
1930 The Big House **F***
1930 Min and Bill
1931 The Secret Six
1931 Hell Divers
1933 Clear All Wires

HILL, Jack
(1933–) Los Angeles, California, USA.
1966 Blood Bath **(Stephanie ROTHMAN)**
1969 Pit Stop
1971 The Big Doll House
1972 The Big Bird Cage
1973 Coffy
1974 Foxy Brown
1974 The Swinging Cheerleaders
1975 Switchblade Sisters

HILL, James
(1919–) England.
1952 The Stolen Plans
1953 The Clue of the Missing Ape
1956 Peril for the Guy
1959 Mystery in the Mine
1961 The Kitchen
1962 The Dock Brief / *Trial and Error*
1962 Lunch Hour
1964 Seaside Swingers / *Every Day's a Holiday*
1966 A Study in Terror
1966 Born Free
1967 The Corrupt Ones / *The Peking Medallion*
1970 Captain Nemo and the Underwater City
1971 An Elephant Called Slowly
1971 Black Beauty
1973 The Belstone Fox / *Free Spirit*
1974 Christian the Lion / *The Lion at World's End*
(also many shorts, documentaries and TV movies)

HILL, Robert F
(1886–1985) American.
1924 The Breathless Moment
1924 The Dangerous Blonde
1924 Dark Stairways
1924 Excitement
1924 Jack O'Clubs
1924 Young Ideas
1929 Melody Lane
1929 Silks and Saddles
1931 Sundown Trail
1932 Love Bound
1932 Come on Danger
1933 Tarzan the Fearless
1933 Cheyenne Kid
1934 A Demon for Trouble
1934 Inside Information
1934 Outlaw's Highway
1934 Frontier Days
1934 Cowboy Holiday
1935 Cyclone Rider
1935 Texas Rambler
1935 Vanishing Riders
1935 Danger Trails
1936 The Idaho Kid
1936 Kelly of the Secret Service
1936 Men of the Plains
1936 Prison Shadows
1936 Put on the Spot
1936 Rio Grande Romance
1936 The Rogue's Tavern
1936 Too Much Beef
1936 West of Nevada
1936 Face in the Fog
1936 Taming the Wild
1936 Rip Roaring Buckaroo
1936 Law and Lead
1936 Phantom of the Range
1937 Two Minutes to Play
1937 Million Dollar Racket
1937 Cheyenne Rides Again
1937 Feud on the Trail
1937 Mystery Range
1937 The Roaming Cowboy
1938 Whirlwind Horseman
1938 Flying Fists
1938 Man's Country
1938 The Painted Trail
1938 Silks and Saddles
1939 Overland Mail
1939 Wild Horse Canyon
1939 Drifting Westward
1940 East Side Kids
1941 Wanderers of the West
(also many serials)

HILL, Sinclair
(1894–1945) British.
1924 The Conspirators
1924 White Slippers
1925 The Squire of Long Hadley
1925 The Presumption of Stanley Hay M.P.
1925 The Qualified Adventurer
1925 The Secret Kingdom
1926 Sahara Love
1926 The Chinese Bungalow
1926 Boadicea
1927 A Woman Redeemed
1927 The King's Highway
1927 The Guns of Loos

1928 The Price of Divorce
1929 The Unwritten Law
1929 Dark Red Roses
1930 Greek Street
1930 Such Is the Law
1931 A Gentleman in Paris
1931 Other People's Sins
1931 The Great Gay Road
1931 The First Mrs Frazer
1932 The Man from Toronto
1933 Britannia of Billingsgate
1934 My Old Dutch
1935 Hyde Park Corner
1936 The Cardinal
1936 The Gay Adventure
1937 Take a Chance
1937 Midnight Menace
1937 Command Performance
1938 Follow Your Star

HILL, Walter
(1942–) Long Beach, California, USA.
1975 Hard Times / *The Streetfighter*
1978 The Driver
1979 The Warriors
1980 The Long Riders
1981 Southern Comfort
1982 48 Hrs
1984 Streets of Fire
1985 Brewster's Millions
1986 Crossroads
1987 Extreme Prejudice
1988 Red Heat
1989 Johnny Handsome

HILLCOAT, John
1988 Ghosts

HILLER, Arthur
(1923–) Edmonton, Alberta, Canada.
1957 The Careless Years
1963 The Miracle of the White Stallions
1963 The Wheeler Dealers / *Separate Beds*
1964 The Americanization of Emily
1966 Promise Her Anything
1966 Penelope
1967 Tobruk
1967 The Tiger Makes Out
1969 Popi
1970 The Out-of-Towners
1970 Love Story **D* F***
1971 Plaza Suite
1971 The Hospital
1972 Man of La Mancha
1974 The Crazy World of Julius Vrooder
1975 The Man in the Glass Booth
1976 WC Fields and Me
1976 Silver Streak
1979 The In-Laws
1979 Nightwing
1981 Making Love
1982 Author! Author!
1983 Romantic Comedy
1984 The Lonely Guy
1984 Teachers
1987 Outrageous Fortune
1989 See No Evil, Hear No Evil

HILLIARD, Richard L
1964 Psychomania

HILLMAN, William Byron
1971 Betta, Betta
1973 The Trail Ride
1974 The Photographer
1977 The Man from Clover Grove
1979 Thetus
1982 Double Exposure
1984 The Master

HILLYER, Lambert
(1889–) Indiana, USA.
1924 Eyes of the Forest
1924 Idle Tongues
1924 Those Who Dance
1925 The Making of O'Malley
1925 I Want My Man
1925 The Knockout
1925 The Unguarded Hour
1926 Her Second Chance
1926 Miss Nobody
1926 The War Horse
1927 Hills of Peril
1927 Chain Lightning
1928 Branded Sombrero
1928 Fleetwing
1930 Beau Bandit
1932 The Deadline
1932 One-Man Law
1932 The Fighting Fool
1932 South of the Rio Grande
1932 White Eagle
1932 Hello, Trouble
1932 The Sundown Rider
1933 The Forbidden Trail
1933 Dangerous Crossroads
1933 The California Trail
1933 Unknown Valley
1933 Police Car 17
1933 Before Midnight
1933 Master of Men
1934 The Fighting Code
1934 Once to Every Woman
1934 One Is Guilty
1934 The Guilty
1934 The Man Trailer
1934 The Defense Rests
1934 Most Precious Thing in Life
1934 Against the Law / *Urgent Call*
1934 Men of the Night
1935 Behind the Evidence
1935 In Spite of Danger
1935 Men of the Hour
1935 The Awakening of Jim Burke / *Iron Fist*
1935 Guard That Girl!
1935 Superspeed
1936 The Invisible Ray
1936 Dangerous Waters
1936 Dracula's Daughter
1936 Speed to Spare
1937 Girls Can Play
1937 Women in Prison
1938 My Old Kentucky Home
1938 All-American Sweetheart
1938 Extortion
1939 Convict's Code
1939 Should a Girl Marry?
1939 Girl from Rio

1940 The Durango Kid / *The Masked Stranger*
1941 The Pinto Kid / *All Square*
1941 North from the Lone Star
1941 The Wildcat of Tucson / *Promise Fulfilled*
1941 The Return of Daniel Boone / *The Mayor's Nest*
1941 Beyond Sacramento / *Power of Justice*
1941 Hands Across the Rockies
1941 The Son of Davy Crockett
1941 The Medico of Painted Springs / *Doctor's Alibi*
1941 King of Dodge City
1941 Prairie Stranger
1941 Thunder Over the Prairie
1941 Roaring Frontiers
1941 The Royal Mounted Patrol / *Giants A'Fire*
1942 North of the Rockies / *False Clues*
1942 The Devil's Trail / *Rogues' Gallery*
1942 Prairie Gunsmoke
1942 Vengeance of the West / *The Black Shadow*
1943 Fighting Frontier
1943 Six-Gun Gospel
1943 The Stranger from Pecos
1943 The Texas Kid
1944 Smart Guy / *You Can't Beat the Law*
1944 Partners of the Trail
1944 Law Men
1944 West of the Rio Grande
1944 Land of the Outlaws
1944 Ghost Guns
1945 Beyond the Pecos / *Beyond the Seven Seas*
1945 Flame of the West
1945 Stranger from Santa Fe
1945 South of the Rio Grande
1945 The Lost Trail
1945 Frontier Feud
1946 Border Bandits
1946 Under Arizona Skies
1946 The Gentleman from Texas
1946 Trigger Fingers
1946 Shadows on the Range
1947 Silver Range
1947 Raiders of the South
1947 Valley of Fear
1947 Trailing Danger
1947 Land of the Lawless
1947 The Law Comes to Gunsight
1947 Flashing Guns
1947 Prairie Express
1947 Gun Talk
1948 Song of the Drifter
1948 Overland Trails
1948 Oklahoma Blues
1948 Crossed Trails
1948 Partners of the Sunset
1948 Frontier Agent
1948 Range Renegades
1948 The Fighting Ranger
1948 The Sheriff of Medicine Bow
1948 Outlaw Brand
1949 Gun Runner
1949 Gun Law Justice
1949 Haunted Trail
1949 Riders of the Dusk
1949 Range Land
1949 Trail Ends

HILTON, Arthur David
1950 The Return of Jesse James
1954 Cat-Women of the Moon / *Rocket to the Moon*

HINZMAN, Bill
1989 Flesh Eater

HIRSCH, Bettina
1987 Munchies

HIRSCH, John
1987 Eye of the Spider

HISCOTT, Leslie
(1894–1968) London, England.
1927 This Marriage Business
1928 The Passing of Mr Quinn
1928 SOS
1929 Ringing the Changes
1929 The Feather
1930 At the Villa Rose
1930 The House of the Arrow
1930 The Call of the Sea
1931 The Sleeping Cardinal / *Sherlock Holmes' Fatal Hour*
1931 Brown Sugar
1931 Alibi
1931 Black Coffee
1932 A Night in Montmartre
1932 Sherlock Holmes and the Missing Rembrandt
1932 Murder at Covent Garden
1932 The Crooked Lady
1932 Once Bitten
1932 Double Dealing
1932 A Safe Proposition
1932 A Tight Corner
1932 The Face at the Window
1932 The Iron Stair
1933 The Stolen Necklace
1933 Out of the Past
1933 The Melody-Maker
1933 Yes Madam
1933 That's My Wife
1933 Cleaning Up
1933 The Stickpin
1933 Great Stuff
1933 Strike It Rich
1933 I'll Stick to You
1933 Flat No 3
1934 The Man I Want
1934 Passing Shadows
1934 Keep It Quiet
1934 Gay Love
1934 Crazy People
1935 The Big Splash
1935 The Triumph of Sherlock Holmes
1935 Annie, Leave the Room!
1935 Death on the Set
1935 Three Witnesses
1935 Inside the Room
1935 Department Store
1935 A Fire Has Been Arranged
1935 She Shall Have Music
1936 Fame
1936 The Interrupted Honeymoon
1936 Millions

1936 Ship's Concert
1936 Fine Feathers
1940 Tilly of Bloomsbury
1941 The Seventh Survivor
1942 Sabotage at Sea
1942 The Lady from Lisbon
1943 The Butler's Dilemma
1944 Welcome Mr Washington
1955 The Time of His Life
1956 Tons of Trouble

HITCHCOCK, Sir Alfred
(1899–1980) Leytonstone, London, England. American. Biographies: Le Cinéma selon Hitchcock by Francois Truffaut; Hitch by John Russell Taylor; The Life of Alfred Hitchcock: The Dark Side of the Genius by Donald Spoto.
1925 The Pleasure Garden
1926 The Mountain Eagle / *Fear o' God*
1926 The Lodger / *The Case of Jonathan Drew*
1927 Downhill / *When Boys Leave Home*
1927 Easy Virtue
1927 The Ring
1928 The Farmer's Wife
1928 Champagne
1929 The Manxman
1929 Blackmail
1929 Murder
1930 Elstree Calling **(Adrian BRUNEL, Andre CHARLOT, Jack HULBERT, Paul MURRAY)**
1930 Juno and the Paycock / *The Shame of Mary Boyle*
1931 The Skin Game
1932 Number Seventeen
1932 Rich and Strange / *East of Shanghai*
1934 The Man Who Knew Too Much
1935 The 39 Steps
1935 Strauss's Great Waltz / *Waltzes from Vienna*
1935 Sabotage / *A Woman Alone*
1936 The Secret Agent
1937 Young Innocent / *A Girl Was Young*
1938 The Lady Vanishes
1939 Jamaica Inn
1940 Rebecca **D* F****
1940 Foreign Correspondent **F***
1941 Mr and Mrs Smith
1941 Suspicion **F***
1942 Saboteur
1943 Shadow of a Doubt
1944 Lifeboat **D***
1945 Spellbound **D* F***
1946 Notorious
1947 The Paradine Case
1948 Rope
1949 Under Capricorn
1950 Stage Fright
1951 Strangers on a Train
1953 I Confess
1954 Dial M for Murder
1954 Rear Window **D***
1955 To Catch a Thief
1955 The Trouble with Harry
1956 The Man Who Knew Too Much
1956 The Wrong Man
1958 Vertigo
1959 North By Northwest
1960 Psycho **D***
1963 The Birds
1964 Marnie
1966 Torn Curtain
1972 Frenzy
1976 Family Plot

HITTLEMAN, Carl K
1955 Kentucky Rifles
1957 Gun Battle at Monterey
1957 The Buckskin Lady

HIVELY, Jack
(1910–) American.
1939 They Made Her a Spy
1939 Panama Lady
1939 The Spellbinder
1939 Three Sons
1939 Two Thoroughbreds
1940 The Saint's Double Trouble
1940 The Saint Takes Over
1940 Anne of Windy Poplars
1940 Laddie
1941 The Saint in Palm Springs
1941 They Met in Argentina **(Leslie GOODWINS)**
1941 Father Takes a Wife
1941 Four Jacks and a Jill
1942 Street of Chance
1945 Appointment in Tokyo
1948 Are You With It?
1976 Starbird and Sweet William

HOBBS, Fredric
1973 Alabama's Ghost
1973 Roseland

HOBBS, Lyndall
1987 Back to the Beach

HODGES, Michael
(1932–) Bristol, Avon, England.
1971 Get Carter
1972 Pulp
1974 The Terminal Man
1980 Flash Gordon
1985 Morons from Outer Space
1987 A Prayer for the Dying
1989 Black Rainbow
(also many TV movies)

HODI, Jeno
1988 Deadly Obsession
1989 Bloody Mary

HOERL, Arthur
1932 Big Town
1933 The Shadow Laughs
1933 Before Morning
1934 Drums o' Voodoo

HOFFMAN, David
1974 Sing Sing Thanksgiving

HOFFMAN, Herman
1951 The MGM Story
1955 The Bar Sinister / *It's a Dog's Life*
1956 The Great American Pastime
1957 Invisible Boy

HOFFMAN, Michael
1982 Privileged
1985 Restless Natives
1987 Promised Land
1988 Some Girls / *Sisters*

HOFFMAN, Peter
1986 Valentino Returns

HOFFS, Tamar Simon
1987 The Allnighter / *Cutting Loose*

HOFSISS, Jack
(1950–) Brooklyn, New York, USA.
1982 I'm Dancing As Fast As I Can

HOGAN, James P
(1891–1943) American.
1924 Unmarried Wives
1924 Black Lightning
1924 Women and Gold
1924 Capital Punishment
1925 Jimmie's Millions
1925 The Mansion of Aching Hearts
1925 SOS
1925 My Lady's Lips
1925 Perils of the Sea
1925 The Bandit's Baby
1925 Steel Preferred
1926 King of the Turf
1926 The Isle of Retribution
1926 Flaming Fury
1927 Mountains of Manhattan
1927 The Final Extra
1927 The Silent Avenger
1927 Finnegan's Ball
1928 Hearts of Men
1928 Top Sergeant Mulligan
1928 The Broken Mask
1928 Burning Bridges
1928 Code of the Air
1928 The Border Patrol
1931 The Sheriff's Secret
1931 Six Shooters in Lariat
1931 Echo of the 45
1935 Desert Gold
1936 The Accusing Finger
1936 Arizona Raiders
1937 Bulldog Drummond Escapes
1937 The Texans
1937 Scandal Street
1938 Sons of the Legion
1939 Arrest Bulldog Drummond
1939 Bulldog Drummond's Bride
1939 Bulldog Drummond's Secret Police
1939 Grand Jury Secrets
1939 1000 Dollars a Touchdown
1940 The Farmer's Daughter
1940 Texas Rangers Ride Again
1940 Queen of the Mob
1941 Ellery Queen and the Murder Ring
1941 Ellery Queen and the Perfect Crime
1941 Ellery Queen's Penthouse Mystery
1941 Power Dive
1942 Close Call for Ellery Queen
1942 Desperate Chance for Ellery Queen
1942 Enemy Agents Meet Ellery Queen / *The Lido Mystery*
1943 The Mad Ghoul
1943 The Strange Death of Adolf Hitler
1943 No Place for a Lady

HOGG, Joanna
1987 Caprice

HOLCOMB, Rod
1985 Stitches
(also many TV movies)

HOLE Jnr,, William
1955 Hell Bound
1959 Speed Crazy
1959 The Ghost of Dragstrip Hollow
1959 Four Fast Guns
1962 The Devil's Hand
1962 The Continental Twist

HOLLAND, Agnieszka
(1948–) Warsaw, Poland.
1979 Provincial Actors
1980 Fever
1981 Woman on Her Own
1985 Angry Harvest
1988 To Kill a Priest

HOLLAND, Savage Steve
1985 Better Off Dead
1986 Summer Vacation / *One Crazy Summer*
1989 How I Got into College

HOLLAND, Tom
1985 Fright Night
1987 Fatal Beauty
1988 Child's Play

HOLLANDER, Eli
1982 Out

HOLLEB, Allen
1974 Candy Stripe Nurses
1985 School Spirit

HOLMES, Ben
1934 Lightning Strikes Twice
1936 We're on the Jury
1936 The Plot Thickens
1936 The Farmer in the Dell
1937 There Goes My Girl
1937 Too Many Wives
1938 Maid's Night Out
1938 The Saint in New York
1938 I'm for the City
1938 Little Orphan Annie
1943 Petticoat Larceny
1943 Coastal Command

HOLT, Seth (James Holt)
(1923–1971) Palestine.
1958 Nowhere to Go
1961 Taste of Fear / *Scream of Fear*
1962 Station Six Sahara
1965 The Nanny
1967 Danger Route
1971 Blood from the Mummy's Tomb

HOLZBERG, Roger
1988 Midnight Crossing

HOLZMAN, Allan
1982 Forbidden World
1985 Out of Control
1985 Grunt! The Wrestling Movie
1987 Retaliator / *Programmed to Kill*

HONDA, Inoshiro (Ishiro Honda)
1954 Godzilla, King of the Monsters **(Terry O MORSE)**
1955 Half Human
1957 Rodan
1958 Varan the Unbelievable
1959 The Mysterians
1959 The H-Man
1960 Battle in Outer Space
1962 Gorath
1962 Mothra
1963 King Kong Versus Godzilla
1964 Godzilla Versus the Thing / *Godzilla Versus Mothra*
1964 Frankenstein Conquers the World
1964 Attack of the Mushroom People
1965 Dagora, the Space Monster
1965 Atragon
1966 Ghidrah, the Three-Headed Monster
1968 King Kong Escapes
1969 Destroy All Monsters
1969 Godzilla's Revenge
1970 Latitude Zero
1971 Yog, Monster from Space

HONG, Elliott
1979 Kill the Golden Goose
1982 They Call Me Bruce! / *A Fistful of Chopsticks*
1983 Hot and Deadly

HONTHANER, Ron
1974 The House on Skull Mountain

HOOK, Harry
1987 The Kitchen Toto
1989 Lord of the Flies

HOOL, Lance
(1948–) Mexico City, Mexico.
1984 Missing in Action II: The Beginning
1987 Desert Warrior
1990 Dark Rain

HOOPER, Tobe
(1943–) Houston, Texas, USA.
1974 The Texas Chainsaw Massacre
1976 Eaten Alive / *Death Trap*
1981 The Funhouse
1982 Poltergeist
1985 Lifeforce
1986 Invaders from Mars
1986 The Texas Chainsaw Massacre II
1988 Entangled

HOPKINS, John
1986 Torment **(Samson ASLANIAN)**

HOPKINS, Steven
1987 Dangerous Game

HOPPER, Dennis
(1936–) Dodge City, Kansas, USA.
1969 Easy Rider
1971 The Last Movie
1982 Out of the Blue
1988 Colors
1989 Backtrack

HOPPER, E Mason
(1885–1966) American.
1924 Janice Meredith / *The Beautiful Rebel*
1925 The Crowded Hour
1929 The Carnation Kid
1929 Square Shoulders
1930 Their Own Desire
1930 Temptation
1930 Wise Girls
1932 Her Mad Night
1932 Shop Angel
1932 Midnight Morals
1932 Alias Mary Smith
1932 No Living Witness
1932 Malay Nights
1933 Sister to Judas
1933 One Year Later
1934 Curtain at Eight
1935 Hong Kong Nights

HOPPER, Jerry
(1907–) Guthrie, Oklahoma, USA.
1952 The Atomic City
1952 Hurricane Smith
1953 Pony Express
1954 Alaska Seas
1954 Secret of the Incas
1954 Naked Alibi
1955 Smoke Signal
1955 The Private War of Major Benson
1955 One Desire
1956 The Square Jungle
1956 Never Say Goodbye
1956 Everything But the Truth
1956 The Sharkfighters
1956 Toy Tiger
1961 The Missouri Traveller
1961 Blueprint for Murder
1970 Madron
(also many TV shorts)

HORIAN, Richard
1987 Student Confidential / *The Counsellor*

HORN, Leonard
(1926–1975) American.
1968 Rogue's Gallery
1970 The Magic Garden of Stanley Sweetheart
1971 Corky

HORNE, James W
(1880–1942) American.
1927 College
1928 The Big Hop
1935 Bonnie Scotland
1936 The Bohemian Girl **(Charles ROGERS)**
1937 Way Out West
1937 All Over Town
(also many series)

HORNER, Harry
(1910–) Czechoslovakian.
1952 Red Planet Mars
1952 Beware, My Lovely

1953 Vicki
1954 New Faces
1955 A Life in the Balance
1956 Man from Del Rio
1956 The Wild Party

HOROWITZ, Irving
1974 Slapshots

HOSKINS, Bob
(1942–) London, England.
1988 The Raggedy Rawney

HOUCK Jnr., Joy N
1975 Night of the Strangler
1976 The Creature from the Black Lake

HOUGH, John
(1941–) London, England.
1970 Wolfhead
1971 Eyewitness / *Sudden Terror*
1971 The Practice
1972 Twins of Evil
1972 Treasure Island
1974 The Legend of Hell House
1974 Dirty Mary, Crazy Larry
1974 Escape to Witch Mountain
1978 Return from Witch Mountain
1978 Brass Target
1980 The Watcher in the Woods **(Vincent McEVEETY)**
1982 The Incubus
1983 Triumphs of a Man Called Horse
1986 Biggles: Twice Upon a Time
1987 American Gothic
1988 A Hazard of Hearts
1988 Howling IV: The Original Nightmare
1989 Say Anything

HOUGH, R L
1928 Wild West Romance
1928 Girl Shy Cowboy
1932 The Silent Witness **(Marcel VARNEL)**

HOUSTON, Robert
1980 Shogun Assassin
1984 Bad Manners / *Growing Pains*
1989 Trust Me

HOVDE, Ellen
1985 Enormous Changes at the Last Minute **(Mirra BANKS)**

HOWARD, Cy
(1915–) Milwaukee, Wisconsin, USA.
1969 Lovers and Other Strangers
1972 Every Little Crook and Nanny

HOWARD, David
(1896–1941) American.
1932 The Rainbow Trail
1932 Mystery Ranch
1932 The Golden West
1933 Smoke Lightning
1934 The Marines Are Coming
1934 Crimson Romance
1934 In Old Santa Fe
1935 Whispering Smith Speaks
1935 Hard Rock Harrigan
1935 Thunder Mountain
1935 O'Malley of the Mounted
1936 Border Patrol
1936 The Mine with the Iron Door
1936 Daniel Boone
1936 Conflict
1937 Park Avenue Logger
1938 The Stadium Murders
1938 Gun Law
1938 Painted Desert
1938 Border G-Man
1938 Lawless Valley
1938 Hollywood Stadium Mystery
1939 The Renegade Ranger
1939 Arizona Legion
1939 The Fighting Gringo
1939 The Marshal of Mesa City
1939 Timber Stampede
1939 Trouble in Sundown
1939 The Rookie Cop
1940 Bullet Code
1940 Legion of the Lawless
1940 Prairie Law
1940 Triple Justice
1941 Dude Cowboy
1942 Six Gun Gold

HOWARD, James
1974 Welcome Home Johnny

HOWARD, Leslie (Leslie Stainer)
(1890–) London, England.
Autobiography: Trivial Fond Records.
1938 Pygmalion **(Anthony ASQUITH)** F*
1941 Pimpernel Smith / *Mister V*
1942 The First of the Few / *Spitfire*
1943 The Gentle Sex **(Maurice ELVEY)**

HOWARD, Noël
(1920–1987) Paris, France.
1966 Marco the Magnificent **(Denys DE LA PATELLIERE)**
1975 Don't You Hear the Dogs Bark? **(François REICHENBACH)**

HOWARD, Ron
(1954–) Duncan, Oklahoma, USA.
1978 Grand Theft Auto
1982 Night Shift
1984 Splash
1985 Cocoon
1986 Gung Ho
1988 Willow
1989 Parenthood
(also TV movies)

HOWARD, William K (William Kerrigan Howard)
(1899–1954) St Mary's, Ohio, USA.
1924 The Border Legion
1924 East of Broadway
1925 The Thundering Herd
1925 Code of the West
1925 The Light of Western Stars
1926 Red Rice
1926 Bachelor Brides
1926 Volcano
1926 Gigolo
1927 The Main Event
1927 White Gold
1928 A Ship Comes In / *His Country*

1928 The River Pirate
1928 Love, Live and Laugh
1928 The Valiant
1928 Christina
1930 Good Intentions
1930 Scotland Yard / *'Detective Clive' Bart*
1931 Don't Bet on Women
1931 Transatlantic
1931 Surrender
1932 The First Year
1932 Sherlock Holmes
1932 The Trial of Vivienne Ware
1933 The Power and the Glory
1934 The Cat and the Fiddle
1934 Evelyn Prentice
1934 This Side of Heaven
1935 Mary Burns, Fugitive
1935 Rendezvous
1935 Vanessa, Her Love Story
1936 The Princess Comes Across
1936 Fire Over England
1937 Murder on Diamond Row / *The Squeaker*
1937 Over the Moon **(Thornton FREELAND)**
1939 Back Door to Heaven
1940 Money and the Woman
1941 Bullets for O'Hara
1942 Klondike Fury
1943 Johnny Come Lately / *Johnny Vagabond*
1944 When the Lights Go On Again
1946 A Guy Could Change

HOWE, James Wong (Wong Tung Jim)
(1899–1976) China.
1953 The World of Dong Kingman
1954 Go Man, Go
1958 Invisible Avenger **(John SLEDGE)**

HU, King (Hu Chin Ch'uan)
(1931–) Peking, China.
1963 Eternal Love
1964 Sons of the Good Earth
1966 Come Drink with Me
1967 Dragon Gate Inn
1968 A Touch of Zen
1970 Four Moods
1973 The Fate of Lee Kahn
1974 The Valiant Ones
1977 Raining on the Mountain
1978 Legend of the Mountain
1981 The Rejuvenator
1983 All the King's Men
1983 The Wheel of Life **(Pai CHING-JUI, Li HSING)**
1984 The World's Best Men

HUBBARD, Lucien
(1888–1971) American.
1927 Rose Marie
1929 The Mysterious Island
1936 Sworn Enemy **(Edwin L MARIN)**
1936 Moonlight Murder **(Edwin L MARIN)**
1936 Speed **(Edwin L MARIN)**
1936 All American Chump **(Edwin L MARIN)**

HUCKABEE, Tom
(1955–) Fort Worth, Texas, USA.
1983 Taking Tiger Mountain **(Ken SMITH)**

HUCKERT, John W
1982 Ernie and Rose
1983 The Passing

HUDSON, Gary
1986 Thunder Run

HUDSON, Hugh
(1936–) British.
1981 Chariots of Fire **D* F****
1984 Greystoke: The Legend of Tarzan, Lord of the Apes
1985 Revolution
1988 Reversal of Fortune
1989 Lost Angels / *Wall Time*

HUGGINS, Roy
(1914–) Litelle, Washington, USA.
1952 Hangman's Knot

HUGHES, Howard
(1905–1976) Houston, Texas, USA. Biographies: Howard Hughes by John Keats; Bashful Millionaire, the Story of Howard Hughes by Albert B Gerber.
1928 The Mating Call
1930 Hell's Angels
1943 The Outlaw **(Howard HAWKS)**
1950 Vendetta
1957 Jet Pilot **(Joseph Von STERNBERG)**

HUGHES, John
1984 Sixteen Candles
1985 The Breakfast Club
1985 Weird Science
1986 Ferris Bueller's Day Off
1987 Plains, Trains and Automobiles
1988 She's Having a Baby
1989 Uncle Buck

HUGHES, Ken
(1922–1987) Liverpool, England.
1952 Wide Boy
1954 Heatwave / *The House Across the Lake*
1954 Black 13
1955 The Brain Machine
1955 The Case of the Little Red Monkey
1955 Confession / *The Deadliest Sin*
1955 The Atomic Man / *Timeslip*
1956 Joe Macbeth
1957 Wicked As They Come / *Portrait in Smoke*
1957 The Long Haul
1960 Jazz Boat
1960 In the Nick
1960 The Trials of Oscar Wilde / *The Man with the Green Carnation*
1961 Play It Cooler
1963 The Small World of Sammy Lee
1964 Of Human Bondage **(Henry HATHAWAY)**
1966 Drop Dead Darling / *Arrivederci Baby*
1967 Casino Royale **(Val GUEST, John HUSTON, Joseph McGRATH, Robert PARRISH)**
1968 Chitty, Chitty, Bang, Bang
1970 Cromwell
1974 The Internecine Project
1975 Alfie, Darling

1978 Sextette
1981 Night School / *Terror Eyes*
(also many documentaries)

HUGHES, Robert C
1986 Hunter's Blood

HUI, Ann
(1947–) Manchuria, China.
1979 The Secret
1980 The Spooky Bunch
1981 The Story of Woo Viet
1983 Boat People
1984 Love in a Fallen City
1987 The Book and the Sword

HULBERT, Jack
(1892–1978) Ely, Cambridgeshire, England.
Autobiography: The Little Woman's Always Right.
1930 Elstree Calling **(Adrian BRUNEL, André CHARLOT, Alfred HITCHCOCK, John MURRAY)**
1933 Falling for You **(Robert STEVENSON)**
1936 Jack of All Trades **(Robert STEVENSON)**

HULETTE, Donald
(1937–) Los Angeles, California, USA.
1978 Breaker, Breaker
1979 A Great Ride
1982 Tennessee Stallion
1986 The Eagle
1988 S.W.A.T.

HULL, Norman
1989 Ladder of Swords

HUMBERSTONE, H Bruce (Lucky Humberstone)
(1903–1984) American.
1932 Strangers of the Evening
1932 The Crooked Circle
1932 If I Had a Million **(James CRUZE, Ernst LUBITSCH, Norman Z McLEOD, Stephen ROBERTS, William A SEITER, Norman TAUROG)**
1933 King of the Jungle **(Max MARCIN)**
1934 The Merry Wives of Reno
1934 Goodbye Love
1934 The Dragon Murder Case
1935 Ladies Love Danger
1935 Silk Hat Kid
1935 Three Live Ghosts
1936 Charlie Chan at the Race Track
1936 Charlie Chan at the Opera
1937 Charlie Chan at the Olympics
1937 Checkers
1938 In Old Chicago **(Henry KING)**
1938 Rascals
1938 Time Out for Murder
1938 Charlie Chan in Honolulu
1938 While New York Sleeps
1939 Pack Up Your Troubles / *We're in the Army Now*
1939 Pardon Our Nerve
1940 Lucky Cisco Kid
1940 The Quarterback
1941 Tall, Dark and Handsome
1941 Sun Valley Serenade
1941 I Wake Up Screaming / *Hot Spot*
1942 To the Shores of Tripoli
1942 Iceland / *Katina*
1943 Hello, Frisco, Hello
1944 Pin-Up Girl
1945 Wonder Man
1945 Within These Walls
1946 Three Little Girls in Blue
1947 The Homestretch
1948 Fury at Furnace Creek
1950 South Sea Sinner / *East of Java*
1951 Happy Go Lovely
1952 She's Working Her Way Through College
1953 The Desert Song
1955 Ten Wanted Men
1955 The Purple Mask
1957 Tarzan and the Lost Safari
1958 Tarzan's Fight for Life
1962 Madison Avenue

HUNSICKER, Jackson
1987 The Frog Prince

HUNT, Ed
1985 King of the Streets
1988 The Brain

HUNT, Peter
(1928–1970) London, England.
1969 On Her Majesty's Secret Service
1974 Gold
1976 Shout at the Devil
1977 Gulliver's Travels
1981 Death Hunt
1985 Wild Geese II
1986 Hyper Sapien: People from Another Star
1987 Assassination / *The President's Wife*
1988 Twisted Nightmare

HUNT, Peter H
(1938–) Pasadena, California, USA.
1972 1776
1978 Bully
(also many TV movies)

HUNTER, T Hayes
(1881–1944) American.
1919 Desert Gold
1920 Earthbound
1929 The Triumph of the Scarlet Pimpernel
1929 The Silver King
1932 The Frightened Lady
1933 Sally Bishop
1933 The Ghoul

HUNTER, Tim
1982 Tex
1985 Sylvester
1986 River's Edge
1989 Paint It Black

HUNTINGTON, Lawrence
(1900–1968) British.
1929 After Many Years
1934 Romance in Rhythm
1936 Full Speed Ahead

1936 Café Mascot
1936 Strange Cargo
1936 Two on a Doorstep
1936 Bad Boy
1937 Screen Struck
1937 Passage to London
1937 The Bank Messenger Mystery
1938 Dial 999
1938 Twin Faces
1941 This Man Is Dangerous / *The Patient Vanishes*
1941 The Tower of Terror
1941 Women Aren't Angels
1942 Suspected Person
1943 Warn That Man
1945 Night Boat to Dublin
1946 Wanted for Murder
1947 When the Bough Breaks
1947 The Upturned Glass
1948 Mr Perrin and Mr Traill
1949 Man on the Run
1951 The Franchise Affair
1952 There Was a Young Lady
1955 Contraband Spain
1959 Deadly Record
1962 Stranglehold
1962 The Fur Collar
1962 Death Drums Along the River
1966 The Vulture

HUPPERT, Caroline
1985 Sincerely Charlotte

HURLEY, Maury
1972 It Ain't Easy

HURST, Brian Desmond
(1900–1986) Republic of Ireland.
1934 Irish Hearts / *Norah O'Neale*
1934 The Tell-Tale Heart
1935 Riders to the Sea
1936 Sensation
1936 The Tenth Man
1937 Glamorous Night
1938 Prison Without Bars
1939 The Lion Has Wings **(Adrian BRUNEL, Michael POWELL)**
1939 On the Night of the Fire / *The Fugitive*
1941 Dangerous Moonlight / *Suicide Squadron*
1942 Alibi
1943 The Hundred Pound Window
1946 Hungry Hill
1947 The Mark of Cain
1949 Trottie True / *The Gay Lady*
1951 Scrooge
1953 The Malta Story
1955 Simba
1956 The Black Tent
1957 Dangerous Exile
1958 Behind the Mask
1960 His and Hers
1962 The Playboy of the Western World

HURWITZ, Harry
Pseudonym: Harry Tampa.
1971 The Projectionist
1971 The Comeback Trail
1972 Richard **(Lorees YERBY)**
1972 Chaplinesque, My Life and Hard Times
1978 Fairy Tales
1979 Nocturna
1982 Safari 3000
1985 The Rosebud Beach Hotel
1987 That's Adequate

HUSSEIN, Waris
(1938–) Lucknow, India.
1969 A Touch of Love / *Thank You All Very Much*
1970 Quackser Fortune Has a Cousin in the Bronx
1971 Melody / *S.W.A.L.K.*
1971 The Possession of Joe Delaney
1972 Henry VIII and His Six Wives
(also many TV movies)

HUSTON, Danny
1988 Mr North

HUSTON, Jimmy
1977 River Death
1978 Dark Sunday
1978 Buckstone County Prison
1978 Seabo
1981 Final Exam
1984 The Sleuth Slayer
1988 My Best Friend Is a Vampire / *I Was a Teenage Vampire*

HUSTON, John (John Marcellus Huston)
(1906–1987) Nevada, Missouri, USA.
Autobiography: An Open Book.
1941 The Maltese Falcon **F***
1942 In This Our Life
1942 Across the Pacific
1948 The Treasure of the Sierra Madre **D** F***
1948 Key Largo
1949 We Were Strangers
1950 The Asphalt Jungle **D***
1951 The Red Badge of Courage
1952 The African Queen **D***
1952 Moulin Rouge **D* F***
1954 Beat the Devil
1956 Moby Dick
1957 Heaven Knows, Mr Allison
1958 The Barbarian and the Geisha
1958 The Roots of Heaven
1960 The Unforgiven
1961 The Misfits
1963 Freud
1963 The List of Adrian Messenger
1964 Night of the Iguana
1966 The Bible..In the Beginning
1967 Reflections in a Golden Eye
1967 Casino Royale **(Val GUEST, Ken HUGHES, Joseph McGRATH, Robert PARRISH)**
1969 A Walk with Love and Death
1969 Sinful Davey
1970 The Kremlin Letter
1972 Fat City
1973 The Life and Times of Judge Roy Bean
1973 The Mackintosh Man
1975 The Man Who Would Be King
1979 Wise Blood
1981 Phobia
1981 Victory
1982 Annie

1984 Under the Volcano
1985 Prizzi's Honor **D* F***
1987 The Dead

HUTCHINSON, Charles
1931 Women Men Marry
1931 Private Scandal
1932 Bachelor Mother
1932 Out of Singapore
1933 Found Alive
1934 House of Danger
1934 Pals of the Prairie
1935 Circus Shadows
1935 Judgement Book
1935 On Probation
1935 Riddle Ranch
1936 Born to Fight
1936 Desert Guns
1936 Night Cargo
1936 Phantom Patrol
1938 Topa Topa **(Vin MOORE)**
1940 Killers of the Wild **(Vin MOORE)**

HUTH, Harold
(1892–1967) British.
1939 Hell's Cargo
1940 East of Piccadilly / *The Strangler*
1948 My Sister and I
1948 Look Before You Love
1948 Night Beat
1956 The Hostage

HUTTON, Brian G
(1935–) New York, New York, USA.
1965 Wild Seed / *Fargo*
1966 The Pad and How to Use It
1968 Sol Madrid / *The Heroin Gang*
1969 Where Eagles Dare
1970 Kelly's Heroes
1972 X,Y and Z / *Zee and Co*
1973 Night Watch
1980 The First Deadly Sin
1983 High Road to China
1989 The Pushovers

HUTTON, Robert (Robert Bruce Winne)
(1920–) Kingston, New York, USA.
1962 The Slime People

HUYCK, Willard
1975 Messiah of Evil
1979 French Postcards
1984 Best Defense
1986 Howard the Duck

HYAMS, Nessa
1987 Leader of the Band

HYAMS, Peter
(1943–) New York, New York, USA.
1973 Busting
1974 Our Time
1976 Peeper
1978 Capricorn One
1979 Hanover Street
1981 Outland
1983 The Star Chamber
1984 2010
1986 Running Scared
1988 Presidio

ICHASO, Leon
1979 El Super **(Orlando JIMENEZ-LEAL)**
1985 Crossover Dreams

ICHIKAWA, Kon
(1915–) Uji Yamada, Ise, Mie Prefecture.
1946 A Girl at Dojo Temple
1948 A Flower Blooms
1948 365 Nights
1949 Design of a Human Being / *Human Patterns*
1949 Endless Passion / *Passion Without End*
1950 Sanshiro of Ginza
1950 The Hot Marshland / *Heat and Mud*
1950 Pursuit at Dawn
1951 Nightshade Flower
1951 The Lover / *The Sweetheart*
1951 The Man Without a Nationality
1951 Stolen Love
1951 River Solo Flows
1951 Wedding March
1952 Mr Lucky
1952 The Young Generation / *Young People*
1952 The Woman Who Touched the Legs
1952 This Way, That Way
1953 Mr Pu
1953 The Blue Revolution
1953 The Youth of Heiji Zenigata
1953 The Lover
1954 All of Myself
1954 A Billionaire
1954 Twelve Chapters on Women
1955 Ghost Story of Youth
1955 The Heart
1956 Harp of Burma
1956 Punishment Room
1956 Bridge of Japan
1957 The Crowded Streetcar
1957 The Hole / *The Pit*
1957 The Men of Tohoku
1958 Conflagration
1958 Money and Three Bad Men
1959 Goodbye, Good Day
1959 Odd Obsession / *The Key*
1959 A Woman's Testament Part II: Women Who Sell Things at High Prices **(Yasuzo MASAMURA, Kozaburo YOSHIMURA)**
1959 Fires on the Plain
1959 Police and Small Gangsters
1960 A Ginza Veteran
1960 Bonchi
1960 Her Brother
1961 Ten Dark Women
1962 The Sin / *The Outcast* / *The Broken Commandment*
1962 Being Two Isn't Easy
1963 An Actor's Revenge / *The Revenge of Yukinojo*
1963 Alone on the Pacific / *My Enemy the Sea*
1964 Money Talks / *The Money Dance*
1971 To Love Again
1975 I Am a Cat
1976 Between Wife and Lady / *Between Women and Wives* **(Shiro TOYODA)**
1976 The Inugami Family
1977 The Devil's Bouncing Ball Song / *A Rhyme of Vengeance*

1978 The Devil's Island / *Island of Horror*
1978 Queen Bee
1980 The Phoenix
1980 The Ancient City of Koto
1982 Lonely Hearts / *Happiness*
1983 The Makioka Sisters
1983 Fine Snow
1985 The Harp of Burma

IHNAT, Steve
(1934–1972) Czechoslovakia.
1971 The Honkers

IMAMURA, Shohei
(1926–) Tokyo, Japan.
1958 The Stolen Desires
1958 Lights of Night / *Nishi Ginza Station*
1958 The Endless Desire
1959 My Second Brother
1961 Pigs and Battleships
1963 The Insect Woman
1964 Intentions of Murder / *Unholy Desire*
1966 The Pornographer
1967 A Man Vanishes
1968 The Profound Desire of the Gods
1979 Vengeance Is Mine
1981 Eijanaika
1983 The Ballad of Narayama
1987 Lord of the Bordello

IMBERMAN, Shmuel
1988 I Don't Give a Damn

INCE, Ralph
(1882–1937) Boston, Massachusetts, USA.
1924 The Moral Sinner
1924 The House of Youth
1924 The Uninvited Guest
1924 Dynamite Smith
1924 The Chorus Lady
1925 Alias Mary Flynn
1925 Playing with Susie
1925 Smooth As Satin
1925 Lady Robin Hood
1926 Bigger Than Barnum's
1926 Breed of the Sea
1926 The Lone Wolf Returns
1926 The Sea Wolf
1926 The Better Way
1926 Yellow Fingers
1927 Home Struck
1927 Wandering Girls
1927 Molders of Men
1927 Not for Publication
1927 Shanghaied
1928 Hit of the Show
1928 South Sea Love
1928 Coney Island
1928 Chicago After Midnight
1929 Danger Street
1929 The Singapore Mutiny / *The Wreck of the Singapore*
1929 Hurricane
1929 Hardboiled / *A Real Girl*
1932 Men of America / *Great Decision*
1933 Lucky Devils
1933 Flaming Gold
1934 No Escape
1934 What's in a Name?
1934 A Glimpse of Paradise
1935 Murder at Monte Cristo
1935 Mr What's His Name
1935 Unlimited
1935 Black Mask
1935 Blue Smoke
1935 Rolling House
1936 Jury's Evidence
1936 It's You I Want
1936 Jail Break
1936 Twelve Good Men
1936 Fair Exchange
1936 Hail and Farewell
1937 The Vulture
1937 Side Street Angel
1937 It's Not Cricket
1937 The Perfect Crime
1937 The Man Who Made Diamonds
(also many shorts)

INGRAHAM, Lloyd
(1885–1956) American.
1923 The Beauty Prize
1927 Jesse James
1928 Kit Carson **(Alfred WERKER)**
1928 Pioneer Scout
1928 The Sunset Legion **(Alfred WERKER)**
1930 Take the Heir

INGRAM, Rex (Reginald Ingram Montgomery Hitchcock)
(1893–1950) Dublin, Republic of Ireland.
Biography: Rex Ingram by Liam O'Leary.
1921 The Four Horsemen of the Apocalypse
1921 The Conquering Power
1921 Turn to the Right
1922 The Prisoner of Zenda
1922 Trifling Women
1923 Where the Pavement Ends
1923 Scaramouche
1924 The Arab
1925 Mare Nostrum
1926 The Magician
1927 The Garden of Allah
1929 The Three Passions
1931 Baroud
1933 Love in Morocco

INGRIA, Robert
1987 Hammerhead Jones

INGSTER, Boris
(1913–1978) American.
1940 Stranger on the Third Floor
1947 The Judge Steps Out / *Indian Summer*
1950 South Side 1–1000

INGVORDSEN, J Christian
1988 Hangmen
1988 Covert Action
1988 Search and Destroy
1988 Shock Troop
1988 Mob War

IRELAND, John
(1914–) Vancouver, British Columbia, Canada.
1953 Outlaw Territory **(Lee GARMES)**

IRVIN, John
(1940–) British.
1980 The Dogs of War
1981 Ghost Story
1983 Champions
1985 Turtle Diary
1986 Raw Deal
1987 Hamburger Hill
1989 Signs of Conquest
1989 Next of Kin
(also many TV movies)

IRVIN, Sam
1988 Stiff

IRVING, David
1982 Goodbye Cruel World
1987 Rumpelstiltskin
1987 Sleeping Beauty
1987 The Emperor's New Clothes
1987 Young Robinson Crusoe
1988 B.U.D. / *C.H.U.D. II*

IRWIN, Jack
1931 Lightnin' Smith's Return / *Valley of the Badmen*
1931 White Renegade / *The Empire Builders*

ISAAC, James
1989 Horror Show

ISASI, Anthony
1966 That Man in Istanbul
1973 Summertime Killer

ISHII, Sogo
(1957–) Hakata, Fukuoka, Japan.
1978 Panic in High School
1980 Crazy Thunder Road
1981 Shuffle
1982 Burst City
1983 Revenge of Asia
1984 The Crazy Family

ISRAEL, Neil
1976 Tunnelvision **(Brad SWIRNOFF)**
1979 Americathon
1984 Bachelor Party
1985 Moving Violations

ITAMI, Juzo
(1933–) Kyoto, Japan.
1984 The Funeral
1986 Dandelion

IVORY, James
(1928–) Berkeley, California, USA.
1963 The Householder
1966 Shakespeare Wallah
1969 The Guru
1970 Bombay Talkie
1972 Savages
1973 Mahatma and the Mad Boy
1975 The Wild Party
1976 Sweet Sounds
1977 Roseland
1979 Hullabaloo Over Georgia and Bonnie's Pictures
1979 The Europeans
1980 Jane Austen in Manhattan
1981 Quartet
1983 Heat and Dust
1984 The Bostonians
1986 A Room with a View **D* F***
1987 Maurice
1989 Slaves of New York
(also documentaries and TV movies)

JACCARD, Jacques
1930 The Cheyenne Kid
1936 Señor Jim
1937 Phantom of Santa Fe

JACK, Del
1969 A Session with the Committee

JACKSON, Donald G
1988 Hell Comes to Frogtown **(R J KIZER)**
1989 Rollerblade III

JACKSON, Horace
1974 Tough

JACKSON, Lewis
1980 You Better Watch Out / *Christmas Evil*

JACKSON, Pat
(1916–) London, England.
1944 Western Approaches / *The Raider*
1949 Shadow on the Wall
1951 Encore **(Harold FRENCH, Anthony PELISSIER)**
1951 White Corridors
1952 Something Money Can't Buy
1956 The Feminine Touch / *The Gentle Touch*
1957 The Birthday Present
1958 Virgin Island
1960 Snowball
1961 What a Carve Up! / *No Place Like Homicide*
1962 Seven Keys
1962 Don't Talk to Strange Men
1964 Seventy Deadly Pills
1969 On the Run
(also many war documentaries)

JACKSON, Peter
1989 Meet the Feebles
1989 Brain Dead

JACKSON, Richard
1973 The Big Bustout

JACOBSON, Arthur
1935 Home on the Range

JACOBY, Irving
1968 Snow Treasure

JACOBY, Joseph
(1942–) Brooklyn, New York, USA.
1970 Shame, Shame, Everybody Knows Her Name
1973 Hurry Up or I'll Be Thirty
1978 The Great Bank Hoax / *Shenanigans*

JACOVES, Felix
(1907–) American.
1948 Embraceable You

1949 Homicide

JAECKIN, Just
1974 Emmanuelle
1975 The Story of O
1979 The French Woman / *Madame Claude*
1980 The Last Romantic Lover
1980 Girls
1980 Collections Privées **(Walerian BOROWCZYK, Shuji TERAYAMA)**
1982 Lady Chatterley's Lover
1984 The Perils of Gwendoline

JAFFE, Stanley
(1940–) New Rochelle, New York, USA.
1983 Without a Trace

JAFFE, Steve Charles
1982 Scarab

JAGLOM, Henry
(1941–) London, England.
1971 A Safe Place
1977 Tracks
1978 Sitting Ducks
1981 National Lampoon's Movie Madness **(Bob GIRALDI)**
1983 Can She Bake a Cherry Pie?
1985 Always
1987 Is It You?
1988 Someone to Love

JAKOBS, Harry
1987 Rebel High

JAMES, Alan
1932 Come On, Tarzan
1932 Fargo Express
1932 Tombstone Canyon
1933 Gun Justice
1933 King of the Arena
1933 The Lone Avenger
1933 Phantom Thunderbolt
1933 The Strawberry Roan
1933 Trail Drive
1934 Honour on the Range
1934 Smoking Guns
1934 Wheels of Destiny
1934 When a Man Sees Red
1935 Valley of Wanted Men
1935 Men of Action
1935 Arizona Trails
1936 Lucky Terror
1936 Swifty
1938 Call of the Rockies
1938 Two Gun Justice
1938 West of Rainbow's End
1938 Land of Fighting Men
1939 Trigger Smith
1943 The Law Rides Again
1943 Wild Horse Stampede
(also many serials)

JAMES, Rian
1933 Best of Enemies

JAMESON, Jerry
1971 Brute Corps
1972 The Dirt Gang
1974 The Bat People
1977 Airport '77
1980 Raise the Titanic
1987 Capitol Hell
(also many TV movies)

JANCSO, Miklos *
(1921–) Vac, Hungary.
1958 The Bells Have Gone to Rome
1960 Three Stars
1964 My Way Home
1965 The Round-Up
1967 The Red and the White
1967 Silence and Cry
1969 The Confrontation
1969 Winter Wind / *Sirokko*
1972 Red Psalm
1976 Private Vices, Public Virtue
1977 Masterwork
1978 Hungarian Rhapsody
1981 Heart of a Tyrant
1986 Dawn
(also many shorts)

JANKEL, Annabel
1988 D.O.A. **(Rocky MORTON)**

JARMAN, Derek
(1943–) Northwood, London, England.
Autobiography: Dancing Ledge.
1977 Sebastiane **(Paul HUMFRESS)**
1978 Jubilee
1980 The Tempest
1981 In the Shadow of the Sun
1981 The Angelic Conversation
1986 Caravaggio
1987 Aria **(Robert ALTMAN, Bruce BERESFORD, Bill BRYDEN, Jean-Luc GODARD, Franc RODDAM, Nicolas ROEG, Ken RUSSELL, Charles STURRIDGE, Julien TEMPLE)**
1987 The Last of England
1989 The War Requiem

JARMUSCH, Jim
(1953–) American.
1982 Permanent Vacation
1984 Stranger Than Paradise
1986 Down By Law

JARROTT, Charles
(1927–) London, England.
1969 Anne of a Thousand Days **F***
1971 Mary, Queen of Scots
1972 Lost Horizon
1974 The Dove
1977 Escape from the Dark / *The Littlest Horse Thieves*
1977 The Other Side of Midnight
1980 The Last Flight of Noah's Ark
1981 Condorman
1981 The Amateur
1985 The Boy in Blue
1987 Poor Little Rich Girl

JASON, Leigh (L. Jacobson)
(1904–1979) American.
1928 The Price of Fear
1929 The Body Punch

1929 Wolves of the City
1929 Eyes of the Underworld
1929 The Tip Off / *Underworld Love*
1933 High Gear / *The Big Thrill*
1936 Love on a Bet
1936 The Bride Walks Out
1936 That Girl from Paris
1937 Wise Girl
1938 The Mad Miss Manton
1939 The Flying Irishman
1939 Career
1941 Model Wife
1941 Three Girls About Town
1941 Lady for a Night
1943 Dangerous Blondes
1944 Nine Girls
1944 Carolina Blues
1946 Meet Me on Broadway
1947 Lost Honeymoon
1947 Out of the Blue
1947 Man from Texas
1952 Okinawa

JASON, Will
(1899–1970) American.
1944 The Soul of a Monster
1945 Eve Knew Her Apples
1945 Tahiti Nights
1945 Ten Cents a Dance
1946 Blonde Alibi
1946 The Dark Horse
1946 Ideal Girl
1946 Slightly Scandalous
1947 Sarge Goes to College
1948 Campus Sleuth
1948 Music Man
1948 Rusty Leads the Way
1951 Chain of Circumstance
1951 Disc Jockey
1952 Thief of Damascus

JEFFRIES, Lionel
(1926–) London, England.
1970 The Railway Children
1972 The Amazing Mr Blunden
1973 Baxter!
1978 The Water Babies
1979 Wombling Free

JENKINS, Michael
1986 Rebel

JESSOP, Clytie
1987 Emma's War

JEWISON, Norman
(1926–) Toronto, Canada.
1962 40 Pounds of Trouble
1963 The Thrill of It All
1964 Send Me No Flowers
1965 The Art of Love
1965 The Cincinnati Kid
1966 The Russians Are Coming, the Russians Are Coming **F***
1967 In the Heat of the Night **D* F****
1968 The Thomas Crown Affair
1969 Gaily, Gaily / *Chicago, Chicago*
1971 Fiddler on the Roof **D* F***
1973 Jesus Christ Superstar
1975 Rollerball
1978 F.I.S.T.
1979 ...And Justice for All
1982 Best Friends
1984 A Soldier's Story **F***
1985 Agnes of God
1988 Moonstruck **D* F***
1989 In Country

JIRAS, Robert
1983 I Am the Cheese

JITTLOV, Mike
1988 The Wizard of Speed and Time

JOANOU, Phil
1987 3 O'Clock High

JODRELL, Steve
1988 Shame

JOFFE, Arthur
1986 Harem

JOFFE, Mark
1988 Watch the Shadows Dance
1989 Grievous Bodily Harm

JOFFE, Roland
1984 The Killing Fields **D* F***
1986 The Mission **D* F***
1989 Fat Man and Little Boy

JOHNSON, Alan
1983 To Be or Not to Be
1986 Solarbabies

JOHNSON, Emory
1927 The Lone Eagle
1927 The Shields of Honour
1927 The Fourth Commandment
1927 The Third Alarm
1932 The Phantom Express

JOHNSON, Jed
1977 Andy Warhol's Bad

JOHNSON, Kenneth
1988 Short Circuit II

JOHNSON, Lamont
(1920–) Stockton, California, USA.
1961 Thin Ice
1966 A Covenant with Death
1968 Kona Coast
1970 The Mackenzie Break
1971 A Gunfight
1972 The Groundstar Conspiracy
1972 You're Like My Mother
1973 The Last American Hero / *Hard Driver*
1974 Visit to a Chief's Son
1976 Lipstick
1977 One on One
1978 Somebody Killed Her Husband
1981 Cattle Annie and Little Britches
1983 Spacehunter: Adventures in the Forbidden Zone
(also many TV movies)

JOHNSON, Mick
1989 Chattahoochee

JOHNSON, Nunnally
(1897–1977) Columbia, Georgia, USA. Biography: The Letters of Nunnally Johnson by Dorris Johnson.
1954 Night People
1954 Black Widow
1955 How to Be Very, Very Popular
1956 The Man in the Gray Flannel Suit
1957 Oh, Men! Oh Women!
1957 The Three Faces of Eve
1959 The Man Who Understood Women
1960 The Angel Wore Red

JOHNSON, Patrick Read
1989 Martians

JOHNSON, Raymond K
1931 Call of the Rockies
1935 Kentucky Blue Streak
1935 Skybound
1936 I'll Name the Murderer
1936 Suicide Squad
1939 Daughter of the Tong
1939 In Old Montana
1939 The Code of the Fearless
1939 The Two Gun Troubador
1940 Covered Wagon Trails
1940 The Kid from Santa Fe
1940 Land of Six Guns
1940 Wild Horse Range
1940 The Cheyenne Kid
1940 Pinto Canyon
1940 Riders from Nowhere
1941 Riding the Trail
1941 Law of the Wild
1941 Law of the Wolf

JOHNSON, Terry
1989 Way Upstream

JOHNSTON, Joe
1989 Honey I've Shrunk the Kids

JONES, Amy
1982 Slumber Party Massacre
1983 Love Letters
1987 Maid to Order

JONES, Brian
1988 The Rejuvenator / *Juvenatrix / Skindeep*
1989 Bloodscape / *Inferno in Safehaven*

JONES, Buck (Charles Gebhardt)
(1889–1942) Vincennes, Indiana, USA.
1937 Black Aces
1937 For the Service
1937 Law of the Tombstone

JONES, David
(1934–) Poole, Dorset, England.
1983 Betrayal
1987 84, Charing Cross Road
1988 Jacknife

JONES, Don
1988 Lethal Pursuit
1988 Murderlust

JONES, F Richard
1928 The Big Killing
1928 Someone to Love
1928 The Water Hole
1929 Bulldog Drummond

JONES, Harmon C
(1911–1972) Canadian.
1951 As Young As You Feel
1952 The Pride of St Louis
1952 Bloodhounds of Broadway
1953 The Silver Ship
1953 City of Bad Men
1953 The Kid from Left Field
1954 Gorilla at Large
1954 Princess of the Nile
1955 Target Zero
1956 A Day of Fury
1956 Canyon River
1958 The Beast of Budapest
1958 Bullwhip
1958 Wolf Larsen
1966 Don't Worry, We'll Think of a Title

JONES, L Q (Justus Ellis McQueen)
(1927–) Beaumont, Texas, USA.
1975 A Boy and His Dog

JONES, Peter Frazer
(1920–) British.
1980 George and Mildred

JONES, Robert
(1942–) Boston, Massachusetts, USA.
1983 Mission Hill

JONES, Terry
(1942–) Colwyn Bay, Wales.
1975 Monty Python and the Holy Grail **(Terry GILLIAM)**
1979 Monty Python's Life of Brian
1983 Monty Python's the Meaning of Life
1987 Personal Services
1989 Erik the Viking

JORDAN, Glenn
(1936–) San Antonio, Texas, USA.
1981 Neil Simon's Only When I Laugh
1984 The Buddy System
1984 Mass Appeal
(also many TV movies)

JORDAN, Neil
(1950–) Irish.
1983 Angel / *Danny Boy*
1984 The Company of Wolves
1986 Mona Lisa
1988 High Spirits
1989 We're No Angels

JUDGE, Fred
1954 The Golden Mistress

JULIAN, Rupert
(1879–1943) Auckland, New Zealand.
1923 Merry-Go-Round **(replaced Erich VON STROHEIM)**
1924 Love and Glory
1924 Hell's High Road

1926 The Phantom of the Opera
1926 Three Faces East
1926 Silence
1927 The Yankee Clipper
1927 The Country Doctor
1928 The Leopard Lady
1928 Walking Back
1930 Love Comes Along
1930 The Cat Creeps

JURAN, Nathan (Nathan Hertz Juran)
(1907–) Austria.
1952 The Black Castle
1953 Gunsmoke
1953 Law and Order
1953 The Golden Blade
1953 Tumbleweed
1954 Highway Dragnet
1954 Drums Across the River
1955 The Crooked Web
1957 The Deadly Mantis
1957 Hellcats of the Navy
1957 Twenty Million Miles to Earth
1958 The Seventh Voyage of Sinbad
1959 Good Day for a Hanging
1961 Flight of the Lost Balloon
1962 Jack the Giant Killer
1963 Siege of the Saxons
1964 First Men in the Moon
1964 East of Sudan
1970 Land Raiders
1973 The Boy Who Cried Werewolf

JUST, Jon
1977 Angel City

JUSTMAN, Paul
1984 Gimme an F

JUTRA, Claude
(1930–1987) Montreal, Quebec, Canada.
1981 Surfacing
1982 By Design
(also many TV movies)

KACZENDER, George
(1933–) Budapest, Hungary.
1968 Don't Let the Angels Fall
1974 The Girl in Blue / *U-Turn*
1978 In Praise of Older Women
1980 Agency
1981 Your Ticket Is No Longer Valid
1981 Chanel Solitaire
1987 Prettykill / *Tomorrow's a Killer*
1988 The Last Island

KADAR,Ján (János Kadár)
(1918–1979) Budapest, Hungary. Czechoslovakian.
1952 Kidnap **(Elmar KLOS)**
1953 Music from Wars **(Elmar KLOS)**
1957 The House at the Terminus **(Elmar KLOS)**
1958 Three Wishes **(Elmar KLOS)**
1959 The Magic Lantern II **(Elmar KLOS)**
1963 Death Is Called Engelchen **(Elmar KLOS)**
1964 The Accused / *The Defendant* **(Elmar KLOS)**
1965 The Shop in the High Street **(Elmar KLOS)**
1969 Adrift **(Elmar KLOS)**
1970 The Angel Levine
1975 Lies My Father Told Me
1978 Freedom Road
(also many documentaries)

KADISON, Ellis
1965 Git
1966 The Cat

KAGAN, Jeremy Paul
(1945–) Mt. Vernon, New York, USA.
1977 Heroes
1977 Scott Joplin
1978 The Big Fix
1982 The Chosen
1983 Sting II
1985 The Journey of Natty Gann
1988 Honor Bright
1989 Big Man on Campus / *The Hunchback of UCLA*

KAHN, Jeff
1988 Astonished

KAHN, Richard C
1931 Secret Menace
1934 Children of Loneliness
1939 The Bronze Buckaroo
1939 Harlem Rides Again
1939 Two-Gun Man from Harlem
1940 Son of Ingagi **(Herbert MEYER)**
1940 Buzzy Rides the Range
1941 Buzzy and the Phantom Pinto

KAISERMAN, Constance
1987 My Little Girl

KAMEN, Jay
1988 Transformations

KAMPMANN, Steven
1988 Stealing Home **(Will ALDIS)**

KANE, Joseph
(1894–1975) American.
1935 Tumbling Tumbleweeds
1935 Melody Trail
1935 The Sagebrush Troubadour
1936 The Lawless Nineties
1936 King of the Pecos
1936 The Lonely Trail
1936 Guns and Guitars
1936 Oh, Susanna!
1936 Ride Ranger Ride
1937 Paradise Express
1937 Git Along Little Dogies / *Serenade of the West*
1937 Ghost Town Gold
1937 Round-Up Time in Texas
1937 The Old Corral / *Texas Serenade*
1937 Come on Cowboys!
1937 Gunsmoke Ranch
1937 Public Cowboy No. One
1937 Yodelin' Kid from Pine Ridge / *The Hero of Pine Ridge*
1937 Boots and Saddles
1937 Springtime in the Rockies

1938 The Old Barn Dance
1938 Born to Be Wild
1938 Arson Gang Busters / *Fire Fighters*
1938 Under Western Skies
1938 Gold Mine in the Sky
1938 Man from Music Mountain
1938 Billy the Kid Returns
1938 Come On, Rangers!
1938 Shine on Harvest Moon
1939 Rough Riders' Round-Up
1939 Frontier Pony Express
1939 Southward Ho!
1939 In Old Caliente
1939 In Old Monterey
1939 Wall Street Cowboy
1939 The Arizona Kid
1939 Days of Jesse James
1939 Saga of Death Valley
1940 Young Buffalo Bill
1940 The Carson City Kid
1940 The Ranger and the Lady
1940 Colorado
1940 Young Bill Hickok
1940 The Border Legion
1941 Robin Hood of the Pecos
1941 In Old Cheyenne
1941 Sheriff of Tombstone
1941 The Great Train Robbery
1941 Nevada City
1941 Rags to Riches
1941 Bad Man of Deadwood
1941 Jesse James at Bay
1941 Red River Valley
1941 The Man from Cheyenne
1942 South of Santa Fe
1942 Sunset on the Desert
1942 Romance of the Range
1942 Sons of the Pioneers
1942 Sunset Serenade
1942 Heart of the Golden West
1942 Ridin' Down the Canyon
1943 Idaho
1943 King of the Cowboys
1943 Song of Texas
1943 Silver Spurs
1943 The Man from Music Mountain
1943 Hands Across the Border
1944 The Cowboy and the Señorita
1944 The Yellow Rose of Texas
1944 Song of Nevada
1945 Flame of the Barbary Coast
1945 The Cheaters
1945 Dakota
1946 In Old Sacramento
1946 The Plainsman and the Lady
1947 Wyoming
1948 Old Los Angeles
1948 The Gallant Legion
1948 The Plunderers
1949 The Last Bandit
1949 Brimstone
1950 Rock Island Trail / *Transcontinental Express*
1950 The Savage Horde
1950 California Passage
1951 Oh, Susanna
1951 Fighting Coast Guard
1951 The Sea Hornet
1952 Hoodlum Empire
1952 Woman of the North Country
1952 Ride the Man Down
1953 San Antone
1953 Fair Wind to Java
1953 Sea of Lost Ships
1954 Jubilee Trail
1955 Hell's Outpost
1955 Timberjack
1955 The Road to Denver
1955 The Vanishing American
1956 The Maverick Queen
1956 Accused of Murder
1957 Duel at Apache Wells
1957 Spoilers of the Forest
1957 Last Stagecoach West
1957 The Crooked Circle
1958 Gunfire at Indian Gap
1958 The Notorious Mr Monks
1958 The Lawless Eighties
1958 The Man Who Died Twice
1966 Here Comes the Nashville Sound
1967 Search for the Evil One
1968 Track of Thunder
1971 Smoke in the Wind

KANEW, Jeff
1979 Natural Enemies
1983 Eddie Macon's Run
1984 Revenge of the Nerds
1985 Gotcha
1986 Tough Guys
1989 Troop Beverly Hills / *Be Prepared*

KANIEVSKA, Marek
1984 Another Country
1987 Less Than Zero

KANIN, Garson
(1912–) Rochester, New York, USA. Autobiographies: Hollywood; It Takes a Long Time to Become Young.
1938 A Man to Remember
1938 Next Time I Marry
1939 The Great Man Votes
1939 Bachelor Mother
1940 My Favourite Wife
1940 They Knew What They Wanted
1941 Tom, Dick and Harry
1945 The True Glory **(Carol REED)**
1969 Where It's At
1969 Some Kind of Nut
(also many documentaries)

KANIN, Michael
(1910–) American.
1951 When I Grow Up

KANNER, Alexis
(1942–) British.
1981 Kings and Desperate Men

KANTER, Hal
(1918–) Savannah, Georgia, USA.
1956 I Married a Woman
1957 Loving You
1958 Once Upon a Horse

KAPLAN, Henry
1962 The Girl on the Boat

KAPLAN, Jonathan
(1947–) Paris, France.
1973 The Student Teachers
1973 The Slams
1974 Truck Turner
1974 Night Call Nurses
1975 White Line Fever
1976 Mr Billion
1979 Over the Edge
1983 Heart Like a Wheel
1987 Project X
1988 Reckless Endangerment
1989 Immediate Family

KAPLAN, Nelly
(1934–) Buenos Aires, Argentina.
1970 A Very Curious Girl / *La Fiancée du Pirate*
1976 Nea, A Young Emmanuelle
1980 Charles et Lucie

KARANOVIC, Srdan
1987 Something in Between

KARDOS, Leslie
1940 Dark Streets of Cairo
1951 The Strip
1953 Small Town Girl
1957 The Man Who Turned to Stone
1957 The Tijuana Story

KARES, Peter
1975 The Night They Robbed Big Bertha's

KARLSON, Phil (Philip N. Karlstein)
(1908–1986) Chicago, Illinois, USA.
1944 A Wave, a Wac and a Marine
1945 There Goes Kelly
1945 G.I. Honeymoon
1945 The Shanghai Cobra
1946 Dark Alibi
1946 Live Wires
1946 The Missing Lady
1946 Swing Parade of 1946
1946 Behind the Mask
1946 Bowery Bombshell
1946 Wife Wanted
1947 Black Gold
1947 Kilroy Was Here
1947 Louisiana
1948 Adventures in Silverado / *Above All Laws*
1948 Rocky
1948 Thunderhoof / *Fury*
1948 The Ladies of the Chorus
1949 Down Memory Lane
1949 The Big Cat
1950 The Iroquois Trail / *The Tomahawk Trail*
1951 Lorna Doone
1951 The Texas Rangers
1951 Mask of the Avenger
1952 Scandal Sheet / *The Dark Page*
1952 Kansas City Confidential / *The Secret Four*
1952 The Brigand
1953 99 River Street
1954 They Rode West
1955 Hell's Island
1955 Tight Spot
1955 Five Against the House
1955 The Phenix City Story
1957 The Brothers Rico
1958 The Gunman's Walk
1960 Hell to Eternity
1960 Key Witness
1961 The Secret Ways
1962 The Scarface Mob
1962 Kid Galahad
1963 Rampage
1966 The Silencers
1967 A Time for Killing / *The Long Ride Home*
1968 The Wrecking Crew
1970 Hornets' Nest
1972 Ben
1973 Walking Tall
1974 Framed

KARN, Bill
1955 Gang Busters
1960 Ma Barker's Killer Brood

KARSON, Eric
1979 Dirt **(Cal NAYLOR)**
1980 The Octagon
1986 Hell Camp / *Opposing Forces*
1988 Black Eagle
1989 Angel Town

KASDAN, Lawrence
(1949–) Miami Beach, Florida, USA.
1981 Body Heat
1983 The Big Chill **F***
1985 Silverado
1988 The Accidental Tourist **F***
1989 I Love You to Death

KASTLE, Leonard
(1929–) American.
1970 The Honeymoon Killers

KASZUBOWSKI, Jerzy
1987 The Road Home

KATAKOUZINOS, George
1982 Angelos

KATSELAS, Milton
(1933–) Pittsburgh, Pennsylvania, USA.
1972 Butterflies Are Free
1973 Forty Carats
1974 Report to the Comissioner / *Operation Undercover*
1979 When You Comin' Back, Red Ryder?

KATZ, Gloria
1975 Messiah of Evil

KATZIN, Lee H
(1935–) Detroit, Michigan, USA.
1967 Hondo and the Apaches
1969 Heaven with a Gun
1969 What Ever Happened to Aunt Alice?
1970 The Phynx
1970 Le Mans
1972 The Salzburg Connection
1988 World Gone Wild
(also many TV movies)

KATZMAN, Sam
(1901–1973) American.
1937 Orphan of the Pecos
1937 Brothers of the West
1937 Lost Ranch

KAUFER, Jonathan
(1955–) Los Angeles, California, USA.
1982 Soup for One

KAUFMAN, Charles
1977 The Secret Dreams of Mona Q
1980 Mother's Day
1984 When Nature Calls / *The Outdoorsters*
1988 Jakarta / *Triangle Invasion*

KAUFMAN, George S
(1889–1961) Pittsburgh, Pennsylvania, USA.
Biographies: George S Kaufman by Howard Teichman; George S Kaufman, His Life, His Theatre by Malcolm Goldstein.
1947 The Senator Was Indiscreet

KAUFMAN, Lloyd
1971 The Battle of Love's Return

KAUFMAN, Millard
(1917–) American.
1962 Convicts Four / *Reprieve*

KAUFMAN, Philip
(1936–) Chicago, Illinois, USA.
1965 Goldstein **(Benjamin MANASTER)**
1969 Fearless Frank
1972 The Great Northfield Minnesota Raid
1974 The White Dawn
1978 Invasion of the Body Snatchers
1979 The Wanderers
1983 The Right Stuff **F***
1987 The Unbearable Lightness of Being

KAWADRI, Anwar
(1953–) Damascus, Syria.
1977 Paulina
1980 Waiting Room
1980 Sex with the Stars
1982 Nutcracker
1985 Claudia's Story
1989 Out of Time

KAY, Gilbert L
1956 Three Bad Sisters
1964 The Secret Door

KAY, Roger
1962 The Cabinet of Dr Caligari

KAYLOR, Robert
1980 Carny

KAZAN, Elia (Elia Kazanjoglou)
(1909–) Kadi-Keu, Constantinople, Turkey.
Biography: Kazan on Kazan by Michel Ciment.
1941 It's Up to You
1945 A Tree Grows in Brooklyn
1947 Sea of Grass
1947 Boomerang!
1947 Gentleman's Agreement **D** F****
1949 Pinky
1950 Panic in the Streets
1951 A Streetcar Named Desire **D* F***
1952 Viva Zapata!
1953 Man on a Tightrope
1954 On the Waterfront **D** F****
1955 East of Eden **D***
1956 Baby Doll
1957 A Face in the Crowd
1960 Wild River
1961 Splendor in the Grass
1963 America, America / *The Anatolian Smile* **D* F***
1969 The Arrangement
1972 The Visitors
1975 The Last Tycoon
1989 Beyond the Aegean

KAZANJIAN, Howard
1987 Dream Machine

KEATON, Buster (Joseph Francis Keaton)
(1895–1966) Piqua, Kansas, USA.
Autobiography: My Wonderful World of Slapstick.
Biographical Film: 1957 The Buster Keaton Story.
1923 The Balloonatic
1923 The Love Nest **(Edward F CLINE)**
1923 The Three Ages
1923 Our Hospitality **(John G BLYSTONE)**
1924 Sherlock Junior
1924 The Navigator **(Donald CRISP)**
1925 Seven Chances
1925 Go West
1926 Battling Butler
1926 The General **(Clyde BRUCKMAN)**
1938 Life in Sometown USA
1938 Hollywood Handicap
1938 Streamlined Swing

KEAYS, Vernon
1942 Strictly in the Groove
1942 Arizona Trail
1944 Trigger Law
1944 The Utah Kid
1944 Marshal of Gunsmoke
1945 Rockin' in the Rockies
1945 Blazing the Western Trail
1945 Lawless Empire
1945 Dangerous Intruder
1946 Landrush
1948 Whirlwind Raiders

KEENAN, Haydn
1987 Pandemonium

KEESLAR, Don
1978 Bog

KEGLEVIC, Peter
1987 Magic Sticks

KEIGHLEY, William
(1893–1984) Philadelphia, Pennsylvania, USA.
1932 The Match King **(Howard**

BRETHERTON)
1933 Ladies They Talk About **(Howard BRETHERTON)**
1934 Easy to Love
1934 Journal of a Crime
1934 Dr Monica
1934 Kansas City Princess
1934 Big Hearted Herbert
1934 Babbitt
1934 The Right to Live / *The Sacred Flame*
1935 G-Men
1935 Mary Jane's Pa / *Wanderlust*
1935 Special Agent
1935 Stars Over Broadway
1935 The Singing Kid
1936 Bullets or Ballots
1936 The Green Pastures **(Marc CONNELLY)**
1936 God's Country and the Woman
1936 The Prince and The Pauper
1937 Varsity Show
1938 The Adventures of Robin Hood **(Michael CURTIZ)** F*
1938 Brother Rat
1938 Secrets of an Actress
1938 Valley of the Giants
1939 Each Dawn I Die
1939 Yes, My Darling Daughter
1939 The Fighting 69th
1940 Torrid Zone
1940 No Time for Comedy
1941 Four Mothers
1941 The Bride from C.O.D.
1942 George Washington Slept Here
1942 The Man Who Came to Dinner
1942 Honeymoon / *Two Men and a Girl*
1948 The Street with No Name
1950 Rocky Mountain
1953 The Master of Ballantrae

KEITH, David
(1954–) Knoxville, Tennessee, USA.
1987 The Farm / *The Curse*
1987 Sacrifice
1988 Further Adventures of Tennessee Buck

KEITH, Harvey
1988 Mondo New York

KELLER, Frederick King
1981 Tuck Everlasting
1984 Vamping
1987 My Dark Lady

KELLER, Harry
(1913–1987) Los Angeles, California, USA.
1949 The Blonde Bandit
1950 Tarnished
1951 Fort Dodge Stampede
1951 Desert of Lost Men
1952 Rose of Cimarron
1952 Leadville Gunslinger
1952 Black Hills Ambush
1952 Thundering Caravans
1953 Marshal of Cedar Rock
1953 Savage Frontier
1953 Bandits of the West
1953 El Paso Stampede
1954 Red River Shore
1954 Phantom Stallion
1956 The Unguarded Moment
1957 Man Afraid
1957 Quantez
1958 The Day of the Bad Man
1958 The Female Animal
1958 Voice in the Mirror
1958 Step Down to Terror / *The Silent Stranger*
1960 Seven Ways from Sundown
1961 Tammy Tell Me the Truth
1962 Six Black Horses
1963 Tammy and the Doctor
1964 The Brass Bottle
1968 In Enemy Country

KELLETT, Bob
(1927–) British.
1965 A Home of Your Own
1969 Futtock's End
1971 Girl Stroke Boy
1971 Up Pompeii
1971 Up the Chastity Belt
1972 The Alf Garnett Saga
1972 Our Miss Fred
1972 Up the Front
1973 Don't Just Lie There, Say Something!
1975 Spanish Fly
1977 Are You Being Served?

KELLEY, Albert
1930 Woman Racket **(Robert OBER)**
1933 Jungle Bride **(Harry HOYT)**
1941 Double Cross
1943 Submarine Base
1948 Street Corner
1948 Slippery McGee

KELLINO, Roy
(1912–1956) British.
1937 The Last Adventurers
1937 Catch As Catch Can / *Atlantic Episode*
1939 I Met a Murderer
1952 Lady Possessed **(William SPIER)**
1953 Charade
1955 The Silken Affair

KELLINO, W P
(1875–1958) British.
1930 Alf's Button
1935 Royal Cavalcade **(Thomas BENTLEY, Herbert BRENON, Thomas LEE, Walter SUMMERS, Marcel VARNEL)**

KELLJAN, Bob (Robert Kelljchian)
(1930–1982) American.
1969 Little Sister
1970 Count Yorga Vampire
1971 Return of Count Yorga
1973 Scream, Blacula, Scream
1974 Act of Vengeance
1977 Black Oak Conspiracy

KELLMAN, Barnet
(1947–) New York, New York, USA.
1985 Key Exchange

KELLOGG, Ray
(1900–1976) American.
1959 The Giant Gila Monster
1959 The Killer Shrews

1960 My Dog Buddy
1968 The Green Berets **(John WAYNE)**
1970 Tora! Tora! Tora! **(Richard FLEISCHER, Kinji FUKASAKU, Toshio MASUDA)**

KELLY, Duke
1976 My Name Is Legend

KELLY, Gene (Eugene Curran Kelly)
(1912–) Pittsburgh, Pennsylvania, USA.
Biography: Gene Kelly: A Biography by Clive Hirschhorn.
1949 On the Town **(Stanley DONEN)**
1952 Singin' in the Rain **(Stanley DONEN)**
1955 It's Always Fair Weather **(Stanley DONEN)**
1956 Invitation to a Dance
1957 The Happy Road
1958 The Tunnel of Love
1962 Gigot
1967 A Guide for the Married Man
1969 Hello, Dolly! **F***
1970 The Cheyenne Social Club
1976 That's Entertainment, Part II

KELLY, James
(1931–1978) British.
1970 The Beast in the Cellar
1971 Night Hair Child

KELLY, Patrick
1985 Beer

KELLY, Ron
1970 King of the Grizzlies

KEMP, Ron
1948 Miracle in Harlem

KENNEDY, Burt
(1923–) Muskegon, Michigan, USA.
1961 The Canadians
1963 Mail Order Bride / *West of Montana*
1965 The Rounders
1966 The Money Trap
1966 Return of the Seven
1967 Welcome to Hard Times / *Killer on a Horse*
1967 The War Wagon
1969 Support Your Local Sheriff
1969 Young Billy Young
1969 The Good Guys and the Bad Guys
1970 Dirty Dingus Magee
1971 Support Your Local Gunfighter
1971 Hannie Caulder
1973 The Train Robbers
1976 The Killer Inside Me
1980 More Wild Wild West
1981 Wolf Lake / *The Honour Guard*
1987 Trouble with Spies
1989 Killer Inside Me
1989 Big Bad John
(also many TV movies)

KENNEDY, Michael
1988 Erik

KENNEDY, Tom
1983 Time Walker

KENNY, Joseph
1967 Gunfight in Abilene

KENT, Gary
1985 Rainy Day Friends

KENT, Larry
1987 High Stakes

KENT, Willis
1940 Mad Youth

KENTON, Erle C
(1896–1980) American.
1924 Danger Signal
1925 Red Hot Tires
1925 A Fool and His Money
1926 Palm Beach Girl
1926 The Love Toy
1926 The Sap
1926 Other Women's Husbands
1927 The Girl in the Pullman / *The Girl on the Train*
1927 Wedding Bills
1927 The Rejuvenation of Aunt Mary
1928 Golf Widows
1928 Bare Knees / *Short Skirts*
1928 Name the Woman
1928 The Companionate Marriage / *The Jazz Bride*
1928 The Side Show
1928 Nothing to Wear
1928 The Sporting Age / *The Stronger Love*
1928 The Street of Illusion
1929 Father and Son
1929 Trial Marriage
1929 Song of Love
1930 Mexicali Rose / *The Girl from Mexico*
1930 A Royal Romance
1930 The Last Parade
1931 Lover Come Back
1931 Leftover Ladies / *Broken Links*
1931 X Marks the Spot
1932 Stranger in Town
1932 Guilty As Hell
1933 Island of Lost Souls
1933 From Hell to Heaven
1933 Disgraced!
1933 Big Executive
1934 Search for Beauty
1934 You're Telling Me
1935 The Best Man Wins **(E R DAVISON)**
1935 Party Wire
1935 The Public Menace
1935 Grand Exit
1936 Devil's Squadron
1936 Counterfeit
1936 End of the Trail / *Revenge*
1937 Devil's Playground
1937 Racketeers in Exile
1937 She Asked for It
1938 The Lady Objects
1938 Little Tough Guys in Society
1939 Everything's on Ice
1939 Escape to Paradise
1940 Remedy for Riches
1941 Petticoat Politics
1941 Melody for Three
1941 Naval Academy
1941 They Meet Again

1941 Flying Cadets
1942 Frisco Lil
1942 North to the Klondike
1942 The Ghost of Frankenstein
1942 Pardon My Sarong
1942 Who Done It?
1943 How's About It?
1943 It Ain't Hay / *Money for Jam*
1943 Always a Bridesmaid
1945 House of Frankenstein
1945 She Gets Her Man
1945 House of Dracula
1946 The Cat Creeps
1946 Little Miss Big
1948 The Story of Bob and Sally / *Should Parents Tell?*
1950 One Too Many / *Killer with a Label*
(also many shorts)

KERN, James V
(1909–1966) American.
1944 The Doughgirls
1946 Never Say Goodbye
1947 Stallion Road
1948 April Showers
1951 The Second Woman / *Ellen*
1951 Two Tickets to Broadway

KERR, Frank
1989 True Blood / *Edge of Darkness*

KERRIGAN, George
1988 L.A.B.C.

KERSHNER, Glenn
1937 Island Captives

KERSHNER, Irvin (I. Kerschner)
(1923–) Philadelphia, Pennsylvania, USA.
1958 Stakeout on Dope Street
1959 The Young Captives
1961 The Hoodlum Priest
1963 A Face in the Rain
1964 The Luck of Ginger Coffey
1966 A Fine Madness
1967 The Flim-Flam Man / *One Born Every Minute* **(Yakima KANUTT)**
1970 Loving
1972 Up the Sandbox
1974 S*P*Y*S
1976 The Return of a Man Called Horse
1978 Eyes of Laura Mars
1980 The Empire Strikes Back
1983 Never Say Never Again
1988 Puccini
1988 In Dubious Battle

KERWIN, Harry E
1975 God's Bloody Acre
1979 Barracuda

KESLER, Henry S
1943 Three Russian Girls **(Fedor OZEP)**
1957 Five Steps to Danger

KESSLER, Bruce
(1936–) California, USA.
1968 Angels from Hell
1968 Killers Three

1969 The Gay Deceivers
1971 Simon, King of the Witches
(also TV movies)

KIBBEE, Roland
(1914–) American.
1974 The Midnight Man **(Burt LANCASTER)**

KIDD, Michael (Milton Greenwald)
(1919–) Brooklyn, New York, USA.
1958 Merry Andrew

KIDRON, Beeban
1988 Vroom

KIERSCH, Fritz
1984 Children of the Corn
1985 Tuff Turf
1987 Winners Take All
1987 Gor
1988 Under the Boardwalk / *Wipeout*

KIESLOWSKI, Krzysztof
1986 No End
1988 Thou Shalt Not Kill

KIKOINE, Gerard
1987 Treasure Island
1987 Dragonard
1987 Master of Dragonard Hill
1988 Edge of Sanity / *Dr Jekyll and Mr Hyde — Journey in Fear*
1989 Edgar Allan Poe's Buried Alive

KILLY, Edward
1935 Freckles **(William HAMILTON)**
1935 Seven Keys to Baldpate **(William HAMILTON)**
1936 Murder on the Bridal Path **(William HAMILTON)**
1936 Bunker Bean **(William HAMILTON)**
1936 Second Wife
1936 Wanted, Jane Turner
1937 China Passage
1937 The Big Shot
1937 Saturday's Heroes
1938 Quick Money
1940 The Fargo Kid
1940 Stage to Chino
1940 Wagon Train
1941 Along the Rio Grande
1941 The Bandit Trail
1941 Cyclone on Horseback
1941 Robbers of the Range
1942 Come On, Danger
1942 Land of the Open Range
1942 Riding the Wind
1944 Nevada
1945 West of the Pecos
1945 Wanderer of the Wasteland **(Wallace GRISSELL)**

KIMBERLIN, Bill
1979 American Nitro

KIMBRO, Clinton
1973 The Young Nurses

KIMMEL, Bruce
(1947–) Los Angeles, California,

USA.
1976 The First Nudie Musical **(Mark HAGGARD)**
1982 Spaceship / *The Creature Wasn't Nice*

KIMMINS, Anthony
(1901–1964) British.
1934 By-Pass to Happiness
1934 How's Chances?
1935 Once in a New Moon
1935 His Majesty and Co
1935 All at Sea
1937 Keep Fit
1938 I See Ice
1938 It's in the Air
1939 Come on George
1939 Trouble Brewing
1947 Mine Own Executioner
1948 Bonnie Prince Charlie
1951 Flesh and Blood
1951 Mr Denning Drives North
1952 Who Goes There? / *The Passionate Sentry*
1953 The Captain's Paradise
1954 Aunt Clara
1956 Smiley
1958 Smiley Gets a Gun
1962 The Amorous Prawn / *The Playgirl and the War Minister*

KINCADE, John
1987 Terminal Entry
1989 Back to Back

KINCAID, Tim
1985 Escape from Bad Girls Dormitory
1986 Breeders
1987 Robot Holocaust
1987 Mutant Hunt
1987 Maximum Thrust
1988 Riot on 42nd Street
1989 She's Back / *Dead and Married*

KING, Allan
(1930–) Vancouver, Canada.
1977 Who Has Seen the Wind?
1978 One-Night Stand
1981 Silence of the North
(also many documentaries)

KING, Christopher
1989 The Manageress

KING, George
(1899–1966) American.
1930 Too Many Crooks
1930 Leave It to Me
1931 Midnight Deadlock!
1931 Number Please
1931 The Professional Guest
1932 Self Made Lady
1932 Two Way Street
1932 Men of Steel
1932 To Brighton with Gladys
1933 The Matinee Idol
1933 Too Many Wives
1933 High Finance
1933 Beware of Women
1933 Mayfair Girl / *Society Girl*
1933 Enemy of the Police
1933 Smithy
1933 Her Imaginary Lover
1933 I Adore You
1934 The Silver Spoon
1934 Murder at the Inn
1934 The Office Wife
1934 To Be a Lady
1934 Guest of Honour
1934 Nine Forty Five
1934 The Blue Squadron
1934 Adventure Limited
1934 Oh No Doctor
1934 The Little Stranger
1935 The Man Without a Face
1935 Full Circle
1935 Windfall
1935 Gay Old Dog
1936 Sweeney Todd, the Demon Barber of Fleet Street
1936 The Crimes of Steven Hawks
1936 Reasonable Doubt
1937 Wanted
1937 Merry Comes to Town
1937 Under a Cloud
1937 The Ticket of Leave Man
1937 Silver Top
1938 Sexton Blake and the Hooded Terror
1938 John Halifax Gentleman
1939 The Face at the Window
1939 The Chinese Bungalow / *The Chinese Den*
1940 Crimes at the Dark House
1940 The Case of the Frightened Lady
1940 George and Margaret
1940 Two for Danger
1942 Tomorrow We Live / *At Dawn We Die*
1945 Candlelight in Algeria
1946 Gaiety George / *Showtime*
1946 The Shop at Sly Corner / *Code of Scotland Yard*
1948 Forbidden

KING, Henry
(1888–1982) Christianburg, Virginia, USA.
1924 Romola
1925 Any Woman
1925 Sack Cloth and Scarlet
1925 Stella Dallas
1926 Partners Again
1926 The Winning of Barbara Worth
1927 The Magic Flame
1929 She Goes to War
1929 Hell Harbour
1930 Eyes of the World
1930 Lightnin'
1930 The Concentratin' Kid
1931 Merely Mary Ann
1931 Over the Hill
1932 The Woman in Room 13
1933 State Fair **F***
1933 I Loved You Wednesday **(William Cameron MENZIES)**
1934 Carolina / *The House of Connelly*
1934 Marie Galante
1935 Way Down East
1935 One More Spring
1936 Lloyds of London
1936 Ramona
1936 The Country Doctor

1937 Seventh Heaven
1938 In Old Chicago **F***
1938 Alexander's Ragtime Band **F***
1939 Jesse James
1939 Stanley and Livingstone
1940 Chad Hanna
1940 Little Old New York
1940 Maryland
1941 Remember the Day
1941 A Yank in the R.A.F.
1942 The Black Swan
1943 The Song of Bernadette **D* F***
1944 Wilson **D* F***
1945 A Bell for Adano
1946 Margie
1947 Captain from Castille
1948 Deep Waters
1949 Prince of Foxes
1949 12 O'Clock High **F***
1950 The Gunfighter
1951 David and Bathsheba
1951 I'd Climb the Highest Mountain
1952 The Snows of Kilimanjaro
1952 Wait 'Til the Sun Shines
1952 Nellie
1953 King of the Khyber Rifles
1955 Love Is a Many-Splendored Thing **F***
1955 Untamed
1956 Carousel
1957 The Sun Also Rises
1958 The Bravados
1959 Beloved Infidel
1959 This Earth Is Mine
1962 Tender Is the Night

KING, Louis
(1898–1962) American.
1923 Sun Dog Trails
1923 Peaceful Peters
1923 Devil's Door Yard
1923 Spawn of the Desert
1923 Law Rustlers
1927 The Boy Rider
1927 The Slingshot Kid
1927 Wizard of the Saddle
1928 The Pinto Kid
1928 The Little Buckaroo
1928 The Bantam Cowboy
1928 The Fightin' Redhead
1928 Young Whirlwind
1928 Rough Ridin' Red
1928 Terror Mountain / *Tom's Vacation*
1928 Orphan of the Sage
1929 The Vagabond Cub
1929 The Freckled Rascal
1929 The Little Savage
1929 Pals of the Prairie
1930 The Lone Rider
1930 Shadow Ranch
1930 Men Without Law
1931 Desert Vengeance
1931 The Fighting Sheriff
1931 Border Law
1931 The Deceiver
1932 Police Court
1932 The County Fair
1932 Arm of the Law
1932 Drifting Souls
1933 Robbers' Roost
1933 Life in the Raw
1934 Murder in Trinidad
1934 Pursued
1934 Bachelor of Arts
1935 Charlie Chan in Egypt
1936 Road Gang
1936 Special Investigator
1936 Song of the Saddle
1936 The Bengal Tiger
1937 Melody for Two
1937 That Man's Here Again
1937 Draegerman Courage / *The Cave-In*
1937 Wild Money
1937 Bulldog Drummond Comes Back
1937 Wine, Women and Horses
1937 Bulldog Drummond's Revenge
1938 Prison Farm
1938 Tip-Off Girls
1938 Hunted Men
1938 Bulldog Drummond in Africa
1938 Illegal Traffic
1938 Tom Sawyer, Detective
1939 Persons in Hiding
1939 Undercover Doctor
1940 Seventeen
1940 Typhoon
1940 The Way of All Flesh
1940 Moon Over Burma
1942 Young America
1943 Chetniks / *Underground Guerillas*
1944 Ladies of Washington
1945 Thunderhead, Son of Flicka
1946 Smoky
1947 Thunder in the Valley / *Bob, Son of Battle*
1948 Green Grass of Wyoming
1949 Sand
1949 Mrs Mike
1950 Frenchie
1952 The Lion and the Horse
1953 Powder River
1954 Sabre Jet
1954 Dangerous Mission
1956 Massacre

KING, Rick
1977 Off the Wall
1986 Hard Choices
1987 Hotshot / *Hang Tough*
1987 The Killing Time
1989 Forced March

KING, Stephen
(1947–) Maine, USA.
1986 Maximum Overdrive

KING, Woodie
1976 The Long Night

KING, Zalman
1988 Wildfire
1988 Two Moon Junction
1989 Wild Orchid

KIRK, Robert
1988 Destroyer / *Edison Effect / Shadow of Death*

KIRKLAND, David
1931 Riders of the Cactus
1932 Soul of Mexico

KIRKLAND, John
1974 Curse of the Headless Horseman

KIRTMAN, Leonard
1976 Carnival of Blood

KISHON, Ephraim
1963 Sallah
1969 The Big Dig
1972 The Policeman
1974 Ervinka
1978 Fox in the Chicken Coop

KIZER, R J
1988 Hell Comes to Frogtown **(Donald G JACKSON)**

KJELLIN, Alf
(1920–1988) Lund, Sweden.
1955 Girl in the Rain
1957 Seventeen Years Old
1957 Encounters at Dusk
1959 Swinging at the Castle
1960 Only a Waiter
1961 Pleasure Garden
1962 Siska
1969 Midas Run / *A Run on Gold*
1970 The McMasters

KLANE, Robert
1978 Thank God It's Friday

KLEIN, Charles
(1898–) German.
1928 Blindfold
1929 The Sin Sister
1929 Pleasure Crazed

KLEIN, Dennis
1986 One More Saturday Night / *Datenight*

KLEIN, Larry
1970 The Adversary

KLEIN, William
(1926–) New York, New York, USA.
1970 Mister Freedom
(also many documentaries)

KLEISER, Randal
(1946–) American.
1978 Grease
1980 The Blue Lagoon
1982 Summer Lovers
1984 Grandview USA
1986 Flight of the Navigator
1988 Big Top Pee-Wee
1989 Getting It Right
(also TV movies)

KLEVEN, Max
1988 Deadly Stranger / *Mixtec*
1988 W.B., Blue and the Beaner

KLICK, Roland
1988 Let It Rock / *White Star*

KLIMOV, Elem
(1933–) Volgograd, USSR.
1964 Welcome, Or No Entry for Unauthorised Persons
1965 Adventures of a Dentist
1970 Sport, Sport, Sport
1974 And Nonetheless I Believe
1975 Rasputin
1982 Welcome to Majorca
1983 The Farewell
1985 Come and See

KLINE, Benjamin
1943 Cowboy in the Clouds
1944 Cowboy from Lonesome River
1944 Cyclone Prairie Rangers
1944 Saddle Leather Law
1944 Sagebrush Heroes
1944 Sundown Valley

KLINE, Herbert
(1909–) Chicago, Illinois, USA.
1949 The Kid from Cleveland
1952 The Fighter
(also many shorts and documentaries)

KLOVES, Steve
1989 The Fabulous Baker Boys

KNIGHT, Castleton
(1894–1972) British.
1929 The Flying Scotsman
1930 Kissing Cup's Race

KNOPF, Edwin H
(1899–1981) American.
1930 Slightly Scarlet **(Louis GASNIER)**
1930 The Light of Western Stars **(Otto BROWER)**
1930 The Border Legion **(Otto BROWER)**
1930 The Santa Fe Trail **(Otto BROWER)**
1930 Only Saps Work **(Cyril GARDNER)**
1932 Nice Women
1933 The Rebel **(Luis TRENKER)**
1951 The Law and the Lady

KNOWLES, Bernard
(1900–) British.
1944 A Piece of One's Own
1946 The Magic Bow
1947 The Man Within / *The Smugglers*
1947 The White Unicorn / *Bad Sister*
1947 Jassy
1948 Easy Money
1949 The Lost People
1949 The Perfect Woman
1950 The Reluctant Widow
1953 Park Plaza 605 / *Norman Conquest*
1954 Barbados Quest / *Murder on Approval*
1964 Frozen Alive
1965 Space Flight IC-1
1968 Hell Is Empty

KOBAYASHI, Masaki
(1916–) Otaru, Hokkaido, Japan.
1952 My Sons' Youth
1953 Sincere Heart
1953 Room with Thick Walls
1954 Three Loves
1954 Somewhere Beneath the Wide Sky
1955 Beautiful Days
1956 The Fountainhead / *The Spring*
1956 I'll Buy You

1957 Black River
1959 The Human Condition, Part I: No Greater Love
1959 The Human Condition, Part II: Road to Eternity
1961 The Human Condition, Part III: A Soldier's Prayer
1962 The Inheritance / *The Entanglement*
1962 Harakiri / *Seppuku*
1964 Kwaidan
1967 Samurai Rebellion
1968 Hymn to a Tired Man / *The Youth of Japan*
1971 Inn of Evil / *At the Risk of My Life*
1979 Glowing Autumn
1985 The Empty Table

KOCH, Howard W
(1916–) New York, New York, USA.
1954 Shield for Murder **(Edmund O'BRIEN)**
1955 Big House, USA
1957 Untamed Youth
1957 Bop Girl
1957 Jungle Heat
1957 The Girl in Black Stockings
1958 Fort Bowie
1958 Violent Road
1958 Frankenstein — 1970
1958 Andy Hardy Comes Home
1959 The Last Mile
1959 Born Reckless
1973 Badge 373

KOHNER, Pancho
(1939–) Los Angeles, California, USA.
1971 The Bridge in the Jungle
1975 Mr Sycamore

KOLLEK, Amos
1980 Worlds Apart
1985 Goodbye New York
1987 Forever Lulu
1988 Melanie Rose

KOMACK, James
(1930–) New York, New York, USA.
1985 Porky's Revenge

KONCHALOVSKY, Andrei (Andrei Mikhalkov-Konchalovsky)
(1937–) Moscow, Russia.
1965 The First Teacher
1967 Asya's Happiness
1969 A Nest of Gentlefolk
1971 Uncle Vanya
1974 A Lover's Romance
1979 Siberiade
1984 Maria's Lovers
1986 Runaway Train
1987 Duet for One
1987 Shy People
1988 Homer and Eddie

KONG, Jackie
1983 The Being
1984 Night Patrol
1987 Blood Diner
1987 Nightschool / *Underachievers*

KORDA, Sir Alexander (Sàndor Làszlo Kellner)
(1893–1956) Puszta, Turposzto, near Turkeye, Hungary.
Pseudonyms: Sàndor Korda; Jozsef Neumann.
Biographies: Alexander Korda: The Man Who Could Work Miracles by Karol Kulik; Charmed Lives: A Family Romance by Michael Korda.
1927 Madame Wants No Children
1927 A Modern Dubarry
1927 The Stolen Bride
1927 The Private Life of Helen of Troy
1928 Yellow Lily
1928 The Night Watch
1929 The Squall
1929 Love and the Devil
1929 Her Private Life
1929 Lilies of the Field
1930 The Princess and the Plumber
1930 Women Everywhere
1932 Wedding Rehearsal
1932 Service for Ladies / *Reserved for Ladies*
1932 The Girl from Maxim's
1933 The Private Lives of Henry VIII **F***
1934 The Private Life of Don Juan
1937 Rembrandt
1941 That Hamilton Woman
1945 Perfect Strangers / *Vacation from Marriage*
1947 An Ideal Husband

KORDA, Sandor see **Alexander KORDA**

KORDA, Zoltan (Zoltan Kellner)
(1895–1961) Puszta, Turposzto, near Turkeye, Hungary.
1934 Forget-Me-Not / *Forever Yours* **(Stanley IRVING)**
1935 Sanders of the River / *Bosambo*
1936 Conquest of the Air
1937 Elephant Boy **(Robert FLAHERTY)**
1938 The Drum
1939 The Four Feathers
1942 The Jungle Book **(André DE TOTH)**
1943 Sahara
1945 Counterattack / *One Against Seven*
1947 The Macomber Affair
1948 A Woman's Revenge
1951 African Fury / *Cry the Beloved Country*
1955 Storm Over the Nile **(Terence YOUNG)**

KORTY, John
(1936–) Lafayette, Indiana, USA.
1965 Crazy Quilt
1969 Funnyman
1970 Riverrun
1974 Silence
1976 Alex and the Gypsy
1978 Oliver's Story
1984 Caravan of Courage
(also many TV movies)

KOSTER, Henry (Hermann Kosterlitz)
(1905–1988) Berlin, Germany.
1932 Thea Roland
1933 Peter
1934 Little Mother

1936 Three Smart Girls
1937 100 Men and a Girl **F***
1938 The Rage of Paris
1939 Three Smart Girls Grow Up
1939 First Love
1940 Spring Parade
1941 It Started with Eve
1942 Between Us Girls
1944 Music for Millions
1946 Two Sisters from Boston
1947 The Unfinished Dance
1947 The Bishop's Wife **D* F***
1948 The Luck of the Irish
1949 Come to the Stable
1949 The Inspector General / *Happy Times*
1950 Wabash Avenue
1950 My Blue Heaven
1950 Harvey
1951 No Highway in the Sky
1951 Mr Belvedere Rings the Bell
1951 Elopement
1952 Stars and Stripes Forever / *Marching Along*
1953 My Cousin Rachel
1953 The Robe **F***
1954 Desirée
1955 A Man Called Peter
1955 The Virgin Queen
1955 Good Morning, Miss Dove
1956 D-Day, The Sixth of June
1956 The Power and the Prize
1957 My Man Godfrey
1958 Fräulein
1959 The Naked Maja
1960 The Story of Ruth
1961 Flower Drum Song
1962 Mr Hobbs Takes a Vacation
1963 Take Her, She's Mine
1965 Dear Brigitte
1966 The Singing Nun

KOTANI, Tom
1982 The Bushido Blade

KOTCHEFF, Ted (William Theodore Kotcheff)
(1931–) Toronto, Canada.
1962 Tiara Tahiti
1965 Life at the Top
1969 Two Gentlemen Sharing
1971 Outback / *Wake in Fright*
1974 Billy Two Hats / *The Lady and the Outlaw*
1974 The Apprenticeship of Duddy Kravitz
1977 Fun with Dick and Jane
1978 Who Is Killing the Great Chefs of Europe? / *Too Many Chefs*
1979 North Dallas Forty
1982 Split Image
1982 First Blood
1983 Uncommon Valour
1985 Joshua, Then and Now
1988 Switching Channels
1988 The Winter People
1989 Hot and Cold / *Heatwave*

KOTTO, Yaphet
(1937–) New York, New York, USA.
1972 The Limit / *Speed Limit 65*

KOUF, Jim
1985 Miracles
1989 Disorganized Crime / *Bank Job / Waiting for Salazar*

KOVACS, Steven
1988 68

KOWALSKI, Bernard L
(1929–) Brownsville, Texas, USA.
1958 Hot Car Girl
1958 Night of the Blood Beast
1959 The Giant Leeches
1959 Blood and Steel
1969 Krakatoa, East of Java
1969 Stiletto
1970 Macho Callahan
1973 Sssssss

KOWALSKI, Lech
1985 Gringo
1987 Story of a Junkie

KOZINTSEV, Grigori
(1905–1973) Kiev, Russia.
Biography: Grigori Kozintsev by Barbara Leaming.
1924 The Adventures of Octyabrina **(Leonid TRAUBERG)**
1925 Mishka Against Yudenitch **(Leonid TRAUBERG)**
1926 The Devil's Wheel **(Leonid TRAUBERG)**
1926 The Cloak **(Leonid TRAUBERG)**
1927 Little Brother **(Leonid TRAUBERG)**
1927 The Club of the Big Dead **(Leonid TRAUBERG)**
1929 The New Babylon **(Leonid TRAUBERG)**
1931 Alone **(Leonid TRAUBERG)**
1935 The Youth of Maxim **(Leonid TRAUBERG)**
1939 New Horizons / *The Vyborg Side*
1945 Simple People, Plain People
1947 Pirogov
1953 Belinski
1957 Don Quixote
1963 Hamlet
1971 King Lear

KRAMER, Jerry
1986 Modern Girls
1988 Moonwalker **(Colin CHILVERS)**

KRAMER, Remi
1977 High Velocity

KRAMER, Robert
(1939–) New York, New York, USA.
1968 In the Country
1968 The Edge
1970 Ice
1975 Milestone **(John DOUGLAS)**
1980 Guns
1982 Birth
1985 Diesel
1989 Doc's Kingdom

KRAMER, Stanley
(1913–) New York, New York, USA.
1955 Not As a Stranger

1957 The Pride and the Passion
1958 The Defiant Ones **D* F***
1959 On the Beach
1960 Inherit the Wind
1961 Judgement at Nuremberg **D* F***
1963 It's a Mad, Mad, Mad, Mad World
1965 Ship of Fools **F***
1965 Guess Who's Coming to Dinner **D* F***
1969 The Secret of Santa Vittoria
1970 R.P.M.
1971 Bless the Beasts and the Children
1973 Oklahoma Crude
1977 The Domino Principle
1979 The Runner Stumbles

KRASILOVSKY, Alexis
1979 Beale Street

KRASNA, Norman
(1909–1984) Corona, New York, USA.
1943 Princess O'Rourke
1950 The Big Hangover
1956 The Ambassador's Daughter

KRASNY, Paul
(1935–) Cleveland, Ohio, USA.
1974 Christina
1976 Joe Panther
(also many TV movies)

KRESS, Harold F
(1913–) American.
1945 Purity Squad
1951 No Questions Asked
1951 The Painted Hills
1952 Apache War Smoke

KRIMS, Milton
1954 Crossed Swords / *Il Maestro di Don Giovanni*

KRISH, John
(1923–) British.
1958 The Salvage Gang
1963 The Wild Affair
1964 The Unearthly Stranger
1969 Decline and Fall of a Birdwatcher
1971 The Man Who Had Power Over Women
1979 Jesus **(Peter SYKES)**
1986 Out of the Darkness

KROEKER, Allan
1987 Tramp at the Door

KRONSBERG, Jeremy Joe
1981 Going Ape!

KRUEGER, Michael
1987 Mind Killer
1988 Night Vision

KUBRICK, Stanley
(1928–) Bronx, New York, USA.
Biographies: Stanley Kubrick Directs by Alexander Walker; Cinema of Stanley Kubrick by Norman Kagan; Kubrick, Inside a Film Artist's Maze by T.A. Nelson.
1954 Fear and Desire
1955 Killer's Kiss
1956 The Killing
1957 Paths of Glory
1960 Spartacus
1962 Lolita
1964 Dr Strangelove or: How I Learned to Stop Worrying and Love the Bomb **D* F***
1968 2001: A Space Odyssey **D***
1971 A Clockwork Orange **D* F***
1975 Barry Lyndon **D* F***
1980 The Shining
1987 Full Metal Jacket

KULIK, Buzz (Seymour Kulik)
(1923–) New York, New York, USA.
1961 The Explosive Generation
1963 The Yellow Canary
1964 Ready for the People
1968 Warning Shot
1968 Sergeant Ryker / *The Case Against Paul Ryker*
1968 Villa Rides!
1969 Riot
1972 To Find a Man / *Sex and the Teenager / The Boy Next Door*
1973 Shamus
1980 The Hunter
(also many TV movies)

KULL, Edward
1935 Man's Best Friend

KUROSAWA, Akira
(1910–) Tokyo, Japan.
Autobiography: Something Like an Autobiography.
1943 Sanshiro Sugata
1944 The Most Beautiful
1945 Those Who Tread on the Tiger's Tail
1945 Sanshiro Sugata, Part II
1946 No Regrets for Our Youth
1946 Those Who Make Tomorrow
1947 One Wonderful Sunday
1948 Drunken Angel
1949 The Quiet Duel
1949 Stray Dog
1950 Scandal
1950 Rashomon
1951 The Idiot
1952 Ikiru
1954 Seven Samurai
1955 I Live in Fear
1957 The Lower Depths
1957 The Castle of the Spider's Web / *Throne of Blood*
1958 Three Bad Men in a Hidden Fortress
1960 The Bad Sleep Well
1963 High and Low / *Heaven and Hell*
1965 Red Beard
1980 Kagemusha: The Shadow Warrior
1985 Ran **D***

KURYS, Diane
(1948–) French.
1977 Peppermint Soda / *Diabolo Menthe*
1980 Cocktail Molotov
1983 Coup de Foudre / *Entre Nous*
1987 A Man in Love

KUSTURICA, Emir
(1955–) Sarajevo, Yugoslavia.
1981 Do You Remember Dolly Bell?
1985 When Father Was Away on Business

KUZUI, Franni
1988 Tokyo Pop

KWAPIS, Ken
1985 Sesame Street Presents: Follow That Bird
1988 Vibes

KYRIAZI, Paul
1976 Death Machines
1987 One Way Out

LA CAVA, Gregory
(1892–1949) Towanda, Pennsylvania, USA.
1924 Restless Wives
1924 The New Schoolteacher
1925 Womanhandled
1926 Let's Get Married
1926 Say It Again
1926 So's Your Old Man
1927 Paradise for Two
1927 Running Wild
1927 The Gay Defender
1927 Tell It to Sweeney
1928 Feel My Pulse
1928 Half a Bride
1928 Big News
1929 Saturday's Children
1930 His First Command
1931 Laugh and Get Rich
1931 Smart Woman
1932 The Age of Consent
1932 The Half-Naked Truth
1932 Symphony of Six Million / *Melody of Life*
1933 Gabriel Over the White House
1933 Bed of Roses
1933 Gallant Lady
1934 Affairs of Cellini
1934 What Every Woman Knows
1935 Private Worlds
1935 She Married Her Boss
1936 My Man Godfrey **D***
1937 Stage Door **D***
1939 Fifth Avenue Girl
1940 The Primrose Path
1941 Unfinished Business
1942 Lady in a Jam
1947 Living in a Big Way

LACHMAN, Harry
(1886–1975) American.
1929 Weekend Wives
1930 Under the Greenwood Tree
1930 Song of Soho
1930 The Yellow Mask
1931 The Love Habit
1932 Aren't We All?
1933 The Face in the Sky
1933 The Outsider
1933 Paddy, the Next Best Thing
1934 George White's Scandals **(Thornton FREELAND, George WHITE)**
1934 I Like It That Way
1934 Baby Take a Bow
1935 Dante's Inferno
1935 Dressed to Thrill
1936 Charlie Chan at the Circus
1936 Our Relations
1936 The Man Who Lived Twice
1937 The Devil Is Driving
1937 It Happened in Hollywood / *Once a Hero*
1938 No Time to Marry
1939 They Came By Night
1940 Murder Over New York
1941 Dead Men Tell
1941 Charlie Chan in Rio
1942 Castle in the Desert
1942 Dr Renault's Secret
1942 The Loves of Edgar Allan Poe

LAEMMLE, Edward
1925 Spook Ranch
1925 A Woman's Faith
1926 The Still Alarm
1927 Cheating Cheaters
1927 Held By the Law
1927 The Thirteenth Juror
1929 Man, Woman and Wife
1929 The Drake Case
1931 Lasca of the Rio Grande
1932 Texas Bad Man
1934 Embarrassing Moments
1935 A Notorious Gentleman

LAEMMLE, Ernest
1926 Prowler of the Night
1927 The Bronco Buster
1927 Hands Off
1927 A One Man Game
1927 Range Courage
1927 Red Clay
1928 The Grip of the Yukon
1928 Phyllis of the Follies
1930 What Men Want

LAFIA, John
1988 The Blue Iguana

LAHIFF, Craig
1988 Fever

LAING, John
1986 Other Halves
1987 Dangerous Orphans

LAIRD, Marlena
(1949–) London, England.
1979 Friendship, Secrets and Lies **(Anne Zane SHANKS)**

LaLOGGIAFrank
1981 Fear No Evil
1988 Lady in White

LAMAC, Karel *
1943 It Happened One Saturday
1943 They Met in the Dark
1943 Schweik's New Adventure

LAMAS, Fernando (Fernando Alvaro Lamas)
(1915–1982) Buenos Aires, Argentina.
1967 The Violent Ones

LAMB, André
1950 The Texan Meets Calamity Jane

LAMBERSON, Gregory
1988 Slime City

LAMBERT, Mary
1987 Siesta
1989 Pet Sematary

LAMONT, Charles Fred
(1898–) San Francisco, California, USA.
1934 The Curtain Falls
1935 Tomorrow's Youth
1935 The World Accuses
1935 Son of Steel
1935 False Pretenses
1935 Gigolette / *Night Club*
1935 A Shot in the Dark
1935 Circumstantial Evidence
1935 The Girl Who Came Back
1935 Happiness C.O.D.
1935 The Lady in Scarlet
1936 Ring Around the Moon
1936 Little Red Schoolhouse / *Schoolboy Penitentiary*
1936 Below the Deadline
1936 August Weekend
1936 The Dark Hour
1936 Lady Luck
1936 Bulldog Edition / *Lady Reporter*
1937 Wallaby Jim of the Island
1938 International Crime
1938 Shadows Over Shanghai
1938 Slander House
1938 Cipher Bureau
1938 The Long Shot
1939 Pride of the Navy
1939 Panama Patrol
1939 Inside Information
1939 Unexpected Father / *Sandy Takes a Bow*
1939 Little Accident
1940 Oh Johnny, How You Can Love!
1940 Sandy Is a Lady
1940 Love Honour and Oh Baby!
1940 Give Us Wings
1941 San Antonio Rose
1941 Sing Another Chorus
1941 Moonlight in Hawaii
1941 Melody Lane
1941 Road Agent
1942 Don't Get Personal
1942 You're Telling Me
1942 Almost Married
1942 Hi, Neighbour!
1942 Get Hep to Love / *She's My Lovely*
1942 When Johnny Comes Marching Home
1943 It Comes Up Love / *A Date with an Angel*
1943 Mr Big
1943 Hit the Ice
1943 Fired Wife
1943 Top Man
1944 Chip Off the Old Block
1944 Her Primitive Man
1944 The Merry Monahans
1944 Bowery to Broadway
1945 Salome, Where She Danced
1945 That's the Spirit
1945 Frontier Gal / *The Bride Wasn't Willing*
1946 She Wrote the Book
1946 The Runaround
1947 Slave Girl
1948 The Untamed Breed
1949 Ma and Pa Kettle
1949 Bagdad
1950 Ma and Pa Kettle Go to Town
1950 I Was a Shoplifter
1950 Curtain Call at Cactus Creek / *Take the Stage*
1950 Abbott and Costello in the Foreign Legion
1951 Abbott and Costello Meet the Invisible Man
1951 Comin' Round the Mountain
1951 Flame of Araby
1952 Abbott and Costello Meet Captain Kid
1953 Abbott and Costello Go to Mars
1953 Ma and Pa Kettle on Vacation / *Ma and Pa Kettle Go to Paris*
1953 Abbott and Costello Meet Dr Jekyll and Mr Hyde
1954 Ma and Pa Kettle at Home
1954 Untamed Heiress
1954 Ricochet Romance
1955 Carolina Cannonball
1955 Abbott and Costello Meet the Keystone Cops
1955 Abbott and Costello Meet the Mummy
1955 Lay That Rifle Down
1956 The Kettles in the Ozarks
1956 Francis in the Haunted House
(also a multitude of shorts 1923–1935)

LANCASTER, Burt
(1913–) New York, New York, USA. Biography: Burt Lancaster by Minty Clinch.
1955 The Kentuckian
1974 The Midnight Man **(Roland KIBBEE)**

LANDERS, Lew (Louis Friedlander)
(1901–1962) American.
1935 The Raven
1935 Stormy
1936 Parole!
1936 Without Orders
1936 Night Waitress
1937 They Wanted to Marry
1937 The Man Who Found Himself
1937 You Can't Buy Luck
1937 Border Café
1937 Flight from Glory
1937 Living on Love
1937 Danger Patrol
1938 The Affairs of Annabel
1938 Crashing Hollywood
1938 Double Danger
1938 Condemned Women
1938 Law of the Underworld
1938 Blind Alibi
1938 Sky Giants
1938 Smashing the Rackets
1938 Annabel Takes a Tour
1939 Pacific Liner
1939 Twelve Crowded Hours
1939 Fixer Dugan / *Double Daring*
1939 The Girl and the Gambler

1939 Bad Lands
1939 Conspiracy
1940 Honeymoon Deferred
1940 Enemy Agent
1940 La Conga Nights
1940 Sky Patrol
1940 Wagons Westward
1940 Sing, Dance, Plenty Hot / *Melody Girl*
1940 Girl from Havana
1940 Slightly Tempted
1941 Ridin' on a Rainbow
1941 Lucky Devils
1941 Back in the Saddle
1941 The Singing Hill
1941 I Was a Prisoner on Devil's Island
1941 Mystery Ship
1941 The Stork Pays Off
1942 The Man Who Returned to Life
1942 Alias Boston Blackie
1942 Canal Zone
1942 Harvard, Here I Come
1942 Not a Ladies' Man
1942 Submarine Raider
1942 Cadets on Parade
1942 Atlantic Convoy
1942 Sabotage Squad
1942 The Boogie Man Will Get You
1942 Smith of Minnesota
1942 Junior Army
1943 After Midnight with Boston Blackie
1943 Redhead from Manhattan
1943 Murder in Times Square
1943 Power of the Press
1943 Doughboys in Ireland
1943 Deerslayer
1944 Cowboy Canteen / *Close Harmony*
1944 The Ghost That Walks Alone
1944 The Return of the Vampire
1944 Two-Man Submarine
1944 Stars on Parade
1944 The Black Parachute
1944 U-Boat Prisoner / *Dangerous Mists*
1944 Swing in the Saddle / *Swing and Sway*
1944 I'm from Arkansas
1945 Crime, Inc.
1945 The Power of the Whistler
1945 Trouble Chasers
1945 Follow That Woman
1945 Arson Squad
1945 Shadow of Terror
1945 The Enchanted Forest
1945 Tokyo Rose
1945 Hot Cargo
1946 The Mask of Dijon
1946 A Close Call for Boston Blackie / *Lady of Mystery*
1946 The Truth About Murder / *The Lie Detector*
1946 Death Valley
1947 Secrets of a Sorority Girl / *Secret of Linda Hamilton*
1948 My Dog Rusty
1948 Adventures of Gallant Bess
1948 Inner Sanctum
1949 Stagecoach Kid
1949 Law of the Barbary Coast
1949 Air Hostess
1949 Barbary Private
1950 Davy Crockett, Indian Scout
1950 Girls' School / *Dangerous Inheritance*
1950 Dynamite Pass
1950 Tyrant of the Sea
1950 State Penitentiary
1950 Beauty on Parade
1950 Chain Gang
1950 Last of the Buccaneers
1950 Revenue Agent
1951 Blue Blood
1951 A Yank in Korea
1951 When the Redskins Rode
1951 The Big Gusher
1951 Hurricane Island
1951 The Magic Carpet
1951 Jungle Manhunt
1952 Aladdin and His Lamp
1952 Jungle Jim in Forbidden Land
1952 California Conquest
1952 Arctic Flight
1953 Torpedo Alley
1953 Tangier Incident
1953 Man in the Dark
1953 Run for the Hills
1953 Captain John Smith and Pocahontas / *Burning Arrows*
1954 Captain Kidd and the Slave Girl
1956 The Cruel Tower
1958 Hot Rod Gang / *Fury Unleashed*
1963 Terrified

LANDIS, James
1964 The Nasty Habit
1971 Deadwood '76

LANDIS, John
(1950–) Chicago, Illinois, USA.
1973 Schlock
1977 The Kentucky Fried Movie
1978 National Lampoon's Animal House
1980 The Blues Brothers
1981 An American Werewolf in London
1983 Twilight Zone — The Movie **(Joe DANTE, George MILLER, Steven SPIELBERG)**
1983 Trading Places
1985 Into the Night
1985 Spies Like Us
1986 The Three Amigos
1987 Amazon Women on the Moon **(Joe DANTE, Carl GOTTLIEB, Peter HORTON, Robert K WEISS)**
1988 Coming to America

LANDON, Michael (Eugene Orowitz)
(1937–) Forest Hills, New York, USA.
1984 Sam's Son
(also many TV movies and shorts)

LANDRES, Paul
(1912–) American.
1949 Grand Canyon
1949 Square Dance Jubilee
1950 Hollywood Varieties
1950 A Modern Marriage
1951 Rhythm Inn
1951 Navy Bound
1952 Army Bound
1953 Eyes of the Jungle
1957 Chain of Evidence
1957 Hell Canyon Outlaws
1957 Last of the Badmen

1957 New Day at Sundown
1957 Oregon Passage
1957 The Vampire
1957 The Return of Dracula / *The Fantastic Disappearing Man*
1958 The Flame Barrier
1958 Johnny Rocco
1958 Man from God's Country

LANE, Andrew
1986 Jake Speed

LANFIELD, Sidney
(1900–1972) Chicago, Illinois, USA.
1930 Cheer Up and Smile
1931 Three Girls Lost
1931 Hush Money
1932 Dance Team
1932 Society Girl
1932 Hat Check Girl / *Embassy Girl*
1933 Broadway Bad / *Her Reputation*
1934 Moulin Rouge
1934 The Last Gentleman
1935 Hold 'Em, Yale / *Uniform Lovers*
1935 Red Salute / *Runaway Daughter / Arms and the Girl*
1935 King of Burlesque
1936 Half Angel
1936 Sing, Baby Sing
1936 One in a Million
1936 Wake Up and Live
1937 Thin Ice / *Lovely to Look At*
1937 Love and Hisses
1938 Always Goodbye
1939 The Hound of the Baskervilles
1939 Second Fiddle
1939 Swanee River
1941 You'll Never Get Rich
1942 The Lady Has Plans
1942 My Favourite Blonde
1943 The Meanest Man in the World
1943 Let's Face It
1944 Standing Room Only
1945 Bring on the Girls
1946 The Well-Groomed Bride
1947 The Trouble with Women
1947 Where There's Life
1948 Station West
1949 Sorrowful Jones
1951 The Lemon Drop Kid
1951 Follow the Sun
1952 Skirts Ahoy!

LANG, Fritz
(1890–1976) Vienna, Austria. Biographies: Fritz Lang in Hollywood by Cornelius Schnauber; Fritz Lang in America by Peter Bogdanovich; Fritz Lang: The Image and the Look edited by Stephen Jenkins.
1924 Kriemhilde's Revenge / *Die Nibelungen Part II: Kriemhildes Rache*
1927 The Spy
1928 The Girl in the Moon / *By Rocket to the Moon*
1931 M
1932 The Testament of Dr Mabuse
1935 Liliom
1936 Fury
1937 You Only Live Once
1938 You and Me
1940 The Return of Frank James
1941 Man Hunt
1941 Western Union
1941 Confirm or Deny **(Archie MAYO)**
1942 Moontide **(Archie MAYO)**
1943 Hangmen Also Die / *Lest We Forget*
1944 Ministry of Fear
1945 Scarlet Street
1945 The Woman in the Window
1946 Cloak and Dagger
1948 Secret Beyond the Door
1950 American Guerilla in the Philippines / *I Shall Return*
1950 House By the River
1952 Clash By Night
1952 Rancho Notorious
1953 The Big Heat
1953 The Blue Gardenia
1954 Human Desire
1955 Moon Fleet
1956 Beyond a Reasonable Doubt
1956 While the City Sleeps
1960 The Thousand Eyes of Dr Mabuse

LANG, Richard
1980 The Mountain Men
1980 A Change of Season
(also many TV movies)

LANG, Rocky
1989 All's Fair / *Skirmish*

LANG, Walter
(1896–1972) Memphis, Tennessee, USA.
1925 The Red Kimono
1926 The Carnival Girl
1926 The Golden Web
1926 The Earth Woman
1926 Money to Burn
1927 By Whose Hand?
1927 The College Hero
1927 Sally in Our Alley
1927 The Satin Woman
1927 The Ladybird
1928 The Desert Bride
1928 The Night Flyer
1928 Shadows of the Past
1929 Spirit of Youth
1929 Brothers / *Two Sons*
1930 Hello, Sister
1930 Cock o' the Walk **(William Roy NEILL)**
1930 The Big Fight
1930 The Costello Murder Case
1930 Command Performance
1931 Hell Bound
1931 Women Go on Forever
1932 Meet the Baron
1932 No More Orchids
1933 The Warrior's Husband
1934 Whom the Gods Destroy
1934 The Mighty Barnum
1935 Carnival Nights
1935 Hooray for Love
1936 Love Before Breakfast
1937 Wife, Doctor and Nurse
1937 Second Honeymoon
1938 The Baroness and the Butler

1938 I'll Give a Million
1939 The Little Princess
1940 The Blue Bird
1940 Star Dust
1940 The Great Profile
1940 Tin Pan Alley
1941 Moon Over Miami
1941 Weekend in Havana
1942 Song of the Islands
1942 Magnificent Dope
1943 Coney Island
1944 Greenwich Village
1945 State Fair / *It Happened One Summer*
1946 Sentimental Journey
1946 Claudia and David
1947 Mother Wore Tights
1948 Sitting Pretty
1948 When My Baby Smiles at Me
1949 You're My Everything
1950 Cheaper By the Dozen
1950 The Jackpot
1951 On the Riviera
1952 With a Song in My Heart
1953 Call Me Madam
1954 There's No Business Like Show Business
1956 The King and I **D* F***
1957 Desk Set / *His Other Woman*
1959 But Not for Me
1960 Can-Can
1960 The Marriage-Go-Round
1961 Snow White and the Three Stooges

LANGLEY, Noel
(1911–) South African.
1952 The Pickwick Papers
1953 Our Girl Friday
1954 Svengali
1955 The Adventures of Sadie
1956 The Search for Bridey Murphy

LANGTON, Simon
(1941–) Amersham, Buckinghamshire, England.
1987 The Whistle Blower

LANSBURGH, Larry
1964 The Tattooed Police Horse

LANZA, Anthony M
1967 The Glory Stompers
1970 The Incredible Two-Headed Transplant

LARKIN, Christopher
1974 A Very Natural Thing

LARKIN, John
1943 Quiet Please, Murder
1945 Circumstantial Evidence

LARRY, Sheldon
(1949–) Canadian.
1985 Terminal Choice
1988 Our Boy Badenov
1988 Boardwalk

LARSEN, Keith
(1925–) American.
1969 Mission Batangas

LATHAN, Stan
1974 Amazing Grace
1984 Beat Street
(also many TV movies)

LATTUADA, Alberto *
(1914–) Milan, Italy.
1947 Flesh Will Surrender
1948 Without Pity
1949 The Mill on the Po
1950 Variety Lights **(Federico FELLINI)**
1951 Anna
1952 The Overcoat
1953 Love in the City **(Michelangelo ANTONIONI, Federico FELLINI, Carlo LIZZANI, Francesco MASELLI, Dino RISI)**
1954 The Beach
1958 Tempest
1960 Rita
1962 Mafioso
1965 The Love Root
1966 Matchless
1967 Don Giovanni in Sicilia
1970 Come Have Coffee with Us
1971 White Sister / *Bianco, Rosso e ...*
1976 Oh Serafina!

LAUGHLIN, Frank
1974 The Trial of Billy Jack
1975 The Master Gunfighter

LAUGHLIN, Michael
1981 Strange Behavior / *Dead Kids*
1983 Strange Invaders
1985 Mesmerized

LAUGHLIN, Tom
(1938–) Minneapolis, Minnesota, USA.
Pseudonyms: T.C. Frank; Donald Handerson; Lloyd James.
1960 The Proper Time
1965 The Young Sinner
1967 Born Losers
1971 Billy Jack
1978 Billy Jack Goes to Washington
1986 The Return of Billy Jack

LAUGHTON, Charles
(1889–1962) Scarborough, Yorkshire, England.
Biographies: Charles Laughton and I by Elsa Lancaster; The Charles Laughton Story by Kurt Singer; Charles Laughton by Charles Higham.
1955 The Night of the Hunter

LAUNDER, Frank
(1907–) Hitchin, Hertfordshire, England.
Biography: Launder and Gilliat by Geoffrey Brown.
1943 Millions Like Us **(Sidney GILLIAT)**
1944 Two Thousand Women
1945 I See a Dark Stranger / *The Adventuress*
1947 Captain Boycott
1949 The Blue Lagoon
1950 The Happiest Days of Your Life

1951 Lady Godiva Rides Again
1952 Folly to Be Wise
1954 The Belles of St Trinians
1955 Wee Geordie
1957 Blue Murder at St Trinians
1959 The Bridal Path
1960 The Pure Hell of St Trinians
1965 Joey Boy
1966 The Great St Trinians Train Robbery **(Sidney GILLIAT)**
1980 The Wildcats of St Trinians

LAUTNER, Georges *
(1926–) French.
1983 My Other Husband
1986 La Cage aux Folles III: The Wedding
1989 The Murdered House

LAVEN, Arnold
(1922–) Chicago, Illinois, USA.
1952 Without Warning
1953 Vice Squad / *The Girl in Room 17*
1954 Down Three Dark Streets
1956 The Rack
1957 The Monster That Challenged the World
1957 Slaughter on Tenth Avenue
1958 Anna Lucasta
1962 Geronimo
1965 The Glory Guys
1967 Rough Night in Jericho
1969 Sam Whiskey

LAW, Harold
1936 Neighbourhood House

LAWRENCE, Denny
1987 House Broken
1988 Afraid to Dance / *Kick Start*
1988 Army Wives

LAWRENCE, Edmund
1929 The House of Secrets

LAWRENCE, Marc (Max Goldsmith)
(1910–) New York, New York, USA.
1963 Nightmare in the Sun

LAWRENCE, Quentin
(c1920–1980) British.
1955 The Trollenberg Terror
1962 The Man Who Finally Died
1963 Cash on Demand
1964 The Secret of Blood Island

LAWRENCE, Ray
1986 Bliss

LAYTON, David
1989 Demon Hunters

LAZARUS, Ashley
1976 Forever Young, Forever Free / *E' Lollipop*
1977 Golden Rendezvous

LEACH, Wilford
1969 The Wedding Party **(Brian DePALMA, Cynthia MUNROE)**
1983 The Pirates of Penzance

LEACOCK, Philip
(1917–) London, England.
1946 Riders of the New Forest
1952 The Brave Don't Cry
1953 Assignment in London
1954 The Kidnappers
1955 Escapade
1956 The Spanish Gardener
1957 High Tide at Noon
1958 Innocent Sinners
1959 The Rabbit Trap
1960 Let No Man Write My Epitaph
1960 Take a Giant Step
1960 Hand in Hand
1962 Reach for Glory
1962 13 West Street
1962 The War Lover
1964 Tamahine
1970 Adam's Woman
(also many documentaries and TV movies)

LEADER, Tony
1964 Children of the Damned
1969 The Cockney Cowboys of Calico County

LEAN, David
(1908–) Croydon, Surrey, England.
1941 Major Barbara **(Harold FRENCH, Gabriel PASCAL)**
1942 In Which We Serve **(Noel COWARD)** **F***
1944 This Happy Breed
1945 Blithe Spirit
1946 Brief Encounter **D***
1947 Great Expectations **D* F***
1948 Oliver Twist
1949 The Passionate Friends / *One Woman's Story*
1950 Madeleine
1952 The Sound Barrier
1954 Hobson's Choice
1956 Summertime / *Summer Madness* **D***
1957 The Bridge Over the River Kwai **D** F****
1962 Lawrence of Arabia **D** F****
1965 Doctor Zhivago **D* F***
1970 Ryan's Daughter
1984 A Passage to India **D* F***
1987 Nostromo

LEAR, Norman
(1922–) New Haven, Connecticut.
1953 Scared Stiff **(George MARSHALL, Ed SIMMONS)**
1970 Cold Turkey

LeBORG, Reginald
(1902–) Vienna, Austria.
1943 She's for Me
1943 Calling Dr Death
1944 Weird Woman
1944 The Mummy's Ghost
1944 Jungle Woman
1944 San Diego, I Love You
1944 Dead Man's Eyes
1944 Destiny **(Julien DUVIVIER)**
1945 Honeymoon Ahead
1946 Joe Palooka, Champ

1946 Little Iodine
1946 Susie Steps Out
1947 Fall Guy
1947 The Adventures of Don Coyote
1947 Philo Vance's Secret Mission
1947 Joe Palooka in the Knockout
1948 Port Said
1948 Joe Palooka in Winner Take All
1948 Trouble Makers
1948 Joe Palooka in Fighting Mad
1949 Fighting Fools
1949 Hold That Baby!
1949 Joe Palooka in the Counterpunch
1950 Young Daniel Boone
1950 Wyoming Mail
1950 Joe Palooka in the Squared Circle
1951 G.I. Jane
1951 Joe Palooka in the Triple Cross
1952 Models Inc.
1953 The Flanagan Boy / *Bad Blonde*
1953 The Great Jesse James Raid
1953 Sins of Jezebel
1954 The White Orchid
1956 The Black Sheep
1957 Voodoo Island
1957 War Drums
1957 The Dalton Girls
1961 The Flight That Disappeared
1962 Deadly Duo
1963 Diary of a Madman
1964 The Eyes of Annie Jones
1973 So Evil My Sister
(also many shorts)

LEDER, Herbert J
1960 Pretty Boy Floyd
1966 The Frozen Dead
1967 It
1968 The Candy Man

LEDER, Paul
1974 I Disremember Mama
1976 A*P*E
1987 The Education of Allison Tate
1987 Jade Dragon Connection
1988 The 11th Commandment
1989 Twenty Dollar Star

LEDERER, Charles
(1911–1976) American.
1942 Fingers at the Windows
1951 On the Loose
1951 Never Steal Anything Small

LEDERMAN, D Ross
(1895–1972) American.
1927 A Dog of the Regiment
1928 A Race for Life
1928 Rinty of the Desert
1928 Shadows of the Night
1929 The Million Dollar Collar
1930 The Man Hunter
1931 The Texas Ranger
1931 Branded
1931 Range Feud
1932 Ridin' for Justice
1932 The Fighting Marshal
1932 High Speed
1932 Riding Tornado
1932 The Texas Cyclone
1932 Daring Danger
1932 Two-Fisted Law
1932 McKenna of the Mounted
1933 Speed Demon
1933 End of the Trail
1933 Whirlwind
1933 The State Trooper
1933 Soldiers of the Storm
1933 Rusty Rides Alone
1933 Silent Men
1934 Hell Bent for Love
1934 The Crime of Helen Stanley
1934 A Man's Game
1934 Beyond the Law
1934 Girl in Danger
1934 Murder in the Clouds
1934 Red Hot Tires
1935 Dinky **(Howard BRETHERTON)**
1935 Moonlight on the Prairie
1935 The Case of the Missing Men
1935 Too Tough to Kill
1936 Hell-Ship Morgan
1936 Panic on the Air
1936 Pride of the Marines
1936 The Final Hour
1936 Alibi for Murder
1936 Come Close, Folks
1937 Counterfeit Lady
1937 I Promise to Pay
1937 Motor Madness
1937 The Frame-Up
1937 The Game That Kills
1938 Juvenile Court
1938 The Little Adventuress
1938 Adventure in Sahara
1939 North of Shanghai
1939 Racketeers of the Range
1940 Military Academy
1940 Thundering Frontier
1940 Glamour for Sale
1941 Across the Sierras
1941 Father's Son
1941 Strange Alibi
1941 Shadows on the Stairs
1941 Passage from Hong Kong
1942 The Body Disappears
1942 Bullet Scars
1942 I Was Framed
1942 Escape from Crime
1942 Busses Roar
1942 The Gorilla Man
1943 Adventure in Iraq
1943 Find the Blackmailer
1943 The Racket Man
1944 The Last Ride
1946 The Phantom Thief
1946 Out of the Depths
1946 The Notorious Lone Wolf
1946 Dangerous Business
1946 Sing While You Dance
1946 Boston Blackie and the Law
1947 The Lone Wolf in Mexico
1947 Key Witness
1948 The Return of the Whistler
1950 Military Academy with That 10th Avenue Gang
1951 The Tanks Are Coming **(Lewis SEILER)**

LEE, Damien
1987 Circle Man

1988 After Food of the Gods / *Gnaw: Food of the Gods II*

LEE, Jack
(1913–) Stroud, England.
1947 The Woman in the Hall
1948 Once a Jolly Swagman / *Maniacs on Wheels*
1950 The Wooden Horse
1952 South of Algiers / *The Golden Mask*
1953 Turn the Key Softly
1956 A Town Like Alice / *The Rape of Malaya*
1957 Robbery Under Arms
1958 The Captain's Table
1960 Circle of Deception
(also many documentaries)

LEE, Norman
1933 Money Talks
1935 Royal Cavalcade **(Thomas BENTLEY, Herbert BRENON, W P KELLINO, Walter SUMMERS, Marcel VARNEL)**
1937 Bulldog Drummond at Bay
1938 Yes, Madam
1938 Kathleen
1940 The Door with Seven Locks / *Chamber of Horrors*
1949 The Case of Charles Peace
1950 The Girl Who Couldn't Quite

LEE, Rowland V
(1891–1975) Findlay, Ohio, USA.
1924 Gentle Julia
1924 In Love with Love
1925 Man Without a Country
1925 Havoc
1925 As No Man Has Loved
1926 The Silver Treasure
1926 The Outsider
1927 The Whirlwind of Youth
1928 The Secret Hour
1928 Doomsday
1928 Three Sinners
1928 The First Kiss
1928 Loves of an Actress
1929 Wolf of Wall Street
1929 A Dangerous Woman
1929 Mysterious Mr Fu Manchu
1930 The Return of Fu Manchu
1930 Ladies Love Brutes
1930 A Man from Wyoming
1930 Derelict
1931 The Ruling Voice
1931 The Guilty Generation
1931 Upper Underworld
1932 That Night in London / *Over Night*
1932 The Sign of Four **(Graham CUTTS)**
1933 Zoo in Budapest
1934 I Am Suzanne
1934 The Count of Monte Cristo
1934 Gambling
1935 Cardinal Richelieu
1935 The Three Musketeers
1936 One Rainy Afternoon
1937 Love from a Stranger
1937 The Toast of New York
1938 Mother Carey's Chickens
1938 Service De Luxe
1939 Son of Frankenstein
1939 The Sun Never Sets
1939 Tower of London
1940 The Son of Monte Cristo
1942 Powder Town
1944 The Bridge of San Luis Rey
1945 Captain Kidd

LEE, Spike (Shelton Jackson Lee)
1983 Joe's Bed-Study Barbershop: We Cut Heads
1986 She's Gotta Have It
1988 School Daze
1989 Do the Right Thing

LEEDS, Herbert I (Herbert I Levy)
(c1900–1954) American.
1938 Love on a Budget
1938 Island in the Sky
1938 Keep Smiling
1938 Five of a Kind
1938 Arizona Wildcat
1939 Mr Moto in Danger Island
1939 The Return of the Cisco Kid
1939 Chicken Wagon Family
1939 Charlie Chan in City in Darkness
1940 Cisco Kid and the Lady
1940 Yesterday's Heroes
1941 Romance of the Rio Grande
1941 Ride on Vaquero
1941 Blue White and Perfect
1942 The Man Who Wouldn't Die
1942 Just Off Broadway
1942 Manilla Calling
1942 Time to Kill
1946 It Shouldn't Happen to a Dog
1948 Let's Live Again
1950 Bunco Squad
1950 Father's Wild Game

LEEWOOD, Jack
1961 20,000 Eyes
1963 Thunder Island

LEGRAND, Michel
1988 Blind Love

LEHMAN, Ernest
(1920–) New York, New York, USA.
1972 Portnoy's Complaint

LEHMANN, Michael
1988 Lethal Attraction / *Heathers*
1989 Meet the Applegates

LEHRMAN, Henry (Pathé Lehrman)
(1886–1946) Vienna, Austria.
1926 The Fighting Edge
1927 Sailor Izzy Murphy
1927 Husbands for Rent
1928 Chicken à la King
1928 Homesick
1929 New Year's Eve

LEIFER, Neil
1988 Trading Hearts

LEIGH, Mike
1971 Bleak Moments
1989 High Hopes / *Winter*

LEISEN, Mitchell
(1898–1972) Menominee, Michigan, USA.
1933 Cradle Song
1934 Death Takes a Holiday
1934 Murder at the Vanities
1935 Behold My Wife
1935 Hands Across the Table
1935 Four Hours to Kill
1936 The Big Broadcast of 1937
1936 13 Hours By Air
1937 Easy Living
1937 Swing High, Swing Low
1938 Artists and Models Abroad / *Stranded in Paris*
1938 The Big Broadcast of 1938
1939 Midnight
1940 Arise My Love
1940 Remember the Night
1941 Hold Back the Dawn **F***
1941 I Wanted Wings
1942 The Lady Is Willing
1942 Take a Letter, Darling / *Green-Eyed Woman*
1943 No Time for Love
1944 Frenchman's Creek
1944 Lady in the Dark
1945 Practically Yours
1945 Masquerade in Mexico
1945 Kitty
1946 To Each His Own
1947 Golden Earrings
1947 Suddenly It's Spring
1948 Dream Girl
1949 Bride of Vengeance
1949 Song of Surrender
1950 Captain Carey, USA / *After Midnight*
1950 No Man of Her Own
1951 Darling, How Could You! / *Rendezvous*
1951 The Mating Season
1952 Young Man with Ideas
1953 Tonight We Sing
1955 Bedevilled
1957 The Girl Most Likely

LEITCH, Christopher
1979 The Hitter
1987 Teen Wolf Too
1989 Courage Mountain

LELAND, David
1987 Wish You Were Here
1989 Checking Out

LeLOUCH, Claude
(1937–) Paris, France.
1960 Le Propre de L'Homme
1963 L'Amour avec des Si
1964 La Femme Spectacle
1965 To Be a Crook / *The Decadent Influence / Une Fille et des Fusils*
1965 Les Grands Moments
1966 A Man and a Woman **D***
1967 Live for Life
1969 Life Love Death
1970 Love Is a Funny Thing / *Un Homme qui me Plait*
1971 The Crook
1971 Smic, Smac, Smoc
1972 Money Money Money / *L'Aventure c'est l'Aventure*
1973 Happy New Year
1975 And Now My Love / *Toute une Vie*
1975 Mariage
1975 Cat and Mouse
1976 The Good and the Bad
1976 Second Chance / *Si C'Etait à Refaire*
1977 Another Man, Another Chance
1978 Robert and Robert
1979 An Adventure for Two
1982 Bolero / *Within Memory / The Ins and Outs*
1983 Edith and Marcel
1984 Viva la Vie
1985 Partir Revenir
1986 A Man and a Woman (20 Years Later)
1987 Attention Bandits
(also many documentaries)

LEMAY, Alan
(1899–) American.
1950 High Lonesome

LEMMON, Jack
(1925–) Boston, Massachusetts, USA.
Biographies: Lemmon by Don Widener; Jack Lemmon by Michael Freedland.
1971 Kotch

LEMONT, John
(1914–) British.
1954 The Green Buddha
1959 The Shakedown
1960 And Women Shall Weep
1961 Konga
1961 Frightened City

LEMORANDE, Rusty
1988 Journey to the Center of the Earth

LENI, Paul
(1885–1929) Stuttgart, Germany.
1924 Waxworks / *Three Wax Men*
1927 The Cat and the Canary
1927 The Chinese Parrot
1928 The Man Who Laughs
1929 The Last Warning

LEONARD, Arthur
1939 Straight to Heaven
1940 Pocomania
1947 Boy! It's a Girl
1947 Sepia Cinderella

LEONARD, Brett
1988 The Dead Pit

LEONARD, Herbert B
(1922–) New York, New York, USA.
1967 The Perils of Pauline **(Joshua SHELLEY)**
1971 Going Home

LEONARD, Robert Z (Robert Zigler Leonard)
(1889–1968) Chicago, Illinois, USA.
1924 Circe the Enchantress
1924 Mademoiselle Midnight
1924 Love's Wilderness

1925 Cheaper to Marry
1925 Bright Lights
1925 Time, the Comedian
1926 Dance Madness
1926 The Waning Sex
1926 Mademoiselle Modiste
1927 A Little Journey
1927 The Demi-Bride
1927 Adam and Evil
1927 Tea for Two
1928 Baby Mine
1928 The Cardboard Lover
1928 A Lady of Chance
1929 Marianne
1930 In Gay Madrid
1930 The Divorcee **D* F***
1930 Let Us Be Gay
1931 The Bachelor Father
1931 It's a Wise Child
1931 Five and Ten / *Daughter of Luxury*
1931 Susan Lennox, Her Rise and Fall / *The Rise of Helga*
1932 Lovers Courageous
1932 Strange Interlude
1933 Peg o' My Heart
1933 Dancing Lady
1934 Outcast Lady / *A Woman of the World*
1935 Riff Raff
1935 After Office Hours
1935 Escapade
1936 The Great Ziegfeld **D* F****
1936 Piccadilly Jim
1937 Maytime
1937 Firefly
1938 The Girl of the Golden West
1939 Broadway Serenade
1940 New Moon
1940 Pride and Prejudice
1940 Third Finger, Left Hand
1941 Ziegfeld Girl
1941 When Ladies Meet
1942 We Were Dancing
1942 Stand By for Action / *Cargo of Innocence*
1943 The Man from Down Under
1944 Marriage Is a Private Affair
1945 Weekend at the Waldorf
1947 The Secret Heart
1948 Cynthia / *The Rich Full Life*
1948 B.F.'s Daughter / *Polly Fulton*
1949 The Bribe
1949 In the Good Old Summertime
1950 Nancy Goes to Rio
1950 Duchess of Idaho
1950 Grounds for Marriage
1951 Too Young to Kiss
1952 Everything I Have Is Yours
1953 The Clown
1953 The Great Diamond Robbery
1954 Her Twelve Men
1955 The King's Thief
1955 Beautiful But Dangerous
1957 Kelly and Me

LEONARD, Terry
1987 Death Before Dishonour

LEONE, John
1978 The Great Smokey Roadblock / *The Last of the Cowboys*

LEONE, Sergio
(1929–1989) Rome, Italy.
1960 The Colossus of Rhodes
1964 A Fistful of Dollars
1965 For a Few Dollars More
1966 The Good, the Bad and the Ugly
1969 Once Upon a Time in the West
1971 A Fistful of Dynamite / *Duck, You Sucker*
1984 Once Upon a Time in America

LEONG, Po-Chih (Liang Puzhi)
(1939–) London, England.
1976 Jumping Ash
1977 Foxbat
1977 Itchy Fingers
1979 No Big Deal
1981 Super Fool
1982 He Lives By Night
1984 Banana Cop
1985 Hong Kong 1941
1985 Time Traveller
1985 The Island
1985 Ping Pong

LERNER, Carl
(c1905–1975) American.
1964 Black Like Me

LERNER, Irving
(1909–1976) New York, USA.
1953 Man Crazy
1958 Murder By Contract
1958 Edge of Fury
1959 City of Fear
1960 Studs Lonigan
1963 Cry of Battle
1969 Royal Hunt of the Sun

LERNER, Joseph
1947 The Fight Never Ends
1949 C-Man
1950 Guilty Bystander
1950 Mr Universe

LERNER, Richard
1976 Revenge of the Cheerleaders

LeROY, Mervyn
(1900–1987) San Francisco, California, USA.
Autobiography: Take One.
1927 No Place to Go
1928 Flying Romeos
1928 Harold Teen
1928 Oh Kay!
1929 Naughty Baby / *Reckless Rosie*
1929 Hot Stuff
1929 Broadway Babies / *Broadway Daddies*
1929 Little Johnny Jones
1929 Playing Around
1930 Showgirl in Hollywood
1930 Numbered Men
1930 Top Speed
1931 Gold Dust Gertie
1931 Little Caesar
1931 Gentleman's Fate
1931 Too Young to Marry
1931 Broad Minded
1931 Five Star Final **F***

1931 Local Boy Makes Good
1931 Tonight or Never
1932 Heart of New York
1932 Two Seconds
1932 Big City Blues
1932 Three on a Match
1932 I Am a Fugitive from a Chain Gang **F***
1932 Hard to Handle
1933 Elmer the Great
1933 Gold Diggers of 1933
1933 Tugboat Annie
1933 The World Changes
1934 Hi, Nellie!
1934 Heat Lightning
1934 Happiness Ahead
1935 Sweet Adeline
1935 Oil from the Lamps of China
1935 Page Miss Glory
1935 I Found Stella Parrish
1935 Anthony Adverse
1935 Three Men on a Horse
1936 Road Gang
1937 The King and the Chorus Girl / *Romance Is Sacred*
1937 They Won't Forget
1937 Fools for Scandal
1938 The Marriage Business
1940 Waterloo Bridge
1940 Escape / *When the Door Opened*
1941 Blossoms in the Dust **F***
1941 Unholy Partners
1941 Johnny Eager
1942 Random Harvest **D* F***
1943 Madame Curie **F***
1944 Thirty Seconds Over Tokyo
1946 Without Reservations
1947 Desire Me **(Jack CONWAY, George CUKOR)**
1948 Homecoming
1949 Little Women
1949 Any Number Can Play
1950 East Side, West Side
1951 Quo Vadis **F***
1952 Lovely to Look At
1952 Million Dollar Mermaid / *The One Piece Bathing Suit*
1953 Latin Lovers
1954 Rose Marie
1955 Strange Lady in Town
1955 Mister Robert **(John FORD)** **F***
1956 The Bad Seed
1956 Toward the Unknown / *Brink of Hell*
1958 No Time for Sergeants
1958 Home Before Dark
1959 The FBI Story
1960 Wake Me When It's Over
1961 The Devil at 4 O'Clock
1962 A Majority of One
1962 Gypsy
1963 Mary, Mary
1966 Moment to Moment
1969 Downstairs at Ramsey's
1970 The 13 Clocks

LESTER, Mark L
(1946–) Cleveland, Ohio, USA.
1972 Tricia's Wedding
1973 Steel Arena
1974 Truck Stop Women
1975 White House Madness
1976 Bobbi Jo and the Outlaw
1977 Stunts / *Who Is Killing the Stuntmen?*
1979 Roller Boogie
1982 Class of 1984
1984 Firestarter
1985 Commando
1986 Armed and Dangerous
1989 Class of 1999
1990 Prime Directive

LESTER, Richard
(1932–) Philadelphia, Pennsylvania, USA.
1962 Ring-a-Ding Rhythm / *It's Trad, Dad*
1963 The Mouse on the Moon
1964 A Hard Day's Night
1965 The Knack. . And How to Get It
1965 Help!
1966 A Funny Thing Happened on the Way to the Forum
1967 Teenage Rebellion / *Mondo Teeno*
1967 How I Won the War
1968 Petulia
1969 The Bed Sitting Room
1974 The Three Musketeers / *The Queen's Diamonds*
1974 Juggernaut
1974 The Four Musketeers / *Milady's Revenge*
1976 Royal Flash
1976 Robin and Marion
1976 The Ritz
1979 Butch and Sundance: The Early Days
1979 Cuba
1981 Superman II
1983 Superman III
1984 Finders Keepers
1989 The Return of the Musketeers

LEVERING, Joseph
1931 Sea Devils
1931 Defenders of the Law
1933 Cheating Blondes
1938 Frontiers of '49
1938 In Early Arizona
1938 Pioneer Trail
1938 Phantom Gold
1938 Rolling Caravans
1938 Stagecoach Days
1939 The Law Comes to Texas
1939 Lone Star Pioneers

LEVESQUE, Michel
1971 Werewolves on Wheels
1973 Sweet Sugar

LEVEY, William A
1973 Blackenstein
1974 To Be a Rose
1975 Wam Bam Thank You Spaceman
1977 Slumber Party 157
1977 The Happy Hooker Goes to Washington
1979 Skatetown USA
1986 Lightning — The White Stallion
1988 Committed
1989 Hellgate

LEVIGARD, Joseph
1929 Born to the Saddle
1929 Grit Wins
1929 Slim Fingers
1929 The Smiling Terror

LEVIN, Henry
(1909–1980) Trenton, New Jersey, USA.
1944 Cry of the Werewolf
1944 Sergeant Mike
1945 Dancing in Manhattan
1945 I Love a Mystery
1946 The Fighting Guardsman
1946 The Bandit of Sherwood Forest **(George SHERMAN)**
1946 Night Editor
1946 The Unknown
1946 The Devil's Mask
1946 The Return of Monte Cristo
1947 The Guilt of Janet Ames
1947 The Corpse Came C.O.D.
1948 The Mating of Millie
1948 The Gallant Blade
1948 The Man from Colorado
1949 Mr Soft Touch / *House of Settlement* **(Gordon DOUGLAS)**
1949 Jolson Sings Again
1950 And Baby Makes Three
1950 Convicted
1950 The Petty Girl / *Girl of the Year*
1950 The Flying Missile
1951 Two of a Kind
1951 The Family Secret
1952 Belles on Their Toes
1953 The President's Lady
1953 The Farmer Takes a Wife
1953 Mister Scoutmaster
1954 Three Young Texans
1954 The Gambler from Natchez
1955 The Warriors / *The Dark Avenger*
1957 The Lonely Man
1957 Let's Be Happy
1957 Bernadine
1957 April Love
1958 A Nice Little Bank That Should Be Robbed
1959 The Remarkable Mr Pennypacker
1959 Holiday for Lovers
1959 Journey to the Center of the Earth
1960 Where the Boys Are
1962 The Wonderful World of the Brothers Grimm **(George PAL)**
1962 If a Man Answers
1963 Come Fly with Me
1964 Honeymoon Hotel
1965 Genghis Khan
1966 Murderers' Row
1967 The Ambushers
1969 The Desperadoes
1973 That Man Bolt **(David Lowell RICH)**
1978 Run for the Roses

LEVIN, Jack (Jack Jevne)
1935 The Ghost Rider

LEVIN, Sidney
1978 The Great Brain

LEVINSON, Barry
(1932–) New York, New York, USA.
1982 Diner
1984 The Natural
1985 Young Sherlock Holmes
1987 Tin Men
1988 Good Morning, Vietnam
1988 Rainman **D** F****

LEVINSON, Fred
1973 Hail to the Chief
1979 Washington B.C.

LEVITT, Gene
(1920–) New York, New York, USA.
1974 The Phantom of Hollywood
(also many TV movies)

LEVY, Ralph
(1919–) American.
1964 Bedtime Story
1965 Do Not Disturb

LEWIN, Albert
(1894–1968) Newark, New Jersey, USA.
1943 The Moon and Sixpence
1945 The Picture of Dorian Gray
1947 The Private Affairs of Bel Ami
1950 Pandora and the Flying Dutchman
1953 Saadia
1956 The Living Idol

LEWIN, Robert
1961 Third of a Man

LEWIS, Al
1955 Our Miss Brooks

LEWIS, Cecil
1932 Arms and the Man

LEWIS, David
1988 Dangerous Curves

LEWIS, Edgar
1927 One Glorious Scrap
1928 Made to Order Hero
1928 Put 'Em Up
1928 Arizona Cyclone
1928 The Fearless Rider
1929 Unmasked
1930 Ladies in Love
1930 Love at First Sight

LEWIS, Herschell Gordon
(1926–) American.
Pseudonyms: Lewis H Gordon; Mark Hanson; Armand Pays.
Sheldon Seymour; R.L. Smith.
1960 Living Venus
1961 The Adventures of Lucky Pierre
1962 Daughter of the Sun
1962 Nature's Playmates
1963 Boin-n-g
1963 Blood Feast
1963 Goldilocks and the Three Bears / *Goldilocks' Three Chicks*
1963 Bell, Bare and Beautiful
1963 Scum of the Earth / *Devil's Camera*

1964 2000 Maniacs
1964 Moonshine Mountain
1965 Colour Me Blood Red
1965 Monster a Go-Go / *Terror at Halfday*
1965 Sin, Suffer and Repent
1966 Jimmy, the Wonder Boy
1966 Alley Tramp
1966 An Eye for an Eye
1967 Santa Claus Visits the Land of Mother Goose
1967 Suburban Roulette
1967 Something Weird
1967 A Taste of Blood
1967 The Gruesome Twosome
1967 The Girl, the Body and the Pill
1967 Blast-Off Girls
1969 The Ecstasies of Women
1969 Linda and Abilene
1970 Miss Nymphet's Zap-In
1970 The Wizard of Gore
1971 This Stuff'll Kill Ya!
1972 Year of the Yahoo!
1972 Black Love
1972 The Gore-Gore Girls

LEWIS, Jay
(1914–1969) British.
1956 The Baby and the Battleship
1961 Invasion Quartet
1962 Live Now Pay Later
1965 Home of Your Own

LEWIS, Jerry (Joseph Levitch)
(1926–) Newark, New Jersey, USA. Biography: The Story of Jerry Lewis by Richard Gehman.
1960 The Bellboy
1961 The Ladies' Man
1962 The Errand Boy
1963 The Nutty Professor
1964 The Patsy
1965 The Family Jewels
1966 Three on a Couch
1967 The Big Mouth
1970 One More Time
1970 Which Way to the Front?
1981 Hardly Working
1983 Smorgasbord

LEWIS, Joseph H
(1900–) New York, New York, USA.
1937 Navy Spy **(Wilbur CRANE)**
1937 The Singing Outlaw
1937 Courage of the West
1938 The Spy Ring
1938 Border Wolves
1938 The Last Stand
1940 Two-Fisted Rangers / *Forestalled*
1940 Blazing Six Shooters / *Stolen Wealth*
1940 Texas Stage-Coach / *Two Roads*
1940 The Man from Tumbleweeds
1940 The Return of Wild Bill / *False Evidence*
1940 Boys of the City
1940 That Gang of Mine
1941 Pride of the Bowery / *Here We Go Again*
1941 The Invisible Ghost
1941 Criminals Within
1941 Arizona Cyclone
1942 Bombs Over Burma
1942 The Silver Bullet
1942 Secrets of a Co-Ed / *Silent Witness*
1942 The Boss of Hangtown Mesa
1942 The Mad Doctor of Market Street
1944 Minstrel Man
1945 The Falcon in San Francisco
1945 My Name Is Julia Rose
1946 So Dark the Night
1946 The Jolson Story
1947 The Swordsman
1948 The Return of October / *A Date with Destiny*
1949 The Undercover Man
1949 Gun Crazy / *Deadly Is the Female*
1950 A Lady Without Passport
1952 Retreat Hell!
1952 Desperate Search
1953 Cry of the Hunted
1955 The Big Combo
1955 A Lawless Street
1956 The Seventh Cavalry
1957 The Halliday Brand
1958 Terror in a Texan Town

LEWIS, Robert
1956 Anything Goes

LEWIS, Vance
1975 The Silent Stranger

LEWISTON, Dennis
1985 Hot Target

LEYTES, Josef
1952 Faithful City
1967 Valley of Mystery
1968 The Counterfeit Killer

LIEBERMAN, Art
1975 Up Your Alley
1979 The Melon Affair

LIEBERMAN, Jeff
1976 Squirm
1979 Blue Sunshine
1980 Just Before Dawn
1988 Remote Control

LIEBERMAN, Robert
1983 Table for Five
1989 Honeymoon

LILIENTHAL, Peter
(1929–) German.
1976 Er herrscht Ruhe im Land
1979 David
1981 The Uprising
1982 Dear Mr Wonderful
1984 The Autograph
1986 Das Schweigen des Dichters

LILLEY, Edward C
(1896–1974) American.
1942 Cross Your Fingers
1942 Never a Dull Moment
1943 Honeymoon Lodge
1943 Larceny with Music
1943 Moonlight in Vermont
1944 Allergic to Love

1944 Babes on Swing Street
1944 Hi, Good Lookin'
1944 My Gal Loves Music
1944 Sing a Jingle
1945 Her Lucky Night
1945 Swing Out Sister

LINDSAY, Lance
1986 Star Crystal

LINDSAY-HOGG, Michael
(1940–) New York, New York, USA.
1976 Nasty Habits

LINK, John F
1947 Call of the Forest
1948 Devil's Cargo

LINSON, Art
1980 Where the Buffalo Roam
1984 The Wild Life

LIPPERT, Robert L
(1909–) American.
1948 Last of the Wild Horses

LIPSTADT, Aaron
(1952–) Southington, Connecticut, USA.
1982 Arnold
1984 City Limits

LISBERGER, Steven
(1951–) Rye, New York, USA.
1982 Tron
1987 Hot Pursuit
1989 Slipstream

LITTLE, Dwight
1984 Lethal / *KGB — The Secret War*
1986 Getting Even
1987 Night Crawler
1988 Bloodstone
1988 Halloween IV: The Return of Michael Myers
1989 The Phantom of the Opera

LITTLEWOOD, Joan
(1914–) British.
1962 Sparrows Can't Sing

LITTMAN, Lynne
1983 Testament

LITVAK, Anatole (Mikhail Anatol Litvak)
(1902–1974) Kiev, Russia.
1924 Hearts and Dollars
1930 Dolly Gets Ahead
1931 No More Love
1932 Be Mine Tonight
1932 Lilac
1933 Sleeping Car
1935 Flight into Darkness
1936 Mayerling
1937 Tovarich
1937 The Woman I Love / *The Woman Between*
1938 The Amazing Mr Clitterhouse
1938 The Sisters
1939 Confessions of a Nazi Spy
1940 Castle on the Hudson / *Years Without Days*
1940 All This and Heaven Too **F***
1940 City for Conquest
1941 Out of the Fog
1941 Blues in the Night
1942 This Above All
1947 The Long Night
1948 Sorry, Wrong Number
1948 The Snake Pit **D* F***
1952 Decision Before Dawn **F***
1953 Act of Love
1955 The Deep Blue Sea
1956 Anastasia
1959 The Journey
1961 Goodbye Again / *Aimez-Vous Brahms?*
1963 Five Miles to Midnight
1967 The Night of the Generals
1970 The Lady in the Car with Glasses and a Gun
(also many documentaries)

LIZZANI, Carlo *
(1917–) Rome, Italy.
Pseudonym: Lee W. Beaver.
1953 Love in the City **(Michaelangelo ANTONIONI, Federico FELLINI, Alberto LATTUADA, Francesco MASELLI, Dino RISI)**
1966 The Dirty Game / *Guerre Secrète* **(Christian JACQUE, Werner KLINGER, Terence YOUNG)**
1966 Thrilling **(Dino De LAURENTIIS, Gian Luigi POLIDORI, Ettore SCOLA)**
1966 The Hills Run Red / *Un Fiume di Dollari*
1967 Requiescant
1968 The Violent Four
1974 Crazy Joe
1974 The Last Four Days / *Mussolini: Ultimo Atto*

LLOSA, Luis
1987 Hour of the Assassin

LLOYD, Frank
(1889–1960) Glasgow, Scotland.
1924 Black Oxen
1924 The Sea Hawk
1924 The Silent Watcher
1925 The Winds of Chance
1925 The Splendid Road
1925 Her Husband's Secret
1926 The Wise Guy
1926 The Eagle of the Sea
1927 Children of Divorce
1928 Adoration
1929 Weary River
1929 The Divine Lady **D****
1929 Drag / *Parasites*
1929 Young Nowheres
1929 Dark Streets
1930 Son of the Gods
1930 The Way of All Men
1931 The Lash / *Adios*
1931 East Lynne **F***
1931 The Right of Way
1931 The Age of Love
1932 A Passport to Hell

1933 Cavalcade **D** F****
1933 Berkeley Square
1933 Hoopla
1934 Servants' Entrance
1935 Mutiny on the Bounty **D* F****
1936 Under Two Flags
1937 Maid of Salem
1937 Wells Fargo
1937 Arizona Mahoney
1938 If I Were King
1939 Rulers of the Sea
1940 The Howards of Virginia / *The Tree of Liberty*
1941 The Lady from Cheyenne
1941 This Woman Is Mine
1943 Forever and a Day **(René CLAIR, Edmund GOULDING, Cedric HARDWICKE, Victor SAVILLE, Robert STEVENSON, Herbert WILCOX)**
1945 Blood on the Sun
1954 The Shanghai Story
1955 The Last Command
(also many silent shorts)

LOACH, Chris
1988 The 13th Floor

LOACH, Kenneth
(1936–) Nuneaton, Warwickshire, England.
1967 Poor Cow
1969 Kes
1971 Wednesday's Child / *Family Life*
1979 Black Jack
1980 The Gamekeeper
1981 Looks and Smiles
1986 Fatherland
(also many British TV movies)

LO BIANCO, Tony
1984 Too Scared to Scream

LOCKE, Peter
1971 You've Got to Walk It Like You Talk It or You'll Lose That Beat

LOCKE, Sondra
(1947–) Shelbyville, Indiana, USA.
1986 Ratboy
1989 Impulse

LOCKWOOD, Roy
1937 The Mutiny of the Elsinore
1957 Jamboree

LODEN, Barbara
(1932–1980) Marion, North Carolina, USA.
1971 Wanda

LOGAN, Bruce
1986 Vendetta / *Angel Behind Bars*

LOGAN, Joshua (Joshua Lockwood Logan)
(1908–) Texarkana, Texas, USA. Autobiographies: Josh, My Up and Down, In and Out Life: Movie Stars, Real People and Me.
1938 I Met My Love Again **(Arthur RIPLEY)**
1956 Picnic **D* F***
1956 Bus Stop / *The Wrong Kind of Girl*
1957 Sayonara **D* F***
1958 South Pacific
1960 Tall Story
1961 Fanny **F***
1964 Ensign Pulver
1967 Camelot
1969 Paint Your Wagon

LOGAN, Stanley
1937 First Lady
1938 Love, Honour and Behave
1938 Women Are Like That
1942 The Falcon's Brother

LOGOTHETIS, Dimitri
1987 Pretty Smart / *The Bentley Academy*
1988 Slaughterhouse Rock

LOMA, José Antonio de la
1987 Counterforce
1988 Fine Gold
1989 A Man of Passion

LOMBARDO, Louis
1975 Russian Roulette
1987 P.K. and the Kid

LOMMEL, Ulli
(1944–) German.
1973 Tenderness of the Wolves
1976 Der Mann von Oberzalberg — Adolf und Marlene
1979 Black Generation
1979 Cocaine Cowboys
1980 The Boogey Man
1983 A Taste of Sin
1983 Brainwaves
1983 The Devonsville Terror
1984 Strangers in Paradise
1985 Revenge of the Stolen Stars
1986 IFO
1988 Warbirds

LONCRAINE, Richard
(1946–) Cheltenham, Gloucestershire, England.
1972 Radio Wonderful
1975 Flame
1976 The Haunting of Julia / *Full Circle*
1982 Brimstone and Treacle
1982 The Missionary
1988 Bellman and True

LONDON, Jerry
(1937–) Los Angeles, California, USA.
1987 Rent-a-Cop
(also many TV movies)

LORD, Del
(1895–) American.
1929 Barnum Was Right
1936 Trapped By Television
1937 What Price Vengeance?
1944 Kansas City Kitty
1944 She's a Sweetheart
1945 I Love a Bandleader
1945 Rough, Tough and Ready

1945 Blonde from Brooklyn
1945 Hit the Hay
1946 In Fast Company
1946 It's Great to Be Young
1946 Singin' in the Corn

LORD, Jean-Claude *
(1943–) Montreal, Quebec, Canada.
1982 Visiting Hours
1984 Covergirl
1985 Frankenstein '88 / *The Vindicator*
1986 Toby McTeague

LORING, Thomas Z
1942 Who Is Hope Schuyler?
1943 Thru Different Eyes
1943 He Hired the Boss

LOSEY, Joseph
(1909–1984) La Crosse, Wisconsin, USA.
Pseudonyms: Andrea Forzano; Victor Hanbury; Joseph Walton.
Biography: Losey on Losey edited by Tom Milne.
1948 The Boy with Green Hair
1950 The Lawless / *The Dividing Line*
1951 M
1951 The Big Night
1951 The Prowler
1952 Stranger on the Prowl / *Encounter*
1954 The Sleeping Tiger
1955 Finger of Guilt / *The Intimate Stranger*
1956 Time Without Pity
1957 The Gypsy and the Gentleman
1958 Blind Date / *Chance Meeting*
1962 The Criminal / *The Concrete Jungle*
1962 These Are the Damned
1962 Eve / *Eva*
1963 The Servant
1964 King and Country
1966 Modesty Blaise
1967 Accident
1968 Boom!
1968 Secret Ceremony
1970 Figures in the Landscape
1971 The Go-Between
1972 The Assassination of Trotsky
1973 A Doll's House
1975 Galileo
1975 The Romantic Englishwoman
1977 Mr Klein
1978 The Roads to the South
1979 Don Giovanni
1982 The Trout
1984 Steaming

LOTEANU, Emil
(1936–) Bukovina, Russia.
1963 Wait for Us at Dawn
1966 Red Meadows
1968 Frescos on the White
1969 This Instant
1972 Lautary
1973 My White City
1976 Into the Sunset
1978 The Shooting Party
1985 Anna Pavlova: A Woman for All Time

LOURIE, Eugène
(1905–) French.
1953 The Beast from Twenty Thousand Fathoms
1958 The Colossus of New York
1959 The Giant Behemoth **(Douglas HICKOK)**
1960 Gorgo
1978 An Enemy of the People

LOUZIL, Eric
1987 Lust for Freedom / *Georgia County Lockup*

LOVENTHAL, Charlie
1983 The First Time
1987 My Demon Lover

LOVER, Anthony
1975 Distance

LOVERING, Otho
1936 Wanderer of the Wasteland
1936 Border Flight
1936 Drift Fence
1936 The Sky Parade

LOVITT, Bert
1984 Prince Jack

LOWENSTEIN, Richard
1987 Dogs in Space

LOWRY, Dick
1983 Smokey and the Bandit, Part III
(also many TV movies)

LOY, Nanni *
(1925–) Cagliari, Sardinia, Italy.
1962 The Four Days of Naples
1965 Made in Italy
1971 Why / *Detenuto in Attesta di Giudizio*
1980 Café Express
1984 Where's Picone?

LUBIN, Arthur
(1901–) California, USA.
1934 A Successful Failure
1935 Great God Gold
1935 Honeymoon Limited
1935 Two Sinners
1935 Frisco Waterfront / *When We Look Back*
1936 The House of a Thousand Candles
1936 Yellowstone
1937 Mysterious Crossing
1937 California Straight Ahead
1937 I Cover the War
1937 Idol of the Crowds
1937 Adventure's End
1938 Midnight Intruder
1938 Beloved Brat / *A Dangerous Age*
1938 Prison Break
1938 Secrets of a Nurse
1938 Risky Business
1939 Big Town Czar
1939 Mickey the Kid
1939 Call a Messenger
1940 The Big Guy
1940 Black Friday

1940 Gangs of Chicago
1940 I'm Nobody's Sweetheart Now
1940 Meet the Wildcat
1940 Who Killed Aunt Maggie?
1941 San Francisco Docks
1941 Where Did You Get That Girl?
1941 Buck Privates / *Rookies*
1941 In the Navy
1941 Hold That Ghost
1941 Keep 'Em Flying
1942 Ride 'Em Cowboy
1942 Eagle Squadron
1943 White Savage / *White Captive*
1943 The Phantom of the Opera
1944 Ali Baba and the Forty Thieves
1945 Delightfully Dangerous
1946 The Spider Woman Strikes Back
1946 A Night in Paradise
1947 New Orleans
1949 Impact
1949 Francis
1951 Queen for a Day
1951 Francis Goes to the Races
1952 It Grows on Trees
1952 South Sea Woman / *Pearl of the South Pacific*
1953 Francis Covers the Big Time
1954 Francis Joins the WACS
1955 Francis in the Navy
1955 Footsteps in the Fog
1955 Lady Godiva of Coventry
1955 Star of India
1956 The First Travelling Saleslady
1957 Escapade in Japan
1961 Thief of Baghdad
1964 The Incredible Mr Limpet
1966 Hold On!
1971 Rain for a Dusty Summer
(also many TV comedy shorts)

LUBITSCH, Ernst
(1892–1947) Berlin, Germany.
1924 The Marriage Circle
1924 Forbidden Paradise
1924 Three Women
1924 Montmartre
1925 Kiss Me Again
1925 Lady Windermere's Fan
1926 So This Is Paris
1927 The Student Prince in Old Heidelberg
1928 The Patriot **D* F***
1929 The Love Parade **D* F***
1929 Eternal Love
1930 Monte Carlo
1932 Broken Lullaby / *The Man I Killed*
1932 The Smiling Lieutenant **F***
1932 One Hour with You **(George CUKOR) F***
1932 Trouble in Paradise
1932 If I Had a Million **(James CRUZE, H Bruce HUMBERSTONE, Norman Z LEONARD, Stephen ROBERTS, William A SEITER, Norman TAUROG)**
1933 Design for Living
1934 The Merry Widow
1937 Angel
1938 Bluebeard's Eighth Wife
1939 Ninotchka **F***
1940 The Shop Around the Corner
1941 That Uncertain Feeling
1942 To Be or Not to Be
1943 Heaven Can Wait **D* F***
1945 A Royal Scandal / *Czarina* **(Otto PREMINGER)**
1946 Cluny Brown
1948 That Lady in Ermine **(Otto PREMINGER)**
(also many foreign shorts)

LUBY, S Roy
1935 Outlaw Rule
1935 Range Warfare
1935 Lightning Triggers
1936 The Crooked Trail
1936 The Desert Phantom
1936 Rogue of the Range
1937 Border Phantom
1937 Race Suicide
1937 The Red Rope
1937 Tough to Handle
1940 The Range Busters
1940 Trailing Double Trouble
1940 West of Pinto Basin
1941 Fugitive Valley
1941 The Kid's Last Ride
1941 Trail of the Silver Spurs
1941 Tumbledown Ranch in Arizona
1941 Wrangler's Roost
1941 Saddle Mountain Roundup
1941 Tonto Basin Outlaws
1941 Underground Rustlers
1942 Pride of the Army
1942 Boot Hill Bandits
1942 Rocky River Renegades
1942 Texas Trouble Shooters
1942 Thunder River Feud
1942 Arizona Stagecoach
1943 Black Market Rustlers
1943 Cowboy Commandos
1943 Land of Hunted Men

LUCAS, George
(1944–) Modesto, California, USA. Biography: Skywalking, The Life and Films of George Lucas by Dale Pollach.
1970 THX 1138
1973 American Graffiti **D* F***
1977 Star Wars **D* F***

LUCENTE, Francesco
1987 The Virgin Queen of St Francis High / *Paradise Bungalows*

LUDMAN, Larry
1983 Thunder

LUDWIG, Edward
(1895–1982) Russia.
1932 Steady Company
1933 They Just Had to Get Married
1934 A Woman's Man
1934 Let's Be Ritzy / *Millionaire for a Day*
1934 Friends of Mr Sweeney
1935 The Man Who Reclaimed His Head
1935 Age of Indiscretion
1935 Old Man Rhythm
1935 Three Kids and a Queen / *The Baxter Millions*
1936 Fatal Lady

1936 Adventure in Manhattan / *Manhattan Madness*
1937 Her Husband Lies
1937 The Last Gangster
1938 That Certain Age
1939 Coast Guard
1940 Swiss Family Robinson
1941 The Man Who Lost Himself
1942 Born to Sing **(Busby BERKELEY)**
1943 They Came to Blow Up America
1944 The Fighting Seabees
1944 Three Is a Family
1947 The Fabulous Texan
1948 Wake of the Red Witch
1949 The Big Wheel
1951 Smuggler's Island
1952 Caribbean
1952 Big Jim McLain
1952 The Blazing Forest
1953 The Vanquished
1953 Sangaree
1954 Jivaro / *Lost Treasure of the Amazon*
1955 Flame of the Islands
1957 The Black Scorpion
1963 The Gun Hawk

LUMET, Sidney
(1924–) Philadelphia, Pennsylvania, USA.
1957 Twelve Angry Men **D* F***
1958 Stage Struck
1959 That Kind of Woman
1960 The Fugitive Kind
1961 A View from the Bridge
1962 Long Day's Journey into Night
1964 Fail-Safe
1965 The Pawnbroker
1965 The Hill
1965 The Group
1967 The Deadly Affair
1968 Bye Bye Braverman
1968 The Seagull
1969 The Appointment
1970 Last of the Mobile Hot-Shots
1971 The Anderson Tapes
1972 Child's Play
1973 The Offense
1973 Serpico
1974 Lovin' Molly
1974 Murder on the Orient Express
1975 Dog Day Afternoon **D* F***
1976 Network **D* F***
1977 Equus
1977 The Wiz
1980 Just Tell Me What You Want
1981 Prince of the City
1982 Deathtrap
1982 The Verdict **D* F***
1983 Daniel
1984 Garbo Talks
1986 Power
1987 The Morning After
1988 Running on Empty
1989 Family Business
1990 Q & A

LUPINO, Ida
(1918–) London, England.
1950 Outrage
1951 Never Fear
1951 Hard, Fast and Beautiful
1951 On Dangerous Ground **(Nicholas RAY)**
1953 The Hitch-Hiker
1953 The Bigamist
1956 The Trouble with Angels
(also many TV shorts)

LURASCHI, Tony
1980 The Outsider

LUSTGARDEN, Steven
(1951–) American.
1983 American Taboo
1986 American Hero

LUSTIG, William
(1955–) Bronx, New York, USA.
1977 The Violation of Claudia
1981 Maniac
1983 Vigilante
1988 Maniac Cop
1988 Hit List
1989 Relentless

LYNCH, David
(1946–) Missoula, Montana, USA.
1978 Eraserhead
1980 The Elephant Man **D* F***
1984 Dune
1986 Blue Velvet **D***
1988 One Saliva Bubble
1988 Running Rocket

LYNCH, Paul
(1946–) Canadian.
1974 The Hard Part Begins
1978 Blood and Guts
1980 Prom Night
1982 Humongous
1983 Cross-Country
1985 Flying
1986 Bullies
1987 Mania **(David M ROBERTSON, John SHEPPARD)**
1987 Blindside

LYNE, Adrian
1980 Foxes
1983 Flashdance
1985 9½ Weeks
1987 Fatal Attraction **D* F***
1987 Diversion

LYNN, Henry
1939 Mothers of Today

LYNN, Jonathon
1985 Clue
1989 Nuns on the Run

LYNN, Robert
(1918–1982) British.
1961 Postman's Knock
1962 Dr Crippen
1965 Victim Five
1966 Change Partners

LYNWOOD, Burt
1935 Motive for Revenge
1935 The Firetrap

1935 Reckless Roads
1937 Shadows of the Orient

LYON, Francis D
(1905–) American.
1953 Crazylegs
1954 The Bob Mathias Story / *The Flaming Torch*
1955 The Cult of the Cobra
1956 The Great Locomotive Chase
1957 The Oklahoman
1957 Bailout at 43,000
1957 Gunsight Ridge
1958 South Seas Adventure **(many others)**
1959 Escort West
1961 Tomboy and the Champ
1963 The Young and the Brave
1966 Destination Inner Space
1967 Castle of Evil
1968 The Destructors
1968 The Money Jungle
1969 The Girl Who Knew Too Much

LYTELL, Bert
(1888–1954) American.
1936 Along Came Love **(Duncan MANSFIELD)**

MAAS, Dick
1983 The Lift
1988 Amsterdamned

MACARTHUR, Charles
(1895–1956) Cranton, USA.
Biography: Charlie: The Improbable Life and Times of Charlie Macarthur by Ben Hecht.
1934 Crime Without Passion **(Ben HECHT)**
1935 The Scoundrel **(Ben HECHT)**
1935 Soak the Rich **(Ben HECHT)**
1936 Once in a Blue Moon **(Ben HECHT)**

MACDONALD, David
(1904–1983) Scottish.
1936 Double Alibi
1937 The Lost Curtain
1937 Riding High
1937 It's Never Too Late to Mend
1937 Death Croons the Blues
1937 When the Poppies Bloom Again
1938 Make It Three
1938 Dead Men Tell No Tales
1938 Meet Mr Penny
1938 This Man Is News
1938 A Spot of Bother
1939 Spies of the Air / *Law and Disorder*
1939 This Man in Paris
1939 The Midas Touch
1940 This England
1947 The Brothers
1948 Good Time Girl
1948 Snowbound
1949 Diamond City
1949 Christopher Columbus
1949 The Bad Lord Byron
1950 Cairo Road
1950 The Adventurers
1952 The Big Frame / *The Lost Hours*
1953 Tread Softly
1954 Devil Girl from Mars
1956 Alias John Preston
1957 Small Hotel
1958 Moonraker
1958 A Lady Mislaid
1961 Petticoat Pirates
1962 The Golden Rabbit

MacDONALD, Peter
1988 Rambo III
1989 Colossus

MacDOUGALL, Ranald
(1916–1973) American.
1955 Queen Bee
1956 Hot Cars
1957 Man on Fire
1959 The World, the Flesh and the Devil
1960 The Subterraneans
1961 Go Naked in the World

MacFADDEN, Hamilton
(1901–) American.
1930 Harmony at Home
1930 Crazy That Way
1930 Oh, For a Man!
1930 Are You There?
1931 Charlie Chan Carries On
1931 The Black Camel
1931 Riders of the Purple Sage
1931 Their Mad Moment **(Chandler SPRAGUE)**
1932 Cheaters at Play
1933 Second Hand Wife
1933 The Fourth Horseman
1933 Trick for Trick
1933 The Man Who Dared
1933 Charlie Chan's Greatest Case
1934 As Husbands Go
1934 Hold That Girl
1934 Stand Up and Cheer
1934 She Was a Lady
1935 Elinor Norton
1935 Fighting Youth
1937 Three Legionnaires
1937 It Can't Last Forever
1937 Sea Racketeers
1937 Escape By Night
1942 Inside the Law

MACHATY, Gustav *
(1901–1963) Prague, Czechoslovakia.
1938 The Wrong Way Out
1939 Within the Law
1945 Jealousy

MACK, Brice
1978 Jennifer
1979 Half a House
1979 Swap Meet

MACK, Ray
1942 Hillbilly Blitzkrieg

MACK, Russell
(1892–1972) American.
1930 Second Wife
1930 Big Money
1930 Night Work
1931 Lonely Wives
1931 The Spirit of Notre Dame

1931 Heaven on Earth
1932 Once in a Lifetime
1932 The All American
1932 Scandal for Sale
1933 Private Jones
1934 The Band Plays On
1934 Meanest Girl in Town

MACK, Willard
1929 The Voice of the City
1933 What Price Innocence?
1933 Broadway to Hollywood / *Ring Up the Curtain*

MACKENDRICK, Alexander (Sandy Mackendrick)
(1912–) Boston, Lincolnshire, England.
1948 Whisky Galore! / *Tight Little Island*
1951 The Man in the White Suit
1952 Mandy / *The Crash of Silence*
1954 The Maggie / *High and Dry*
1956 The Ladykillers
1957 Sweet Smell of Success
1963 Sammy Going South / *A Boy Ten Feet Tall*
1965 A High Wind in Jamaica
1967 Don't Make Waves

MacKENNA, Kenneth (Leo Mielziner)
(1899–1962) American.
1931 Always Goodbye **(William Cameron MENZIES)**
1931 The Spider **(William Cameron MENZIES)**
1932 Good Sport
1932 Careless Lady
1933 Walls of Gold
1934 Sleepers East

MACKENZIE, John
(1932–) Edinburgh, Scotland.
1970 One Brief Summer
1971 Unman, Wittering and Zigo
1975 Made
1980 The Long Good Friday
1983 The Honorary Consul / *Beyond the Limit*
1985 The Innocent
1987 The Fourth Protocol
1989 Street Legal
(also many TV movies)

MACKENZIE, Peter
1988 Mission Manila / *Web*
1989 Merchants of War

MACKENZIE, Will
1988 A Hobo's Christmas
1989 Worth Winning

MACKEY, Clarke
1987 Taking Care / *Prescription for Murder*

MacLAINE, Shirley (Shirley Maclean Beaty)
(1934–) Richmond, Virginia, USA. Autobiographies: Don't Fall Off the Mountain; You Can't Get There from Here; Out on a Limb.
1975 The Other Half of the Sky

MacNAUGHTON, Ian
1971 And Now for Something Completely Different

MACRAE, Henry
(1888–) American.
1927 Wild Beauty
1928 The Danger Rider
1928 Guardians of the Wild
1928 The Two Outlaws
1929 Burning the Wind
1929 The Harvest of Hate
1929 Hoofbeats of Vengeance
1929 Plunging Hoofs
1929 Smilin' Guns
1929 Wild Blood

MADDEN, Lee
1969 Hell's Angels of '69
1970 Angel Unchained
1973 The Manhandlers
1973 The Night God Screamed
1978 Out of the Darkness / *Night Creatures*
1984 Ghost Fever / *Benny and Buford*

MADDEN, Paul
1989 Medium Rare
1989 Summer Job

MADDOW, Ben (David Wolff)
1963 An Affair of the Skin

MAGAR, Guy
1988 Retribution

MAGDER, Murray
1988 Galucci Brothers / *The Brothers Spaghetti*

MAGNATTA, Constantino
1987 The Darkside
1988 Freakshow

MAGNOLI, Albert
1984 Purple Rain
1986 American Anthem

MAGWOOD, Paul
1971 Chandler

MAHARAJ, Anthony
1987 Mission Terminate / *Cooper*
1987 Not Another Mistake

MAILER, Norman
(1923–) Long Branch, New Jersey, USA.
1968 Wild 90
1968 Beyond the Law
1971 Maidstone
1987 Tough Guys Don't Dance

MAJEWSKI, Lech
1986 The Flight of the Spruce Goose
1987 Prisoner of Rio

MAJOR, Anthony
1974 Super Spook

MAK, Johnny (Mai Dangxiong)
(1949–) Hong Kong.
1984 Long Arm of the Law
1987 Red Guards in Hong Kong

MAKAVEJEV, Dusan
(1932–) Belgrade, Yugoslavia.
1965 Man Is Not a Bird
1966 Love Affair, Or the Case of the Missing Switchboard Operator
1968 Innocence Unprotected
1971 WR, Mysteries of the Organism
1975 Sweet Movie
1981 Montenegro, or Pigs and Pearls
1985 The Coca Cola Kid
1988 For a Night of Love
1989 Manifesto

MAKELIM, Hal
1953 Man of Conflict

MAKK, Karoly
(1925–) Hungarian.
1954 Lilomfi
1955 Ward No 9
1958 The House Under the Rocks
1961 The Fanatics
1962 The Lost Paradise
1963 The Last But One
1968 Before God and Man
1971 Love
1974 Cat's Play
1978 A Very Moral Night
1980 Behind the Brick Wall
1983 Another Way
1985 Lily in Love

MALDEN, Karl (Mladen Sekulovich)
(1914–) Gary, Indiana, USA.
1957 Time Limit

MALICK, Terence (Terence Maliek)
(1943–) Ottawa. Illinois, USA.
1973 Badlands
1978 Days of Heaven

MALLE, Louis
(1932–) Thumeries, Nord, France.
Autobiography: Louis Malle edited by Jacques Mallecot.
1953 Fontaine de Vaucluse
1955 Station 307
1957 Frantic / *Ascenseur pour l'Echafaud*
1958 The Lovers
1960 Zazie
1962 A Very Private Affair
1963 The Fire Within / *Will o' the Wisp*
1965 Viva Maria!
1967 The Thief of Paris
1969 Spirits of the Dead / *Histoires Extraordinaires* **(Federico Fellini, Roger VADIM)**
1971 Murmur of the Heart / *Dearest Love*
1975 Black Moon
1978 Pretty Baby
1981 Atlantic City USA **D* F***
1981 My Dinner with André
1984 Crackers
1985 Alamo Bay
(also many documentaries)

MALLON, James
1986 Bloodhook

MALMUTH, Bruce
(1937–) Brooklyn, New York, USA.
1975 Fore Play **(John G AVILDSEN, Robert McCARTY)**
1981 Nighthawks
1983 The Man Who Wasn't There
1986 Where Are the Children?
1989 Dance at My Weddings

MALONE, William
1982 Scared to Death
1985 Creature

MALONEY, Leo
1929 Overland Bound

MAMET, David
1987 House of Games
1988 Things Change

MAMOULIAN, Rouben
(1897–1987) Tiflis, Caucasus, Russia.
Biography: Rouben Mamoulian by Tom Milne.
1929 Applause
1931 City Streets
1932 Dr Jekyll and Mr Hyde
1932 Love Me Tonight
1933 Song of Songs
1933 Queen Christina
1934 We Live Again
1935 Becky Sharp
1936 The Gay Desperado
1937 High, Wide and Handsome
1939 Golden Boy
1940 The Mark of Zorro
1941 Blood and Sand
1942 Rings on Her Fingers
1948 Summer Holiday
1957 Silk Stockings

MANASSE, George
1973 Blade

MANDEL, Howie
1987 The Delivery Boy

MANDEL, Robert
1983 Independence Day
1986 Touch and Go
1986 FX — Murder By Illusion
1987 Big Shots

MANDER, Miles (Lionel Mander)
(1888–1946) Wolverhampton, Staffordshire, England.
1928 The First Born
1929 Loose Ends
1932 Fascination
1932 The Woman Decides
1935 The Morals of Marcus
1936 The Flying Doctor

MANDUKE, Joseph
1971 Jump
1975 Cornbread, Earl and Me
1977 Kid Vengeance

1981 Beatlemania
1987 Omega Syndrome

MANGINE, Joseph
1987 Neon Maniacs
1988 Voodoo Dawn

MANKIEWICZ, Francis
1988 The Revolving Doors

MANKIEWICZ, Joseph L
(1909–) Wilkes-Barre, Pennsylvania, USA.
Biography: Pictures Will Talk: The Life and Films of Joseph L Mankiewicz by Kenneth L Geist.
1946 Dragonwyck
1946 Somewhere in the Night
1947 The Late George Apley
1947 The Ghost of Mrs Muir
1948 Escape
1949 A Letter to Three Wives **D** F***
1949 House of Strangers
1950 No Way Out
1950 All About Eve **D** F****
1951 People Will Talk
1952 Five Fingers **D***
1953 Julius Caesar **F***
1954 The Barefoot Contessa
1955 Guys and Dolls
1958 The Quiet American
1960 Suddenly Last Summer
1963 Cleopatra **F***
1967 The Honey Pot
1970 There Was a Crooked Man
1972 Sleuth **D***

MANKIEWICZ, Tom
(1942–) Los Angeles, California, USA.
1987 Dragnet

MANN, Anthony (Emile Anton Bundesmann)
(1906–1967) San Diego, California, USA.
Biography: Anthony Mann by Jeanine Basinger.
1942 Dr Broadway
1942 Moonlight in Havana
1943 Nobody's Darling
1944 Strangers in the Night
1944 My Best Gal
1945 The Great Flamarion
1945 Sing Your Way Home
1945 Two O'Clock Courage
1946 Strange Impersonation
1946 The Bamboo Blonde
1947 T-Men
1947 Desperate
1947 Railroaded
1948 Raw Deal
1949 Border Incident
1949 The Black Book / *Reign of Terror*
1949 Side Street
1950 Devil's Doorway
1950 The Furies
1951 The Tall Target
1951 Winchester 73
1952 Bend of the River
1953 The Naked Spur
1953 Thunder Bay
1954 The Glenn Miller Story
1955 The Far Country
1955 The Last Frontier / *Savage Wilderness*
1955 The Man from Laramie
1955 Strategic Air Command
1956 Serenade
1957 Men in War
1957 The Tin Star
1958 God's Little Acre
1958 Man of the West
1960 Cimarron
1961 El Cid
1964 The Fall of the Roman Empire
1965 The Heroes of Telemark
1968 A Dandy in Aspic *(completed by* **Laurence HARVEY)**

MANN, Daniel
(1912–) New York, New York, USA.
1952 Come Back, Little Sheba
1954 About Mrs Leslie
1955 The Rose Tattoo **F***
1955 I'll Cry Tomorrow
1956 Teahouse of the August Moon
1958 Hot Spell
1959 The Last Angry Man
1959 The Mountain Road
1960 Butterfield 8
1961 Ada
1962 Five Finger Exercise
1962 Who's Got the Action?
1963 Who's Been Sleeping in My Bed?
1965 Judith
1966 Our Man Flint
1968 For Love of Ivy
1969 A Dream of Kings
1971 Willard
1972 The Revengers
1973 Interval
1973 Maurie
1974 Lost in the Stars
1976 Journey into Fear
1978 Matilda
(also TV movies)

MANN, Delbert
(1920–) Lawrence, Kansas, USA.
1955 Marty **D** F****
1957 The Bachelor Party
1958 Desire Under the Elms
1959 Separate Tables **F***
1959 Middle of the Night
1960 The Dark at the Top of the Stairs
1961 The Outsider
1962 Lover Come Back
1962 That Touch of Mink
1963 A Gathering of Eagles
1964 Dear Heart
1965 Quick Before It Melts
1966 Mister Buddwing / *Woman Without a Face*
1967 Fitzwilly
1968 The Pink Jungle
1971 Kidnapped
1976 Birch Interval
1982 Night Crossing
1983 Bronte
(also many TV movies)

MANN, Edward
1956 Scandal Incorporated
1966 Hallucination Generation
1971 Cauldron of Blood
1971 Who Says I Can't Ride a Rainbow!
1972 Hot Pants Holiday

MANN, Michael
1981 Thief / *Violent Streets*
1983 The Keep
1986 Manhunter / *Red Dragon*
1989 Hanna

MANN, Ron
1984 Listen to the City

MANNING, Bruce
1943 The Amazing Mrs Holiday

MANNING, Michelle
1986 Blue City

MANOOGIAN, Peter
1985 The Dungeonmaster / *Ragewar* **(David ALLEN, Charles BAND, John BUECHLER, Ted NICOLAOU, Stephen STAFFORD, Rose-Marie TURKO)**
1986 Eliminators
1987 Enemy Territory
1988 Arena

MANSFIELD, Duncan
1936 Along Came Love **(Bert LYTELL)**
1937 Girl Loves Boy
1937 Sweetheart of the Navy

MANTIS, Costa
1987 Time of Tears / *Uncle*

MANUPELLI, George
1971 Cry Dr Chicago

MARCEL, Terry
(1942–) Oxford, England.
1979 Why Not Stay for Breakfast
1980 There Goes the Bride
1980 Hawk, the Slayer
1987 Jane and the Lost City of Gold

MARCH, Alex
1968 Paper Lion
1969 The Big Bounce
1977 Mastermind

MARCIN, Max
1930 The Shadow of the Law **(Louis GASNIER)**
1931 The Lawyer's Secret **(Louis GASNIER)**
1931 Silence **(Louis GASNIER)**
1932 The Strange Case of Clara Deane **(Louis GASNIER)**
1933 King of the Jungle **(H Bruce HUMBERSTONE)**
1933 Gambling Ship **(Louis GASNIER)**
1934 The Love Captive

MARCUM, Gary
1988 Through the Fire

MARCUS, James
1989 Tank Malling

MARGOLIN, Stuart
1988 Paramedics
(also many TV movies)

MARIN, Edwin L
(1901–1951) American.
1933 The Death Kiss
1933 A Study in Scarlet
1933 The Avenger
1933 The Sweetheart of Sigma Chi / *Girl of My Dreams*
1934 Bombay Mail
1934 The Crosby Murder Case
1934 Affairs of a Gentleman
1934 Paris Interlude
1935 The Casino Murder Case
1935 Pursuit
1936 Absolute Quiet
1936 Moonlight Murder **(Lucien HUBBARD)**
1936 Speed **(Lucien HUBBARD)**
1936 Sworn Enemy **(Lucien HUBBARD)**
1936 I'd Give My Life
1936 All American Chump **(Lucien HUBBARD)**
1936 The Garden Murder Case
1937 Man of the People
1937 Married Before Breakfast
1938 Everybody Sing
1938 Hold That Kiss
1938 The Chaser
1938 Listen, Darling
1938 A Christmas Carol
1939 Fast and Loose
1939 Society Lawyer
1939 Maisie
1940 Henry Goes to Arizona / *Spats to Spurs*
1940 Florian
1940 Gold Rush Maisie
1940 Hullabaloo
1941 Maisie Was a Lady
1941 Ringside Maisie / *Cash and Carry*
1941 Paris Calling
1942 A Gentleman After Dark
1942 Miss Annie Rooney
1942 Invisible Agent
1943 Two Tickets to London
1944 Show Business
1944 Tall in the Saddle
1945 Johnny Angel
1946 Abilene Town
1946 Young Widow
1946 Lady Luck
1946 Mr Ace
1946 Nocturne
1947 Christmas Eve / *Sinners' Holiday*
1947 Intrigue
1948 Race Street
1949 Canadian Pacific
1949 The Younger Brothers
1949 Fighting Man of the Plains
1950 Colt 45 / *Thundercloud*
1950 The Cariboo Trail
1951 Sugarfoot / *Swirl of Glory*
1951 Raton Pass / *Canyon Pass*
1951 Fort Worth

MARINO, Jack
1989 Forgotten Heroes

MARINOS, Lex
1986 An Indecent Obsession
1988 Boundaries of the Heart

MARIS, Peter
1979 Delirium
1988 Viper
1988 Terror Squad

MARKHAM, Monte
(1935–) American.
1988 Defense Play
1989 The Tree People

MARKLE, Fletcher
(1921–) Canadian.
1949 Jigsaw
1951 The Man with a Cloak
1951 Night into Morning
1963 The Incredible Journey

MARKLE, Peter
1982 The Personals
1984 Hot Dog.. The Movie
1986 Young Blood
1988 Bat 21

MARKOWITZ, Robert
1979 Voices
(also many TV movies)

MARKS, Arthur
(1927–) Los Angeles, California, USA.
1972 Class of '74 **(Mack BING)**
1973 Bonnie's Kids
1973 The Room Mates
1973 Detroit 9000
1975 A Woman for All Men
1975 Bucktown
1975 Friday Foster
1976 J.D.'s Revenge
1976 The Monkey Hustle

MARNER, Eugene
1987 Beauty and the Beast
1987 Puss in Boots

MARNHAM, Christian
1988 Most Dangerous Woman Alive

MARQUAND, Christian
(1927–) Marseille, France.
1968 Candy

MARQUAND, Richard
(1937–1987) Wales.
1978 The Legacy
1981 Eye of the Needle
1983 Return of the Jedi
1984 Until September
1985 Jagged Edge
1987 Hearts of Fire

MARR, Leon
1986 Dancing in the Dark
1989 Caprice

MARSH, Ray
1974 The Mad, Mad Movie Makers
1975 Lord Shango

MARSHALL, Andrew
1988 Happy Birthday **(David RENWICK)**

MARSHALL, Anthony
1943 Bullets and Saddles

MARSHALL, Don
1971 Cycles South

MARSHALL, Garry
(1934–) New York, New York, USA.
1982 Young Doctors in Love
1984 The Flamingo Kid
1986 Nothing in Common
1987 Overboard
1988 Friends / *Beaches*

MARSHALL, George
(1891–1975) Chicago, Illinois, USA.
1932 Their First Mistake
1932 Towed into a Hole
1932 Pack Up Your Troubles / *We're in the Army Now* **(Ray McCAREY)**
1934 Ever Since Eve
1934 Wild Gold
1934 She Learned About Sailors
1934 365 Nights in Hollywod
1935 Life Begins at Forty
1935 Ten Dollar Raise / *Mr Faintheart*
1935 In Old Kentucky
1935 Music Is Magic
1935 Show Them No Mercy / *Tainted Money*
1936 A Message to Garcia
1936 The Crime of Dr Forbes
1936 Can This Be Dixie?
1937 Nancy Steele Is Missing
1937 Love Under Fire
1938 The Goldwyn Follies
1938 The Battle of Broadway
1938 Hold That Co-Ed / *Hold That Girl*
1939 You Can't Cheat an Honest Man
1939 Destry Rides Again
1940 The Ghost Breakers
1940 When the Daltons Rode
1941 Pot o' Gold / *The Golden Hour*
1941 Texas
1942 Valley of the Sun
1942 The Forest Rangers
1942 Star Spangled Rhythm
1943 True to Life
1943 Riding High / *Melody Inn*
1944 And the Angels Sing
1945 Murder, He Says
1945 Incendiary Blonde
1945 Hold That Blonde
1946 The Blue Dahlia
1946 Monsieur Beaucaire
1947 The Perils of Pauline
1947 Variety Girl
1948 Hazard
1948 Tap Roots
1949 My Friend Irma
1950 Fancy Pants
1950 Never a Dull Moment
1951 A Millionaire for Christy

1952 The Savage
1953 Off Limits / *Military Policeman*
1953 Scared Stiff **(Norman LEAR, Ed SIMMONS)**
1953 Houdini
1953 Money from Home
1954 Red Garters
1954 Duel in the Jungle
1954 Destry
1955 The Second Greatest Sex
1956 Pillars of the Sky / *The Tomahawk and the Cross*
1957 The Guns of Fort Petticoat
1957 Beyond Mombasa
1957 The Sad Sack
1958 The Sheepman
1958 Imitation General
1959 The Mating Game
1959 It Started with a Kiss
1959 The Gazebo
1961 Cry for Happy
1962 The Happy Thieves
1962 How the West Was Won **(John FORD, Henry HATHAWAY) F***
1963 Papa's Delicate Condition
1964 Dark Purpose
1964 Advance to the Rear / *Company of Cowards*
1966 Boy, Did I Get a Wrong Number!
1967 Eight on the Lam
1968 The Wicked Dreams of Paul Schultz
1969 Hook, Line and Sinker
(also many shorts)

MARSHALL, Noel
1981 Roar

MARSHALL, Penny
(1942–) Bronx, New York, USA.
1986 Jumpin' Jack Flash
1988 Big

MARSHALL, William
(1917–) American.
1951 The Adventures of Captain Fabian
1961 The Phantom Planet

MARTELL, Alphonse
1933 Gigolettes of Paris

MARTIN, Charles
(1916–1986) Newark, New Jersey, USA.
1946 No Leave to Love
1948 My Dear Secretary
1956 Death of a Scoundrel
1968 If He Hollers, Let Him Go
1974 How to Seduce a Woman
1978 One Man Jury
1979 Dead on Arrival

MARTIN, Eugenio *
(1925–) Spanish.
1971 Badman's River
1972 Horror Express / *Pànico en el Transiberiano*

MARTIN, Francis
1933 Tillie and Gus

MARTIN, Paul
1932 Happy Ever After **(Robert STEVENSON)**
1934 Orient Express

MARTIN, Richard
1973 The Bengal Tiger
1989 Midnight Matinée

MARTINEZ, Chuck
1987 Nice Girls Don't Explode

MARTINI, Richard
1988 You Can't Hurry Love / *Lovestruck / Greetings from L.A.*
1989 Limit Up

MARTINO, Sergio *
(1938–) Italian.
1985 After the Fall of New York
1986 Hands of Steel

MARTINSON, Leslie H
1954 The Atomic Kid
1956 Hot Rod Girl
1957 Hot Rod Rumble
1961 Lad: A Dog **(Aram AVAKIAN)**
1963 PT 109
1963 Black Gold
1964 F.B.I. Code 98
1964 For Those Who Think Young
1966 Batman
1967 Fathom
1971 Mrs Pollifax — Spy
1976 Escape from Angola
1978 Cruise Missile
(also many TV movies)

MARTON, Andrew (Endre Marton)
(1904–) Budapest, Hungary.
1929 Two O'Clock in the Morning / *The Hour of Fear*
1932 S.O.S. Iceberg / *Nordpol Ahoi!*
1934 Beast of the Himalayas
1935 Miss President
1936 Wolf's Clothing
1936 The Secret of Stamboul / *The Spy in White*
1937 School for Husbands
1940 A Little Bit of Heaven
1944 Gentle Annie
1946 Gallant Bess
1950 King Solomon's Mines **(Compton BENNETT) F***
1951 Storm Over Tibet
1951 The Wild North
1952 The Devil Makes Three
1954 Gypsy Colt
1954 Prisoner of War
1954 Men of the Fighting Lady
1955 Green Fire
1956 Seven Wonders of the World **(many others)**
1958 Underwater Warrior
1962 The Longest Day **(Ken ANNAKIN, Bernard WICKI) F***
1962 It Happened in Athens
1964 The Thin Red Line
1965 Crack in the World
1965 Clarence, the Cross-Eyed Lion

1966 Around the World Under the Sea
1966 Birds Do It
1967 Africa Texas Style!
(Andrew Marton was second-unit director on **Ben Hur (Willian WYLER) D** F**)**

MARVIN, Mike
1986 Hamburger..The Motion Picture
1986 The Wraith

MARX, Gerard
1987 Fatale

MASCELLI, Joseph
1964 Monstrosity

MASLANSKY, Paul
(1933–) New York, New York, USA.
1974 Sugar Hill

MASON, Herbert
(1891–1960) British.
1936 First Offense
1936 East Meets West
1936 His Lordship / *Man of Affairs*
1937 Take My Tip
1938 Strange Boarders
1938 A Window in London / *Lady in Distress*
1939 The Silent Battle
1939 Dr O'Dowd
1940 The Briggs Family
1940 Fingers
1941 Once a Crook
1942 Back Room Boy
1942 The Night Invader
1942 When We Are Married
1943 It's in the Bag
1944 Flight from Folly

MASSARO, Francesco
1987 Quite By Chance

MASTERS, Quentin
(1946–) Australian.
1972 Thumb Tripping
1978 The Stud
1981 The PSI Factor
1982 A Dangerous Summer
1983 Midnite Spares

MASTERSON, Peter
(1934–) Houston, Texas, USA.
1986 The Trip to Bountiful
1987 Blood Red
1988 Full Moon in Blue Water
1989 Night Game
1989 Convicts

MASTORAKIS, Nico
1982 The Next One
1984 Blind Date
1985 Skyhigh
1986 The Zero Boys
1987 The Wind / *Terror's Edge*
1987 Terminal Exposure / *Double Exposure*
1988 Nightmare at Noon
1988 Glitch!
1989 Stranger on a Plane

MASTROIANNI, Armand
1980 He Knows You're Alone
1982 The Clairvoyant / *The Killing Hour*
1985 The Supernaturals
1987 Distortions
1988 Cameron's Closet
1988 Double Revenge
1989 Skins

MATE, Rudolph (Rudolf Matheh)
(1898–1964) Cracow, Austria. Polish.
1947 It Had to Be You **(Don HARTMAN)**
1948 D.O.A.
1949 The Dark Past
1950 No Sad Songs for Me
1950 Union Station
1950 Branded
1951 The Prince Who Was a Thief
1951 When Worlds Collide
1952 The Green Glove
1952 Paula / *The Silent Voice*
1952 Sally and Saint Anne
1953 The Mississippi Gambler
1953 Second Chance
1953 Forbidden
1954 The Siege at Red River
1954 The Black Shield of Falworth
1955 The Violent Man / *Rough Company*
1955 The Far Horizons
1956 Miracle in the Rain
1956 The Rawhide Years
1956 Port Afrique
1956 Three Violent People
1958 The Deep Six
1959 For the First Time
1961 Seven Seas to Calais
1962 The 300 Spartans
1963 Aliki — My Love

MATHER, Ted
1988 Dance Academy

MATTEI, Bruno
1983 The Seven Magnificent Gladiators
1988 Appointment in Trieste

MATTER, Alex
1967 The Drifter

MATTHAU, Charles
1987 Doin' Time on Planet Earth

MATTHAU, Walter (Walter Matuschanskayasky)
(1920–) New York, New York, USA. Biography: Walter Matthau by Allan Hunter.
1960 Gangster Story

MATTISON, Frank S
1929 Broken Hearted
1929 Bye-Bye Buddy

MAURER, Norman
1963 The Three Stooges Go Around the World in a Daze
1965 The Outlaws Is Coming

MAXWELL, Ronald F
(1947–) American.

1980 Little Darlings
1981 The Night the Lights Went Out in Georgia
1983 Kidco

MAY, Elaine (Elaine Berlin)
(1932–) Philadelphia, Pennsylvania, USA.
1970 A New Leaf
1972 The Heartbreak Kid
1977 Mickey and Nicky
1987 Ishtar

MAY, Joe (Joseph MANDEL)
(1880–1954) Vienna, Austria.
1934 Music in the Air
1936 One Hour of Romance
1937 Confession
1939 House of Fear
1939 Society Smugglers
1940 The House of the Seven Gables
1940 The Invisible Man Returns
1940 You're Not So Tough
1941 Hit the Road
1944 Johnny Doesn't Live Here Anymore

MAYBERRY, Russ
1971 The Jesus Trip
1979 The Spaceman and King Arthur / *Unidentified Flying Oddball*
(also many TV movies)

MAYER, Gerald
(1919–) American.
1950 Dial 1119 / *The Violent Hour*
1951 Inside Straight
1951 The Sellout
1952 Holiday for Sinners
1953 Bright Road
1955 The Marauders
1958 Diamond Safari

MAYERSBERG, Paul
1986 Captive / *Heroine*
1988 Nightfall
1989 Last Samurai

MAYLAM, Tony
(1943–) London, England.
1978 The Riddle of the Sands
1982 The Burning
1989 Across the Lake

MAYNARD, Ken
(1895–1973) Vevay, Indiana, USA.
1933 Fiddlin' Buckaroo

MAYO, Archie L
(1891–1968) New York, New York, USA.
1926 Christine of the Big Tops
1926 Money Talks
1926 Unknown Treasures
1926 Johnny Get Your Hair Cut **(B Reeves EASON)**
1927 Dearie
1927 Quarantined Rivals
1927 Slightly Used
1927 The College Widow
1928 The Crimson City
1928 Beware of Married Men
1928 On Trial
1928 My Man
1928 State Street Sadie / *The Girl from State Street*
1929 Sonny Boy
1929 The Sap
1929 The Sacred Flame
1929 Is Everybody Happy?
1930 Vengeance
1930 Wide Open
1930 Courage
1930 Oh, Sailor Behave!
1930 The Doorway to Hell / *A Handful of Clouds*
1931 Illicit
1931 Svengali
1931 Bought
1931 Under Eighteen
1932 The Expert
1932 Street of Women
1932 Two Against the World
1932 Night After Night
1933 The Life of Jimmy Dolan / *The Kid's Last Fight*
1933 The Mayor of Hell
1933 Ever in My Heart
1933 Convention City
1934 Gambling Lady
1934 The Man with Two Faces
1934 Desirable
1935 Bordertown
1935 Go into Your Dance
1935 The Case of the Lucky Legs
1936 The Petrified Forest
1936 I Married a Doctor
1936 Give Me Your Heart / *Sweet Aloes*
1936 Black Legion
1937 Call It a Day
1937 It's Love I'm After
1938 The Adventures of Marco Polo
1938 Youth Takes a Fling
1939 They Shall Have Music / *Melody of Youth*
1940 The House Across the Bay
1940 Four Sons
1941 The Great American Broadcast
1941 Charley's Aunt
1941 Confirm or Deny
1942 Moontide
1942 Orchestra Wives
1943 Crash Dive
1944 Sweet and Lowdown
1946 Angel on My Shoulder
1946 A Night in Casablanca
(also many silent shorts)

MAZURSKY, Paul
(1930–) Brooklyn, New York, USA.
1969 Bob & Carol & Ted & Alice
1970 Alex in Wonderland
1973 Blume in Love
1974 Harry and Tonto
1975 Next Stop Greenwich Village
1977 An Unmarried Woman **F***
1980 Willie and Phil
1982 Tempest
1984 Moscow on the Hudson
1986 Down and Out in Beverly Hills
1988 Moon Over Parador

McBRIDE, Jim
1967 David Holzman's Diary
1968 My Girlfriend's Wedding
1971 Glen and Randa
1983 A Hard Day for Archie
1983 Breathless
1987 The Big Easy / *Nothing But the Truth*
1989 Great Balls of Fire

McCAHON, Robert
1973 Running Wild
1975 Deliver Us From Evil

McCALMONT, James
1989 Underground Terror / *An Urban Nightmare*

McCAREY, Leo
(1898–1969) Los Angeles, California, USA.
1929 The Sophomore
1929 Red Hot Rhythm
1930 Wild Company
1930 Let's Go Native
1930 Part-Time Wife
1931 Indiscreet
1932 The Kid from Spain
1933 Duck Soup
1934 Belle of the Nineties
1934 Six of a Kind
1935 Ruggles of Red Gap **F***
1936 The Milky Way
1937 The Awful Truth **D** F***
1937 Make Way for Tomorrow
1939 Love Affair **F***
1942 Once Upon a Honeymoon
1944 Going My Way **D** F****
1945 The Bells of St Mary's **D* F***
1948 Good Sam
1952 My Son John
1957 An Affair to Remember
1958 Rally 'Round the Flag, Boys!
1962 Satan Never Sleeps
(also many shorts)

McCAREY, Ray
(1904–1948) American.
1932 Pack Up Your Troubles / *We're in the Army Now* **(George MARSHALL)**
1934 Girl of My Dreams
1935 Millions in the Air
1935 Sunset Range
1935 Mystery Range
1935 Hot Tip **(James GLEASON)**
1936 Three Cheers for Love
1937 Oh, Doctor
1937 Let's Make a Million
1937 Love in a Bungalow
1938 Goodbye, Broadway
1938 The Devil's Party
1939 Torchy Runs for Mayor
1940 You Can't Fool Your Wife
1940 Millionaires in Prison
1940 Little Orvie
1941 Accent on Love
1941 Cadet Girl
1941 The Cowboy and the Blonde
1941 The Perfect Snob
1941 Murder Among Friends
1942 A Gentleman at Heart
1942 It Happened in Flatbush
1942 That Other Woman
1943 So This Is Washington
1944 Passport to Adventure
1944 Atlantic City
1946 The Falcon's Alibi
1946 Strange Triangle
1948 The Gay Intruders

McCARTHY, John P
(1885–) American.
1927 Diamond Handcuffs
1927 The Lovelorn
1931 Cavalier of the West
1931 Nevada Buckaroo
1931 Rose of the Rio Grande
1931 The Ridin' Fool
1931 Rider of the Plains
1931 Sunrise Trail
1931 God's Country and the Man
1931 Ship of Hate
1931 Mother and Son
1932 The Western Code
1932 The Fighting Champ
1932 The '49ers
1933 Trailin' North
1933 Lucky Larrigan
1933 Return of Casey Jones
1935 The Lawless Border
1936 Song of the Gringo
1944 Marked Trails
1944 Raiders of the Border
1945 The Cisco Kid Returns

McCARTHY, Michael
(1917–1959) British.
1951 Assassin for Hire
1951 Mystery Junction
1952 Crow Hollow
1954 Shadow of a Man
1956 It's Never Too Late
1957 Smoke Screen
1957 The Traitor
1958 Operation Amsterdam

McCARTHY, Mike
1989 May the Best Man Win

McCARTY, Robert
1965 Light Fantastic
1973 I Could Never Have Sex with a Man Who Has So Little Regard for My Husband
1975 Fore Play **(John G AVILDSEN, Bruce MALMUTH)**

McCAULEY, John
1976 Rattlers

McCLATCHY, Gregory
1988 Vampire at Midnight

McCLINTIC, Guthrie
1930 On Your Back
1931 Once a Sinner
1931 Once a Lady

McCLORY, Kevin
(1926–) Irish.
1956 Around the World in Eighty Days

(Michael ANDERSON) D* F**
1959 The Boy and the Bridge

McCOWAN, George
(1931–) Canadian.
1972 The Magnificent Seven Ride!
1972 Frogs
1976 Shadow of the Hawk
1979 The Shape of Things to Come
(also many TV movies)

McCOY, Denys
1971 The Last Rebel

McCULLOUGH Snr., Jim
1983 Mountaintop Motel Masscre
1986 Aurora Encounter
1989 Teen Vamp

McCUNE, Hank
1956 Wetbacks

McDONALD, Frank
(1899–1980) American.
1935 Broadway Hostess
1936 The Murder of Dr Harrigan
1936 Boulder Dam
1936 The Big Noise
1936 Love Begins at Twenty
1936 Treachery Rides the Range
1936 Murder By an Aristocrat
1936 Smart Blonde
1936 Isle of Fury
1937 Midnight Court
1937 Her Husband's Secretary
1937 Fly-Away Baby
1937 Dance, Charlie, Dance
1937 The Adventurous Blonde
1938 Blondes at Work
1938 Reckless Living
1938 Over the Wall
1938 Freshman Year
1938 Flirting with Fate
1939 First Offenders
1939 They Asked for It
1939 Jeepers Creepers
1940 Rancho Grande
1940 In Old Missouri
1940 Gaucho Serenade
1940 Carolina Moon
1940 Ride, Tenderfoot, Ride
1940 Grand Ole Opry
1940 Barnyard Follies
1941 Arkansas Judge
1941 Country Fair
1941 Flying Blind
1941 Under Fiesta Stars
1941 Tuxedo Junction
1941 No Hands on the Clock
1942 Shepherd of the Ozarks
1942 The Old Homestead
1942 Mountain Rhythm
1942 Wildcat
1942 Wrecking Crew
1942 The Traitor Within
1943 High Explosive
1943 Swing Your Partner
1943 Alaska Highway
1943 Submarine Alert
1943 Hoosier Holiday
1943 O, My Darling Clementine
1944 Timber Queen
1944 Take It Big
1944 Sing, Neighbour, Sing
1944 One Body Too Many
1944 Lights of Old Santa Fe
1944 Gambler's Choice
1945 Scared Stiff
1945 Bells of Rosarita
1945 The Chicago Kid
1945 The Man from Oklahoma
1945 Tell It to a Star
1945 Sunset in El Dorado
1945 Along the Navajo Trail
1946 Song of Arizona
1946 Rainbow Over Texas
1946 My Pal Trigger
1946 Sioux City Sue
1947 Hit Parade of 1947
1947 Twilight on the Rio Grande
1947 Under Nevada Skies
1947 Bulldog Drummond Strikes Back
1947 When a Girl's Beautiful
1947 Linda Be Good
1948 Mr Reckless
1948 13 Lead Soldiers
1948 French Leave
1948 Gun Smugglers
1949 The Big Sombrero
1949 Ringside
1949 Apache Chief
1950 Snow Dog
1950 Call of the Klondike
1951 Sierra Passage
1951 Texans Never Cry
1951 Father Takes the Air
1951 Yukon Manhunt
1951 Yellow Fin
1951 Northwest Territory
1952 Sea Tiger
1952 Yukon Gold
1953 Son of Belle Starr
1953 Border City Rustlers
1954 Thunder Pass
1955 The Treasure of Ruby Hills
1955 The Big Tip-Off
1960 The Purple Gang
1960 Raymie
1962 The Underwater City
1963 Gunfight at Comanche Creek
1965 Mara of the Wilderness

McDONELL, Fergus
(1910–) British.
1948 The Small Voice / *The Hideout*
1950 Prelude to Fame
1952 Private Information

McDOWALL, Roddy
(1928–) London, England.
1971 Tam-Lin / *The Devil's Widow*

McEVEETY, Bernard
1966 Ride Beyond Vengeance
1970 The Brotherhood of Satan
1972 Napoleon and Samantha
1973 One Little Indian
1974 The Bears and I
(also many TV movies)

McEVEETY, Vincent
1968 Firecreek
1971 The Million Dollar Duck
1972 The Biscuit Eater
1972 Charley and the Angel
1972 Superdad
1974 The Castaway Cowboy
1975 The Strongest Man in the World
1976 The Treasure of Matecumbe
1976 Gus
1976 Herbie Goes to Monte Carlo
1979 The Apple Dumpling Gang Rides Again
1980 Herbie Goes Bananas
1980 The Watcher in the Woods **(John HOUGH)**
1981 Amy
(also many TV movies)

McEVOY, Earl
1950 Cargo to Capetown
1950 The Killer That Stalked New York / *Frightened City*
1951 The Barefoot Mailman

F McGAHA, William
1972 J.C.

H McGANN, William
(1895–1977) American.
1928 The Home Towners
1930 On the Border
1931 I Like Your Nerve
1932 Illegal
1932 Murder on the Second Floor
1932 The Silver Greyhound
1932 Little Fella
1932 Her Night Out
1933 Long Live the King
1935 Maybe It's Love
1935 A Night at the Ritz
1935 Man of Iron
1936 Freshman Love
1936 Brides Are Like That
1936 Times Square Playboy
1936 Two Against the World / *The Case of Mrs Pembroke*
1936 Hot Money
1936 Polo Joe
1936 The Case of the Black Cat
1937 Penrod and Sam
1937 Marry the Girl
1937 Sh! The Octopus
1938 Alcatraz Island
1938 Penrod and His Twin Brother
1938 When Were You Born?
1938 Girls on Probation
1939 Blackwell's Island
1939 Sweepstakes Winner
1939 Everybody's Hobby
1939 Pride of the Blue Grass
1940 Wolf of New York
1940 Dr Christian Meets the Women
1941 A Shot in the Dark
1941 The Parson of Panamint
1941 Highway West
1941 We Go Fast
1942 In Old California
1942 Tombstone, the Town Too Tough to Die
1942 American Empire / *My Son Alone*
1943 Frontier Badman

McGAVIN, Darren
(1922–) Spokane, Washington, USA.
1973 Happy Mother's Day, Love George / *Run, Stranger, Run*

McGOOHAN, Patrick
(1928–) New York, New York, USA.
1974 Catch My Soul

McGOWAN, Dorrell
1950 The Showdown **(Stuart McGOWAN)**
1951 Tokyo File 212 **(Stuart McGOWAN)**
1958 Snow-Fire **(Stuart McGOWAN)**
1962 The Bashful Elephant **(Stuart McGOWAN)**

McGOWAN, J P
(1880–1952) American.
1929 The Cowboy and the Outlaw
1929 The Invaders
1929 The Riders of the Rio Grande
1930 Breezy Bill
1930 Call of the Desert
1930 The Canyon of Missing Men
1930 The Oklahoma Sheriff
1930 Beyond the Law
1930 Code of Honour
1930 Covered Wagon Trails
1930 Hunted Men
1930 The Man from Nowhere
1930 Near the Rainbow's End
1930 O'Malley Rides Alone
1930 The Parting of the Trails
1930 Pioneers of the West
1930 Western Honour
1930 'Neath Western Skies
1931 Shotgun Pass
1931 Under Texan Skies
1931 Riders of the North
1931 Headin' for Trouble
1931 Quick Trigger Lee
1931 Cyclone Kid
1932 Human Target
1932 Mark of the Spur
1932 Tangled Fortunes
1932 Scarlet Brand
1932 Man from New Mexico
1933 Drum Taps
1933 When a Man Rides Alone
1933 Deadwood Pass
1933 War of the Range
1936 The Outlaw Tamer
1937 Rough Riding Rhythm
1938 Roaring Six Guns

McGOWAN, Robert A
(1901–) American.
1935 Frontier Justice
1936 Too Many Parents
1940 The Haunted House
1940 The Old Swimmin' Hole
1940 Tomboy

McGOWAN, Stuart
1950 The Showdown **(Dorrell McGOWAN)**
1951 Tokyo File 212 **(Dorrell McGOWAN)**
1958 Snow-Fire **(Dorrell McGOWAN)**

1962 The Bashful Elephant **(Dorrell McGOWAN)**
1968 The Billion Dollar Hobo

McGOWAN, Tom
1956 The Amazon Trader
1958 Manhunt in the Jungle
1960 The Hound That Thought He Was a Raccoon

McGRATH, Joseph
(1930–) Scotland.
1967 Casino Royale **(Val GUEST, Ken HUGHES, John HUSTON, Robert PARRISH)**
1968 30 Is a Dangerous Age, Cynthia
1969 The Bliss of Mrs Blossom
1970 The Magic Christian
1974 Digby, the Biggest Dog in the World
1975 The Great McGonagall
1976 I'm Not Feeling Myself Tonight
1980 Rising Damp

McGREGOR, Sean
1974 People Toys

McGUANE, Thomas
(1939–) American.
1975 92 in the Shade

McGUIRE, Dennis
1974 Shoot It: Black, Shoot It: Blue

McGUIRE, Don
(1919–) American.
1955 Break to Freedom
1956 Johnny Concho
1956 The Delicate Delinquent
1957 Hear Me Good

McKAY, Cole
1989 The Game

McLACHLAN, Duncan
1988 Scavengers

McLAGLEN, Andrew V
(1920–) London, England.
1956 Gun the Man Down
1956 Man in the Vault
1957 The Abductors
1960 Freckles
1961 The Little Shepherd of Kingdom Come
1963 McLintock!
1965 Shenandoah
1966 The Rare Breed
1967 Monkeys, Go Home!
1967 The Way West
1968 The Ballad of Josie
1968 The Devil's Brigade
1968 Bandolero!
1969 Hellfighters
1969 The Undefeated
1970 Chisum
1971 One More Train to Rob
1971 Fools' Parade / *Dynamite Man from Glory Jail*
1971 Something Big
1973 Cahill, US Marshal
1975 Mitchell
1976 The Last Hard Men
1978 Breakthrough
1979 The Wild Geese
1980 North Sea Hijack / *Ffolkes*
1981 The Sea Wolves
1984 Sahara
1989 Return from the River Kwai
(also many TV movies)

McLAUGHLIN, Sheila
1983 Committed
1988 She Must Be Seeing Things

McLENNAN, Don
1987 Slate, Wyn and Me
1989 Mullaway

McLEOD, Norman Z (Norman Zenos McLeod)
(1898–1964) Grayling, Michigan, USA.
1929 Taking a Chance
1931 Along Came Youth **(Lloyd CORRIGAN)**
1931 Finn and Hattie **(Norman TAUROG)**
1931 Monkey Business
1931 Touchdown / *Playing the Game*
1932 The Miracle Man
1932 Horse Feathers
1932 If I Had a Million **(James CRUZE, H Bruce HUMBERSTONE, Ernst LUBITSCH, Steven ROBERTS, William A SEITER, Norman TAUROG)**
1933 A Lady's Profession
1933 Mama Loves Papa
1933 Alice in Wonderland
1934 Melody in Spring
1934 Many Happy Returns
1934 It's a Gift
1935 Redheads on Parade
1935 Here Comes Cookie / *The Plot Thickens*
1935 Coronado
1936 Early to Bed
1936 Pennies from Heaven
1936 Mind Your Own Business
1937 Topper
1938 Merrily We Live
1938 There Goes My Heart
1939 Topper Takes a Trip
1939 Remember?
1940 Little Men
1941 The Trial of Mary Dugan
1941 Lady Be Good
1942 Jackass Mail
1942 Panama Hattie
1942 The Powers Girl / *Hello Beautiful*
1943 Swing Shift Maisie / *The Girl in Overalls*
1946 The Kid from Brooklyn
1947 The Secret Life of Walter Mitty
1947 The Road to Rio
1948 Isn't It Romantic?
1948 The Paleface
1950 Let's Dance
1951 My Favourite Spy
1952 Never Wave at a WAC / *The Private Wore Skirts*
1954 Casanova's Big Night
1957 Public Pigeon No. 1
1959 Alias Jesse James

McLOUGHLIN, Tom
1982 One Dark Night
1986 Friday the 13th Part VI - Jason Lives
1987 Date with an Angel

McMULLEN, Ken
1986 Zina

McMURRAY, Mary
1985 The Assam Garden

McNAUGHT, Bob
(1915–1976) British.
1953 Grand National Night / *The Wicked Wife*

McNAUGHTON, John
1987 Henry, Portrait of a Serial Killer
1988 The Borrower

McTIERNAN, John
(1951–) Albany, New York, USA.
1985 Nomads
1987 Predator
1988 Die Hard
1989 The Hunt for Red October

MEDAK, Peter
1968 Negatives
1971 A Day in the Death of Joe Egg
1971 The Ruling Class
1974 Ghost in the Noonday Sun
1978 The Odd Job
1980 The Changeling
1981 Zorro, the Gay Blade
1986 The Men's Club
1988 Servants' Entrance
1989 Fatal Charm
(also many TV movies)

MEDFORD, Don
(1917–) American.
1965 To Trap a Spy
1971 The Hunting Party
1971 The Organization
1976 The November Plan
(also many TV movies)

MEDOWAY, Cary
(1949–) Philadelphia, Pennsylvania, USA.
1985 Paradise Motel
1985 The Heavenly Kid

MEGAHY, Francis
1988 Taffin

MEINERT, Rudolph
1930 Strange Case of District Attorney M

MEINS, Gus
1934 Babes in Toyland / *March of the Wooden Soldiers / Laurel and Hardy in Toyland* **(Charles ROGERS)**
1936 Kelly the Second
1936 Nobody's Baby
1936 The Hit Parade
1937 The Californians
1937 Roll Along, Cowboy
1938 Ladies in Distress
1938 The Higgins Family
1938 His Exciting Night
1938 Romance on the Run
1939 My Wife's Relatives
1939 Money to Burn
1939 The Mysterious Miss X
1939 The Covered Trailer
1939 Should Husbands Work?
1940 Earl of Puddlestone
1940 Grandpa Goes to Town
1940 Scatterbrain

MELANCON, André
1987 Bach and Broccoli

MELCHOIR, Ib
(1917–) Copenhagen, Denmark.
1959 The Angry Red Planet
1961 Reptilicus
1964 The Time Travellers

MELFORD, George
(1899–1961) American.
1921 The Sheik
1924 The Dawn of a Tomorrow
1924 Flaming Barriers
1924 Tiger Love
1925 Friendly Enemies
1925 The Top of the World
1927 A Man's Past
1928 Freedom of the Press
1929 The Charlatan
1929 Love in the Desert
1929 Sea Fury
1930 The Poor Millionaire
1931 East of Borneo
1931 Homicide Squad **(Edward L CAHN)**
1931 The Viking
1932 Boiling Point
1932 The Cowboy Counsellor
1932 A Scarlet Weekend
1932 The Penal Code
1933 The Dude Bandit
1933 Man of Action
1933 Officer 13
1933 Eleventh Commandment
1934 Hired Wife
1935 East of Java

MENDE, Roger
1988 Open Fire

MENDELUK, George
(1948–) Augsburg, Germany.
1979 Stone Cold Dead
1980 The Kidnapping of the President
1985 Doin' Time
1987 Meatballs III: Summer Job

MENDES, Lothar
(1894–1974) German.
1925 Love Blinds Us
1926 The Prince of Tempters
1928 A Night of Mystery
1928 Adventure Mad
1929 Dangerous Curves
1929 Interference **(Roy POMEROY)**
1929 The Four Feathers **(Merian C COOPER, Ernest B SCHOEDSACK)**
1929 Illusion

1929 Marriage Playground
1931 Ladies' Man
1932 Strangers in Love
1932 Payment Deferred
1933 Luxury Liner
1934 Power / *Jew Süss*
1937 The Man Who Could Work Miracles
1938 Moonlight Sonata
1941 Flight for Freedom
1944 Tampico
1946 The Walls Came Tumbling Down

MENENDEZ, Ramon
1988 Stand and Deliver / *Walking in Water*

MENGES, Chris
1988 A World Apart

MENZIES, William Cameron
(1896–1957) New Haven, Connecticut, USA.
1931 Always Goodbye **(Kenneth McKENNA)**
1931 The Spider **(Kenneth McKENNA)**
1932 Almost Married
1932 Chandu, the Magician **(Marcel VARNEL)**
1933 I Love You Wednesday **(Henry KING)**
1934 Wharf Angel **(George SOMNES)**
1936 Things to Come
1937 The Green Cockatoo / *Four Dark Hours / Race Gang*
1944 Address Unknown
1951 Drums in the Deep South
1951 The Whip Hand
1953 The Maze
1953 Invaders from Mars

MEREDITH, Burgess (George Burgess)
(1908–) Cleveland, Ohio, USA.
1948 The Man on the Eiffel Tower

MERRICK, George M
1933 Secrets of Hollywood
1937 Angkor
1942 Today I Hang **(Oliver DRAKE)**

MERRICK, Ian
1977 The Black Panther

MERRILL, Keith
(1940–) Utah, USA.
1978 Three Warriors
1979 Take Down
1980 Windwalker
1981 Harry's War

MERTZ, Arthur
1935 Off the Dole

METTER, Alan
1985 Girls Just Want to Have Fun
1986 Back to School
1988 Moving
1989 Cold Dog Soup

METZGER, Radley H
(1930–) American.
Pseudonym: Henry Paris.
1961 Dark Odyssey **(William KYRIASKYS)**
1964 Dictionary of Sex
1965 The Dirty Girls
1966 The Alley Cats
1967 Carmen, Baby
1968 Therese and Isabelle
1969 Camille 2000
1970 The Lickerish Quartet
1972 Little Mother
1973 Score
1975 Naked Came the Stranger
1975 The Private Afternoons of Pamela Mann
1975 Esotika, Erotika, Psicotika Fab
1975 The Punishment of Anne
1976 The Image
1976 The Opening of Misty Beethoven
1977 Barbara Broadcast
1978 Maraschino Cherry
1978 The Cat and the Canary
1981 The Tales of Tiffany Lust
1984 The Princess and the Call Girl

MEYER, Andrew
1970 The Sky Pirate
1974 Night of the Cobra Woman

MEYER, Herbert
1939 Bad Boy
1939 Son of Ingagi **(Richard KAHN)**

MEYER, Nicholas
(1945–) New York, New York, USA.
1980 Time After Time
1982 Star Trek II: The Wrath of Khan
1985 Volunteers
1988 The Deceivers

MEYER, Russ
(1922–) Oakland, California, USA.
1959 The Immoral Mr Teas
1961 Eve and the Handyman
1961 Erotica
1961 The Immoral West and How It Was Lost
1963 Europe in the Raw
1963 Heavenly Bodies
1964 Kiss Me Quick!
1965 Lorna
1965 Rope of Flesh
1965 Fanny Hill: Memoirs
1965 Motor Psycho
1965 Faster Pussycat, Kill! Kill!
1966 Mondo Topless
1967 How Much Loving Does a Normal Couple Need?
1967 Good Morning.. and Goodbye / *The Lust Seekers*
1967 Common Law Cabin
1968 Finders Keepers, Lovers Weepers
1968 Russ Meyer's Vixen
1969 Cherry, Harry and Raquel
1970 Beyond the Valley of the Dolls
1971 The Seven Minutes
1975 Sweet Suzie / *Blacksnake*
1975 Supervixens
1976 Russ Meyer's Up!
1979 Beneath the Valley of the Ultravixens
1983 The Breast of Russ Meyer

MEYERS, Byron
1985 Sword of Heaven

MICHAELS, Richard
(1936–) American.
1975 How Come Nobody's on Our Side
1976 Death Is Not the End
1983 Blue Skies Again
(also many TV movies)

MICHAEUX, Oscar
1924 A Son of Satan
1925 Body and Soul
1926 The Devil's Disciple
1927 The Broken Violin
1927 The Spider's Web
1929 Wages of Sin
1929 Daughter of the Congo
1930 Easy Street
1931 Darktown Review
1931 The Exile
1932 Black Magic
1932 Ten Minutes to Live
1932 Veiled Aristocrats
1933 The Girl from Chicago
1933 Ten Minutes to Kill
1934 Harlem After Midnight
1935 Len Hawkin's Confession
1936 Temptation
1936 Underworld
1937 God's Stepchildren
1948 The Betrayal

MIHALKA, George
1981 My Bloody Valentine
1981 Pick-Up Summer / *Pinball Summer*
1982 Scandals
1987 The Blue Man / *Eternal Evil*
1989 Office Party

MIKELS, Ted V
1966 The Black Klansman / *I Crossed the Colour Line*
1966 The Undertaker and His Pals
1968 Up Your Teddy Bear
1968 The Girl in Gold Boots
1969 The Astro-Zombies
1972 The Corpse Grinders
1973 Blood Orgy of the She-Devils
1974 The Doll Squad
1975 The Worm Eaters
1982 Ten Violent Women
1987 Angel of Vengeance

MIKHALKOV, Nikita
(1945–) Russian.
1974 At Home Among Strangers
1976 A Slave to Love
1977 An Unfinished Piece for Player Piano
1979 Five Evenings
1981 Oblomov
1983 Family Relations
1984 Without Witness
1987 Black Eyes

MILES, Sir Bernard (Lord Miles)
(1907–) Uxbridge, Middlesex, England.
1944 Tawny Pipit **(Charles SAUNDERS)**
1950 Chance of a Lifetime

MILES, Christopher
(1939–) London, England.
1966 Up Jumped a Swagman
1970 The Virgin and the Gypsy
1971 Time for Loving
1974 The Maids
1975 That Lucky Touch
1981 Priest of Love
(also many TV movies)

MILESTONE, Lewis (Lewis Milstein)
(1895–1980) Chisinau, near Odessa, Russia.
Biography: Lewis Milestone by Joseph Millichap.
1925 Seven Sinners
1926 The Caveman
1926 Fascinating Youth **(Malcolm St CLAIR)**
1926 The New Klondike
1927 Two Arabian Knights **D****
1927 The Kid Brother **(Ted WILDE)**
1928 The Garden of Eden
1928 The Racket **F***
1929 Betrayal
1929 New York Nights
1930 All Quiet on the Western Front **D** F****
1931 The Front Page **D* F***
1932 Rain
1933 Hallelujah, I'm a Bum / *Lazy Bones*
1934 The Captain Hates the Sea
1935 Paris in Spring / *Paris Love Song*
1936 Anything Goes / *Tops Is the Limit*
1936 The General Died at Dawn
1939 Of Mice and Men **F***
1939 The Night of Nights
1940 Lucky Partners
1941 My Life with Caroline
1943 Edge of Darkness
1943 The North Star / *Armoured Attack*
1944 The Purple Heart
1946 The Strange Love of Martha Ivers
1946 A Walk in the Sun
1947 No Minor Vices
1948 Arch of Triumph
1949 The Red Pony
1950 Halls of Montezuma
1952 Kangaroo
1952 Les Misérables
1953 Melba
1953 They Who Dare
1955 The Widow
1959 Pork Chop Hill
1960 Ocean's Eleven
1961 Mutiny on the Bounty **F***

MILFORD, Gene
1960 The Pusher

MILICEVIC, Djordje
1987 Riding Fast

MILIUS, John
(1944–) St Louis, Missouri, USA.
1973 Dillinger
1975 The Wind and the Lion
1978 Big Wednesday
1981 Conan the Barbarian
1984 Red Dawn
1987 Farewell to the King
1988 Capone

MILLAIS, Warren
1933 Her Secret

MILLAND, Ray (Reginald Truscott-Jones)
(1905–1986) Neath, Wales.
Autobiography: Wide-Eyed in Babylon.
1955 A Man Alone
1956 Lisbon
1958 The Safecracker
1962 Panic in the Year Zero
1968 Hostile Witness

MILLAR, Catherine
1987 A Difficult Woman

MILLAR, Gavin
(1938–) Clydebank, Scotland.
1983 Secrets
1985 Dreamchild
1987 Irons of Wrath
1989 Danny the Champion of the World
(also many TV movies)

MILLAR, Stuart
(1929–) New York, New York, USA.
1972 When the Legend Dies
1975 Rooster Cogburn

MILLARDE, Harry
1925 The Fool
1926 The Taxi Driver
1927 On Ze Boulevard

MILLER, David
(1909–) Paterson, New Jersey, USA.
1941 Billy the Kid
1942 Sunday Punch
1942 Flying Tigers
1948 Top o' the Morning / *Kleptomaniacs*
1949 Love Happy
1950 Our Very Own
1951 Saturday's Hero / *Idols in the Dust*
1952 Sudden Fear
1954 The Beautiful Stranger / *Twist of Fate*
1956 Diane
1956 The Opposite Sex
1957 The Story of Esther Costello / *The Golden Virgin*
1959 Happy Anniversary
1961 Midnight Lace
1961 Back Street
1962 Lonely Are the Brave
1964 Captain Newman. M.D.
1968 Hammerhead
1969 Hail, Hero!
1973 Executive Action
1976 Bittersweet Love
(also many shorts and TV movies)

MILLER, George
(1945–) Cinchilla, Queensland, Australia.
1979 Mad Max
1981 Mad Max II / *The Road Warrior*
1983 Twilight Zone — The Movie **(Joe DANTE, John LANDIS, Steven SPIELBERG)**
1985 Mad Max III: Beyond Thunderdome
1987 The Witches of Eastwick

MILLER, George
1982 The Man from Snowy River
1985 The Aviator
1986 Cool Change
1987 Les Patterson Saves the World
(also many TV mini-series)

MILLER, Gilbert
1933 The Lady Is Willing

MILLER, Harvey
(1935–) New York, New York, USA.
1985 Bad Medicine

MILLER, Jason
(1939–) Long Island City, New York, USA.
1982 That Championship Season

MILLER, J C
1987 No Dead Heroes

MILLER, Jonathan
(1936–) London, England.
1970 Take a Girl Like You

MILLER, Michael
1975 Street Girls
1976 Jackson County Jail
1982 Silent Rage
1983 National Lampoon's Class Reunion
(also many TV movies)

MILLER, Robert Ellis
(1927–) New York, New York, USA.
1966 Any Wednesday / *Bachelor Girl Apartment*
1967 Sweet November
1968 The Heart Is a Lonely Hunter
1970 The Buttercup Chain
1972 Big Truck and Poor Clare
1974 The Girl from Petrovka
1980 The Baltimore Bullet
1983 Reuben, Reuben
1987 Brenda Starr
1988 Hawks
(also many TV movies)

MILLER, Sidney
1959 The 30-Foot Bride of Candy Rock
1964 Get Yourself a College Girl
1967 Tammy and the Millionaire **(Leslie GOODWINS)**

MILLER, Warren
1988 White Winter Heat

MILLS, Sir John
(1908–) North Elmham, Norfolk, England.
Autobiography: Up in the Clouds Gentlemen, Please.
1965 Sky West and Crooked / *Gypsy Girl*

MILLS, Reginald
1971 Peter Rabbit and the Tales of Beatrix Potter

MILNER, Dan
1957 From Hell It Came

MILTON, Robert
(1890–) USA.
1929 The Dummy
1929 Charming Sinners
1930 Behind the Makeup **(Dorothy ARZNER)**
1931 Outward Bound
1931 The Bargain
1932 Devotion
1932 Westward Passage
1932 Husband's Holiday
1932 Strange Evidence
1933 Dance of the Witches
1934 Bella Donna

MINER, Allen H
1956 Ghost Town
1957 Black Patch
1957 The Ride Back
1967 Chubasco

MINER, Michael
1988 Deadly Weapon

MINER, Steve
(1951–) Chicago, Illinois, USA.
1981 Friday the 13th: Part II
1982 Friday the 13th: Part III
1986 House
1986 Soul Man
1989 Warlock
1990 The Fugitive

MINER, Worthington
1933 Let's Try Again
1934 Hat, Coat and Glove

MINGAY, David
1980 Rude Boy **(Jack HAZAN)**

MINNELLI, Vincente
(1910–1986) Chicago, Illinois, USA.
Autobiography: I Remember It Well.
1943 Cabin in the Sky
1943 I Dood It / *By Hook or By Crook*
1944 Meet Me in St Louis
1945 Yolanda and the Thief
1945 The Clock
1946 Ziegfeld Follies
1946 Till the Clouds Roll By **(Richard WHORF)**
1946 Undercurrent
1948 The Pirate
1949 Madame Bovary
1950 Father of the Bride **F***
1951 An American in Paris **D* F****
1951 Father's Little Dividend
1952 The Bad and the Beautiful
1953 The Story of Three Loves **(Gottfried REINHARDT)**
1953 The Band Wagon
1954 The Long, Long Trailer
1954 Brigadoon
1955 The Cobweb
1955 Kismet
1955 Lust for Life
1956 Tea and Sympathy
1957 Designing Woman
1958 Gigi **D** F****
1958 The Reluctant Debutante
1959 Some Came Running
1960 Home from the Hill
1960 Bells Are Ringing
1962 The Four Horsemen of the Apocalypse
1962 Two Weeks in Another Town
1963 The Courtship of Eddie's Father
1964 Goodbye Charlie
1965 The Sandpiper
1970 On a Clear Day You Can See Forever
1976 A Matter of Time

MITA, Merata
1988 Mauri

MITCHELL, Bruce
1927 Sky-High Saunders
1927 Three Miles Up
1928 The Air Patrol
1928 The Cloud Dodger
1928 Won in the Clouds
1929 The Sky Skidder
1930 The Lonesome Trail
1931 Sheer Luck
1932 45 Calibre Echo
1934 The Rainbow Terror

MITCHELL, David
1989 Thunderground

MITCHELL, Oswald
(c1890–1949) British.
1937 Old Mother Riley
1941 Asking for Trouble
1941 Danny Boy
1943 The Dummy Talks
1946 Loyal Heart
1947 The Mysterious Mr Nicholson
1947 Black Memory
1948 The Greed of William Hart
1948 House of Darkness
1949 The Man from Yesterday

MITCHELL, Sollace
1988 Call Me

MIZRAHI, Moshe
(1931–) Egypt.
1973 I Love You Rosa
1974 The House on Chelouche Street
1975 Daughters! Daughters!
1976 Rachel's Man
1978 Madame Rosa / *La Vie devant soi*
1980 I Sent a Letter to My Love / *Chère Inconnue*
1983 Youth
1984 The Children's War / *War and Love*
1986 Everytime We Say Goodbye

MOELLER, Philip
1934 The Age of Innocence
1935 Break of Hearts

MOFFITT, John
1988 Love at Stake / *Burnin' Love*

MOGUY, Leonide (Leonide Maguilevsky) *
(1899–1976) St Petersburg, Russia.
1943 Paris After Dark / *The Night Is Ending*
1944 Action in Arabia
1946 Whistle Stop

MOHR, Hal
(1894–1974) San Francisco, California, USA.
1937 When Love Is Young

MOHR, Hanro
1987 Hostage

MOLINARO, Edouard *
(1928–) Bordeaux, France.
1958 Back to the Wall / *Evidence in Concrete*
1959 Road to Shame
1960 Girls for the Summer
1961 The Passion of Slow Fire / *La Mort de Belle*
1962 Seven Capital Sins **(Claude CHABROL, Philippe DeBROCA, Jacques DEMY, Sylvaine DHOMME, Jean-Luc GODARD, Marie-José NAT, Dominique PATUREL, Perrette PRADIER, Jean-Marc TENNBERG, Roger VADIM)**
1963 A Ravishing Idiot
1965 Male Hunt / *The Gentle Art of Seduction*
1967 To Commit a Murder / *Peau d'Espion*
1968 Oscar
1969 Amorous Adventures of Uncle Benjamin
1969 Hibernatus
1973 A Pain in the A... / *L'Emmerdeur*
1973 The Hostages
1975 The Pink Telephone
1979 La Cage aux Folles D*
1981 Sunday Lovers **(Bryan FORBES, Dino RISI, Gene WILDER)**
1981 La Cage aux Folles II
1984 Just the Way You Are
1985 Palace

MONES, Paul
1987 The Beat / *Conjuror*

MONICELLI, Mario *
(1915–) Viareggio, Tuscany, Italy.
1957 The Tailor's Maid / *Padre e Figli*
1958 Big Deal on Madonna Street / *Persons Unknown*
1959 The Great War
1960 The Passionate Thief
1963 The Organizer
1964 High Fidelity **(Elio PETRI, Franco ROSSI, Luciano SALCE)**
1965 Casanova '70
1966 The Queens / *Le Fate* **(Mauro BOLOGNINI, Antonio PIETRANGELI, Luciano SALCE)**
1971 Lady Liberty / *Mortadella*
1975 My Friends
1978 Viva Italia / *I Nuovi Mostri* **(Dino RISI, Ettore SCOLA)**
1979 Lovers and Liars
1979 Hurricane Rosy
1986 Let's Hope It's a Girl

MONSON, Carl
1988 Savage Harbor / *Raggedy Anne*

MONTAGNE, Edward J
1949 Project X
1950 The Tattooed Stranger
1951 The Man with My Face
1964 McHale's Navy
1965 McHale's Navy Joins the Air Force
1967 The Reluctant Astronaut
1978 They Went That-A-Way and That-A-Way

MONTALDO, Giuliano *
(1930–) Italian.
1968 Grand Slam / *Ad Ogni Costo*
1970 Machine Gun McCain / *Gli Intoccabile*
1977 Closed Circuit
1987 The Day Before
1988 The Gold-Rimmed Glasses

MONTGOMERY, George (George M Letz)
(1916–) Brady, Montana, USA.
1961 The Steel Claw
1962 Samar
1964 From Hell to Borneo
1970 Satan's Harvest

MONTGOMERY, Monty
1981 The Loveless **(Kathryn BIGELOW)**

MONTGOMERY, Robert
(1904–1981) New York, New York, USA.
Biography: The Life of Robert Montgomery by Mary Margaret McBride.
1946 Lady in the Lake
1947 Ride the Pink Horse
1949 Once More, My Darling
1950 Eye Witness / *Your Witness*
1959 The Gallant Hours

MONTON, Vincent
1987 Windrider

MOODY, Titus
1974 The Last of the American Hoboes

MOORE, James
1940 The Secret Seven

MOORE, Michael
1966 An Eye for an Eye
1966 Paradise, Hawaiian Style
1967 Kill a Dragon
1968 Buckskin
1968 The Fastest Guitar Alive

MOORE, Richard
(1925–) Jacksonville, Illinois, USA.
1978 Silent Flute
1979 Circle of Iron

MOORE, Robert
(1927–1984) American.
1976 Murder By Death
1978 The Cheap Detective
1979 Chapter Two

MOORE, Ronald
1985 Future Kill

MOORE, Tara
1986 Fire in Eden
1987 Tusks

MOORE, Tom
1986 'Night Mother

MOORE, Vin
1930 Cohens and Kellys in Africa
1931 Virtuous Husband
1931 Many a Slip
1931 Ex-Bad Boy
1932 Racing Youth
1934 Love Past Thirty
1934 Flirting with Danger
1935 Cheers of the Crowd
1936 The Dragnet
1938 Topa Topa **(Charles HUTCHINSON)**
1940 Killers of the Wild **(Charles HUTCHINSON)**

MOOS, A I
1988 The Expendables

MORA, Philippe
(1949–) Australian.
1972 Trouble in Molopolis
1976 Mad Dog
1982 The Beast Within
1983 The Return of Captain Invincible / *Legend in Leotards*
1983 A Breed Apart
1985 The Howling II: Your Sister Is a Werewolf
1986 The Death of a Soldier / *Leonski*
1987 The Howling III: The Marsupials
1989 Communion

MORAHAN, Christopher
(1929–) London, England.
1968 Diamonds for Breakfast
1969 All Neat in Black Stockings
1985 In the Secret State
1985 Clockwise

MORANIS, Rick
1983 Strange Brew **(Dave THOMAS)**

MORE O'FERRALL, George
(1906–1982) British.
1950 The Woman with No Name / *Her Panelled Door* **(Ladislas VAJDA)**
1952 Angels One Five
1952 The Holly and the Ivy
1953 The Heart of the Matter
1954 The Green Scarf
1954 Three Cases of Murder **(David EADY, Wendy TOYE)**
1955 A Woman for Joe
1956 The March Hare

MORGAN, William
1941 Mr District Attorney
1941 Sierra Sue
1941 Sunset in Wyoming
1941 Mercy Island
1941 Bowery Boy
1941 The Gay Vagabond
1942 Bells of Capistrano
1942 Cowboy Serenade
1942 The Heart of the Rio Grande
1942 Home in Wyoming
1942 Stardust on the Sage
1942 Secrets of the Underground
1943 Headin' for God's Country
1947 Fun and Fancy Free

MORRIS, David Burton
(1948–) Kansas City, Missouri, USA.
1975 Loose Ends
1983 Purple Haze
1988 Patti Rocks

MORRIS, Errol
1988 The Thin Blue Line

MORRIS, Howard
(1919–) New York, New York, USA.
1967 Who's Minding the Mint?
1968 With Six You Get Egg Roll
1969 Don't Drink the Water
1978 Goin' Coconuts

MORRIS, Judy
1989 Luigi's Ladies

MORRISON, Bruce
1984 Constance
1985 Shaker Run
1985 Queen City Rocker

MORRISSEY, Paul
(1939–) New York, New York, USA.
1968 Flesh
1970 Trash
1971 Andy Warhol's Women
1972 Heat
1973 L'Amour **(Andy WARHOL)**
1974 Andy Warhol's Frankenstein / *Flesh for Frankenstein*
1974 Andy Warhol's Dracula / *Blood for Dracula*
1979 The Hound of the Baskervilles
1981 Madame Wang's
1982 Forty-Deuce
1984 Mixed Blood
1985 Beethoven's Nephew
1988 Mafia Kid / *Throwback*

MORROW, Vic
(1932–1982) New York, New York, USA.
1967 Deathwatch
1970 A Man Called Sledge

MORSE, Hollingsworth
1970 Puffnstuff
1972 Daughters of Satan

MORSE, Terry O
(1905–1984) American.
1939 Adventures of Jane Arden
1939 On Trial
1939 Waterfront
1939 Smashing the Money Ring
1939 No Place to Go
1940 British Intelligence / *Enemy Agent*
1940 Tear Gas Squad
1940 Fog Island
1946 Danny Boy

1946 Shadows Over Chinatown
1946 Dangerous Money
1947 Bells of San Fernando
1951 Unknown World
1954 Godzilla, King of the Monsters **(Inoshiro HONDA)**
1965 Taffy and the Jungle Hunter
1965 Young Dillinger

MORTIMER, Edmund
1924 Against All Odds
1924 The Desert Outlaw
1924 Just Off Broadway
1924 That French Lady
1924 The Wolf Man
1925 Arizona Romeo
1925 Scandal Proof
1925 Stardust Trail
1925 Gold and the Girl

MORTON, Rocky
1988 D.O.A. **(Annabel JANKEL)**

MOSES, Gilbert
(1942–) Cleveland, Ohio, USA.
1974 Willie Dynamite
1979 The Fish That Saved Pittsburgh

MOSS, Jack
1945 S N A F U / *Welcome Home*

MOURADIAN, Sarky
1974 Tears of Happiness

MOURIS, Frank
1986 Beginners' Luck

MOWBRAY, Malcolm
1984 A Private Function
1988 Out Cold / *Stiffs*

MOXEY, John Llewellyn
(1920–) Burlingham, England.
1960 City of the Dead / *Horror Hotel*
1960 Foxhole in Cairo
1962 Death Trap
1963 The 20,000 Pound Kiss
1963 Ricochet
1964 Downfall
1964 Face of a Stranger
1965 Strangler's Web
1967 Psycho Circus / *Circus of Fear*
1967 The Tormentor
(also a multitude of TV movies)

MOYLE, Allan
1978 Montreal Main **(Maxine McGILLIVRAY, Frank VITALE)**
1978 The Rubber Gun
1980 Times Square
1989 Lean on Me

MULCAHY, Russell
(1953–) Melbourne, Victoria, Australia.
1984 Razorback
1986 Highlander
1990 Hell Drivers

MULLIGAN, Robert
(1925–) Bronx, New York, USA.
1957 Fear Strikes Out
1960 The Rat Race
1961 The Great Imposter
1961 Come September
1962 The Spiral Road
1962 To Kill a Mockingbird **D* F***
1964 Love with the Proper Stranger
1965 Baby, the Rain Must Fall
1966 Inside Daisy Clover
1969 Up the Down Staircase
1969 The Stalking Moon
1971 The Pursuit of Happiness
1971 Summer of '42
1972 The Other
1979 The Nickel Ride
1979 Bloodbrothers
1979 Same Time, Next Year
1982 Kiss Me Goodbye
1988 Clara's Heart

MUNDHRA, Jag
1987 Open House
1987 Death Mask
1989 Jigsaw Murders

MUNE, Ian
1984 Came a Hot Friday

MUNGER, Chris
1972 Kiss of the Tarantula
1974 Black Scarlet

MURAKAMI, Jimmy T
1980 Battle Beyond the Stars

MURCH, Walter
1985 Return to Oz

MURER, Fredi
1986 Alpine Fire

MURNAU, F W (Friedrich Wilhelm Plumpe)
(1888–1931) Bielefeld, Westphalia, Germany.
Biography: Murnau by Lotte Eisener.
1924 The Last Laugh
1925 Tartuffe
1926 Faust
1927 Sunrise, a Song of Two Humans
1929 Four Devils
1930 City Girl / *Our Daily Bread*

MURO, Jim
1987 Street Trash

MURPHY, Dudley
(1897–) American.
1931 Confessions of a Co-Ed **(David BURTON)**
1932 The Sport Parade
1933 The Emperor Jones
1935 The Night Is Young
1936 Don't Gamble with Love
1939 One Third of a Nation
1939 Main Street Lawyer

MURPHY, Eddie
(1961–) Brooklyn, New York, USA.

1989 Harlem Nights

MURPHY, Edward
1982 Raw Force
1985 The Jungle / *Heated Vengeance*

MURPHY, Geoff
1980 Wildman
1981 Goodbye Pork Pie
1983 Utu
1985 The Quiet Earth
1988 Never Say Die / *007 Down She Goes / The Paranoid Man*

MURPHY, Pat
1985 Anne Devlin

MURPHY, Ralph
(1895–1967) American.
1931 The Big Shot / *The Optimist*
1932 70,000 Witnesses
1932 Panama Flo
1933 Strictly Personal
1933 Song of the Eagle
1933 Girl Without a Room
1933 Golden Harvest
1934 The Notorious Sophie Lang
1934 She Made Her Bed
1934 Private Scandal
1934 The Great Flirtation
1934 Menace
1935 McFadden's Flat
1935 Men Without Names
1935 One Hour Late
1936 Florida Special
1936 Collegiate / *The Charm School*
1936 The Man I Marry
1936 Top of the Town
1937 Night Club Scandal
1937 Partners in Crime
1939 Our Neighbours the Carters
1940 I Want a Divorce
1941 You're the One
1941 Las Vegas Nights
1941 Glamour Boy
1941 Midnight Angel
1942 Mrs Wiggs of the Cabbage Patch
1942 Pacific Blackout
1943 Night Plane from Chungking
1943 Salute for Three
1944 The Man in Half Moon Street
1944 Rainbow Island
1944 The Town Went Wild
1945 Sunbonnet Sue
1945 How Do You Do?
1947 The Spirit of West Point
1948 Mickey
1949 Red Stallion in the Rockies
1951 The Lady and the Bandit / *Dick Turpin's Ride*
1951 Never Trust a Gambler
1951 Stage to Tucson / *Lost Stage Valley*
1952 Lady in the Iron Mask
1955 Mystery of the Black Jungle / *Black Devils of Kali*

MURPHY, Richard
(1912–) American.
1955 Three Stripes in the Sun / *The Gentle Sergeant*
1960 The Wackiest Ship in the Army

MURRAY, Don
(1929–) Hollywood, California, USA.
1970 The Cross and the Switchblade

MUSKER, John
1989 The Little Mermaid **(Ron CLEMENTS)**

MUTRUX, Floyd
1971 Dusty and Sweet McGee
1975 Aloha, Bobby and Rose
1978 American Hot Wax
1980 The Hollywood Knights

MYCROFT, Walter C
(1891–1959) British.
1940 Spring Meeting
1941 My Wife's Family
1941 Banana Ridge

MYERS, Zion
1931 Sidewalks of New York **(Jules WHITE)**
1933 Lucky Dog

MYERSON, Alan
1972 Steelyard Blues
1981 Private Lessons
1988 Police Academy V: Assignment Miami

NADEL, Arthur H
1967 Clambake
1970 Underground

NAGEL, Conrad
(1896–1970) Keokik, Iowa, USA.
1937 Love Takes Flight

NAGY, Ivan
(1938–) Budapest, Hungary.
1973 Bad Charleston Charlie
1973 Money, Marbles and Chalk
1973 Five Minutes of Freedom
1976 Dead Hero
(also many TV movies)

NAHAY, Michael
1976 The Thursday Morning Murders

NANKIN, Michael
(1955–) Los Angeles, California, USA.
1981 Midnight Madness **(David WECHTER)**

NAPOLEON, Arthur
(1923–) American.
1957 Man on the Prowl
1958 Too Much Too Soon
1969 The Activist

NARBY, Leon
1987 Illustrious Energy

NARIZZANO, Silvio
(1928–) Montreal, Quebec, Canada.
1960 Under Ten Flags **(Duilio COLETTI)**
1965 Fanatic / *Die! Die! My Darling*
1967 Georgy Girl
1968 Blue
1972 Loot

1975 Redneck
1976 The Sky Is Falling
1977 Why Shoot the Teacher?
1979 The Class of Miss MacMichael
1981 Choices

NASH, Gene
1970 Dinah East

NAUD, William T
1966 Hot Rod Hullabaloo
1971 Wild in the Sky / *Black Jack*

NAVA, Gregory
(1949–) San Diego, California, USA.
1976 The Confessions of Amans
1984 El Norte
1988 A Time of Destiny

NAZARRO, Ray
(1902–) American.
1945 Outlaws of the Rockies
1945 Texas Panhandle
1945 Song of the Prairie / *Sentiment and Song*
1946 Cowboy Blues / *Beneath Starry Skies*
1946 Desert Horsemen / *Checkmate*
1946 Galloping Thunder / *On Boot Hill*
1946 Gunning for Vengeance / *Jail Break*
1946 Headin' West / *The Cheat's Last Throw*
1946 Roaring Rangers / *False Hero*
1946 Terror Trail / *Hands of Menace*
1946 Two Fisted Stranger
1946 That Texas Jamboree / *Medicine Man*
1946 Throw a Saddle on a Star
1946 Singing on the Trail / *Lookin' for Someone*
1946 Lone Star Moonlight
1947 Buckaroo from Powder River
1947 Last Days of Boot Hill
1947 Law of the Canyon / *The Price of Crime*
1947 The Lone Hand Texan / *The Cheat*
1947 West of Dodge City / *The Sea Wall*
1947 Over the Santa Fe Trail
1947 Rose of Santa Rosa
1948 Blazing Across the River / *Under Arrest*
1948 El Dorado Pass / *Desperate Men*
1948 Phantom Valley
1948 Singing Spurs
1948 Six-Gun Law
1948 Trail to Laredo
1948 West of Senora
1948 Song of Idaho
1948 Smokey Mountain Melody
1949 Bandits of El Dorado / *Tricked*
1949 The Blazing Trail / *The Forged Will*
1949 Challenge of the Range / *Moonlight Raid*
1949 Laramie
1949 Quick on the Trigger
1949 Renegades of the Sage
1949 South of Death Valley / *River of Poison*
1949 The Tougher They Come
1950 Frontier Outpost
1950 Outcast of Black Mesa / *The Clue*
1950 The Palomino / *Hills of the Brave*
1950 Streets of Ghost Town
1950 Texas Dynamo / *Suspected*
1950 Trail of the Rustlers / *Lost River*
1950 David Harding, Counterspy
1950 Hoedown
1951 Al Jennings of Oklahoma
1951 Flame of Stamboul
1951 Cyclone Fury
1951 Fort Savage Raiders
1951 The Kid from Amarillo / *Silver Chains*
1951 War Cry
1952 Cripple Creek
1952 Indian Uprising
1952 Montana Territory
1952 Junction City
1952 Laramie Mountains
1952 The Rough Tough West
1953 The Bandits of Corsica
1953 Gun Belt
1953 Kansas Pacific
1954 The Black Dakotas
1954 The Lone Gun
1954 Southwest Passage / *Camels West*
1955 Top Gun
1956 The White Squaw
1956 The Domino Kid
1957 The Hired Gun
1957 The Phantom Stagecoach
1958 Apache Territory
1958 Return to Warbow
1964 When Strangers Meet / *Dog Eat Dog*
1967 Arrivederci Cowboy

NEAME, Ronald
(1911–) London, England.
1947 Take My Life
1950 The Golden Salamander
1952 The Card / *The Promoter*
1954 The Million Pound Note / *Man with a Million*
1956 The Man Who Never Was
1957 The Seventh Sin
1958 Windom's Way
1959 The Horse's Mouth
1960 Tunes of Glory
1962 Escape from Zahrain
1963 I Could Go on Singing
1964 The Chalk Garden
1965 Mister Moses
1966 A Man Could Get Killed **(Cliff OWEN)**
1966 Gambit
1969 The Prime of Miss Jean Brodie
1970 Scrooge
1972 The Poseidon Adventure
1974 The Odessa File
1979 Meteor
1980 Hopscotch
1981 First Monday in October
1986 Foreign Body

NEAT, Timothy
1989 Play Me Something

NEEDHAM, Hal
(1931–) Memphis, Tennessee, USA.
1977 Smokey and the Bandit
1978 Hooper
1979 The Villain
1980 Smokey and the Bandit II
1980 The Cannonball Run
1982 Megaforce
1983 Stroker Ace

1984 Cannonball Run II
1986 RAD
1987 Body Slam

NE'EMAN, Judd
1989 Streets of Yesterday

NEFF, Thomas L
1986 Running Mates

NEGRIN, Alberto
1987 Secret of the Sahara

NEGULESCO, Jean
(1900–) Craiova, Romania. Autobiography: Things I Did.. and Things I Think I Did.
1941 Singapore Woman
1944 The Conspirators
1944 The Mask of Dimitrios
1946 Humoresque
1946 Nobody Lives Forever
1946 Three Strangers
1947 Deep Valley
1948 Johnny Belinda **D* F***
1948 Road House
1949 The Forbidden Street / *Britannia Mews*
1950 The Mudlark
1950 Three Came Home
1950 Under My Skin
1951 Take Care of My Little Girl
1952 Phone Call from a Stranger
1952 Lydia Bailey
1952 Lure of the Wilderness
1953 Titanic
1953 How to Marry a Millionaire
1953 Scandal at Scourie
1954 Three Coins in the Fountain **F***
1954 A Woman's World
1955 Daddy Long Legs
1955 The Rains of Ranchipur
1957 Boy on a Dolphin
1958 The Gift of Love
1958 A Certain Smile
1959 Count Your Blessings
1959 The Best of Everything
1962 Jessica
1964 The Pleasure Seekers
1970 Hello, Goodbye
1970 The Invincible Six
(also many shorts)

NEILAN, Marshall ('Micky' Neilan)
(1891–1958) San Bernardino, California, USA.
1924 Dorothy Vernon of Haddon Hall
1924 Tess of the D'Urbervilles
1925 The Sporting Venus
1925 The Great Love
1926 Diplomacy
1926 Everybody's Acting
1926 Wild Oats Lane
1926 Mike
1926 The Skyrocket
1927 Venus of Venice
1927 Her Wild Oat
1928 His Last Haul / *Pious Crooks*
1928 Three Ring Marriage
1928 Take Me Home
1928 Taxi 13
1929 Black Waters
1929 Tanned Legs
1929 The Awful Truth
1929 The Vagabond Lover
1930 Sweethearts on Parade
1934 Chloe
1934 Love Is Calling You
1934 Social Register
1934 The Lemon Drop Kid
1935 This Is the Life
1936 Sing While You're Able
1937 Swing It, Professor
1937 Thanks for Everything / *Partly Confidential*

NEILL, Roy William (Roland W.N. de Gostrie)
(1890–1946) Dublin, Republic of Ireland.
1924 By Divine Right
1924 Broken Laws
1924 Vanity's Price
1925 Greater Than a Crown
1925 Kiss Barrier
1925 Percy
1925 Marriage in Transit
1926 The City
1926 Black Paradise
1926 The Cowboy and the Countess
1926 The Fighting Buckaroo
1926 A Man Four-Square
1927 The Arizona Wildcat
1927 Marriage
1928 Lady Raffles
1928 The Olympic Hero
1928 San Francisco Nights / *Divorce*
1928 The Viking
1929 Behind Closed Doors
1929 Wall Street
1930 The Melody Man
1930 Cock o' the Walk **(Walter LANG)**
1930 Just Like Heaven
1931 The Avenger
1931 The Good Bad Girl
1931 Fifty Fathoms Deep
1932 The Menace
1932 That's My Boy
1933 The Circus Queen Murder
1933 The Whirlpool
1933 As the Devil Commands
1933 Above the Clouds / *Winged Devils*
1934 Fury of the Jungle
1934 The Ninth Guest
1934 Black Moon
1934 Blind Date
1934 I'll Fix It
1934 Jealousy
1935 Mills of the Gods
1935 Eight Bells
1935 The Black Room
1936 The Lone Wolf Returns
1936 Gypsy
1937 Dr Syn
1938 Quiet Please
1938 Thank Evans
1938 Simply Terrific
1938 The Viper
1938 Everything Happens to Me
1938 Many Tanks Mr Atkins
1939 The Good Old Days
1939 Murder Will Out

1939 Hoots Mon!
1939 His Brother's Keeper
1942 Madame Spy
1942 Sherlock Holmes and the Secret Weapon
1943 Eyes of the Underworld
1943 Frankenstein Meets the Wolf Man
1943 Rhythm of the Islands
1943 Sherlock Holmes in Washington
1943 Sherlock Holmes Faces Death
1944 Sherlock Holmes and the Spider Woman
1944 The Scarlet Claw
1944 Gypsy Wildcat
1944 The Pearl of Death
1945 The House of Fear
1945 The Woman in Green
1945 Pursuit to Algiers
1946 Black Angel
1946 Dressed to Kill / *Sherlock Holmes and the Secret Code*
1946 Terror By Night

NEILSON, James
(1918–1979) American.
1957 Night Passage
1962 Moon Pilot
1962 Bon Voyage!
1963 Summer Magic
1963 Dr Syn, Alias the Scarecrow
1966 The Moonspinners
1966 Return of the Gunfighter
1967 The Adventures of Bullwhip Griffin
1967 Gentle Giant
1968 Where Angels Go, Trouble Follows!
1969 The First Time / *You Don't Need Pyjamas at Rosie's*
1969 Flareup
(also many TV movies)

NEIMAN, L E
1987 Morning Terror

NEITZ, Alvin J
1930 Firebrand Jordan
1930 Breed of the West
1930 Trails of Peril
1931 Pueblo Terror
1931 Hell's Valley
1931 Lariats and Six Shooters
1931 Red Fork Range
1931 Flying Lariats
1932 Tex Takes a Holiday

NELSON, David
(1936–) New York, New York, USA.
1981 Death Screams
1983 Last Plane Out
1984 A Rare Breed

NELSON, Dusty
1987 White Phantom
1988 Renegade Knights

NELSON, Gary
1973 Molly and Lawless John
1973 Santee
1976 Freaky Friday
1979 The Black Hole
1983 Jimmy the Kid
1987 Alan Quatermain and the Lost City of Gold
(also many TV movies)

NELSON, Gene (Leander Berg)
(1920–) Seattle, Washington, USA.
1962 Hand of Death
1962 Hootenanny Hoot
1964 Kissin' Cousins
1964 Your Cheatin' Heart
1965 Harum Scarum / *Harem Holiday*
1967 The Cool Ones

NELSON, Jack
1931 Two Gun Caballero
1934 Border Guns
1934 The Border Menace

NELSON, Mervyn
1971 Some of My Best Friends Are...

NELSON, Ozzie
(1907–1975) American.
1965 Love and Kisses

NELSON, Ralph
(1916–1987) New York, New York, USA.
1962 Requiem for a Heavyweight / *Blood Money*
1963 Lilies of the Field **F***
1963 Soldier in the Rain
1964 Fate Is the Hunter
1964 Father Goose
1965 Once a Thief
1966 Duel at Diablo
1968 Counterpoint
1968 Charley
1970 Tick, Tick, Tick
1970 Soldier Blue
1971 Flight of the Doves
1972 The Wrath of God
1975 The Wilby Conspiracy
1976 Embryo
1977 A Hero Ain't Nothing But a Sandwich
(also many TV movies)

NELSON, Sam
1937 Outlaws of the Prairie
1938 Cattle Raiders
1938 The Colorado Trail
1938 Law of the Plains
1938 Rio Grande
1938 South of Arizona
1938 West of Cheyenne
1938 West of Santa Fe
1939 Parents on Trial
1939 Man from Sundown
1939 North of the Yukon
1939 The Stranger from Texas
1939 Texas Stampede
1939 The Thundering West
1939 Western Caravans
1940 Pioneers of the Frontier
1940 Prairie Schooners
1940 Bullets for Rustlers
1940 Outlaws of the Panhandle
1942 Sagebrush Law
1943 The Avenging Rider
(also serials)

NESBITT, Frank
1964 Walk a Tightrope
1971 Dulcima

NESHER, Avi
1978 The Troupe / *Halahaka*
1979 Dizengoff 99
1984 She
1984 Rage and Glory
1985 Breaking

NEUMAN, Lewis
1931 Ubangi

NEUMANN, Jozsef *see* **Alexander ZORDA**

NEUMANN, Kurt
(1906–1958) Germany.
1932 Fast Companions
1932 My Pal, the King
1933 The Big Cage
1933 The Secret of the Blue Room
1933 King for a Night
1934 Let's Talk It Over
1934 Half a Sinner
1934 Wake Up and Dream
1935 Alias Mary Dow
1935 The Affair of Susan
1936 Let's Sing Again
1936 Rainbow on the River
1937 Espionage
1937 Make a Wish
1937 Hold 'Em Navy / *That Navy Spirit*
1938 Wide Open Faces
1938 Touchdown, Army / *Generals of Tomorrow*
1939 Unmarried / *Night Club Hostess*
1939 Island of Lost Men
1939 Ambush
1939 All Women Are Saints
1940 A Night at Earl Carroll's
1940 Ellery Queen, Master Detective
1942 Brooklyn Orchid
1942 About Face
1942 The McGuerins from Brooklyn
1942 Fall In
1942 Taxi, Mister
1943 Yanks Ahoy
1943 The Unknown Guest
1945 Tarzan and the Amazons
1946 Tarzan and the Leopard Woman
1947 Tarzan and the Huntress
1948 The Dude Goes West
1948 Bad Men of Tombstone
1949 Bad Boy
1950 The Kid from Texas
1950 Rocketship X-M
1951 Cattle Drive
1951 Reunion in Rio
1952 Son of Ali Baba
1952 The Ring
1952 Hiawatha
1953 Tarzan and the She-Devil
1954 Carnival Story
1955 They Were So Young
1956 Mohawk
1956 The Desperadoes Are in Town
1957 She Devil
1957 Kronos
1957 The Deerslayer
1958 The Fly
1958 Machete
1959 Watusi
1959 The Counterplot

NEWBROOK, Peter
(1916–) British.
1973 The Asphyx

NEWELL, Mike
(1942–) British.
1977 Ready When You Are, Mr McGill
1980 The Awakening
1983 Bad Blood
1985 Dance with a Stranger
1986 The Good Father
1987 Amazing Grace and Chuck
1988 Soursweet

NEWFIELD, Sam (Sam Neufeld)
(1900–1964) American.
Pseudonyms: Sherman Scott; Peter Stewart.
1933 Reform Girl
1933 Important Witness
1933 Under Secret Orders
1934 Big Time or Bust / *Heaven Bound*
1934 Marrying Widows
1934 Beggar's Holiday
1935 Code of the Mounted
1935 Northern Frontier
1935 Trails of the Wild / *Arrest at Sundown*
1935 Racing Luck
1935 Bulldog Courage
1936 Timber War
1936 Federal Agent
1936 Burning Gold
1936 Border Caballero
1936 Lightnin' Bill Carson
1936 Roarin' Guns
1936 The Lion's Den
1936 Ghost Patrol
1936 Aces and Eights
1936 Go-Get-'Em Haines
1936 The Traitor
1936 Stormy Trails
1937 Melody of the Plains
1937 Doomed at Sundown
1937 Bar Z Bad Man
1937 Roarin' Lead **(Mack V WRIGHT)**
1937 Guns in the Dark
1937 Gun Lords of Stirrup Basin
1937 A Lawman Is Born
1937 Boot Hill Brigade
1937 Arizona Gunfighter
1937 Riding the Lone Trail
1937 The Colorado Kid
1938 Paroled, To Die
1938 Rangers' Roundup
1938 Harlem on the Prairie
1938 Code of the Rangers
1938 Six Gun Trail
1938 Thunder in the Desert
1938 Songs and Bullets
1938 Desert Patrol
1938 The Phantom Ranger
1938 Terror of Tiny Town
1938 Frontier Scout
1938 Lightning Carson Rides Again
1938 Crashin' Thru Danger

1938 Lightnin' Crandall
1938 Durango Valley Raiders
1938 The Feud Maker
1939 Six Gun Rhythm
1939 Trigger Fingers
1939 Trigger Pals
1939 Code of the Cactus
1939 Texas Wildcats
1939 Outlaws' Paradise
1939 The Fighting Renegade
1939 Fighting Mad
1939 Flaming Lead
1939 Sagebrush Family Trails West
1939 The Invisible Killer
1939 Beast of Berlin
1940 Straight Shooter
1940 Secrets of a Model
1940 Hold That Woman!
1940 I Take This Oath
1940 A Fugitive from Justice
1940 Marked Men
1940 Arizona Gang Busters
1940 Billy the Kid in Texas
1940 Billy the Kid Outlawed
1940 Billy the Kid's Gun Justice
1940 Frontier Crusaders
1940 Gun Code
1940 Riders of Black Mountain
1940 Texas Renegades
1941 The Lone Rider Ambushed
1941 The Lone Rider Crosses the Rio
1941 The Lone Rider Fights Back
1941 The Lone Rider in Frontier Fury
1941 The Lone Rider in Ghost Town
1941 The Lone Rider Rides On
1941 Billy the Kid Is Wanted
1941 Billy the Kid's Fighting Pals
1941 Billy the Kid's Roundup
1941 Billy the Kid in Santa Fe
1941 Billy the Kid's Range War
1941 Outlaws of the Rio Grande
1941 The Texas Marshal
1942 The Lone Rider and the Bandit
1942 The Lone Rider in Cheyenne
1942 Along the Sundown Trail
1942 Billy the Kid Trapped
1942 Billy the Kid's Smoking Guns
1942 Law and Order
1942 Raiders of the West
1942 Rolling Down the Great Divide
1942 Jungle Siren
1942 The Lone Rider in Border Roundup
1942 The Lone Rider in Texas Justice
1942 The Mad Monster
1942 Outlaws of Border Pass
1942 Overland Stagecoach
1942 Prairie Pals
1942 The Mysterious Rider
1942 Sheriff of Sage Valley
1942 Texas Manhunt
1942 Tumbleweed Trail
1943 Queen of Broadway
1943 Western Cyclone
1943 Wild Horse Rustlers
1943 The Kid Rides Again
1943 Danger! Men at Work
1943 Harvest Melody
1943 The Renegade
1943 Tiger Fangs
1943 The Black Raven
1943 Blazing Frontier
1943 Dead Men Walk
1943 Death Rides the Plains
1943 Fugitive of the Plains
1943 Cattle Stampede
1943 Wolves of the Range
1943 Raiders of Red Gap
1944 The Contender
1944 The Drifter
1944 Frontier Outlaws
1944 I Accuse My Parents
1944 Fuzzy Settles Down
1944 The Monster Maker
1944 Nabonga
1944 Oath of Vengeance
1944 Rustler's Hideout
1944 Swing Hostess
1944 Thundering Gun Slingers
1944 Valley of Vengeance
1944 Wild Horse Phantom
1945 Apology for Murder
1945 Border Badmen
1945 Fighting Bill Carson
1945 The Lady Confesses
1945 Gangster's Den
1945 His Brother's Ghost
1945 The Kid Sister
1945 The Prairie Rustlers
1945 Stagecoach Outlaws
1945 White Pongo
1946 Lightning Raiders
1946 Outlaw of the Plains
1946 Blonde for a Day
1946 Gashouse Kids
1946 Ghost of Hidden Valley
1946 Lady Chasers
1946 Larceny in Her Heart
1946 Murder Is My Business
1946 Overland Riders
1946 Queen of Burlesque
1946 Terrors on Horseback
1946 The Flying Serpent
1946 Prairie Badmen
1947 Raiders of Red Rock
1947 Three on a Ticket
1947 Frontier Fighters
1947 Code of the Plains
1948 The Counterfeiters
1948 Money Madness
1948 Lady at Midnight
1948 The Strange Mrs Caines
1949 State Department File 649 / *Assignment in China*
1949 The Devil's Weed / *Wild Weed*
1950 Motor Patrol
1950 Radar Secret Service
1950 Western Pacific Agent
1950 Hi-Jacked
1951 The Lost Continent
1951 Skip Along Rosenbloom
1951 Sky High
1951 Fingerprints Don't Lie
1951 Mask of the Dragon
1951 Leave It to the Marines
1951 Three Desperate Men
1952 Outlaw Women **(Ron ORMOND)**
1952 The Gambler and the Lady
1952 Lady in the Fog / *Scotland Yard Inspector*
1954 Thunder Over Sangoland

1955 Last of the Desperados
1956 Frontier Gambler
1956 The Three Outlaws
1956 The Wild Dakotas
1956 Along the Mohawk Trail
1956 The Long Rifle and the Tomahawk **(Sidney SALKOW)**
1956 The Pathfinder and the Mohican
1956 The Redmen and the Renegades
1958 Flaming Frontier
1958 Wolf Dog
(also many shorts)

NEWLAND, John
(1917–) Cincinnati, Ohio, USA.
1957 That Night
1957 The Violators
1966 The Spy with My Face
1970 My Lover, My Son
1974 Who Fears the Devil / *The Legend of Hillbilly John*
(also many TV movies)

NEWLEY, Anthony
(1931–) London, England.
1969 Can Hieronymous Merkin Ever Forget Mercy Humppe and Find True Happiness?
1971 Summertree

NEWMAN, Joseph M
(1909–) Logan, Utah, USA.
1942 Northwest Rangers
1948 Jungle Patrol
1949 The Great Dan Patch
1949 Abandoned
1950 711 Ocean Drive
1951 Lucky Nick Cain / *I'll Get You for This*
1951 The Guy Who Came Back
1951 Love Nest
1952 Red Skies of Montana / *Smoke Jumpers*
1952 The Outcasts of Poker Flat
1952 Pony Soldier / *Macdonald of the Canadian Mounties*
1953 Dangerous Crossing
1954 The Human Jungle
1955 This Island Earth
1955 Kiss of Fire
1956 Flight to Hong Kong
1957 Death in Small Doses
1958 Fort Massacre
1959 The Gunfight at Dodge City
1959 The Big Circus
1959 Tarzan, the Ape Man
1961 King of the Roaring Twenties / *The Big Bankroll*
1961 A Thunder of Drums
1961 The George Raft Story / *Spin of a Coin*
1961 Twenty Plus Two / *It Started in Tokyo*
(also many shorts)

NEWMAN, Paul
(1925–) Cleveland, Ohio, USA.
Biographies: Paul Newman Superstar: A Critical Biography by Lionel Godfrey; Paul Newman by J.C. Landry.
1968 Rachel, Rachel **F***
1971 Sometimes a Great Notion / *Never Give an Inch*
1972 The Effect of Gamma Rays on Man-in-the-Moon Marigolds
1984 Harry and Son
1987 The Glass Menagerie

NEWMEYER, Fred
(1888–) American.
1922 Doctor Jack
1922 Grandma's Boy
1923 Safety Last **(Sam TAYLOR)**
1924 Hot Water **(Sam TAYLOR)**
1925 The Freshman **(Sam TAYLOR)**
1925 Seven Keys to Baldpate
1926 The Quarterback
1927 The Potters
1927 Too Many Crooks
1927 On Your Toes
1928 That's My Daddy
1928 The Night Birds
1928 Warming Up
1929 The Rainbow Man
1929 Sailor's Holiday
1929 It Can Be Done
1930 Fast and Loose
1930 The Grande Parade
1930 Queen High
1931 Subway Express
1932 They Never Come Back
1932 Discarded Lovers
1932 The Fighting Gentlemen
1932 Gambling Sex
1933 Easy Millions
1934 The Big Race
1934 The Moth
1935 No Ransom
1935 Secrets of Chinatown
1936 General Spanky **(Gordon DOUGLAS)**
1942 Rodeo Rhythm

NEWTON, Joel
1953 Jennifer

NIBLO, Fred (Federico Nobile)
(1874–1948) York, Nebraska, USA.
1924 Thy Name Is Woman
1924 The Red Lily
1925 Ben Hur
1926 The Temptress **(Mauritz STILLER)**
1927 Camille
1928 The Enemy
1928 Two Lovers
1928 The Mysterious Lady
1928 Dream of Love
1930 Redemption
1930 Way Out West
1931 Young Donovan's Kid
1931 The Big Gamble
1932 Two White Arms
1932 Diamond Cut Diamond / *Blame the Woman* **(Maurice ELVEY)**
1941 Three Sons o' Guns

NICHOLAS, Paul (Lutz Schaatwaechter)
1982 Bad Blood / *Julie Darling*
1983 Chained Heat
1986 The Naked Cage

NICHOLLS, Allan
1982 Dead Ringer

NICHOLLS Jnr, George
(1897–1940) American.
1934 Anne of Green Gables
1934 Finishing School **(Wanda TUCHOCK)**
1934 The Return of Peter Grimm
1935 Chasing Yesterday
1935 Chatterbox
1936 Witness Chair
1936 M'Liss
1936 The Big Game
1936 The Soldier and the Lady / *Michael Strogoff*
1937 Portia on Trial
1938 Army Girl
1939 Man of Conquest
1940 The Marines Fly High **(Ben STOLOFF)**
1940 High School

NICHOLS, Dudley
(1895–1960) Wapakoneta, Ohio, USA.
1943 Government Girl
1946 Sister Kenny
1947 Mourning Becomes Electra

NICHOLS, Mike (Michael Igor Peschkowsky)
(1931–) Berlin, Germany.
Biography: Mike Nichols by H Wayne Schuth.
1966 Who's Afraid of Virginia Woolf? **D* F***
1967 The Graduate **D** F***
1970 Carnal Knowledge
1973 The Day of the Dolphin
1975 The Fortune
1983 Silkwood **D***
1986 Heartburn
1988 Biloxi Blues
1988 Working Girl **D* F***

NICHOLSON, Arch
1988 Dark Age

NICHOLSON, Jack
(1937–) Neptune, New Jersey, USA.
Biography: Jack Nicholson: The Search for a Superstar by Norman Dickens.
1970 Drive, He Said
1978 Goin' South

NICOL, Alex
(1919–) Ossining, New York, USA.
1958 The Screaming Skull
1961 Then There Were Three
1973 Point of Terror

NICOLAOU, Ted
1985 The Dungeonmaster / *Ragewar* **(David ALLEN, Charles BAND, John BUECHLER, Peter MANOOGIAN, Stephen STAFFORD, Rose-Marie TURKO)**
1986 Terrorvision
1987 I Eat Cannibals

NIERENBERG, George T
1975 The Hollow

NIGH, William
(1881–1955) American.
1926 The Fire Brigade
1926 The Little Giant
1927 Mr Wu
1927 The Law of the Range
1928 Across to Singapore
1928 Four Walls
1929 Thunder
1929 Desert Nights
1930 Lord Byron of Broadway / *What Price Melody?* **(Harry BEAUMONT)**
1930 Fighting Thru
1930 Today
1931 The Single Sin
1931 Lightning Flyer
1931 Sea Ghost
1932 Border Devils
1932 Night Rider
1932 Without Honours
1933 Men Are Such Fools
1933 He Couldn't Take It
1934 City Limits
1934 Monte Carlo Nights
1934 Mystery Liners
1934 Once to Every Bachelor
1934 School for Girls
1934 Two Heads on a Pillow
1934 Without Children
1934 House of Mystery
1935 His Night Out
1935 The Old Homestead
1935 Dizzy Dames
1935 Headline Woman
1935 She Gets Her Man
1935 Mysterious Mr Wong
1935 Sweepstakes Annie
1936 Don't Get Personal
1936 Crash Donovan
1936 North of Nome
1936 Penthouse Party
1936 Steel
1937 The 13th Man
1937 Atlantic Flight
1937 Boy of the Streets
1937 The Hoosier Schoolboy
1937 A Bride for Henry
1937 Bill Cracks Down
1937 The Right to Kill
1937 The Law Commands
1938 Female Fugitive
1938 Rose of the Rio Grande
1938 Gangster Boy
1938 Mr Wong, Detective
1938 I Am a Criminal
1938 Romance of the Limberlost
1939 Streets of New York
1939 Mutiny in the Big House
1939 Mr Wong in Chinatown
1939 The Mystery of Mr Wong
1940 The Ape
1940 Doomed to Die / *The Mystery of the Wentworth Castle*
1940 The Fatal Hour
1940 Son of the Navy
1940 The Under-Dog
1941 The Kid from Kansas
1941 Mob Town
1941 No Greater Sin
1941 Secret Evidence
1941 Zis Boom Bah
1942 Lady from Chungking

1942 Mr Wise Guy
1942 The Strange Case of Dr Rx
1942 Black Dragons
1942 City of Silent Men
1942 Tough As They Come
1942 Escape from Hong Kong
1942 Corregidor
1943 Where Are Your Children?
1943 The Ghost and the Guest
1944 Are These Our Parents?
1944 Forever Yours
1944 Trocadero
1945 Allotment Wives
1945 Divorce
1945 They Shall Have Faith
1946 Beauty and the Bandit
1946 The Gay Cavalier
1946 South of Monterey
1946 Partners in Time
1947 Riding the California Trail
1948 I Wouldn't Be in Your Shoes
1948 Stage Struck

NILSSON, Rob
1979 Northern Lights **(John HUSTON)**
1984 On the Edge
1984 Signal 7
1986 Heat and Sunlight

NIMOY, Leonard
(1931–) Boston, Massachusetts, USA.
1984 Star Trek III: The Search for Spock
1986 Star Trek IV: The Voyage Home
1987 Three Men and a Baby
1988 The Good Mother

NIVELLI, Mickey
1988 Messing Around
1989 Jealous

NOBEL, Jack
1934 At the Sign

NOEL, Jean-Guy
1987 Tinamer

NOFEL, Emil
1987 You Gotta Be Crazy

NOGUEIRA, Helena
1988 Fire in Their Hearts / *Quest for Love*

NOLBANDOV, Sergei
(1895–1971) Russian.
1941 Ships with Wings
1943 Undercover

NOLTE, William
1983 Life Goes On

NORMAN, Leslie
(1911–) London, England.
1954 The Night My Number Came Up
1956 X the Unknown
1958 The Shiralee
1958 Dunkirk
1959 Summer of the Seventeenth Doll / *Season of Passion*
1960 The Long and the Short and the Tall / *Jungle Fighters*
1961 Spare the Rod
1961 Mix Me a Person

NORMAN, Ron
(1950–) New York, New York, USA.
1979 A Death
1980 VT
1982 Rennie
1983 Horizons

NORRIS, Aaron
1988 Braddock Missing in Action III
1988 Platoon Leader
1989 Delta Force II: America's Red Army

NORTON, Bill L (William Lloyd Norton)
(1943–) California, USA.
1971 Cisco Pike
1979 More American Graffiti
1985 Baby — Secret of the Lost Legend
1987 Three for the Road
1988 Nam: Tour of Duty

NORTON, Charles
1989 No Hard Feelings

NOSLER, Lloyd
1931 Man from Death Valley
1932 Galloping Thru
1933 Son of the Border

NOSSECK, Max (Alexander M Morris)
(1902–1972) Polish.
1940 Girls Under 21
1941 Gambling Daughters
1945 Dillinger
1945 The Brighton Strangler
1946 Black Beauty
1947 The Return of Rin-Tin-Tin
1950 Kill or Be Killed
1951 Korea Patrol
1951 The Hoodlum
1951 Body Beautiful
1957 Garden of Evil

NOSSECK, Noel
1973 Best Friends
1976 Las Vegas Lady
1978 Youngblood
1979 Dreamer
1981 King of the Mountain
(also many TV movies)

NOTZ, Thierry
1989 The Terror Within

NOVAK, Blaine
1986 Good to Go

NOYCE, Phillip
(1950–) Griffith, New South Wales, Australia.
1979 Backroads
1982 Newsfront
1982 Heatwave
1987 Shadows of the Peacock
1988 Dead Calm
1989 Echoes of Paradise
1989 Blind Fury

NUCHTERN, Simon
1968 Girl Grabbers
1969 To Hex with Sex
1970 The Cowards
1972 What Do I Tell the Boys at the Station?
1972 The Broad Coalition
1976 The Bodyguard
1984 Silent Madness
1984 New York Nights
1985 Savage Dawn

NUGENT, Elliott
(1900–1980) Dover, Ohio, USA. Autobiography: Events Leading Up to the Comedy.
1932 The Mouthpiece **(James FLOOD)**
1932 Life Begins / *A Dream of Life* **(James FLOOD)**
1933 Three-Cornered Moon
1933 Whistling in the Dark / *Scared!*
1933 If I Were Free
1934 She Loves Me Not
1934 Strictly Dynamite
1934 Two Alone
1935 Enter Madame
1935 Love in Bloom
1935 Splendor
1935 College Scandal / *The Clock Strikes Eight*
1936 And So They Were Married
1936 Wives Never Know
1937 It's All Yours
1938 Give Me a Sailor
1938 Professor Beware
1938 Never Say Die
1939 The Cat and the Canary
1940 Nothing But the Truth
1942 The Male Animal
1943 The Crystal Ball
1944 Up in Arms
1947 My Favourite Brunette
1947 Welcome Stranger
1948 My Girl Tisa
1949 The Great Gatsby
1949 Mr Belvedere Goes to College
1950 The Skipper Surprised His Wife
1951 My Outlaw Brother
1952 Just for You

NUNEZ, Victor
1979 Gal Young Un

NUNN, Trevor
(1940–) Ipswich, Suffolk, England.
1975 Hedda
1985 Lady Jane

NUSSBAUM, Raphael
1974 Pets
1976 The Amorous Adventures of Don Quixote and Sancho Panza
1987 W.A.R. Women Against Rape
1987 Private Road / *No Trespassing*
1988 Deathblow

NUTTER, David
1985 Cease Fire / *In Country*

NYBY, Christian
(1919–) American.
1951 The Thing **(Howard HAWKS)**
1957 Hell on Devil's Island
1965 Operation CIA
1965 Young Fury
1967 First to Fight

NYSWANER, Ron
1988 The Prince of Pennsylvania

O'BANNON, Dan
(1946–) St Louis, Missouri, USA.
1985 Return of the Living Dead

OBOLER, Arch
(1907–1987) Chicago, Illinois, USA.
1945 Bewitched
1946 Strange Holiday
1947 The Arnelo Affair
1951 Five
1952 Bwana Devil
1953 The Twonky
1961 One Plus One: Exploring the Kinsey Reports
1967 The Bubble

O'BRIEN, Edmond
(1915–1985) New York, New York, USA.
1954 Shield for Murder **(Howard W KOCH)**
1961 Mantrap

O'BRIEN, Jim
1988 The Dressmaker

O'BRIEN, John
1925 Daring Days
1925 The Outlaw's Daughter

OBROW, Jeffrey
1982 The Dorm That Dripped Blood / *Pranks* **(Stephen CARPENTER)**
1984 The Power **(Stephen CARPENTER)**
1987 The Kindred **(Stephen CARPENTER)**

O'CONNELL, Jack
1963 Greenwich Village Story
1971 Swedish Fly Girls / *Christa*

O'CONNOLLY, James
(1926–) British.
1964 The Hi-Jackers
1964 Smokescreen
1965 The Little Ones
1968 Berserk!
1969 The Valley of the Gwangi
1969 Crooks and Coronets / *Sophie's Place*
1972 Horror on Snape Island / *Beyond the Fog*
1974 Mistress Pamela

O'CONNOR, Frank
1926 Spangles
1927 Colleen
1930 Call of the Circus
1938 Religious Racketeers
1939 Mystic Circle Murder

O'CONNOR, Pat
1984 Cal
1987 A Month in the Country

1988 Stars and Bars
1989 The January Man

O'CONNOR, William
1930 Chiselers of Hollywood
1931 Ten Nights in a Bar Room
1931 Primrose Path
1931 Playthings of Hollywood
1932 The Drifter
1933 Her Splendid Folly
1935 Cheyenne Tornado

ODELL, David
1988 Martians Go Home

ODETS, Clifford
(1903–1963) Philadelphia, Pennsylvania, USA.
1944 None But the Lonely Heart
1960 The Story on Page One

O'DONOGHUE, Michael
1979 Mr Mike's Mondo Video

OGILVIE, George
1985 Mad Max III: Beyond Thunderdome **(George MILLER)**
1986 Short Changed
1986 The Place at the Coast

O'HANLON, George (George Rice)
(1917–) Brooklyn, New York, USA.
1959 The Rookie

O'HARA, Gerry
(1924–) Boston, Lincolnshire, England.
1963 Models, Inc. / *That Kind of Girl*
1963 A Game for Three Losers
1965 The Pleasure Girls
1966 Maroc 7
1968 Amsterdam Affair
1970 Fidelia
1971 All the Right Noises
1976 The Brute
1978 Leopard in the Snow
1979 The Bitch
1983 Fanny Hill
1984 Strictly for Cash

O'HERLIHY, Michael
(1928–) Dublin, Republic of Ireland.
1966 The Fighting Prince of Donegal
1967 The One and Only Genuine, Original Family Band
1969 Smith!
(also many TV movies)

O'HORGAN, Tom
1969 Futz
1974 Rhinoceros

O'KEEFE, Dennis (Edward 'Bud' Flanagan)
(1908–1968) Fort Madison, Iowa, USA.
1954 The Diamond Wizard
1955 Angela

OLCOTT, Sidney (John S Olcott)
(1897–1949) Toronto, Canada.
Biography: Actor-Soldier-Poet by R. Henderson-Bland.
1924 The Humming Bird
1924 Monsieur Beaucaire
1925 Not So Long Ago
1925 The Best People
1925 The Charmer
1925 Salome of the Tenements
1927 The Claw

OLIANSKY, Joel
(1935–) New York, New York, USA.
1980 The Competition

OLIVER, David
1985 Cavegirl

OLIVER, Richard
1989 A Girl to Kill For

OLIVERA, Hector *
(1931–) Olivos, Argentina.
1983 Funny Dirty Little War
1985 Wizards of the Lost Kingdom
1985 Barbarian Queen
1985 Cocaine Wars
1987 The Night of the Pencils
1988 Two to Tango

OLIVIER, Sir Laurence (Lord Olivier)
(1907–1989) Dorking, Surrey, England.
Autobiography: Confessions of an Actor.
Biography: Laurence Olivier by Melvin Bragg.
1944 Henry V **F***
1945 Hamlet **D* F****
1955 Richard III
1957 The Prince and the Showgirl
1970 The Three Sisters

OLLSTEIN, Marty
1989 Dangerous Love / *Singles*

OLMI, Ermanno
(1931–) Bergamo, Italy.
1959 Time Stood Still
1961 The Sound of Trumpets / *The Job*
1963 The Fiancés / *The Engagement*
1965 And There Came a Man / *A Man Named John*
1969 One Fine Day
1970 The Scavengers
1971 During the Summer
1974 The Circumstance
1979 The Tree of Wooden Clogs
1983 Keep Walking
1987 Lunga Vita alla Signora

OLSEN, Wes
1986 The Dark Side of Midnight

OLSEN, William
1983 Getting It On
1986 Rockin' Road Trip
1988 Private Tutor / *Before God / After School / Return to Eden*

O'MALLEY, David
1978 Mountain Man
1985 Kid Colter

1987 Awesome Lotus: Mistress of the Martial Arts
1989 Easy Wheels / *Women on Wheels*

O'NEAL, Ron
(1937–) Utica, New York, USA.
1973 Superfly T.N.T.

O'NEIL, Robert Vincent
1970 The Loving Touch
1971 Blood Mania
1973 Wonder Women
1975 Paco
1984 Angel
1985 Avenging Angel

O'NEILL, Maurice
1937 A Tenderfoot Goes West

OPHULS, Marcel (M. Oppenheimer)
(1927–) Frankfurt-am-Main, Germany.
1960 Matisse
1962 Love at Twenty **(Shintaro ISHIHARA, Renzo ROSSELLINI, François TRUFFAUT, Andrzej WAJDA)**
1965 Banana Peel
1965 Feu à Volonté
(also many documentaries)

OPHULS, Max (M. Oppenheimer) *
(1902–1957) Saarbrücken, Germany.
Autobiography: Max Ophüls par Max Ophüls.
1932 The Bartered Bride
1938 Werther
1939 There's No Tomorrow
1940 Mayerling to Sarajevo
1948 The Exile
1948 Letter from an Unknown Woman
1948 Caught
1949 The Reckless Moment
1952 House of Pleasure
1953 The Earrings of Madame De...
1955 The Fall of Lola Montes

ORDUNG, Wyott
1956 Walk the Dark Street

ORLANDO, Dominic
1985 Knights of the City

ORLEBECK, Lester
1940 Pioneers of the West
1941 Gauchos of Eldorado
1941 Prairie Pioneers
1941 Pals of the Pecos
1941 Saddlemates
1941 Outlaws of the Cherokee Trail
1941 West of Cimarron
1942 Shadows of the Sage

ORME, Stuart
1989 The Wolves of Willoughby Chase

ORMOND, Ron
1951 Kentucky Jubilee
1951 Varieties on Parade
1951 Yes Sir, Mr Bones
1951 King of the Bullwhip
1952 Outlaw Women **(Sam NEWFIELD)**

ORMOND, Peter
1986 Eat the Peach

OROSS, Emmerich
(1940–) Hungarian.
1985 Last Call

O'ROURKE, Dennis
1986 Half Life

ORR, James
1985 Breaking All the Rules
1987 They Still Call Me Bruce **(Johnny YUNE)**

OSBORNE, Kent
1970 Cain's Way

OSHIMA, Nagisa
(1932–) Kyoto, Japan.
Autobiography: Ecrits (1958–1978): Dissolution et Jaillissement translated by Jean-Paul le Pape.
1959 A Town of Love and Hope
1960 Cruel Story of Youth / *Naked Youth*
1960 The Sun's Burial
1960 Night and Fog in Japan
1961 The Catch
1962 The Revolutionary / *The Rebel*
1964 A Small Child's First Adventure
1964 It's Me Here, Bellett
1965 The Pleasures of the Flesh
1966 Violence at Noon
1967 Band of Ninja
1967 A Treatise in Japanese Bawdy Songs / *Sing a Song of Sex*
1967 Japanese Summer: Double Suicide
1968 Death By Hanging
1968 Three Resurrected Drunkards
1968 Diary of a Shinjuku Burglar
1969 Boy
1970 The Man Who Left His Will on Film / *He Died After the War*
1972 Summer Soldiers
1974 The Ceremony
1977 In the Realm of the Senses
1980 Empire of Passion / *Ai No Corrida*
1983 Merry Christmas, Mr Lawrence
1986 Max, Mon Amour

OSMOND, Cliff
1988 The Penitent

O'STEEN, Sam
(1923–) American.
1976 Sparkle
(also many TV movies)

OSWALD, Gerd
(1916–) Berlin, Germany.
1956 A Kiss Before Dying
1956 The Brass Legend
1957 Crime of Passion
1957 Fury at Showdown
1957 Valerie
1957 Paris Holiday
1958 Screaming Mimi
1959 The Day It Rained

1960 Three Moves to Freedom / *The Royal Game*
1960 Brainwashed
1963 The Scarlet Eye
1966 Agent for H.A.R.M.
1969 80 Steps to Jonah
1971 Bunny O'Hare
1975 To the Bitter End

OSWALD, Richard (R. Ornstein)
(1880–1963) Vienna, Austria.
Biography: Richard Oswald edited by Walter Kaul and Robert Scheuer.
1941 The Captain of Koepenick
1942 Isle of Missing Men
1949 The Loveable Cheat

OTTONI, Filippo
1986 Private Detective / *Detective School Dropouts / Dumb Dicks*
1988 Stray Days

OURY, Gerard (Max-Gerard Houry Tannenbaum) *
(1919–) Paris, France.
1961 The Menace
1962 Crime Does Not Pay
1966 The Sucker
1966 Don't Look Now, We're Being Shot At / *La Grande Vadroville*
1969 The Brain
1971 Delusions of Grandeur
1974 The Mad Adventures of 'Rabbi' Jacob
1986 Levy and Goliath

OVE, Horace
1987 Playing Away

OWEN, Cliff
(1919–) London, England.
1961 Offbeat
1961 A Prize of Arms
1963 The Wrong Arm of the Law
1966 A Man Could Get Killed **(Ronald NEAME)**
1966 That Riviera Touch
1967 The Magnificent Two / *What Happened at Campo Grande?*
1968 The Vengeance of She
1972 Steptoe and Son
1973 Ooh. . You Are Awful / *Get Charlie Tully*
1973 No Sex Please, We're British
1975 The Bawdy Adventures of Tom Jones

OWEN, Don
1964 Nobody Waved Goodbye
1967 The Ernie Game
1967 Partners
1984 Unfinished Business

OZ, Frank (Frank Oznowicz)
(1944–) Hereford, Herefordshire, England.
1982 The Dark Crystal
1984 The Muppets Take Manhattan
1986 Little Shop of Horrors
1988 Dirty Rotten Scoundrels

PACHARD, Henri
1982 The Devil in Miss Jones II

PADGETT, Calvin
1966 Secret Agent Super Dragon

PAGE, Anthony
(1935–) Bangalore, India.
1968 Inadmissible Evidence
1976 Alpha Beta
1977 I Never Promised You a Rose Garden
1978 Absolution
1979 The Lady Vanishes
(also many TV movies)

PAIZS, John
1987 Crimewave

PAKULA, Alan J
(1928–) New York, New York, USA.
1969 The Sterile Cuckoo / *Pookie*
1971 Klute
1973 Love Pain and the Whole Damn Thing
1974 The Parallax View
1976 All the President's Men **D* F***
1978 Comes a Horseman
1979 Starting Over
1981 Rollover
1982 Sophie's Choice
1986 Dream Lover
1987 Orphans
1989 See You in the Morning

PAL, George (Georg Pál)
(1908–1980) Cegled, Hungary.
1958 Tom Thumb
1960 The Time Machine
1961 Atlantis, The Lost Continent
1962 The Wonderful World of the Brothers Grimm **(Henry LEVIN)**
1964 Seven Faces of Doctor Leo
(also many shorts)

PALCY, Euzhan
1983 Sugar Cane Alley
1989 A Dry White Season

PALLENBERG, Rospo
1989 Cutting Class

PALMER, Tony
1971 200 Motels **(Frank ZAPPA)**
1985 George Frederic Handel 1685–1759
1988 Testimony

PALMISANO, Conrad E
1985 A Dollar a Day
1986 Space Rage / *Trackers*
1986 Busted Up

PALTROW, Bruce
(1943–) New York, New York, USA.
1982 A Little Sex

PANAMA, Norman
(1914–) Chicago, Illinois, USA.
1950 The Reformer and the Redhead **(Melvin FRANK)**
1951 Strictly Dishonourable **(Melvin FRANK)**

1951 Callaway Went Thataway / *The Star Said No* **(Melvin FRANK)**
1952 Above and Beyond **(Melvin FRANK)**
1954 Knock on Wood **(Melvin FRANK)**
1956 The Court Jester **(Melvin FRANK)**
1956 That Certain Feeling **(Melvin FRANK)**
1959 Li'l Abner **(Melvin FRANK)**
1959 The Trap
1962 The Road to Hong Kong
1966 Not with My Wife, You Don't!
1969 How to Commit Marriage
1969 The Maltese Bippy
1976 I Will, I Will..For Now
1978 Barnaby and Me

PAPAS, Michael
1988 The Troubleshooter

PAPPAS, Robert K
1989 Now I Know

PARADISE, Michael J
1979 The Visitor

PARIS, Dominic
1980 Dracula's Last Rites
1984 Splitz

PARIS, Henry *see* **Radley H METZGER**

PARIS, Jerry
(1925–1986) San Francisco, California, USA.
1968 Don't Raise the Bridge, Lower the River
1968 Never a Dull Moment
1968 How Sweet It Is!
1969 Viva Max!
1969 The Grasshopper
1971 What's a Nice Girl Like You..?
1971 Star Spangled Girl
1980 Leo and Loree
1985 Police Academy II
1986 Police Academy III: Back in Training
(also many TV movies)

PARK, Richard
1986 Ninja Turf / *LA Streetfighters*
1987 Miami Connection

PARKER, Alan
(1944–) Islington, London, England.
1976 Bugsy Malone
1978 Midnight Express **D* F***
1980 Fame
1981 Shoot the Moon
1982 Pink Floyd, The Wall
1985 Birdy
1987 Angel Heart
1988 Mississippi Burning **D* F***

PARKER, Albert
1926 The Black Pirate
1927 The Loves of Sunya
1936 Blind Man's Buff
1938 Murder in the Family

PARKER, Cary
1986 The Girl in the Picture

PARKER, Clifton
(1905–) British.
1949 Marry Me

PARKER, Joseph
1957 Eighteen and Anxious
1958 The Hot Angel

PARKS, Gordon
(1912–) Fort Scott, Kansas, USA.
1969 The Learning Tree
1971 Shaft
1972 Shaft's Big Score
1974 The Super Cops
1976 Leadbelly

PARKS Jnr., Gordon
(1948–1979) American.
1972 Superfly
1974 Thomasine and Bushrod
1974 Three the Hard Way
1975 Aaron Loves Angela

PARKS, Michael
(1938–) Corona, California, USA.
1988 The Return of Josey Wales

PARMET, Philip
1989 Riders in the Dark

PAROLINI, Billy
1986 Igor and the Lunatics

PARR, Larry
1988 A Soldier's Tale

PARRISH, Robert R
(1916–) Columbus, Georgia, USA. Autobiography: Growing Up in Hollywood.
1951 Cry Danger
1951 The Mob / *Remember That Face*
1952 The San Francisco Story
1952 Assignment, Paris
1952 My Pal Gus
1953 Rough Shoot / *Shoot First*
1954 The Purple Plain
1955 Lucy Gallant
1957 Fire Down Below
1957 Saddle the Wind
1959 The Wonderful Country
1963 In the French Style
1963 Up from the Beach
1967 Casino Royale **(Val GUEST, Ken HUGHES, John HUSTON, Joseph McGRATH)**
1967 The Bobo
1968 Duffy
1969 Journey to the Far Side of the Sun / *Doppelgänger*
1971 A Town Called Bastard
1974 The Marseilles Contract / *The Destructors*
1984 Mississippi Blues **(Bertrand TAVERNIER)**

PARROTT, James (Poll Parrott)
(1892–1939) American.
1931 Pardon Us / *Jailbirds*
(also a multitude of shorts 1920–1935)

PARRY, Gordon
(1908–1981) British.
1947 Bond Street
1948 Third Time Lucky
1949 Now Barabbas Was a Robber..
1949 Golden Arrow / *Three Men and a Girl*
1950 Midnight Episode
1951 Tom Brown's Schooldays
1952 Women of Twilight
1953 Innocents in Paris
1953 Front Page Story
1954 Fast and Loose
1955 A Yank in Ermine
1956 Sailor Beware / *Panic in the Parlour*
1956 Touch of the Sun
1957 The Surgeon's Knife
1958 Tread Softly Stranger
1959 Friends and Neighbours
1959 The Navy Lark

PARRY, Michael
1989 Silver Screen

PARRY, Robert
1957 Tomahawk Trail

PASCAL, Gabriel
(1894–1954) Arad, Hungary.
1941 Major Barbara **(Harold FRENCH, David LEAN)**
1945 Caesar and Cleopatra

PASKALJEVIC, Goran
1976 The Beach Guard in Winter
1978 The Dog That Liked Trains
1980 The Days Are Passing
1982 Special Treatment
1983 Twilight Time
1984 The Illusory Summer of '68
1987 Guardian Angel

PASOLINI, Pier Paolo *
(1922–1975) Bologna, Italy.
Autobiography: Pasolini on Pasolini edited by Oswald Stack.
1964 The Gospel According to St Matthew
1966 Hawks and Sparrows
1967 Oedipus Rex
1968 Theorem
1969 Pigsty
1971 The Decameron
1972 The Canterbury Tales
1974 Arabian Nights
1975 Salo — the 120 Days of Sodom

PASSER, Ivan
(1933–) Prague, Czechoslovakia.
1965 A Boring Afternoon
1965 Intimate Lighting
1971 Born to Win
1974 Law and Disorder
1976 Crime and Passion
1978 Silver Bears
1981 Cutter's Way / *Cutter and Bone*
1985 Creator
1988 Haunted Summer

PATAKI, Michael
1977 Mansion of the Doomed

PATE, Michael
(1920–) Sydney, New South Wales, Australia.
1979 Tim

PATEL, Raju
1984 In the Shadow of Kilimanjaro

PATEL, Sharad
1983 Amin: The Rise and Fall

PATON, Stuart
1927 Fangs of Destiny
1928 The Four Footed Ranger
1928 The Hound of Silver Creek
1931 Air Police
1931 Chinatown After Dark
1931 First Aid
1931 Hell Bent for Frisco
1931 In Old Cheyenne
1931 Is There Justice?
1931 Mounted Fury
1935 The Silent Code
1935 Thunderbolt
1936 Clipped Wings

PATRICK, Matthew
1989 Hider in the House

PATRICK, Nigel (Neigel Wemyss)
(1913–1981) London, England.
1957 How to Murder a Rich Uncle
1960 Johnny Nobody

PATRICK, Robert
1970 Road to Nashville

PATTERSON, John D
1975 The Legend of Earl Durand
1989 Deadly Innocents

PATTINSON, Michael
1988 Ground Zero

PATTISON, Barrie
1988 Zombie Brigade

PAUL, Steven
(1958–) New York, New York, USA.
1980 Falling in Love Again
1983 Slapstick of Another Kind

PAUL, Stuart
1986 Emanon
1987 Street Dreams

PAULSEN, David
1976 Savage Weekend / *The Upstate Murders*
1980 Schizoid

PAVLOU, George
1986 Underworld / *Transmutations*
1987 Rawhead Rex

PAYNE, John
(1912–) American.
1969 They Ran for Their Lives

PAYS, Armand *see* **Herschell G LEWIS**

PEARCE, Leslie A
1929 The Delightful Rogue
1930 The Fall Guy
1931 Meet the Wife

PEARCE, Michael
1985 James Joyce's Women
1987 Initiation

PEARCE, Richard
1979 Heartland
1983 Threshold
1984 Country
1986 No Mercy
(also TV movies)

PEARSON, George
(1875–1973) London, England.
Autobiography: Flashback: The Autobiography of a British Filmmaker.
1924 Reveille
1925 Satan's Sister
1925 Mr Preedy and the Countess
1925 The Little People
1926 Blinkeyes
1927 Huntingtower
1929 Love's Option
1929 Auld Lang Syne
1930 Harry Lauder's Songs
1930 East Lynne on the Western Front
1930 The Third String
1934 A Shot in the Dark
1934 River Wolves
1934 The Pointing Finger
1934 Ace of Spades
1934 Four Masked Men
1934 Whispering Tongues
1935 Open All Night
1935 Jubilee Window
1935 Gentleman's Agreement
1935 Once a Thief
1935 That's My Uncle
1936 Checkmate
1936 The Secret Voice
1936 Wednesday's Luck
1936 Murder By Rope
1937 The Fatal Hour
1937 Midnight at Madame Tussaud's
(also many documentary shorts)

PEARSON, Peter
1987 Paperback Hero

PECK, Ron
1987 Empire State
1990 Forever Yours Montgomery Clift

PECKINPAH, Sam
(1925–1984) Fresno, California, USA.
Biography: Sam Peckinpah by Doug McKinney.
1961 The Deadly Companions
1962 Ride the High Country / *Guns in the Afternoon*
1965 Major Dundee
1969 The Wild Bunch
1970 The Ballad of the Cable Hogue
1972 Straw Dogs
1972 The Getaway
1973 Junior Bonner
1973 Pat Garrett and Billy the Kid
1974 Bring Me the Head of Alfredo Garcia
1975 The Killer Elite
1977 Cross of Iron
1978 Convoy
1983 The Osterman Weekend

PEERCE, Larry
(c1935–) Bronx, New York, USA.
1964 One Potato, Two Potato
1967 The Incident
1969 Goodbye, Columbus
1971 The Sporting Club
1972 A Separate Peace
1973 Ash Wednesday
1975 The Other Side of the Mountain / *A Window to the Sky*
1976 Two-Minute Warning
1978 The Other Side of the Mountain, Part II
1979 The Bell Jar
1980 Why Would I Lie?
1982 Love Child
1984 Hard to Hold
1989 Wired
(also many TV movies)

PEETERS, Barbara
1970 The Dark Side of Tomorrow **(Jacques BEERSON)**
1972 Bury Me an Angel
1975 Summer School Teachers
1975 Just the Two of Us
1978 Starhops
1980 Humanoid from the Deep / *Monster*

PELAEZ, Antonio
1987 Crystalstone

PELISSIER, Anthony
(1912–1988) British.
1949 The History of Mr Polly
1949 The Rocking Horse Winner
1951 Encore **(Harold FRENCH, Pat JACKSON)**
1951 Night Without Stars
1952 Meet Me Tonight
1953 Meet Mr Lucifer
1953 Personal Affair

PEMBROKE, Scott
1929 Should a Girl Marry?
1930 Jazz Cinderella
1930 Last Dance
1930 The Medicine Man
1936 The Oregon Trail
1938 Telephone Operator

PENN, Arthur
(1922–) Philadelphia, Pennsylvania, USA.
Biography: Arthur Penn by Robin Wood.
1958 The Left-Handed Gun
1962 The Miracle Worker **D***
1965 Mickey One
1966 The Chase
1967 Bonnie and Clyde **D* F***
1969 Alice's Restaurant **D***

1970 Little Big Man
1975 Night Moves
1976 The Missouri Breaks
1981 Four Friends / *Georgia's Friends*
1985 Target
1987 Dead of Winter
1989 Penn and Teller Get Killed

PENN, Leo
1966 A Man Called Adam
1987 Judgement in Berlin
(also many TV movies)

PENNELL, Eagle (Glenn Irwin Pennell)
1979 The Whole Shootin' Match
1983 Last Night at the Alamo

PENNINGTON-RICHARDS, C
(1911–) British.
1953 The Oracle
1957 The Hour of Decision
1962 Mystery Submarine / *Decoy*
1963 Ladies Who Do
1967 A Challenge for Robin Hood

PEOPLES, David
1989 The Salute of the Jugger

PEPLOE, Clare
1987 High Season

PEPLOE, Mark
1988 Out of the Blue

PEPPARD, George
(1928–) Detroit, Michigan, USA.
1977 Five Days from Home

PERIER, Etienne
(1931–) French.
1961 Bridge to the Sun
1962 Swordsman of Siena
1971 When Eight Bells Toll
1971 Zeppelin
1972 A Murder Is a Murder, Is a Murder
1978 The Investigation / *Un si joli Village*
1989 Venetian Red

PERISIC, Zoran
(1940–) Yugoslavia.
1986 Gunbus / *Sky Bandits*
1987 The Disc

PERKINS, Anthony
(1932–) New York, New York, USA.
1986 Psycho III
1988 Lucky Stiff / *Mr Christmas Dinner*

PERRY, Frank
(1930–) New York, New York, USA.
1962 David and Lisa **D***
1963 Ladybug, Ladybug
1968 The Swimmer
1969 Last Summer
1969 Trilogy
1970 Diary of a Mad Housewife
1971 Doc
1972 Play It As It Lays
1974 Man on a Swing
1975 Rancho Deluxe
1981 Mommie Dearest
1982 Monsignor
1985 Compromising Positions
1987 Hello Again

PERRY, Peter
1979 The Young Cycle Girls

PERRY, Steve
1989 Nemesis

PERSKY, Bill
(1931–) New Haven, Connecticut, USA.
1980 Serial
(also many TV movies and comedy shorts)

PETERS, Brooke L
1954 The World Dances
1957 The Unearthly
1961 Anatomy of a Psycho

PETERSEN, Wolfgang
(1941–) German.
1973 Einer von Uns Beiden
1976 Vier Gegen die Blank
1977 The Consequence
1978 Black and White Like Night and Day
1981 The Boat **D***
1984 The Neverending Story
1985 Enemy Mine
1988 The Plastic Nightmare

PETERSON, Daniel M
1987 Vampire Knights
1989 The Girlfriend from Hell

PETERSON, Kristine
1989 Deadly Dreams

PETIT, Chris
(1949–) British.
1979 Radio On
1982 An Unsuitable Job for a Woman
1984 Flight to Berlin
1984 Chinese Boxes

PETRIE, Daniel
(1920–) Glace Bay, Nova Scotia, Canada.
1960 The Bramble Bush
1961 A Raisin in the Sun
1962 The Main Attraction
1963 Stolen Hours
1966 The Idol
1966 The Spy with the Cold Nose
1973 The Neptune Factor
1974 Buster and Billie
1976 Lifeguard
1978 The Betsy
1980 Resurrection
1981 Fort Apache, the Bronx
1982 Six Pack
1984 The Dollmaker
1984 The Bay Boy
1987 Square Dance
1988 Rocket Gibraltar
1988 Cocoon: The Return
(also many TV movies)

PETRIE, Donald
1988 Mystic Pizza

PETROFF, Boris
1936 Hats Off
1952 Red Snow
1961 Outcasts of the City

PEVNEY, Joseph
(1920–) New York, New York, USA.
1950 Shakedown
1950 Undercover Girl
1951 Air Cadet / *Jet Men of the Air*
1951 Iron Man
1951 The Lady from Texas
1951 The Strange Door
1952 Meet Danny Wilson
1952 Flesh and Fury
1952 Just Across the Street
1952 Because of You
1953 Desert Legion
1953 It Happens Every Thursday
1953 Back to God's Country
1954 Yankee Pasha
1954 Playgirl
1954 Three Ring Circus
1955 Six Bridges to Cross
1955 Foxfire
1955 Female on the Beach
1956 Away All Boats
1956 Congo Crossing
1956 Istanbul
1957 Tammy and the Bachelor
1957 The Midnight Story / *Appointment with a Shadow*
1957 Man of a Thousand Faces
1958 Twilight for the Gods
1958 Torpedo Run
1960 Cash McCall
1960 The Plunderers
1960 The Crowded Sky
1961 Portrait of a Mobster
1966 The Night of the Grizzly
1985 Prisoners of the Sea

PEYSER, John
(1916–) New York, New York, USA.
1958 Undersea Girl
1964 The Murder Men
1967 The Young Warriors
1970 Massacre Harbour
1974 Centrefold Girls

PFEIFFER, Scott
1987 Firefight

PHELPS, William
1987 The North Shore

PHILIPS, Lee
(1927–) American.
1981 On the Right Track
(also many TV movies)

PHILLIPS, Maurice
1986 The American Way

PICHEL, Irving
(1891–1954) Pittsburgh, Pennsylvania, USA.
1932 The Most Dangerous Game / *The Hounds of Zaroff* **(Ernest B SCHOEDSACK)**
1933 Before Dawn
1935 She **(Lansing C HOLDEN)**
1936 The Gentleman from Louisiana
1936 Larceny on the Air
1937 Beware of Ladies
1937 The Sheik Steps Out
1937 The Duke Comes Back / *The Call of the Ring*
1939 The Great Commandment
1940 Earthbound
1940 The Man I Married / *I Married a Nazi*
1940 Hudson's Bay
1941 Dance Hall
1942 Secret Agent of Japan
1942 The Pied Piper **F***
1942 Life Begins at Eight-Thirty / *The Light of Heart*
1943 The Moon Is Down
1943 Happy Land
1944 And Now Tomorrow
1945 A Medal for Benny
1945 Colonel Effingham's Raid / *Man of the Hour*
1946 Tomorrow Is Forever
1946 The Bride Wore Boots
1946 Temptation
1946 O.S.S.
1947 They Won't Believe Me
1947 Something in the Wind
1948 The Miracle of the Bells
1948 Mr Peabody and the Mermaid
1949 Without Honor
1950 The Great Rupert
1950 Quicksand
1950 Destination Moon
1951 Santa Fe
1953 Martin Luther
1954 Day of Triumph

PIERCE, Charles B
1973 The Legend of Boggy Creek
1974 Bootleggers
1975 Winterhawk
1976 The Winds of Autumn
1977 The Town That Dreaded Sundown
1978 The Norseman
1978 Greyeagle
1979 The Evictors
1983 Sacred Ground
1985 Boggy Creek II
1986 Hawken

PIERCE, Douglas
1954 The Delavine Affair / *Murder Is News*

PIERSON, Arthur
1948 Dangerous Years
1949 Fighting O'Flynn
1951 Home Town Story

PIERSON, Carl
1935 The New Frontier
1935 Paradise Canyon
1935 The Singing Vagabond

PIERSON, Frank
(1925–1988) New York, USA.

1969 The Looking Glass War
1976 A Star Is Born
1978 King of the Gypsies
1989 Black and Blue

PILLSBURY, Sam
1988 Starlight Hotel

PINE, Phillip
(1925–) Hanford, California, USA.
1972 The Cat and the Canary
1975 Pot! Parents! Police!

PINE, William H
(1896–1955) American.
1943 Aerial Gunner
1945 Tokyo Rose
1946 Swamp Fire
1947 Seven Were Saved
1947 Danger Street
1948 Disaster
1949 Dynamite

PINK, Sidney
(1916–) American.
1961 Journey to the Seventh Planet
1965 Finger on the Trigger
1966 The Tall Woman

PINSENT, Gordon
1988 John and the Missus

PINTER, Harold
(1930–) London, England.
1973 Butley

PINTOFF, Ernest
(1931–) Watertown, Connecticut, USA.
1965 Harvey Middleman Fireman
1971 Who Killed Mary What's 'Er Name?
1972 Dynamite Chicken
1979 Jaguar Lives
1981 Lunch Wagon
1981 St Helens

PIPER, Brett
1988 Mutant War

PIROSH, Robert
(1910–) American.
1951 Go for Broke
1952 Washington Story / *Target for Scandal*
1954 Valley of the Kings
1955 The Girl Rush
1956 Spring Reunion

PIRRO, Mark
1987 Deathrow Gameshow

PITRE, Glen
(1955–) Louisiana, USA.
1985 Belizaire the Cajun

PITTMAN, Bruce
1985 The Painted Door
1986 Confidential
1987 The Haunting of Hamilton High / *Hello Mary Lou: Prom Night II*

PLONE, Allen
1987 Night Screams
1989 Phantom of the Ritz

POE, Amos
1980 Unmade Beds
1981 The Foreigner
1981 Subway Riders
1984 Alphabet City

POGOSTIN, S Lee
(1926–) American.
1969 Hard Contract

POITIER, Sidney
(1924–) Miami, Florida, USA.
Autobiography: This Life.
1971 Buck and the Preacher
1972 Warm December
1974 Uptown Saturday Night
1975 Let's Do It Again
1977 A Piece of the Action
1980 Stir Crazy
1982 Hanky Panky
1985 Fast Forward

POLAKOFF, James
1975 Sunburst
1979 Love and the Midnight Auto Supply

POLANSKI, Roman
(1933–) Paris, France.
Autobiography: Roman.
1963 Knife in the Water
1964 The Beautiful Swindlers **(Claude CHABROL, Ugo GRIGORETTI, Hiromichi HORIKAWA)**
1965 Repulsion
1966 Cul-de-Sac
1967 The Fearless Vampire Killers, or Pardon Me But Your Teeth Are in My Neck / *Dance of the Vampires*
1968 Rosemary's Baby
1971 Macbeth
1973 What?
1974 Chinatown **D* F***
1976 The Tenant
1980 Tess **D* F***
1985 Pirates
1988 Frantic
(also shorts)

POLIAKOFF, Stephen
1987 Hidden City

POLLACK, Barry
1972 Cool Breeze
1973 This Is a Hijack

POLLACK, Sydney
(1934–) South Bend, Indiana, USA.
Biography: Sydney Pollack by Jean A. Gili.
1965 The Slender Thread
1966 This Property Is Condemned
1968 The Scalphunters
1969 Castle Keep
1969 They Shoot Horses, Don't They? **D***
1972 Jeremiah Johnson
1973 The Way We Were

1975 The Yakuza
1975 Three Days of the Condor
1977 Bobby Deerfield
1979 The Electric Horseman
1981 Absence of Malice
1982 Tootsie **D* F***
1986 Out of Africa **D** F****

POLLARD, Bud
1930 Danger Man
1931 Alice in Wonderland
1931 Rio's Road to Hell
1931 Voice of the Jungle
1932 Black King
1933 Victims of Persecution
1937 The Death March
1946 Beware
1946 Tall, Tan and Terrific
1947 It Pays to Be Funny
1947 Road to Hollywood

POLLARD, Harry A
(1883–1934) American.
1924 Sporting Youth
1924 K — The Unknown
1924 The Reckless Age
1925 California Straight Ahead
1925 I'll Show You the Town
1925 Oh, Doctor!
1925 The Cohens and the Kellys
1926 Poker Faces
1927 Uncle Tom's Cabin
1929 Show Boat
1929 Tonight at Twelve
1930 Undertow
1930 Great Day
1931 Shipmates
1931 The Prodigal
1932 Fast Life
1932 When a Feller Needs a Friend

POLLEXFEN, Jack
1954 Dragon's Gold **(Aubrey WISBERG)**
1956 The Indestructable Man

POLLOCK, George
(1907–) British.
1957 Stranger in Town
1957 Rooney
1958 The Poacher's Daughter / *Sally's Irish Rogue*
1959 Broth of a Boy
1959 Don't Panic, Chaps!
1960 And the Same to You
1961 Village of Daughters
1961 Murder She Said
1962 Kill or Cure
1963 Murder at the Gallop
1964 Murder Most Foul
1965 Murder Ahoy
1965 Ten Little Indians

POLONSKY, Abraham
(1910–) New York, New York, USA.
1948 The Force of Evil
1969 Tell 'Em Willie Boy Is Here
1971 Romance of a Horsethief

POMEROY, Roy J
1929 Interference **(Lothar MENDES)**
1930 Inside the Lines
1934 Shock

PONTECORVO, Gillo (Gilberto Pontecorvo)
(1919–) Pisa, Italy.
1956 Giovanna
1957 La Grande Strada Azzurra
1960 Kapo
1967 Battle of Algier **D***
1968 Queimada! / *Burn!*
1979 Operation Ogro
1988 The Devil's Bishop

POOLE, Patrick C
1987 Shadows on the Wall

POPESCU, Petru
1985 Death of an Angel

POPKIN, Leo C
1939 One Dark Night
1939 Reform School
1951 The Well **(Russell ROUSE)**

POST, Charles A
1932 Single-Handed Sanders

POST, Ted
(1918–) Brooklyn, New York, USA.
1956 The Peacemaker
1959 The Legend of Tom Dooley
1968 Hang 'Em High
1970 Beneath the Planet of the Apes
1973 The Baby
1973 The Harrad Experiment
1973 Magnum Force
1975 W.H.I.F.F.S. / *C.A.S.H.*
1978 Good Guys Wear Black
1978 Go Tell the Spartans
(also many TV movies)

POTTER, H C (Hank Potter or Henry Codman Potter)
(1904–1977) New York, New York, USA.
1936 Beloved Enemy
1937 Wings Over Honolulu
1938 Romance in the Dark
1938 Shopworn Angel
1938 The Cowboy and the Lady
1939 The Story of Vernon and Irene Castle
1939 Blackmail
1940 Congo Maisie
1940 Second Chorus
1941 Hellzapoppin'
1943 Mr Lucky
1943 Victory Through Air Power
1947 The Farmer's Daughter
1947 A Likely Story
1948 Mr Blandings Builds His Dream House
1948 The Time of Your Life
1948 You Gotta Stay Happy
1950 The Miniver Story
1957 Top Secret Affair / *Their Secret Affair*

POTTER, Sally
1984 The Gold Diggers

POTTERTON, Gerald
1975 The Rainbow Boys

POWELL, Dick
(1904–1963) Mountain View, Arkansas, USA.
1953 Split Second
1955 The Conqueror
1956 You Can't Run Away from It
1957 The Enemy Below
1958 The Hunters

POWELL, Michael
(1905–) Bekesbourne, near Canterbury, Kent, England. Autobiography: A Life in the Movies: An Autobiography.
1931 Two Crowded Hours
1931 My Friend the King
1931 Rynox
1931 The Rasp
1931 The Star Reporter
1932 Hotel Splendide
1932 Born Lucky
1932 C.O.D.
1932 His Lordship
1933 The Fire Raisers
1934 The Night of the Party / *The Murder Party*
1934 Red Ensign / *Strike!*
1934 Something Always Happens
1934 The Girl in the Crowd
1935 The Love Test
1935 Lazybones
1935 Some Day
1935 Her Last Affair
1935 The Price of a Song
1935 The Phantom Light
1936 The Brown Wallet
1936 Crown Versus Stevens
1936 The Man Behind the Mask
1937 The Edge of the World
1939 The Spy in Black / *U-Boat 29*
1939 The Lion Has Wings **(Adrian BRUNEL, Brian Desmond HURST)**
1940 The Thief of Bagdad **(Ludwig BERGER, Tim WHELAN)**
1940 Contraband / *Blackout*
1941 The 49th Parallel / *The Invaders*
1942 One of Our Aircraft Is Missing **(Emeric PRESSBURGER)**
1943 The Volunteer **(Emeric PRESSBURGER)**
1943 The Life and Death of Colonel Blimp **(Emeric PRESSBURGER)**
1944 A Canterbury Tale **(Emeric PRESSBURGER)**
1945 I Know Where I'm Going **(Emeric PRESSBURGER)**
1946 A Matter of Life and Death / *Stairway to Heaven* **(Emeric PRESSBURGER)**
1947 Black Narcissus **(Emeric PRESSBURGER)**
1948 The Red Shoes **(Emeric PRESSBURGER)** **F***
1948 The Small Back Room / *Hour of Glory* **(Emeric PRESSBURGER)**
1950 Gone to Earth / *The Wild Heart* **(Emeric PRESSBURGER)**
1950 The Elusive Pimpernel **(Emeric PRESSBURGER)**
1951 The Tales of Hoffman **(Emeric PRESSBURGER)**
1955 Oh Rosalinda! **(Emeric PRESSBURGER)**
1956 The Battle of the River Plate / *Pursuit of the Graf Spee* **(Emeric PRESSBURGER)**
1956 Ill Met By Moonlight / *Night Ambush* **(Emeric PRESSBURGER)**
1958 Honeymoon
1960 Peeping Tom
1961 The Queen's Guards
1966 They're a Weird Mob
1970 Age of Consent
1972 The Boy Who Turned Yellow **(Emeric PRESSBURGER)**
1974 The Tempest

PRAGER, Stanley
1968 The Bang Bang Kid
1970 Madigan's Millions

PRATT, Gilbert
1934 Elmer and Elsie

PREECE, Michael
(1936–) Los Angeles, California, USA.
1979 The Prize Fighter

PREMINGER, Otto (Otto Ludwig Preminger)
(1906–1986) Vienna, Austria. Autobiography: Preminger: an Autobiography.
1936 Under Your Spell
1937 Danger — Love at Work
1943 Margin for Error
1944 In the Meantime, Darling
1944 Laura **D***
1944 A Royal Scandal / *Czarina* **(Ernst LUBITSCH)**
1945 Fallen Angel
1946 Centennial Summer
1947 Forever Amber
1947 Daisy Kenyon
1948 That Lady in Ermine **(Ernst LUBITSCH)**
1949 The Fan
1950 Whirlpool
1950 Where the Sidewalk Ends
1951 The 13th Letter
1953 Angel Face
1953 The Moon is Blue
1954 River of No Return
1955 Carmen Jones
1955 The Man with the Golden Arm
1955 The Court-Martial of Billy Mitchell / *One Man Mutiny*
1957 Saint Jones
1958 Bonjour Tristesse
1959 Porgy and Bess
1959 Anatomy of a Murder **F***
1960 Exodus
1962 Advise and Consent
1963 The Cardinal **D***
1964 In Harm's Way
1965 Bunny Lake Is Missing
1967 Hurry Sundown
1968 Skidoo
1969 Tell Me That You Love Me, Junie Moon
1971 Such Good Friends
1975 Rosebud

1979 The Human Factor

PRENTISS, Chris
1976 Goin' Home

PRESSBURGER, Emeric
(1902–1988) Miskolc, Hungary.
1941 One of Our Aircraft Is Missing **(Michael POWELL)**
1943 The Volunteer **(Michael POWELL)**
1943 The Life and Death of Colonel Blimp **(Michael POWELL)**
1944 A Canterbury Tale **(Michael POWELL)**
1945 I Know Where I'm Going **(Michael POWELL)**
1946 A Matter of Life and Death / *Stairway to Heaven* **(Michael POWELL)**
1947 Black Narcissus **(Michael POWELL)**
1948 The Red Shoes **(Michael POWELL) F***
1948 The Small Back Room / *Hour of Glory* **(Michael POWELL)**
1950 Gone to Earth / *The Wild Heart* **(Michael POWELL)**
1950 The Elusive Pimpernel **(Michael POWELL)**
1951 The Tales of Hoffman **(Michael POWELL)**
1955 Oh Rosalinda! **(Michael POWELL)**
1956 The Battle of the River Plate / *Pursuit of the Graf Spee* **(Michael POWELL)**
1956 Ill Met By Moonlight / *Night Ambush* **(Michael POWELL)**
1972 The Boy Who Turned Yellow **(Michael POWELL)**

PRESSMAN, Michael
(1950–) New York, New York, USA.
1976 The Great Texas Dynamite Chase
1977 The Bad News Bears in Breaking Training
1979 Boulevard Nights
1980 Those Lips, Those Eyes
1983 Doctor Detroit
(also many TV movies)

PRESTON, Gaylene
1985 Mr Wrong

PREVIN, Steve
1962 Escapade in Florence
1963 The Waltz King

PRICE, Will
1949 Strange Bargain
1950 Tripoli

PRINCE (Rogers Nelson)
(1960–) Minneapolis, Minnesota, USA.
1986 Under the Cherry Moon
1987 Sign of the Times

PRINCE, Harold
(1928–) American.
1970 Something for Everyone / *Black Flowers for the Bride*
1977 A Little Night Music

PRINZ, Leroy
(1895–1983) American.
1941 All American Co-Ed
1941 Fiesta

PRIOR, David A
1987 Death Chase
1987 Deadly Prey
1987 Mankillers / *Twelve Wild Women*
1987 Nightwars
1988 Hell on the Battleground
1988 Jungle Assault
1988 Operation: War Zone
1988 Born to Kill
1988 The Lost Platoon
1989 Rapid Fire
1989 Deadly Dancer
1989 Final Sanction
1989 C.O.P.S. / *Future Force*
1989 Future Force II

PRYOR, Richard
(1940–) Peoria, Illinois, USA. Biography: Richard Pryor, a Man and His Madness: A Biography by Jim Haskins.
1986 Jo Jo Dancer, Your Life Is Calling

PUENZO, Luis
1985 The Official Story
1988 The Old Gringo

PURCELL, Evelyn
1986 Nobody's Fool

PURCELL, Joseph
1987 The Delos Adventure

PURDY, Jim
1989 Destiny to Order

PUZO, Dorothy
1987 Cold Steel / *Stiletto*

PYTKA, Joe
1989 Let It Ride

PYUN, Albert
1982 The Sword and the Sorcerer
1986 Dangerously Close / *Choice Kill*
1986 Radioactive Dreams
1987 Pleasure Planet / *Vicious Lips*
1987 The Treasure of San Lucas / *Down Twisted*
1988 Alien from L.A. / *Odeon*
1988 Cyborg — Attack from the Future
1989 Spiderman the Movie
1989 Masters of the Universe II

QUANDOUR, Mohy
1974 The Spectre of Edgar Allan Poe

QUESTED, John
1971 Philadelphia Here I Come
1971 Here Are the Ladies
1981 Loophole

QUILLEN, Thomas
1975 Pursuit

QUINE, Richard
(1920–1989) Detroit, Michigan, USA.
1948 Leather Gloves **(William ASHER)**
1951 Sunny Side of the Street
1951 Purple Heart Diary
1952 Sound Off
1952 Rainbow 'Round My Shoulder
1953 All Ashore
1953 Siren of Bagdad
1953 Cruising Down the River
1954 Drive a Crooked Road
1954 Pushover
1955 So This Is Paris
1955 My Sister Eileen
1956 The Solid Gold Cadillac
1957 Full of Life
1957 Operation Mad Ball
1958 Bell, Book and Candle
1959 It Happened to Jane
1960 Strangers When We Meet
1960 The World of Suzie Wong
1962 The Notorious Landlady
1964 Paris When It Sizzles
1965 Sex and the Single Girl
1965 How to Murder Your Wife
1965 Synanon / *Get Off My Back*
1967 Oh Dad, Poor Dad, Momma's Hung You in the Closet and I'm Feeling So Bad
1967 Hotel
1969 A Talent for Loving
1970 The Moonshine War
1974 'W'
1979 The Prisoner of Zenda

QUINN, Anthony
(1915–) Chihuahua, Mexico.
Autobiography: The Original Sin: A Self Portrait.
1958 The Buccaneer

QUINN, John
1988 Cheerleader Camp / *Bloody Pom Poms*

QUINNELL, Ken
1983 The City's Edge

QUINTANO, Gene
1989 For Better or for Worse
1989 Why Me?

QUINTERO, Jose
(1924–) Panama City, Panama.
1961 The Roman Spring of Mrs Stone

RADEMAKERS, Fons
(1920–) Roosendaal, Brabant, Belgium.
1958 Village on the River
1960 That Joyous Eve. . .
1961 The Knife
1963 The Spitting Image
1966 The Dance of the Heron
1971 Mira
1973 Because of the Cats
1976 Max Havelaar
1978 Mysteries
1979 My Friend / *The Judge's Friend*
1986 The Assault
1988 An Instant in the Wind
1989 The Rose Garden

RADEMAKERS, Lili
1987 Diary of a Mad Old Man

RADER, Peter
1988 Grandmother's House
1989 The Cold Room

RADFORD, Michael
(1946–) English.
1983 Another Time, Another Place
1984 1984
1988 White Mischief

RAE, Michael
1978 Laserblast

RAEBURN, Michael
(1943–) Cairo, Egypt.
1983 Killing Heat / *The Grass Is Singing*

RAFELSON, Bob
(1935–) New York, New York, USA.
1968 Head
1970 Five Easy Pieces **F***
1972 The King of Marvin Gardens
1976 Stay Hungry
1981 The Postman Always Rings Twice
1987 Black Widow
1989 Mountains of the Moon

RAFFILL, Stewart
(1945–) English.
1971 The Tender Warrior
1975 The Adventures of the Wilderness Family
1976 Across the Great Divide
1978 The Sea Gypsies
1981 High Risk
1983 The Ice Pirates
1984 The Philadelphia Experiment
1988 Mac and Me

RAFKIN, Alan
(1938–) New York, New York, USA.
1965 Ski Party
1966 The Ghost and Mr Chicken
1967 The Ride to Hangman's Tree
1968 Nobody's Perfect
1968 The Shakiest Gun in the West
1969 Angel in My Pocket
1971 How to Frame a Figg

RAGOZZINI, Ed
1978 Sasquatch

RAIMI, Sam
1983 The Evil Dead
1985 Crimewave / *Broken Hearts and Noses*
1987 The Evil Dead II : Dead By Dawn

RAKER, Hugh *see* **C Raker ENDFIELD**

RAKOFF, Alvin
(1927–) Toronto, Ontario, USA.
1959 Treasures of San Teresa / *Hot Money Girl*
1959 Passport to Shame / *Room 43*
1961 On Friday at Eleven

1962 World in My Pocket
1964 The Comedy Man
1969 Crossplot
1971 Hoffman
1971 Say Hello to Yesterday
1978 King Solomon's Treasure
1978 City of Fire!
1980 Death Ship
1981 Dirty Tricks

RAMATI, Alexander
1964 Sands of Beersheba / *Rebel Against the Light*
1985 The Assisi Underground
1987 And the Violins Stopped Playing

RAMIS, Harold
(1944–) Chicago, Illinois, USA.
1980 Caddyshack
1983 National Lampoon's Vacation
1986 Club Paradise

RANDALL, John
(1929–) Oakland, California, USA.
1978 Deadly Reef
1984 J J Garcia
1988 Hellraiser II: Hellbound

RANSEN, Mort
1987 Bayo

RAPP, Joel
1959 High School Big Shot
1960 Battle of Blood Island

RAPPAPORT, Mark
(1941–) American.
1973 Casual Relations
1975 Mozart in Love
1977 Local Colour
1978 Scenic Route
1979 Imposters
1985 Chain Letters

RAPPER, Irving
(1898–) London, England.
1941 Shining Victory
1941 One Foot in Heaven **F***
1942 The Gay Sisters
1942 Now, Voyager
1944 The Adventures of Mark Twain
1945 The Corn Is Green
1945 Rhapsody in Blue
1945 Deception
1947 The Voice of the Turtle / *One for the Book*
1949 Anna Lucasta
1950 The Glass Menagerie
1952 Another Man's Poison
1954 Bad for Each Other
1954 Forever Female
1956 Strange Intruder
1956 The Brave One
1958 Marjorie Morningstar
1959 The Miracle
1970 The Christine Jorgensen Story
1978 Born Again

RASH, Steve
1978 The Buddy Holly Story
1981 Under the Rainbow
1987 Boy Rents Girl / *Can't Buy Me Love*

RASKIN, Jay
1986 I Married a Vampire

RATHBONE, Tina
1988 Zelly and Me / *Phoebe*

RATOFF, Gregory
(1897–1960) St Petersburg, Russia.
1936 Sins of Man **(Otto BROWER)**
1937 The Lancer Spy
1939 Wife, Husband and Friend
1939 Rose of Washington Square
1939 Hotel for Women
1939 Intermezzo: A Love Story / *Escape to Happiness*
1939 Barricade
1939 Daytime Wife
1940 I Was an Adventuress
1940 Public Deb No. One
1941 Adam Had Four Sons
1941 The Men in Her Life
1941 The Corsican Brothers / *Bandits of Corsica*
1942 Two Yanks in Trinidad
1942 Footlight Serenade
1943 Something to Shout About
1943 The Heat's On / *Tropicana*
1943 Song of Russia
1944 Irish Eyes Are Smiling
1945 Where Do We Go from Here?
1945 Paris Underground / *Madame Pimpernel*
1946 Do You Love Me?
1947 Moss Rose
1947 Carnival in Costa Rica
1949 Black Magic
1950 If This Is Sin / *That Dangerous Age*
1951 Operation X / *My Daughter Joy*
1953 Taxi
1954 Abdulla the Great / *Abdulla's Harem*
1960 Oscar Wilde

RAWI, Ousami
(1939–) Baghdad, Iraq.
1987 Judgement in Stone / *The Housekeeper*

RAWLINS, John
(1902–) American.
1932 Lucky Ladies
1933 Going Straight
1938 State Police
1938 Young Fugitives
1938 The Missing Guest
1938 Air Devils
1940 The Leatherpushers
1941 Six Lessons from Madame La Zonga
1941 A Dangerous Game
1941 Mr Dynamite
1941 Mutiny in the Arctic
1941 Men of the Timberland
1941 Raiders of the Desert
1942 Bombay Clipper
1942 Unseen Enemy
1942 Mississippi Gambler
1942 Half Way to Shanghai
1942 Sherlock Holmes and the Voice of

Terror
1942 The Great Impersonation
1942 Arabian Nights
1942 Torpedo Boat
1943 We've Never Been Licked / *Texas to Tokyo*
1944 Ladies Courageous
1945 Sudan
1945 Strange Conquest
1946 Her Adventurous Night
1947 Dick Tracy's Dilemma / *Mark of the Claw*
1947 Dick Tracy Meets Gruesome / *Dick Tracy's Amazing Adventure*
1948 The Arizona Ranger
1948 Michael O'Halloran
1949 Massacre River
1950 The Boy from Indiana / *Blaze of Glory*
1950 Rogue River
1951 Fort Defiance
1953 Shark River
1958 Lost Lagoon
(also serials)

RAY, Albert
1926 More Work, Less Pay
1926 Whispering Wires
1927 Love Makes 'Em Wild
1927 Publicity Madness
1927 Rich But Honest
1928 None But the Brave
1928 Thief in the Dark
1928 Woman Wise
1929 Molly and Me
1930 Call of the West
1930 Her Unborn Child **(Charles McGRATH)**
1930 Kathleen Mavourneen
1932 The Thirteenth Guest
1932 Unholy Love
1932 Guilty or Not Guilty
1933 West of Singapore
1933 A Shriek in the Night
1933 The Intruder
1934 Dancing Man
1935 St Louis Woman
1935 Marriage Bargain
1936 Everyman's Law
1936 Lawless Land
1936 Undercover Man
1939 Desperate Trails

RAY, Bernard B
1934 Rawhide Mail
1934 Mystery Ranch
1934 Loser's End
1935 Fast Bullets
1935 Midnight Phantom
1935 Now or Never
1935 The Silver Bullet
1935 Coyote Trails
1935 Rio Rattler
1935 Silent Valley
1935 Texas Jack
1935 Never Too Late
1936 Ambush Valley
1936 Caryl of the Mountains
1936 Prince of the Rustlers
1936 Riding On
1936 Millionaire Kid
1936 Roamin' Wild
1936 The Speed Reporter
1936 The Test
1936 Santa Fe Trail
1936 Trigger Tom
1936 Step on It
1936 Vengeance of Rannah
1937 The Silver Trail
1938 It's All in Your Mind
1938 Santa Fe Rider
1939 Smoky Trails
1940 Broken Strings
1941 Dangerous Lady
1941 Law of the Timber
1942 Too Many Women
1942 House of Errors
1946 Buffalo Bill Rides Again

RAY, Fred Olen
1984 Scalps
1985 The Tomb
1986 Armed Response / *Jade Jungle*
1987 Cyclone
1987 Commando Squad
1987 Prison Ship: The Adventures of Tara / *Star Slammer*
1987 Deep Space
1988 Demented Death Farm Massacre **(Donn DAVISON)**
1988 Hollywood Chainsaw Hookers
1988 The Phantom Empire
1989 Warlords
1989 Terminal Force
1989 Beverly Hills Vampire

RAY, Nicholas (Raymond Nicholas Kienzle)
(1911–1979) La Crosse, Wisconsin, USA.
Biography: Nicholas Ray by John Kreidl.
1947 Your Red Wagon
1948 They Live By Night / *The Twisted Road*
1949 Knock on Any Door
1949 A Woman's Secret
1950 Born to Be Sad
1950 In a Lonely Place
1951 Flying Leathernecks
1951 On Dangerous Ground **(Ida LUPINO)**
1951 This Man Is Mine
1952 The Lusty Men
1954 Johnny Guitar
1955 Rebel Without a Cause
1955 Run for Cover
1956 Bigger Than Life
1956 Hot Blood
1957 The True Story of Jesse James / *The James Brothers*
1958 Bitter Victory
1958 Party Girl
1958 Wind Across the Everglades
1959 The Savage Innocents
1961 King of Kings
1963 55 Days at Peking
1973 We Can't Go Home Again
1980 Lightning Over Water / *Nick's Movie* **(Wim WENDERS)**

RAY, Satyajit
(1921–) Calcutta, India.
Biography: Portrait of a Director by

1955 Song of the Little Road / *Pather Panchali*
1956 The Unvanquished / *Aparajito*
1957 The Philosopher's Stone / *Paras Pather*
1958 The Music Room / *Jalsaghar*
1959 The World of Apu / *Apu Sansar*
1960 Devi / *The Goddess*
1961 Two Daughters / *Teen Kanya*
1962 Expedition
1963 The Big City / *Mahanagar*
1964 The Lonely Wife / *Charulata*
1966 The Hero / *Nayak*
1967 The Zoo
1968 The Adventures of Goopy and Bagha
1970 Days and Nights in the Forest
1971 The Adversary
1971 Company Limited
1973 Distant Thunder
1975 The Golden Fortress
1976 The Middleman / *The Masse's Music*
1977 The Chess Players
1979 The Elephant God
1980 The Kingdom of Diamonds
1984 The Home and the World

RAYMAKER, Herman C
1925 Tracked in the Snow Country
1925 Below the Line
1926 The Night Cry
1926 His Jazz Bride
1926 Hero of the Big Snows
1926 Millionaires
1927 The Gay Old Bird
1927 Simple Sis
1928 Under the Tonto Rim
1932 Trailing the Killer
1934 Adventure Girl

RAYMOND, Gene (Guion Raymond)
(1908–) New York, New York, USA.
1948 Million Dollar Weekend

RAYMOND, Jack (John Caines)
(1892–1953) British.
1929 Splinters
1930 French Leave
1930 Tilly of Bloomsbury
1931 Mischief
1931 The Speckled Band
1931 Say It with Music
1932 Life Goes On
1932 Just My Luck
1933 Night of the Garter
1933 Sorrell and Son
1933 King of Paris
1934 Where's George?
1936 When Knights Were Bold
1937 The Frog
1937 The Rat
1938 Blondes for Danger
1938 No Parking
1938 A Royal Divorce
1939 The Mind of Mr Reeder
1940 You Will Remember
1951 Reluctant Heroes
1951 Worm's Eye View

READ, Melanie
1984 Trial Run

REBANE, Bill
1975 The Giant Spider Invasion
1979 The Capture of Bigfoot
1987 Blood Harvest

RED, Eric
1988 Cohen and Tate

REDFORD, Robert (Charles R. Redford)
(1937–) Santa Monica, California, USA.
Biographies: Robert Redford: The Superstar Nobody Knows by David Hanna; Robert Redford by David Paige.
1980 Ordinary People **D** F****
1988 The Milagro Beanfield War

REED, Sir Carol
(1906–1976) Putney, London, England.
1935 Midshipman Easy / *Men of the Sea*
1936 Laburnum Grove
1936 Talk of the Devil
1937 Who's Your Lady Friend?
1938 Bank Holiday / *Three on a Weekend*
1938 Penny Paradise
1938 Climbing High
1939 A Girl Must Live
1939 The Stars Look Down
1940 Night Train to Munich / *Gestapo*
1940 The Girl in the News
1941 The Remarkable Mr Kipps
1942 The Young Mr Pitt
1944 The Way Ahead / *Immortal Battalion*
1945 The True Story **(Garson KANIN)**
1946 Odd Man Out / *Gang War*
1948 The Fallen Idol / *The Lost Illusion* **D***
1949 The Third Man **D***
1951 An Outcast of the Islands
1953 The Man Between
1955 A Kid for Two Farthings
1956 Trapeze
1958 The Key
1959 Our Man in Havana
1963 The Running Man
1965 The Agony and the Ecstacy
1968 Oliver **D** F****
1970 Flap / *The Last Warrior*
1971 Follow Me / *The Public Eye*

REED, James
1973 Tarzana, the Wild Girl

REED, Jay Theodore
(1887–1959) American.
1936 Lady, Be Careful
1937 Double or Nothing
1938 Tropic Holiday
1939 I'm from Missouri
1939 What a Life!
1940 Those Were the Days
1941 Life with Henry
1941 Her First Beau

REED, Jerry
(1937–) American.
1987 What Comes Around

REED, Joel M
1972 Career Bed

1975 Dragon Lady

REED, Luther
(1888–1961) American.
1926 The Ace of Cads
1927 New York
1927 Evening Clothes
1927 Honeymoon Hate
1927 Shanghai Bound
1927 The World at Her Feet
1928 The Sawdust Paradise
1929 Rio Rita
1930 Hit the Deck
1930 Dixiana
1935 Convention Girl

REED, Roland
1936 In Paris A.W.O.L.
1937 Red Lights Ahead

REEVE, Geoffrey
(1932–) Tring, Hertfordshire, England.
1970 Puppet on a Chain **(Don SHARP)**
1974 Caravan to Vaccares
1988 Souvenir / *The Pork Butcher*

REEVES, Michael
(1944–1969) British.
1965 Sister of Satan
1967 The Sorcerers
1968 Witchfinder General / *The Conqueror Worm*

REGAN, Patrick
(1939–) Los Angeles, California, USA.
1981 Kiss Daddy Goodbye

REGGIO, Godfrey
1983 Koyaanisqatsi
1988 North South / *Powaqqatsi*

REICHERT, Mark
1980 Union City

REID, Alastair
(1939–) Edinburgh, Scotland.
1969 Baby Love
1971 The Night Digger
1971 Something to Hide
(also TV movies)

REID, Dorothy
(1895–1977) American.
1929 Linda
1933 Sucker Money **(Melville SHYER)**
1934 The Road to Ruin **(Melville SHYER)**
1934 A Woman Condemned

REID, Max
1987 Wild Thing

REINER, Carl
(1922–) Bronx, New York, USA.
1967 Enter Laughing
1969 The Comic
1970 Where's Poppa?
1978 The One and Only
1978 Oh, God!
1979 The Jerk
1979 Dead Men Don't Wear Plaid
1983 The Man with Two Brains
1984 All of Me
1985 Summer Rental
1987 Summer School
1989 Bert Rigby, You're a Fool

REINER, Rob
(1945–) Beverly Hills, California, USA.
1984 This Is Spinal Tap
1985 The Sure Thing
1986 Stand By Me / *The Body*
1987 Princess Bride
1989 Harry, This Is Sally

REINHARDT, Gottfried
(1911–) Austrian.
1952 Invitation
1953 The Story of Three Loves **(Vincente MINNELLI)**
1954 Betrayed
1956 Vor Sonnenuntergang
1959 Grand Hôtel
1959 Abschied der Götter
1961 Town Without Pity
1963 Elf Jahre und ein Tag
1965 Situation Hopeless But Not Serious

REINHARDT, John
1936 Captain Calamity
1947 The Guilty
1947 High Tide
1947 For You I Die
1947 Ambush
1948 Sofia
1948 Open Secret
1951 Chicago Calling

REINHARDT, Max (Maximilian Goldman)
(1873–1943) Baden, Austria.
Biography: The Genius: A Memoir of Max Reinhardt by Gottfried Reinhardt.
1935 A Midsummer Night's Dream **(William DIETERLE)** F*

REIS, Irving
(1906–1953) New York, USA.
1940 One Crowded Night
1940 I'm Still Alive
1941 Footlight Fever
1941 The Gay Falcon
1941 Weekend for Three
1941 A Date with the Falcon
1942 The Big Street
1946 The Crack-Up
1947 The Bachelor and the Bobby-Soxer / *Bachelor Knights*
1948 All My Sons
1948 Enchantment
1949 Roseanna McCoy
1949 Dancing in the Dark
1950 Three Husbands
1950 Of Men and Music **(Alex HAMMID)**
1951 New Mexico
1952 The Four Poster

REISCH, Walter
(1900–1983) Austrian.

1937 Men Are Not Gods
1947 Song of Scheherezade

REISNER, Allen
1956 All Mine to Give / *The Day They Gave Babies Away*
1958 St Louis Blues
(also many TV movies)

REISNER, Charles F (Chuck Riesner)
(1887–1962) Minneapolis, Minnesota, USA.
1925 The Man on the Box
1926 The Better 'Ole
1926 Oh! What a Nurse
1927 What Every Girl Should Know
1927 The Missing Link
1927 The Fortune Hunter
1928 Steamboat Bill Jnr
1928 Fools for Luck
1928 Brotherly Love
1929 Chasing Rainbows
1929 Noisy Neighbours
1929 China Bound
1929 The Hollywood Revue of 1929 **F***
1929 Road Show
1930 Caught Short
1930 Love in the Rough
1931 Reducing
1931 Stepping Out
1931 Politics
1931 Flying High / *Happy Landing*
1932 Divorce in the Family
1933 The Chief / *My Old Man's a Fireman*
1934 You Can't Buy Everything
1934 The Show-Off
1934 Student Tour
1935 The Winning Ticket
1935 It's in the Air
1936 Everybody Dance
1937 Murder Goes to College
1937 Sophie Lang Goes West
1937 Manhattan Merry-Go-Round / *Manhattan Music Box*
1939 Winter Carnival
1941 The Big Store
1942 This Time for Keeps
1943 Harrigan's Child
1944 Meet the People
1944 Lost in a Harem
1948 The Cobra Strikes
1948 In This Corner
1950 The Travelling Saleswoman
(also many shorts)

REISZ, Karel
(1926–) Ostrava, Czechoslovakia. Biography: Karel Reisz by Georg Gaston.
1958 We Are the Lambeth Boys
1961 Saturday Night and Sunday Morning
1964 Night Must Fall
1966 Morgan: A Suitable Case for Treatment
1969 Isadora
1974 The Gambler
1978 Who'll Stop the Rain? / *Dog Soldiers*
1981 The French Lieutenant's Woman
1985 Sweet Dreams
1989 Everybody Wins

REITMAN, Ivan
(1946–) Czechoslovakian.
1971 Foxy Lady
1973 Cannibal Girls
1979 Meatballs
1981 Stripes
1984 Ghostbusters
1986 Legal Eagles
1988 Twins / *Brothers*
1989 The Last of the Ghostbusters

RELPH, Michael
(1915–) Broadstone, Dorset, England.
1948 Saraband for Dead Lovers **(Basil DEARDEN)**
1954 Out of the Clouds **(Basil DEARDEN)**
1955 The Ship That Died of Shame **(Basil DEARDEN)**
1957 Davy
1958 Rockets Galore / *Mad Little Island*
1959 Desert Mice

RENOIR, Jean *
(1894–1979) Paris, France. Autobiography: My Life and My Films.
1924 Whirlpool of Fate / *La Fille de l'Eau*
1926 Nana
1928 The Little Match-Girl
1932 Boudu Saved from Drowning
1934 Madame Bovary
1936 People of France / *La Vie est à Nous*
1937 The Lower Depths
1938 Judas Was a Woman / *La Bête Humaine*
1939 The Rules of the Game
1941 Swamp Water / *The Man Who Came Back*
1943 This Land Is Mine
1945 The Southerner **D***
1946 Diary of a Chambermaid
1947 Woman on the Beach
1951 The River
1952 The Golden Coach
1955 French Can Can
1957 Paris Does Strange Things
1959 Experiment in Evil / *The Doctor's Horrible Experiment*
1959 Lunch on the Grass
1962 The Vanishing Corporal / *The Elusive Corporal*
(also many documentaries)

RESNAIS, Alain *
(1922–) Vannes, Britanny, France. Biography: Alain Resnais by John Francis Kreidl.
1961 Last Year at Marienbad
1963 Muriel
1966 The War Is Over
1977 Providence
1983 Life Is a Bed of Roses
1986 Mélo
1989 I Want to Go Home
(also many documentaries)

REVIER, Harry J
(1889–) American.
1930 The Convict's Code
1936 The Lash of the Penitentes

1938 Child Bride

REYNOLDS, Burt (Burton Reynolds)
(1936–) Waycross, Georgia, USA. Biographies: Burt: The Unauthorised Biography by Marc Eliot; Portrait of a Superstar by Dianna Whitley.
1976 Gator
1978 The End
1981 Sharky's Machine
1985 Stick

REYNOLDS, Christopher
1989 Offerings

REYNOLDS, Clark E
1958 Gunman from Laredo

REYNOLDS, Kevin
(1952–) San Antonio, Texas, USA.
1984 Fandango
1988 The Beast of War

REYNOLDS, Lynn
1926 Chip of the Flying U
1926 The Man in the Saddle
1926 Prisoners of the Storm
1927 Hey! Hey! Cowboy
1927 The Silent Rider

REYNOLDS, Sheldon
(1923–) American.
1956 Foreign Intrigue
1967 Assignment to Kill

REYNOLDS, William H ('Red' Reynolds)
(1910–) American.
1960 Chartroose Caboose

RICE, Ron
1962 The Flower Thief

RICH, David Lowell
(1920–) New York, New York, USA.
1957 No Time to Be Young / *Teenage Delinquents*
1958 Senior Prom
1959 Hey! Boy, Hey! Girl
1959 Have Rocket, Will Travel
1966 Madame X
1966 The Plainsman
1967 Rosie!
1968 A Lovely Way to Die
1968 Three Guns for Texas **(Earl BELLAMY, Paul STANLEY)**
1969 Eye of the Cat
1973 That Man Bolt **(Henry LEVIN)**
1979 The Concorde: Airport '79
1981 Chu Chu and the Philly Flash
(also a multitude of TV movies (1967–)

RICH, John
(1925–) Rockaway Beach, New York, USA.
1963 Wives and Lovers
1964 The New Interns
1964 Roustabout
1965 Boeing-Boeing
1966 Easy Come, Easy Go

RICHARD, Jefferson
1986 In Search of a Golden Sky
1987 Berserker

RICHARDS, Dick
(1936–) American.
1972 The Culpepper Cattle Company
1975 Rafferty and the Gold Dust Twins
1977 March or Die
1981 Death Valley
1983 Man, Woman and Child
1988 Money's Tight / *Goin' to the Chapel*

RICHARDS, R M
1987 Heat

RICHARDSON, Peter
1985 The Supergrass
1987 Eat the Rich
1988 The Strike
1988 Five Go to Hell

RICHARDSON, Sir Ralph
(1902–1983) Cheltenham, Gloucestershire, England. Biography: Ralph Richardson: An Actor's Life by Garry O'Connor.
1952 Home at Seven / *Murder on Monday*

RICHARDSON, Tony (Cecil Antonio Richardson)
(1928–) Shipley, Yorkshire, England.
1958 Look Back in Anger
1960 The Entertainer
1961 Sanctuary
1962 A Taste of Honey
1962 The Loneliness of the Long Distance Runner
1963 Tom Jones **D** F****
1965 The Loved One
1966 Mademoiselle
1967 The Sailor from Gibraltar
1968 The Charge of the Light Brigade
1969 Laughter in the Dark
1969 Hamlet
1970 Ned Kelly
1973 A Delicate Balance
1973 Dead Cert
1977 Joseph Andrews
1982 The Border
1984 The Hotel New Hampshire

RICHERT, William
1979 Winter Kills
1979 The American Success Co.
1988 Jimmy Reardon

RICHMOND, Anthony
(1942–) London, England.
1985 Déjà Vu / *Always*

RICHTER, W D
1984 The Adventures of Buckaroo Banzai: Across the 8th Dimension

RICKMAN, Tom
1984 The River Rat

RIDDIFORD, Richard
1985 Arriving Tuesday

RIEAD, William
1986 Scorpion / *The Summons*

RIESNER, Charles F *see* **Charles F REISNER**

RIESNER, Dean
(c1930–) American.
1947 Bill and Coo

RILLA, Wolf
(1920–) Germany.
1953 Glad Tidings
1953 Marilyn
1953 Noose for a Lady
1953 The Large Rope
1954 The Black Rider
1954 The End of the Road
1955 Stock Car
1955 The Blue Peter
1956 Pacific Destiny
1957 The Scamp
1958 Bachelor of Hearts
1959 Witness in the Dark
1960 Village of the Damned
1961 Piccadilly Third Stop
1961 Watch It Sailor!
1962 Cairo
1963 The World Ten Times Over / *Pussycat Alley*
1973 Secrets of a Door to Door Salesman / *Naughty Wives*
1974 Bedtime with Rosie

RIPLEY, Arthur
(1895–1961) New York, USA.
1937 I Met My Love Again **(Joshua LOGAN)**
1942 Prisoner of Japan
1944 A Voice in the Wind
1947 The Chase
1958 Thunder Road
(also many shorts)

RIPLEY, Jonathan
1989 Spirit

RISAN, Leidulv
1987 Rubicon

RISI, Dino *
(1917–) Milan, Italy.
Biography: Dino Risi by A. Vigano.
1953 Love in the City **(Michelangelo ANTONIONI, Federico FELLINI, Alberto LATTUADA, Carlo LIZZANI, Francesco MASELLI)**
1955 Scandal in Sorrento / *Pan, Amore e . . .*
1956 Poor But Beautiful
1960 Love and Larceny / *Il Mattatore*
1962 The Easy Life / *Il Sorpasso*
1963 15 from Rome / *Il Mostri*
1965 Weekend, Italian Style / *L'Ombrellone*
1966 Treasure of San Gennaro / *Operazione San Gennaro*
1967 The Tiger and the Pussycat
1967 The Prophet
1970 The Priest's Wife
1973 How Funny Can Sex Be? / *Sessomatto*
1976 Scent of a Woman
1978 Viva Italia / *I Nouvi Mostri* **(Maria MONICELLI, Ettore SCOLA)**
1980 Sunday Lovers **(Bryan FORBES, Edouardo MOLINARO, Gene WILDER)**
1981 Ghost of Love
1987 Inspector Lo Gatto

RISKIN, Adam
1988 Never on Tuesday
1989 Tales of Two Sisters

RISKIN, Robert
(1897–1955) New York, New York, USA.
1937 When You're in Love / *For You Alone*

RITCHIE, Michael
(1938–) Waukesha, Wisconsin, USA.
1969 Downhill Racer
1972 Prime Cut
1972 The Candidate
1975 Smile
1976 The Bad News Bears
1978 Semi-Tough
1979 An Almost Perfect Affair
1980 The Island
1983 The Survivors
1985 Fletch
1986 Wildcats / *First and Goal*
1986 The Golden Child
1988 The Couch Trip
1989 Fletch II
1989 The Scout

RITT, Martin
(1920–) New York, New York, USA.
1957 Edge of the City / *A Man Is Ten Feet Tall*
1957 No Down Payment
1958 The Long Hot Summer
1959 The Black Orchid
1959 The Sound and the Fury
1960 Five Branded Women
1961 Paris Blues
1962 Hemingway's Adventures of a Young Man
1962 Hud **D***
1964 The Outrage
1965 The Spy Who Came in from the Cold
1967 Hombre
1968 The Brotherhood
1970 The Molly Maguires
1970 The Great White Hope
1972 Sounder **F***
1972 Pete 'n' Tillie
1974 Conrack
1976 The Front
1978 Casey's Shadow
1979 Norma Rae **F***
1981 Back Roads
1983 Cross Creek
1985 Murphy's Romance
1987 Nuts
1989 Letters / *Stanley and Iris / Union Street*

RITTER, Joe
1988 Beach Balls / *Summertime Fun*

RIVERS, Joan
(1937–) New York, New York, USA.
1978 Rabbit Test

RIVETTE, Jacques *
(1928–) Rouen, France.
1961 Paris Belongs to Us
1966 The Nun
1974 Out 1: Spectre
1974 Celine and Julie Go Boating
1979 Merry-Go-Round
1984 Love on the Ground
1985 Wuthering Heights / *Hurlevent*

ROACH, Sir Hal
(1892–) Elmira, New York, USA.
1930 Man of the North
1930 The Rogue Song **(Lionel BARRYMORE)**
1933 The Devil's Brother / *Fra Diavolo* **(Charles ROGERS)**
1936 Kelly the Second
1939 Captain Fury
1939 The Housekeeper's Daughter
1940 One Million B.C. / *The Cave Dwellers / Man and His Mate* **(D W GRIFFITH, Hal ROACH Jnr)**
1940 Turnabout
1941 Road Show **(Gordon DOUGLAS, Hal ROACH Jnr)**

ROACH Jnr., Hal
(1921–1972) American.
1940 One Million B.C. / *The Cave Dwellers / Man and His Mate* **(D W GRIFFITH, Hal ROACH)**
1941 Road Show **(Gordon DOUGLAS, Hal ROACH)**
1942 Dudes Are Pretty People
1943 Calaboose
1944 Prairie Chickens

ROBBE-GRILLET, Alain *
(1922–) Brest, France.
1968 The Man Who Lies

ROBBIE, Seymour
1970 C.C. and Company
1974 Marco

ROBBINS, Jerome (Jerome RABINOWITZ)
(1918–) Weehawken, New Jersey, USA.
1961 West Side Story **(Robert WISE) D** F****

ROBBINS, Matthew
1979 Corvette Summer / *The Hot One*
1981 Dragonslayer
1985 The Legend of Billie Jean / *Fair Is Fair*
1987 Batteries Not Included

ROBERSON, Arthur
1974 Black Hooker

ROBERSON, James W
1982 The Witch

ROBERT, Genevieve
1988 Casual Sex?

ROBERT, Vincent
1988 The Ghouls

ROBERT, Yves *
(1920–) Saumur, France.
1968 Very Happy Alexander
1972 The Tall Blond Man with One Black Shoe
1974 Return of the Tall Blond Man with One Black Shoe
1976 Pardon mon affaire: Un éléphant ca trompe enormement
1977 Pardon mon affaire, Too!: nous irons tous au Paradis

ROBERTS, Alan
1970 The Zodiac Couples
1974 Panorama Blue
1977 Young Lady Chatterley
1980 The Happy Hooker Goes to Hollywood
1983 Flashdance Fever
1984 Young Lady Chatterley II / *Private Property*

ROBERTS, Charles E
1933 Flaming Signal **(George JESKE)**
1933 Corruption
1935 Adventurous Knights
1941 Hurry, Charlie, Hurry

ROBERTS, Deborah
1988 Frankenstein General Hospital

ROBERTS, Florian *see* **Robert FLOREY**

ROBERTS, Stephen
(1895–1936) West Virginia, USA.
1932 Sky Bride
1932 Lady and Gent
1932 The Night of June 13th
1932 If I Had a Million **(James CRUZE, H Bruce HUMBERSTONE, Ernst LUBITSCH, Norman Z McLEOD, William A SEITER, Norman TAUROG)**
1933 The Story of Temple Drake
1933 One Sunday Afternoon
1934 The Trumpet Blows
1934 Romance in Manhattan
1935 Star of Midnight
1935 The Man Who Broke the Bank at Monte Carlo
1936 The Lady Consents
1936 The Ex Mrs Bradford

ROBERTSON, Cliff
(1925–) La Jolla, California, USA.
1971 J.W. Coop
1981 The Pilot

ROBERTSON, Hugh
1972 Melinda
1976 Bim

ROBERTSON, John S
(1878–1964) Canadian.
1927 The Road to Romance
1927 Captain Salvation
1929 The Single Standard
1929 Shanghai Lady
1930 Night Ride
1930 Captain of the Guard **(Paul FEJOS)**
1930 Madonna of the Streets

1931 Beyond Victory
1931 The Phantom of Paris
1932 Little Orphan Annie
1933 One Man's Journey
1934 The Crime Doctor
1934 His Greatest Gamble
1934 Wednesday's Child
1934 Grand Old Girl
1935 Our Little Girl
1935 Captain Hurricane

ROBINS, John
1973 Love Thy Neighbour
1974 A Man About the House
1985 Hot Resort

ROBINSON, Bruce
(1946–) London, England.
1987 Withnail and I
1989 How to Get Ahead in Advertising
1989 High Rise

ROBINSON, Casey
(1903–1979) American.
1932 Renegades of the West

ROBINSON, Chris
(1938–) West Palm Beach, Florida, USA.
1979 Sunshine Run

ROBINSON, Dick
1975 Brother of the Wind
1975 Poor Pretty Eddie
1979 Redneck Country

ROBINSON, John Mark
1984 Roadhouse 66

ROBINSON, Phil Alden
1987 In the Mood / *The Woo-Woo Kid*
1989 Shoeless Joe

ROBINSON, Ted
1987 Those Dear Departed
1988 Two Brothers Running

ROBSON, Mark
(1913–1978) Montreal, Quebec, Canada.
1943 The Seventh Victim
1943 The Ghost Ship
1944 Youth Runs Wild
1945 Isle of the Dead
1946 Bedlam
1949 Champion
1949 Home of the Brave
1949 Roughshod
1949 My Foolish Heart
1950 Edge of Doom / *Stronger Than Fear*
1950 Bright Victory / *Lights Out*
1951 I Want You
1953 Return to Paradise
1954 Hell Below Zero
1954 Phffft
1954 The Bridges of Toko-Ri
1955 A Prize of Gold
1955 Trial
1955 The Harder They Fall
1957 The Little Hut
1957 Peyton Place **D* F***
1958 The Inn of the Sixth Happiness **D***
1960 From the Terrace
1963 Nine Hours to Rama
1963 The Prize
1965 Von Ryan's Express
1966 Lost Command
1967 Valley of the Dolls
1969 Daddy's Gone a-Hunting
1971 Happy Birthday, Wanda Jane
1972 Limbo / *Chained to Yesterday*
1974 Earthquake
1979 Avalanche Express

ROCCO, Marc
1987 Scenes from the Goldmine
1988 Dream a Little Dream

ROCCO, Pat
1975 Drifter

ROCHAT, Eric
1987 Too Much

RODDAM, Franc
1979 Quadrophenia
1983 The Lords of Discipline
1985 The Bride
1987 Aria **(Robert ALTMAN, Bruce BERESFORD, Bill BRYDEN, Jean-Luc GODARD, Derek JARMAN, Nicolas ROEG, Ken RUSSELL, Charles STURRIDGE, Julien TEMPLE)**
1987 A Prayer for the Dying
1989 War Party

ROEG, Nicolas
(1928–) London, England.
Biography: Nicolas Roeg by Neil Feineman.
1970 Performance **(Donald CAMMELL)**
1971 Walkabout
1972 Nightmare Honeymoon
1974 Don't Look Now
1976 The Man Who Fell to Earth
1980 Bad Timing / *A Sensual Obsession*
1984 Eureka
1985 Insignificance
1987 Castaway
1987 Aria **(Robert ALTMAN, Bruce BERESFORD, Bill BRYDEN, Jean-Luc GODARD, Derek JARMAN, Franc RODDAM, Ken RUSSELL, Charles STURRIDGE, Julien TEMPLE)**
1988 Track 29
1989 The Witches

ROEMER, Michael
(1928–) Berlin, Germany.
1949 A Touch of the Times
1965 Nothing But a Man **(Robert M YOUNG)**
1971 The Plot Against Harry
1980 Pilgrim, Farewell

ROGELL, Albert S
(1901–1988) Oklahoma, USA.
1924 The Mask of Lopez
1924 The Silent Stranger
1924 Fighting for Justice
1924 Galloping Gallagher

1924 North of Nevada
1924 Thundering Hoofs
1924 Lightning Romance
1924 The Fighting Sap
1924 The Dangerous Coward
1925 Easy Money
1925 Super Speed
1925 Youth's Gamble
1925 The Knockout Kid
1925 The Goat Getter
1925 The Snob Buster
1925 The Circus Cyclone
1925 Crack o' Dawn
1925 Pals
1925 The Fear Fighter
1925 Triple Action
1925 The Cyclone Cavalier
1926 Lazy Lightning
1926 The Man from the West
1926 The Unknown Cavalier
1926 The Ridin' Rascal
1926 Rustler's Ranch
1926 Fighting Fate
1926 The Set Up
1926 Red Hot Leather
1926 Sky High Corral
1926 Men of the Night
1926 The Wild Horse Stampede
1926 Señor Daredevil
1927 Overland Stage
1927 Red Raiders
1927 Western Whirlwind
1927 Men of Daring
1927 Western Rover
1927 The Sunset Derby
1927 Grinning Guns
1927 The Devil's Saddle
1927 Rough and Ready
1927 Somewhere in Senora
1928 The Upland Rider
1928 Shepherd of the Hills
1928 Canyon of Adventure
1928 The Glorious Trail
1928 Phantom City
1929 Cheyenne
1929 California Mail
1929 Lone Wolf's Daughter
1929 Flying Marine
1930 Painted Faces
1930 Mamba
1931 Aloha / *No Greater Love*
1931 Sweepstakes
1931 The Tip-Off / *Looking for Trouble*
1931 The Suicide Fleet
1932 Carnival Boat
1932 The Rider of Death Valley
1933 Air Hostess
1933 Below the Sea / *Hell's Cargo*
1933 The Wrecker
1933 East of Fifth Avenue / *Two in a Million*
1934 Fog
1934 No More Women
1934 The Hell Cat
1934 Among the Missing
1934 Name the Woman
1934 Fugitive Lady
1935 Unknown Woman
1935 Air Hawks
1935 Atlantic Adventure
1935 Escape from Devil's Island
1936 Roaming Lady
1936 Grand Jury
1936 You May Be Next! / *Panic in the Air*
1937 Murder in Greenwich Village
1938 Start Cheering
1938 The Lone Wolf in Paris
1938 City Streets
1938 The Last Warning
1939 For Love or Money / *Tomorrow at Midnight*
1939 Hawaiian Nights
1939 Laugh It Off / *Lady Be Gay*
1940 Private Affairs
1940 I Can't Give You Anything But Love, Baby
1940 Argentine Nights
1940 Li'l Abner / *Trouble Chaser*
1941 The Black Cat
1941 Tight Shoes
1941 Public Enemies
1942 Jailhouse Blues
1942 Sleepytime Gal
1942 True to the Army
1942 Butch Minds the Baby
1942 Priorities on Parade
1942 Youth on Parade
1943 Hit Parade of 1943 / *Change of Heart*
1943 In Old Oklahoma / *War of the Wildcats*
1945 Love, Honour and Goodbye
1946 Earl Carroll Sketchbook / *Hats Off to Rhythm*
1946 The Magnificent Rogue
1947 Heaven Only Knows
1948 Northwest Stampede
1949 The Song of India
1950 The Admiral Was a Lady
1956 Shadow of Fear / *Before I Wake*

ROGERS, Charles ('Buddy' Rogers)
(1904–) Olathe, Kansas, USA.
1933 Me and My Pal **(Lloyd FRENCH)**
1933 The Devil's Brother / *Fra Diavolo* **(Hal ROACH)**
1934 Babes in Toyland / *March of the Wooden Soldiers / Laurel and Hardy in Toyland* **(Gus MEINS)**
1936 The Bohemian **(James W HORNE)**

ROGERS, Maclean
(1899–1962) British.
1929 The Third Eye
1935 The Right Age to Marry
1935 Old Faithful
1935 The Shadow of Mike Emerald
1936 A Touch of the Moon
1937 Busman's Holiday
1937 Not So Dusty
1937 To Catch a Thief
1937 Nothing But Publicity
1937 The Heirloom Mystery
1937 All That Glitters
1937 Farewell to Cinderella
1937 Fifty Shilling Boxer
1937 The Strange Adventures of Mr Smith
1937 Father Steps Out
1938 Why Pick on Me?
1938 Easy Riches
1938 Racing Romances
1938 Merely Mr Hawkins
1938 Darts Are Trumps

1938 Romance à la Carte
1938 His Lordship Regrets
1939 Old Mother Riley Joins Up
1939 Weddings Are Wonderful
1939 Shadowed Eyes
1942 Gert and Daisy's Weekend
1942 Variety Jubilee
1944 Give Me the Stars
1945 Don Chicago
1945 The Trojan Brothers
1946 Woman to Woman
1948 The Story of Shirley Yorke
1948 Calling Paul Temple
1950 Something in the City
1950 Paul Temple's Triumph
1951 Madame Louis
1954 Johnny on the Spot
1957 Not Wanted on Voyage
1960 Not a Hope in Hell

ROHMER, Eric (Jean-Marie Maurice Scherer)
(1920–) Tulle, France.
Biographies: Eric Rohmer by G. Angeli.
1959 Le Signe du Lion
1963 La Carrière de Suzanne
1967 La Collectionneuse
1970 My Night at Maud's
1971 Claire's Knee
1972 Chloe in the Afternoon
1976 The Marquise of O..
1978 Perceval
1981 The Aviator's Wife
1982 Le Beau Mariage
1983 Pauline at the Beach
1984 Full Moon in Paris / *Les Nuits de la Pleine Lune*
1985 The Green Ray / *Summer*
1987 My Girlfriend's Friend
1987 Four Adventures of Reinette and Mirabelle

ROLAND, George
1932 Joseph in the Land of Egypt

ROLEY, Sutton
1966 How to Steal the World
1972 The Loners
1974 Chosen Survivors

ROMANEK, Mark
1986 Static

ROMERO, Eddie
(1924–) Negros Oriental, Philippines.
1957 The Day of the Trumpet
1962 Lost Battalion
1963 The Raiders of Leyte Gulf
1964 Moro Witch Doctor
1964 The Kidnappers / *Man on the Run*
1964 The Walls of Hell **(Gerardo DeLEON)**
1965 The Ravagers
1971 Beast of the Yellow Night
1971 Beast of Blood
1972 Twilight People
1973 Black Mama, White Mama
1973 Beyond Atlantis
1974 Savage Sisters
1975 The Woman Hunt
1977 Sudden Death
1980 Aguila
1983 Desire
1983 Ganito Kami Noon, Paano Kayo Hgayon?
1989 A Case of Honor

ROMERO, George A
(1940–) New York, USA.
1968 Night of the Living Dead
1972 There's Always Vanilla
1972 The Crazies / *Code Name: Trixie*
1973 Hungry Wives
1978 Martin
1979 Dawn of the Dead / *Zombies*
1982 Creepshow
1982 Knightriders
1985 Day of the Dead
1988 Apartment Living
1988 Monkey Shines

RONDELL, Ronnie
1987 No Safe Haven

ROODT, Darrell
1986 Place of Weeping
1987 City of Blood
1987 Tenth of a Second
1988 The Stick

ROOKS, Conrad
1968 Chappaqua
1973 Siddhartha

ROOME, Alfred
1948 It's Not Cricket
1948 My Brother's Keeper **(Roy RICH)**

ROONEY, Jack
1988 Pushed Too Far

ROONEY, Mickey (Joe Yule Jnr)
(1920–) Brooklyn, New York, USA.
Autobiography: I.E.
1951 My True Story
1960 The Private Lives of Adam and Eve **(Albert ZUGSMITH)**

ROOT, Wells
1936 The Bold Caballero
1942 Monkey

ROPER, Mark
1988 Dancing in the Forest

ROQUEMORE, Cliff
1976 The Human Tornado

ROSE, Bernard
1989 Paperhouse
1989 Chicago Joe and the Showgirl

ROSE, Les
1977 Three Card Monte
1979 Title Shot
1980 Hog Wild
1981 Gas
1985 Drastic Measures / *Isaac Littlefeathers*
1986 Spooks
1987 The Life and Times of Eddie Boyd

ROSE, Mickey
1981 Student Bodies

ROSE, Sherman A
1955 Target Earth
1956 Magnificent Roughnecks
1958 Tank Battalion

ROSEN, Martin
1988 Stackin' / *Season of Dreams*

ROSEN, Phil (Philippe Rosen)
(1888–1951) Russian.
1924 The Dramatic Life of Abraham Lincoln
1924 This Woman
1924 The Bridge of Sighs
1924 Being Respectable
1925 The Heart of a Siren
1925 The White Monkey
1925 Wandering Footsteps
1926 A Woman's Heart
1926 Stolen Pleasure
1926 Rose of the Tenements
1926 The Adorable Deceivers
1927 Closed Gates
1927 Heaven on Earth
1927 Salvation Jane
1927 The Woman Who Didn't Care
1927 The Cruel Truth
1927 Thumbs Down
1927 Stranded
1927 Pretty Clothes
1927 Cancelled Debts
1928 Marry the Girl / *The House of Deceit*
1928 Burning Up Broadway
1928 Undressed
1928 Modern Mothers
1928 The Apache
1929 Peacock Fan
1929 The Faker
1929 The Phantom in the House
1929 Extravagance
1929 The Rampant Age
1930 The Lotus Lady
1930 Worldly Goods
1931 Second Honeymoon
1931 The Two-Gun Man / *Two's Company*
1931 Alias the Bad Man
1931 The Arizona Terror
1931 Range Law
1931 Branded Men
1931 The Pocatello Kid
1932 The Gay Buckaroo
1932 The Texas Gun Fighter
1932 Whistlin' Dan
1932 Lena Rivers
1932 The Vanishing Frontier
1932 Klondike / *The Doctor's Sacrifice*
1932 A Man's Land
1933 Young Blood / *Lola*
1933 Self Defence
1933 The Phantom Broadcast / *Phantom of the Air*
1933 The Sphinx
1933 Black Beauty
1933 Devil's Mate / *He Knew Too Much*
1934 Hold the Press
1934 Beggars in Ermine
1934 Shadows of Sing Sing
1934 Picture Brides
1934 Cheaters
1934 Take the Stand / *The Great Radio Mystery*
1934 Dangerous Corner
1934 Woman in the Dark
1934 Little Men
1934 West of the Pecos
1935 Death Flies East
1935 Unwelcome Stranger
1935 Born to Gamble
1936 The Calling of Dan Matthews
1936 Tango
1936 The Bridge of Sighs
1936 Three of a Kind
1936 Easy Money
1936 It Couldn't Have Happened
1936 Brilliant Marriage
1936 The President's Mystery / *One for All*
1936 Missing Girls / *When Girls Leave Home*
1936 Ellis Island
1937 Two Wise Maids
1937 Jim Hanvey, Detective
1937 It Could Happen to You
1937 Roaring Timber
1937 Youth on Parole
1938 The Marines Are Here
1939 Ex-Champ / *Golden Gloves*
1939 Missing Evidence
1940 Double Alibi
1940 Forgotten Girls
1940 The Crooked Road
1940 Phantom of Chinatown
1940 Queen of the Yukon
1941 The Roar of the Press
1941 Crime Inc.
1941 Murder By Invitation
1941 The Deadly Game
1941 Spooks Run Wild
1941 I Killed the Man
1942 Road to Happiness
1942 The Man with Two Lives
1942 The Mystery of Marie Roget
1943 You Can't Beat the Law
1943 A Gentle Gangster
1943 Wings Over the Pacific
1944 Charlie Chan in the Secret Service
1944 The Chinese Cat
1944 Return of the Ape Man
1944 Black Magic
1944 Call of the Jungle
1944 The Jade Mask
1944 Army Wives
1945 The Scarlet Clue
1945 The Red Dragon
1945 Captain Tugboat Annie
1945 In Old New Mexico
1946 The Shadow Returns
1946 The Strange Mr Gregory
1946 Step By Step
1949 The Secret of St Ives

ROSEN, Robert L
(1937–) Palm Springs, California, USA.
1984 Courage

ROSENBERG, Stuart
(1925–) New York, New York, USA.
1960 Murder Inc. **(Burt BALABAN)**

1961 Question 7
1967 Cool Hand Luke
1969 The April Fools
1970 Move
1970 Wusa
1972 Pocket Money
1973 The Laughing Policeman / *An Investigation of Murder*
1975 The Drowning Pool
1977 Voyage of the Damned
1979 Love and Bullets
1979 The Amityville Horror
1980 Brubaker
1984 The Pope of Greenwich Village
1986 Let's Get Harry

ROSENTHAL, Mark
1988 The In Crowd / *Dance Party*

ROSENTHAL, Rick
(1950–) New York, New York, USA.
1981 Halloween II
1983 Bad Boys
1984 American Dreamer
1987 Russkies
1988 Distant Thunder

ROSENTHAL, Robert J
1978 Malibu Beach
1982 Zapped!
1989 Zapped Again

ROSI, Francesco *
(1922–) Naples, Italy.
1958 The Challenge
1965 The Moment of Truth
1967 More Than a Miracle / *C'Era una Volta / Cinderella, Italian Style*
1973 The Mattei Affair
1974 Lucky Luciano
1980 Christ Stopped at Eboli
1981 Three Brothers
1984 Bizet's Carmen
1988 Chronicle of a Death Foretold

ROSMAN, Mark
1983 The House on Sorority Row

ROSMER, Milton (Arthur Milton Lunt)
(1881–1971) British.
1930 P.C. Josser
1931 Many Waters
1931 Dreyfus **(F W KRAEMER)**
1932 After the Ball
1933 Channel Crossing
1934 The Secret of the Loch
1934 What Happened to Harkness?
1935 The Guvnor / *Mr Hobo*
1935 Emil and the Detectives
1935 Maria Marten or Murder in the Red Barn
1936 Everything Is Thunder
1938 The Challenge **(Luis TRENKER)**

ROSS, Dick
1971 The Late Liz

ROSS, Frank
(1904–) American.
1951 The Lady Says No

ROSS, Herbert
(1927–) New York, New York, USA.
1969 Goodbye, Mr Chips
1970 The Owl and the Pussycat
1971 T.R. Baskin / *A Date with a Lonely Girl*
1972 Play It Again Sam
1973 The Last of Sheila
1975 Funny Lady
1975 The Sunshine Boys
1976 The Seven-Per-Cent Solution
1977 The Turning Point **D* F***
1977 The Goodbye Girl **F***
1978 California Suite
1980 Nijinsky
1981 Pennies from Heaven
1982 I Ought to Be in Pictures
1983 Max Dugan Returns
1984 Footloose
1984 Protocol
1987 The Secret of My Success
1987 Dancers / *Giselle*
1989 Steel Magnolias

ROSS, Nat
1928 Stop That Man
1929 College Love

ROSSEN, Robert (Robert Rosen)
(1908–1966) New York, New York, USA.
1947 Johnny O'Clock
1947 Body and Soul
1949 All the King's Men **D* F****
1951 The Brave Bulls
1955 Mambo
1956 Alexander the Great
1957 Island in the Sun
1959 They Came to Cordura
1961 The Hustler **D* F***
1964 Lilith

ROSSO, Franco
1988 The Nature of the Beast

ROSSON, Arthur
(1889–1960) American.
1924 The Measure of a Man
1925 The Burning Trail
1925 The Meddler
1925 Straight Through
1925 The Taming of the West
1926 Stranded in Paris
1926 Wet Paint
1926 You'd Be Surprised
1927 Set Free
1927 The Last Outlaw
1927 Silk Legs
1928 The Farmer's Daughter
1928 Play Girl
1929 Show Boat
1929 The Winged Horseman **(B Reeves EASON)**
1929 Points West
1929 The Long, Long Trail
1930 The Roaring Ranch **(B Reeves EASON)**
1930 The Mounted Stranger
1930 Trailing Trouble
1930 The Concentratin' Kid
1933 Hidden Gold
1933 Flaming Guns

1937 Boots of Destiny

ROSSON, Richard
(1894–1953) American.
1926 Fine Manners
1927 Rolled Stockings
1927 Blonde or Brunette
1927 Ritzy
1927 Shootin' Irons
1927 The Wizard
1928 The Escape
1928 Road House
1929 The Very Idea **(William LaBARON)**
1935 West Point of the Air
1937 Behind the Headlines
1937 Hideaway
1943 Corvette K-225 / *The Nelson Touch*

ROTER, Ted
1979 One Page of Love

ROTH, Bobby
1977 Independence Day
1980 The Boss's Son
1983 Circle of Power / *Mystique / Brainwash*
1984 Heartbreakers
1988 Baja Oklahoma

ROTH, Cy
1953 Combat Squad
1955 Air Strike
1956 Five Maidens from Outer Space

ROTH, Joe
(1948–) New York, New York, USA.
1986 Streets of Gold
1987 Revenge of the Nerds II; Nerds in Paradise

ROTH, Murray
1929 Queen of the Night Clubs **(Addison BURKHARD)**
1933 Don't Bet on Love
1934 Million Dollar Ransom
1934 Harold Teen / *Dancing Fool*
1935 Chinatown Squad
1936 Flying Hostess

ROTHA, Paul
(1907–) London, England.
1951 No Resting Place
1952 World Without End **(Basil WRIGHT)**
1958 Cat and Mouse
1962 Silent Road
(also many documentaries)

ROTHMAN, Joseph
1938 Dynamite Delaney

ROTHMAN, Stephanie
1966 Blood Bath **(Jack HILL)**
1967 It's a Bikini World
1970 The Student Nurses
1971 The Velvet Vampire
1972 Group Marriage
1973 Terminal Island
1974 The Working Girls

ROURKE, Adam
1987 Trespasses **(Loren BIVENS)**

ROUSE, Russell
(1916–1987) New York, USA.
1951 The Well **(Leo POPKINS)**
1952 The Thief
1954 Wicked Woman
1955 New York Confidential
1956 The Fastest Gun Alive
1957 House of Numbers
1959 Thunder in the Sun
1964 A House Is Not a Home
1966 The Oscar
1967 The Caper of the Golden Bulls / *Carnival of Thieves*

ROWE, Peter
1987 Lost!
1987 Take Two
1988 Personal Exemptions

ROWLAND, Roy
(1910–) New York, USA.
1934 Hollywood Party **(Richard BOLESLAWSKI, Allan DWAN)**
1943 A Stranger in Town
1943 Lost Angel
1945 A Song for Miss Julie
1945 Our Vines Have Tender Grapes
1946 Boys' Ranch
1947 The Romance of Rosey Ridge
1947 Killer McCoy
1947 Tenth Avenue Angel
1949 Scene of the Crime
1950 The Outriders
1950 Two Weeks with Love
1951 Excuse My Dust
1952 Bugles in the Afternoon
1953 Affair with a Stranger
1953 The 5,000 Fingers of Dr T
1953 The Moonlighter
1954 Witness to Murder
1954 Rogue Cop
1955 Hit the Deck
1955 Many Rivers to Cross
1956 Meet Me in Las Vegas / *Viva Las Vegas!*
1956 These Wilder Years
1956 Slander
1957 Gun Glory
1963 The Girl Hunters
1965 Gunfighters of Casa Grande
1967 The Sea Pirate
(also many shorts)

ROWLAND, William
1939 Perfida
1946 Flight to Nowhere
1948 Woman in the Night
1970 The Wild Scene

RUBBO, Michael
1985 The Peanut Butter Solution

RUBEN, Joseph
1975 The Sister-In-Law
1976 Pom-Pom Girls
1977 Joyride
1978 Our Winning Season
1980 Gorp
1984 Dreamscape
1987 The Stepfather

1988 Cat Chaser
1989 True Believer

RUBEN, Katt Shea
1987 Stripped to Kill / *Deception*
1988 Dance of the Damned / *Half Life*
1989 Live Girls Stripped to Kill II

RUBEN, Walter J
(1899–1942) American.
1931 The Public Defender
1931 Secret Service
1932 The Phantom of Crestwood
1932 Roadhouse Murder
1933 The Great Jasper
1933 No Marriage Ties
1933 Ace of Aces
1933 No Other Woman
1934 Man of Two Worlds
1934 Success at Any Price
1934 Where Sinners Meet
1935 Public Hero Number One
1935 Riff Raff
1935 Java Head
1936 Old Hutch
1936 Trouble for Two / *The Suicide Club*
1937 Good Old Soak
1938 Bad Man of Brimstone

RUBENS, Percival
1969 Strangers at Sunrise
1974 Mr Kingstreet's War
1985 Night Caller / *The Demon*
1986 Hostage
1989 Okavango

RUBIN, Rick
1989 Tougher Than Leather

RUDOLPH, Alan
(1944–) Los Angeles, California, USA.
1972 Premonition
1976 Welcome to LA
1978 Remember My Name
1980 Roadie
1982 Endangered Species
1984 Choose Me
1984 Songwriter
1986 Trouble in Mind
1987 Made in Heaven
1988 The Moderns
1989 Love at Large

RUDOLPH, Oscar
1954 The Rocket Man
1961 Twist Around the Clock
1962 Don't Knock the Twist
1962 The Wild Westerners

RUGGLES, Wesley
(1889–1972) Los Angeles, California, USA.
1924 The Age of Innocence
1925 The Plastic Age
1925 Broadway Lady
1926 A Man of Quality
1926 The Kick-Off
1926 Beware of Widows
1927 Silk Stockings
1928 The Fourflusher
1929 Scandal
1929 Street Girl
1929 Girl Overboard
1929 Condemned
1930 Honey
1930 The Sea Bat
1931 Cimarron **D* F****
1931 Are These Our Children?
1932 Roar of the Dragon
1932 No Man of Her Own
1933 The Monkey's Paw
1933 College Humour
1933 I'm No Angel
1934 Bolero
1934 Shoot the Works / *Thank Your Stars*
1935 The Gilded Lily
1935 Accent on Youth
1935 The Bride Comes Home
1936 Valiant Is the Word for Carrie
1937 I Met Him in Paris
1937 True Confession
1938 Sing You Sinners
1939 Invitation to Happiness
1940 Too Many Husbands / *My Two Husbands*
1940 Arizona
1941 You Belong to Me / *Good Morning Doctor*
1942 Somewhere I'll Find You
1943 Slightly Dangerous
1944 See Here, Private Hargrove
1953 London Town / *My Heart Goes Crazy*

RUNZE, Ottakar
1987 Nonstop Trouble with the Spies

RUSH, Richard
(1930–) New York, New York, USA.
1960 Too Soon to Love
1963 Of Love and Desire
1967 Fickle Finger of Fate
1967 Thunder Alley
1967 Hell's Angels on Wheels
1968 A Man Called Dagger
1968 Psych-Out
1968 The Savage Seven
1970 Getting Straight
1974 Freebie and the Bean
1980 The Stunt Man **D***
1987 Air America

RUSSELL, Chuck
1987 Nightmare on Elm Street III: The Dream Warriors
1988 The Blob

RUSSELL, Jay
1987 End of the Line

RUSSELL, Ken (Henry Kenneth Alfred Russell)
(1927–) Southampton, Hampshire, England.
Autobiography: An Appalling Talent: Ken Russell.
1963 French Dressing
1967 Billion Dollar Brain
1970 Women in Love **D***
1971 The Music Lovers

1971 The Devils
1971 The Boyfriend
1972 Savage Messiah
1974 Mahler
1975 Tommy
1975 Lisztomania
1977 Valentino
1980 Altered States
1984 Crimes of Passion
1985 Hedwic: The Cool Lakes of Death
1986 Gothic
1987 Aria **(Robert ALTMAN, Bruce BERESFORD, Bill BRYDEN, Jean-Luc GODARD, Derek JARMAN, Franc RODDAM, Nicolas ROEG, Charles STURRIDGE, Julien TEMPLE)**
1988 Salome's First Night
1988 St Mawr
1988 The Lair of the White Worm
1988 The Rainbow
1989 The Spectre of Rose

RUSSELL, Rusty
1973 The New York Experience

RUSSELL, William D
(1908–1968) American.
1946 Our Hearts Were Growing Up
1947 Ladies' Man
1947 Dear Ruth
1948 The Sainted Sisters
1949 The Green Promise / *Raging Waters*
1949 Bride for Sale
1951 Best of the Badmen

RUSSO, John
1989 The Awakening

RUSTAM, Mardi
1985 Evils of the Night

RUTLAND, Mark
1989 Prime Suspect

RYAN, Frank
(1907–1947) American.
1942 Call Out the Marines **(William HAMILTON)**
1943 Hers to Hold
1944 Can't Help Singing
1945 Patrick the Great
1946 So Goes My Love / *A Genius in the Family*

RYAN, Terence
1989 Hold My Hand I'm Dying

RYDELL, Mark
(1934–) New York, New York, USA.
1968 The Fox
1970 The Reivers
1972 The Cowboys
1974 Cinderella Liberty
1976 Harry and Walter Go to New York
1979 The Rose
1981 On Golden Pond **D* F***
1984 The River

SACHS, William
1976 Secrets of the Gods
1977 There Is No Thirteen
1977 The Incredible Melting Man
1979 Van Nuys BLVD
1980 Galaxina
1985 Hot Summer / *Hot Chili*
1989 Judgement

SACKHEIM, William A
(1919–) American.
1945 Let's Go Steady

SACKS, Alan
1984 Du Beat-E-O

SAETA, Eddie
1973 Doctor Death, Seeker of Souls

SAFRAN, Henri
(1932–) Paris, France.
1975 Elephant Boy
1976 Storm Boy
1981 Norman Loves Rose
1983 The Wild Duck
1983 Prince and the Great Race
1988 Edge of Power
(also many miniseries)

SAGAL, Boris
(1923–1981) Russian.
1961 The Crimebusters
1963 Dime with a Halo
1963 Twilight of Honour / *The Charge Is Murder*
1964 Guns of Diablo
1965 Girl Happy
1966 Made in Paris
1967 The Helicopter Spies
1969 The Thousand Plane Raid
1970 Mosquito Squadron
1971 Operation Heartbeat
1971 The Omega Man
(also many TV movies)

ST CLAIR, Malcolm
(1897–1952) Los Angeles, California, USA.
1924 Find Your Man
1924 George Washington Jnr.
1925 Lighthouse by the Sea
1925 On Thin Ice
1925 Are Parents People?
1925 A Woman of the World
1925 The Trouble with Wives
1926 Fascinating Youth **(Lewis MILESTONE)**
1926 Grand Duchess and the Waiter
1926 The Show-Off
1926 Good and Naughty
1926 The Social Celebrity
1927 The Popular Sin
1927 Knockout Riley
1928 Gentlemen Prefer Blondes
1928 The Fleet's In
1928 Sporting Goods
1928 Beau Broadway
1929 Side Street
1929 Night Parade / *Sporting Life*
1930 The Canary Murder Case
1930 Montana Moon
1930 Dangerous Nan McGrew
1930 The Boudoir Diplomat

1930 Remote Control **(Nick GRINDE)**
1933 Goldie Gets Along
1933 Olsen's Big Moment
1937 Crack-Up
1937 Time Out for Romance
1937 She Had to Eat
1937 Born Reckless
1937 Dangerously Yours
1938 A Trip to Paris
1938 Safety in Numbers
1938 Down on the Farm
1938 Everybody's Baby
1939 Quick Millions
1939 The Jones Family in Hollywood
1940 Young As You Feel
1940 Meet the Missus
1941 The Bashful Bachelor
1942 Over My Dead Body
1942 The Man in the Trunk
1943 The Dancing Masters
1943 Jitterbugs
1943 Two Weeks to Live
1943 Swing Out the Blues
1944 The Big Noise
1945 The Bullfighters
1948 Arthur Takes Over
1948 Fighting Back

ST JACQUES, Raymond (James Arthur Johnson)
(1930–) Hartford, Connecticut, USA.
1973 Book of Numbers

ST JOHN, Christopher
1972 Top of the Heap

SAKS, Gene
(1921–) New York, New York, USA.
1967 Barefoot in the Park
1968 The Odd Couple
1969 Cactus Flower
1972 Last of the Red Hot Lovers
1974 Mame
1986 Brighton Beach Memoirs

SALA, Henry
1986 Nightmare Weekend

SALCE, Luciano *
(1922–) Italy.
1962 Crazy Desire / *La Voglia Matta*
1963 The Hours of Love
1963 The Little Nuns
1964 High Fidelity **(Mario MONICELLI, Elio PETRI, Franco ROSSI)**
1965 Kiss the Other Sheik / *Oggi, Domani e Dopodomani* **(Edouardo DE FILIPPO. Marco FERRERI)**
1965 Slalom
1966 The Queens / *Le Fate* **(Mauro BOLOGNINI, Maria MONICELLI, Antonio PIETRANGELI)**

SALE, Richard
(1911–) American.
1947 Spoilers of the North
1948 Campus Honeymoon
1950 I'll Get By
1950 A Ticket to Tomahawk
1951 Half Angel
1951 Let's Make It Legal
1951 Meet Me After the Show
1952 My Wife's Best Friend
1953 The Girl Next Door
1954 Fire Over Africa / *Malaga*
1955 Gentlemen Marry Brunettes
1957 Abandon Ship! / *Seven Waves Away*

SALKOW, Sidney
(1909–) American.
1937 Four Days' Wonder
1937 Girl Overboard
1937 Behind the Mike
1938 That's My Story
1938 The Night Hawk
1939 Storm Over Bengal
1939 Fighting Thoroughbreds
1939 Woman Doctor
1939 Street of Missing Men
1939 The Zero Hour
1939 She Married a Cop
1939 Flight at Midnight
1939 Café Hostess
1940 The Lone Wolf Strikes Back
1940 The Lone Wolf Meets a Lady
1940 Girl from God's Country
1940 The Lone Wolf Keeps a Date
1941 The Lone Wolf Takes a Chance
1941 Time Out for Rhythm
1941 Tillie the Toiler
1942 The Adventures of Martin Eden
1942 Flight Lieutenant
1943 City Without Men
1943 The Boy from Stalingrad
1946 Faithful in My Fashion
1947 Millie's Daughter
1947 Bulldog Drummond at Bay
1948 Sound of the Avenger
1952 Scarlet Angel
1952 The Golden Hawk
1952 The Pathfinder
1953 Prince of Pirates
1953 Jack McCall, Desperado
1953 Raiders of the Seven Seas
1954 Sitting Bull
1955 Robber's Roost
1955 Las Vegas Shakedown
1955 Shadow of the Eagle
1955 Toughest Man Alive
1956 The Long Rifle and the Tomahawk **(Sam NEWFIELD)**
1956 Gun Brothers
1957 The Iron Sheriff
1957 Gun Duel in Durango
1957 Chicago Confidential
1960 The Big Night
1963 Twice Told Tales
1964 The Quick Gun
1964 Blood on the Arrow
1965 The Great Sioux Massacre
1966 The Murder Game

SALMONSEN, Grete
1987 Camilla and the Thief

SALTER, James
1969 Three

SANDERS, Denis
(1929–1987) New York, USA.

1958 Crime and Punishment USA
1961 War Hunt
1964 One Man's Way
1964 Shock Treatment
1973 Invasion of the Bee Girls

SANDOR, Pal *
(1939–) Hungarian.
1987 Miss Arizona

SANDRICH, Jay
(1932–) Los Angeles, California, USA.
1980 Neil Simon's Seems Like Old Times
(also many TV movies and comedy shorts)

SANDRICH, Mark
(1900–1945) New York, USA.
1930 The Talk of Hollywood
1933 Melody Cruise
1933 Aggie Appleby
1933 Maker of Men / *Cupid in the Rough*
1934 Hips, Hips Hooray
1934 Cockeyed Cavaliers
1934 The Gay Divorcee **F***
1935 Top Hat **F***
1936 Follow That Fleet
1936 A Woman Rebels
1937 Shall We Dance
1938 Carefree
1939 Man About Town
1940 Buck Benny Rides Again
1940 Love Thy Neighbour
1941 Skylark
1942 Holiday Inn
1943 So Proudly We Hail
1944 Here Come the Waves
1944 I Love a Soldier
(also many shorts)

SANFORTH, Clifford
1938 I Demand Payment

SANGER, Jonathan
1985 Code Name: Emerald

SANGSTER, Jimmy
(1927–) England.
1970 The Horror of Frankenstein
1970 Lust for a Vampire
1972 Fear in the Night

SANTEAN, Antonio
1964 The Glass Cage / *Den of Doom*

SANTELL, Alfred
(1895–1981) American.
1929 Twin Beds
1929 Romance of the Rio Grande
1930 The Arizona Kid
1930 The Sea Wolf
1931 Body and Soul
1931 Daddy Long Legs
1931 Sob Sister / *The Blonde Reporter*
1932 Polly of the Circus
1932 Rebecca of Sunnybrook Farm
1932 Tess of the Storm Country
1933 Bondage
1933 The Right to Romance
1934 The Life of Vergie Winters
1935 The Dictator / *For Love of a Queen* **(Victor SAVILLE)**
1935 People Will Talk
1935 A Feather in Her Hat
1936 Winterset
1937 Interns Can't Take Money / *You Can't Take Money*
1937 Breakfast for Two
1938 Cocoanut Grove
1938 Having a Wonderful Time
1938 The Arkansas Traveller
1939 Our Leading Citizen
1941 Aloma of the South Seas
1942 Beyond the Blue Horizon
1943 Jack London
1944 The Hairy Ape
1945 Mexicana
1946 That Brennan Girl

SANTIAGO, Cirio H
1972 Women in Cages
1974 Bamboo Gods and Iron Men
1975 TNT Jackson
1975 Cover Girl Models
1976 The Muthers
1978 Vampire Hookers
1978 Death Force
1981 Firecracker
1984 Caged Fury
1985 Desert Warrior / *Wheels of Fire*
1985 The Destroyers / *The Devastator*
1986 Naked Vengeance / *Satin Vengeance*
1986 Silk
1987 Equalizer 2000
1987 Demon of Paradise
1987 Eye of the Eagle
1987 The Spear
1988 The Sisterhood
1988 Behind Enemy Lines / *Killer Instinct*
1989 Nam Angels

SANTLEY, Joseph (Joseph Mansfield)
(1889–1911) Utah, USA.
1925 The Man Who Played Square
1929 The Cocoanuts **(Robert FLOREY)**
1930 Swing High
1934 The Loud Speaker
1934 Young and Beautiful
1935 Million Dollar Baby
1935 Harmony Lane
1935 Waterfront Lady
1936 Dancing Feet
1936 Her Master's Voice
1936 Laughing Irish Eyes
1936 The Harvester
1936 We Went to College / *The Old School Tie*
1936 Walking on Air
1936 The Smartest Girl in Town
1937 Meet the Missus
1937 There Goes the Groom
1937 The Life of the Party
1938 She's Got Everything
1938 Blonde Cheat
1938 Always in Trouble
1938 Swing, Sister, Swing
1939 Spirit of Culver / *Man's Heritage*
1939 The Family Next Door

1939 Two Bright Boys
1940 Music in My Heart
1940 Melody and Moonlight
1940 Melody Ranch
1940 Behind the News
1941 Dancing on a Dime
1941 Sis Hopkins
1941 Rookies on Parade
1941 Puddin' Head / *Joan Goes to Town*
1941 Ice-Capades
1941 A Tragedy at Midnight
1942 Yokel Boy / *Hitting the Headlines*
1942 Remember Pearl Harbour
1942 Joan of Ozark / *The Queen of Spies*
1943 Call of the Canyon
1943 Chatterbox
1943 Shantytown
1943 Thumbs Up
1943 Sleepy Lagoon
1943 Here Comes Elmer
1944 Rosie, the Riveter
1944 Jamboree
1944 Goodnight Sweetheart
1944 Three Little Sisters
1944 Brazil
1945 Earl Carroll Vanities
1945 Hitchhike to Happiness
1946 Shadow of a Woman
1949 Make Believe Ballroom
1950 When You're Smiling
(also many shorts)

SAPERSTEIN, David
1987 Monday, Tuesday, Wednesday / *My Sister's Keeper*
1989 Personal Choice

SARAFIAN, Deran
1986 Alien Predators / *The Falling*
1987 Interzone
1989 To Die For

SARAFIAN, Richard C.
(1925–) New York, New York, USA.
1962 Terror at Black Falls
1965 Andy
1969 Run Wild, Run Free
1971 Fragment of Fear
1971 Man in the Wilderness
1971 Vanishing Point
1973 Lolly-Madonna XXX / *The Lolly Madonna War*
1973 The Man Who Loved Cat Dancing
1976 The Next Man
1979 Sunburn
1984 The Bear
1986 Eye of the Tiger
1987 Street Justice
(also many TV movies)

SARGENT, Joseph (Giuseppe Danielle Sorgente)
(1925–) Jersey City, New Jersey, USA.
1966 One Spy Too Many
1968 The Hell with Heroes
1970 Colossus: The Forbin Project
1972 The Man
1973 White Lightning
1974 The Taking of Pelham 1–2–3
1977 MacArthur / *The Rebel General*
1979 Goldengirl
1980 Coast to Coast
1983 Nightmares
1987 Jaws — The Revenge
(also many TV movies)

SARIN, Vic
1987 The Corner
1989 Cold Comfort

SARNE, Michael
(1939–) London, England.
1966 The Road to St Tropez
1968 Joanna
1970 Myra Breckinridge
1972 Intimidade
1986 Trouble with a Battery

SARNO, Joe
1968 Moonlighting Wives

SASDY, Peter
(1934–) Budapest Hungary.
1970 Taste the Blood of Dracula
1972 Countess Dracula
1972 Hands of the Ripper
1972 Doomwatch
1975 Nothing But the Night
1976 I Don't Want to Be Born / *The Devil Within Her*
1977 Welcome to Blood City
1983 The Lonely Lady

SAUNDERS, Charles
(1904–) British.
1944 Tawny Pipit **(Bernard MILES)**
1947 Fly Away Peter
1951 One Wild Oat
1951 Dark Interval
1951 Chelsea Story
1954 Meet Mr Callaghan
1955 The Narrowing Circle
1957 The Man Without a Body **(W Lee WILDER)**
1958 Kill Her Gently
1958 Womaneater
1962 Danger By My Side

SAURA, Carlos *
(1932–) Huesca, Spain.
1966 The Hunt
1968 Peppermint Frappé
1969 Honeycomb / *La Madriguera*
1970 The Garden of Delights
1974 Cousin Angelica
1981 Blood Wedding
1982 Sweet Hours
1983 Carmen
1988 Mama Turns 100

SAUTET, Claude *
(1924–) Montrouge, Paris, France.
1960 The Big Risk
1970 The Things of Life
1972 Cesar and Rosalie
1974 Vincent, François, Paul and Others
1979 A Simple Story

SAVAGE, Peter
1970 House in Naples

SAVALAS, Telly (Aristotle Savalas)
(1925–) Garden City, New York, USA
Biography: Telly Savalas by Marsh Daly.
1982 Beyond Reason

SAVIC, Bosko
1987 Strangler v Strangler

SAVILLE, Philip
(1929–) London, England.
1966 Stop the World, I Want to Get Off
1968 The Best House in London
1971 Oedipus the King
1971 Secrets
1985 Shadey
1988 The Fruit Machine

SAVILLE, Victor (Victor Salberg)
(1897–1979) Birmingham, England.
Biography: Victor Saville by Cyril Rollins.
1927 The Arcadians / *Land of Heart's Desire*
1928 Tesha / *A Woman in the Night*
1928 Kitty
1930 The W Plan
1931 Sunshine Susie / *The Office Girl*
1931 The Sport of Kings
1931 Michael and Mary
1932 The Good Companions
1932 Love on Wheels
1933 Friday the Thirteenth
1933 I Was a Spy
1934 Evergreen
1934 Evensong
1934 The Iron Duke
1935 First a Girl
1935 Me and Marlborough
1935 The Dictator / *For Love of a Queen* **(Alfred SANTELL)**
1936 It's Love Again
1937 Dark Journey
1937 Storm in a Teacup **(Ian DALRYMPLE)**
1937 South Riding
1943 Forever and a Day **(René CLAIR, Edmund GOULDING, Cedric HARDWICKE, Frank LLOYD, Robert STEVENSON, Herbert WILCOX)**
1945 Tonight and Every Night
1946 The Green Years
1947 Green Dolphin Street
1948 If Winter Comes
1949 Conspirators
1950 Kim
1951 Calling Bulldog Drummond
1952 Twenty-Four Hours of a Woman's Life / *Affair in Monte Carlo*
1954 The Long Wait
1955 The Silver Chalice

SAXON, John (Carmen Orrico)
(1935–) Brooklyn, New York, USA.
1988 Death House

SAYLES, John
(1950–) Schenectady, New York, USA.
1980 Return of the Secaucus Seven
1983 Lianna
1983 Baby It's You
1984 The Brother from Another Planet
1987 Matewan
1988 Eight Men Out

SCANLAN, Joseph L
1983 Spring Fever
1987 Night Stick / *Nightstalk / Calhoun*

SCHAAF, Allen
(1942–) San Francisco, California, USA.
1984 Dracula's Disciple

SCHAEFER, Armand
(1898–) American.
1931 Hurricane Horsemen
1931 Reckless Riders
1932 Law and the Lawless
1932 Wyoming Whirlwind
1932 Cheyenne Cyclone
1932 Sinister Hands
1933 Terror Trail
1933 Fighting Texans
1933 Sagebrush Trail
1933 Outlaw Justice
1934 Sixteen Fathoms Deep
(also many serials)

SCHAEFER, George
(1920–) Wallingford, Connecticut, USA.
1961 Macbeth
1969 Pendulum
1969 Generation / *A Time for Giving*
1970 Doctors' Wives
1974 Once Upon a Scoundrel
1977 An Enemy of the People
(also many TV movies)

SCHAEFFER, Francis
1986 Wired to Kill
1988 Headhunter
1989 Rebel Waves

SCHAERTL, Michael L
1988 High Spirits

SCHAFFNER, Franklin J
(1920–) Tokyo, Japan.
1963 The Stripper / *Woman of Summer*
1964 The Best Man
1965 The War Lord
1968 Planet of the Apes
1968 The Double Man
1970 Patton / *Lust for Glory* **D** F****
1971 Nicholas and Alexandra **F***
1973 Papillon
1977 Islands in the Stream
1978 The Boys from Brazil
1980 Sphinx
1982 Yes, Giorgio
1987 Lionheart
1989 Welcome Home

SCHAIN, Don
1971 Ginger
1972 The Abductors

1972 A Place Called Today
1973 Girls Are for Loving
1978 Too Hot to Handle
1987 Taken By Force

SCHARY, Dore (Isidore Schary)
(1905–1980) Newark, New Jersey, USA.
Autobiography: Heyday: An Authobiography.
1963 Act One

SCHATZBERG, Jerry
(1927–) Bronx, New York, USA.
1970 Puzzle of a Downfall Child
1971 Panic in Needle Park
1973 Scarecrow
1976 Dandy, The All-American Girl / *Sweet Revenge*
1979 The Seduction of Joe Tynan
1980 Honeysuckle Rose
1984 Misunderstood
1984 No Small Affair
1987 Street Smart
1988 Blood Money / *Clinton and Nadine*
1989 Reunion

SCHEEPSMAKER, Hans
1987 Field of Honour

SCHEERER, Robert
1970 Adam at 6.00am
1973 The World's Greatest Athlete
1980 How to Beat the High Cost of Living
(also TV movies)

SCHELL, Maximilian
(1930–) Vienna, Austria.
1970 First Love
1974 The Pedestrian
1976 End of the Game
1979 Tales from the Vienna Woods
1989 An American Place

SCHELLERUP, Henning
1973 The Black Bunch
1973 Sweet Jesus, Preacher Man
1974 The Black Alleycats
1979 In Search of Historic Jesus
1979 Beyond Death's Door
1979 The Legend of Sleepy Hollow
1984 Camp-Fire Girls

SCHENCK, George
1972 Superbeast

SCHENKEL, Carl
1984 Out of Order / *Abwärts*
1989 The Mighty Quinn / *Finding Maubee*
1989 Lady Killer

SCHEPISI, Fred
(1939–) Melbourne, Victoria, Australia.
1973 Libido **(David BAKER, Tim BURSTALL, John B MURRAY)**
1976 The Devil's Playground
1978 The Chant of Jimmy Blacksmith
1981 Barbarosa
1984 Iceman
1985 Plenty
1987 Roxanne
1988 A Cry in the Dark / *Guilty By Suspicion / Evil Angels*

SCHERBERGER, Aiken
1987 Whodunnit

SCHERER, Gene
1987 See You Tomorrow

SCHERTZINGER, Victor
(1880–1941) Pennsylvania, USA.
1924 Bread
1925 Man and Maid
1925 Thunder Mountain
1925 The Wheel
1926 Siberia
1926 The Golden Strain
1926 The Lily
1926 Return of Peter Grimm
1927 Heart of Salome
1927 Secret Studio
1927 Stage Madness
1928 Forgotten Faces
1928 The Showdown
1929 Redskin
1929 Nothing But the Truth
1929 The Wheel of Life
1929 Fashions in Love
1930 The Laughing Lady
1930 Safety in Numbers
1930 Heads Up
1931 The Woman Between / *Madame Julie*
1931 Friends and Lovers
1932 Strange Justice
1932 Uptown New York
1933 The Constant Woman
1933 The Cocktail Hour
1933 My Woman
1934 Beloved
1934 One Night of Love **D* F***
1935 Let's Live Together
1935 Love Me Forever / *On Wings of Song*
1936 The Music Goes 'Round
1937 Something to Sing About
1939 The Mikado
1940 Road to Singapore
1940 Rhythm on the River
1941 Road to Zanzibar
1941 Kiss the Boys Goodbye
1941 Birth of the Blues
1942 The Fleet's In

SCHEUER, Tom
1974 Gosh

SCHILLER, Lawrence L
(1936–) New York, New York, USA.
1982 The Executioner's Song

SCHILLER, Tom
1984 Nothing Lasts Forever

SCHLAMME, Thomas
1989 Miss Firecracker

SCHLATTER, George
(1931–) American.
1976 Norman, Is That You?

SCHLESINGER, John
(1926–) London, England.
Biography: John Schlesinger by Gene D. Phillips.
1962 A Kind of Loving
1963 Billy Liar
1965 Darling **D*.F***
1967 Far from the Madding Crowd
1969 Midnight Cowboy **D** F****
1970 Sunday Bloody Sunday **D***
1975 The Day of the Locust
1976 Marathon Man
1979 Yanks
1981 Honky Tonk Freeway
1985 The Falcon and the Snowman
1987 The Believers
1988 First and Last
1988 Madame Sousatzka
(also many documentaries)

SCHLONDORFF, Volker
(1939–) Wiesbaden, Germany.
1966 Young Törless
1967 A Degree of Murder / *Mordung Totschlag*
1969 Michael Kohlhaas
1970 The Sudden Wealth of the Poor People of Komback
1971 Die Moral der Ruth Halbfass
1971 A Free Woman / *Strohfeuer*
1975 The Lost Honour of Katharina Blum
1976 Coup de Grâce
1980 The Tin Drum
1982 Circle of Deceit / *Die Fälschung*
1984 Swann in Love
1987 A Gathering of Old Men
1989 The Handmaid's Tale
(also many TV movies)

SCHMIDT, Thomas
1973 Hot Summer Week

SCHMITT, Richard
1989 Spinning Wheels

SCHMITZ, Oliver
1988 Mapantsula / *One Look Shook the World*

SCHMOELLER, David
1979 Tourist Trap
1981 The Seduction
1986 Crawlspace
1987 Ghost Town
1988 Catacombs
1989 Puppetmaster

SCHMULEVICH, Michael
1987 Just Married

SCHNEIDER, Paul
1986 Something Special / *Willy Milly*

SCHNITZER, Robert Allen
1975 No Place to Hide
1976 The Premonition
1987 Kandyland

SCHOEDSACK, Ernest Beaumont
(1893–1979) Council Bluffs, Ohio, USA.
1925 Grass **(Merian C COOPER)**
1927 Chang **(Merian C COOPER)**
1929 The Four Feathers **(Merian C COOPER, Lothar MENDES)**
1931 Rango
1932 The Most Dangerous Game / *The Hounds of Zaroff* **(Irving PICHEL)**
1933 King Kong **(Merian C COOPER)**
1933 Blind Adventure
1933 Son of Kong
1934 Long Lost Father
1935 The Last Days of Pompeii **(Merian C COOPER)**
1937 Trouble in Morocco
1937 Outlaws of the Orient
1940 Dr Cyclops
1949 Mighty Joe Young
(also many documentaries)

SCHOLES, Roger
1987 The Tale of Ruby Rose

SCHOLL, Jack
1950 Holiday Rhythm

SCHOOLNIK, Stuart
1987 Hide and Go Shriek

SCHOTTEN, Wayne A
1950 Friday on My Mind

SCHRADER, Paul
(1946–) Grand Rapids, Michigan, USA.
1978 Blue Collar
1978 Hardcore
1980 American Gigolo
1982 Cat People
1985 Mishima: A Life in Four Chapters
1987 Light of Day
1988 Patty Hearst

SCHREIBAN, Myrl
1979 The Italian
1982 Angel of H.E.A.T.

SCHREINER, William
1989 A Sinful Life / *The Immaculate Conception of Baby Bump*

SCHROEDER, Barbet
(1941–) Teheran, Iran.
1969 More
1972 The Valley...Obscured By Clouds
1987 Barfly
1989 Reversal of Fortune

SCHROEDER, Michael
1988 Mortuary Academy
1988 Out of the Dark
1989 The Devil's Odds
1989 Damned River

SCHULTZ, Carl
(1939–) Budapest, Hungary.
1978 Blue Fin
1982 Goodbye Paradise
1983 Careful, He Might Hear You
1987 Bullseye
1988 Travelling North

1988 The Seventh Sign / *The Boarder*

SCHULTZ, Michael
(1938–) Milwaukee, Wisconsin, USA.
1973 Together for Days
1974 Honeybaby, Honeybaby
1975 Cooley High
1976 Car Wash
1977 Greased Lightning
1978 Which Way Is Up?
1978 Sergeant Pepper's Lonely Hearts Club Band
1979 Scavenger Hunt
1981 Carbon Copy
1985 The Last Dragon
1985 Krush Groove / *Rap Attack*
1987 Disorderlies

SCHUMACHER, Joel
(1942–) New York, New York, USA.
1981 The Incredible Shrinking Woman
1983 D.C. Cab
1985 St Elmo's Fire
1987 The Lost Boys
1989 Cousins

SCHUNZEL, Reinhold
(1886–1954) Hamburg, Germany.
1933 Victor Victoria
1938 Rich Man, Poor Girl
1939 Balalaika
1939 Ice Follies of 1939
1941 New Wine / *The Great Awakening*

SCHUSTER, Harold D
(1902–1986) American
1937 Dinner at the Ritz
1937 Wings of the Morning
1938 Swing That Cheer
1938 Exposed
1939 One Hour to Live
1940 Zanzibar
1940 Ma! He's Making Eyes at Me
1940 South to Karanga
1940 Diamond Frontier
1940 Framed
1941 A Very Young Lady
1941 Small Town Deb
1941 A Modern Monte Cristo
1942 Girl Trouble
1942 The Postman Didn't Ring
1942 On the Sunny Side
1943 My Friend Flicka
1944 Marine Raiders
1946 Breakfast in Hollywood / *The Mad Hatter*
1947 The Tender Years
1948 So Dear to My Heart
1952 Kid Monk Baroni / *Young Paul Baroni*
1953 Jack Slade
1954 Loophole
1954 Port of Hell
1954 Security Risk
1955 Finger Man
1955 The Return of Jack Slade
1955 Tarzan's Hidden Jungle
1957 Courage of Black Beauty
1957 Dragoon Wells Massacre
1957 Portland Exposé

SCHWAB, Lawrence
1933 Take a Chance **(Monte BRICE)**
1933 Follow Thru **(Lloyd CORRIGAN)**

SCHWARTZ, Douglas
1971 The Peace Killers
1973 Your Three Minutes Are Up

SCOLA, Ettore *
(1931–) Trevico, Avellino, Italy.
1964 Let's Talk About Women / *Se permette, Parliamo di Donne*
1965 Thrilling **(Dino DeLAURENTIIS, Carlo LIZZANI, Gian Luigi POLIDORI)**
1966 The Devil in Love / *L'Arcidiavolo*
1970 The Pizza Triangle / *Dramma della Gelosia - Tutti Particolari Incronica*
1971 My Name Is Rocco Papaleo
1975 We All Loved Each Other So Much
1976 Down and Dirty / *Brutti, Sporchi e Cattivi*
1977 A Special Day
1979 Viva Italia / *I Nuovi Mostri* **(Mario MONICELLI, Dino RISI)**
1985 Macaroni
1987 The Family

SCORSESE, Martin
(1942–) Flushing, New York, USA.
1968 Who's That Knocking at My Door?
1972 Boxcar Bertha
1973 Mean Streets
1974 Alice Doesn't Live Here Anymore
1976 Taxi Driver **F***
1977 New York, New York
1978 The Last Waltz
1978 Raging Bull **D* F***
1983 The King of Comedy
1985 After Hours
1986 The Color of Money
1988 The Last Temptation of Christ **D***
1989 New York Stories **(Woody ALLEN, Francis Ford COPPOLA)**

SCOTT, Ewing
1934 Renegade
1937 Hollywood Cowboy
1937 Windjammer
1937 Headin' West
1937 Hollywood Roundup
1947 Untamed Fury
1948 Harpoon
1949 Arctic Manhunt

SCOTT, George C
(1927–) Wise, Virginia, USA.
1972 Rage
1974 The Savage Is Loose

SCOTT, James
1989 Loser Takes All

SCOTT, Oz
1981 Bustin' Loose
1983 Dreamland **(Nancy BAKER. Joel SCHULMAN)**
1988 Driving Academy

SCOTT, Peter Graham
(1923–) British.

1957 Account Rendered
1962 Captain Clegg / *Night Creatures*
1963 Bitter Harvest
1963 The Cracksman
1963 Father Came Too

SCOTT, Ridley
(1939–) South Shields, County Durham, England.
1977 The Duellists
1979 Alien
1982 Blade Runner
1985 Legend
1987 Someone to Watch Over Me
1989 Black Rain

SCOTT, Robert
1987 The Video Dead

SCOTT, Sherman *see* **Sam NEWFIELD**

SCOTT, Tony
1983 The Hunger
1986 Top Gun
1987 Beverly Hills Cop II
1989 Revenge

SCOTTO, Aubrey H
1932 Divorce Racket
1932 Uncle Moses
1934 Three Loves
1934 I Hate Women
1935 1,000 Dollars a Minute
1935 Hitch-Hike Lady
1935 Smart Girl
1936 Ticket to Paradise
1936 Follow Your Heart
1936 Happy Go Lucky
1936 Palm Springs
1937 Blazing Barriers
1938 Gambling Ship
1938 I Was a Criminal
1938 Little Miss Roughneck

SEARLE, Francis
(1909–) British.
1936 Someone at the Door
1946 A Girl in a Million
1951 Cloudburst
1951 Whispering Smith Hits London / *Whispering Smith Versus Scotland Yard*
1952 Never Look Back
1952 Love's a Luxury
1953 Murder at 3.00am
1954 Wheel of Fate
1954 The Profile
1956 The Gelignite Gang
1958 The Undercover Girl
1959 Murder at Site 3
1960 Trouble with Eve
1960 Ticket to Paradise
1961 Freedom to Die
1962 Emergency
1962 Gaolbreak
1963 Dead Man's Evidence
1963 Night of the Prowler
1963 The Marked One
(also many documentaries)

SEARS, Fred F
(1913–1957) Massachusetts, USA.
1949 Desert Vigilante
1949 Horsemen of the Sierras / *Remember Me*
1950 Across the Badlands / *The Challenge*
1950 Raiders of Tomahawk Creek / *Circle of Fear*
1950 Lightning Guns / *Taking Sides*
1951 Prairie Roundup
1951 Ridin' the Outlaw Trail
1951 Snake River Desperadoes
1951 Bonanza Town / *Two Fisted Agent*
1951 Pecos River / *Without Risk*
1952 Smokey Canyon
1952 The Hawk of Wild River
1952 The Kid from Broken Gun
1952 Last Train from Bombay
1952 Target Hong Kong
1953 Ambush at Tomahawk Gap
1953 The 49th Man
1953 Mission Over Korea / *Eyes of the Skies*
1953 Sky Commando
1953 The Nebraskan
1954 El Alamein / *Desert Patrol*
1954 Overland Pacific
1954 The Miami Story
1954 Massacre Canyon
1954 The Outlaw Stallion
1955 Wyoming Renegades
1955 Cell 2455, Death Row
1955 Chicago Syndicate
1955 Apache Ambush
1955 Teenage Crimewave
1955 Inside Detroit
1956 Fury at Gunsight Pass
1956 Rock Around the Clock
1956 Earth Versus the Flying Saucers
1956 The Werewolf
1956 Miami Exposé
1956 Cha-Cha-Cha Boom!
1956 Rumble on the Docks
1956 Don't Knock the Rock
1957 Utah Blaine
1957 Calypso Heatwave
1957 The Night the World Exploded
1957 The Giant Claw
1957 Escape from San Quentin
1958 The World was His Jury
1958 Going Steady
1958 Crash Landing
1958 Badman's Country
1958 Ghost of the China Seas

SEATON, George (George Stenius)
(1911–1979) South Bend, Indiana, USA.
1945 Diamond Horseshoe
1945 Junior Miss
1946 The Shocking Miss Pilgrim
1947 Miracle on 34th Street / *The Big Heart* **F***
1948 Apartment for Peggy
1949 Chicken Every Sunday
1950 The Big Lift
1950 For Heaven's Sake
1952 Anything Can Happen
1953 Little Boy Lost
1954 Chief Crazy Horse
1954 The Country Girl **D* F***

1956 The Proud and the Profane
1957 Williamsburg
1958 Teacher's Pet
1961 The Pleasure of His Company
1962 The Counterfeit Traitor
1963 The Hook
1965 36 Hours
1968 What's So Bad About Feeling Good?
1970 Airport F*
1973 Showdown

SEBASTIAN, Beverly
1974 Gator Bait **(Ferd SEBASTIAN)**
1974 The Single Girls **(Ferd SEBASTIAN)**
1979 Delta Fox **(Ferd SEBASTIAN)**
1979 On the Air with Captain Midnight **(Ferd SEBASTIAN)**

SEBASTIAN, Ferd
1974 Gator Bait **(Beverly SEBASTIAN)**
1974 The Single Girls **(Beverly SEBASTIAN)**
1979 Delta Fox **(Beverly SEBASTIAN)**
1979 On the Air with Captain Midnight **(Beverly SEBASTIAN)**

SEDGWICK, Edward
(1893–1953) American.
1924 Broadway or Bust
1924 40-Horse Hawkins
1924 Hit and Run
1924 Hook and Ladder
1924 Ride for Your Life
1924 The Ridin' Kid from Powder River
1924 The Sawdust Trail
1925 The Hurricane Kid
1925 Let 'Er Buck
1925 Lorraine of the Lions
1925 The Saddle Hawk
1925 Two-Fisted Jones
1926 The Flaming Frontier
1926 The Runaway Express
1926 Under Western Skies
1926 Tin Hats
1926 Slide Kelly Slide
1927 The Bugle Call
1927 West Point
1927 Spring Fever
1928 The Cameraman
1928 Circus Rookies
1929 Spite Marriage
1930 Free and Easy
1930 Dough Boys / *Forward March*
1931 Parlour, Bedroom and Bath / *Romeo in Pyjamas*
1931 A Dangerous Affair
1931 Maker of Men
1932 The Passionate Plumber
1932 Speak Easily
1933 What! No Beer?
1933 Saturday's Millions
1933 Horseplay
1934 The Poor Rich
1934 I'll Tell the World
1934 Here Comes the Groom
1934 Death on the Diamond
1935 Father Brown, Detective
1935 Murder in the Fleet
1935 The Virginia Judge
1936 Mister Cinderella
1937 Pick a Star
1937 Riding on Air
1937 Fit for a King
1938 The Gladiator
1939 Bring 'Em Up O'Connor
1939 Beware Spooks!
1940 So You Won't Talk?
1943 Air Raid Wardens
1948 A Southern Yankee / *My Hero*
1951 Ma and Pa Kettle Back on the Farm

SEDLEY, Gerri
1975 Teenage Hitch-Hikers

SEGAL, Alex
(1915–1977) American.
1955 Ransom
1963 All the Way Home
1965 Joy in the Morning
1965 Harlow

SEIDELMAN, Arthur Allen
1970 Hercules in New York / *Hercules Goes Bananas*
1975 Children of Rage
1983 Echoes
1987 The Caller

SEIDELMAN, Susan
1982 Smithereens
1985 Desperately Seeking Susan
1987 Making Mr Right
1989 Cookie
1990 The Life and Loves of a She-Devil

SEILER, Lewis
(1891–1963) New York, USA.
1924 Darwin Was Right
1926 The Great A and K Train Robbery
1926 No Man's Trail
1927 Outlaws of Red River
1927 Tumbling River
1927 The Wolf's Fangs
1928 The Air Circus
1928 Square Crooks
1929 The Ghost Talks
1929 Girls Gone Wild
1929 A Song of Kentucky
1932 No Greater Love / *Divine Love*
1934 Deception
1935 Charlie Chan in Paris
1935 Ginger
1935 Paddy O'Day
1936 Here Comes Trouble
1936 The First Baby
1936 Star for a Night
1936 Career Woman
1937 Turn Off the Moon
1938 He Couldn't Say No
1938 Crime School
1938 Penrod's Double Trouble
1938 Heart of the North
1939 King of the Underworld
1939 You Can't Get Away with Murder
1939 The Kid from Kokomo / *The Orphan of the Ring*
1939 Hell's Kitchen **(E A DUPONT)**
1939 Dust Be My Destiny
1940 It All Came True
1940 Flight Angels
1940 Murder in the Air

1940 Tugboat Annie Sails Again
1940 South of the Suez
1941 Kisses for Breakfast
1941 The Smiling Ghost
1941 You're in the Army Now
1941 International Squadron
1942 The Big Shot
1942 Pittsburgh
1943 Guadalcanal Diary
1944 Something for the Boys
1945 Molly and Me
1945 Doll Face / *Come Back to Me*
1946 If I'm Lucky
1948 Whiplash
1950 Breakthrough
1951 The Tanks Are Coming **(D Ross LEDERMAN)**
1952 The Winning Team
1952 Operation Secret
1953 The System
1954 The Bamboo Prison
1955 Battle Stations
1955 Woman's Prison
1956 Over-Exposed
1958 The True Story of Lynn Stuart
(also many shorts)

SEITER, William A
(1891–1964) American.
1924 Daddies
1924 The Family Secret
1924 The Fast Worker
1925 Where Was I?
1925 Dangerous Innocence
1925 The Teaser
1925 The Mad Whirl
1926 What Happened to Jones
1926 Skinner's Dress Suit
1926 Rolling Home
1926 Take It from Me
1927 The Cheerful Fraud
1927 Out All Night
1927 The Small Bachelor
1927 Thanks for the Buggyride
1928 Good Morning Judge
1928 Outcast
1929 Synthetic Sin
1929 Why Be Good?
1929 Smiling Irish Eyes
1929 Prisoners
1929 Footlights and Fools
1929 Love Racket / *Such Things Happen*
1930 Strictly Modern
1930 Back Pay
1930 The Flirting Widow
1930 The Truth About Youth
1930 Sunny
1931 Kiss Me Again / *Toast of the Legion*
1931 Going Wild
1931 Big Business Girl
1931 Too Many Cooks
1931 Caught Plastered
1931 Peach O'Reno
1931 Full of Notions
1932 Way Back Home / *Old Greatheart*
1932 Girl Crazy
1932 Young Bride
1932 Is My Face Red?
1932 Hot Saturday
1932 If I Had a Million **(James CRUZE. H Bruce HUMBERSTONE, Ernst LUBITSCH, Norman Z McLEOD, Norman TAUROG)**
1933 Hello Everybody!
1933 Diplomaniacs
1933 Professional Sweetheart / *Imaginary Sweetheart*
1933 Chance at Heaven
1934 Sons of the Desert / *Fraternally Yours*
1934 Rafter Romance
1934 Sing and Love It
1934 Love Birds
1934 We're Rich Again
1934 The Richest Girl in the World
1935 Roberta
1935 The Darling Young Man
1935 Orchids to You
1935 In Person
1935 If You Could Only Cook
1936 The Moon's Our Home
1936 The Case Against Mrs Ames
1936 Dimples
1936 Stowaway
1937 This Is My Affair
1937 The Life of the Party
1937 Life Begins in College / *The Joy Parade*
1938 Sally, Irene and Mary
1938 Three Blind Mice
1938 Room Service
1938 Thanks for Everything
1939 Susannah of the Mounties
1939 Allegheny Uprising / *The First Rebel*
1940 It's a Date
1940 Hired Wife
1941 Nice Girl?
1941 Appointment for Love
1942 Broadway
1942 You Were Never Lovelier
1943 Four Jills in the Jeep
1943 Destroyer
1943 A Lady Takes a Chance / *The Cowboy and the Girl*
1944 Belle of the Yukon
1945 It's a Pleasure
1945 The Affairs of Susan
1945 That Night with You
1946 Little Giant / *On the Carpet*
1946 Lover Come Back
1947 I'll Be Yours
1948 Up in Central Park
1948 One Touch of Venus
1950 Borderline
1952 Dear Brat
1953 The Lady Wants Mink
1953 Champ for a Day
1954 Make Haste to Live

SEITZ, George B (George Brackett Seitz)
(1888–1944) Boston, Massachusetts, USA.
1925 The Vanishing American
1925 Wildhorse Mesa
1926 Pals in Paradise
1926 The Last Frontier
1926 The Ice Flood
1926 Desert Gold
1927 Jim the Conqueror
1927 The Blood Ship
1927 The Great Mail Robbery

1927 The Tigress
1927 The Warning
1928 Ransom
1928 Beware of Blondes
1928 Hey Rube! / *High Stakes*
1928 Court Martial
1928 The Circus Kid
1928 Blockade
1929 The Thirteenth Chair
1929 Black Magic
1930 The Murder on the Roof
1930 Guilty
1930 Midnight Mystery
1930 Danger Lights
1931 Drums of Jeopardy / *The Virtuous Wife*
1931 The Lion and the Lamb
1931 Arizona
1931 Shanghaied Love
1931 The Night Beat
1932 Docks of San Francisco
1932 Sally of the Subway
1932 Sin's Pay Day
1932 Passport to Paradise
1932 The Widow in Scarlet
1933 Treason
1933 The Thrill Hunt
1933 The Woman in His Life
1934 Lazy River
1934 The Fighting Rangers
1935 Only Eight Hours
1935 Society Doctor
1935 Shadow of Doubt
1935 Times Square Lady
1935 Calm Yourself
1935 Woman Wanted
1935 Kind Lady / *House of Menace*
1936 Exclusive Story
1936 Absolute Quiet
1936 The Three Wise Guys
1936 The Last of the Mohicans **(Wallace FOX)**
1936 Mad Holiday
1937 Under Cover of Night
1937 A Family Affair
1937 The Thirteenth Chair
1937 Mama Steps Out
1937 Between Two Women / *Surrounded By Women*
1937 My Dear Miss Aldrich
1938 You're Only Young Twice
1938 Judge Hardy's Children
1938 Yellow Jack
1938 Love Finds Andy Hardy
1939 Six Thousand Enemies
1939 Thunder Afloat
1939 Judge Hardy and Son
1940 Judge Hardy Meets Debutante
1940 Kit Carson
1940 Sky Murder
1940 Gallant Sons
1941 Andy Hardy's Private Secretary
1941 A Yank on the Burma Road / *China Caravan*
1941 Life Begins for Andy Hardy
1942 The Courtship of Andy Hardy
1942 Pierre of the Plains
1942 Andy Hardy's Double Life
1944 Andy Hardy's Blonde Trouble
(also many serials)

SEKELY, Steve (Istvan Szekely)
(1899–1979) Hungary.
1940 A Miracle on Main Street
1943 Behind Prison Walls
1943 Revenge of the Zombies
1943 Women in Bondage
1944 Lady in the Death House
1944 Waterfront
1944 My Buddy
1944 Lake Placid Serenade
1946 The Fabulous Suzanne
1947 Blonde Savage
1948 Hollow Triumph / *The Scar*
1949 Amazon Quest
1952 Stronghold
1959 Desert Desperadoes
1963 The Day of the Triffids
1969 Kenner

SELANDER, Lesley
(1900–1980) California, USA.
1936 Sandflow
1936 Ride 'Em Cowboy
1936 Empty Saddles
1936 Boss Rider of Gun Creek
1937 Left-Handed Law
1937 Smoke Tree Range
1937 Hopalong Rides Again
1937 The Barrier
1937 Partners of the Plains
1938 Cassidy of Bar 20
1938 The Heart of Arizona
1938 Bar 20 Justice
1938 Pride of the West
1938 The Mysterious Rider
1938 Sunset Trail
1938 The Frontiersman
1939 Silver on the Sage
1939 Heritage of the Desert
1939 Renegade Trail
1939 Range War
1940 Santa Fe Marshal
1940 Knights of the Range
1940 The Light of Western Stars
1940 Hidden Gold
1940 Stagecoach War
1940 Three Men from Texas
1940 Cherokee Strip / *Fighting Marshal*
1941 Doomed Caravan
1941 The Round Up
1941 Pirates on Horseback
1941 Wide Open Town
1941 Riders of the Timberline
1941 Stick to Your Guns
1941 Thundering Hoofs
1942 Undercover Man
1942 Bandit Ranger
1942 Red River Robin Hood
1943 Lost Canyon
1943 Buckskin Frontier / *The Iron Road*
1943 Border Patrol
1943 Colt Comrades
1943 Bar 20
1943 Riders of the Deadline
1944 Lumberjack
1944 Call of the Rockies
1944 Forty Thieves
1944 Bordertown Trail
1944 Sheriff of Sundown
1944 Firebrands of Arizona

1944 Sheriff of Las Vegas
1944 Stagecoach to Monterey
1944 Cheyenne Wildcat
1945 The Great Stagecoach Robbery
1945 The Vampire's Ghost
1945 The Trail of Kit Carson
1945 Three's a Crowd
1945 The Fatal Witness
1945 Phantom of the Plains
1946 The Catman of Paris
1946 Passkey to Danger
1946 Traffic in Crime
1946 Night Train to Memphis
1946 Out California Way
1947 The Pilgrim Lady
1947 The Last Frontier Uprising
1947 Saddle Pals
1947 Robin Hood of Texas
1947 The Red Stallion
1947 Blackmail
1948 Panhandle
1948 Guns of Hate
1948 Belle Starr's Daughter
1948 Indian Agent
1948 Strike It Rich
1949 Brothers in the Saddle
1949 Rustlers
1949 Stampede
1949 Sky Dragon
1949 The Mysterious Desperado
1949 Masked Raiders
1949 Riders of the Range
1950 Dakota Lil
1950 Storm Over Wyoming
1950 Rider from Tucson
1950 The Kangaroo Kid
1950 Rio Grande Patrol
1950 Short Grass
1950 Law of the Badlands
1951 Saddle Legion
1951 I Was an American Spy
1951 Gunplay
1951 Cavalry Scout
1951 Pistol Harvest
1951 The Highwayman
1951 Flight to Mars
1951 Overland Telegraph
1952 Fort Osage
1952 Trail Guide
1952 Road Agent
1952 Desert Passage
1952 The Raiders / *Riders of Vengeance*
1952 Battle Zone
1952 Flat Top / *Eagles of the Fleet*
1953 Fort Vengeance
1953 Cow Country
1953 War Paint
1953 Fort Algiers
1953 The Royal African Rifles / *Storm Over Africa*
1953 Fighter Attack
1954 Shotgun
1954 Tall Man Riding
1954 Desert Sands
1954 Fort Yuma
1954 Tomahawk Trail / *Mark of the Apache*
1956 Revolt at Fort Laramie
1956 Outlaw's Son
1956 Taming Sutton's Gal
1956 The Wayward Girl
1958 The Lone Ranger and the Lost City of Gold
1965 War Party
1965 Fort Courageous
1965 Convict Stage
1965 Town Tamer
1966 The Texican
1967 Fort Utah
1968 Arizona Bushwackers

SELIGNAC, Arnaud
1984 Dream One

SELL, Jack M
(1954–) Albany, Georgia, USA.
1980 The Psychotronic Man
1984 Outtakes

SELLAR, Ian
1989 Venus Peter

SELLERS, Peter (Richard Sellers)
(1925–1980) Southsea, Hampshire, England.
Biographies: P.S. I Love You: Peter Sellers 1925–1980 by Michael Sellers; Peter Sellers, the Authorised Biography by Alexander Walker.
1961 Mr Topaze / *I Like Money*

SELLIER jnr, Charles E
1983 In Search of a Golden Sky / *Children of the North Woods*
1984 Smooth Moves / *Snowballing*
1984 Silent Night, Deadly Night
1986 The Annihilators

SELMAN, David
1934 The Prescott Kid
1934 The Westerner
1935 Fighting Shadows
1935 Gallant Defender
1935 Justice on the Range
1935 The Revenge Rider
1935 Riding Wild
1935 Square Shooter
1936 Shakedown
1936 Killer at Large
1936 The Cowboy Star
1936 The Mysterious Avenger
1936 Secret Patrol
1936 Dangerous Intrigue
1936 Tugboat Princess
1937 The Texas Trail
1937 Find the Witness
1937 Thunder Trail
1938 Women Against the World

SELTZER, David
1986 Lucas
1988 Punchline

SELWYN, Edgar
(1875–1944) American
1930 War Nurse
1930 Girl in the Show
1931 Men Call It Love
1931 The Sin of Madelon Claudet / *The Lullaby*

Lullaby
1932 Skyscraper Souls
1933 Men Must Fight
1933 Turn Back the Clock
1934 The Mystery of Mr X
1940 The Golden Fleecing

SENNETT, Mack (Mikall Sinnott)
(1880–1960) Danville, Quebec, Canada.
Autobiography: Mack Sennett: King of Comedy as told to Cameron Shipp.
Biography: Father Goose: The Story of Mack Sennett by Gene Fowler.
1923 The Extra Girl
1928 The Goodbye Kiss
1929 Midnight Daddies
1933 Hypnotized
(also a multitude of shorts 1910–1935)

SERESIN, Michael
1988 Homeboy

SERIOUS, Yahoo
1988 Young Einstein

SERREAU, Coline *
(1947–) French.
1986 Three Men and a Cradle
1989 Romauld and Juliet

SESSA, Alejandro (Alex Sessa)
1987 Amazons
1988 Stormquest

SEWELL, Vernon
(1903–) British.
1943 The Silver Fleet **(Gordon WELLESLEY)**
1944 The World Owes Me a Living
1945 Latin Quarter / *Frenzy*
1947 The Ghost of Berkeley Square
1948 Uneasy Terms
1951 The Black Widow
1952 The Ghost Ship
1953 Counter Spy / *Undercover Agent*
1953 The Floating Dutchman
1954 Dangerous Voyage
1955 Where There's a Will
1956 Soho Incident / *Spin a Dark Web*
1956 Home and Away
1956 Johnny You're Wanted
1957 Rogue's Yarn
1958 The Battle of the V1 / *Missiles from Hell / Unseen Heroes*
1959 Wrong Number
1960 Urge to Kill
1961 The Man in the Back Seat
1961 Strongroom
1961 House of Mystery
1961 The Wind of Change
1963 A Matter of Choice
1967 The Bloodbeast Terror
1967 Some May Live
1968 Curse of the Crimson Altar / *Crimson Cult*
1971 Burke and Hare
(also documentaries)

SEYMOUR, Sheldon *see* **Herschell G LEWIS**

SGARRO, Nicholas
1975 The Happy Hooker

SHADBURNE, Susan
1986 Shadow Play

SHAFTEL, Josef
1955 The Naked Hills
1956 No Place to Hide

SHAH, Krishna
(1938–) India.
1972 Rivals
1976 The River Niger
1978 Shalimar
1984 Hard Rock Zombies
1984 American Drive-In
1988 Strictly Personal

SHANE, Maxwell
(1905–1983) American.
1947 Fear in the Night
1949 City Across the River
1952 The Glass Wall
1955 The Naked Street
1956 Nightmare

SHANKLIN, Lina
1983 Summerspell

SHANKS, Don
1987 The Legend of Grizzly Adams

SHAPIRO, Ken
(1943–) New Jersey, USA.
1974 The Groove Tube
1981 Modern Problems
1988 Forbidden Fruit

SHARMAN, Jim
1972 Shirley Thompson Versus the Aliens
1976 The Rocky Horror Picture Show
1976 Summer of Secrets
1978 The Night of the Prowler
1981 Shock Treatment

SHARON, Yoel
1989 Shell Shock

SHARP, Alan
1985 Little Treasure

SHARP, Don
(1922–) Hobart, Tasmania.
1955 The Golden Airliner
1958 The Adventures of Hal.5
1958 The In-Between Age / *The Golden Disc*
1960 The Professionals
1961 Linda
1963 It's All Happening / *The Dream Maker*
1963 Kiss of the Vampire / *Kiss of Evil*
1964 The Devil-Ship Pirates
1964 Witchcraft
1965 The Face of Fu Manchu
1965 Curse of the Fly
1966 Rasputin, The Mad Monk / *I Killed Rasputin*
1966 Bang Bang You're Dead / *Our Man in Marrakesh*
1966 The Brides of Fu Manchu

1967 Those Fantastic Flying Fools / *Blast Off / Jules Verne's Rocket to the Moon*
1968 Taste of Excitement
1969 The Violent Enemy
1972 Puppet on a Chain **(Geoffrey REEVE)**
1973 Psychomania / *The Death Wheeler*
1974 Dark Places
1975 Hennessy
1975 Callan
1978 The 39 Steps
1980 Bear Island
1984 What Waits Below
1988 Tears in the Rain

SHARP, Ian
(1946–) Clitheroe, Lancashire, England.
1979 The Music Machine
1983 Who Dares Wins / *The Final Option*

SHATNER, William
(1931–) Montreal, Canada.
1989 Star Trek V: Final Frontier

SHAUGHNESSY, Alfred
(1916–) British.
Autobiography: Both Ends of the Candle.
1961 The Impersonator

SHAVELSON, Melville
(1917–) Brooklyn, New York, USA.
1955 The Seven Little Foys
1957 Beau James
1958 Houseboat
1959 The Five Pennies
1960 It Started in Naples
1961 On the Double
1962 The Pigeon That Took Rome
1963 A New Kind of Love
1966 Cast a Giant Shadow
1968 Yours, Mine and Ours
1972 The War Between Men and Women
1974 Mixed Company
(also many TV movies)

SHAW, Tom
1988 Operation: Take No Prisoners

SHAYNE, Linda
1989 Purple People Eater

SHEA, Jack
(1928–) New York, New York, USA.
1968 Dayton's Devils
1969 The Monitors

SHEA, William
1936 Girl of the Ozarks

SHEAR, Barry
(1923–1979) American.
1967 The Karate Killers
1968 Wild in the Streets
1970 The Todd Killings
1972 Across 110th Street
1973 The Deadly Trackers

SHEBIB, Donald
(1938–) Toronto, Canada.
Pseudonym: D.S. Everett.
1970 Goin' Down the Road
1971 Rip-Off
1973 Between Friends
1976 Second Wind
1981 Fish Hawk
1982 Heartaches
1983 Running Brave
1987 The Climb

SHELACH, Riki
1983 The Last Winter
1987 Freedom Fighters

SHELDON, Forrest
1931 Law of the Rio Grande **(Bennett COHEN)**
1932 Between Fighting Men
1932 Dynamite Ranch
1932 Hellfire Austin
1932 Lone Trail
1935 Wilderness Mail

SHELDON, Norman
1949 Rio Grande

SHELDON, Sidney
(1917–) Chicago, Illinois, USA.
1953 Dream Wife
1957 The Buster Keaton Story

SHELTON, Ron
1988 Bull Durham
1990 Blaze

SHEPARD, Sam
1988 Far North

SHEPHARD, Mark
1987 Dark Romances

SHEPPARD, John
1987 Mania **(Paul LYNCH, D M ROBERTSON)**
1988 Higher Education

SHER, Jack
(1913–) Minneapolis, Minnesota, USA.
1956 Four Girls in Town
1958 Kathy O
1959 The Wild and the Innocent
1959 The Three Worlds of Gulliver
1961 Love in a Goldfish Bowl

SHERIN, Edwin
(1930–) Danville, Pennsylvania, USA.
1971 Valdez Is Coming
1972 My Old Man's Place / *Glory Boy*

SHERMAN, Gary A
1973 Raw Meat / *Death Line*
1981 Dead and Buried
1982 Vice Squad
1986 Wanted: Dead or Alive
1988 Poltergeist III

SHERMAN, George
(1908–) New York, New York, USA.

1938 Wild Horse Rodeo
1938 The Purple Vigilantes / *The Purple Riders*
1938 Outlaws of Sonora
1938 Riders of the Black Hills
1938 Pals of the Saddle
1938 Overland Stage Raiders
1938 Rhythm of the Saddle
1938 Santa Fe Stampede
1938 Red River Range
1939 Mexicali Rose
1939 The Night Riders
1939 Three Texan Steers / *Danger Rides the Range*
1939 Wyoming Outlaw
1939 Colorado Sunset
1939 New Frontier
1939 Cowboys from Texas
1939 The Kansas Terrors
1939 Rovin' Tumbleweeds
1939 South of the Border
1940 Ghost Valley Raiders
1940 One Man's Law
1940 The Tulsa Kid
1940 Texas Terrors
1940 Covered Wagon Days
1940 Rocky Mountain Rangers
1940 Under Texas Skies
1940 The Trail Blazers
1940 Lone Star Raiders
1940 Frontier Vengeance
1941 Wyoming Wildcat
1941 The Phantom Cowboy
1941 Two Gun Sheriff
1941 Desert Bandit
1941 Kansas Cyclone
1941 Death Valley Outlaws
1941 A Missouri Outlaw
1941 Citadel of Crime / *Outside the Law*
1941 The Apache Kid
1942 Arizona Terrors
1942 Stagecoach Express
1942 Jesse James Jnr
1942 The Cyclone Kid
1942 The Sombrero Kid
1942 X Marks the Spot
1942 London Blackout Murders / *Secret Motive*
1943 The Purple V
1943 The Mantrap
1943 The West Side Kid
1943 Mystery Broadcast
1944 The Lady and the Monster / *The Lady and the Doctor*
1944 Storm Over Lisbon
1945 The Crime Doctor's Courage
1946 The Gentleman Misbehaves
1946 Renegades
1946 Talk About a Lady
1946 The Bandit of Sherwood Forest **(Henry LEVIN)**
1947 Personality Kid
1947 Secrets of the Whistler
1947 Last of the Redmen
1948 Relentless
1948 Black Bart
1948 River Lady
1948 Larceny
1949 Red Canyon
1949 Calamity Jane and Sam Bass
1949 Yes Sir, That's My Baby
1949 Sword in the Desert
1950 Spy Hunt / *Panther's Moon*
1950 The Sleeping City
1950 Feudin', Fussin' and a-Fightin'
1950 Comanche Territory
1951 Tomahawk / *Battle of Powder River*
1951 Target Unknown
1951 The Raging Tide
1951 The Golden Horde
1952 Steel Town
1952 Against All Flags
1952 The Battle at Apache Pass
1952 Back at the Front / *Willie and Joe in Tokyo*
1953 The Lone Hand
1953 War Arrow
1953 Veils of Bagdad
1954 Border River
1954 Dawn at Socorro
1955 Johnny Dark
1955 Chief Crazy Horse / *Valley of Fury*
1955 Count Three and Pray
1955 The Treasure of Pancho Villa
1956 Comanche
1956 Reprisal!
1957 The Hard Man
1958 The Last of the Fast Guns
1958 Ten Days to Tulara
1959 The Son of Robin Hood
1959 The Flying Fontaines
1960 Hell Bent for Leather
1960 For the Love of Mike / *None But the Brave*
1960 The Enemy General
1960 The Wizard of Bagdad
1961 The Fiercest Heart
1964 Panic Button
1964 Murieta / *Vendetta*
1966 Smoky
1971 Big Jake

SHERMAN, Lowell
(1885–1934) American.

1930 The Pay-Off
1930 Lawful Larceny
1931 Bachelor Apartment
1931 The Royal Bed / *The Queen's Husband*
1931 High Stakes
1932 The Greeks Have a Word for Them
1932 False Faces
1932 Ladies of the Jury
1933 Morning Glory
1933 She Done Him Wrong **F***
1933 Broadway Thru a Keyhole
1934 Born to Be Bad
1935 Night Life of the Gods

SHERMAN, Vincent (Abram Orovitz)
(1906–) Vienna, Georgia, USA.

1939 The Return of Doctor X
1940 Saturday's Children
1940 The Man Who Talked Too Much
1941 Flight from Destiny
1941 Underground
1942 All Through the Night
1942 The Hard Way
1943 Old Acquaintance
1944 In Our Time
1945 Mr Skeffington

1945 Pillow to Post
1947 Nora Prentiss
1947 The Unfaithful
1949 The Adventures of Don Juan
1949 The Hasty Heart
1950 Backfire
1950 The Damned Don't Cry
1950 Harriet Craig
1951 Goodbye Mr Fancy
1952 Lone Star
1952 Affair in Trinidad
1959 The Garment Jungle
1959 The Naked Earth
1959 The Young Philadelphians / *The City Jungle*
1960 Ice Palace
1961 A Fever in the Blood
1961 The Second Time Around
1969 The Young Rebel / *Cervantes*
(also many TV movies)

SHERMANN, Arthur
1989 ZITS

SHERWOOD, Bill
(1952–) Washington, USA.
1986 Parting Glances

SHERWOOD, John
1956 Raw Edge
1956 The Creature Walks Among Us
1957 The Monolith Monsters

SHIELDS, Frank
1987 The Surfer

SHIELDS, Pat
1973 Frasier, the Sensuous Lion

SHILLINGFORD, Peter
1970 Today Mexico, Tomorrow the World
1979 The English Abroad

SHINDO, Kaneto
(1922–) Hiroshima, Prefecture, Japan.
1951 Story of My Loving Wife
1952 Avalanche
1952 Children of the Atom Bomb
1953 Epitome
1953 A Life of a Woman
1954 Gutter
1955 Wolves
1956 Silver Double Suicide
1956 Bank of Departure
1956 An Actress
1957 Guys of the Sea
1957 Sorrow Is Only for Women
1959 The World's Best Bride
1959 Graffiti Blackboard
1960 The Island
1962 Human Being
1962 Mother
1964 Onibaba — The Hole / *The Demon*
1964 Passion
1965 Conquest
1965 A Scoundrel
1966 Instinct
1966 Monument of Totsuseki
1966 Four Seasons of Tateshina
1967 Origin of Sex
1968 A Black Cat in the Bush
1968 Strong Woman and Weak Man
1969 Heat Haze
1970 Tentacles
1970 Naked Nineteen Year Old
1972 Iron Ring
1972 A Paean
1973 Heart
1974 My Way
1977 Life of Chikuzan
1982 Hokusai, Ukiyoe Master
1984 The Horizon

SHINODA, Masahiro
(1931–) Gifu, Prefecture, Japan.
1960 One Way Ticket to Love
1960 Dry Lake
1961 My Face Red in the Sunset
1961 Epitaph to My Love
1961 Shamisen and Motorcycle
1962 Our Marriage
1962 Glory on the Summit: Burning Youth
1962 Tears on the Lion's Mane
1963 Pale Flower
1964 Assassination
1965 With Beauty and Sorrow
1965 Samurai Spy
1966 Punishment Island
1969 Clouds at Sunset
1969 Double Suicide
1970 The Scandalous Adventures of Buraikan
1971 Silence
1973 The Petrified Forest
1975 Under the Cherry Blossoms
1977 The Ballad of Orin
1979 Demon Pond
1980 Devil's Island
1984 MacArthur's Children
1986 Gonza, the Spearman

SHOLDER, Jack
1982 Alone in the Dark
1986 A Nightmare on Elm Street II: Freddy's Revenge
1987 Hidden
1989 Lakota

SHOLEM, Lee
(1900–) American.
1949 Tarzan's Magic Fountain
1950 Tarzan and the Slave Girl
1952 The Redhead from Wyoming
1953 The Stand at Apache River
1954 Cannibal Attack
1954 Jungle Man-Eaters
1954 Tobor the Great
1955 Ma and Pa Kettle at Waikiki
1956 Crime Against Joe
1956 Emergency Hospital
1957 Hell Ship Mutiny **(Elmo WILLIAMS)**
1957 The Pharaoh's Curse
1957 Sierra Stranger

SHORE, Sig
1975 That's the Way of the World / *Shining Star*
1984 The Act
1985 Sudden Death

1987 Jack Tillman: The Survivalist

SHORES, Lynn
1929 The Delightful Rogue
1936 The Glory Trail
1936 Million to One
1936 Rebellion
1936 Woman in Distress
1937 The Shadow Strikes
1937 Here's Flash Casey
1940 Charlie Chan at the Wax Museum
1941 Golden Hoofs

SHORT, Robert
(1950–) Santa Monica, California, USA.
1987 Goblins

SHOURDS, Sherry
1948 The Big Punch

SHUMLIN, Herman
(1898–1979) American.
1943 Watch on the Rhine **F***
1945 Confidential Agent

SHYER, Charles
(1941–) Los Angeles, California, USA.
1984 Irreconcilable Differences
1987 Baby Boom

SHYER, Melville
1933 Sucker Money **(Dorothy REID)**
1933 Murder in the Museum
1934 The Road to Ruin **(Dorothy REID)**

SIDARIS, Andy
(1933–) Chicago, Illinois, USA.
1973 Stacey
1979 Seven
1984 Malibu Express
1987 Hard Ticket to Hawaii
1988 Picasso Trigger

SIDNEY, George
(1916–) Long Island City, New York.
1941 Free and Easy
1942 Pacific Rendezvous
1943 Pilot No.5
1943 Thousands Cheer
1944 Bathing Beauty
1945 Anchors Aweigh **F***
1946 The Harvey Girls
1946 Holiday in Mexico
1947 Cass Timberlane
1948 The Three Musketeers
1949 The Red Danube
1950 Key to the City
1950 Annie Get Your Gun
1951 Show Boat
1952 Scaramouche
1953 Young Bess
1953 Kiss Me Kate
1955 Jupiter's Darling
1956 The Eddie Duchin Story
1957 Jeanne Eagels
1957 Pal Joey
1960 Who Was That Lady?
1960 Pepe
1963 Bye Bye Birdie
1963 A Ticklish Affair
1964 Viva Las Vegas / *Love in Las Vegas*
1966 The Swinger
1968 Half a Sixpence
(also many shorts)

SIEGEL, Don
(1912–) Chicago, Illinois, USA.
Pseudonym: Allen Smithee.
Biography: Don Siegel: Director by Stuart M. Kaminsky.
1946 The Verdict
1949 Night Unto Night
1949 The Big Steal
1952 Duel at Silver Creek
1952 No Time for Flowers
1953 Count the Hours / *Every Minute Counts*
1953 China Venture
1954 Riot in Cell Block 11
1954 Private Hell 36
1955 An Annapolis Story / *The Blue and the Gold*
1956 Invasion of the Body Snatchers
1956 Crime in the Streets
1957 Baby Face Nelson
1958 Spanish Affair
1958 The Line Up
1958 The Gun Runners
1959 Hound Dog Man
1959 Edge of Eternity
1960 Flaming Star
1962 Hell Is for Heroes
1964 The Killers
1968 Madigan
1968 Coogan's Bluff
1969 Death of a Gunfighter **(Robert TOTTEN)**
1970 Two Mules for Sister Sara
1971 The Beguiled
1972 Dirty Harry
1974 Charley Varrick
1974 The Black Windmill
1976 The Shootist
1977 Telefon
1979 Escape from Alcatraz
1980 Rough Cut
1982 Jinxed

SIEGEL, Robert J.
1972 Parades

SIGNORELLI, James
1983 Easy Money
1988 Elvira, Mistress of the Dark

SIJAN, Slobodan *
1988 Secret Ingredient

SILBERG, Joel (Yoel Zilberg)
1976 The Rabbi and the Shikse
1978 Millionaire in Trouble
1979 Marriage, Tel Aviv Style
1981 My Mother, the General
1984 Breakdancin'
1985 Rappin'
1986 Bad Guys
1987 Feel the Heat

SILVER, Joan Micklin
(1935–) Omaha, Nebraska, USA.
1974 Hester Street
1977 Between the Lines
1980 Head Over Heels / *Chilly Scenes of Winter*
1988 Crossing Delancey
1989 Loverboy

SILVER, Marcel
1929 Married in Hollywood
1929 William Fox Movietone Follies of 1929 **(David BUTLER)**
1930 One Mad Kiss

SILVER, Marisa
(1960–) Cleveland, Ohio, USA.
1984 Old Enough
1988 Permanent Record

SILVER, Raphael D
1979 On the Yard
1988 A Walk on the Moon

SILVERSTEIN, Elliot
(1927–) Boston, Massachusetts, USA.
1962 Belle Sommers
1965 Cat Ballou
1967 The Happening
1970 A Man Called Horse
1974 Deadly Honeymoon / *Nightmare Honeymoon*
1977 The Car

SIMMONS, Anthony
(c1924–) British.
1960 Your Money or Your Wife
1965 Four in the Morning
1973 The Optimists of Nine Elms
1977 Black Joy
1988 Little Sweetheart

SIMON, Francis
1977 The Chicken Chronicles

SIMON, Juan Piquer
1988 Slugs
1989 The Rift

SIMON, Roger
1985 My Man Adam

SIMON, Sylvan S
(1910–1951) American.
1937 A Girl with Ideas
1937 A Prescription for Romance
1938 The Crime of Dr Hallet
1938 Nurse from Brooklyn
1938 The Road to Reno
1938 Spring Madness
1939 Four Girls in White
1939 The Kid from Texas
1939 These Glamour Girls
1939 Dancing Co-Ed / *Every Other Inch a Lady*
1940 Two Girls on Broadway / *Choose Your Partner*
1940 Sporting Blood
1940 Dulcy
1941 Keeping Company
1941 Washington Melodrama
1941 Whistling in the Dark
1941 The Bugle Sounds
1942 Rio Rita
1942 Grand Central Murder
1942 Tish
1942 Whistling in Dixie
1943 Salute to the Marines
1943 Whistling in Brooklyn
1944 Son of Lassie
1944 Abbott and Costello in Hollywood
1946 Bad Bascomb
1946 The Cockeyed Miracle / *Mr Griggs Returns*
1946 The Thrill of Brazil
1947 Her Husband's Affairs
1948 I Love Trouble
1948 The Fuller Brush Man / *That Mad Mr Jones*
1949 Lust for Gold

SIMPSON, Michael A
1986 Impure Thoughts
1987 Funland
1988 Unhappy Campers / *Sleepaway Camp II*
1988 Mace
1989 Sleepaway Camp III / *Teenage Wasteland*
1989 Fast Food

SINATRA, Frank
(1915–) Hoboken, New Jersey, USA. Biographies: Sinatra by Alan Frank. Frank Sinatra My Father by Nancy Sinatra.
1965 None But the Brave

SINCLAIR, Andrew
(1935–) British.
1971 The Breaking of Bumbo
1971 Under Milk Wood
1973 Blue Blood

SINCLAIR, Robert B
(1905–1970) American.
1938 Dramatic School
1938 Woman Against Woman
1939 Joe and Ethel Turp Call on the President
1940 The Captain Is a Lady
1940 And One Was Beautiful
1941 The Wild Man of Borneo
1941 I'll Wait for You
1941 Down in San Diego
1942 Mr and Mrs North
1947 Mr District Attorney
1958 That Wonderful Urge

SINDELL, Gerald Seth
(1944–) Cleveland, Ohio, USA.
1967 Double-Stop
1974 Teenager
1979 H.O.T.S.

SINESE, Gary
1988 Farm of the Year / *Miles from Home*

SINGER, Alexander
(1932–) New York, New York, USA.
1960 A Cold Wind in August
1964 Love Has Many Faces
1964 Psyche 59
1971 Captain Apache
1972 Glass Houses
(also many TV movies)

SINGER, Stanford
1987 I Was a Teenage TV Terrorist / *Amateur Hour*

SIODMAK, Curt
(1902–) Germany.
1951 Bridge of the Gorilla
1953 The Magnetic Monster
1956 Curuco, Beast of the Amazon
1957 Love Slaves of the Amazon
1959 Ski Fever

SIODMAK, Robert
(1900–1973) Memphis, Tennessee, USA.
Autobiography: Zwischen Berlin und Hollywood: Erinnerungen eines Grossen Filmregisseurs.
1929 People on Sunday
1931 Looking for His Murderer
1931 Inquest
1931 Tempest
1932 Quick
1933 The Burning Secret
1933 The Weaker Sex
1936 Mister Flow
1936 Woman Racket / *Traffic in Souls*
1937 Hatred
1939 Snares / *Personal Column*
1941 West Point Widow
1942 Fly By Night / *Secrets of 632*
1942 The Night Before the Divorce
1942 My Heart Belongs to Daddy
1943 Someone to Remember
1943 Son of Dracula
1944 Phantom Lady
1944 Cobra Woman
1944 Christmas Holiday
1944 The Suspect
1944 Uncle Harry
1945 The Spiral Staircase
1946 The Killers / *A Man Alone*
1946 The Dark Mirror
1947 Time Out of Mind
1948 Cry of the City
1949 Criss Cross
1949 The Great Sinner
1949 Thelma Jordan
1949 The Crimson Pirate
1950 Deported
1951 The Whistle at Eaton Falls / *Richer Than the Earth*
1954 Flesh and the Woman / *Le Grand Jeu*
1957 The Devil Strikes at Night
1959 The Rough and the Smooth / *Portrait of a Sinner*
1960 The Magnificent Sinner / *Katja*
1962 Tunnel 28 / *Escape from East Berlin*
1964 The Yellow Devil
1968 Custer of the West

SIRK, Douglas (Claus Detlev Sierk or Hans Detlef Sierck)
(1900–1987) Hamburg, Germany.
1935 April, April
1935 The Pillars of Society
1936 Final Accord / *Ninth Symphony*
1937 To New Shores / *Life Begins Anew*
1939 Wilton's Zoo
1943 Hitler's Madmen
1944 Summer Storm
1946 Thieves' Holiday / *A Scandal in Paris*
1947 Lured / *Personal Column*
1948 Sleep My Love
1949 Shock Proof
1949 Slightly French
1950 Mystery Submarine
1951 The First Legion
1951 The Lady Pays Off
1951 Thunder on the Hill / *Bonaventure*
1951 Weekend with Father
1952 Has Anybody Seen My Gal?
1952 Meet Me at the Fair
1952 No Room for the Groom
1953 All I Desire
1953 Take Me to Town
1954 Magnificent Obsession
1954 Sign of the Pagan
1954 Taza, Son of Conchise
1955 Captain Lightfoot
1955 All That Heaven Allows
1956 Battle Hymn
1956 There's Always Tomorrow
1956 Written on the Wind
1957 Interlude
1957 The Tarnished Angels
1958 A Time to Love and a Time to Die
1959 Imitation of Life

SJOMAN, Vilgot (David Harald Vilgot Sjöman)
(1924–) Stockholm, Sweden.
1962 The Swedish Mistress
1964 491
1964 The Dress
1965 Stimulantia
1966 My Sister My Love / *Syskonbadd 1782*
1967 I Am Curious — Yellow
1968 I Am Curious — Blue
1969 You're Lying
1970 Blushing Charlie
1971 Till Sex Do Us Part / *Troll*
1972 The Karlsson Brothers
1974 A Handful of Love
1975 The Garage
1977 Tabu
1979 Linus and the Mysterious Red Brick House
1982 I Am Blushing

SJOSTROM, Victor (Victor Seastrom)
(1879–1960) Silbodal, Sweden.
1924 He Who Gets Slapped
1925 Confessions of a Queen
1925 The Tower of Lies
1926 The Scarlet Letter
1927 The Divine Woman
1927 The Wind
1928 Masks of the Devil
1930 A Lady to Love
1931 Father and Son

1937 Under the Red Robe

SKOLIMOWSKI, Jerzy (Yurek Skolimowski)
(1938–) Warsaw, Poland.
1964 Identification Marks: None
1965 Walkover
1966 Barrier
1967 Hands Up!
1968 Dialogue
1969 The Adventures of Girard
1971 Deep End
1972 King, Queen, Knave
1979 The Shout
1982 Moonlighting
1984 Success Is the Best Revenge
1985 The Lightship

SKOTAK, Bob
1988 Invasion Earth: They Came from Outer Space

SLATE, Lane
1971 Clay Pigeon **(Tom STERN)**

SLATZER, Robert F
1973 Big Foot

SLOANE, Paul H
(1893–) American
1925 A Man Must Live
1925 The Shock Punch
1925 Too Many Kisses
1926 The Clinging Vine
1929 Hearts in Dixie **(A H Van BUREN)**
1930 The Cuckoos
1930 Half Shot at Sunrise
1930 Three Sisters
1931 Travelling Husbands
1931 Consolation Marriage
1932 War Correspondent
1933 The Woman Accused
1933 Terror Abroad
1934 Straight Is the Way
1934 The Lone Cowboy
1934 Down to Their Last Yacht
1935 Here Comes the Band
1940 Geronimo!
1951 The Sun Sets at Dawn

SLOANE, Rick
1987 The Visitants

SLOMAN, Edward
(1887–) American.
1925 The Price of Pleasure
1925 The Stormbreaker
1925 Up the Ladder
1926 The Beautiful Cheat
1926 Butterflies in the Rain
1926 The Old Soak
1927 Alias the Deacon
1928 The Foreign Legion
1928 We Americans
1929 The Girl on the Barge
1929 The Kibitzer
1930 The Lost Zeppelin
1930 Puttin' on the Ritz
1930 Hell's Island
1930 Soldiers and Women
1931 His Woman
1931 The Conquering Horde
1931 Gun Smoke
1931 Murder By the Clock
1931 Caught
1932 Wayward
1934 There's Always Tomorrow
1935 A Dog of Flanders
1938 The Jury's Secret

SLUZIER, George
1987 Red Desert Penitentiary

SMALLCOMBE, John
1989 An African Dream

SMART, Ralph
(1908–) British.
1947 A Boy, a Girl and a Bike
1947 Bush Christmas
1949 Quartet **(Ken ANNAKIN, Arthur CRABTREE, Harold FRENCH)**
1950 Bitter Springs
1952 Curtain Up
1954 Always a Bride

SMAWLEY, Robert
1988 Murphy's Fault

SMIGHT, Jack
(1926–) Minneapolis, Minnesota, USA.
1964 I'd Rather Be Rich
1965 The Third Day
1966 Harper / *The Moving Target*
1966 Kaleidoscope / *The Bank Breaker*
1968 The Secret War of Harry Frigg
1968 No Way to Treat a Lady
1969 Strategy of Terror / *In Darkness Waiting*
1969 The Illustrated Man
1970 Rabbit, Run
1970 The Travelling Executioner
1974 Airport 1975
1976 Midway
1977 Damnation Alley
1979 Fast Break
1980 Loving Couples
1987 Number One with a Bullet
1988 The Favourite
(also many TV movies)

SMITH, Bud
1988 Johnny Be Good / *Quarterback Sneak*

SMITH, Charles Martin
(1954–) Los Angeles, California, USA.
1986 Trick or Treat
1989 Boris and Natasha in Our Boy Badenov

SMITH, Clifford
(1894–1937) American.
1916 The Aryan **(William S HART)**
1924 Sing Jim McKee
1924 The Back Trail
1924 Fighting Fury
1924 Ridgeway of Montana
1924 The Western Wallop
1924 Daring Changes

1924 The Call of Courage
1925 Don Dare Devil
1925 Flying Hoofs
1925 The Red Rider
1925 Ridin' Pretty
1925 Ridin' Thunder
1925 A Roaring Adventure
1925 The Sign of the Cactus
1925 The White Outlaw
1926 The Arizona Sweepstakes
1926 The Demon
1926 The Fighting Pacemaker
1926 The Phantom Bullet
1926 The Ridin' Rascal
1926 Rustler's Ranch
1926 The Scrappin' Kid
1926 A Shootin' Romance
1926 The Set Up
1926 Sky High Corral
1926 The Terror
1926 The Valley of Hell
1926 The Desert's Toll
1927 The Open Range
1932 Riders of Golden Gulch
1932 The Texan
1935 Devil's Canyon
1935 Five Bad Men
(also many serials)

SMITH, Harry W
1953 Louisiana Territory

SMITH, Kent
1983 Taking Tiger Mountain **(Tom HUCKABEE)**

SMITH, Mel
1989 The Tall Guy / *Camden Town Boy*

SMITH, Noel Mason
(c1890–) American
1925 Clash of Wolves
1929 Bachelor Club
1929 Back from Shanghai
1930 Heroic Lover
1931 Yankee Don
1931 Dancing Dynamite
1931 Scareheads
1935 Fighting Pilot
1936 Trailin' West
1936 King of Hockey
1937 California Mail
1937 Guns of the Pecos
1937 Blazing Sixes
1937 The Cherokee Strip
1937 Over the Goal
1938 Mystery House
1939 Secret Service of the Air
1939 Code of the Secret Service
1939 Torchy Plays with Dynamite
1939 Cowboy Quarterbacks
1940 Ladies Must Live
1940 Calling All Husbands
1940 Always a Bride
1940 Father Is a Prince
1941 The Case of the Black Parrot
1941 The Nurse's Secret
1941 Burma Convoy
1941 Here Comes Happiness
1952 Cattle Town

SMITH, Peter
1986 No Surrender

SMITH, R L *see* **Herschell G LEWIS**

SMITH, Richard
1988 Trident Force

SMITH, Robert
1988 The Love Child

SMITHEE, Allen *see* **Don SIEGEL**

SNODY, Robert R
1930 Love Kiss

SOBEL, Mark S
(1956–) Toronto, Ontario, Canada.
1984 Access Code
1987 Sweet Revenge

SOHMER, Steve
1988 Dead Heat

SOKAL, Henry
1937 A Smile in the Storm **(Bernard VORHAUS)**
1940 They Met on Skis

SOLDAY, Paul
1973 The Devil's Wedding Night

SOLE, Alfred
(1943–) Paterson, New Jersey, USA.
1977 Alice, Sweet Alice / *Communion / Holy Terror*
1981 Tanya's Island
1982 Pandemonium

SOLUM, Ola
1985 Orion's Belt
1987 Turnaround / *Deadly Illusion*

SOMMERS, Stephen
1989 Catch Me If You Can

SOMNES, George
1933 The Girl in 419 **(Alexander HALL)**
1933 Midnight Club **(Alexander HALL)**
1933 Torch Singer **(Alexander HALL)**
1934 Wharf Angel **(William Cameron MENZIES)**

SONTAG, Susan
1969 Duet for Cannibals
1972 Brother Carl

SORIN, Carlos
1989 Eversmile, New Jersey

SOS, Maria
1987 Tandem

SOTOS, Jim (Dimitri Sotirakis)
(1935–) New York, New York, USA.
1975 The Last Victim
1980 Forced Entry
1982 Sweet Sixteen
1984 Hot Moves
1988 The Silencer

1989 Beverly Hills Brats

SPANGLER, Larry G
1973 The Soul of Nigger Charley
1974 A Knife for the Ladies
1974 The Life and Times of Xaviera Hollander
1976 Joshua
1983 Silent Sentence

SPARKS, Teresa
(1952–) Kentucky, USA.
1984 Over the Summer

SPARR, Robert
1968 More Dead Than Alive
1969 Once You Kiss a Stranger

SPENCER, James H
1988 Sounds Kinda Risky

SPENCER, Norman
1935 Rainbow's End

SPERLING, Karen
1971 Make a Face

SPHEERIS, Penelope
1984 Suburbia / *Wild Side*
1985 No Apparent Motive / *The Boys Next Door*
1986 Hollywood Vice Squad
1987 Dudes
1988 The Decline of Western Civilization Part II: The Metal Years

SPIELBERG, Steven
(1947–) Cincinnati, Ohio, USA.
1971 Duel
1974 Sugarland Express
1975 Jaws **F***
1977 Close Encounters of the Third Kind **D***
1979 1941
1981 Raiders of the Lost Ark **D* F***
1982 E.T. — Extra Terrestrial **D* F***
1983 Twilight Zone — The Movie **(Joe DANTE, John LANDIS, George MILLER)**
1984 Indiana Jones and the Temple of Doom
1986 The Color Purple **F***
1987 Empire of the Sun
1989 Indiana Jones and the Last Crusade

SPITZER, Nat
1931 Monsters of the Deep

SPOTTISWOODE, Roger
(1943–) American.
1980 Terror Train
1982 The Pursuit of D.B. Cooper
1983 Under Fire
1986 The Best of Times
1988 Shoot to Kill / *Deadly Pursuit / The Mountain King*
1989 Turner and Hooch

SPRADLIN, G D
1972 The Only Way Home

SPRAGUE, Chandler
1930 Not Damaged
1930 The Dancers
1931 Their Mad Moment **(Hamilton MacFADDEN)**

SPRING, Tim
1989 A Reason to Die

SPRINGSTEEN, R G (Buddy Springsteen)
(1904–) Tacoma, Washington, USA.
1945 Marshal of Laredo
1945 Colorado Pioneers
1945 Wagon Wheels Westward
1946 California Goldrush
1946 Sheriff of Redwood Valley
1946 Home on the Range
1946 Man from Rainbow Valley
1946 Conquest of Cheyenne
1946 Santa Fe Uprising
1946 Stagecoach to Denver
1947 Vigilantes of Boomtown
1947 Homesteaders of Paradise Valley
1947 Oregon Trail Scouts
1947 Rustlers of Devil's Canyon
1947 Marshal of Cripple Creek
1947 Along the Oregon Trail
1947 Under Colorado Skies
1948 The Main Street Kid
1948 Heart of Virginia
1948 Secret Service Investigator
1948 Out of the Storm
1948 Son of God's Country
1948 Sundown in Santa Fe
1948 Renegades of Sonora
1949 Sheriff of Wichita
1949 Death Valley Gunfighter
1949 The Red Menace / *The Enemy Within*
1949 Hellfire
1949 Flame of Youth
1949 Navajo Trail Raiders
1950 Belle of Old Mexico
1950 Singing Guns
1950 Harbour of Missing Men
1950 The Arizona Cowboy
1950 Hills of Oklahoma
1950 Covered Wagon Raid
1950 Frisco Tornado
1951 Million Dollar Pursuit
1951 Honeychile
1951 Street Bandits
1952 The Fabulous Señorita
1952 Oklahoma Annie
1952 Gobs and Gals / *Cruising Casanovas*
1952 Tropical Heatwave
1952 Toughest Men in Arizona
1953 A Perilous Journey
1953 Geraldine
1955 I Cover the Underworld
1955 Double Jeopardy
1955 Cross Channel
1955 Secret Venture
1956 Track Down the Man
1956 Come Next Spring
1956 When Gangland Strikes
1957 Affair in Reno
1958 Cole Younger, Gunfighter
1958 Revolt in the Big House
1959 Battle Flame
1959 King of the Wild Stallions

1961 Operation Eichmann
1963 Showdown
1964 He Rides Tall
1964 Bullet for a Badman
1964 Taggart
1965 Black Spurs
1966 Apache Uprising
1966 Johnny Reno
1966 Waco
1967 Red Tomahawk
1967 Hostile Guns
1968 Tiger By the Tail

SPRY, Robin
(1939–) Toronto, Ontario, Canada.
1969 Prologue
1977 One Man
1978 Drying Up the Streets
1981 Hit and Run
1982 Suzanne
1984 Stress and Emotions
1986 Keeping Track
1987 Hit and Run
1988 Obsessed / *Hitting Home*

SROUR, Heiny
1984 Leila and the Wolves

STAHL, John M
(1886–1950) New York, New York, USA.
1927 The Gay Deceiver
1927 Old Kentucky
1930 A Lady Surrenders / *Blind Wives*
1931 Seed
1931 Strictly Dishonourable
1932 Back Street
1933 Only Yesterday
1934 Imitation of Life **F***
1935 Magnificent Obsession
1937 Parnell
1938 Freshman Year
1938 Letter of Introduction
1939 When Tomorrow Comes
1941 Our Wife
1942 The Immortal Sergeant
1943 Holy Matrimony
1944 The Eve of St Mark
1944 Keys of the Kingdom
1945 Leave Her to Heaven
1947 The Foxes of Harrow
1948 The Walls of Jericho
1949 Father Was a Fullback
1949 Oh, You Beautiful Doll

STALLONE, Sylvester (Michael Sylvester Stallone)
(1946–) New York, New York, USA. Biography: Stallone! A Hero's Story: An Unauthorised Story by Jeff Rovin.
1978 Paradise Alley
1979 Rocky II
1982 Rocky III
1983 Staying Alive
1985 Rocky IV

STANLEY, Paul
1959 Cry Tough
1968 Three Guns for Texas **(Earl BELLAMY, David Lowell RICH)**
(also many TV movies)

STARRETT, Jack
(1936–) Refugio, Texas, USA.
1969 Run, Angel, Run!
1970 The Losers
1970 Cry Blood Apache
1972 The Strange Vengeance of Rosalie
1972 Slaughter
1973 Cleopatra Jones
1974 Gravy Train / *The Dion Brothers*
1975 Race with the Devil
1976 A Small Town in Texas
1977 Final Chapter, Walking Tall
1982 Kiss My Grits / *A Texas Legend / Summer Heat*
(also many TV movies)

STAUB, Ralph
(1899–1969) American.
1936 Country Gentleman
1936 Sitting on the Moon
1937 Join the Marines
1937 Navy Blues
1937 The Mandarin Mystery
1937 Affairs of Cappy Ricks
1937 Meet the Boyfriend
1937 Mama Runs Wild
1938 Prairie Moon
1938 Western Jamboree
1940 Chip of the Flying U
1940 Yukon Flight
1940 Danger Ahead
1940 Sky Bandits
1957 The Heart of Show Business

STECKLER, Ray Dennis
(1939–) American.
1962 Wild Guitar
1962 The Incredibly Strange Creatures Who Stopped Living and Became Mixed Up Zombies
1964 The Thrill Killers
1964 Rat Pfink A-Boo-Boo
1965 Scream of the Butterfly
1967 Sinthia, The Devil's Doll
1972 Body Fever
1975 Lemon Grove Kids Meet the Monsters
1984 The Hollywood Strangler Meets the Skid Row Slasher

STEIN, Paul L
(1891–1952) Austrian.
1926 My Official Wife
1927 Forbidden Woman
1927 Don't Tell the Wife
1927 The Climber
1929 This Thing Called Love
1929 Her Private Affair
1929 The Official Scandal
1930 The Lottery Bride
1930 One Romantic Night
1931 Sin Takes a Holiday
1931 The Common Law
1931 Born to Love
1932 Breach of Promise
1932 A Woman Commands
1932 Lily Christine
1933 Red Wagon
1934 The Song You Gave Me

1934 Blossom Time / *April Romance*
1935 Mimi
1935 Heart's Desire
1936 Faithful
1938 Black Limelight
1939 The Outsider
1939 Poison Pen
1941 It Happened to One Man
1942 Talk About Jacqueline
1943 The Saint Meets the Tiger
1944 Kiss the Bride Goodbye
1944 The Twilight Hour
1945 Waltz Time
1946 The Lisbon Story
1948 Counterblast
1949 The Twenty Questions Murder Mystery

STEINBERG, David
(1942–) Winnipeg, Canada.
1981 Paternity
1983 Going Berserk
1989 Severance

STEINBERG, Ziggy
1986 The Boss's Wife

STEINMANN, Daniel
1984 Savage Streets
1985 Friday the 13th Part V — A New Beginning
1988 Subterraneans

STELLMAN, Martin
1988 For Queen and Country

STEPHENS, Peter
1959 Mustang

STERLING, William
1972 Alice's Adventures in Wonderland

STERN, Leonard
(1923–) New York, New York, USA.
1979 Just You and Me, Kid

STERN, Steven Hillard
(1937–) Ontario, Canada.
1970 B.S. I Love You
1972 Neither by Day Nor by Night
1974 The Harrad Summer
1979 Running
1981 The Devil and Max Devlin
1982 Rona Jaffe's Mazes and Monsters
1987 Rolling Vengeance
(also many TV movies)

STEVENS, David
1982 The Clinic
1983 Undercover
1988 Kansas
(also many TV movies)

STEVENS, George
(1904–1975) Oakland, California, USA. Biography: George Stevens: An American Romantic by Donald Richie.
1933 The Cohens and the Kellys in Trouble
1934 Bachelor Bait
1934 Kentucky Kernels / *Triple Trouble*
1934 Alice Adams **F***
1934 Annie Oakley
1935 The Nitwits
1935 Laddie
1935 The Rainmakers
1936 Swing Time
1937 A Damsel in Distress
1937 Quality Street
1938 Vivacious Lady
1939 Gunga Din
1940 Vigil in the Night
1941 Penny Serenade
1942 The Talk of the Town **F***
1942 Woman of the Year
1943 The More the Merrier **D* F***
1948 I Remember Mama
1951 A Place in the Sun **D** F***
1952 Something to Live for
1953 Shane **D* F***
1956 Giant **D** F***
1959 The Diary of Anne Frank
1965 The Greatest Story Ever Told
1970 The Only Game in Town
(also many shorts)

STEVENS, Leslie
(1924–) Washington DC, USA.
1960 Private Property
1961 Incubus
1962 Hero's Island
1964 Della
1967 Fanfare for a Death Scene
1987 Three Kinds of Heat

STEVENS, Mark (Richard Stevens)
(1915–) Cleveland, Ohio, USA.
1954 Cry Vengeance
1955 Timetable
1958 Gun Fever

STEVENS, Robert
(c1925–) American.
1957 The Big Caper
1958 Never Love a Stranger
1962 I Thank a Fool
1962 In the Cool of the Day
1969 Change of Mind

STEVENSON, Robert
(1905–1986) London, England.
1932 Happily Ever After **(Paul MARTIN)**
1933 Falling for You **(Jack HULBERT)**
1936 Jack of All Trades / *The Two of Us* **(Jack HULBERT)**
1936 Tudor Rose / *Nine Days a Queen*
1936 The Man Who Changed His Mind / *The Man Who Lived Again*
1937 King Solomon's Mines
1937 Non-Stop New York
1938 Owd Bob / *To the Victor*
1939 The Ware Case
1939 A Young Man's Fancy
1939 Return to Yesterday
1940 Tom Brown's Schooldays
1941 Back Street
1942 Joan of Paris
1944 Forever and a Day **(René CLAIR, Edmund GOULDING, Cedric HARDWICKE, Frank LLOYD, Victor SAVILLE, Herbert WILCOX)**

1944 Jane Eyre
1947 Dishonoured Lady
1948 To the Ends of the Earth
1949 The Woman on Pier 13 / *I Married a Communist*
1950 Walk Softly, Stranger
1951 My Forbidden Past
1952 The Las Vegas Story
1957 Johnny Tremain
1957 Old Yeller
1959 Darby O'Gill and the Little People
1960 Kidnapped
1960 The Absent-Minded Professor
1962 In Search of the Castaways
1963 Son of Flubber
1964 The Misadventures of Merlin Jones
1964 Mary Poppins **D* F***
1965 The Monkey's Uncle
1965 That Darn Cat
1967 The Gnome-Mobile
1968 Blackbeard's Ghost
1969 The Love Bug
1971 Bedknobs and Broomsticks
1974 Herbie Rides Again
1974 The Island at the Top of the World
1975 One of Our Dinosaurs Is Missing
1976 The Shaggy D.A.

STEWART, Alan
1989 Ghettoblasters

STEWART, Douglas Day
1984 Thief of Hearts
1989 Charlie's Kids / *Mismatch*

STEWART, John
1989 Action USA
1989 Smash Hit

STEWART, Larry
1984 The Initiation

STEWART, Peter *see* **Sam NEWFIELD**

STILLER, Mauritz (Mosche Stiller)
(1883–1928) Helsinki, Finland.
1924 The Atonement of Gosta Berling
1927 The Woman on Trial
1927 The Temptress **(Fred NIBLO)**
1927 Barbed Wire **(Lee ROWLAND)**
1928 The Street of Sin

STIX, John
(1920–) St Louis, Missouri, USA.
1959 The Great St Louis Bank Robbery **(Charles GUGGENHEIM)**

STOCKWELL, John
(1961–) Texas, USA.
1987 Undercover

STOLOFF, Benjamin
(1895–) American.
1926 The Canyon of Light
1927 The Circus Age
1927 The Gay Retreat
1927 Silver Valley
1928 Horseman of the Plains
1928 Plastered in Paris
1929 Speakeasy
1929 The Girl from Havana
1929 Protection
1930 Happy Days
1930 New Movietone Follies of 1930
1930 Soup to Nuts
1931 Three Rogues
1931 Goldie
1931 Not Exactly Gentlemen
1932 The Night Mayor
1932 The Devil Is Driving
1932 Destry Rides Again
1932 By Whose Hands?
1933 Obey the Law
1933 Night of Terror
1934 Palooka
1934 Transatlantic Merry-Go-Round
1935 To Beat the Band
1935 Swell Head
1936 Sea Devils
1936 Two in the Dark
1937 Don't Turn 'Em Loose
1937 Super-Sleuth
1937 Fight for Your Lady
1938 Radio City Revels
1938 The Affairs of Annabel
1939 The Lady and the Mob
1940 The Marines Fly High **(George NICHOLLS Jnr)**
1941 The Great Mr Nobody
1941 Three Sons o' Guns
1942 The Hidden Hand
1942 Secret Enemies
1943 The Mysterious Doctor
1944 Take It or Leave It
1944 Bermuda Mystery
1946 Johnny Comes Flying Home
1947 It's a Joke, Son

STOLOFF, Victor
1965 Intimacy
1971 Three Hundred Year Weekend

STONE, Andrew L
(1902–) Oakland, California, USA.
1930 Sombras de Gloria
1932 Hell's Headquarters
1937 The Girl Said No
1938 Stolen Heaven
1938 Say It in French
1939 The Great Victor Herbert
1941 There's Magic in Music
1943 Stormy Weather
1943 Hi Diddle Diddle / *Try and Find It*
1944 Sensations of 1945
1945 Bedside Manner
1946 The Bachelor's Daughter / *Bachelor Girl*
1946 Fun on a Weekend
1950 Highway 301
1951 Confidence Girl
1952 The Steel Trap
1953 A Blueprint for Murder
1955 The Night Holds Terror
1956 Julie
1958 Cry Terror!
1958 The Decks Ran Red
1960 The Last Voyage
1961 Ring of Fire
1963 The Password Is Courage
1964 Never Put It in Writing

1965 The Secret of My Success
1970 Song of Norway
1972 The Great Waltz

STONE, Marshall
1967 Come Spy with Me

STONE, Oliver
(1946–) New York, New York, USA.
1974 Seizure
1981 The Hand
1986 Salvador
1987 Platoon **D** F****
1988 Wall Street
1988 Talk Radio
1989 Born on the 4th July

STONE, Phil
1937 Damaged Goods

STONE, Virginia
1976 Evil in the Deep
1987 Run If You Can

STOPPARD, Tom
1989 Rosencrantz and Guildenstern

STORM, Howard
1985 Once Bitten

STORM, Jerome
1924 The Brass Bowl
1930 Courtin' Wildcats
1932 The Racing Strain

STORY, Mark
1986 Odd Jobs

STOUFFER, Mark
1987 Man Outside

STOUMEN, Louis Clyde
1965 The Image of Love

STRAYER, Frank R
(1891–1964) American.
1927 Rough-House Rosie
1927 Now We're in the Air
1928 Just Married
1928 Moran of the Marines
1928 Partners in Crime
1929 The Fall of Eve
1929 Acquitted
1930 Let's Go Places
1930 Borrowed Wives
1931 Murder at Midnight
1931 Caught Cheating
1931 Anybody's Blonde
1931 Soul of the Slums
1932 The Crusader
1932 Dragnet Patrol
1932 The Monster Walks
1932 Love in High Gear
1932 Gorilla Ship
1932 Dynamite Denny
1932 Tangled Destinies
1932 Manhattan Tower
1932 Behind Stone Walls
1933 Dance, Girl Dance
1933 The Vampire Bat
1933 By Appointment Only
1934 In Love with Life
1934 Fugitive Road
1934 In the Money
1934 Twin Husbands
1934 Cross Streets
1934 Fifteen Wives
1934 Once in a Million
1935 The Ghost Walks
1935 Death from a Distance
1935 Port of Lost Dreams
1935 Symphony of Living
1935 Public Opinion
1935 Society Fever
1936 Hitch-Hike to Heaven
1936 Murder at Glen Athol
1936 Sea Spoilers
1937 Off to the Races
1937 Big Business
1937 Hot Water
1937 Borrowing Trouble
1937 Laughing at Trouble
1938 Blondie
1939 Blondie Meets the Boss
1939 Blondie Brings Up Baby
1939 Blondie Takes a Vacation
1940 Blondie on a Budget
1940 Blondie Has Servant Trouble
1940 Blondie Plays Cupid
1941 Blondie Goes Latin
1941 Go West, Young Lady
1941 Blondie in Society
1942 Blondie's Blessed Event
1942 Blondie Goes to College
1942 Blondie For Victory
1943 The Daring Young Man
1943 Footlight Glamour
1943 It's a Great Life
1945 Mama Loves Papa
1945 Señorita from the West
1946 I Ring Doorbells
1950 Messenger of Peace
1951 The Sickle and the Cross

STREISAND, Barbra
(1942–) Brooklyn, New York, USA. Biographies: Barbra Streisand: An Illustrated Biography by Frank Brady; Barbra Streisand: The Woman, The Myth, The Music by Shaun Considine.
1983 Yentil

STRICK, Joseph
(1923–) Pittsburgh, Pennsylvania, USA.
1963 The Balcony
1967 Ulysses
1970 Tropic of Cancer
1974 Road Movie
1979 A Portrait of the Artist as a Young Man

STROCK, Herbert L
(1918–) **American.**
1954 Gog
1955 Battle Taxi
1956 Blood of Dracula
1957 I Was a Teenage Frankenstein
1958 How to Make a Monster
1962 Rider on a Dead Horse
1962 The Devil's Messenger

1964 The Crawling Hand
1973 Brother on the Run

STROMBERG, William B
1977 The Crater Lake Monster

STRYKER, Jonathon
1986 Curtains

STUART, Allen
1938 Unashamed

STUART, Brian
1982 Sorceress

STUART, Mark
1971 Please Sir

STUART, Mel
(1928–) American.
1969 If It's Tuesday, This Must Be Belgium
1970 I Love My Wife
1971 Willy Wonka and the Chocolate Factory
1972 One Is a Lonely Number
1978 Mean Dog Blues
1979 The White Lions
(also many TV movies and documentaries)

STURGES, John
(1911–) Oak Park, Illinois, USA.
1945 Thunderbolt **(William WYLER)**
1946 The Man Who Dared
1946 Shadowed
1946 Alias Mr Twilight
1947 For the Love of Rusty
1947 Keeper of the Bees
1948 Best Man Wins
1948 The Sign of the Ram
1949 The Walking Hills
1950 The Capture
1950 Mystery Street
1950 Right Cross
1950 The Magnificent Yankee / *The Man with Thirty Sons*
1951 Kind Lady
1951 The People Against O'Hara
1952 It's a Big Country **(Clarence BROWN, Don HARTMAN, Richard THORPE, Charles VIDOR, Don WEIS, William A WELLMAN)**
1952 The Girl in White / *So Bright the Flame*
1953 Jeopardy
1953 Fast Company
1953 Escape from Fort Bravo
1955 Bad Day at Black Rock **D***
1955 Underwater!
1955 The Scarlet Coat
1956 Backlash
1957 Gunfight at the OK Corral
1958 The Law and Jake Wade
1958 The Old Man and the Sea
1959 Last Train from Gun Hill
1959 Never So Few
1960 The Magnificent Seven
1961 By Love Possessed
1962 Sergeants 3
1963 A Girl Named Tamiko
1963 The Great Escape
1965 The Satan Bug
1965 The Hallelujah Trail
1967 Hour of the Gun
1968 Ice Station Zebra
1969 Marooned
1972 Joe Kidd
1973 Chino / *The Valdez Horses*
1974 McQ
1977 The Eagle Has Landed

STURGES, Preston (Edmund P. Biden)
(1898–1959) Chicago, Illinois, USA. Biography: Between Flops: A Biography of Preston Sturges by James Curtis.
1940 Christmas in July
1940 The Great McGinty
1941 The Lady Eve
1941 Sullivan's Travels
1942 The Palm Beach Story
1944 The Great Moment
1944 Hail the Conquered Hero
1944 The Miracle of Morgan's Creek
1947 The Sin of Harold Diddlebock
1948 Unfaithfully Yours
1949 The Beautiful Blonde from Bashful Bend
1950 Mad Wednesday
1957 The French, They Are a Funny Race / *The Diary of Major Thompson*

STURRIDGE, Charles
(1951–) London, England.
1983 Runners
1987 Aria **(Robert ALTMAN, Bruce BERESFORD, Bill BRYDEN, Jean-Luc GODARD, Derek JARMAN, Franc RODDAM, Nicolas ROEG, Ken RUSSELL, Julien TEMPLE)**
1988 A Handful of Dust

STYLES, Richard
1987 Shallow Grave
1988 Escape
1989 Payoff

SUGARMAN, Andrew
1985 Basic Training / *Up the Pentagon*
1988 Dangerous Curves / *Tan Lines*

SUMMERS, Jeremy
(1931–) British.
1960 Depth Charge
1962 The Punch and Judy Man
1964 Crooks in Cloisters
1965 Ferry Cross the Mersey
1966 San Ferry Ann
1966 Dateline Diamonds
1967 House of 1,000 Dolls
1968 Five Golden Dragons
1968 The Vengeance of Fu Manchu
(also TV movies)

SUMMERS, Walter
(1896–1973) British.
1926 Nelson
1927 The Battles of Coronel and the Falkland Islands
1928 The Betrayal
1929 The Lost Patrol

1929 Chamber of Horrors
1930 Raise the Roof
1930 The Man from Chicago
1930 Suspense
1931 The Flying Fool
1931 Men Like These / *Trapped in a Submarine*
1932 The House Opposite
1932 Deeds Men Do
1934 The Return of Bulldog Drummond
1934 The Warren Case
1934 What Happened Then?
1935 Music Hath Charms **(Thomas BENTLEY, Alex ESWAY, Arthur WOODS)**
1935 Royal Cavalcade **(Thomas BENTLEY, Herbert BRENON, William KELLINO, Norman LEE, Marcel VARNEL)**
1935 McGlusky, the Sea Rover
1936 Mutiny on the Elsinore
1936 The Limping Man
1937 The Price of Folly
1938 Premier
1938 At the Villa Rose
1939 Dark Eyes of London / *The Human Monster*
1940 Traitor Spy

SUTHERLAND, Edward A (Albert Edward Sutherland)
(1895–1973) London, England.
1925 Coming Through
1925 A Regular Fellow
1925 Wild, Wild Susan
1926 Behind the Front
1926 It's the Old Army Game
1926 We're in the Navy Now
1927 Fireman, Save My Child
1927 Love's Greatest Mistake
1928 Figures Don't Lie
1928 Tillie's Punctured Romance / *Marie's Millions*
1928 What a Night
1928 The Baby Cyclone
1929 Close Harmony **(John CROMWELL)**
1929 The Dance of Life **(John CROMWELL)**
1929 Fast Company
1929 The Saturday Night Kid
1929 Pointed Heels
1930 Burning Up
1930 The Social Lion
1930 The Sap from Syracuse / *The Sap Abroad*
1931 Palmy Days
1931 The Gang Bust
1931 June Moon
1931 Up Pops the Devil
1932 Mr Robinson Crusoe
1932 Secrets of the French Police
1932 Sky Devils
1933 International House
1933 Murder in the Zoo
1933 Too Much Harmony
1935 Diamond Jim
1935 Mississippi
1936 Poppy
1937 Champagne Waltz
1937 Every Day's a Holiday
1939 The Flying Deuces
1940 Beyond Tomorrow
1940 The Boys from Syracuse
1940 One Night in the Tropics
1941 The Invisible Woman
1941 Steel Against the Sky
1941 Nine Lives Are Not Enough
1942 The Navy Comes Through
1942 Sing Your Worries Away
1942 Army Surgeon
1943 Dixie
1944 Follow the Boys
1944 Secret Command
1945 Having Wonderful Crime
1946 Abie's Irish Rose
1956 Bermuda Affair

SWACKHAMER, E W
1972 Man and Boy
1981 Longshot
(also many TV movies)

SWAIM, Bob
(1943–) Evanston, Illinois, USA.
1986 Half Moon Street
1988 Masquerade / *Dying for Love*

SWIFT, David
(1919–) Minneapolis, Minnesota, USA.
1960 Pollyanna
1961 The Parent Trap
1962 The Interns
1962 Love Is a Ball / *All This and Money Too*
1963 Under the Yum Yum Tree
1964 Good Neighbour Sam
1967 How to Succeed in Business Without Really Trying

SWIMMER, Saul
1961 Force of Impulse
1968 Mrs Brown, You've Got a Lovely Daughter
1971 Come Together
1977 The Black Pearl

SWIRNOFF, Brad
1976 Tunnelvision **(Neil ISRAEL)**
1980 American Raspberry

SYKES, Peter
(1939–) Melbourne, Victoria, Australia.
1968 The Committee
1972 Demons on My Mind
1973 Steptoe and Son Ride Again
1973 The House in Nightmare Park
1974 Legend of Spider Forest / *Venom*
1975 To the Devil a Daughter
1977 Crazy House
1979 Jesus **(John KRISH)**

SYLBERT, Paul
1971 The Steagle

SZABO, Istvan
(1938–) Budapest, Hungary.
1964 Age of Illusions
1966 Father
1970 Love Film
1970 25, Fireman's Street

1976 Budapest Tales
1979 Confidence
1979 The Green Bird
1980 Mephisto
1985 Colonel Redl
1988 Hanussen

SZWARC, Jeannot
(1936–) Paris, France.
1973 Extreme Close-Up
1975 Bug
1978 Jaws II
1980 Somewhere in Time
1982 Enigma
1984 Supergirl
1985 Santa Claus — The Movie
1989 Honor Bound
(also many TV movies)

TACCHELLA, Jean-Charles
(1925–) Cherbourg, France.
1973 Voyage to Grande Tartarie
1975 Cousin Cousine
1977 The Blue Country
1979 It's a Long Time That I've Loved You / *Soupçon*
1981 Croque la Vie
1985 Escalier C

TAFT, Gene
1984 Blame It on the Night

TAGGART, Errol
1936 Women Are Trouble
1936 The Longest Night
1936 Sinner Takes All
1937 The Women Men Marry
1937 Song of the City
1938 Strange Faces

TAICHER, Bob
1986 Inside Out

TAKACS, Tibor
1977 Metal Messiah
1979 The Tomorrow Man / *Prisoner 984*
1987 The Gate
1988 I, Madman / *Hardcover*
1989 The Gate II

TAKITA, Yojiro
1987 Comic Magazine

TALAN, Len
1987 Hansel and Gretel

TALLAS, Greg
1948 Siren of Atlantis
1951 Prehistoric Woman
1956 Barefoot Battalion
1957 Bed of Grass
1957 Bikini Paradise
1966 007 Espionnage à Tanger
1980 Cataclysm

TALMADGE, Richard (Ricardo Metzertti)
(1896–1981) Munich, Germany.
1950 Border Outlaws
1953 Project Moonbase
1956 I Killed Wild Bill Hickok

1967 Casino Royale **(Val GUEST, Ken HUGHES, John HUSTON, Joe McGRATH, Robert PARRISH)**

TAMPA, Harry *see* **Harry HURWITZ**

TAN, Fred
1984 Lovers
1986 Storm of Youth
1986 Dark Night

TANNEN, William
1984 Flashpoint
1987 Deadly Illusion / *Love You to Death* **(Larry COHEN)**
1988 Hero and the Terror

TANNER, Alain *
(1929–) Geneva, Switzerland.
1969 Charles, Dead or Alive
1974 The Middle of the World
1976 Jonah Who Will Be 25 in the Year 2000
1981 Light Years Away
1983 In the White City
1985 No Man's Land
1988 A Flame in My Heart

TANSEY, James
1930 Romance of the West **(Robert E TANSEY)**

TANSEY, Robert E
1930 Romance of the West **(James TANSEY)**
1931 Riders of Rio
1932 Galloping Kid
1941 The Driftin' Kid
1941 Dynamite Canyon
1941 Riding the Sunset Trail
1941 Lone Star Lawmen
1942 Texas to Bataan
1942 Trail Riders
1942 Two Fisted Justice
1942 Arizona Roundup
1942 Where the Trail Ends
1943 Blazing Guns
1943 Death Valley Rangers
1944 Arizona Whirlwind
1944 Outlaw Trail
1944 Senora Stagecoach
1944 Westward Bound
1944 Harmony Trail
1945 Song of Wyoming
1946 God's Country
1946 Colorado Serenade
1946 Driftin' River
1946 Stars Over Texas
1946 Tumbleweed Trail
1946 Wild West
1946 The Caravan Trail
1946 Romance of the West
1948 The Enchanted Valley
1948 Prairie Outlaws
1948 Shaggy
1950 The Fighting Stallion
1950 Forbidden Jungle
1950 Federal Man
1951 Badman's Gold

TARADASH, Daniel
(1913–) Louisville, Kentucky, USA.
1956 Storm Centre

TARKOVSKY, Andrei
(1932–1987) Moscow, Russia.
1960 The Steam Roller and the Violin
1962 My Name Is Ivan / *Ivan's Childhood*
1968 Andrei Rublev
1972 Solaris
1974 The Mirror
1979 Stalker
1983 Nostalghia
1986 The Sacrifice

TASHLIN, Frank
(1913–1972) Weehawken, New Jersey, USA.
1951 The Lemon Drop Kid
1952 The First Time
1952 Son of Paleface
1953 Marry Me Again
1954 Susan Slept Here
1955 Artists and Models
1956 The Girl Can't Help It
1956 Hollywood or Bust
1956 The Lieutenant Wore Skirts
1957 Will Success Spoil Rock Hunter? / *Oh! For a Man!*
1958 The Geisha Girl
1958 Rock-a-Bye Baby
1959 Say One for Me
1960 Cinderfella
1961 Bachelor Flat
1962 It's Only Money
1963 The Man from the Diner's Club
1963 Who's Minding the Store?
1964 The Disorderly Orderly
1966 The Glass Bottom Boat
1966 The Alphabet Murders
1967 Caprice
1968 The Private Navy of Sgt. O'Farrell

TASS, Nadia
1986 Malcolm
1988 Rikky and Pete

TATI, Jacques (Jacques Tatischeff)
(1908–1982) Le Pecq, France.
Biography: Jacques Tati by Penelope Gilliatt.
1949 Jour de Fête
1951 Monsieur Hulot's Holiday
1958 Mon Oncle
1967 Playtime
1971 Traffic

TAUROG, Norman
(1899–1981) Chicago, Illinois, USA.
1929 Lucky Boy **(Charles C WILSON)**
1930 Troopers Three **(B Reeves EASON)**
1930 Sunny Skies
1930 Hot Curves
1930 Follow the Leader
1931 Finn and Hattie **(Norman Z McLEOD)**
1931 Skippy **D** F***
1931 Newly Rich
1931 Huckleberry Finn
1931 Sooky
1932 Hold 'Em Jail!
1932 The Phantom President
1932 If I Had a Million **(James CRUZE, H Bruce HUMBERSTONE, Ernst LUBITSCH, Norman Z McLEOD, Stephen ROBERTS, William A SEITER)**
1933 A Bedtime Story
1933 The Way to Love
1934 We're Not Dressing
1934 Mrs Wiggs of the Cabbage Patch
1934 College Rhythm
1935 The Big Broadcast of 1936
1936 Strike Me Pink
1936 Rhythm on the Range
1936 Reunion
1937 Fifty Roads to Town
1937 You Can't Have Everything
1938 The Adventures of Tom Sawyer
1938 Mad About Music
1938 Boys Town **D* F***
1939 The Girl Downstairs
1939 Lucky Night
1940 Young Tom Edison
1940 Broadway Melody of 1940
1940 Little Nellie Kelly
1941 Men of Boys Town
1941 Design for Scandal
1942 Are Husbands Necessary?
1942 A Yank at Eton
1943 Presenting Lily Mars
1943 Girl Crazy / *When the Girls Meet the Boys*
1946 The Hoodlum Saint
1947 The Beginning of the End?
1948 The Bride Goes Wild
1948 The Big City
1948 Words and Music
1949 That Midnight Kiss
1950 Please Believe Me
1950 The Toast of New Orleans
1950 Mrs O'Malley and Mr Malone
1951 Rich, Young and Pretty
1952 Room for One More
1952 Jumping Jacks
1952 The Stooge
1953 The Stars Are Singing
1953 The Caddy
1954 Living It Up
1955 You're Never Too Young
1956 The Birds and the Bees
1956 Pardners
1956 Bundle of Joy
1957 The Fuzzy Pink Nightgown
1958 Onionhead
1959 Don't Give Up the Ship
1960 Visit to a Small Planet
1960 G.I. Blues
1961 All Hands on Deck
1961 Blue Hawaii
1962 Girls! Girls! Girls!
1963 It Happened at the World's Fair
1963 Palm Springs Weekend
1965 Tickle Me
1965 Sergeant Deadhead
1965 Dr Goldfoot and the Bikini Machine
1966 Spinout / *California Holiday*
1967 Double Trouble
1968 Speedway
1968 Live a Little, Love a Little
(also many shorts)

TAVERNIER, Bertrand
(1941–) Lyons, France.
1963 Les Baisers
1974 The Clockmaker of St Paul
1975 Let Joy Reign Supreme / *Que la Fête Commence*
1976 The Judge and the Assassin
1977 Spoiled Children
1979 Femmes Fatales
1980 Death Watch
1982 A Week's Vacation
1982 Clean Slate
1984 Mississippi Blues **(Robert PARRISH)**
1984 A Sunday in the Country
1986 'Round Midnight
1988 Passion Beatrice
1989 La Vie et Rien d'Autre

TAVIANI, Paolo *
(1931–) San Miniato, Pisa, Italy.
1979 The Meadow **(Vittorio TAVIANI)**
1981 The Night of the Shooting Stars / *La Notte di San Lorenzo* **(Vittorio TAVIANI)**
1985 Kaos **(Vittorio TAVIANI)**
1987 Good Morning Babylon **(Vittorio TAVIANI)**

TAVIANI, Vittorio *
(1929–) San Miniato, Pisa, Italy.
1979 The Meadow **(Paolo TAVIANI)**
1981 The Night of the Shooting Stars / *La Notte di San Lorenzo* **(Paolo TAVIANI)**
1985 Kaos **(Paolo TAVIANI)**
1987 Good Morning Babylon **(Paolo TAVIANI)**

TAYLOR, Donald
(1920–) Freeport, Pennsylvania, USA.
1943 Battle for Music
1961 Everything's Ducky
1964 Ride the Wild Surf
1967 Jack of Diamonds
1970 The Five Man Army
1971 Escape from the Planet of the Apes
1973 Tom Sawyer
1976 Echoes of a Summer
1976 The Great Scout and Cathouse Thursday / *Wildcat*
1977 The Island of Dr Moreau
1978 Damien — Omen II
1980 The Final Countdown
(also many TV movies)

TAYLOR, Jud
(1940–) American.
1968 Fade In
(also a multitude of TV movies 1970–)

TAYLOR, Ray
(1888–1952) American.
1928 Beauty and Bullets
1928 The Clean-Up Man
1928 The Crimson Canyon
1928 Greased Lightning
1928 Quick Triggers
1929 Come Across
1929 The Border Wildcat
1929 The Ridin' Demon
1931 The One Way Trail
1934 Return of Chandu
1934 Fighting Trooper
1935 The Ivory Handled Gun
1935 Outlawed Guns
1935 The Throwback
1935 Fang and Claw
1935 Sunset of Power
1935 Call of the Savage
1936 The Cowboy and the Kid
1936 Silver Spurs
1936 The Three Mesquiteers
1936 Tex Rides with the Boy Scouts
1937 The Mystery of the Hooded Horseman
1937 Sudden Bill Dorn
1937 Drums of Destiny
1937 Boss of Lonely Valley
1938 Frontier Town
1938 Rawhide
1938 Hawaiian Buckaroo
1938 Panamint's Bad Man
1940 West of Carson City
1940 Bad Man from Red Butte
1940 Law and Order
1940 Pony Post
1940 Ragtime Cowboy Joe
1940 Riders of Pasco Basin
1941 Arizona Cyclone
1941 The Masked Rider
1941 Fighting Bill Fargo
1941 Boss of Bullion City
1941 Bury Me Not on the Lone Prairie
1941 Law of the Range
1941 The Man from Montana
1941 Rawhide Rangers
1941 Lucky Ralston
1942 Destination Unknown
1942 Treat 'Em Rough
1942 Mountain Justice
1942 Stagecoach Buckaroo
1943 Mug Town
1943 Cheyenne Round-Up
1943 The Lone Star Trail
1944 Boss of Boomtown
1945 The Daltons Ride Again
1946 The Michigan Kid
1947 The Vigilantes Return
1947 Range Beyond the Blue
1947 Border Feud
1947 Law of the Lash
1947 Wild Country
1947 West to Glory
1947 Ghost Town Renegades
1947 Pioneer Justice
1947 Black Hills
1947 Return of the Lash
1947 The Fighting Vigilantes
1947 Stage to Mesa City
1947 Cheyenne Takes Over
1948 Gunning for Justice
1948 Hidden Danger
1948 The Return of Wildfire
1948 The Hawk of Powder River
1948 Tornado Range
1948 The Tioga Kid
1948 The Westland Trail
1948 Check Your Guns
1949 Law of the West

1949 Range Justice
1949 West of El Dorado
1949 Son of Billy the Kid
1949 Son of a Badman
1949 Outlaw Country
1949 Crashing Thru
1949 Shadows of the West
(also many serials)

TAYLOR, Richard
1978 Stingray

TAYLOR, Rod
1988 Lucky Strike

TAYLOR, Sam
(1895–1958) American.
1923 Safety Last **(Fred NEWMEYER)**
1923 Why Worry?
1924 Hot Water **(Fred NEWMEYER)**
1925 The Freshman **(Fred NEWMEYER)**
1926 Exit Smiling
1926 For Heaven's Sake
1926 My Best Girl
1929 The Taming of the Shrew
1929 Coquette
1930 Du Barry, Woman of Passion
1931 Kiki
1931 Skyline
1931 Ambassador Bill
1932 Devil's Lottery
1933 Out All Night
1934 The Cat's Paw
1935 Vagabond Lady
1944 Nothing But Trouble

TAYLOR, Samuel A
1957 The Monte Carlo Story

TEAGUE, Lewis
(1941–) American.
1974 Dirty O'Neil **(Howard FREEN)**
1979 The Lady in Red
1980 Alligator
1982 Fighting Back / *Death Vengeance*
1983 Cujo
1985 Stephen King's Cat's Eye
1986 The Jewel of the Nile
1988 Collision Course

TECHINE, André *
(1943–) French.
1985 Rendezvous
1986 Scene of the Crime

TEMPLE, Julien
(1953–) London, England.
1980 The Great Rock 'n' Roll Swindle
1985 Running Out of Luck
1986 Absolute Beginners
1987 Aria **(Robert ALTMAN, Bruce BERESFORD, Bill BRYDEN, Jean-Luc GODARD, Derek JARMAN, Franc RODDAM, Nicolas ROEG, Ken RUSSELL, Charles STURRIDGE)**
1988 Earth Girls Are Easy

TEMPLEMAN, Conny
1986 Nanou

TEMPLETON, George
1950 The Sundowners
1951 Quebec

TENNEY, Del
1964 The Horror of Party Beach
1964 The Curse of the Living Corpse

TENNEY, Kevin S
1987 Witchboard
1988 Night of the Demons / *Halloween Party*
1989 The Cellar

TENNYSON, Pen (Penrose Tennyson)
(1912–1941) American.
1939 The Proud Valley
1941 Convoy

TENZER, Bert
1969 2,000 Years Later

TETZLAFF, Ted (Theodore Tetzlaff)
(1903–) Los Angeles, California, USA.
1941 World Premiere
1947 Riff Raff
1948 Fighting Father Dunne
1949 The Window
1949 Johnny Allegro / *Hounded*
1949 A Dangerous Profession
1950 The White Tower
1950 Under the Gun
1950 Gambling House
1952 The Treasure of Lost Canyon
1953 Terror on a Train / *Time Bomb*
1955 Son of Sinbad
1959 The Young Land

TEUBER, Monica
1989 Magdalene / *Silent Night*

TEWKESBURY, Joan
(1937–) Redlands, California, USA.
1979 Old Boyfriends

TEWKESBURY, Peter
(1924–) American.
1963 Sunday in New York
1964 Emil and the Detectives
1967 Doctor You've Got to Be Kidding
1968 Stay Away Joe
1969 The Trouble with Girls

THEW, Anna
1986 Hilda Was a Goodlooker

THIELE, William (Wilhelm Thiele)
(1890–1975) Vienna, Austria.
1933 Waltz Time
1935 Lottery Lover
1936 The Jungle Princess
1937 London By Night
1937 Beg, Borrow or Steal
1939 Bridal Suite
1939 Bad Little Angel
1940 The Ghost Comes Home
1943 Tarzan Triumphs
1943 Tarzan's Desert Mystery
1946 The Madonna's Secret

THOMAS, Anna
(1948–) Stuttgart, Germany.
1981 The Haunting of M

THOMAS, Anthony
1989 S.P.O.O.K.S

THOMAS, Dave
1983 Strange Brew **(Rick MORANIS)**
1988 The Experts

THOMAS, Gerald
(1920–) Hull, Humberside, England.
1956 Circus Friends
1957 Timelock
1957 The Vicious Circle / *The Circle*
1958 The Duke Wore Jeans
1958 The Solitary Child
1958 Chain of Events
1958 Carry On Sergeant
1959 Carry On Nurse
1959 Carry On Teacher
1959 Please Turn Over
1960 Watch Your Stern
1960 Beware of Children / *No Kidding*
1960 Carry On Constable
1961 Raising the Wind / *Roommates*
1961 Carry On Regardless
1962 Twice Round the Daffodils
1962 Carry On Cruising
1962 The Iron Maiden / *The Swingin' Maiden*
1963 Nurse on Wheels
1963 Carry On Cabby
1964 Carry On Jack / *Carry On Venus*
1964 Carry On Spying
1964 Carry On Cleo
1966 The Big Job
1966 Carry On Cowboy
1966 Carry On Screaming
1966 Carry On Don't Lose Your Head
1967 Follow That Camel
1968 Carry On Doctor
1969 Carry On . . Up the Khyber
1969 Carry On Camping
1970 Carry On Up the Jungle
1970 Carry On Again, Doctor
1971 Carry On at Your Convenience
1971 Carry On Henry
1971 Carry On Loving
1972 Carry On Abroad
1972 Carry On Matron
1973 Bless This House
1973 Carry On Girls
1974 Carry On Dick
1976 Carry On Behind
1976 Carry On England
1978 That's a Carry On *(partly compilation)*
1978 Carry On Emmanuelle
1985 The Second Victory

THOMAS, John
1987 Arizona Heat
1989 Maximum Security

THOMAS, Ralph
(1915–) Hull, Humberstone, England.
1949 Helter Skelter
1949 Once Upon a Dream
1949 Traveller's Joy
1950 The Clouded Yellow
1951 Appointment with Venus / *Island Rescue*
1952 The Venetian Bird / *The Assassin*
1953 The Dog and the Diamonds
1953 A Day to Remember
1954 Doctor in the House
1954 Mad About Men
1955 Doctor at Sea
1955 Above Us the Waves
1956 The Iron Petticoat
1956 Checkpoint
1956 Doctor at Large
1957 Campbell's Kingdom
1958 A Tale of Two Cities
1958 The Wind Cannot Read
1959 The 39 Steps
1959 Upstairs and Downstairs
1960 Conspiracy of Hearts
1960 Doctor in Love
1961 No Love for Johnnie
1961 No, My Darling Daughter
1962 A Pair of Briefs
1962 The Wild and the Willing / *Young and Willing*
1963 Doctor in Distress
1963 Hot Enough for June / *Agent 8¾*
1964 The High Bright Sun / *McGuire Go Home*
1965 Doctor in Clover / *Carnaby M.D.*
1966 Deadlier Than the Male
1968 Some Girls Do
1968 The High Commissioner / *Nobody Runs Forever*
1970 Doctor in Trouble
1971 Percy
1971 Quest for Love
1972 It's a 2' 6" Above the Ground World / *The Love Ban*
1974 Percy's Progress
1980 A Nightingale Sang in Berkeley Square

THOMAS, Ralph L
1981 Ticket to Heaven
1988 The Long Lost Friend / *Apprentice to Murder*
(also many TV movies)

THOMAS, William C
(1903–) American.
1945 Midnight Manhunt
1945 One Fascinating Night
1946 They Made Me a Killer
1946 I Cover Big Town
1947 Big Town
1947 Big Town After Dark
1948 Big Town Scandal
1949 Special Agent

THOMASIN, Harry
1975 The Great Lester Boggs
1975 So Sad About Gloria
1975 Encounter with the Unknown
1979 The Day It Came to Earth

THOMPSON, Brett
1989 Not Since Casanova

THOMPSON, Ernest
1988 1969

THOMPSON, Harlan
1934 The Past of Mary Holmes **(Slavko VORKAPICH)**
1934 Kiss and Make Up

THOMPSON, Harry
1989 After the Rain / *The Passage*

THOMPSON, J Lee
(1914–) Bristol, Avon, England.
1950 Murder Without Crime
1952 The Yellow Balloon
1954 The Weak and the Wicked
1954 For Better For Worse / *Cocktails in the Kitchen*
1955 As Long As They're Happy
1955 An Alligator Named Daisy
1956 Yield to the Night / *Blonde Sinner*
1957 The Good Companions
1957 Woman in a Dressing Gown
1958 Ice Cold in Alex / *Desert Attack*
1959 No Trees in the Street
1959 Tiger Bay
1959 North West Frontier / *Flame Over India*
1960 I Aim at the Stars
1961 The Guns of Navarone **D* F***
1962 Cape Fear
1962 Taras Bulba
1963 Kings of the Sun
1964 What a Way to Go!
1965 John Goldfarb, Please Come Home
1965 Return from the Ashes
1967 Eye of the Devil
1969 Before Winter Comes
1969 The Chairman / *The Most Dangerous Man in the World*
1969 Mackenna's Gold
1970 Country Dance / *Brotherly Love*
1973 Conquest of the Planet of the Apes
1973 Battle of the Planet of the Apes
1974 Huckleberry Finn
1975 The Reincarnation of Peter Proud
1976 St Ives
1977 The White Buffalo
1978 The Greek Tycoon
1979 The Passage
1981 Cabo Blanco
1981 Happy Birthday to Me
1983 10 to Midnight
1984 The Evil That Men Do
1984 The Ambassador
1985 King Solomon's Mines
1986 Murphy's Law
1986 Firewalker
1987 Death Wish IV: The Crackdown
1988 Messenger of Death / *Avenging Angels*
1989 Kinjite / *Forbidden Subjects*

THOMPSON, Marshall (James Marshall Thompson)
(1925–) Peoria, Illinois, USA.
1964 A Yank in Viet Nam

THOMPSON, William L
1935 The Irish Gringo

THORNHILL, Michael
1987 The Everlasting Secret Family

THORPE, Jerry
(1930–) American.
1968 The Venetian Affair
1968 The Day of the Evil Gun
1972 Company of Killers / *The Protectors*
(also many TV movies)

THORPE, Richard (Rollo Smolt Thorpe)
(1896–) Hutchinson, Kansas, USA.
1925 The Desert Demon
1925 Saddle Cyclone
1925 Full Speed
1926 Rawhide
1926 The Bandit Buster
1926 The Fighting Cheat
1926 Double Daring
1926 College Days
1926 Josselyn's Wife
1927 The Cyclone Cowboy
1927 Between Dangers
1927 The Desert of the Lost
1927 The Soda Water Cowboy
1927 White Pebbles
1927 The First Night
1928 The Galloping Gobs
1928 Valley of the Hunted Men
1928 The Cowboy Cavalier
1928 Desperate Courage
1929 The Bachelor Girl
1930 Border Romance
1930 The Dude Wrangler
1930 Wings of Adventure
1930 The Thoroughbred
1930 Under Montana Skies
1930 The Utah Kid
1931 The Lawless Woman
1931 The Lady from Nowhere
1931 Wild Horse **(Sidney ALGIER)**
1931 The Sky Spider
1931 Grief Street
1931 Neck and Neck
1931 The Devil Plays
1932 Cross Examination
1932 Forgotten Women
1932 Murder at Dawn / *The Death Ray*
1932 Probation
1932 Midnight Lady / *Dream Mother*
1932 Escapade / *Dangerous Ground*
1932 Forbidden Company
1932 The Beauty Parlour
1932 The King Murder
1932 Thrill of Youth
1932 Slightly Married
1933 Women Won't Tell
1933 The Secrets of Wu Sin
1933 Love Is Dangerous / *Women Are Dangerous*
1933 Forgotten
1933 Strange People
1933 I Have Lived
1933 Notorious But Nice
1933 Man of Sentiment
1933 Rainbow Over Broadway
1934 Murder on the Campus / *At the Stroke of Nine*
1934 The Quitter
1934 City Park

1934 Stolen Sweets
1934 Green Eyes
1934 Cheating Cheaters
1935 Secret of the Chateau
1935 Strange Wives
1935 Last of the Pagans
1936 The Voice of Bugle Ann
1936 Tarzan Escapes
1937 Dangerous Number
1937 Night Must Fall
1937 Double Wedding
1938 Man-Proof
1938 Love Is a Headache
1938 The First Hundred Years
1938 The Toy Wife / *Frou, Frou*
1938 The Crowd Roars
1938 Three Loves Has Nancy
1939 The Adventures of Huckleberry Finn
1939 Tarzan Finds a Son!
1940 The Earl of Chicago
1940 Twenty-Mule Team
1940 Wyoming
1941 The Bad Man / *Two Gun Cupid*
1941 Barnacle Bill
1941 Tarzan's Secret Treasure
1942 Joe Smith, American / *Highway to Freedom*
1942 Tarzan's New York Adventure
1942 Apache Trail
1942 White Cargo
1943 Three Hearts for Julia
1943 Above Suspicion
1943 Cry Havoc
1944 Two Girls and a Sailor
1944 The Thin Man Goes Home
1945 Thrill of a Romance
1945 Her Highness and the Bellboy
1945 What Next, Corporal Hargrove?
1946 Fiesta
1947 This Time for Keeps
1949 The Sun Comes Up
1949 Big Jack
1949 Challenge to Lassie
1949 Malaya / *East of the Rising Sun*
1950 The Black Hand
1950 Three Little Words
1951 Vengeance Valley
1951 The Great Caruso
1951 The Unknown Man
1951 It's a Big Country **(Clarence BROWN, Don HARTMAN, John STURGES, Charles VIDOR, Don WEIS, William A WELLMAN)**
1952 Carbine Williams
1952 Ivanhoe **F***
1952 The Prisoner of Zenda
1953 The Girl Who Had Everything
1953 All the Brothers Were Valiant
1953 Knights of the Round Table
1953 The Student Prince
1954 Athena
1955 The Prodigal
1955 Quentin Durward
1957 Ten Thousand Bedrooms
1957 Tip on a Dead Jockey / *Time for Action*
1957 Jailhouse Rock
1959 The House of the Seven Hawks
1960 The Killers of Kilimanjaro / *Adam Son of Africa*
1961 The Honeymoon Machine
1962 The Horizontal Lieutenant
1963 Follow the Boys
1963 Fun in Acapulco
1965 The Truth About Spring
1965 That Funny Feeling
1965 The Golden Head
1967 The Last Challenge / *The Pistolero of Red River*
1968 The Scorpio Letters
(also many shorts)

THURN-TAXIS, Alexis
(1891–1979) Austrian.
1942 A Night of Crime
1942 The Yanks Are Coming
1943 Man of Courage
1945 Hollywood and Vine

TILL, Eric
(1929–) Canadian.
1967 A Great Big Thing
1968 Hot Millions
1970 The Walking Stick
1972 A Fan's Notes
1978 It Shouldn't Happen to a Vet / *All Things Bright and Beautiful*
1979 Wild Horse Hawk
1981 Improper Channels
1982 If You Could See What I Hear
(also many TV movies)

TILTON, Roger
1985 Spiker

TINLING, James
(1889–1955) American.
1927 Very Confidential
1928 Soft Living
1928 Don't Marry
1929 True Heaven
1929 The Exalted Flapper
1929 Words and Music
1930 For the Love o' Lil
1931 The Flood
1933 Arizona to Broadway
1933 The Last Trail
1933 Jimmy and Sally
1934 Three on a Honeymoon
1934 Call It Luck
1934 Love Time
1935 Under the Pampas Moon
1935 Welcome Home
1935 Charlie Chan in Shanghai
1936 Every Saturday Night
1936 Champagne Charlie
1936 Educating Father
1936 Pepper
1936 Back to Nature
1937 The Holy Terror
1937 Angel's Holiday
1937 Sing and Be Happy
1937 The Great Hospital Mystery
1937 45 Fathers
1938 Change of Heart
1938 Mr Moto's Gamble
1938 Passport Husband
1938 Sharpshooters
1939 Boy Friend
1941 Last of the Duanes
1941 Riders of the Purple Sage

1942 Sundown Jim
1942 The Lone Star Ranger
1943 Cosmo Jones, Crime Smasher
1946 Rendezvous 24
1946 Deadline for Murder
1946 Strange Journey
1946 Dangerous Millions / *The House of Tao Lin*
1947 Second Chance
1947 Roses Are Red
1948 Night Wind
1948 Trouble Preferred
1951 Tales of Robin Hood

TOBACK, James
(1944–) American.
1972 Fingers
1982 Love and Money
1983 Exposed
1987 The Pick-Up Artist

TOBEROFF, Marc
1987 Zombie High

TOKAR, Norman
(1920–1979) American.
1962 Big Red
1963 Savage Sam
1964 A Tiger Walks
1964 Those Calloways
1966 The Ugly Dachshund
1966 Follow Me, Boys!
1967 The Happiest Millionaire
1968 The Horse in the Grey Flannel Suit
1969 Rascal
1970 The Boatniks
1972 Snowball Express
1974 Where the Red Fern Grows
1975 Apple Dumpling Gang
1976 No Deposit, No Return
1977 Candleshoe
1978 The Cat from Outer Space

TOPPER, Burt
(1928–) New York, New York, USA.
1958 Hell Squad
1959 Tank Commandos
1959 The Diary of a High School Bride
1964 War Is Hell
1964 The Strangler
1968 The Devil's 8
1971 The Hard Ride
1976 The Day the Lord Got Busted

TORN, Rip (Elmore Rual Torn)
(1931–) Temple, Texas, USA.
1987 The Telephone

TORNATORE, Joseph
1986 Code Name: Zebra
1988 The Crystal Eye
1988 Grotesque

TORRANCE, Robert
1989 Mutant on the Bounty

TORRINI, Cinzia H
1987 Hotel Colonial

TORS, Ivan
(1916–1983) Hungarian.
1964 Rhino!
1965 Zebra in the Kitchen

TOTTEN, Robert
(1937–) Los Angeles, California, USA.
1963 The Quick and the Dead
1969 Death of a Gunfighter **(Don SIEGEL)**
1970 The Wild Country
1976 Pony Express Rider
1989 Dark Before Dawn

TOURNEUR, Jacques
(1904–1977) Paris, France.
Biography: Jacques Tourneur by Michael Henry.
1939 They All Come Out
1939 Nick Carter, Master Detective
1940 Phantom Raiders
1941 Doctors Don't Tell
1942 The Cat People
1943 I Walked with a Zombie
1943 The Leopard Man
1944 Days of Glory
1944 Experiment Perilous
1946 Canyon Passage
1947 Out of the Past / *Build My Gallows High*
1948 Berlin Express
1949 Easy Living
1950 Stars in My Crown
1950 The Flame and the Arrow
1951 Circle of Danger
1951 Anne of the Indies
1952 Way of a Gaucho
1953 Appointment in Honduras
1955 Stranger on Horseback
1955 Wichita
1956 Great Day in the Morning
1956 Nightfall
1958 Curse of the Demon
1958 The Fearmakers
1959 Timbuktu
1959 Frontier Rangers
1959 Fury River
1959 Mission of Danger
1960 The Giant Marathon
1963 The Comedy of Terrors
1965 War Gods of the Deep / *City Under the Sea*
(also many shorts)

TOWNE, Robert
(1936–) American.
1982 Personal Best
1988 Tequila Sunrise

TOWNSEND, Bud
1969 Nightmare in Wax
1972 The Folks at the Red Wolf Inn / *Terror Inn*
1976 Alice in Wonderland
1978 Coach
1984 Love Scenes

TOWNSEND, Pat
1982 The Beach Girls

TOWNSEND, Robert
1987 Hollywood Shuffle

TOYE, Wendy
(1917–) London, England.
1954 The Teckman Mystery
1954 Three Cases of Murder **(David EADY, George O'FERRALL)**
1955 Raising a Riot
1956 All for Mary
1956 True As a Turtle
1962 We Joined the Navy
(also many shorts and TV shorts)

TRAMONT, Jean-Claude
(1934–) Brussels, Belgium.
1977 Le Point de Mire
1981 All Night Long

TRAUBE, Shepard
1940 Street of Memories
1941 The Bride Wore Crutches
1941 For Beauty's Sake

TRAVERS, Thomas
1988 A Time to Remember / *Miracle in a Manger*

TRBOVICH, Tom
1986 Free Ride

TRENCHARD-SMITH, Brian
(1946–) British.
1975 The Love Epidemic
1975 The Man from Hong Kong
1976 Deathcheaters
1978 Stunt Rock
1981 The Day of the Assassin
1982 Turkey Shoot
1983 BMX Bandits
1985 Jenny Kissed Me
1985 Frog Dreaming / *The Quest*
1986 The Spirit Chaser
1986 Dead End Drive-In
1987 The Day of the Panther
1987 The Strike of the Panther
1988 Out of the Body
1989 Forward Firebase Gloria

TRENKER, Luis *
(1893–) St Ulrich, Südtirol, Germany.
1933 The Rebel **(E A KNOPF)**
1935 The Prodigal Son
1939 The Challenge **(Milton ROSMER)**

TRENT, John
1970 Homer
1980 Middle Age Crazy

TREVILLION, Dale
1989 One Man Force

TRIESCHMANN, Charles
1974 Two

TRIKONIS, Gus
1969 Five the Hard Way
1975 The Swinging Barmaids
1975 Supercock
1976 Nashville Girl
1977 Moonshine County Express
1977 New Girl in Town
1978 The Evil
1978 Touched By Love
1981 Take This Job and Shove It
1983 Dance of the Dwarfs
(also many TV movies)

TROELL, Jan
(1931–) Limhamn, Skåne, Sweden.
1966 Here Is Your Life
1968 Who Saw Him Die? / *Eeny, Meeny, Miny, Mo*
1972 The Emigrants / *Utvandrarna* D* F*
1973 The New Land / *Nybyggarna*
1974 Zandy's Bride
1977 Bang!
1979 Hurricane
1982 The Flight of the Eagle

TRONSON, Robert
(1924–) British.
1962 The Man at the Carlton Tower
1962 The Traitors
1963 On the Run
1963 Ring of Spies / *Ring of Treason*

TROPIA, Marc C
1986 Miami Beach Bug Police **(Tano TROPIA)**
1986 Friars Road

TRUFFAUT, François
(1932–1984) Paris, France.
Biography: Finally Truffaut by Don Allen.
1959 The 400 Blows
1960 Shoot the Pianist
1961 Jules and Jim
1962 Love at Twenty **(Shintaro ISHIHARA, Marcel OPHULS, Renzo ROSSELLINI, Andrzej WAJDA)**
1964 Silken Skin
1966 Fahrenheit 451
1967 The Bride Wore Black
1968 Stolen Kisses
1969 The Wild Child
1969 Mississippi Mermaid
1970 Bed and Board
1972 Anne and Muriel / *Two English Girls*
1972 A Gorgeous Bird Like Me / *Such a Gorgeous Kid Like Me*
1973 Day for Night / *La Nuit Américaine* D*
1975 The Story of Adèle H
1976 Small Change
1977 The Man Who Loved Women
1978 The Green Room
1979 Love on the Run
1980 The Woman Next Door
1983 The Long Saturday Night

TRUMAN, Michael
(1916–) British.
1955 Touch and Go / *The Light Touch*
1961 Go to Blazes
1963 The Girl in the Headlines / *The Model Murder Case*

TRUMBO, Dalton
(1905–1976) Montrose, USA.
1971 Johnny Got His Gun

TRUMBULL, Douglas
(1942–) Los Angeles, California, USA.
1971 Silent Running
1983 Brainstorm

TRYON, Glenn
(1894–1970) American.
1934 Gridiron Flash
1936 Two in Revolt
1936 Easy to Take
1937 Small Town Boy
1938 The Law West of Tombstone
1939 Beauty for the Asking
1941 Double Date
1943 That Nazty Nuisance
1944 Meet Miss Bobby Socks
1949 Miss Mink of 1949

TSUKERMAN, Slava
1983 Liquid Sky

TUCHNER, Michael
(1934–) Berlin, Germany.
1971 Villain / *Cactus Jack*
1972 Fear Is the Key
1975 Mister Quilp / *The Old Curiosity Shop*
1976 The Likely Lads
1983 Trenchcoats
(also many TV movies)

TUCKER, Phil
1953 Robot Master

TUGGLE, Richard
(1948–) Coral Gables, Florida, USA.
1984 Tightrope
1986 Out of Bounds

TULLY, Montgomery (Geoffrey M. Tully)
(1904–) British.
1945 Murder in Reverse
1946 Spring Song
1947 Mrs Fitzherbert
1949 Boys in Brown
1951 A Tale of Five Cities
1952 Girdle of Gold
1953 Small Town Story
1954 The Diamond
1954 Paid to Kill / *Five Days*
1954 36 Hours / *Terror Street*
1954 Devil's Harbour
1955 The Glass Cage
1956 The Way Out / *Dial 999*
1957 The Counterfeit Plan
1957 No Road Back
1957 The Hypnotist / *Scotland Yard Dragnet*
1957 The Key Man
1957 Man in the Shadow
1958 Escapement
1958 Strange Awakening / *Female Friends*
1958 The Long Knife
1958 Man with a Gun
1958 Diplomatic Corpse
1958 I Only Asked!
1959 Man Accused
1960 Dead Lucky
1960 Jackpot
1960 The Price of Silence
1960 The House in Marsh Road
1960 The Man Who Was Nobody
1961 The Middle Course
1961 The Third Alibi
1961 Two Wives at One Wedding
1962 She Knows Y'Know!
1962 Out of the Fog
1963 Master Spy
1963 Clash By Night / *Escape By Night*
1964 Who Killed the Cat?
1967 The Terrornauts
1967 Battle Beneath the Earth
1968 The Hawks

TUNG, Sandy
1983 Broken Promise / *A Marriage*

TURKIEWICZ, Sophia
1984 Silver City
1988 I've Come About the Suicide

TURKO, Rose-Marie
(1951–) Orleans, France.
1983 Scarred / *Street Love*
1985 The Dungeonmaster / *Ragewar* **(David ALLEN, Charles BAND, John BUECHLER, Peter MANOOGIAN, Ted NICOLAOU, Stephen STAFFORD)**

TURMAN, Lawrence
(1926–) Los Angeles, California, USA.
1971 Marriage of a Young Stockbroker
1983 Second Thoughts

TURNER, Brad
1987 Goofballs

TURNER, Dean
1973 Valley of Blood

TUTTLE, Frank
(1892–1963) New York, USA.
1924 Grit
1924 Dangerous Money
1925 Kiss in the Dark
1925 Lovers in Quarantine
1925 The Lucky Devil
1925 The Manicure Girl
1925 Miss Bluebeard
1926 The American Venus
1926 Love 'Em and Leave 'Em
1926 Kid Boots
1926 The Untamed Lady
1926 Blind Alleys
1927 One Woman to Another
1927 The Spotlight
1927 Time to Love
1928 Easy Come, Easy Go
1928 Varsity
1928 His Private Life
1928 Love and Learn
1928 Something Always Happens
1929 The Canary Murder Case
1929 Marquis Preferred
1929 The Studio Murder Mystery

1929 The Greene Murder Case
1929 Sweetie
1929 Men Are Like That
1930 Only the Brave
1930 The Benson Murder Case
1930 True to the Navy
1930 Love Among the Millionaires
1930 Her Wedding Night
1931 No Limit
1931 It Pays to Advertise
1931 Dude Ranch
1932 This Reckless Age
1932 This Is the Night
1932 The Big Broadcast
1933 Dangerously Yours
1933 Pleasure Cruise
1933 Roman Scandals
1934 Ladies Should Listen
1934 Springtime for Henry
1934 Here Is My Heart
1935 All the King's Horses
1935 The Glass Key
1935 Two for Tonight
1936 College Holiday
1937 Waikiki Wedding
1937 Doctor Rhythm
1939 Paris Honeymoon
1939 I Stole a Million
1939 Charlie McCarthy, Detective
1942 This Gun for Hire
1942 Lucky Jordan
1943 Hostages
1944 The Hour Before Dawn
1945 The Great John L / *A Man Called Sullivan*
1945 Don Juan Quilligan
1946 Suspense
1946 Swell Guy
1951 The Magic Face
1955 Hell on Frisco Bay
1956 A Cry in the Night
1959 Island of Lost Women

TWIST, Derek
(1905–1979) British.
1947 The End of the River
1949 All Over Town
1951 Green Grow the Rushes
1955 Police Dog
1957 Family Doctor / *R X Murder*

ULLMAN, Daniel B
(1918–1979) American.
1957 Badlands of Montana

ULLMANN, Liv
(1939–) Tokyo, Japan.
Autobiography: Changing.
1982 Love **(Annette COHEN, Nancy DOWD, Mai ZETTERLING)**

ULMER, Edgar Georg
(1904–1972) Vienna, Austria.
Pseudonym: John Warner.
1929 People on Sunday **(Robert SIODMAK)**
1933 Mister Broadway
1933 Damaged Lives
1934 The Black Cat / *House of Doom*
1934 Thunder Over Texas
1935 From Nine to Nine
1935 Green Fields **(Jacob BENAMI)**
1938 The Singing Blacksmith
1939 Cossacks Across the Danube
1939 The Light Ahead
1939 The Marriage Broker
1939 Moon Over Harlem
1942 Tomorrow We Live / *The Man with a Conscience*
1943 My Son, My Hero
1943 Girls in Chains
1943 Isle of Forgotten Sins
1943 Jive Junction
1944 Bluebeard
1945 Strange Illusion / *Out of the Night*
1946 Club Havana
1946 Detour
1946 The Wife of Monte Carlo
1946 Her Sister's Secret
1946 The Strange Woman
1947 Carnegie Hall
1948 Ruthless
1949 The Pirates of Capri / *The Masked Pirate*
1951 The Man from Planet X
1951 St. Benny the Dip / *Escape If You Can*
1952 Babes in Bagdad
1955 Murder Is My Beat
1955 The Naked Dawn
1957 Daughter of Dr Jekyll
1957 The Perjurer
1960 Hannibal **(Carlo Ludovico BRAGAGLIA)**
1960 The Amazing Transparent Man
1960 Beyond the Time Barrier
1961 Journey Beneath the Desert / *Atlantis, the Lost Continent*
1965 The Cavern

USTINOV, Peter
(1921–) London, England.
Autobiography: Dear Me.
1946 School for Secrets / *Secret Flight*
1947 Vice Versa
1949 Private Angelo **(Michael ANDERSON)**
1961 Romanoff and Juliet / *Dig That Juliet*
1962 Billy Bud
1965 Lady L
1972 Hammersmith Is Out
1984 Memed, My Hawk

UYS, Jamie
(1921–) South American.
1965 Dingaka
1967 After You, Comrade
1971 Lost in the Desert
1979 The Gods Must Be Crazy
1983 The Gods Must Be Crazy II

VADIM, Roger (Roger Vadim Plémiannicov)
(1928–) Paris, France.
Autobiography: Memoirs of the Devil translated by Peter Beglan.
1956 And God Created Woman
1957 No Sun in Venice / *When the Devil Drives*
1957 The Night Heaven Fell / *Les Bijoutiers du Clair de Lune*
1959 Les Liaisons Dangereuses
1960 Blood and Roses / *Et Mourir de Plaisir*
1961 Please, Not Now! / *La Bride sur le Cou*

1962 Seven Capital Sins **(Claude CHABROL, Philippe DeBROCA, Jacques DEMY, Sylvaine DHOMME, Jean-Luc GODARD, Edouard MOLINARO, Marie-José NAT, Dominique PATUREL, Perrette PRADIER, Jean-Marc TENNBERG)**
1962 Love on a Pillow / *Warrior's Rest*
1963 Of Flesh and Blood / *Les Grands Chemins*
1963 Vice and Virtue
1963 Nutty, Naughty Château / *Château en Suède*
1964 Circle of Love
1966 The Game Is Over / *La Curée*
1968 Spirits of the Dead **(Federico FELLINI, Louis MALLE)**
1968 Barbarella
1971 Pretty Maids All in a Row
1972 Hellé
1973 Don Juan, or If Don Juan Were a Woman
1974 Charlotte / *La Jeune Fille Assassinée*
1976 When a Woman in Love. .
1980 Night Games
1981 The Hot Touch
1982 Surprise Party
1983 Come Back
1987 And God Created Woman

VALDEZ, Luis
(1940–) Delano, California, USA.
1981 Zoot Suit
1987 La Bamba

VANCE, Daniel J
1975 Trained to Kill

VANDERBILT, William K
1933 Over the Seven Seas

VANDERKLOOT, William
1987 The Sofia Conspiracy / *Mace*

VAN DER MERWE, Tonie
1987 Operation: Hit Squad

VAN DUSEN, Bruce
1984 Cold Feet

VAN DYKE, W S (Woodbridge Strong Van Dyke II)
(1889–1943) San Diego, California, USA.
1923 The Girl Next Door
1923 The Destroying Angel
1923 The Miracle Workers
1923 Half-a-Dollar
1923 Loving Lies
1923 The Battling Fool
1924 The Beautiful Sinner
1924 Winner Takes All
1924 The Desert's Price
1925 Gold Heels
1925 The Chicago Fire / *Barriers Burned Away*
1925 Ranger of the Big Pines
1925 The Trail Rider
1925 Heart and Spurs
1925 The Timber Wolf
1925 Eyes of the Totem
1925 The Heart of the Yukon
1926 The Gentle Cyclone
1926 War Paint
1926 Winners of the Wilderness
1927 White Shadows in the South Seas
1927 California
1927 Spoilers of the West
1927 Foreign Devils
1928 Wyoming / *The Rock of Friendship*
1928 Under the Black Eagle
1929 The Pagan
1931 Trader Horn **F***
1931 Guilty Hands
1931 Never the Twain Shall Meet
1931 The Cuban Love Song
1932 Tarzan the Ape Man
1932 Night Court / *Justice for Sale*
1933 Penthouse / *Crooks in Clover*
1933 The Prizefighter and the Lady / *Every Woman's Man*
1934 Laughing Boy
1934 Eskimo / *Mala the Magnificent*
1934 Manhattan Melodrama
1934 The Thin Man **D* F***
1934 Hide-Out
1934 Forsaking All Others
1935 I Live My Life
1935 Naughty Marietta **F***
1936 After the Thin Man
1936 The Devil Is a Sissy / *The Devil Takes the Count*
1936 His Brother's Wife / *Lady of the Tropics*
1936 Love on the Run
1936 San Francisco **D* F***
1937 Personal Property / *The Man in Possession*
1937 They Gave Him a Gun
1937 Rosalie
1938 Marie Antoinette
1938 Sweethearts
1939 Andy Hardy Gets Spring Fever
1939 Another Thin Man
1939 It's a Wonderful World
1939 Stand Up and Fight
1940 Bitter Sweet
1940 I Love You Again
1940 I Take This Woman
1940 Dr Kildare's Victory / *The Doctor and the Debutante*
1941 The Feminine Touch
1941 Rage in Heaven
1941 Shadow of the Thin Man
1942 I Married an Angel
1942 Journey for Margaret
1942 Cairo
(also many serials)

VANE, Norman Thaddens
1983 Frightmare
1984 The Black Room **(Elly KENNER)**
1986 Club Life / *King of the City*
1989 Midnight

VAN HEMERT, Ruud
1988 Honeybunch

VAN HORN, Buddy
1980 Any Which Way You Can

1988 The Dead Pool
1989 Pink Cadillac

VAN PEEBLES, Melvin (Melvin Peebles)
(1932–) Chicago, Illinois, USA.
1968 The Story of a Three-Day Pass
1970 Watermelon Man
1971 Sweet Sweetback's Baadass Song

VARDA, Agnes
(1928–) Brussels, Belgium.
1954 La Pointe Courte
1962 Cleo from 5 to 7
1965 Le Bonheur
1966 Les Créatures
1969 Lions Love
1977 One Sings, the Other Doesn't
1981 Documenteur: An Emotion Picture
1985 Vagabond / *Sans Toit ni Loi*
1989 Don't Say It! / *Kung Fu Master*
(also many documentaries)

VARDY, Mike
1973 Man at the Top

VARNEL, Marcel
(1894–1947) Paris, France.
1932 The Silent Witness **(R L HOUGH)**
1932 Chandu, the Magician **(William Cameron MENZIES)**
1933 Infernal Machine
1934 Freedom of the Seas
1935 Dance Band
1935 Girls Will Be Boys
1936 All In
1936 I Give My Heart
1936 No Monkey Business
1936 Public Nuisance No. 1
1937 Good Morning Boys
1937 Oh Mr Porter
1937 Okay for Sound
1938 The Love of Madame DuBarry
1938 Alf's Button Afloat
1938 Ask a Policeman
1938 Convict 99
1938 Hey! Hey! USA
1938 Old Bones of the River
1939 Band Wagon
1939 The Frozen Limits
1939 Where's That Fire?
1940 Gasbags
1940 Let George Do It
1940 Neutral Port
1941 The Ghost of St Michaels
1941 Hi Gang
1941 I Thank You
1941 South American George
1941 Turned Out Nice Again
1942 Get Cracking
1942 King Arthur Was a Gentleman
1942 Much Too Shy
1943 Bell Bottom George
1944 He Snoops to Conquer
1945 I Didn't Do It
1946 George in Civvy Street
1946 This Man Is Mine

VARNEL, Max
(1925–) Paris, France.
1958 A Woman Possessed
1959 The Great Van Robbery
1960 A Taste of Money
1961 Return of a Stranger
1962 Enter Inspector Duval
1963 The Silent Invasion

VEBER, Francis *
1976 The Toy
1988 Three Fugitives

VEILLER, Bayard
1929 The Trial of Mary Dugan

VENTURINI, Edward D
1939 In Old Mexico
1939 The Llano Kid

VERBRUGGE, Caspar
1987 The Performer

VERHOEVEN, Paul *
(1938–) Dutch.
1974 Turkish Delight
1979 Soldier of Orange
1981 Spetters
1983 The 4th Man
1985 Flesh and Blood
1987 Robocop
1989 Total Recall

VERNEUIL, Henri (Achod Malakian) *
(1920–) Rodosto, Turkey.
1951 The Village Feud / *Les Tables aux Crevés*
1952 Forbidden Fruit
1953 The Most Wanted Man in the World / *Public Enemy No.1*
1953 The Wild Oat
1954 The Sheep Has Five Legs
1955 Lovers' Net
1956 Paris Hotel
1957 What Price Murder? / *Une Manche et la Belle*
1958 Maxime
1959 The Big Chief
1959 The Cow and I
1959 It Happened All Night
1961 The Lions Are Loose
1962 A Monkey in Winter / *It's Hot in Hell*
1963 Any Number Can Win / *The Big Snatch*
1964 Greed in the Sun
1965 Weekend at Dunkirk
1967 The 25th Hour
1968 Guns for San Sebastian
1970 The Sicilian Clan
1972 The Burglars
1973 The Serpent / *Night Flight to Moscow*
1975 The Night Caller / *Peur sur la Ville*

VERNON, Harry
1987 The Danger Zone

VERONA, Stephen F
(1940–) Illinois, USA.
1974 The Lords of Flatbush **(Martin DAVIDSON)**
1976 Pipe Dream
1979 Boardwalk
1984 Talking Walls

VICAS, Victor *
(1918–) Franco-Russian.
1954 Double Destiny
1955 No Way Back
1957 Count Five and Die
1967 The Wayward Bus

VIDOR, Charles
(1900–1959) Budapest, Hungary.
1932 The Music of Fu Manchu **(Charles BRABIN)**
1934 Sensation Hunters
1934 Double Door
1934 Strangers All
1935 The Arizonian
1935 His Family Tree
1935 Muss 'Em Up
1937 A Doctor's Diary
1937 The Great Gambini
1937 She's No Lady
1939 Romance of the Redwoods
1939 Blind Alley
1939 Those High Grey Walls
1940 My Son, My Son
1941 New York Town
1941 Ladies in Retirement
1942 The Tuttles of Tahiti
1943 The Desperadoes
1944 Cover Girl
1944 Together Again
1945 A Song to Remember
1945 Over 21
1946 Gilda
1946 The Loves of Carmen
1951 It's a Big Country **(Clarence BROWN, Don HARTMAN, John STURGES Richard THORPE, Don WEIS, William A WELLMAN)**
1952 Hans Christian Andersen
1953 Thunder in the East
1954 Rhapsody
1955 Love Me or Leave Me
1956 The Swan
1957 The Joker Is Wild
1957 A Farewell to Arms
1960 Song Without End **(George CUKOR)**

VIDOR, King (King Wallis Vidor)
(1894–1982) Galveston, Texas, USA. Autobiographies: La Grande Parade: Autobiographie; A Tree Is a Tree.
1923 Peg o' My Heart
1923 The Woman of Bronze
1923 Three Wise Fools
1924 Wild Oranges
1924 Wine of Youth
1924 Happiness
1924 His Hour
1924 Wife of the Centaur
1925 Proud Flesh
1925 The Big Parade
1926 La Bohème
1927 The Patsy / *The Politic Flapper*
1928 The Crowd **D***
1928 Show People
1929 Hallelujah **D***
1930 Billy the Kid
1930 Not So Dumb
1931 The Champ **D* F***
1931 Street Scene
1932 Bird of Paradise
1932 Cynara
1933 The Stranger's Return
1934 Our Daily Bread / *The Miracle of Life*
1935 So Red the Rose
1935 The Wedding Night
1936 The Texas Rangers
1937 Stella Dallas
1938 The Citadel **D* F***
1940 Comrade X
1940 Northwest Passage
1941 H.M. Pulham Esq.
1944 An American Romance
1946 Duel in the Sun *(also many others)*
1948 On Our Merry Way / *A Miracle Can Happen* **(Leslie FENTON)**
1949 Beyond the Forest
1949 The Fountainhead
1951 Lightning Strikes Twice
1952 Japanese War Bride
1952 Ruby Gentry
1955 Man Without a Star
1956 War and Peace **D***
1959 Solomon and Sheba

VIERTEL, Berthold
(1885–1953) Austrian.
1929 Seven Faces
1929 The One Woman Idea
1930 Man Trouble
1931 The Magnificent Lie
1931 The Spy
1932 The Wiser Sex
1932 The Man from Yesterday
1934 Little Friend
1936 Rhodes of Africa
1936 The Passing of the 3rd Floor Back

VIGNE, Daniel
(1942–) French.
1973 Les Hommes
1983 The Return of Martin Guerre
1986 One Woman or Two

VIGNOLA, Robert G
(1882–1953) American.
1924 Married Flirts
1924 The Way of a Girl
1927 The Cabaret
1933 Broken Dreams
1934 The Scarlet Letter
1935 The Perfect Clue
1937 The Girl from Scotland Yard

VILA, Camilio
1988 Options

VILLIERSVILA, François (François Salomons) *
(1920–) French.
1989 Monica: The Girl Who Lived Twice

VINCENT, Chuck
1971 Blue Summer
1971 While the Cat's Away
1971 The Appointment
1972 Mrs Barrington
1974 Letcher
1975 Heavy Load
1976 American Tickler

1976 Bang Bang / *Porn Flakes*
1976 Farewell Scarlet
1977 Visions
1978 Dirty Lilly
1979 Hot T-Shirts
1979 Bad Penny
1980 Jack and Jill
1981 Summer Camp
1981 Bon Appetit
1981 Misbehavin'
1981 That Lucky Stiff
1982 C.O.D.
1982 Games Women Play
1982 Roommates
1982 This Lady Is a Tramp
1982 Dirty Looks
1983 Puss 'n Boots
1984 Jack and Jill II
1984 Preppies
1984 Hollywood Hot Tubs
1985 House of the Rising Sun
1986 Sex Appeal
1987 Pompeii / *Warrior Queen*
1987 Slammer Girls
1987 Wimps
1987 If Looks Could Kill
1987 Deranged
1987 Student Affairs / *High School*
1987 Young Nurses in Love
1988 New York's Finest
1988 Wildest Dreams
1988 Beyond Deranged
1988 Sensations
1988 Sexpot
1989 Thrilled to Death
1989 Bad Blood / *Son*
1989 Cleo
1989 Party Girls

VINT, Jesse
1987 Another Chance

VIOLA, Albert T
1970 Interplay
1988 Preacher Man

VISCONTI, Luchino (Count Don Luchino Visconti di Modrone)
(1906–1976) Milan, Italy.
Biographies: Visconti by Geoffrey Nowell-Smith; Luchino Visconti by Gala Servido.
1942 Ossessione
1948 The Earth Trembles
1951 Bellissima
1954 The Wanton Countess / *Senso*
1957 White Nights
1960 Rocco and His Brothers
1963 The Leopard
1965 Of a Thousand Delights / *Sandra*
1967 The Stranger
1969 The Damned
1971 Death in Venice
1973 Ludwig
1975 Conversation Piece
1976 The Innocent Intruder

VOGEL, Virgil W
1956 The Mole People
1957 The Kettles on Old MacDonald's Farm
1957 The Land Unknown
1958 Terror in the Midnight Sun
1962 Invasion of the Animal People **(Jerry WARREN)**
1965 The Sword of Ali Baba
(also many TV movies)

VON STERNBERG, Josef (Josef Stern or Jonas Sternberg)
(1894–1969) Vienna, Austria.
Autobiography: Fun in a Chinese Laundry.
1925 The Salvation Hunters
1926 The Exquisite Sinner
1927 Underworld / *Paying the Penalty*
1928 Docks of New York
1928 The Dragnet
1928 The Last Command **F***
1929 The Case of Lena Smith
1929 Thunderbolt
1930 The Blue Angel
1930 Morocco **D***
1931 Dishonoured
1931 An American Tragedy
1932 Blonde Venus
1932 Shanghai Express **D* F***
1934 The Scarlet Empress
1934 Crime and Punishment
1935 The Devil Is a Woman
1936 The King Steps Out
1937 I, Claudius *(not completed)*
1939 Sergeant Madden
1941 The Shanghai Gesture
1946 Duel in the Sun *(also many others)*
1952 Macao
1953 The Saga of Anatahan
1957 Jet Pilot
1962 Forever My Love

VON STROHEIM, Erich (Hans Erich Maria Stroheim von Nordenwall or Erich Oswald Stroheim)
(1885–1957) Vienna, Austria.
Biographies: The Man You Loved to Hate: Erich Von Stroheim and Hollywood by Richard Koszarski; Erich Von Stroheim by Thomas Quinn Curtiss.
1918 Blind Husbands
1920 The Devil's Pass Key
1921 Foolish Wives
1923 Merry-Go-Round *(replaced by* **Rupert JULIAN)**
1923 Greed
1925 The Merry Widow
1928 Queen Kelly *(not completed)*
1928 The Wedding March
1933 Hello Sister / *Walking Down Broadway*

VON TROTTA, Margarethe
(1942–) Berlin, Germany.
1975 The Lost Honour of Katharina Blum **(Volker SCHLONDORFF)**
1977 The Second Awakening of Christa Klages
1979 Schwestern oder die Balance des Glücks
1981 Marianne and Julianne / *Die Bleirne Zeit*
1983 Sheer Madness

1986 Rosa Luxembourg

VORHAUS, Bernard
(c1898–) German.
1933 The Ghost Camera
1935 The Last Journey
1935 Street Song
1937 A Smile in the Storm **(Henry SOKAL)**
1937 Hideout in the Alps
1938 King of the Newboys
1938 Tenth Avenue Kid
1939 Vagabond Violinist
1939 Meet Dr Christian
1939 Fisherman's Wharf
1939 Way Down South
1940 The Courageous Dr Christian
1940 Three Faces West
1940 The Refugee
1941 Lady from Louisiana
1941 Mr District Attorney in the Carter Case
1941 Angels with Broken Wings
1941 Hurricane Smith
1942 Affairs of Jimmy Valentine
1942 Ice Capades Revue
1947 Bury Me Dead
1947 Winter Wonderland
1948 The Amazing Mr X / *The Spiritualist*
1950 So Young, So Bad
1951 Pardon My French

VORKAPICH, Slavko
(1892–1976) Dobrinci, Serbia, Yugoslavia.
1927 The Life and Death of a Hollywood Extra **(Robert FLOREY)**
1931 I Take This Woman **(Marion GERING)**
1933 The Past of Mary Holmes **(Harlan THOMPSON)**

WACHSBERG, Orin
1986 Starlight

WACHSMANN, Daniel
1979 Transit
1982 Hot Wind / *Hamsin*

WACKS, Jonathan
1988 The Powwow Highway

WADLEIGH, Michael
1981 Wolfen

WAGGNER, George (George Waggoner)
(1894–1984) Philadelphia, Pennsylvania, USA.
1938 Border Wolves
1938 Western Trails
1938 Outlaw Express
1938 Guilty Trails
1938 Prairie Justice
1938 The Black Bandit
1938 Ghost Town Riders
1939 Honour of the West
1939 The Mystery Plane
1939 Wolf Call
1939 Stunt Pilot
1939 The Phantom Stage
1940 Drums of the Desert
1941 Man-Made Monster / *The Electric Man*
1941 Horror Island
1941 South of Tahiti / *White Savage*
1941 Sealed Lips
1941 The Wolf Man
1944 The Climax
1945 Frisco Sal
1946 Tangier
1947 The Gunfighters / *The Assassin*
1949 The Fighting Kentuckian
1951 Operation Pacific
1957 Destination 60,000
1957 Pawnee / *Pale Arrow*

WAGNER, Jane
(1935–) Morristown, Tennessee, USA.
1978 Moment By Moment

WAITE, Ralph
(1928–) White Plains, New York, USA.
1980 On the Nickel

WAJDA, Andrzej
(1926–) Suwalki, Poland.
1954 A Generation
1955 Je Vais vers le Soleil
1957 Kanal
1958 Ashes and Diamonds
1959 Lotna
1960 Innocent Sorcerers
1961 Samson
1961 The Siberian Lady Macbeth / *Fury Is a Woman*
1962 Love at Twenty **(Shintaro ISHIHARA, Marcel OPHULS, Renzo ROSSELLINI, François TRUFFAUT)**
1965 Ashes
1967 Gates to Paradise
1968 Everything for Sale
1969 Hunting Flies
1970 Landscape After Battle
1971 The Birch-Wood
1972 The Wedding
1974 The Promised Land
1976 The Shadow Line
1977 Man of Marble
1979 Without Anaesthetic
1979 The Girls from Wilko
1980 The Conductor
1980 Rough Treatment
1981 Man of Iron
1983 Danton
1983 A Love in Germany
1986 Chronicle of a Love Affair
1988 The Possessed

WALAS, Chris
1989 The Fly II: The Insect Awakens

WALDRON, Gy
1974 Moonrunners

WALKER, Dorian
1984 Making the Grade
1988 Teen Witch

WALKER, Giles
1985 90 Days

WALKER, Hal
(1896–1972) American.
1945 Out of This World
1945 Duffy's Tavern
1945 Stork Club
1945 Road to Utopia
1950 My Friend Irma Goes West
1950 At War with the Army
1951 That's My Boy
1951 Sailor Beware
1952 Road to Bali

WALKER, Nancy (Ann Myrtle Swoyer Barto)
(1921–) Philadelphia, Pennsylvania, USA.
1980 Can't Stop the Music

WALKER, Norman
(1892–) British.
1927 Tommy Atkins
1931 The Middle Watch
1935 Turn of the Tide
1937 Our Fighting Navy / *Torpedoed*
1940 The Man at the Gate
1942 The Great Mr Handel
1942 Hard Steel / *What Shall It Profit?*
1945 They Knew Mr Knight

WALKER, Peter
(1935–) American.
1966 I Like Birds
1967 Girls for Men Only
1968 School for Sex
1969 Strip Poker
1970 Cool It Carol!
1971 Man of Violence
1971 Die Screaming, Marianne
1972 The Flesh and Blood Show
1972 The Four Dimensions of Greta
1973 Tiffany Jones
1974 House of Whipcord
1975 Frightmare
1976 House of Mortal Sin
1976 Schizo
1978 The Comeback
1979 Home Before Midnight
1983 House of the Long Shadows

WALKER, Robert
1958 Street of Darkness

WALKER, Stuart
(1887–1941) American.
1931 The Secret Call
1932 The False Madonna / *The False Idol*
1932 The Misleading Lady
1932 Evenings for Sale
1933 Tonight Is Ours
1933 The Eagle and the Hawk
1933 White Woman
1934 Romance in the Rain
1934 Great Expectations
1935 The Mystery of Edwin Drood
1935 The Werewolf of London
1935 Manhattan Moon / *Sing Me a Love Song*
1939 Bulldog Drummond's Bride
1940 Emergency Squad

WALLACE, Richard
(1894–1951) American.
1926 Syncopating Sue
1927 American Beauty / *The Beautiful Fraud*
1927 McFadden's Flat
1927 A Texas Steer
1927 The Poor Nut
1928 Lady Be Good
1928 The Butter and Egg Man / *Actress and Angel*
1929 Shopworn Angel
1929 Innocents of Paris
1929 River of Romance
1930 Seven Days' Leave / *Medals* **(John CROMWELL)**
1930 Anybody's War
1930 The Right to Love
1931 Man of the World
1931 Kick In
1931 The Road to Reno
1932 Tomorrow and Tomorrow
1932 Thunder Below
1933 The Masquerader
1934 Eight Girls in a Boat
1934 The Little Minister
1935 Wedding Present
1937 John Meade's Woman
1937 Blossoms on Broadway
1938 The Young in Heart
1939 The Under-Pup
1940 Captain Cautious
1941 A Girl, a Guy and a Gob / *The Navy Steps Out*
1941 She Knew All the Answers
1941 Obliging Young Lady
1942 The Wife Takes a Flyer / *A Yank in Dutch*
1943 Bombardier
1943 A Night to Remember
1943 The Fallen Sparrow
1943 My Kingdom for a Cook
1944 Bride By Mistake
1945 It's in the Bag / *The Fifth Chair*
1945 Kiss and Tell
1946 Because of Him
1947 Sinbad the Sailor
1947 Framed / *Paula*
1947 Tycoon
1948 Let's Live a Little
1949 Adventure in Baltimore / *Bachelor Bait*
1949 A Kiss for Corliss / *Almost a Bride*

WALLACE, Steven
1986 The Boy Who Had Everything
1987 For Love Alone

WALLACE, Tommy Lee
1982 Halloween III: Season of the Witch
1985 Hanauma Bay / *Made in Hawaii*
1988 Fright Night II

WALLS, Tom
(1883–1949) Kingsthorpe, Northamptonshire, England.
1930 Canaries Sometimes Sing
1930 Tons of Money
1930 Plunder
1930 Rookery Nook
1932 A Night Like This
1932 Thark

1933 Leap Year
1933 A Cuckoo in the Nest
1933 Turkey Time
1933 Just Smith
1933 The Blarney Stone
1934 A Cup of Kindness
1934 Lady in Danger
1934 Dirty Work
1935 Fighting Stock
1935 Stormy Weather
1935 Foreign Affairs
1936 Dishonour Bright
1936 Pot Luck
1937 For Valour
1938 Second Best Bed
1939 Old Iron

WALSH, Raoul
(1887–1981) New York, USA.
Autobiography: Each Man in His Time: the Life Story of a Director.
1925 East of Suez
1925 The Spaniard
1925 The Wanderer
1926 The Lucky Lady
1926 Lady of the Harem
1926 What Price Glory?
1927 The Loves of Carmen
1927 Me, Gangster
1928 Red Dance / *The Red Dancer of Moscow*
1928 Sadie Thompson
1929 In Old Arizona **(Irving CUMMINGS) D* F***
1929 The Cockeyed World
1929 Hot for Paris
1930 The Big Trail
1931 The Man Who Came Back
1931 Women of All Nations
1931 The Yellow Ticket / *The Yellow Passport*
1932 Me and My Gal / *Pier 13*
1932 Wild Girl
1933 The Bowery
1933 Going Hollywood
1933 Sailor's Luck
1935 Under Pressure
1935 Every Night at Eight
1935 Baby Face Harrigan
1936 Big Brown Eyes
1936 Klondike Annie
1936 Spendthrift
1937 Artists and Models
1937 Hitting a New High
1937 You're in the Army Now / *O.H.M.S.*
1937 When Thief Meets Thief / *Jump for Glory*
1938 College Swing / *Swing, Teacher, Swing*
1939 The Roaring Twenties
1939 St Louis Blues
1940 Dark Command
1940 They Drive By Night / *The Road to Frisco*
1941 High Sierra
1941 Manpower
1941 The Strawberry Blonde
1941 They Died with Their Boots On
1942 Desperate Journey
1942 Gentleman Jim
1943 Background to Danger
1943 Northern Pursuit
1944 Uncertain Glory
1945 The Horn Blows at Midnight
1945 Objective Burma!
1945 Salty O'Rourke
1946 The Man I Love
1947 Cheyenne / *The Wyoming Kid*
1947 Pursued
1948 Fighter Squadron
1948 One Sunday Afternoon
1948 Silver River
1949 Colorado Territory
1949 White Heat
1951 Along the Great Divide
1951 Captain Horatio Hornblower
1951 Distant Drums
1952 Blackbeard the Pirate
1952 Glory Alley
1952 The Lawless Breed
1952 The World in His Arms
1953 Gun Fury
1953 A Lion Is in the Streets
1953 Sea Devils
1954 Saskatchewan / *O'Rourke of the Royal Mounted*
1955 Battle Cry
1955 The Tall Men
1956 The King and Four Queens
1956 The Revolt of Mamie Stover
1957 Band of Angels
1958 The Naked and the Dead
1959 A Private's Affair
1959 The Sheriff of Fractured Jaw
1960 Esther and the King
1961 Marines, Let's Go!
1964 A Distant Trumpet

WALTERS, Charles
(1911–1982) Pasadena, California, USA.
1947 Good News
1948 Easter Parade
1949 The Berkeleys of Broadway
1950 Summer Stock / *If You Feel Like Singing*
1951 Texas Carnival
1951 Three Guys Named Mike
1952 The Belle of New York
1953 Dangerous When Wet
1953 Easy to Love
1953 Lili **D***
1953 Torch Song
1955 The Glass Slipper
1955 The Tender Trap
1956 High Society
1957 Don't Go Near the Water
1959 Ask Any Girl
1960 Please Don't Eat the Daisies
1960 Cimarron **(Anthony MANN)**
1961 Two Loves / *Spinster*
1962 Billy Rose's Jumbo
1964 The Unsinkable Molly Brown
1966 Walk Don't Run

WALTON, Fred
1979 When a Stranger Calls
1984 Hadley's Rebellion
1986 April Fool's Day
1987 The Rosary Murders

WALTON, Joseph *see* **Joseph LOSEY**

WANAMAKER, Sam
(1919–) Chicago, Illinois, USA.
1969 The File of the Golden Goose
1970 The Executioner
1971 Catlow
1977 Sinbad and the Eye of the Tiger

WANG, Peter (Wang Zhengfang)
1986 A Great Wall
1988 The Laserman

WANG, Wayne
(1949–) Hong Kong.
1975 A Man, a Woman and a Killer **(Rick SCHMIDT)**
1982 Chan Is Missing
1984 Dim Sum: A Little Bit of Heart
1987 Slam Dance
1989 Eat a Bowl of Tea

WARD, David S
(1945–)
1982 Cannery Row
1989 Major League

WARD, Vincent
(1956–) New Zealand.
1984 Vigil
1987 The Navigator

WARE, Clyde
(1934–) West Virginia, USA.
1971 No Drums, No Bugles
1985 When the Line Gets Through

WARHOL, Andy (Andrew Warhola)
(1928–1987) McKeesport, Pennsylvania, USA.
Autobiography: The Philosophy of Andy Warhol.
1963 Kiss
1963 Eat
1963 Sleep
1963 Haircut
1964 Tarzan and Jane. . Sort Of
1964 Dance Movie
1964 Blow Job
1964 Batman Dracula
1964 Salome and Delilah
1964 Soap Opera
1964 Couch
1964 Thirteen Most Beautiful Women
1964 Harlot
1965 The Life of Juanita
1965 Empire
1965 Poor Little Rich Girl
1965 Screen Test
1965 Vinyl
1965 Beauty 2
1965 Bitch
1965 Space
1965 The Closet
1965 Henry Geldzahler
1965 Taylor Mead's Ass
1965 Face
1965 My Hustler
1965 Camp
1965 Suicide
1965 Drunk
1966 Outer and Inner Space
1966 Hedy, the Shoplifter
1966 Paul Swan
1966 More Milk, Evette / *Lana Turner*
1966 The Velvet Underground and Nico
1966 Kitchen
1966 Lupe
1966 Eating Too Fast
1966 The Chelsea Girls
1967 I, a Man
1967 Bike Boy
1967 Nude Restaurant
1967 Four Stars / *24-Hour Movie*
1967 Imitation of Christ
1968 The Loves of Ondine
1968 Lonesome Cowboys
1969 Blue Movie
1972 Woman in Revolt
1973 L'Amour **(Paul MORRISSEY)**
(filmography contains shorts)

WARNER Jnr, Jack
(1916–) American.
1961 Brushfire!

WARNER, John *see* **Edgar Georg ULMER**

WARREN, Charles Marquis
(1912–) Baltimore, Maryland, USA.
1951 Little Big Horn / *The Fighting Seventh*
1952 Hellgate
1953 Arrowhead
1953 Flight to Tangier
1955 Seven Angry Men
1956 Tension at Table Rock
1956 The Black Whip
1957 Trooper Hook
1957 Back from the Dead
1957 The Unknown Terror
1957 Copper Sky
1957 Ride a Violent Mile
1958 Desert Hell
1958 Cattle Empire
1958 Blood Arrow
1969 Charro!

WARREN, Jerry
1958 The Incredible Petrified World
1962 Invasion of the Animal People **(Virgil W VOGEL)**
1963 Attack of the Mayan Mummy

WARREN, Mark
1972 Come Back Charleston Blue
1981 Tulips **(Rex BROMFIELD, Al WAXMAN)**
1981 The Kinky Coaches and the Pom Pom Pussycats / *Crunch*

WARREN, Norman J
1987 Gunpowder
1987 Bloody New Year

WATERS, John
1926 Born to the West
1926 Forlorn River
1926 Man of the Forest
1927 Arizona Bound
1927 Drums of the Desert

1927 The Mysterious Rider
1927 Nevada
1927 Two Flaming Youths
1928 The Vanishing Pioneer
1928 Beau Sabreur
1929 The Overland Telegraph
1929 Sioux Blood
1946 The Mighty McGurk

WATERS, John
(1945–) American.
1970 Mondo Trasho
1974 Pink Flamingos
1975 Female Trouble
1977 Desperate Living
1981 Polyester
1988 Hairspray

WATKINS, Peter
(1935–) Norbiton, Surrey, England.
1966 The War Game
1967 Privilege
1969 Gladiators
1971 Punishment Park
1974 Edvard Munch
1975 Fallen
1977 Evening Land

WATSON, John
1983 Deathstalker
1985 The Zoo Gang **(Pen DENSHAM)**

WATSON, William
1939 Heroes in Blue

WATT, Harry
(1906–) Edinburgh, Scotland.
Autobiography: Don't Look at the Camera.
1936 Night Mail **(Basil WRIGHT)**
1941 Target for Tonight
1943 Nine Men
1944 Fiddlers Three
1946 The Overlanders
1949 Eureka Stockade / *Massacre Hill*
1951 Where No Vultures Fly / *Ivory Hunter*
1954 West of Zanzibar
1959 The Siege of Pinchgut / *Four Desperate Men*
(also many documentaries)

WATTS, Roy
1984 Hambone and Hillie

WAYNE, John (Marion Michael Morrison)
(1907–1979) Winterset, Iowa, USA.
Biography: Duke: the Life and Times of John Wayne by Donald Sheppard and Dave Grayson.
1960 The Alamo **F***
1968 The Green Berets **(Ray KELLOGG)**

WEBB, Harry S
1929 Dark Skies
1930 Bar L Ranch
1930 Ridin' Law
1930 Beyond the Rio Grande
1930 Phantom of the Desert
1931 West of Cheyenne
1931 Westward Bound
1932 Lone Trail
1932 Riot Squad
1934 Wolf Rides
1934 Fighting Hero
1934 Riding Thru
1934 Tracy Rides
1934 The Cactus Kid
1935 Unconquered Bandit
1936 Pinto Rustlers
1936 Santa Fe Bound
1939 Port of Hate
1939 Mesquite Buckaroo
1939 Riders of the Sage
1939 The Pal from Texas
1940 Pioneer Days

WEBB, Jack
(1920–1982) California, USA.
1954 Dragnet
1955 Pete Kelly's Blues
1957 The D.I.
1959 -30- / *Deadline Midnight*
1961 The Last Time I Saw Archie

WEBB, Millard
(1893–1935) American.
1924 Her Marriage Vow
1924 The Dark Swan
1925 My Wife and I
1925 The Golden Cocoon
1926 The Sea Beast
1927 The Love Trail
1928 Honeymoon Flats
1929 The Painted Angel
1929 Gentlemen of the Press
1929 Glorifying the American Girl **(John HARKRIDER)**
1930 Her Golden Calf
1934 The Woman Who Dared

WEBB, Nate
1936 Hopalong Cassidy Returns
1936 Navy Born
1936 Trail Dust
1937 Borderland
1937 Hills of Old Wyoming
1937 North of the Rio Grande
1937 Rustler's Valley
1937 Carnival Queen
1939 Law of the Pampas
1940 Frontier Vengeance
1940 Oklahoma Renegade

WEBB, Peter
1984 Give My Regards to Broad Street

WEBB, Robert D
(1903–) American.
1945 The Caribbean Mystery
1945 The Spider
1953 The Glory Brigade
1953 Beneath the 12-Mile Reef
1955 White Feather
1955 Seven Cities of Gold
1956 On the Threshold of Space
1956 The Proud Ones
1956 Love Me Tender
1957 The Way to the Gold
1960 Guns of the Timberland
1961 Pirates of Tortuga

1961 Seven Women from Hell
1967 The Capetown Affair

WEBB, William
1987 Dirty Laundry
1987 Delta Fever
1988 Party Line
1989 The Banker

WEBER, Bruce
1989 Let's Get Lost

WEBER, Lois
(1882–1939) Allegheny, Pennsylvania, USA.
1926 The Marriage Clause
1927 Sensation Seekers
1934 White Heat
(also many silent shorts)

WEBSTER, Nicholas
(1922–) Spokane, Washington, USA.
1961 Dead to the World
1963 Gone Are the Days / *Purlie Victorious*
1964 Santa Claus Conquers the Martians
1968 Mission Mars
1978 No Longer Alone

WECHTER, David
(1956–) Los Angeles, California, USA.
1980 Midnight Madness **(Michael NANKIN)**
1986 The Bikini Shop

WEEKS, Stephen
(1948–) British.
1970 I, Monster
1973 Gawain and the Green Knight
1974 Ghost Story
1984 Clash of the Swords
1988 The Avalon Awakening

WEIGHT, F Harmon
1928 Jazz Mad
1929 Frozen River
1929 Hardboiled Rose
1929 The Careless Age
1929 A Most Immoral Lady

WEIL, Sam
(1945–) New York, New York, USA.
1980 Squeeze Play!
1982 Waitress! **(Michael HERZ)**
1983 Stuck on You! **(Michael HERZ)**
1984 The First Turn On! **(Michael HERZ)**
1984 The Toxic Avenger **(Michael HERZ)**
1986 The Class of Nuke 'Em High **(Richard HAINES)**
1988 Troma's War! **(Michael HERZ)**
1989 The Toxic Avenger II **(Michael HERZ)**

WEILAND, Paul
1987 Leonard Part VI

WEILL, Claudia
(1947–) New York, New York, USA.
1978 Girlfriends
1980 It's My Turn

WEINER, Hal
1986 The Imagemaker
1988 K-2

WEINRIB, Lennie
1965 Beach Ball
1965 Wild, Wild Winter
1966 Out of Sight

WEINSTEIN, Bob
1986 Playing for Keeps **(Harvey WEINSTEIN)**

WEINSTEIN, Harvey
1986 Playing for Keeps **(Bob WEINSTEIN)**

WEINTRAUB, Sandra
1987 The Women's Club

WEIR, Peter
(1944–) Sydney, New South Wales, Australia.
1971 Three to Go **(Brian HANNANT, Oliver HOWES)**
1974 The Cars That Ate Paris
1975 Picnic at Hanging Rock
1977 The Last Wave
1978 The Plumber
1981 Gallipoli
1982 The Year of Living Dangerously
1985 Witness **D* F***
1986 The Mosquito Coast
1989 Dead Poets' Society

WEIS, Don
(1922–) Milwaukee, Wisconsin, USA.
1951 Bannerline
1951 It's a Big Country **(Clarence BROWN, Don HARTMAN, John STURGES, Richard THORPE, Charles VIDOR, William A WELLMAN)**
1952 Just This Once
1952 You for Me
1953 I Love Marvin
1953 Remains to Be Seen
1953 A Slight Case of Larceny
1953 The Affairs of Dobie Gillis
1953 Half a Hero
1954 The Adventures of Hajji Baba
1957 Ride the High Iron
1959 Mr Pharaoh and His Cleopatra
1960 The Gene Krupa Story / *Drum Crazy*
1963 Critic's Choice
1964 Looking for Love
1964 Pajama Party
1964 Billie
1966 The Ghost in the Invisible Bikini
1967 The King's Pirate
1968 Did You Hear the One About the Travelling Saleslady?
1978 Zero to Sixty
(also many TV movies)

WEIS, Gary
1980 Wholly Moses
1982 Young Lust

WEIS, Jack
1972 Quadroon

WEISS, Adrian
1953 The Bride and the Beast

WEISS, Barbara N
1977 On the Line

WELLES, Mel
1973 Lady Frankenstein

WELLES, Orson (George Orson Welles)
(1916–1985) Kenosha, Wisconsin, USA.
Biographies: This Is Orson Welles by Peter Bogdanovich and Orson Welles; Orson Welles: a Biography by Barbara Leaming.
1941 Citizen Kane **D* F***
1942 It's All True *(not completed)*
1942 The Magnificent Ambersons **F***
1942 Journey into Fear **(Norman FOSTER)**
1946 The Stranger
1948 The Lady from Shanghai
1948 Macbeth
1951 Othello
1955 Confidential Report / *Mr Arkadin*
1955 Don Quixote *(not completed)*
1958 Touch of Evil
1962 The Trial
1966 Chimes at Midnight / *Falstaff*
1968 The Immortal Story
1969 The Deep *(not completed)*
1972 The Other Side of the Wind *(not completed)*
1973 F for Fake

WELLINGTON, David
1989 The Carpenter

WELLMAN, William A
(1896–1975) Brookline, Massachusetts, USA.
Autobiography: A Short Time for Insanity.
1924 The Circus Cowboy
1924 Cupid's Fireman
1924 Not a Drum Was Heard
1924 The Vagabond Trail
1926 You Never Know Women
1926 The Cat's Pajamas
1926 The Boob / *The Yokel*
1926 Wings **F****
1927 Ladies of the Mob
1928 Legion of the Condemned
1928 Beggars of Love
1929 Chinatown Nights
1929 The Man I Love
1929 Woman Trap
1930 Maybe It's Love
1930 Dangerous Paradise
1930 Young Eagles
1930 Steel Highway
1931 Night Nurse
1931 Other Men's Women
1931 Public Enemy
1931 Safe in Hell / *The Lost Lady*
1932 Star Witness
1932 The Hatchet Man / *The Honourable Mr Wong*
1932 Love Is a Racket
1932 Purchase Price
1932 The Conquerors / *Pioneer Builders*
1932 So Big
1933 College Coach / *Football Coach*
1933 Heroes for Sale
1933 Central Airport
1933 Frisco Jenny / *Common Ground*
1933 Lilly Turner
1933 Wild Boys of the Road / *Dangerous Days*
1933 Midnight Mary
1933 Lady of the Night
1934 Looking for Trouble
1934 Stingaree
1934 The President Vanishes / *Strange Conspiracy*
1935 Call of the Wild
1935 Robin Hood of El Dorado
1936 Small Town Girl
1937 Nothing Sacred
1937 A Star Is Born **D* F***
1938 Men with Wings
1939 Beau Geste
1939 The Light That Failed
1940 Reaching for the Sun
1942 The Great Man's Lady
1942 Roxie Hart
1942 Thunder Birds
1943 Lady of Burlesque / *Striptease Lady*
1943 The Ox-Bow Incident / *Strange Incident* **F***
1944 Buffalo Bill
1945 The Story of G.I. Joe / *War Correspondent*
1945 This Man's Navy
1946 Gallant Journey
1947 Magic Town
1948 The Happy Years
1948 The Iron Curtain
1948 The Next Voice You Hear
1949 Battleground **D* F***
1950 Across the Wide Missouri
1951 It's a Big Country **(Clarence BROWN, Don HARTMAN, John STURGES, Richard THORPE, Charles VIDOR, Don WEIS)**
1951 Westward the Women
1951 Yellow Sky
1952 My Man and I
1953 Island in the Sky
1954 The High and the Mighty **D***
1954 Track of the Cat
1955 Blood Alley
1956 Goodbye, My Lady
1958 Darby's Rangers / *The Young Invaders*
1958 Lafayette Escadrille / *Hell Bent for Glory*

WENDERS, Wim (Wilheim Wenders)
(1945–) Düsseldorf, Germany.
1970 Summer in the City *(dedicated to the kinks)*
1972 The Goalkeepers' Anxiety at the Penalty Kick
1973 The Scarlet Letter
1974 Alice in the Cities
1975 The Wrong Move
1976 Kings of the Road / *Lauf der Zeit*
1977 The American Friend
1980 Lightning Over Water / *Nick's Movie* **(Nicholas RAY)**

1982 The State of Things
1982 Hammett
1984 Paris, Texas
1987 The Sky Above Berlin
1988 Wings of Desire

WENDKOS, Paul
(1922–) Philadelphia, Pennsylvania, USA.
1957 The Burglar
1958 The Case Against Brooklyn
1958 Tarawa Beachhead
1959 Gidget
1959 Face of a Fugitive
1959 Battle of the Coral Sea
1960 Because They're Young
1961 Gidget Goes Hawaiian
1961 Angel Baby **(Hubert CORNFIELD)**
1961 Temple of the Swinging Doll
1963 Gidget Goes to Rome
1963 Recoil
1966 Johnny Tiger
1968 Attack on the Iron Coast
1969 Guns of the Magnificent Seven
1970 Cannon for Cordoba
1971 The Mephisto Waltz
1976 Special Delivery
(also a multitude of TV movies 1970–)

WENK, Richard
1986 Vamp

WERKER, Alfred Louis
(1896–) American.
1928 Kit Carson **(Lloyd INGRAHAM)**
1928 The Sunset Legion **(Lloyd INGRAHAM)**
1929 The Blue Skies
1929 Chasing Through Europe **(David BUTLER)**
1930 Double Cross Roads **(George MIDDLETON)**
1930 The Last of the Duanes
1931 Fair Warning
1931 Annabelle's Affairs
1931 Heartbreak
1932 The Gay Caballero
1932 Bachelor's Affairs
1932 Rackety Rax
1932 It's Great to Be Alive
1933 Advice to the Lovelorn
1934 The House of Rothschild **F***
1934 You Belong to Me
1935 Stolen Harmony
1936 Love in Exile
1937 We Have Our Moments
1937 Wild and Wooly
1937 City Girl
1937 Big Town Girl
1938 Kidnapped
1938 Gateway
1938 Up the River
1939 It Could Happen to You
1939 News Is Made at Night
1939 The Adventures of Sherlock Holmes
1941 Moon Over Her Shoulder
1941 The Reluctant Dragon
1942 Whispering Ghosts
1942 The Mad Martindales
1942 A-Haunting We Will Go
1944 My Pal Wolf
1946 Shock
1947 Repeat Performance
1947 Pirates of Monterey
1948 He Walked By Night
1949 Lost Boundaries
1951 Sealed Cargo
1952 Walk East on Beacon / *The Crime of the Century*
1953 The Last Posse
1953 Devil's Canyon
1954 Three Hours to Kill
1955 Canyon Crossroads
1955 At Gunpoint
1956 Rebel in Town
1957 The Young Don't Cry

WERNER, Jeff
1979 Cheerleader's Wild Weekend
1980 Die Laughing

WERNER, Peter
(1947–) New York, New York, USA.
1981 Don't Cry It's Only Thunder
1984 Prisoners
1987 No Man's Land
(also many TV movies)

WERTMULLER, Lina (Arcangela Felice Assunta Wertmuller von Elgg Spanol von Braueich)
1963 I Basilischi
1965 Let's Talk About Men
1966 Rita la Zanzara
1967 Non Stuzzicate la Zanzara
1972 The Seduction of Mimi
1974 Love and Anarchy
1974 All Screwed Up / *Tutto a Poste è Niente in Ordine*
1974 Swept Away by an Unusual Destiny in the Blue Sea of August
1976 Seven Beauties / *Pasqualino Settebellezze* **D***
1978 The End of the World in Our Usual Bed in a Night Full of Rain
1980 Blood Feud
1983 A Joke of Destiny, Lying in Wait Around the Corner Like a Street Bandit
1984 Sotto, Sotto
1986 Camorra
1987 Summer Night with a Greek Profile, Almond Coloured Eyes and the Scent of Basil

WESLEY, William
1988 Scarecrows

WEST, Robert D
1973 The Wednesday Children

WEST, Roland
(1887–1952) American.
1925 The Monster
1929 Alibi **F***
1930 The Bat Whispers
1931 Corsair

WEST, William
1940 The Last Alarm

1940 Flying Wild

WESTMAN, Jim
1974 The Wrestler

WESTON, Eric
1979 They Went That-A-Way and That-A-Way
1982 Evilspeak
1983 Marvin and Tige / *Like Father and Son*
1985 Dreams of Gold **(John AGRAS)**
1986 Birds of Prey
1988 Iron Triangle

WEXLER, Haskell
(1926–) Chicago, Illinois, USA.
1969 Medium Cool
1986 Latino

WHALE, James
(1889–1957) Dudley, Worcestershire, England.
1930 Journey's End
1931 Waterloo Bridge
1931 Frankenstein
1932 Impatient Maiden
1932 The Old Dark House
1933 The Kiss Before the Mirror
1933 The Invisible Man
1933 By Candlelight
1934 One More River
1935 The Bride of Frankenstein
1935 Remember Last Night?
1936 Showboat
1937 The Road Back
1937 The Great Garrick
1938 Sinners in Paradise
1938 Wives Under Suspicion
1938 Port of Seven Seas
1939 The Man in the Iron Mask
1940 Green Hell
1941 They Dare Not Love

WHATHAM, Claude
1973 That'll Be the Day
1974 Swallows and Amazons
1980 Sweet William
1981 Hoodwink

WHEAT, Jim
1983 Lies **(Ken WHEAT)**

WHEAT, Ken
1983 Lies **(Jim WHEAT)**

WHEELER, Anne
1987 Loyalties
1988 Cowboys Don't Cry

WHEELER, David
1989 Night Watcher

WHELAN, Tim
(1893–1957) American.
1928 Adam's Apple
1929 When Knights Were Bold
1933 Aunt Sally / *Along Came Sally*
1933 It's a Boy
1934 The Camels Are Coming
1935 The Murder Man
1935 The Perfect Gentleman / *The Imperfect Lady*
1936 Two's Company
1937 Action for Slander
1937 The Divorce of Lady X
1937 Farewell Again / *Troop Ship*
1937 The Mill on the Floss
1937 Smash and Grab
1938 St Martin's Lane / *Sidewalks of London*
1939 Q Planes / *Clouds Over Europe*
1939 Ten Days in Paris / *Missing Ten Days / Spy in the Pantry*
1940 The Thief of Bagdad **(Ludwig BERGER, Michael POWELL)**
1941 International Lady
1941 The Mad Doctor / *A Date with Destiny*
1942 Nightmare
1942 Seven Days Leave
1942 Twin Beds
1943 Higher and Higher
1943 Swing Fever
1944 Step Lively
1945 Badman's Territory
1948 This Was a Woman
1955 Rage at Dawn
1955 Texas Lady

WHITE, George
1934 George White's Scandals **(Thornton FREELAND, Harry LACHMAN)**
1935 George White's 1935 Scandals
1957 My Gun Is Quick **(Phil VICTOR)**

WHITE, Jules
(1900–1985) American.
1931 Sidewalks of New York **(Zion MYERS)**
1960 Stop! Look! and Laugh!
(also many shorts)

WHITE, Merrill C
(c1895–1959) American.
1957 Ghost Driver **(Richard ENFIELD)**

WHITE, Sam
1941 The Officer and the Lady
1942 I Live on Danger
1945 People Are Funny

WHITMAN, Phillip H
1930 Fourth Alarm
1931 Mystery Train
1931 Air Eagles
1932 Stowaway
1932 The Girl from Calgary **(Leon D'USSEAU)**
1933 Police Call
1933 His Private Secretary
1933 Strange Adventure

WHORF, Richard
(1906–1966) American.
1944 Blonde Fever
1945 The Hidden Eye
1945 The Sailor Takes a Wife
1946 Till the Clouds Roll By **(Vincente MINNELLI)**
1947 It Happened in Brooklyn
1947 Love for a Stranger / *A Stranger Walked In*

1948 Luxury Liner
1950 Champagne for Caesar
1951 The Groom Wore Spurs
(also many TV shorts)

WIARD, William
1980 Tom Horn
(also many TV movies)

WICKES, David
1977 Sweeney
1980 Silver Dream Racer

WICKI, Bernhard *
(1919–) St Polten, Austria.
1959 The Bridge
1962 The Longest Day **(Ken ANNAKIN, Andrew MARTON) F***
1964 The Visit
1965 The Saboteur, Code Name Morituri
1966 Transit
1967 Quadriga
1987 Spider's Web

WIDERBERG, Bo
(1930–) Malmö, Sweden.
1962 The Baby Carriage / *The Pram*
1963 Raven's End
1965 Love 65
1965 Thirty Times Your Money
1967 Elvira Madigan
1968 The White Game
1971 Adalen '31 / *The Adalen Riots*
1971 Joe Hill
1974 Stubby
1977 Man on the Roof
1979 Victoria
1985 The Man from Majorca
1987 The Serpent's Way

WIEDERHORN, Ken
1977 Shock Waves
1979 King Frat
1981 Eyes of a Stranger
1984 Meatballs II
1988 Return of the Living Dead: Part II
1988 Spurting Blood

WIEMER, Robert
1984 Somewhere, Tomorrow
1986 Night Train to Katmandu
(also TV movies)

WIEZYCKI, Joe
1975 Satan's Children

WILBOR, Robert
1976 Mark Twain, American

WILBUR, Crane
(1887–1973) American.
1934 Tomorrow's World
1935 High School Girl
1935 The People's Enemy
1935 The Rest Cure
1936 Devil on Horseback
1936 Romance of Robert Burns
1936 We're in the Legion Now
1936 Yellow Cargo
1937 Navy Spy **(Joseph H LEWIS)**
1938 The Patient in Room 18 **(Robert CONNELLY)**
1939 The Man Who Dared
1939 I Am Not Afraid
1947 The Devil on Wheels
1948 Canon City
1949 The Story of Molly X
1950 Outside the Wall
1951 Inside the Walls of Folsom Prison
1959 The Bat

WILCOX, Fred Mcleod
(1905–1964) Tazewell, Virginia, USA.
1943 Lassie Come Home
1946 Blue Sierra
1946 Courage of Lassie
1948 Hills of Home / *Master of Lassie*
1948 Three Daring Daughters / *The Birds and the Bees*
1949 The Secret Garden
1951 Shadow in the Sky
1953 Code Two
1954 Tennessee Champ
1956 Forbidden Planet
1960 I Passed for White

WILCOX, Herbert
(1891–1977) Cork, Republic of Ireland. Autobiography: Twenty-Five Thousand Sunsets: the autobiography of Herbert Wilcox.
1926 London / *Limehouse*
1927 Madame Pompadour
1927 Tiptoes
1927 Mumsie
1933 Bitter Sweet
1933 Goodnight Vienna / *Magic Night*
1933 The Little Damozel
1934 The Queen's Affair / *Runaway Queen*
1934 Nell Gwyn
1935 Limelight / *Backstage*
1935 Peg of Old Dury
1937 London Melody / *Girls in the Street*
1937 The Three Maxims / *The Show Goes On*
1937 Our Fighting Navy / *Torpedoed!*
1937 Victoria the Great
1938 Sixty Glorious Years / *Queen of Destiny*
1939 Nurse Edith Cavell
1940 Irene
1940 No No Nanette
1941 Sunny
1941 They Flew Alone / *Wings and the Woman*
1943 Forever and a Day **(René CLAIR, Edmund GOULDING, Cedric HARDWICKE, Frank LLOYD, Robert STEVENSON)**
1943 Yellow Canary
1945 I Live in Grosvenor Square / *A Yank in London*
1946 Piccadilly Incident
1947 The Courtneys of Curzon Street
1948 Elizabeth of Ladymead
1948 Spring in Park Lane
1949 Maytime in Mayfair
1950 Into the Blue / *Man in a Dinghy*
1950 Odette
1952 Derby Day / *Four Against Fate*

1952 Trent's Last Case
1954 Lilacs in Spring / *Let's Make Up*
1954 Trouble in the Glen
1955 King's Rhapsody
1956 My Teenage Daughter / *Teenage Bad Girl*
1957 The Man Who Wouldn't Talk
1957 These Dangerous Years / *Dangerous Youth*
1958 The Lady Is a Square
1961 The Lady with a Lamp

WILDE, Cornel (Cornelius Wilde)
(1915–) New York, New York, USA.
1955 Storm War
1957 The Devil's Hairpin
1958 Maracaibo
1962 Lancelot and Guinevere / *Sword of Lancelot*
1966 The Naked Prey
1967 Beach Red
1970 No Blade of Grass
1974 Shark's Treasure

WILDER, Ted
1927 The Kid Brother **(Lewis MILESTONE)**
1928 Speedy **D***
1930 Loose Ankles
1930 Clancy in Wall Street

WILDER, Billy (Samuel Wilder)
(1906–) Sucha, Austro-Hungary. (Poland)
Biography: Billy Wilder in Hollywood by Maurice Zolotow.
1942 The Major and the Minor
1943 Five Graves to Cairo
1944 Double Indemnity **D* F***
1945 The Lost Weekend **D** F****
1948 The Emperor Waltz
1948 A Foreign Affair
1950 Sunset Boulevard **D* F***
1951 Ace in the Hole / *The Big Carnival*
1953 Stalag 17 **D***
1954 Sabrina **D***
1955 The Seven Year Itch
1957 The Spirit of St Louis
1957 Love in the Afternoon
1958 Witness for the Prosecution **D* F***
1959 Some Like It Hot **D***
1960 The Apartment **D** F****
1961 One, Two, Three
1963 Irma La Douce
1964 Kiss Me, Stupid
1966 The Fortune Cookie / *Meet Whiplash Willie*
1970 The Private Life of Sherlock Holmes
1972 Avanti!
1974 The Front Page
1981 Buddy Buddy

WILDER, Gene (Jerome Silberman)
(1935–) Milwaukee, Wisconsin, USA.
1975 The Adventures of Sherlock Holmes' Smarter Brother
1977 The World's Greatest Lover
1981 Sunday Lovers **(Bryan FORBES, Edouard MOLINARO, Dino RISI)**
1984 The Woman in Red
1985 Haunted Honeymoon

WILDER, W Lee
(1904–) Austro-Hungarian.
1946 The Glass Alibi
1947 The Pretender
1947 Yankee Pasha
1948 The Vicious Circle
1950 Once a Thief
1951 Three Steps North
1953 Phantom from Space
1954 Killers from Space
1954 The Snow Creature
1955 The Big Bluff
1956 Manfish
1957 The Man Without a Body **(Charles SAUNDERS)**
1958 Spy in the Sky
1960 Bluebeard's Ten Honeymoons

WILES, Gordon
1936 Blackmailer
1936 Charlie Chan's Secret
1936 Two-Fisted Gentleman
1936 Lady from Nowhere
1937 Women of Glamour
1937 Venus Makes Trouble
1938 Prison Train
1938 Mr Boggs Steps Out
1941 Forced Landing
1947 The Gangster
1973 Ginger in the Morning

WILEY, Ethan
1987 House II: The Second Story

WILLAT, Irvin
(1892–1976) American.
1924 The Heritage of the Desert
1924 North of '36
1924 The Story Without a Name
1924 Wanderer of the Wasteland
1925 The Air Mail
1925 The Ancient Highway
1925 Rugged Water
1926 The Enchanted Hill
1927 Back to God's Country
1928 The Michigan Kid
1929 The Isle of Lost Ships
1931 Damaged Love
1937 Luck of Roarin' Camp
1937 Old Louisiana
1937 South of Senora
1937 Under Strange Flags

WILLETT, Paul B
1933 Home on the Range
1933 Western Skies

WILLIAMS, Douglas
1987 Overdrawn at the Memory Bank

WILLIAMS, Elmo
(1913–) Lone Wolf, Oklahoma, USA.
1953 The Tall Texan
1957 Apache Warrior
1957 Hell Ship Mutiny **(Lee SHOLEM)**
1960 The Big Gamble **(Richard O FLEISCHER)**

WILLIAMS, Emlyn (George E Williams)
(1905–1987) Mostyn, Wales.

Autobiography: Emlyn: an Early Autobiography 1927–1935.
1949 The Last Days of Dolwyn / *Woman of Dolwyn*

WILLIAMS, Oscar
(1944–) St Croix, Virgin Islands.
1972 The Final Comedown
1973 Five on the Black Hand Side
1976 Hot Potato
1988 Death Drug

WILLIAMS, Paul
(1943–) New York, New York, USA.
1969 Out of It
1970 Revolutionary
1972 Dealing: Or the Berkeley-to-Boston Forty Brick Lostbag Blues
1978 Nunzio
1981 Miss Right
1986 A Light in the Afternoon

WILLIAMS, Spencer
1941 Blood of Jesus
1944 Go Down Death
1945 The Girl in Room 20
1946 Beale Street Mama
1946 Dirty Gertie from Harlem, USA
1947 Jivin' in Be Bop
1947 Juke Joint

WILLIAMSON, Fred
(1938–) Gary, Indiana, USA.
1976 Adios Amigo
1976 Mean Johnny Barrows
1976 Death Journey
1976 No Way Back
1977 Mr Mean
1982 One Down Two to Go
1983 The Last Fight
1983 The Big Score
1986 Foxtrap
1987 The Messenger

WILLIS, Gordon
1979 Windows

WILLS, J Elder
1936 Song of Freedom
1937 Big Fella

WILSON, Bruce
1981 Doubles
1985 Bombs Away

WILSON, Frank Arthur
1976 Blast

WILSON, Frederick
1949 Floodtide
1949 Poet's Pub

WILSON, Hugh
(1943–) Miami, Florida, USA.
1984 Police Academy
1985 Rustler's Rhapsody
1987 Burglar

WILSON, James
1976 Death Riders
1979 Screams of a Winter Night

WILSON, Jim
1986 Smart Alec
1987 Hollywood Dreaming

WILSON, Richard
(1915–) McKeesport, Pennsylvania, USA.
1955 Man with the Gun / *The Trouble Shooter*
1957 The Big Boodle / *A Night in Havana*
1958 Raw Wind in Eden
1959 Al Capone
1960 Pay or Die
1963 Wall of Noise
1964 Invitation to a Gunfighter
1968 Three in the Attic

WILSON, Sandy
1986 My American Cousin
1989 California Dreaming

WINCER, Simon
1979 The Day After Halloween / *Snapshot*
1980 Harlequin
1983 Phar Lap
1985 D.A.R.Y.L.
1988 The Lighthorseman

WINDON, Lawrence C
1931 Enemies of the Law

WINDUST, Bretaigne
(1906–1960) American.
1948 Winter Meeting
1948 June Bride
1950 Perfect Strangers / *Too Dangerous to Love*
1950 Pretty Baby
1951 The Enforcer / *Murder Inc.*
1952 Face to Face **(John BRAHM)**

WINER, Harry
1986 Spacecamp
(also many TV movies)

WINER, Robert
1974 The Devil's Triangle

WINKLER, Charles
1987 You Talkin' to Me?

WINKLER, Henry
(1945–) New York, New York, USA.
Autobiography: The Other Side of Henry Winkler.
1988 Memories of Me

WINKLESS, Terence H
1988 The Nest

WINNER, Michael
(1935–) London, England.
1958 The Clock Strikes Eight
1960 Climb Up the Wall
1960 Shoot to Kill
1961 Old Mac
1961 Some Like It Cool
1961 Out of the Shadow / *Murder on the*

Campus
1962 Play It Cool
1962 The Cool Mikado
1963 West 11
1964 The System / *The Girl Getters*
1965 You Must Be Joking!
1965 The Jokers
1968 I'll Never Forget What's 'Is Name
1969 Hannibal Brooks
1969 The Games
1971 Lawman
1972 Chato's Land
1972 The Nightcomers
1972 The Mechanic / *Killer of Killers*
1973 Scorpio
1973 The Stone Killer
1974 Death Wish
1976 Won Ton Ton, The Dog Who Saved Hollywood
1977 The Sentinel
1978 The Big Sleep
1979 Firepower
1982 Death Wish II
1983 The Wicked Lady
1984 Scream for Help
1985 Death Wish III
1987 Appointment with Death
1989 A Chorus of Disapproval

WINNING, David
1988 The Storm

WINOGRAD, Peter
1987 Flicks / *Loose Joints*

WINSOR, Terry
1983 Party Party

WINSTON, Ron
1966 Ambush Bay
1967 Banning
1967 Don't Just Stand There
1970 The Gamblers

WINSTON, Stan
1988 Pumpkinhead / *Vengeance, the Demon*
1989 Upworld

WINTERS, David (David Weizer)
(1939–) London, England.
1979 Racquet
1981 Jayne Mansfield — An American Tragedy
1983 The Last Horror Film / *Fanatic*
1984 Mission Kill
1986 Thrashin'
1988 The Lost Platoon
1988 Rage to Kill
1988 Mutiny in Space
1989 Code Name: Vengeance

WINTERS, Paul
1987 The Freeway Maniac / *Breakdown*

WISBAR, Frank
(1899–1967) German.
1945 Strangler of the Swamp
1946 Devil Bat's Daughter
1946 Lighthouse
1946 Secrets of a Sorority Girl
1947 The Prairie
1948 The Mozart Story
1964 Commando

WISCO, Victor
1987 The Demon Princes: Genesis of the Vampire

WISE, Herbert (Herbert Weisz)
(1924–) Vienna, Austria.
1962 Alone Against Rome **(Riccardo FREDA)**
1963 To Have and to Hold
1972 The Lovers!
(also many TV movies)

WISE, Robert
(1914–) Winchester, Indiana, USA.
1944 The Curse of the Cat People **(Gunther VON FRITSCH)**
1944 Mademoiselle Fifi
1945 The Body Snatcher
1945 A Game of Death
1946 Criminal Court
1947 Born to Kill / *Lady of Deceit*
1948 Mystery in Mexico
1948 Blood on the Moon
1949 The Set-Up
1950 Two Flags West
1950 Three Secrets
1951 The House on Telegraph Hill
1951 The Day the Earth Stood Still
1952 The Captive City
1953 Something for the Birds
1953 The Desert Rats
1953 Destination Gobi
1953 So Big
1954 Executive Suite
1956 Tribute to a Bad Man
1957 Somebody Up There Likes Me
1957 This Could Be the Night
1957 Until They Sail
1958 Run Silent, Run Deep
1958 I Want to Live! **D***
1959 Odds Against Tomorrow
1961 West Side Story **(Jerome ROBBINS) D** F****
1962 Two for the Seesaw
1963 The Haunting
1965 The Sound of Music **D** F****
1966 The Sand Pebbles **F***
1968 Star! / *Those Were Happy Times*
1971 The Andromeda Strain
1973 Two People
1975 The Hindenburg
1977 Audrey Rose
1979 Star Trek — The Motion Picture
1987 I, Zorba
1989 Rooftops

WITNEY, William
(1910–) Lawton, Oklahoma, USA.
1937 The Trigger Trio
1940 Hi-Yo Silver
1940 Heroes of the Saddle
1942 Outlaws of Pine Ridge
1942 The Yukon Patrol **(John ENGLISH)**
1946 Helldorado
1947 Apache Rose
1947 Bells of San Angelo

1947 Springtime in the Sierras
1947 On the Spanish Trail
1948 The Gay Ranchero
1948 Under California Skies
1948 Eyes of Texas
1948 Nightmare in Nevada
1948 Grand Canyon Trail
1948 The Far Frontier
1949 Susanna Pass
1949 Down Dakota Way
1949 The Golden Stallion
1950 Bells of Coronado
1950 Twilight in the Sierras
1950 Trigger, Jr.
1950 Sunset in the West
1950 North of the Great Divide
1950 Trail of Robin Hood
1951 Spoilers of the Plains
1951 Heart of the Rockies
1951 In Old Amarillo
1951 South of Caliente
1951 Pals of the Golden West
1951 Night Riders of Montana
1951 Colorado Sundown
1952 The Last Musketeer
1952 Border Saddlemates
1952 Old Oklahoma Plains
1952 South Pacific Trail
1952 Army Capers / *The WAC from Walla Walla*
1953 Down Loredo Way
1953 Iron Mountain Trail
1954 The Outcast / *The Fortune Hunter*
1955 Headline Hunters
1955 City of Shadows
1955 Santa Fe Passage
1955 The Fighting Chance
1956 A Strange Adventure
1956 A Stranger at My Door
1957 Panama Sal
1958 Young and Wild
1958 Juvenile Jungle
1958 The Cool and the Crazy
1958 The Bonnie Parker Story
1959 Paratroop Command
1960 Secret of the Purple Reef
1961 Master of the World
1961 The Long Rope
1964 Apache Rifles
1965 The Girls on the Beach
1965 Arizona Raiders
1967 Forty Guns to Apache Pass
1973 I Escaped from Devil's Island
1975 Darktown Strutters / *Get Down and Boogie*
(also many serials)

WITTLIFF, William
1987 Red-Headed Stranger

WITTMAN, Peter
1981 Play Dead
1984 Ellie

WOHL, Ira
1987 Only Child

WOLF, Tom
1970 Wilbur and the Baby Factory

WOLFOND, Henry
1987 Mr Nice Guy

WOLFSEN, P J
(1903–1979) American.
1939 Boy Slaves

WOLLEN, Peter
1987 Friendship's Death

WOLMAN, Dan
(1941–) Jerusalem, Israel.
1969 The Morning Before Sleep
1970 The Dreamer
1972 Floch
1976 My Michael
1980 Hide and Seek
1983 Nana
1983 Baby Love — Lemon Popsicle V
1983 Soldier of the Night
1984 Up Your Anchor — Lemon Popsicle VI
1986 Contract for Love

WOOD, Duncan
1964 The Bargee
1969 Some Will, Some Won't

WOOD Jnr, Edward D
(1924–1978) American.
1953 Glen or Glenda? / *I Led Two Lives*
1954 Jail Bait
1954 Bride of the Monster
1958 Plan Nine from Outer Space
1959 Revenge of the Dead
1961 The Sinister Urge
1970 Take It Out in Trade

WOOD, Peter
1969 In Search of Gregory

WOOD, Sam
(1884–1949) Philadelphia, Pennsylvania, USA.
1924 Bluff
1924 The Female
1924 The Next Corner
1927 Rookies
1927 The Fair Co-Ed
1927 The Latest from Paris
1928 Telling the World
1929 So This Is College
1929 It's a Great Life
1930 Way for a Sailor
1930 The Girl Said No
1930 Sins of the Children
1930 The Richest Man in the World
1930 Paid / *Within the Law*
1930 They Learned About Women **(Jack CONWAY)**
1931 A Tailor-Made Man
1931 The Man in Possession
1931 New Adventures of Get-Rich-Quick Wallingford
1932 Prosperity
1932 Huddle / *The Impossible Lover*
1933 Hold Your Man
1933 The Barbarian / *A Night in Cairo*
1933 Christopher Bean
1934 Stamboul Quest
1935 A Night at the Opera

1935 Whipsaw
1935 Let 'Em Have It / *False Faces*
1936 The Unguarded Hour
1937 Navy Blue and Gold
1937 Madame X
1937 A Day at the Races
1938 Lord Jeff / *The Boy from Barnado's*
1938 Stablemates
1939 Goodbye Mr Chips **D* F***
1939 Gone with the Wind **(George CUKOR, Victor FLEMING) D** F****
1940 Kitty Foyle **D* F***
1940 Our Town **F***
1940 Raffles
1940 Rangers of Fortune
1941 The Devil and Miss Jones
1942 The Pride of the Yankees
1942 King's Row **D* F***
1943 For Whom the Bell Tolls **F***
1944 Casanova Brown
1945 Guest Wife
1946 Heartbeat
1946 Saratoga Trunk
1947 Ivy
1949 Ambush
1949 The Stratton Story
1949 Command Decision

WOODRUFF, Frank
1940 Play Girl
1940 Curtain Call
1940 Cross Country Romance
1940 Wildcat Bus
1941 Lady Scarface
1943 Cowboy in Manhattan
1943 Two Señoritas from Chicago
1943 Pistol Packin' Mama
1944 Lady, Let's Dance

WOODS, Arthur B
(1904–1942) British.
1930 Stark Nature
1933 On Secret Service / *Spy 77*
1934 Give Her a Ring
1934 Radio Parade of 1935
1935 Drake of England / *Elizabeth of England*
1935 Music Hath Charms **(Thomas BENTLEY, Alexander ESWAY, Walter SUMMERS)**
1936 Where's Sally?
1936 Irish for Luck
1937 Mayfair Melody
1937 Don't Get Me Wrong **(Reginald PURDELL)**
1937 The Windmill
1937 The Compulsory Wife
1937 You Live and Learn
1938 They Drive By Night
1938 The Dark Stairway
1938 The Singing Cop
1938 Mr Satan
1938 Glamour Girl
1938 Thistledown
1938 Dangerous Medicine
1938 The Return of Carol Deane
1939 Confidential Lady
1939 The Nursemaid Who Disappeared
1940 Busman's Honeymoon / *Haunted Honeymoon*

WORKMAN, Carl (Chuck Workman)
1977 The Money
1985 Stoogemania

WORNE, Duke
1929 Bride of the Desert
1929 Handcuffed
1930 Midnight Special
1932 The Last Ride

WORSDALE, Andrew
1987 Shotdown

WORSWICK, Clark
1986 Agent on Ice

WORTH, David
1979 Hollywood Knight
1989 Kickboxer

WRANGELL, Basil
1947 Philo Vance's Gamble
1958 South Seas Adventure **(many others)**

WRAY, John Griffith (John Malloy)
(1890–1940) American.
1925 The Winding Star
1926 The Gilded Butterfly
1926 Hells 400
1927 Singed
1928 Gateway of the Moon
1929 The Careless Age
1929 A Most Immoral Lady

WREDE, Caspar
(1929–) Finnish.
1962 Private Potter
1971 One Day in the Life of Ivan Denisovich
1975 Ransom / *The Terrorists*

WRIGHT, Mack V
(1895–1963) American.
1932 Haunted Gold
1933 The Man from Monterey
1933 Somewhere in Senora
1935 Cappy Rick Returns
1936 The Big Show
1936 Comin' Round the Mountain
1936 Roarin' Lead **(Sam NEWFIELD)**
1936 The Singing Cowboy
1936 Winds of the Wasteland
1937 Hit the Saddle
1937 Rootin' Tootin' Rhythm
1937 Riders of the Whistling Trail
1937 Range Defenders
1940 The Man from Tascosa
(also many serials)

WRIGHT, Patricia
(1939–) San Francisco, California, USA.
1976 Hollywood High

WRIGHT, Ralph
1957 Perri **(Paul KENWORTHY Jnr)**

WRIGHT, Tenny
1932 The Big Stampede
1933 The Telegraph Trail

WRIGHT, Tom
1984 Torchlight

WRYE, Donald
1979 Ice Castles
1981 The House of God / *H.O.G.*
(also many TV movies)

WURLITZER, Rudolph
1988 Candy Mountain **(Robert FRANK)**

WYLER, William
(1902–1981) Mulhouse, Alsace-Lorraine, France.
Biographies: William Wyler: the Authorised Biography by Axel Madsen; William Wyler by Michael A. Anderegg.
1926 Lazy Lightning
1926 The Stolen Ranch
1927 Blazing Days
1927 Border Cavalier
1927 Desert Dust
1927 Hard Fists
1927 Straight Shootin' / *Range Riders*
1928 Thunder Rides
1928 Has Anybody Here Seen Kelly?
1929 The Shakedown
1929 Hell's Heroes
1929 The Love Trap
1930 The Storm
1932 A House Divided
1932 Tom Brown of Culver
1933 Her First Mate
1933 Counsellor-at-Law
1934 Glamour
1935 The Good Fairy
1935 The Gay Deception
1936 Come and Get It **(Howard HAWKS)**
1936 Dodsworth **D* F***
1936 These Three
1937 Dead End **F***
1938 Jezebel **F***
1939 Wuthering Heights **D* F***
1940 The Letter **D* F***
1940 The Westerner
1941 The Little Foxes **D* F***
1942 Mrs Miniver **D** F****
1946 The Best Years of Our Life **D** F****
1949 The Heiress **D* F***
1951 Detective Story **D***
1951 Carrie
1953 Roman Holiday **F***
1955 The Desperate Hours
1956 The Friendly Persuasion **D* F***
1958 The Big Country
1959 Ben Hur **D** F****
1962 The Children's Hour / *The Loudest Whisper*
1965 The Collector **D***
1966 How to Steal a Million
1968 Funny Girl **F***
1970 The Liberation of L.B. Jones
(also many shorts)

WYNORSKI, Jim
(1950–) Long Island, New York, USA.
1984 The Lost Empire
1986 Killbots / *R.O.B.O.T.* / *Chopping Mall*
1987 Deathstalker II
1987 Big Bad Mama II
1988 Not on This Earth
1989 The Return of the Swamp Thing

XIE, Jin
(1923–) Shaoxing, China.
1954 A Crisis
1954 A Wave of Unrest
1954 Rendezvous at Orchard Bridge
1957 Woman Basketball Player Number Five
1960 The Red Detachment of Women
1962 Big Li, Young Li and Old Li
1964 Two Stage Sisters
1977 Youth
1980 Ah, Cradle
1981 The Legend of Tianyuan Mountain
1982 The Herdsman
1983 Qiu Jin
1984 Reeds at the Foot of the Mountain
1987 Hibiscus Town

YABLONSKY, Yablo
1971 B.J. Presents

YANAGIMACHI, Mitsuo
(1944–) Ibaraki, Japan.
1979 A Nineteen Year Old's Plan
1982 Farewell to the Land
1985 Fire Festival

YARBROUGH, Jean
(1900–) American.
1940 The Devil Bat
1941 Caught in the Act
1941 South of Panama
1941 King of the Zombies
1941 The Gang's All Here / *In the Night*
1941 Father Steps Out
1941 Let's Go Collegiate / *Farewell to Fame*
1941 Top Sergeant Mulligan
1941 City Limits
1942 Freckles Come Home
1942 Man from Headquarters
1942 Law of the Jungle
1942 So's Your Aunt Emma!
1942 She's in the Army
1942 Police Bullets
1942 Criminal Investigator
1942 Lure of the Islands
1942 Silent Witness / *The Attorney for the Defence*
1943 Follow the Band
1943 Good Morning Judge
1943 Get Going
1943 Hi Ya Sailor
1943 So's Your Uncle
1944 Weekend Pass
1944 Moon Over Las Vegas
1944 South of Dixie
1944 In Society
1944 Twilight on the Prairie
1945 Under Western Skies
1945 Here Come the Co-Eds
1945 The Naughty Nineties
1945 On Stage Everybody
1946 She Wolf of London / *The Curse of the Ellanbys*
1946 House of Horrors / *Joan Medford Is*

Missing
1946 Inside Job
1946 Cuban Pete / *Down Cuba Way*
1946 The Brute Man
1948 The Challenge
1948 Shed No Tears
1948 The Creeper
1948 Triple Threat
1949 Henry the Rainmaker
1949 The Mutineers
1949 Leave It to Henry
1949 Angels in Disguise
1949 Holiday in Havana
1949 Master Minds
1950 Joe Palooka Meets Humphrey
1950 Square Dance Katy
1950 Father Makes Good
1950 Joe Palooka in Humphrey Takes a Chance
1950 Sideshow
1950 Triple Trouble
1950 Big Timber
1951 Casa Mañana
1951 According to Mrs Hoyle
1952 Jack and the Beanstalk
1952 Lost in Alaska
1955 Night Freight
1956 Crashing Las Vegas
1956 Yaqui Drums
1956 The Women of Pitcairn Island
1956 Hot Shots
1957 Footsteps in the Night
1961 Saintly Sinners
1967 Hillbillys in a Haunted House
(also many shorts)

YAREMA, Neil
1973 A Taste of Hell **(Basil BRADBURY)**

YATES, Peter
(1929–) Aldershot, Hampshire, England.
1963 Summer Holiday
1964 One Way Pendulum
1967 Robbery
1968 Bullitt
1969 John and Mary
1971 Murphy's War
1972 The Hot Rock / *How to Steal a Diamond in Four Uneasy Lessons*
1973 The Friends of Eddie Coyle
1974 For Pete's Sake
1976 Mother, Jugs and Speed
1977 The Deep
1979 Breaking Away **D* F***
1981 Eyewitness / *The Janitor*
1983 Krull
1983 The Dresser **D* F***
1985 Eleni
1987 Suspect
1988 The House on Carroll Street / *Jigsaw*
1989 Hard Rain

YARI, Bob
1989 Mind Games

YEAWORTH Jnr, Irvin S
1958 The Blob
1959 4D Man
1960 Dinosaurs
1967 Way Out

YELLEN, Linda
1969 Come Out, Come Out!
1977 Looking Up

YOLLES, Dave
1987 That's My Baby **(John BRADSHAW)**

YORKIN, Bud (Alan David Yorkin)
(1926–) Washington, Pennsylvania, USA.
1962 Come Blow Your Horn
1965 Never Too Late
1967 Divorce American Style
1968 Inspector Clouseau
1969 Start the Revolution Without Me
1973 The Thief Who Came to Dinner
1985 Twice in a Lifetime
1988 Arthur on the Rocks
1989 Love Hurts

YOSHA, Yaky
1973 Shalom
1978 Rockinghorse
1981 The Vulture
1982 Dead End Street
1984 Sunstroke

YOUNG, Frederick
(1902–) British.
1983 Arthur's Hallowed Ground

YOUNG, Harold
(1897–1970) American.
1934 Leave It to Blanche
1934 The Scarlet Pimpernel
1934 Too Many Millions
1935 Without Regret
1936 Woman Trap
1936 My American Wife
1937 Let Them Live
1937 52nd Street
1938 The Storm
1938 Little Tough Guy
1939 The Forgotten Woman
1939 Newsboys' Home
1939 Sabotage / *Spies at Work*
1939 Hero for a Day
1940 Code of the Streets
1940 Dreaming Out Loud
1941 Bachelor Daddy
1941 Swing It Soldier
1942 The Mummy's Tomb
1942 There's One Born Every Minute
1942 Juke Box Jennie
1942 Robber Racketeers
1943 Hi Ya Chum / *Everything Happens to Us*
1943 I Escaped from the Gestapo
1943 Hi Buddy
1943 Spy Train
1944 Machine Gun Mama
1945 The Frozen Ghost
1945 I'll Remember April
1945 Jungle Captive
1945 Song of the Sarong
1948 Citizen Saint
1948 One Night with You
1954 Roogie's Bump / *The Kid Colossus*

YOUNG, Jeffrey
1971 Been Down So Long, It Looks Like Up to Me

YOUNG, Robert M
(1924–) New York, New York, USA.
1965 Nothing But a Man **(Michael ROEMER)**
1977 Alambrista!
1978 Short Eyes
1979 Rich Kids
1980 One-Trick Pony
1983 The Ballad of Gregorio Cortez
1985 Saving Grace
1986 Extremities
1987 Dominick and Eugene
1989 Triumph of the Spirit

YOUNG, Roger
(1942–) Champaign, Illinois, USA.
1984 Lassiter
1987 The Squeeze / *Skip-Tracer*
(also many TV movies)

YOUNG, Terence (Shaun T Young)
(1915–) Shanghai, China.
1940 Corridor of Mirrors
1948 One Night with You
1948 Woman Hater
1950 They Were Not Divided
1951 Valley of the Eagles
1952 The Tall Headlines / *The Frightened Bride*
1953 The Red Beret / *Paratrooper*
1953 That Lady
1955 Storm Over the Nile **(Zoltan KORDA)**
1956 Safari
1956 Zarak
1957 Action of the Tiger
1958 Tank Force
1959 Serious Charge / *A Touch of Hell*
1960 Black Tights
1960 Too Hot to Handle / *Playgirl After Dark*
1960 Dr No
1962 From Russia with Love
1965 The Amorous Adventures of Moll Flanders
1965 Thunderball
1966 The Dirty Game **(Christian JAQUE, Werner KLINGER, Carlo LIZZANI)**
1966 Triple Cross
1966 The Poppy Is Also a Flower / *Danger Grows Wild*
1967 Wait Until Dark
1967 The Rover
1969 Mayerling
1969 The Christmas Tree
1970 Cold Sweat
1972 Red Sun
1972 The Valachi Papers
1972 War Goddess
1974 The Klansman
1979 Sidney Sheldon's Bloodline
1984 The Jigsaw Man
1987 Sweet Revenge / *Run for Your Life*

YOUNGSON, Robert
(1917–1974) American.
1950 Fifty Years Before Your Eyes
1957 The Golden Age of Comedy
1962 Thirty Years of Fun
1965 Laurel and Hardy's Laughing Twenties
1967 The Further Perils of Laurel and Hardy

YUEN, Corey
1986 No Retreat, No Surrender

YUST, Larry
1973 Trick Baby
1974 Homebodies
1986 Say Yes!

YUVAL, Peter
1987 Streetfighters
1988 Time Burst: The Final Alliance
1988 Dead End City
1989 Shooters
1989 Fatal Skies

ZACHARIAS, Alfredo
1979 The Bees

ZAGGARRIO, Vito
1988 Night of the Full Moon

ZAMPI, Mario
(1903–1963) Italian.
1938 Thirteen Men and a Gun
1939 Spy for a Day
1948 The Fatal Night
1951 Laughter in Paradise
1952 Top Secret / *Mr Potts Goes to Moscow*
1954 Happy Ever After / *Tonight's the Night*
1955 Now and Forever
1957 The Naked Truth / *Your Past Is Showing*
1958 Too Many Crooks
1960 Bottoms Up
1960 Five Golden Hours

ZANUCK, Darryl Francis (Mark Canfield)
(1902–) Wahoo, Nebraska, USA. Biographies: Zanuck: The Rise and Fall of Hollywood's Last Tycoon by Leonard Mosley; Zanuck: Don't Say Yes Until I Finish Talking by Mel Gussow.
1933 Advice to the Lovelorn

ZANUSSI, Krzysztof
(1939–) Warsaw, Poland.
1969 The Structure of Crystals
1971 Family Life
1971 Behind the Wall
1973 Illumination
1974 The Catamount Killing
1975 A Woman's Decision
1977 Camouflage
1978 The Spiral
1980 Ways in the Night
1980 The Constant Factor
1981 Contract
1982 The Unapproachable
1984 The Year of the Quiet Sun
1985 Paradigme / *Le Pouvoir du Mal*
1988 Wherever You Are
(also many TV movies)

ZAPPA, Frank
(1940–) Baltimore, Maryland, USA.
1971 200 Motels **(Tony PALMER)**

1979 Baby Snakes

ZARINDAST, Tony
1987 Deathflash
1987 Hard Case and Fist

ZEFFIRELLI, Franco (Gianfranco Corsi)
(1923–) Florence, Italy.
1957 Camping
1967 The Taming of the Shrew
1968 Romeo and Juliet **D* F***
1973 Brother Sun, Sister Moon
1979 The Champ
1981 Endless Love
1982 La Traviata
1986 Otello
1988 Young Toscanini

ZEISLER, Alfred
1936 The Amazing Quest of Ernest Bliss / *Romance and Riches*
1944 Enemy of Women
1946 Fear
1949 Parole, Inc.
1949 Alimony

ZELNICK, Fred
(1885–1950) Romania.
1932 Happy
1934 Mr Cinders
1937 The Lilac Domino
1939 I Killed the Count
1943 Heaven Is Round the Corner

ZEMECKIS, Robert
(1952–) Chicago, Illinois, USA.
1978 I Wanna Hold Your Hand
1980 Used Cars
1984 Romancing the Stone
1985 Back to the Future
1988 Who Framed Roger Rabbit?
1989 Back to the Future II
1990 Back to the Future III

ZENS, William
1974 Hot Summer in Barefoot County
1975 Truckin' Man

ZETTERLING, Mai
(1925–) Vasteras, Sweden.
Autobiography: All Those Tomorrow.
1964 Loving Couples
1966 Night Games
1968 Doctor Glas
1969 The Girls
1972 Vincent the Dutchman
1976 We Have Many Names
1982 Love **(Annette COHEN, Nancy DOWD, Liv ULLMANN)**
1983 Scrubbers
1986 Amorosa

ZIEFF, Howard
(1943–) Los Angeles, California, USA.
1972 Slither
1975 Hearts of the West / *Hollywood Cowboy*
1978 House Calls
1979 The Main Event
1980 Private Benjamin
1984 Unfaithfully Yours
1989 The Dream Team

ZIELINSKI, Rafal
1980 Hey Babe!
1983 Screwballs
1985 Screwballs II: Loose Screws
1986 Recruits
1987 Valet Girls
1987 Spellcaster
1987 State Park
1988 Screwball Hotel

ZILLER, Paul
1988 Pledge Night / *Hazing in Hell*

ZIMMERMAN, Vernon
(1940–) American.
1963 The College
1971 Deadhead Miles
1972 Unholy Rollers
1980 Fade to Black

ZINMAN, Zoe
1983 City News **(David FISHELSON)**

ZINNEMANN, Fred
(1907–) Vienna, Austria.
1942 Kid Glove Killer
1942 Eyes in the Night
1944 The Seventh Cross
1946 Little Mr Jim
1947 My Brother Talks to Horses
1947 The Search **D***
1949 Act of Violence
1950 The Men / *Battle Stripe*
1951 Teresa
1952 High Noon **D* F***
1953 The Member of the Wedding
1953 From Here to Eternity **D** F****
1955 Oklahoma!
1957 A Hatful of Rain
1959 The Nun's Story **D* F***
1960 The Sundowners **D* F***
1964 Behold a Pale Horse
1966 A Man for All Seasons **D** F****
1973 The Day of the Jackal
1977 Julia **D* F***
1982 Five Days One Summer
(also many shorts)

ZINNER, Peter
(1919–) Vienna, Austria.
1981 The Salamander

ZIOLKOWSKI, Fabrice
(1954–) Charleville, France.
1980 L.A.X.

ZITO, Joseph
(1946–) New York, New York, USA.
1981 Abduction
1982 The Prowler
1984 Friday the 13th Part IV — The Final Chapter
1984 Missing in Action
1985 Invasion USA
1989 Red Scorpion

ZUCKER, David
(1947–) Milwaukee, Wisconsin, USA.
1980 Airplane **(Jim ABRAHAMS, Jerry ZUCKER)**
1984 Top Secret **(Jim ABRAHAMS, Jerry ZUCKER)**
1986 Ruthless People **(Jim ABRAHAMS, Jerry ZUCKER)**
1988 The Naked Gun / *Police Squad*

ZUCKER, Jerry
(1950–) Milwaukee, Wisconsin, USA.
1980 Airplane **(Jim ABRAHAMS, David ZUCKER)**
1984 Top Secret **(Jim ABRAHAMS, David ZUCKER)**
1986 Ruthless People **(Jim ABRAHAMS, David ZUCKER)**

ZUGSMITH, Albert
(1910–) Atlantic City, New Jersey, USA.
1960 College Confidential
1960 Sex Kittens Go to College
1960 The Private Lives of Adam and Eve **(Mickey ROONEY)**
1960 Dondi
1962 Confessions of an Opium Eater / *Evils of Chinatown*
1965 The Incredible Sex Revolution
1966 Movie Star American Style, or LSD I Hate You
1966 On Her Bed of Roses
1969 The Very Friendly Neighbours
1969 Two Roses and a Golden Rod

ZUNIGA, Frank
1978 Further Adventures of the Wilderness Family Part II
1983 Heartbreaker
1983 The Golden Seal
1984 What Colour Is the Wind?
1989 Fistfighter

ZWEIBACK, Martin
1971 Cactus in the Snow / *You Can't Have Everything*

ZWERIN, Charlotte
1989 Thelonious Monk / *Straight No Chaser*

ZWICK, Edward
(1952–) Winnetka, Illinois, USA.
1986 About Last Night / *Sexual Perversity in Chicago*
1989 Glory

ZWICK, Joel
1989 Second Sight

ZWICKY, Karl
1989 Vicious

INDEX TO FILMS